The Lutheran Theology of the Holy Spirit

"Far from the supposition that the Holy Spirit has no 'organic place' in Lutheran theology, Fred Hall demonstrates that in early Lutheran theology the Holy Spirit is the indispensable and efficacious agent who, through the word and sacraments, brings Christ to those desperate for the gospel and unites believers with Christ in his death and resurrection. This book is a welcome addition to Lutheran theology which to date has insufficiently reflected on the person and work of the Spirit."

—**Mark Mattes**, chair in theology, Grand View University

"Fred Hall has provided readers with an accessible and clarifying study of the theology of the Holy Spirit in Luther and early Lutheranism. Engaging the work of Regin Prenter, Oswald Bayer, and others, Hall's contribution is unique in that he traces the trajectory of Luther's confession of the unity of the Word and Spirit in Lutheran thinkers in the later part of the sixteenth century. Not only Reformation scholars, but also pastors and involved laity will appreciate this volume."

—**John T. Pless**, assistant professor of pastoral ministry and missions, Concordia Theological Seminary

"Lutheranism is known for its Christology, but it is often misinterpreted as having no significant pneumatology. *The Lutheran Theology of the Holy Spirit* clearly illustrates that this is the farthest from the truth. Beginning with the great reformer, Rev. Dr. Martin Luther, to the framers of the Lutheran Formula of Concord, Fred Hall strikingly clarifies, through detailed research, the deep and faithful Lutheran doctrine of the Holy Spirit that originates from the inerrant and infallible word of God."

—**Cary G. Larson**, presiding pastor, American Association of Lutheran Churches

"Fred Hall's study of the Lutheran doctrine of the Holy Spirit fills a significant gap in the literature on early modern Lutheran theology. Hall contrasts Luther's teaching with Melanchthon's and shows a greater continuity between Luther's own thought and the doctrine of the Holy Spirit both in closer followers like Brenz, Rhegius, and Spangenberg and in the later formulators of the Concord, Andreae, Chemnitz, and Chytraeus. This is a significant addition to our understanding of patterns of Lutheran thought in the sixteenth century."

—**Richard A. Muller**, professor emeritus of historical theology, Calvin Theological Seminary

The Lutheran Theology of the Holy Spirit

From Luther to the Writers of the *Formula of Concord*

Fred Perry Hall

Foreword by Robert Kolb

WIPF & STOCK · Eugene, Oregon

THE LUTHERAN THEOLOGY OF THE HOLY SPIRIT
From Luther to the Writers of the *Formula of Concord*

Copyright © 2024 Fred Perry Hall. All rights reserved. Except for brief quotations in critical publications or reviews, no part of this book may be reproduced in any manner without prior written permission from the publisher. Write: Permissions, Wipf and Stock Publishers, 199 W. 8th Ave., Suite 3, Eugene, OR 97401.

Wipf & Stock
An Imprint of Wipf and Stock Publishers
199 W. 8th Ave., Suite 3
Eugene, OR 97401

www.wipfandstock.com

PAPERBACK ISBN: 978-1-4982-8220-8
HARDCOVER ISBN: 978-1-4982-8222-2
EBOOK ISBN: 978-1-4982-8221-5

VERSION NUMBER 011024

For Sandy

Contents

Foreword by Robert Kolb | ix
Preface | xiii
Abbreviations | xvii

1. Introduction | 1
   Background—Purpose—Methodology

2. Martin Luther's Theology of the Holy Spirit | 19
   "Pigtails on the Pillow"

3. Philip Melanchthon's Theology of the Holy Spirit | 184
   "The Dynamic Will of God"

4. The Early Reformers' Theology of the Holy Spirit | 234
   Johannes Brenz, Urbanus Rhegius, Johann Spangenberg
   "Co-Workers in the Vineyard of the Lord"

5. The *Formula of Concord* Writers' Theology of the Holy Spirit | 275
   Jakob Andreae, Martin Chemnitz, David Chytraeus
   "The Late Lutheran Reformation"

6. Comparisons—Contrasts—Conclusions | 331

Bibliography | 345
Subject Index | 359
Scripture Index | 381

Foreword

Nearly sixty years ago Hermann Sasse commented that just as the church had formulated its doctrine of God in the fourth century and its Christology in the fifth century, and as it had refined its public formulation of the salvation of the sinner in justification by faith in the sixteenth century, so in the years to come the students in his seminar would see the church expressing anew the biblical teaching on the Holy Spirit.[1] He believed that Lutheran theology had much to contribute to that ecumenical conversation. Whether his prediction is coming true or not remains questionable. With its portrayal of sixteenth-century Lutheran proclamation regarding the work of the Holy Spirit this volume certainly helps lay the foundation for further thinking. Fred Hall's study invites further working on apt expression of what the Bible says about the person and activity of the Holy Spirit in our age.

Martin Luther himself had a rich doctrine of the Holy Spirit.[2] Though often accused of being "Christomonic"—if not Christomanic—Luther's preaching and teaching rested upon a perception of God as creator that explored and proclaimed God's nature as a person who created all things by speaking, as reported in Gen 1. He proclaimed God the Holy Spirit, who continues to employ his Word (in several senses) both to uphold all of creation and to recreate sinners into his children. Luther based this activity of re-creation on Christ's death and resurrection, but he ascribed its execution to the Holy Spirit, who continues to use as his medium for this re-creative work the Word of God in oral, written, and sacramental forms. In his catechisms Luther labeled the work of the Holy Spirit "sanctification." He makes sinners into the holy reborn children of God through the Word,

1. In a seminar in which the author of this foreword took part at Concordia Seminary, Saint Louis, in the winter quarter 1964–65.
2. Silcock, "Luther on the Holy Spirit," 294–309.

and he leads them into lives of new obedience as they make his love present in the world into which he has called them.

Luther insisted that the Holy Spirit is truly present in the pages of Scripture and in written works that convey its message purely. The Spirit is indeed to be heard in absolution, sermon, lecture, and Christian conversation which present the gospel. As the genius with media that the Spirit is, he also comes promising forgiveness, life, and salvation in the sacraments, which convey the promise with words and material elements. As the *Spiritus Creator*, the Holy Spirit has no anxiety regarding his created material order. He readily takes in hand human language and other selected elements of the created order to serve as the instruments of his re-creative activity (John 3:3–8). The result is that he creates and sustains trust in Christ in his chosen people, and he moves them to live as the justified children of God in doing all good works (2 Tim 3:16–17; Eph 2:10). He does that, according to Luther in his Small Catechism, through his church, in which he restores people to their original human fellowship designed by God (Gen 2:18), by gathering them together into the congregations of his trusting and worshipping people, where his Word reigns.[3] Luther recognized that the Holy Spirit remains the master of his activities. As his Wittenberg colleague Philip Melanchthon formulated it in the Augsburg Confession, God bestows his Holy Spirit "who produces faith" where and when he wills, in those who hear the gospel."[4] Human speakers and writers of his Word remain under the Spirit's lordship. No magical recital of the words which he gave originally to the prophets and apostles is automatically effective; believers remain his tools, unable to manipulate him. The Spirit creates and sustains the trust in Christ that forms the heart and foundation of the truly human life.

Luther was, of course, not alone in his reforming efforts. His colleagues in Wittenberg, especially Melanchthon, formed a team, dividing the tasks before them, enriching and cultivating each other's thinking, even if Luther remained the leading thinker in the group. Particularly Melanchthon's contributions to the Wittenberg way of practicing theology dare not be ignored. The Wittenberg Reformation spread also through the preaching and publications of others, among whom Johannes Brenz, reformer in southwestern German lands, chiefly the duchy of Württemberg; Urbanus Rhegius, reformer in Augsburg and the duchy of Braunschweig-Lüneburg; and Johann Spangenberg, active in reform in Nordhausen and the county of Mansfield, typify their generation. They composed some of the leading printed works that conveyed the message being broadcast from Wittenberg, each from the

---

3. *BSELK*, 872–73, 1058–71; *BC*, 355–56, 435–39.
4. *BSELK*, 100–101; *BC*, 41.

author's specific point of departure, to many in the mid-sixteenth century. The next generation of Wittenberg students and adherents also included many talented theologians. Among them are certainly three of the authors of the Formula of Concord of 1577, which brought together adherents of the Wittenberg Reformation who had for a generation engaged in controversy over the interpretations of elements of Luther's and Melanchthon's legacy. Jakob Andreae of Tübingen, Martin Chemnitz of Braunschweig, and David Chytraeus typify this generation at its best.

In this volume Fred Hall traces the unfolding of the Lutheran teaching on the Holy Spirit, his person and his work, during the course of the first two generations of the Lutheran Reformation. His study demonstrates that this understanding of the Holy Spirit's person and activity is fundamental to the Lutheran exposition of the biblical message. Luther's teaching on the third person of the Holy Trinity holds an integral place in the Wittenberg proclamation of justification by faith and the living of the justified life. With an open ear to the previous scholarly treatment of aspects of his subject—and there is tragically little—Hall continues and expands the conversation about the sanctifying action of the Holy Spirit, as Luther defined his transformation of doubting sinners into trusting children of God.

This volume enables twenty-first-century readers to listen to the fruit of Hall's extensive study as he probes the Reformation era's proclamation of the Holy Spirit. These Wittenberg reformers strove to echo the voice of the Holy Spirit as they heard it from the pages of the Bible, where the Holy Spirit, they insisted, conveys all we need to know about him. Hall's presentation of their views of his person and work should open up larger conversations regarding the Holy Spirit and how the church can best proclaim who he is and what he does in twenty-first-century environments. This conversation dare not take place only among Lutherans talking to each other. The witness of Luther and his students and disciples can enrich the exchange of perspectives and ideas with other traditions, as the Lutheran churches of today give witness to their historic confession of the faith.

Robert Kolb
Concordia Seminary, Saint Louis
Easter 2023

Preface

This volume finds its roots and inspiration in the church where my wife Sandy and I were members from 1960 until 1993—Trinity Lutheran Church, San Pedro, California. Our pastor at Trinity, until 1982, was Pastor Larry Christenson, a leader in the renewal of the Holy Spirit among Lutherans. His gifted and diligent Scripture-based teaching and preaching on the Holy Spirit during those years was a remarkable ministry and example to us, as was his personal life in Christ. He entrusted a wide range of responsibility and ministry to church members, developing skills and motivation that served to propel many into ordained ministry, including me.

While still serving at Trinity, in the midst of this environment of the Holy Spirit and being convinced of its biblical authenticity, I sought to find a Lutheran base by which to understand it. I found a wide spectrum of attitudes among Lutherans. Some moved into various degrees of Pentecostalism. In reaction, others took strong, conservative Confessional positions rejecting any experience of the Holy Spirit. Many Lutherans between these poles accepted Charismatic gifts for today, while holding to traditional Confessional Lutheranism.

For a number of years I served as a teaching elder, teaching catechism and adult Bible classes and overseeing the home group program. Eventually Pastor Christenson and his wife, Nordis, pressed me to pursue theological training and prepare for the possibility of teaching in a seminary. (At that time I was an electrical engineer working in the aerospace industry. Some of the projects I worked on sent data back to Earth for a number of years.) I began taking courses at Fuller Theological Seminary, Pasadena, California and the goal of teaching in a seminary was finally reached through my PhD, with the dissertation concentrating on the Lutheran theology of the Holy Spirit and teaching at the American Lutheran Theological Seminary

(TAALC) in St. Paul, Minnesota. Though the interpretation in this volume may not be in exact agreement with Pastor Christenson's, I am indebted to him for his guidance and his caring ministry.

My primary mentor in the doctoral program at Fuller Seminary was Dr. Richard A. Muller (ultimately of Calvin Seminary, Grand Rapids, Michigan), a world-class Reformation and post-Reformation scholar in the Heiko Oberman and David Steinmetz tradition. Dr. Muller directed the research of my Lutheran project in the "non-Lutheran" academics of Fuller. When I began the doctoral program he stated that he was my guarantee that I would successfully finish. He set up a program of research that plunged me into Lutheran studies of theology that taught how research was done. He sent me off to the Library of Claremont Colleges in Claremont, California, the Folger Shakespeare Library in Washington, DC, The Huntington Library in San Marino, California, and the University of California Library in Riverside, California. As I moved through the research I was impressed that the Holy Spirit was such a dynamic part of Luther's life experience and his theology, and how he courageously called people to follow his Scriptural teaching and experience into what we call in this volume his "theology of reality." Dr. Muller's introduction to appropriate Lutheran sources ultimately shaped the dissertation and its presentation of the topic. I am indebted to him.

Dr. Robert Kolb, Concordia Seminary, St. Louis, Missouri, was the external reader of my dissertation and my mentor for this current upgrade of that project. Dr. Kolb raised questions regarding the revised manuscript and provided a new road map for enhancing the work, pointing to numerous additional relevant resources. I am overwhelmingly grateful for his valuable contributions, without which this task could not have been completed. I also value his writing the foreword, providing a meaningful and significant historical setting for the book.

I also thank Mr. Bruce Eldevik and Mr. Peter Watter of Luther Seminary Library, St. Paul, Minnesota, who provided creative resource support during the long time of revising the project. Scott Mulinex's willing, expert, and expeditious computer support has been invaluable.

Most importantly, I dedicate this work to my wife and life partner in Christ, Sandra Sue Thompson Hall. Over the years we have backed each other's intense personal and professional commitments, requiring loving sacrifice and mutual support, literally living out Luther's "theology of reality." Sandy has proofread this work and made significant contributions to its tone and organization. Most of all, Sandy's personal commitment to our Lord Jesus helps to keep my own life in Christ an honest relationship of repentance and faith. Sandy has shared life in the Holy Spirit with me for

PREFACE

over sixty-five years. I am immeasurably indebted to her, and so dedicate this work to her.

Fred Perry Hall
Easter 2023

Abbreviations

BC	Kolb, Robert, and Timothy J. Wengert, eds. *The Book of Concord: The Confessions of the Evangelical Lutheran Church.* Minneapolis: Fortress, 2000.
BCT	Tappert, Theodore, et al., trans. and ed. *Book of Concord.* Philadelphia: Fortress, 1959.
BEMCT	McGrath, Alister E., ed. *The Blackwell Encyclopedia of Modern Christian Thought.* Oxford: Blackwell, 1993.
BHS	Kittel, R., et al., eds. *Biblia Hebraica Stuttgartensa.* 3rd ed. Stuttgart: Deutsche Bibelstiftung, 1977.
BSELK	Dingle, Irene, ed. *Die Bekenntnisschriften der Evangelisch-Lutheranischen Kirche.* Vollständige Neuedition. Göttingen: Vandenhoeck & Ruprecht, 2014.
BSLK	*Die Bekenntnisschriften der evangelisch-lutheranischen Kirche.* 12th ed. Göttingen: Vandenhoeck & Ruprecht, 1998.
Church History	*Church History: Studies in Christianity and Culture*
CLTP	Chemnitz, Martin. *Loci Theologici.* 2 vols. Translated by J. A. O. Preus. Saint Louis: Concordia, 1989.
CLT53	Chemnitz, Martin. *Loci Theologici, quibus et loci communes D. Philippi Melanchthons Perspicue Explicantur, & quasi integrum Christianae doctrinae corpus, Ecclesiae Dei sincere proponitur.* 3 vols. Editi opera & studio, Polycarpi Leyser D. Frankfort & Wittenberg: Mævii & Schumacheri, 1653.

ABBREVIATIONS

CR	Melanchthon, Philipp. *Philippi Melanchthonis Opera quae supersunt omnia*. Edited by C. G. Bretschneider and H. E. Bindseil. *Corpus Reformatorum*, vols. 1–28. N.p.: Halle and Braunschwig, 1834–60.
CR21	*Loci communes rerum theologicarum, seu hypostases theologicae*, 21:59–225. Wittenberg: N.p., 1521.
CR22	Melanchthon, Philipp. *Heubtarticel Christlicher Lere, im Latin genandt, Loci theologici, Etwa von Doctor Justo Jona in Deutsche Sprach gebracht, je kund aber im MDLV jar, von Philippo Melanthon widerumb durchsehen*, 46–751. Wittenberg: N.p., 1558.
CRR3	*Center for Reformation Research*. Sixteenth-Century Bibliography 3. Saint Louis: N.p., 1975.
CTQ	*Concordia Theological Journal*
DCT	Richardson, Alan, ed. *A Dictionary of Christian Theology*. Philadelphia: Westminster, 1969.
DLLT	Wengert, Timothy J., gen. ed. *Dictionary of Luther and the Lutheran Traditions*. Grand Rapids: Baker, 2017.
DNC	Chemnitz, Martin. *De duabus naturis in Christo de Hypostatica earum unione: de communicatione idiomatum, et aliis questionibus inde dependentibus* . . . Frankfort & Wittenberg: Mævii & Schumacher, 1653.
ELC	*The Encyclopedia of the Lutheran Church*. 3 vols. Edited by Julius Bodensieck for LWF. Minneapolis: Augsburg, 1965.
ERK	*The New Schaff-Herzog Encyclopedia of Religious Knowledge*, 13 Vols. [Reprint] Grand Rapids: Baker, 1950.
FSD	Chemnitz, Martin. *Fundamenta Sanae Doctrinae de Vera et Substantiali Praesentia, Exhibitione et Sumptione Corporis & Sanguinis Domini in Coena*. Frankfort & Wittenberg: Mævii & Schumacher, 1653.
Germ.	Both German-speaking territories previous to 1870 and today's country of Germany.
IDPC	Burgess, Stanley M., ed. *International Dictionary of Pentecostal and Charismatic Movements*. Grand Rapids: Zondervan, 2003.

ABBREVIATIONS

JEH	*Journal of Ecclesiastical History*, Cambridge University Press.
K&D	Keil, C. F., and Franz Delitzsch. *Commentary on the Old Testament*. 10 vols. 1866–91. Reprint, Peabody: Hendrickson, 1996.
LC	Large Catechism
LCy	Lueker, Erwin Luther, ed. *Lutheran Cyclopedia*. Saint Louis: Concordia, 1954.
LQ	Lutheran Quarterly
LS	Chemnitz, Martin. *The Lord's Supper*. Translated by J. A. O. Preus. Saint Louis: Concordia, 1979. (*Fundamenta Sanae Doctrinae de . . . corporis & sanguinis Domini in coena*. Jena: Ritzenhain, 1590.)
Lu J. 25 (1958)	*Luther = Jahrbuch 1958*. Jahrbuch der Luther-Gesellschaft. Edited by Professor D. Franz Lau. Markkleeberg bei Leipzig: N.p.
Lu J. 47 (1980)	*Luther = Jahrbuch 1980*. Jahrbuch der Luther-Gesellschaft. Edited by Helmar Junghans. Leipzig: Dozent an der Karl-Marx-Universität.
LW	*Works of Martin Luther, American Edition*. 55 vols. Philadelphia: Fortress, 1955–86. Lutherisches Verlagshaus Berlin.
LWF	Lutheran World Federation
MLC21	Melanchthon, Philip. "Loci communes, 1521." In *Melanchthon and Bucer*, edited by Wilhelm Pauck, translated by Lowell J. Satre, 18–152. Philadelphia: Westminster, 1969.
MLC43	Melanchthon, Philip. *Loci communes, 1543*. Translated by J. A. O. Preus. Saint Louis: Concordia, 1992.
MLC55	Melanchthon, Philip. *Loci communes 1555*. Translated and edited by Clyde L. Manschreck. Grand Rapids: Baker, 1982.
MPG	Migne, J. P. *Patrologia Graeca*. 165 vols. Paris: Atelier catholiques, 1857–58.
MPL	Migne, J. P. *Patrologia Latina*. 224 vols. Paris: Atelier catholiques, 1844–55.

ABBREVIATIONS

MSA	*Melanchthons Werke in Auswahl [Studienausgabe]*. Edited by Robert Stupperich. 7 vols. Gütersloh, Germ.: Gerd Hohn, 1951–75.
NDT	Ferguson, Sinclair, et al., eds. *The New Dictionary of Theology*. Downers Grove: InterVarsity Press, 1988.
ODCC	Cross, F. L., and E. A. Livingstone, eds. *The Oxford Dictionary of the Christian Church*. 2nd ed. Oxford: Oxford University Press, 1997.
OHMLT	Kolb, Robert, et al., eds. *The Oxford Handbook of Martin Luther's Theology*. Oxford: Oxford University Press, 2014.
PE	*Works of Martin Luther*. 6 vols. 1915–43. Reprint, Grand Rapids: Baker, 1982.
RW	*Reformation Writings*. Translated by Bertram Lee Woolf. New York: Philosophical Library, 1953–.
Schaff	Schaff, Philip. *History of the Christian Church*. 8 vols. Grand Rapids: Eerdmans, 1987 (Reprint).
Schmid	Schmid, Heinrich. *The Doctrinal Theology of the Evangelical Lutheran Church*. 3rd ed. Revised and translated by Charles A. Hay and Henry E. Jacobs. Minneapolis: Augsburg, 1961.
Schmidt	Schmidt, Kürt Dietrich. "Luthers Lehre vom Heiligen Geist." In *Schrift und Beketnisstnis, Zeugnisse LutherischerTheologie*, edited by Volkmar Herntrich and Theodor Knolle, 145–64. Hamburg and Berlin: Im Furche-Verlag, 1950.
StA	Philipp Melanchthon. *Melanchthons Werke in Auswahl (Studiensgabe)*. 7 vols. Edited by Robert Stupperich. Gütersloh, Germ.: Bertelsmann, 1951–.
Suggestions	Kolb, Robert. Suggestions for preparing this Manuscript, 2003.
Tappert	*Book of Concord*. Translated and edited by Theodore Tappert et al. Philadelphia: Fortress, 1959.
TNC	Chemnitz, Martin. *The Two Natures in Christ*. Translated by J. A. O. Preus. Saint Louis: Concordia, 1971. (*De duabus naturis in Christo*. Leipzig: N.p., 1578.)

ABBREVIATIONS

Triglotta	Bente, Gerhard Frederick, ed. *Historical Introductions to the Symbolical Books of the Evangelical Lutheran Church.* Saint Louis: Concordia, 1921.
WA	*Luthers Werke: Kritische Gesamtausgabe (Schriften).* 83 vols. Weimar, Germ. N.p., 1883–.
WABr	*Luthers Werke: Kritische Gesamtausgabe: Briefwechsel.* 18 vols. Weimar, Germ. N.p., 1930–.
WADB	*Kritische Gesamtausgabe (Deutsche Bibel).* 15 vols. Weimar, Germ.: N.p., 1906–.
WATR	*Luthers Werke: Kritische Gesamtausgabe. Tischreden.* 6 vols. Weimar, Germ.: N.p., 1912–21.
ZPEB	Tenney, Merrill C., ed. *The Zondervan Pictorial Encyclopedia of the Bible.* 5 vols. Grand Rapids: Zondervan, 1977.

1

Introduction

Background—Purpose—Methodology

What did Martin Luther experience and teach about the Holy Spirit and how did his teachings extend to the writing of the *Formula of Concord*? This volume presents research intended to enhance Reformation studies of this question.

The research examines the work of eight leaders of the Lutheran Reformation from about 1517–77, a formative period for Lutheran theology: Martin Luther, Philip Melanchthon, Johann Brenz, Urbanus Rhegius, Johann Spangenberg, Jakob Andreae, Martin Chemnitz, and David Chytraeus. Their commonality regarding the Holy Spirit is assessed and their contributions to the *Formula of Concord* are noted.

These theologians represent the position of Lutheran theology in the *Augsburg Confession* (1530) sourced in the "true Catholic"[1] tradition according to the Holy Scripture in accordance with divine truth.[2] This position is described in the introduction to the *Book of Concord* (1580):

> A short confession was assembled [in 1530] out of the divine, apostolic, and prophetic Scripture. . . . Subsequently, many churches and schools professed this confession as the

---

1. "True Catholic" tradition is a term that reflects the position of this volume that the conservative reformers—primarily Lutheran, reformed, and Anglican—sought to return the church to the "true Catholic" track of historic biblical Christianity rather than to scrap the entire enterprise.

2. *BC*, 32, 8, 11.

contemporary Symbol of their faith ... [it contained] teaching that was well founded in the divine Scripture and briefly summarized in the time-honored, ancient Symbols; teaching that was recognized as that ancient, united consensus believed in by the universal, orthodox churches of Christ and fought for and reaffirmed against many heresies and errors.[3]

This was the stance of the Lutheran theologians of the period considered in this volume. Rather than invent a "new Christianity" they sought to draw from Scripture according to those who had gone before in the church and who authentically explicated the message of Scripture. Early writers of Lutheran theology considered this to be the true Catholic tradition.

Obviously, Luther (chapter 2), and Melanchthon (chapter 3), must be included in such a study since they worked together at Wittenberg from 1518 until 1546 to express their understanding of Christian theology through writing, teaching, organization, churchmanship, and prayer. Their massive record of foundational formulations of Lutheran theology is the basis for Lutheran theologians who followed them for centuries.

Of the remaining six, Brenz, Rhegius, and Spangenberg represent the diverse leadership of the church in three different German regions beyond Wittenberg (chapter 4). They were contemporary with Luther and Melanchthon and supported their Wittenberg Reformation work. From the generation after Luther and Melanchthon the following are included: Andreae, foremost representative of the Brenz school in Württemberg, and Chemnitz and Chytraeus, two of the foremost representatives of the Lutheran school of the Melanchthonians (chapter 5). These three were prominent leaders in theological and ecclesiastical affairs of that time and in the 1570's they and others combined and edited documents that ultimately became the *Formula of Concord* (1577).[4] These six churchmen encountered crises of debate, division, and sometimes reconciliation. They represent what could be called the mediating or emerging mainstream Lutheranism that culminated in the preparation and presentation of the *Formula of Concord* and the *Book of Concord* (1580). Fortunately, for this present study, sufficient materials from the works of these theologians and pastors are available.

Chapter 6 compares and contrasts the writings of the Reformers concerning the Holy Spirit and includes a summary of results.

---

3. *BC*, 5, 2–3.
4. Jungkuntz, *Formulators*, 82–83; *BC*, 8–9n17.

INTRODUCTION

The Word and the Holy Spirit

Lutheran theology is usually identified as a theology of the word.[5] Kolb and Arand state, "Luther's way of thinking is framed and permeated by his multifaceted understanding of the word of God."[6] Confusion can arise if this is interpreted as a separation of the work of the word from that of the Spirit. In his Ps 51:6 lecture Luther saw them connected in bringing, "A most certain persuasion or truth and an infallible light, by which God through the word and his Spirit fortifies, confirms, and assures our consciences."[7] One purpose of this volume is to confirm that in Lutheran theology the Word and the Spirit are inseparably intertwined in the Triune God's mission to reconcile his creation to himself. The Son (Word) and the Spirit have different functions but are interrelated in the outworking of God's overall plan of salvation and sanctification. The gospels declare this interrelationship of Word and Spirit, "And Jesus, full of the Holy Spirit, returned from the Jordan and was led by the Spirit in the wilderness." Immediately after his baptism the Spirit led Jesus to the temptation and then on to his next encounters, "And Jesus returned in the power of the Spirit to Galilee, and a report about him went out through all the surrounding country." (Luke 4:1, 14). In the parallel passages, Matt 4 and Mark 1:9–45, his ministry in the power of the Spirit includes many miracles of healings and exorcisms.

The *Augsburg Confession* (III, V, and VI)[8] defines the gospel: God's incarnate Son suffered and died for the sins of humankind, descended to hell, and ascended into heaven to rule forever. Through the public office of the word, the church proclaims this message through preaching and the administration of the sacraments. By these means the Spirit brings life and produces faith. All who hear and believe will be forgiven and receive eternal life. Kolb has suggested that the Holy Spirit is in charge of all three forms of the word—oral, written, and sacramental—the basis for the theology of the means of grace.[9]

Several twentieth-century theologians point to Luther's and Lutherans' views that the word of God and the Holy Spirit are inseparably related.

Hermann Sasse, commenting on 1 Cor 2:6–10, noted that "Luther's understanding of Scripture can be understood only if one remembers this

---

5. Althaus, *Theology*, 20n1 citing Luther on Ps 51:6, "Every word of Scripture comes from the revealed God. We are able to grasp him in a specific place to which he is bound by his words." *LW* 12:352.

6. Kolb and Arand. *Genius of Luther's Theology*, 130.

7. *LW* 12:352.

8. *BC*, 38–41.

9. Kolb, *Manuscript Suggestion #3*.

function of the Spirit, that God has revealed the hidden things to us through the Spirit." "For the Spirit searches everything, even the depths of God (verse 10)." The external word—Scripture and preaching—"is the means through which the Spirit imparts divine revelation."[10] Luther's insight describes how, as Sasse said, "The Spirit and the word always belong together."[11] Sasse summarized his thoughts on Luther's *Smalcald Articles*:

> God speaks to man His word of revelation only in the "external word" that comprises the Scripture and the oral proclamation of the content of Holy Scripture. These two forms of the word always go together . . . they belong together because in both the Holy Spirit communicates to us in Jesus Christ the Savior, who is the content of the Word.[12]

The following twentieth-century writers echo Sasse's interpretation. *Regin Prenter* described the only road to God for the church confessing faith in the Triune God, is to come to him through the word and the Spirit. The Spirit calls and gathers believers into the fellowship of faith in Christ for salvation. Jesus Christ is the Word, present in the Word of baptism, of the Lord's Supper, and of preaching. The Spirit leads us to this Word and binds us to every one of the faithful and to the Word.[13] In *Spiritus Creator*, Prenter points to Luther's 1519 Galatians commentary in which Luther maintains that the word is the means of the Holy Spirit; the Spirit's presence in the word brings understanding to hearers and the divine reality of life in Jesus Christ. The word without the Spirit is lifeless legalism, but the inner Spirit outwardly manifests divine revelation through the external word.[14]

Paul Althaus presented Luther's idea that God is found only as the divine nature is clothed in Scripture and revealed in Jesus Christ. The external word comprises both the written word and the spoken word. The Holy Spirit works through the external word to bring the inner word whereby God speaks his truths to our hearts. Therefore, the word and the Spirit are intimately connected and the Spirit comes only when preceded by the external word.[15] In the *Smalcald Articles* Luther insisted on the external word preceding the presence of the Holy Spirit.[16]

10. Sasse, "Luther and the Word of God," 76.
11. Sasse, "Luther and the Word of God," 77. Sasse also refers to Luther's comments in *Smalcald Articles* (VIII, 3–6, 9) on this topic.
12. Sasse, "Luther and the Word of God," 78.
13. Prenter, *Word and the Spirit*, 14–15.
14. Prenter, *Spiritus Creator*, 101–2; LW 27:249; WA 2:509, 13 (Gal 3:2–3).
15. Althaus, *Theology*, 35; LW 12:312–13; WA 40^{II}:329–30 (Ps 51:1 [1532]).
16. BC, 322–23 (*Smalcald Articles* [1537], III, [8], 3, 10–11).

Bernard Lohse wrote that "For Luther 'the human word itself becomes bearer of the divine Spirit,' indeed, is 'actually wrapped in the swaddling cloth of the human word.'"[17]

Oswald Bayer, under the heading of "Where the word is, there is the church," identifies Luther's foundational principal of the priority of the word. However, he links the external word of Scripture and the gospel to the Spirit who brings salvation through the external word.[18] Bayer notes that the marks of the church (*notae ecclesiae*)—preaching, baptism, and the supper (Luther also called them *Heiltümer*)—are expressions of the external word[19] through which the Holy Spirit works faith, salvation, and sanctification.[20] Regarding baptism, Bayer interprets Luther to say, "Faith does not make the sacrament, but the Holy Spirit creates faith by use of the sacrament. All who desire forgiveness of their guilt are admitted to the sacrament, not only those who have achieved a certain level of confidence."[21]

These twentieth-century writers confirm the Lutheran understanding that the "efficacy of the means of grace" is the result of the Holy Spirit working in the church through the word in preaching and in administration of the sacraments.

The *Locus* Method[22]

Before the Lutheran Reformation emerged in the early sixteenth century, the *Locus* method was an established academic technique used by medieval scholars to organize and describe philosophical and theological principles. At the beginning of the Reformation Luther's close associate, Philip Melanchthon, began to write systematically following the *loci communes*[23] method he learned at Heidelberg University. *Loci communes*, or *common places*, are the "collection of basic scriptural *loci* and their interpretations into an ordered body of Christian doctrine." His purposes for his readers:

17. Lohse, *Luther's Theology*, 191, citing Meinhold, *Luthers Sprachphilosophie*, 56.
18. Bayer, *Luther's Theology*, 255.
19. Bayer, *Luther's Theology*, 259–63.
20. Bayer, *Luther's Theology*, 263–64.
21. Bayer, *Luther's Theology*, 265.
22. Melanchthon was not consistent in numbering the *loci* in his different editions from 1521 to 1555. Chemnitz, in his *Loci Theologici* (1554–84), used numbering different from any of Melanchthon's, though he was commenting on the successive texts of Melanchthon's 1543 *Loci*. Therefore this brief discussion numbers the elements of the *loci* pertaining to the Holy Spirit as they appear and follows neither Melanchthon nor Chemnitz.
23. Muller, *Dictionary*, 179.

1. To know and to understand the primary teachings of Scripture.
2. To understand how biblical teachings were irreconcilable with the Aristotelianism taught in the scholastic theology of Roman Catholicism.[24]

It must be noted, however, that Melanchthon, Luther, and their followers continually taught the biblical faith that they maintained was the "true Catholic"[25] tradition of the church. This was represented in the *Loci Theologici* (1591) of Martin Chemnitz who, as an early historical theologian, provided comprehensive backup to show the biblical theology of the fathers of the church through history, as well as the discussions of heresies, controversies, councils, *et cetera*.

Robert Preus used Hyperius's *De Theologo, seu de Ratione Studii Theologici Libris IIII* to show the criteria for the use of the *loci* method in dogmatics:

> Book III Hyperius ... points out that the *loci communes* method is simply thematic treatment of a subject, whether in law, natural science, or theology. Typical *loci* that could be considered in theology are Scripture, God, Trinity, Creation, angels, man, the church, the Fall, etc. ... Such *loci* Hyperius calls the rudiments and general principles of theology ... and unless these are placed and handled in their proper order, "you will never gain certainty concerning the questions proposed in theology."[26]

Melanchthon's 1521 *loci communes* was the first work of Lutheran systematic theology and is sometimes called the first Protestant dogmatic or apologetic writing. In this first *loci*, Melanchthon laid out the fundamentals of traditional Christian theology advocated by the theologians of Wittenberg. Since Luther did not write as systematically as Melanchthon, Melanchthon's students and succeeding generations of scholars continued the *loci* method as the prevailing way to organize Lutheran theology through the seventeenth century.[27]

Writing *loci* requires knowledge of the contents of Scripture as well as the works of other commentators, fathers of the church, and writers of theology and philosophy. Thus the traditional Lutheran *locus* of the Holy

---

24. *MLC21*, 18–19.

25. See footnote 1 on "true Catholic" above.

26. Preus, *Post-Reformation Lutheranism*, 1:86–87. For a brief summary of Hyperius's life and work see Achelis, "Hyperius," 432–33.

27. Preus, *Post-Reformation Lutheranis*, 1:32, 46–53, 77–83, 86–87, 90–98, 107–9, 423–25. Preus points to the *loci* of Hypeiras (1556), Chemnitz (1591), Matthias Hafenfeffer (1603), Leonard Hutter (1619), with their application reaching its peak in John Gerhard's *Loci Theologici* (1622).

Spirit provides some guidance for research on the theologians whose work is analyzed and presented in this volume.

This volume references several editions of Melanchthon's *loci*, from the beginning of the period of this study to the *Loci Theologici* of his student, Martin Chemnitz, who worked at the end of the period. Also included are notes from Luther's writing that he may have contributed to a *loci* (had he written one).[28] These works of Luther, Melanchthon, and Chemnitz are representative of their times and are reasonably accessible to the reader for further reference.

Melanchthon's and Chemnitz's *loci* cover topics concerning the Holy Spirit that pertain to understanding of the Triune God, of the Spirit's functions according to Melanchthon's identification of the Holy Spirit as "the living will of God,"[29] and of the Holy Spirit's role in bringing God's grace to believers through the means of the word and the sacraments.

The *Locus* of the Person of the Holy Spirit

When describing the Holy Spirit, Lutheran dogmaticians emphasize that the Holy Spirit is the Third Divine Person of the Trinitarian Godhead. The Spirit fully and equally shares in the one divine substance—*homoousia*—of God while having particular functions that are distinguished from those of the Father and of the Son.[30] In his 1521 *Loci* Melanchthon did not have a *locus* entitled "God," "The Triune God," or "The Holy Spirit." He felt that "It is better to adore the mysteries of Deity than to explain them,"[31] that is, the "incomprehensible" triune nature of God and his work in creation.

---

28. Kolb, *Prophet, Teacher, and Hero*, 195–223. In chapter 8, "The Loci Communes Lutheri, *Luther Systemized for Teaching the Faith*," Kolb identifies the post-Luther writers who assembled the topics of his writing in the *loci* method developed by Melanchthon. The writers of the first complete *Loci* of Luther's works included Johannes Corvinus (1564) and Timotheus Kirchner (1564–68) who gathered materials from Luther's works and passed them along according to Melanchthon's *Loci* method of organization. So the works of Luther were preserved for subsequent generations (197). Kolb describes the variety of *Loci Communes Lutheri* of those who followed Corvinus and Kirchner for more than a hundred years.

29. See discussion in the next section.

30. Althaus, *Theology*, 8–9. Althaus notes that while Luther was committed to the substance of the Trinitarian concepts of the early fathers he was not bound to use their terminologies provided that he held to concepts derived by the councils from Scripture. WA 39^{II}:305; WA 8:117; LW 32:244.

31. CR21, 83 (MLC21, 21), "*Mysteria divinitatis rectius adoraverimus, quam vestigaverimus.*"

However, in 1521 he did describe the Spirit-human relationship in Eden after the creation, and then after the fall:

> When God Almighty had created man without sin, he was near him through his Spirit, who stirred him to pursue the right. The same Spirit would have guided all the posterity of Adam if Adam had not fallen. Now, after Adam fell, God opposed man so that the Spirit of God was not with him as a leader.[32]

After redemption the relationship of God with humans was restored and changed:

> Those who have been renewed by the Spirit of Christ now conform voluntarily even without the law to what the law used to command. The law is the will of God; the Holy Spirit is nothing else than the living will of God and its being in action.[33]

Thus Melanchthon, in 1521, defined what could be called "the Lutheran *locus* of the Triune God" by a tightly knit view of the Trinity with each person—Father, Son, and Spirit—sharing in the divine essence. To receive one of the persons is to receive the fullness of God—Father, Son, and Holy Spirit. The subtopics of the Lutheran *loci* include this idea in all their elements.

In the remaining two major revisions of his *loci* (in Latin, 1535 and 1543, and several German translations of the three from 1521–55)[34] Melanchthon extensively expanded his presentation of God in *Locus I*, in which he discussed the aspects of God and his revelation: The three persons, eternal Father, eternal Son, and eternal Holy Spirit, are one united divine being. God is one with three distinct eternal persons participating in the same divine substance. Each unique person has his own distinctive functions and yet they are interrelated. The Holy Spirit, sharing in the divine essence of the Godhead, proceeds from the Father and the Son. As the "living will of God," the Holy Spirit is the dynamic power of God that is the interface between God and his creation, including all of humanity, to set things in motion in the minds and lives of those faithful ones who are heirs of eternal life.[35] In

---

32. CR21, 97, 14–21 (*MLC21*, 31), "*Deus Opt. Max. cum condidisset hominem sine peccato, aderat ei per spiritum suum, qui hominem ad recta inflammaret. Idem spiritus gubernaturus erat omnem Adae posteritatem, nisi lapsus fuisset Adam. Iam posteaquam deliquit Adam, aversatus est deus hominem, ut non adsit ei gubernator dei spiritus.*"

33. CR21, 195 (*MLC21*, 123) "*Qui spiritu Christi innovate sunt, ii iam sua sponte, etiam non praeeunte lege, feruntur ad ea quae lex iubebat. Voluntas dei lex est. Nec aliud spiritus sanctus est, nisi viva dei voluntas, et agitation*" (1521 *Loci*).

34. CR22, 11–44 (*MLC43*, 7–8).

35. CR21, 614 (*MLC43*, 21).

all his *loci* versions from 1521 to 1555 Melanchthon consistently presented the same teaching concerning the Holy Spirit.

Martin Chemnitz, in his *Locus III*, "The Person of the Holy Spirit," defined the Holy Spirit based on the trinitarian passages of the Old Testament, the New Testament, and the fathers of the church, and he discussed the trinitarian disputes concerning the divinity and personhood of the Holy Spirit. The Spirit refers to the moving power and winds of God—*ruach*—that can also mean inner life, messengers, emotions, etc. Chemnitz noted the different names of the Holy Spirit that relate his being and his work to the Triune God. In agreement with Luther and Melanchthon, Chemnitz emphasized the understanding of Western Christianity of the eternal procession of the Holy Spirit from the Father and the Son (*filioque*).[36]

The *Locus* of the Work of the Holy Spirit

In his *Locus III*, "The Person of the Holy Spirit," Chemnitz provided charts to show the work of the Holy Spirit by outlining the Spirit's benefits and activities.[37] Chemnitz showed how the Holy Spirit is involved with the creation, humankind, the church, and individual Christians. The Spirit works through creation, preservation, and his gifts and fruit to bring sinners to conviction, repentance, faith, and salvation, and he preserves the whole church through the word and sacraments. In this *locus* Chemnitz outlined how the Holy Spirit is the active person of the Triune God who brings about the action of the remaining *loci* of his *Loci Theologici*.

In his 1543 *Loci*, Melanchthon cited Ps 33:6 to describe how, in creation, the Spirit of God, the breath of his mouth, made the powers of the heavens.[38] Chemnitz maintained that "Creation is an action of . . . the undivided Trinity . . . by which the Father, together with the coeternal Son and the coeternal Holy Spirit, established all things . . . out of nothing," thus holding that the Holy Spirit was acting in the creation according to Gen 1:2; Pss 33:6; and 104:30.[39]

---

36. *CLTP* 1:133–47.
37. *CLTP* 1:147, 148–49.
38. *MLC43*, 33.
39. *CLTP* 1:156–57.

Luther's Theology of the Cross
(*Theologia Crucis*)

Luther's theology of the cross, an important theological topic influencing this research, keys on Christ's call for believers to take up their crosses and follow him as he goes to his cross (Matt 16:24–26, Mark 8:34–35), and on Paul's discussion of the wisdom of the world and the foolishness of God (1 Cor 1–2). This way of faith is possible only by the creative companionship, guidance, power, and enabling of the Holy Spirit.

"The Cross Alone Is Our Theology"
(*Crux sola est nostra theologia*)

Gerhard Forde noted "that the cross *is* 'theo-logy,' the word of the cross on the attack." "The word of the cross kills and makes alive. It crucifies the old being in anticipation of the resurrection of the new."[40] Therefore, as Luther declared, "The cross alone is our theology,"[41] and it informs and influences all his work. Alister McGrath agrees, saying that *Operationes in Psalmos* (Luther's *Commentary on Psalms 1–22* [1518–21]) is permeated with *theologia crucis*, "the hallmark of the work (in *Operationes*)." McGrath concludes:

> Far from representing a "pre-reformation" element in Luther's thought (contra O. Ritschl[42]), the *theologia crucis* encapsulates the very essence of his "reformation" thought.[43]

Robert Kolb rejects the idea of some theologians that Luther's theology under the cross is obsolete and instead, declares its application for all eras:

> Luther's theology of the cross reproduces for every age the biblical message regarding who God is and what he does—and regarding the characteristics his human creatures have—beneath the superficial fluctuations of history and culture. The theology of the cross does more than address the fleeting problems of and miseries of one age. It refines the Christian's focus on God and on what it means to be human.[44]

---

40. Forde, *Theologian of the Cross*, 3.
41. Forde, *Theologian of the Cross*, 3; WA 5:176, 32. "*Crux sola est nostra theologia, Operationes in Psalmos*" (1519–21).
42. Ritschl, *Dogmengeschichte des Protestantismus*, 40–84.
43. McGrath, *Theology of the Cross*, 178.
44. Kolb, "Theology of the Cross," 445.

INTRODUCTION

Walter von Loewenich argued that *theologia crucis* is "a persistent, abiding principle in Luther's theology. This thesis (of Loewenich's study) has . . . nowhere been seriously challenged in the literature to date (1954)."[45]

Two Kinds of Theology—Theology of Glory, Theology of the Cross

While the cross of Christ is primary, the crosses believers must take up to follow Christ are also important for Luther. Forde noted that because we are at odds with God, Christ entered into our suffering and death through his own suffering and death. As a result, he suffered and died alone, apart from God.[46] Hopeless in our sin, it is also true that we passively suffer the working of God, as he opposes the claims we may make based on the pretensions of our good works in a theology of glory.[47]

Therefore, Forde maintained,

> There are . . . only two types of theology, glory theology and cross theology. "The theology of glory" is a catchall for virtually all theologies and religions. The cross sets itself apart from and over against all of these.[48]

With regard to Luther's Heidelberg Disputation, Forde noted,

> The argument proceeds by constantly setting the way of glory over against the way of the cross. In every instance all loop holes are closed so that the believer will in the end simply be cast on that creative love of God, which makes the object of its love out of the nothing to which the sinner has been reduced.[49]

McGrath contrasts the theology of the cross with the theology of glory regarding the revelation of God:

> This revelation is to be recognized in the sufferings and the cross of Christ, rather than in human moral activity or the created order (i.e., the theology of glory). . . . This . . . is a matter of faith.[50]

---

45. Loewenich, *Theology of the Cross*, 219.
46. Forde, *Theologian of the Cross*, viii–ix.
47. Forde, *Theologian of the Cross*, 2.
48. Forde, *Theologian of the Cross*, 2.
49. Forde, *Theologian of the Cross*, 12.
50. McGrath, *Theology of the Cross*, 150.

Forde's analysis of the Heidelberg Disputation shows how the foolishness of preaching the cross overcomes even the wisdom of the theologians of glory to save them.[51]

Theology of Glory

THE GLORY STORY

Human souls who originally lived in fellowship with God in glory are trapped in bodies of sinful flesh. They can be restored to glory by moral and intellectual means of works, strength, wisdom, and goodness that claim to see the invisible things of God in the visible things of creation, works, and philosophy. Therefore the return of the lost souls comes through *gnosis*, an intellectual awakening of the soul to its intended place of glory while the desires of the flesh are cast aside as evil encumbrances. In this view, the cross of Christ makes reparation for sin and separation from God but there is no taking up one's cross by the restored sinners. Therefore, the sinners who have not endured the suffering of their own crosses do not know Christ and do not know God, contrary to what Christ has promised "He who has seen me has seen the Father."[52]

THE THEOLOGIAN OF GLORY

Theologians of glory claim that one can know God by looking through the created world and the acts of God to see "the invisible realm of glory behind it." This means there is a glory road to God, "a way of law, which the fallen creature can traverse by willing and working and thus gain the necessary merit eventually to arrive at glory."[53] The theologian of glory fits the cross into a system of works to alleviate failures along the glory road. He misreads reality and calls evil good and good evil. Works are good and suffering is evil. God is not really causally involved but merely "good."

---

51. Forde, *Theologian of the Cross*, 2–3.

52. Forde, *Theologian of the Cross*, 5–9; LW 31:53 (*Heidelberg Disputation*), Theses 21–23 (1518).

53. Forde, *Theologian of the Cross*, 12.

INTRODUCTION

The Theology of the Cross

THE CROSS STORY

The cross story starts with Christ's obedience to the will of the Father to take on our humanity and to assume our sin. Luther, in *A Meditation on Christ's Passion*, reminds us that the nails that pierced Christ's hands should have pierced ours. The horror of his execution is our horror because we have caused it for him. All of humankind, by their sin, have killed and crucified God's Son.[54] Luther explained the purpose:

> The real and true work of Christ's passion is to make man conformable to Christ, so that man's conscience is tormented by his sins in like measure as Christ was pitiably tormented in body and soul for our sins.[55]

The cross draws us into its story so we are part of the story (moving from Matt 16:24–25 to Rom 6:3–11 and Gal 2:20). We are crucified with Jesus. The cross has become our story.[56] Forde both warned and gave hope:

> Unless the cross story does claim us and become our story, we shall not escape the clutches of the glory story. It is not a matter of choice. . . . One of the decisive questions in the battle between a theology of glory and a theology of the cross will always be the question of the human will. A theology of glory always leaves the will in control. It must make its theology attractive to the supposed "free will." A theology of the cross assumes that the will is bound and must be set free. The cross story does that.[57]

The human will is set aside by the working of God's Spirit in our lives through his love. The New Testament consistently teaches that God is love (*agape*) that is, giving self-sacrificially to his creation even unto death on the cross. Jesus calls us to follow him in such love. As we follow him we go through repentance (change of mind and attitude) to give ourselves to him and to those whom he gives us to love. This entails the suffering of self-denial and the death of the self-serving demands of our wills. This is the cross of self-sacrificing love Christians are called to bear. In our crosses Jesus is with us and draws us into the fellowship of love with the Triune God. We see God (who is love) in the love expressed in Jesus through the

---

54. *LW* 42:9–10.
55. *LW* 42:9–10 (*A Meditation of Christ's Passion*, 1519).
56. Forde, *Theologian of the Cross*, 7.
57. Forde, *Theologian of the Cross*, 9.

suffering and death of his cross. We see God through our own crosses as we live out his call on our lives to follow him.

The cross story only becomes our story as we hear the word of Christ proclaimed and the Holy Spirit applies it into our hearts to bring us to repentance and faith. The Holy Spirit works the obedience of faith in us to follow the call of Christ to take up our crosses daily to follow him in trusting faith. Here we see how Luther's understanding of the cross is at the heart of understanding the reality of the Holy Spirit and his work. This theological perspective of the cross provides the hermeneutic to grasp Luther's teaching of the intertwining of the word and the Spirit in God's work to reconcile his creation with himself.

The Theologian of the Cross

Theologians of the cross view life realistically as seen in the cross, the only thing that matters. "Faith means to live *in* the Christ of the story (of the cross)"; therefore they look on everything that happens in life's realities "through suffering and the cross."[58] All circumstances are under God's control and he resolves the problem of his creation's rebellion and sin in Christ's cross and resurrection. Believers live in Christ and will be raised with him. Therefore, for theologians of the cross, the only place to find God and the things of God is in the cross story.[59] In the *Heidelberg Disputation*, a thoroughgoing exposition and refutation of the theology of glory, Luther, as a theologian of the cross, expressed his cross-ward focus of life in God.[60] A passage in Luther's *Operationes in Psalmos* puts these ideas in perspective:

> By the kingdom, the rule, or the dominion of his humanity, or as the Apostle calls it, of his "flesh," which is carried on in the kingdom of faith, he renders us deformed and crucifies us, making us, from having been securely satisfied proud gods, miserable and wretched sinners. For as, in our old Adam, we proudly ascend in self-opinion, so as to imagine ourselves to be like God himself; therefore he descends into our likeness, that he may bring us back to the true knowledge of ourselves. All this is done by his incarnation, that is, in the kingdom faith in which the cross of Christ rules, which casts down all that divinity that we perversely aspired to in our imaginations and brings

---

58. Forde, *Theologian of the Cross*, 13, referring to *LW* 31:52–53, *Heidelberg Disputation*, Thesis 20.
59. Forde, *Theologian of the Cross*, 14.
60. Forde, *Theologian of the Cross*, 14.

back the true sense of our humanity and of the contemptible infirmity of our flesh which we had as perversely left behind.[61]

Life in the Spirit under the Cross

As this volume intends to demonstrate, Luther and his followers declared that the faith of God's kingdom is only possible when the Holy Spirit works God's reality through word and sacrament to bring people to repentance and trust in the truth of God in Christ—suffering, crucified, and resurrected—reconciling the world to himself. And as the Creator breathed his breath of life into his new human creatures that they might live unto him (Gen 2:7), he breathes the breath of his Holy Spirit into his redeemed, resurrected, and restored human creatures that they might live unto him (Acts 2:38; Rom 8:11).

As believers daily hear the word of Christ, the Spirit enables them to renew their repentance and walk of faith and trust in the powerful promises of God's word.[62] This is what it means to be a disciple of Christ. Kolb summarizes Luther's concept of the realization of God's original intention for humankind to live in trust:

> Luther insisted that trust alone—total dependence and reliance on God and what he promises in his incarnation and in Scripture—is the center of life . . . of genuine human living. To recognize trust as the core of our humanity is to perceive the true form of being human as God created his human creature. . . . [It is] not trust in self . . . God has designed life to center upon trust in him.[63]

---

61. Forde, *Theologian of the Cross*, 14; WA 5:128, 36–129.4. "*Humanitatis seu (ut Apostolus loquitur) carnis regno, quod in fide agitur, nos sibi conformes facit et crucifigit, faciens ex infoelicibus et superbis diis homines veros, idest miseros et peccatores. Quia enim ascendimus in Adam ad similitudinem dei, ideo descendit ille in similitudinem nostrum, ut reduceret nos ad nostri cognitionem. Atque hoc agitur sacramento incarnationis. Hoc est regnum fidei, in quo Crux Christi dominator, divinitatem perverse petitam deiiciens et humanitate carnisque contemptam infirmitatem perverse desertam revocans*"; cf. Luther, *Luther's Commentary*, 1:204.

62. Kolb, "Theology of the Cross," 450.

63. Kolb, "Theology of the Cross," 450.

Post-Reformation Issues Regarding the Theology of the Cross

Mark Mattes notes, "Post-Reformation Lutheran theology separated Luther's theology of the cross from his theology of the word and in the process lost the theology of the cross."[64] To lose Luther's theology of the cross is to lose an essential aspect of his theology of the Holy Spirit and of his overall theology.

Nineteenth-century philosophers, such as G. W. F. Hegel (1770–1831), attempting to reestablish the theology of the cross, transformed it into a metaphysic that Oswald Bayer dismissed as a "natural theology of the cross,"[65]

The suffering and horror of two World Wars caused German theologians (some imprisoned and/or executed for their faith) to search for an answer to what seemed like abandonment by God. In his final writing shortly before his execution, Karl Goerdeler despaired, "And yet through Christ I am still looking for the merciful God. I have not yet found him. O Christ, where is truth? Where is there any consolation?"[66]

The repeated failure of the optimism of liberal Protestant theology could not address the central question posed by Goerdeler. Therefore, Luther's theology of the cross, including the crucified and hidden God, "assumed a new relevance and urgency."[67] McGrath points to Jürgen Moltmann's assessment:

> The theology of the cross . . . is the basic theme of my theological thought . . . [since] my first . . . questions concerning Christian faith and theology in real life, as a prisoner of war behind barbed wire. . . . Shattered and broken, the survivors of my generation were then returning from camps and hospitals to the lecture room. A theology which did not speak of God in terms of the abandoned and crucified one would not have got through to us then.[68]

After the war, the desperate need for understanding suffering drove theologians back to Luther's theology of the cross. "Rarely, if ever, has

---

64. S.v. Mattes, "Theology of the Cross," in *DLLT*, 736.
65. S.v. Mattes, "Theology of the Cross," in *DLLT*, 736.
66. McGrath, *Theology of the Cross*, 179–80.
67. McGrath, *Theology of the Cross*, 180.
68. McGrath, *Theology of the Cross*, 180, citing Moltmann, *Der gekreuzigte Gott*, 7.

a sixteenth century idea found such a powerful response in twentieth-century man."[69]

Mattes concludes:

> Only in the twentieth Century has Luther's theology of the cross begun to be fully articulated by Lutherans and others. This is due in part to the renewal in Luther studies begun in the late nineteenth Century but also especially to the study of Walter von Loewenich.... Some theologians have returned to a theology of the cross in recognition of God's judgment on human pride but also in confident trust in God's life-giving word of promise and renewal.[70]

This volume follows a host of nineteenth- and twentieth-century scholars searching out Luther's theology of the cross, seeking to understand how Luther and Lutheran theologians to the Formula of Concord understood the person and work of the Holy Spirit.

Prominent Themes

This volume investigates the early determinative period of Lutheran theology, from Luther to the *Formula of Concord*, and demonstrates how Lutheran theologians of that period viewed the person and the work of the Holy Spirit. First it shows that:

1. Contrary to the impression frequently given in the extant scholarship, the Holy Spirit is prominent in Martin Luther's theology.

2. In Luther's theology, the means of the Holy Spirit are the word of God—the Holy Scriptures—and the sacraments.

3. Luther's theology is an expression of the reality of his own release from his terror of the wrath of God, his salvation in Christ, and his personal experience of the inner testimony of the Holy Spirit.

Secondly, although the theological formulations of Luther's followers to the *Formula of Concord* may differ from his in form, or are more systematized, or address unique issues, the Holy Spirit was also prominent in their theologies demonstrating agreement and continuity with Luther's theology.

---

69. McGrath, *Theology of the Cross*, 180.
70. Mattes, "Theology of the Cross," in *DLLT*, 736–37.

Research Method

Luther's theology is analyzed and informed by the concepts discussed in this chapter: the dynamic of the word and the Spirit, the *loci* of the Holy Spirit, and the theology of the cross. The results are assembled relative to the following principle topics: the person and work of the Holy Spirit, the means of the Holy Spirit, the inner testimony of the Holy Spirit, the Holy Spirit's impact on the church and its ministry, and the Christians' experience of new life in the Spirit.

The results of the analysis of Luther's theology are used as a grid to compare the work of his contemporaries and of later theologians to demonstrate consensus among Luther and his followers on the theology of the Holy Spirit. Extensive block citations are used throughout this work. The purpose is to allow the theologians and historians to "speak for themselves."

2

Martin Luther's Theology of the Holy Spirit

"Pigtails on the Pillow"

Introduction–Luther's Theology of Reality

As quite a surprise to himself and to almost everyone else, Martin Luther married Katherine von Bora on June 27, 1525. Married life was a shock of reality to Luther.

> There is a lot to get used to in the first year of marriage. One wakes up in the morning and finds a pair of pigtails on the pillow, which were not there before.[1]

This statement generally expresses the mood of Luther's theology. His is a theology of reality. Bernard Lohse maintained that Luther drew his practice of theology from the reality of his own walk with God,

> Luther was not only able to speak of God in uncommonly lively fashion but quite clearly had his own, deep experience of God. What is unique about his speaking of God is that it is never theoretical. It is always clear that where God is concerned we have to do with the Lord of the world and history, thus of our own life. There is thus an incomparable concreteness and directness about Luther's speaking of God. There is no mere doctrine of God, but a statement of faith in ever-new variations to the effect

---

1. Bainton, *Here I Stand*, 290.

that God calls to life, that he judges and pardons his creatures, and takes them again to himself."[2]

Luther expressed his theology of reality in day-to-day events in the Christian life. When the baby is immersed into the water of baptism, he comes out a new creature—a real child of God, born from above.[3] When he breathes in that first gasp out of the water he breathes in the Holy Spirit who really dwells within him. When we receive the bread and wine in the Lord's Supper, the whole Jesus Christ—God and man—is truly present in his flesh and blood in and under the bread and wine, just as when Luther awoke in the morning to find pigtails on the pillow belonging to a real flesh and blood Katie.

Luther's theology of the Holy Spirit flowed from the Reformation Principles: justification by faith (*sola fide*), authority of Scripture (*sola scriptura*), unmerited grace (*sola gratia*), and the priesthood of believers, demonstrating positions that comprise the main thrusts of this volume:

1. The reality of the Holy Spirit pervades Luther's theology as expressed in his theology of the cross.

2. Luther maintained that the Holy Spirit works through the physical means of word and sacrament.

3. Luther's theology expressed his personal experiences of conviction of sin, of forgiveness, and of his assurance that he was rescued by faith in Christ—the inner testimony of the Holy Spirit.

In his explanation to the third article of the Apostles' Creed, Luther declared the reality of the work of the Holy Spirit:

> I believe that by my own understanding or strength I cannot believe in Jesus Christ, my Lord, or come to him, but instead the Holy Spirit has called me through the gospel, enlightened

---

2. Lohse, *Theology*, 209.

3. *PE* 1:56, "Baptism (1519)." Luther preferred the form of baptismal immersion, including infants, and since this was the generally accepted form for the church of his time, he was likely immersed as an infant when he was baptized on Saint Martin's Day, 11 November 1483, the day following his birth. Schwiebert, *Luther and His Times*, 104. Luther opens the treatise (56): "Baptism [German, die Taufe, Gk. baptismos, Lat. mersio] . . . means to plunge something entirely into the water, so that the water closes over it. And although in many places it is the custom no longer to thrust and plunge into the font of baptism, but only to pour the baptismal water upon them out of the font, nevertheless the former is what should be done; and it would be right according to the meaning of the word Taufe, that the child, or whoever is baptised is sunk deep into the water. This usage is also demanded by the significance of baptism . . . that the old man and sinful birth of flesh and blood are to be wholly drowned by the grace of God."

me with his gifts, made me holy and kept me in the true faith, just as he calls, gathers, enlightens, and makes holy the whole Christian Church on earth and keeps it with Jesus Christ in the one common, true faith. Daily in this Christian church, the Holy Spirit abundantly forgives all sins—mine and those of all believers. On the Last Day, the Holy Spirit will raise me and all the dead and will give to me and all believers in Christ eternal life. This is most certainly true.[4]

Luther's experience of the power of the person and the work of the Holy Spirit determined his theology. Like the reality of Katie's pigtails on the pillow, the Holy Spirit in Luther's understanding evokes a theology of reality. Not merely ideas, theories, or remembrances of past events, the matters proclaimed and the actions taken portray events that actually happen.

In his article "Luther on the the Holy Spirit and His Use of God's Word," Jeffrey Silcock notes some key milestones in research of Luther's opinion of the Holy Spirit from the 1890's to the present. In his 1898 dissertation, *Die Auschauung vom heiligen Geiste bei Luther* (*Luther's View of the Holy Spirit*), Rudolf Otto (1869–1937), one of the most prominent German Lutheran theologians of the early twentieth century, concluded that the Holy Spirit had little significance in Luther's theology. Otto maintained that Luther chose a psychological understanding of the Spirit and his work. Otto said, however, that Luther did hold to the church's accepted doctrine of the Holy Spirit as the third person of the Trinity.[5] A Luther scholar contemporary with Otto, Erich Seeburg (1888–1945), simply stated Luther's pneumatology, as "The eternal is present in the finite."[6]

In *Spiritus Creator* (English 1953), Regin Prenter produced the twentieth century's foremost presentation of Luther's theology of the Holy Spirit. Silcock notes, "His [Prenter's] emphasis on Luther's pneumatic realism is a necessary corrective to the earlier research of Otto and Seeberg, which saw Luther's thought very much in line with the psychological and moral spiritualism of the modern age."[7]

Prenter declared,

> The concept of the Holy Spirit completely dominates Luther's theology. In every decisive matter, whether it be the study of Luther's doctrine of justification, of his doctrine of the sacraments,

---

4. Luther, *Small Catechism*, 8.
5. Silcock, "Luther on the Holy Spirit," 294–95.
6. Seeberg, *Theologie Luthers*, 52–53.
7. Silcock, "Luther on the Holy Spirit," 295.

of his ethics, or of any other fundamental teaching, we are forced to take into consideration this concept of the Holy Spirit.[8]

While Prenter opened his work on Luther and the Spirit with the above cited statement, he also commented that some nineteenth-century scholarship, such as Rudolf Otto, have reached a "rather disappointing conclusion" that Luther's doctrine of the Spirit is traditional, has "no organic place" in his theology, and is not worth any additional work.[9] Much more than having "no organic place" with Luther, Prenter believed that while Luther had no systematic "doctrine" of the Holy Spirit, he experienced a powerful living testimony of the Spirit.

> We have come to a conclusion . . . diametrically opposed to that of Rudolf Otto. Without the idea of the Holy Spirit, all Luther's thoughts . . . are changed to a great ideology under the law. For only the real presence of the Spirit . . . leads from the domain of the law into that of the gospel.[10]

Larry Christenson called Luther's explanation of the Third Article of the Apostle's Creed the "Lutheran Magna Carta" of church renewal that brings Christians to radical dependence on the Holy Spirit under Christ[11]—from law to gospel!

Bernard Lohse (in 1995/1999) noted that Prenters's work "is still a foundational investigation."[12] Prenter's work finds application in Lutheran churches today amidst various attitudes concerning the Holy Spirit and his work.

Because the development of Luther's theology draws strongly from his personal understanding and experience of the Holy Spirit, a review of his background and some influences on his life follows.

Background and Influences

Martin Luther was born into late Medieval/Renaissance Roman Catholicism. As he matured through the church's training system, the teachings and demands terrified him. Coincidentally he encountered the Vulgate Bible and often found it at odds with teachings of the church. Franz Lau called his education and life experience, as well as the Holy Spirit working through

8. Prenter, *Spiritus Creator*, ix.
9. Prenter, *Spiritus Creator*, ix, citing Otto, *Anschauung vom Heiligen Geiste*.
10. Prenter, *Spiritus Creator*, 201–2.
11. Christenson, *Welcome, Holy Spirit*, 173.
12. Lohse, *Theology*, 232; Malcolm, "Holy Spirit," 340.

Scripture, the "midwives" of Luther's spiritual birth, which brought him to peace with God, as he became a Reformer of the church and of education.[13]

Home

Martin Luther was born November 10, 1483, to Hans and Margaretta in Eisleben, and grew up in Mansfeld in Anhalt Saxony, Germany. Luther's paternal grandfather, Heine Luder (d. ca. 1510) owned a farm in Möhra, near Eisenach.[14] Heine had four sons: Gross-Hans, Klein-Hans, Veit, and Heinz, by his wife Margaret, nee Lindemann (d. 1521 in Mansfeld). According to the customs of that region, Heinz, the youngest, had claim to the paternal farm. Veit acquired a share of another farm by marriage. Therefore, Gross-Hans left his family and region for good and, with his young wife, Margaret (nee Ziegler, Boehmer says of Möhra, Methuen says of a respected family in Eisenach[15]) and his firstborn infant son, they migrated to the county of Mansfeld, to explore the copper mines near Möhra. They started at Eisleben, where on November 10, 1483, his second son, Martin, was born.[16] Luther's parents sought success for their family through thrifty living and hard work. Hans succeeded in copper mining and in the community:[17] Throughout his life, Luther's speech and writing reflected the popular peasant dialect and folklore of his hometown.[18]

> Many never became more than common laborers. But Hans Luder did. Within seven years he ... started his ... enterprise in the copper business ... [Later] ... he became a member of Mansfeld's [town] council ... 25 years after Martin's birth, Hans and his partners owned at least six mineshafts and two copper smelters.[19]

Hans was also involved in church leadership. Hans's and Margaretta's home included the typical late medieval religiosity and severitiy.[20] They raised Martin with harsh discipline that often estranged parents and children,[21] but as a result of his parents' determination and work ethic, Martin gained

---

13. Lau, *Luther*, 58–60.
14. Boehmer, *Road to Reformation*, 4.
15. Methuen, "Luther's Life," 7.
16. Boehmer, *Road to Reformation*, 4–5; see also Methuen, "Luther's Life," 7.
17. Oberman, *Luther*, 83–85; Brecht, *Road to Reformation*, 3–5.
18. Köstlin, *Life of Luther*, 21–23.
19. Kittelson, "Luther the Educational Reformer," 32–34.
20. Brecht, *Luther*, 11.
21. Boehmer, *Road to Reformation*, 6.

the character traits required for his life calling.[22] Though not highly educated, themselves, they gave Martin a good education, compelling him to be a good student and to succeed in life beyond their achievements.[23] After God, Luther said, he owed all to their love in the home and their gift of his education.[24]

Luther's culture included superstitions of Medieval Catholicism and the devil's dark realm.[25] "Hans's mines and woods and home were, he believed, inhabited by elves, gnomes, witches, and spirits. Always the other world and the next life were close at hand."[26] From childhood, Luther sensed the reality of the devil that strongly appeared in his later views.[27] "Hell was described . . . to frighten men into seeking God . . . Christ was not only the merciful redeemer but also the terrible judge who condemned the wicked to the eternal fires of hell. . . . To help the penitent there was purgatory . . . a . . . temporary suffering before one was finally admitted to heaven."[28] This fear, induced by medieval Catholicism, tormented him until his theological breakthrough.[29]

Early Education

Preparing for advanced education, Luther attended the Mansfeld *Trivialschule* until 1496. There he studied Latin, prayers, confessions, the Creed, the Decalogue, the Latin Vulgate Bible, the liturgy, grammar, classical literature, and music theory, which prepared him for studies at Magdeburg, Eisenach, and Erfurt.[30]

In 1497, at Magdeburg, Luther continued his preparation for university study while living with the Brethren of the Common Life—a community of disciplined service. Luther was shamed by the devotion of Prince Wilhelm of Anhalt, a frail Franciscan begging monk, who wasted away to die through fasts and self-flagellation.[31]

---

22. Oberman, *Luther*, 87.
23. Lohse, *Theology*, 28–30.
24. Brecht, *Luther*, 7.
25. Atkinson, *Birth of Protestantism*, 19–21.
26. Deitz, *Luther and the Reformation*, 33–35.
27. Lohse, *Theology*, 29.
28. Boehmer, *Road to Reformation*, 20.
29. Brecht, *Luther*, 11–13.
30. Schwiebert, *Luther and His Times*, 110–17; Brecht, *Luther*, 15.
31. Boehmer, *Road to Reformation*, 17.

After a year, Luther left Magdeburg to complete his pre-university schooling at Eisenach in Thuringia, near relatives of his parents.[32] He lived with Heinrich Schalbe—"The most pious home in Eisenach."[33] Through the Schalbes Luther met supporters of the Franciscans, known as "Schalbe's *collegium*," and Vicar Johannes Braun. There "Luther came to know joyful piety. In the group gathered about Braun, songs and motets for various voices were sung, giving Luther access to the world of music."[34] Luther called Braun "his very closest friend."[35]

Luther continued *Trivialschule* at the school of St. George with his best teacher of Latin, Rector John Trebonius, and another teacher, Wiegand Geldennupf. These teachers motivated their students beyond rote memorization and strict discipline, so that Luther could read ancient authors, give speeches, and write essays and poetry in Latin. Luther was fortunate to have teachers who recognized his ability, gave him a quality education, and recommended him for university.[36] Eisenach was a

> congenial, comfortable atmosphere dominated by strong religious conviction and . . . stimulating conversations with distinguished guests. One of the most frequent . . . was the vicar of *St. Marien* [Braun], who was in charge of the Franciscan monastery at the foot of the Wartburg, the *Barfuesser Kloster*. . . . Luther . . . recalled his stay in Eisenach as one of the happiest periods of his life. Amidst . . . sympathetic friends, and . . . excellent teachers . . . Luther later spoke of Eisenach as his "beloved town."[37]

Perhaps this genuine Christian witness assisted Luther in his anguish over the next four years as he desperately sought the assurance of God's acceptance.[38]

University

As Luther's university studies were integrated with his previous experiences, Luther encountered challenges that wrought significant changes in his life and attitudes. The University of Erfurt was Germany's premium

---

32. Brecht, *Luther*, 15–18.
33. Boehmer, *Road to Reformation*, 19.
34. Lohse, *Theology*, 31.
35. Oberman, *Luther*, 100–102.
36. Kittelson, "Luther the Educational Reformer," 39.
37. Schwiebert, *Luther and His Times*, 127–29.
38. Kittelson, "Luther the Educational Reformer," 40.

school. Located midway between Mainz and Saxony, Erfurt never achieved political or ecclesiastical autonomy because the city lay in an area in which the interests of the archdiocese of Mainz and those of Saxony overlapped.[39] In his *Ninety-Five Theses* (1517) against the indulgences sponsored by the Archbishop of Mainz, Luther, of Saxon Wittenberg, tripped into this theo-political strife. In April 1501, "*Martinus Ludher ex Mansfelt*" (age seventeen) entered the liberal arts department at the University of Erfurt, joining the *bursa* of Saint George at Lehmann's Bridge. "As long as he was a member of the *bursa* . . . he was constantly under . . . the strict oversight of the master of the *bursa* as well as of the instructors and proctors of the university."[40]

Luther worked toward the master's degree while preparing for the bachelor's examination. He passed the bachelor's examination in fall 1502, finishing thirtieth in a class of fifty-seven. In early 1505, he completed his master's degree, ranking second of seventeen students.

Luther's university studies equipped him with the philosophical form and theological methods that he later utilized to apply Scriptural teaching against the religious establishment of his day. His later work benefited more from the methods of his education than from its content. In his Reformation work, Luther applied the methods skillfully, using various languages in his expositions and translations of Scripture, in disputations, theology, philosophy, ethics, and education, and in comments on ecclesiastical and societal matters.[41] Luther held

> that disputation was in itself the best method for the development of the logical faculties. In his own case . . . this method was eminently successful. He had already gained a reputation among his fellow-students as a sharp dialectician and ready disputant, and had on this account been nicknamed the "philosopher."[42]

Philosophy

Luther's education emphasized scholastic philosophy and theology.[43] However, he later exited scholasticism to become its strongest critic.

---

39. Brecht, *Luther*, 23–29.
40. Boehmer, *Road to Reformation*, 22–24.
41. Boehmer, *Road to Reformation*, 23–25; Oberman, *Luther*, 114.
42. Boehmer, *Road to Reformation*, 24.
43. Grane, "Luther and Scholasticism," 52.

Scholasticism

Late-medieval scholastic theology included two schools: *via antiqua*, tracing from Thomas Aquinas (d. 1274) through Duns Scotus (d. 1308), and *via moderna*, issuing from the English scholar, William of Occam (d. 1349) and Gabriel Biel (d. 1495), a protagonist of Occam and the *via moderna*. A sort of "second Occam,"[44] Biel affiliated with the Brethren of the Common life and was influential at the University of Tübingen from 1484 until his retirement in 1489.

Via antiqua was called *realist* because it maintained "universals have real substantial existence."[45] *Via antiqua* emphasized logic and dialectic to analyze everything using Aristotelian syllogistic reasoning to penetrate even the mysteries of God and the world beyond this life. It subordinated biblical revelation to human reason. Aristotle reigned supreme.[46]

In contrast, *via moderna*, or Ockhamism, maintained that universals have no existence independent of being thought, and are merely names (hence "nominalism") representing nothing that really exists.[47] Reality is the experience of the universal principles in the lives of individuals. Thus, "*Via Moderna* maintained that humans cannot penetrate the mysterious realms of God by logic, but held that divine truth was only revealed by the Holy Scriptures, which must be accepted through faith."[48] At Erfurt, a *via moderna* stronghold, nominalism influenced Luther's scholastic education. The "leading lights" at Erfurt, Jodocus Trutfetter von Eisenach (1460(?)-1519) and Bartholomaeus Arnoldi von Usingen (ca. 1464-1532) introduced their students directly to Aristotle's texts instead of using commentaries. They interpreted Aristotle more critically and with more understanding than elsewhere in Germany. Luther was fortunate to complete his liberal arts studies in one of the most dynamic faculties in Europe.[49]

Trutfetter taught at Erfurt and Wittenberg. By 1504, he was a distinguished doctor of theology at Erfurt, dedicated to the philosophy of Occam and Biel.[50] Bartholomaeus Arnoldi von Usingen received his MA at Erfurt

---

44. Oberman, *Luther*, 118.
45. Flew, *Dictionary of Philosophy*, 299.
46. Schwiebert, *Luther and His Times*, 245.
47. Flew, *Dictionary of Philosophy*, 250.
48. Schwiebert, *Luther and His Times*, 245.
49. Oberman, *Luther*, 114, 116.
50. Schwiebert, *Luther and His Times*, 245.

in 1491. He was highly esteemed among his colleagues and was Luther's close friend.[51] His teaching followed Biel obediently.[52] He maintained that,

> Christ has redeemed the faithful from the servitude of sin and the power of the devil, but not from the law. Christ . . . has given his Holy Spirit to the church to establish the new ceremonial and judicial laws, and he has retained the moral law. Christ has fulfilled and perfected the law of Moses in order that he (Christ) be imitated.[53]

Thus, the New Law is the *Lex imitationis*, necessary for salvation. This linked Usingen through Biel to the *Imitatio Christi* spirituality of the Brethren. Usingen's understanding of salvation as solely a gift of God referred only to an outer structure. "Salvation is unmerited: but God has obliged himself to accept man's virtuous acts. Man provides the substructure, the substance of the act; its meritoriousness is a gift of God."[54]

Usingen maintained that man's free will takes "the initiative to open the door of his heart for God's gracious assistance."[55] In late-medieval scholastic theology, this action of human initiative is summarized with the expression: *facere quod in se est* (to those who do what is in them), God will not deny grace.[56] Scholastics immediately preceding the Reformation taught that God recognizes the natural human capacity to turn to him by doing the best they can and honors that with grace to bring one to repentance, confession, forgiveness, and justification. This was Erasmus's view that Luther opposed in *The Bondage of the Will* (1525).

Trutfetter and Usingen applied the fundamental principles of *via moderna*: "all philosophical speculation must be tested by . . . experience and reality-based reason," while "All theological speculation must be tested by the authority of the Scriptures as interpreted by the church."[57] By its tests of experience and Scripture, nominalism became a key factor in the development of natural science and theology. Trutfetter and Usingen formulated the common core of nominalism, consolidating its fundamental principles into a cohesive program at Erfurt. They wrote handbooks and philosophies to introduce students to the application of nominalistic criteria.[58]

51. Kolde, "Arnoldi," 304.
52. Oberman, *Harvest*, 4, 180.
53. Oberman, *Harvest*, 118.
54. Oberman, *Harvest*, 179; cf. McSorley, *Right or Wrong?*, 198–200.
55. Oberman, *Harvest*, 180–82.
56. Muller, *Dictionary*, 113.
57. Oberman, *Harvest*, 118–20.
58. Oberman, *Harvest*, 118.

Luther's scholastic training had diverse effects. On the one hand, "this challenging climate of intellectual innovation,"[59] in which his study was pursued "under gifted professors, for whom he maintained high esteem, Luther received an excellent introduction to medieval scholasticism."[60] He "learned to think in a scholastic way according to . . . *via moderna*, and mastered the subject of theology according to late medieval standards."[61] On the other hand, the aspect of nominalism that depended upon doing one's best to qualify for grace increased his terror and his spiritual assaults (*Anfechtungen*).[62]

Humanism

Humanism brought classical anthropology, including form, style, and substance, from the Renaissance to the Reformation. Desiderius Erasmus of Rotterdam, Martin Luther, and Philip Melanchthon were key formulators of Christian humanism.[63] The influence of humanism stretched from Luther's early university attendance through his translation work in the middle 1530s. At Erfurt, Luther discovered the humanists and treasured their literature.[64] Later, humanism gave Luther access to biblical Greek and Hebrew, classical literature, Scripture, and the early Fathers, as he returned to the original sources—*ad fonts*—of Christianity. He demonstrated astonishing knowledge of the classics; e.g., during the Leipzig debate (1519), he used Scriptural and patristic sources and classical rhetoric to express basic Christian concepts.[65]

At Wittenberg (from 1513 on), Luther used the classics, the Fathers, and acclaimed language scholars, Reuchlin (Hebrew) and Erasmus (Greek).[66] He encouraged exegetes to drink deeply from the Scriptures and to criticize the Fathers and classics when they neglected the theology of the Scriptures.[67] This principle was foundational for Wittenberg's "New Theology,"[68] and

---

59. Oberman, *Luther*, 119.
60. Schwiebert, *Luther and His Times*, 429.
61. Grane, "Luther and Scholasticism," 53.
62. Lau, *Luther*, 55–57.
63. Spitz, "Luther and Humanism," 69–71; Fleischer, *Harvest of Humanism*, 28–30.
64. Spitz, "Luther and Humanism," 74.
65. Spitz, *Luther and German Humanism*, vii.
66. Oberman, *Luther*, 123–25.
67. Schwiebert, *Luther and His Times*, 438.
68. Schwiebert, *Luther and His Times*, 259.

transformed Wittenberg into a center of biblical humanism.[69] His writings during that period show that "theological depth resulted from years of study of the Holy Scriptures and the history of early Christianity. He did not wish to found a new church but to cleanse and reform Christianity by a return to its original standards of doctrinal teachings."[70]

Monastery[71]

From childhood through university, Luther experienced heightened *Anfechtungen* concerning his acceptance before God, exacerbated by the gruesome deaths of several colleagues. His fear of sudden death terrorized him. At Erfurt, he searched Scripture to find peace. When lightning struck nearby, he saw God calling him to become a monk to resolve his aggravations.[72] His purpose: "I took the vow not for the sake of my belly, but for the sake of my salvation, and observed all of our statutes very strictly."[73] The Augustinian requirement, humbly to love God and neighbor, exposed his self-centeredness. This root of sin hopelessly entwined him.[74] The Erfurt Augustinian monastery introduced several influences: discipline, scriptural orientation, the mentorship of Johann von Staupitz, Saint Augustine, and ordination.

Discipline

Luther entered the monastery fearing God's punishment and feeling he must live out God's law. Since monasteries enable such performance, he willingly submitted to the Augustinians who, he perceived, practiced the monastic life most rigorously. His discipline included stringent submission and obedience to Christ, the pope, the church, her teachings, his order, and

---

69. Schwiebert, *Luther and His Times*, 450.

70. Schwiebert, *Luther and His Times*, 426–28.

71. Robrt Kolb comment in MS review, "Ken Hagen always insisted that Luther was NOT a monk but a frater, and I always said, well he called himself a monk, and it is not that big a deal. But it is. Ken is right. The difference is that monks lived their lives within monastery walls, and fratres or brothers were members of mendicant orders and were to spend much of their lives in parish service in nearby congregations. That imposed on Luther duties of preaching and confession and absolution, and that meant the development of his pastoral touch."

72. Brecht, *Luther*, 46–49.

73. *LW* 54:338, No. 4444.

74. Loewenich, *Luther's Theology*, 73.

his superiors. His character, rooted in his home, school, and university experiences, served him well in the monastery. Luther followed the directives of the Augustinians in prayer, confession, study, mortifications and Bible memorization—often exceeding the requirements; for example, when Staupitz directed Luther to prepare for ordination, and later for the doctorate in Holy Scriptures, Luther obeyed, although not without protestations.[75]

Scripture

The day Luther entered the Monastery he received a red leather-bound copy of the Latin Vulgate Bible—a significant event. Shortly afterward, Johann von Staupitz, vicar of Augustinian convents, mandated "that the Holy Scriptures were to be read zealously, heard piously, and fervently made one's own."[76] Armed with his new Bible under these requirements, Luther's biblical theological formation began.[77] Observing Luther's interest in Scripture, Staupitz directed him to memorize the Bible.[78] Luther learned the book; reading it as directed; knowing every page,[79] "practically by heart, and could quote it freely in his lectures without verification, and even cite the Bible passages, in which reference, scholars claim he seldom made a mistake."[80]

Johann von Staupitz

While in the cloister, Luther's mentor was Dr. Johann von Staupitz, vicar-general of the *Observant* Augustinian order and first professor of Bible at the University of Wittenberg.[81] "Staupitz's earliest influence seems to have been exclusively through pastoral conversations, [as] a skilled counselor who enabled Luther to face what he feared and resolve . . . his acute theological anxieties."[82]

Staupitz valued Augustine and biblical exposition.[83] He focused on human redemption: "The dialogue between heaven and earth, between the

- 75. Oberman, *Luther*, 122.
- 76. Brecht, *Luther*, 60.
- 77. Boehmer, *Road to Reformation*, 39.
- 78. Oberman, *Luther*, 136.
- 79. LW 54:14, No. 116.
- 80. Schwiebert, *Luther and His Times*, 438.
- 81. Steinmetz, *Misericordia*, 5
- 82. Steinmetz, *Context*, 13
- 83. Brecht, *Road to Reformation*, 54.

the self-giving *misericordia* [mercy] of God and the dire *miseria* of man." Luther called him "a preacher of grace and the cross." Staupitz's goal: "The task of the theologian is the confession of the praise of God."[84] As Luther's superior, Staupitz directed him to study Scripture, to become a priest, to become a vicar of monasteries, to journey to Rome, to earn his theological doctorate, and to assume the teaching position at Wittenberg. As Luther's spiritual counsel,[85] Staupitz helped him know that behind the authority of the church, with futile religious attempts of contrition or heroic devotion, stands the prior grace of the electing God who shows his mercy in the wounds of Christ. Luther clung to this hope for the rest of his life.[86] Staupitz protected Luther following the indulgence controversy, and introduced him to like-minded communities.[87] He helped Luther understand penance and forgiveness and set him on the path to the Reformation.[88] Luther proclaimed that he received everything from Staupitz, "being my father in the doctrine and having given birth [to me] in Christ."[89] For Luther, Staupitz was God's agent to initiate his life work on all fronts.

Augustine

During his time of development, Luther mined Augustine's *corpus* and respected his authority. His knowledge of Augustine increased rapidly from 1513 to 1518 as he struggled to interpret the Psalms and the writings of Saint Paul.[90] As David Steinmetz observed, "Regarding Romans 9, Luther is not drawn to the position in the *Expositio*, though he knows it, but stays with the [harsher] *Enchiridion*, however much he may fear that Augustine's mature position is too strong a drink for the immature."[91] Though informed by Augustine's *Expositio* of Romans, Luther maintained the primacy of Scripture as needed for his hearers, and did not merely echo the writings of even Augustine. Discussing the Fathers, Luther noted, "It's necessary to stick to the clear word of God and not to human opinions."[92]

84. Steinmetz, *Misericordia*, 1.
85. Brecht, *Road to Reformation*, 54.
86. Steinmetz, *Context*, 9–11, 19.
87. Grane, *Martinus Noster*, 18, 28, 151.
88. Steinmetz, *Luther and Staupitz*, 3.
89. Oberman, *Luther*, 152; WABr, 11:67.
90. Steinmetz, *Context*, 12.
91. Steinmetz, *Context*, 20.
92. *LW* 54:260, No. 3695.

Ordination

Recognizing Luther's capabilities, the order called him to the priesthood when he had completed his noviate and monastic profession (1506). After his ordination (1507), he began teaching philosophy at the Erfurt order (April 1508) and later at Wittenberg (1508-9). Luther's studies included Gabriel Biel's work on the mass and his expansive commentary on Lombard's *Sentences* (*Collectorium*), Occam's *Questiones,* and other scholastic scholars covering Scripture and church practices.[93] Later he worked through Biel's dogmatics and history. This work reinforced Luther's nominalist theology to prepare him for his early lectures on Lombard's *Sentences*.

Doctoral Studies and Early Teaching

Luther's graduate studies, following *via moderna,* concentrated on Lombard's *Sentences* and the Holy Scriptures. Luther taught at Erfurt and Wittenberg while completing the stages of certification for the Doctor of Theology (1507-12):[94] *Biblicus* (Erfurt 1509), *Sententiarius* (Wittenberg 1509), *Formatus* (Erfurt 1510), *Licentiatus* (Erfurt 1511), and Doctor of Theology (Wittenberg 1512). Staupitz recommended Luther as professor of Bible at Wittenberg in 1512. Frederick the Wise paid the fee. The chancellor granted the license, Andreas Bodenstein von Karlstadt conferred the degree on October 19, 1512, and Luther was received onto the faculty of the University of Wittenberg on October 21.[95]

Luther was appointed director of studies in May 1513 and began his first lectures at Wittenberg in the 1513/14 academic fall of that year. These lectures from 1513 to March 1517, included Psalms, Romans, and Galatians. Luther's method of teaching began by listening to the text, which moved to meditation, prayer, submission, and humility. He was essentially teaching his own developing personal relationship of faithful obedience to God through the word. In contrast to the papal scholastic theology that strove to reach God through man's righteousness, good works, and philosophy, Luther lived and taught a theology of humility depending on God's grace and righteousness through faith in and nearness to Christ.[96] Oswald Bayer notes that this theology of humility is a life experience of God's initiation,

---

93. Brecht, *Road to Reformation*, 71.

94. Brecht, *Road to Reformation*, 90-92, 125-27; Schwiebert, *Luther and His Times*, 230-32, 429-31; Oberman, *Luther*, 139-45.

95. Brecht, *Road to Reformation*, 127.

96. Brecht, *Luther*, 130-36.

a passive life—*vita passiva*—of the righteousness of faith,[97] or, according to Bengt Hoffman, the "Theology of the heart." Hoffman maintained, "that Luther's theological thinking was deeply influened by his heart-felt experiences of life in God."[98]

Mysticism

During his early years of teaching, Luther became acquainted with several mystical writers who shared his meditational approach to the Scripture and personal piety as a means of experiencing God.[99] The sermons of the German, Johan Tauler (d. 1361), derived from Tauler's experience and personal suffering and leading to his loving relationship with God, struck Luther for their practical wisdom. In his 1959 essay, "The Theology of the Cross," Hans Iwand notes the opinion held by Rischl, Gyllenkrok, Bizer, and Barth that Luther's theology of the cross was drawn from the pre-Reformation humility-piety drawn from mysticism. Iwand contents that this opinion is incorrect as demonstrated by Walther von Loewenich's analysis in *Luther's Theology of the Cross* (first three editions).[100] However, in his fourth and fifth editions of *Luther's Theology of the Cross*, Loewenich softens his statements, concluding that while there "is an antithesis between Luther's theology of the cross and mysticism," that "Luther was deeply touched by the piety of a Tauler."[101] Thus, while Iwand's overall theological distinctions between mysticism and Luther's Reformation are correct he does not discuss Loewenich's modification to include the possibility of the influence of the piety of medieval mysticism on Luther's theology of reality that involves one's personal relationship to his crucified Lord and Savior through the Holy Spirit.

Bayer observes,

> Luther's revolutionary new way to conceive of faith as a *vita Passiva* found Luther sharing something in common with a

---

97. Bayer, *Theology the Lutheran Way*, 42–43.
98. Hoffman, *Theology*, 8.
99. Brecht, *Road to Reformation*, 137.
100. Iwand, "Theology of the Cross," 1; Loewenich, *Luther's Theology*, 145–66. Until the work of Leowenich, Luther's *theologia crucis* went relatively unnoticed as evidenced in the standard Julius Köstlin, *Theology of Luther* (1897), which, while explicating Luther's Reformation principles thoroughly, does not mention *theologia crucis*.
101. Loewenich, *Luther's Theology*, 221–22; cf. Hoffman, *Theology*, 184.

particular form of mysticism, which he came to know in Tauler's preaching and which he had learned to esteem highly.[102]

In 1516, Luther came upon and published a fragment of an anonymous document written in German about 160 years before. The work emulated the style of Tauler, which Luther claimed was "the right way to distinguish and understand what the old and new man is, who is a child of God, and how Adam must die in us and Christ arise."[103] Later, in 1518, when the rest of the material appeared, Luther published the entire document under the name *A German Theology* (*Theologia Deutsch*). Its themes of the necessity of God working death in the sinner and the rise of the new man in Christ were themes Luther had been working with since his Wittenberg teaching began in 1513. This was the basis of his "Wittenberg Theology," "Theology of Humility," "Theology of the Heart," or "Theology of the Cross," that was emerging at this time and led to his personal theological breakthrough. These two, Johan Tauler and *A German Theology*, coming from 100 to 160 years before Luther, and within the the framework of the church's theology, seemed to confirm Luther's work at this critical time.[104]

Heiko Oberman summarized Luther's view:

> Luther was enthusiastic about Tauler and the *Theologia Germania*; . . . but he read [them] . . . as striking examples of genuine, personal, living theology, not as exponents of mysticism. Tauler became a signpost in Luther's search for life by faith [while living] in the world.[105]

And,

> Luther found the language and the model for a graphic description of this state of dual existence (e.g., *simul justus et peccator*—simultaneously just and sinner) in Tauler and the *Theologia Germanica*.[106]

In these contacts, Luther distinguished between aspects of mysticism that feature human works of piety and experiences apart from Christ and the external word of God and of mysticism that is submissive to Christ and his word and trusts the work of the Holy Spirit. This contributed to the progress of his developing work.

102. Bayer, *Theology the Lutheran Way*, 43.
103. Brecht, *Road to Reformation*, 139.
104. Brecht, *Road to Reformation*, 141; cf. Colinson, *Reformation*, 22.
105. Oberman, *Luther*, 180.
106. Oberman, *Luther*, 184.

Carter Lindberg, using a citation from Luther's Romans Lectures, notes Luther's identification of his own experiences with those of Tauler and the *Theologia Germanica*:

> One of Luther's earliest references to Tauler is in his scholia or commentary on the passage in Romans 8:26: "Likewise the Spirit helps us in our weakness. For we do not know what to pray for as we ought, but the Spirit himself intercedes for us with groanings too deep for words." Here Luther reflects upon the response of God to our prayers which contravenes our conceptions and "renders us capable of receiving His gifts and His works. And we are capable of receiving His works and His counsels only when our own counsels have ceased and our works have stopped and we are made purely passive before God, both with regard to our inner as well as our outward activities." God thus patiently works with us as an artist with new material. "Concerning this patience and endurance of God see Tauler, who has shed more light than others on this matter in the German language."[107]

Effects of Background and Influences

Luther experienced radical changes while serving as *Lectura in Biblia* at the University of Wittenberg. From 1513 to 1518, he lectured on the Psalms, Romans, Galatians, and Hebrews, and experienced his personal, spiritual, and theological breakthrough. He became the Reformer who, through biblical humanism, transformed the university curricula and dethroned Aristotle. With the support and assistance of the Wittenberg faculty, he developed his theology of the cross. With the assistance of his colleague, Philip Melanchthon, Luther introduced Greek and Hebrew. Reflecting the influence of humanism, Wittenberg became the center of the German Reformation from which streamed thousands of students and Reformers to spread Wittenberg's "New Theology" throughout the continent.[108]

David Steinmetz, in *Luther and Staupitz*, reflects on his findings about Luther and his influences,

> This study set out to measure the degree of influence John Staupitz exercised on the theological formation of the young Martin Luther. What it succeeded in demonstrating was the astonishing degree of independence from his teachers Luther exhibited

---

107. Lindberg, *Third Reformation?*, 28, citing *Lectures on Romans* (1516), LW 25:365, 368; WA 56:376, 378. Luther thought Tauler had written *Theologia Germanica*.

108. Schwiebert, *Luther and His Times*, 481.

from the very beginning. Luther is always more than the sum of the parts of his theological heritage. His first lectures on the Psalms comprise a highly original work, unified in theme if not in development, which neither John Staupitz nor John of Paltz—nor even Gregory of Rimini—could have written. Luther learned from Staupitz, Trutfetter, Biel, and Paltz. . . . But [his] first work . . . carries an original and unforgettable stamp.[109]

Sola Scriptura

In *Martin Luther and the Enduring Word of God*, Kolb traces Luther's path from being a loyal son of the Catholic Church, serving under the bishop of Rome, the pope, to maintaining Scripture's authority over all other authorities of his day. These authorities included the traditions of secular and religious philosophy, the religious hierarchies and leadership of rabbinical Judaism and Roman Catholicism, the early church fathers, the councils, the Catholic magisterium, and the pope.[110]

Luther grew up in the Germany of the late Middle Ages in which Christian theology and traditions and Scriptural content had been imposed upon underlying paganism and dubbed "Christian." Therefore, much of "Christianity" of that time taught that human beings must reach fellowship with God by their own performance of religious rituals and sacred works flowing from humankind to the Divine. From his early life, Luther was terrified by such demands set upon individual Christians to qualify for God's grace and approval for his forgiveness.[111] However, as he continued his devotional reading of the Vulgate Bible and pursued his preparation for teaching the Bible in his doctoral studies under the Erfurt Occamism of his scholastic teachers, and through study of Augustine and Bernard, he began to discover that reconciliation with God does not rest on the religious authority and teachings of the church but on God's Spirit working through his word. Saving faith is due to the Bible alone[112]—the work of reconciling God with humankind does not flow from sinful people to God but from God to the people. As Kolb observes, "God talks his way through the entire Scriptures, from his creative Word in Genesis . . . [to] Revelation."[113] God spoke and the

---

109. Steinmetz, *Luther and Staupitz*, 141–42.

110. Kolb, *Enduring Word of God*, 2–6.

111. Kolb, *Enduring Word of God*, 2–3, citing Hendrix, *Recultivating the Vineyard*, 1–35.

112. Lohse, *Theology*, 26, 123, 187.

113. Kolb, *Enduring Word of God*, 46.

creation happened. He spoke through the patriarchs, prophets, evangelists, apostles, and Jesus Christ himself to deal with sin and rebellion and to establish life in his people and his church. "Luther's concept of reality, his ontology, arises from his perception that God's creative word, as recorded in Genesis 1, .brought all created reality into existence.... That... creative word keeps on working in human words, selected by God the Holy Spirit as his instruments for accomplishing the re-creation of the sinners who had destroyed the center of their own lives by not listening to God."[114] Thus, sinners are restored to the substance of a new being—a living relationship with God the Creator through his living and enduring word. Moreover, the word of God comes from the beginning, speaking the mind and intentions of God by the Holy Spirit. This word reigns alone—*Sola Scriptura*—over all the created people and their words of the Old and New Testaments, and of the church, and her contradicting councils, and the pope and his hierarchical system of philosophers, teachers and bishops.[115]

Kolb summarizes the reign of God's word in the context of salvation history, which Luther saw as the LORD's primary purpose for all creation:

> God's most important word for sinners came in Jesus. Luther's practical and pastoral way of practicing theology soberly but unabashedly confronted the reality of sin and evil, which mysteriously remained even in the lives of those whom God had chosen and made his faithful people on this earth. Therefore, what God had to say to human beings throughout biblical history and the history of the church delivered both his call to repentance and his promise of salvation through Jesus Christ, his death, and his resurrection.[116]

Teaching

As Luther began to teach and comment on Scripture he discovered that the righteousness of God is not dependent on the contact from man to God through philosophy and works but is a "righteousness of God, through grace and sheer mercy, that makes a sinful man who believes and trusts in God righteous apart from the curse of the work of law."[117] His discovery took shape in the Romans lectures (1516) and resulted in the full formulation

---

114. Kolb, *Enduring Word of God*, 46
115. Kolb, *Enduring Word of God*, 46–47.
116. Kolb, *Enduring Word of God*, 46.
117. Koyama, *What Does It Mean?*, 10.

of his theology of the cross by the time of the Diet of Worms (1521). As Kosuke Koyama noted, "Luther is no more a medieval man."[118]

During his early teaching, Luther presented his rejection of scholastic theology and introduced his theology of the cross. He considered the Psalms to be the prayers of Christ and his interpretation concentrated on the message of Christ. He was not a theological analyst but a listener of the Holy Spirit and one who proclaimed the message he heard. This listening was the beginning of his theological work.[119] Luther became aware of the Spirit's work through the word, which brings one under the will of God and into union with Christ. His teaching was not from a prescribed curriculum but from the understanding of Christ he gained from prayerful listening to the Holy Spirit through the word.[120]

Luther also listened to the message of the church and her teachers and compared them with Scripture using nominalist methods. Where the authorities and teachers differed from the word of God, he called for disputations to present the differences for discussion. Through his Christo-centric approach, Luther emphasized the issues of humility, pride, judgment, trust, and one's personal relationship with God. Christ's humility on the cross, for example, showed how all must humble themselves under God's judgment to receive his grace. Lohse writes,

> Luther was particularly concerned with questions about the righteousness of God and the justification of people. . . Even these early lectures, . . . considered every question from the standpoint of damnation and salvation, from sin and grace, or from the attempt to realize oneself in contrast to receiving the "alien" righteousness of Christ.[121]

Luther stated the basis of his lectures in Ps 69:

> For surfeit now reigns to such an extent that there is much worship of God everywhere, but it is only going through the motions, without love and spirit, and there are very few with any fervor. And all this happens because we think we are something and are doing enough. Consequently we try nothing, and we hold to no strong emotion, and we do much to ease the way to heaven, by means of indulgences, by means of eastern doctrines, feeling that one sigh is enough. And here God properly chose the things that are not to destroy the things that are. For

---

118. Koyama, *What Does It Mean?*, 10.
119. *LW* 10:4–10; Lohse, *Luther*, 29.
120. Brecht, *Road to Reformation*, 130; *LW* 10:160; *WA* 3:189.
121. Lohse, *Luther*, 29.

> one who from a sincere heart considers himself to be nothing without a doubt is fervent and hastens toward progress and that which is good.[122]

The emphasis was obedience, humbly submitting to God's judgment. This is the life of continual repentance.[123] The contrite sinner, in union with the righteous Christ in his suffering and death, God's Spirit raises with Christ in his resurrection and ascension.[124] Luther's "theology of humility" became his theology of the cross and justification by faith. As he had experienced, he applied the Psalms to those with *Anfechtungen* to affirm them in their despair, and to give them hope.

In Romans, Luther encountered the "obedience of faith" (Rom 1:5; 16:16).[125] As in the Psalms, the disciple is humbled in union with Christ's humility. Trusting the promises of God leads to justification by faith and life in the Spirit. This trust was crucial as Luther came to his Reformation breakthrough, discovering the power of God hidden under the contrary and not expressed through the obvious—the theology of the cross rather than the theology of glory.

Breakthrough and Conversion

From his university days until ca. 1518, Luther continued to be troubled regarding his assurance of salvation. As he learned more of Augustine and his teaching of predestination, Luther's *Anfechtungen* heightened his dread that, despite his monkery, God had not elected him.[126] Humanistic research led him to the Fathers and to Scriptures through which the Holy Spirit led him to his theological and spiritual breakthrough. His breakthrough occurred incrementally from 1509 to 1519.

In her volume, *Luther on Conversion*, Marilyn Harran correlates Luther's understanding of Christian conversion with his own theological breakthrough. Harran deals with the development of Luther's understanding and experience of Christian conversion that "not only changed the course of his own life, but had profound consequences for history."[127] The

---

122. *LW* 10:351; *WA* 3:415–16.
123. Oberman, *Luther*, 162; *LW* 31:25; *WA* 1:236.
124. *LW* 10:351–84; *WA* 3:415–41.
125. *LW* 25:5; *WA* 56:5–6.
126. Lau, *Luther*, 59.
127. Harran, *Conversion*, 9.

development of Luther's breakthough and his understanding of Christian conversion of sinners to life in Christ under the Holy Spirit are intertwined.

> Luther's concept of conversion...is...important for understanding both his developing theology and his personal transition from obsession with his own unworthiness before God and fear of Him to trust in God's mercy and reliance on His saving act in Christ. As early as the *Dictata*, Luther emphasizes the incarnation as the decisive conversion event in history.... When we push to the very center of Luther's perception of conversion, we encounter the incarnated Christ on the Cross. To understand fully Luther's *theologia crucis* we must consider his concept of conversion.[128]

From his pre-1513 writings through the *Dictata super Psalterium* (1515) to 1517 and on to 1519 Luther reached the foundations of his mature theology. Through perseverance, anguish, and opposition, Luther experienced the full meaning of Christian conversion in his own theological breakthrough.[129]

In 1509, Luther completed his theological studies and continued teaching. Scholars have questioned whether he followed the church's teachings that faith and humility were preparations one made to obtain conversion and justification.[130] Harran notes, "This issue of humility as preparation for grace was to haunt... Luther's early efforts to understand how a person is converted to God."[131] Harran also notes that Luther intertwined the medieval concept of faith and humility with conversion as an act of God becoming man in the incarnation of Jesus Christ. Thus, conversion was always due, not to human acts, but to the acts of God in Christ, as, for example, in the conversions of Saul of Tarsus and Augustine of Hippo.[132] Luther's early experience of conversion, however, was more akin to Benedict's Rule—*conversatio morum*—a change from secular to monastic life, adopting the monastic disciplines, and actually living them out, yet without experiencing the spiritual transformation of becoming a monk. The goal of such a both punctiliar and progressive moral conversion was to move from the initial state of moral imperfection to perfection in living.[133] With Bernard of Clairvaux, the steps of the conversion of souls were works of God alone.[134] Later,

---

128. Harran, *Conversion*, 21.
129. Harran, *Conversion*, 19.
130. Harran, *Conversion*, 17.
131. Harran, *Conversion*, 20.
132. Harran, *Conversion*, 23–24.
133. Harran, *Conversion*, 32–33.
134. Harran, *Conversion*, 39, citing Bernard of Clairvaux, *Sermo ad clericos*.

Thomas Aquinas maintained that God began conversion to change human hearts so people could come to faith and repentance. In contrast, Biel held that the first grace of God–justification or conversion–was given as a result of the best human effort. Biel "affirmed that man by his own efforts can attain . . . , 'the habit of faith acquired by natural means through the *facere quod in se est.*'"[135] With such a jumbled tradition of conversion definitions confronting him, the already terrified Luther began his teaching and writing career with continued *Anfechtungen* over whether he would stand or be condemned before the righteous judgment of God. Harran introduces a helpful perspective:

> All of these meanings must have been familiar to the young monk and teacher Martin Luther. As he developed his theology and agonized over his own relationship with God, his concept of conversion changed and matured until at last understanding and experience became one.[136]

Luther's marginal comments on Augustine's works indicate both his interest in Augustine and his realization of the contradiction between Aristotle and the church's teaching. Integrating Augustine's arguments into his lectures, Luther depended on Scripture against the arguments of reason—human philosophy cannot comprehend Scripture. Faith's questions must be resolved through Scripture; otherwise, philosophy has violated the word of God.[137]

From 1513 to 1515, in his *Dictata super Psalterium*, Luther learned obedience, repentance, faith, and trust. He employed a negative example of how conversion can be lost without confession and repentance. Commenting on Ps 1:1, he used Isa 55:7: "Let the wicked forsake his ways . . . and the Lord will have mercy on him." But "sins of weakness against the Father . . . of ignorance against the Son, and . . . of evil or concupiscence against the Holy Spirit . . . cause the person to stand in [is own] way with a very stiff neck. . . . Therefore he is not converted and cannot be converted, because he directly shuts the door of mercy to himself and resists the Holy Spirit."[138] Thus, the Spirit works through God's word to oppose the way of the flesh and human intellect[139] eventually to defeat the claims of philosophy itself.

In Romans, from 1515 to 1516, Luther identified two parts of conversion "as the decisive event that begins Christian pilgrimage and as the

---

135. Harran, *Conversion*, 47, citing Oberman, *Harvest*, 152.
136. Harran, *Conversion*, 53.
137. Oberman, *Luther*, 159–61.
138. *LW* 10:12; *WA* 3:16, *Dictata*, Ps 1:1; *cf.* Harran, *Conversion*, 61–62.
139. *LW* 10:4; *WA* 4:10–11.

repeatable event that occurs after the Christian has fallen away from God," the latter being the result of the constant battle with sin.[140] In Rom 3:27 Paul declared, "Then what becomes of our boasting? It is excluded. By what kind of law? By a law of works? No, but by the law of faith." Luther comments,

> Isaiah 65:1 says, "I was ready to be sought by those who did not ask for me; I was ready to be found by those who did not seek me." cf. Romans 10:20, are we not to seek him but only to wait for him until he is found by chance? This passage is understood in the first place as being directed against the stupid search by those who seek God by a way which they themselves have devised, not the one by which God wishes to be sought and found.
>
> In the second place, the passage is understood as meaning that the righteousness of God is brought to us without our merits and our works, while we are doing and looking for many other things rather than the righteousness of God. For who has ever sought, or would have sought, the incarnate Word, if he had not revealed himself? Therefore, he was found when he was not looked for. However, having been found, he now wills to be sought and found over and over again. He is found when we are converted to him from our sins, but he is sought when we continue in this conversion.[141]

Elsewhere, Paul noted in Rom 8:26, "Likewise the Spirit helps us in our weakness. For we do not know what to pray for as we ought, but the Spirit himself intercedes for us with groanings too deep for words." Luther commented,

> Therefore, these people who do not have the Spirit flee and do not want the works of God to be done but want to form themselves. But those who have the Spirit are helped by him. Thus they do not lose hope but have confidence, even though they are aware of what goes contrary to what they have so sincerely prayed for. For the work of God must be hidden and never understood, even when it happens. But it is never hidden in any other way than under that which appears contrary to our conceptions and ideas.[142]

From this Luther further described the second aspect of conversion, "I call 'first grace' not that which is poured into us at the beginning of conversion,

---

140. Harran, *Conversion*, 87–88.
141. *LW* 25:253–54; *WA* 56:265, 31–266, 4 (Rom 3:27).
142. *LW* 2:366; *WA* 56:376 (Rom 8:26).

as in the case of Baptism, contrition, or remorse, but rather all that grace which follows and is new, which we call a degree and increase of grace."[143]

In Romans, Luther found his "breakthrough" regarding the righteousness of God (1:17): "Only in the gospel is the righteousness of God revealed (that is, who is and becomes righteous before God and how this takes place) by faith alone, by which the word of God is believed. . . . For the righteousness of God is the cause of salvation. And, here again, by the righteousness of God we must not understand the righteousness by which he is righteous in himself but the righteousness by which we are made righteous by God. This happens through faith in the gospel (Rom 3:20)."[144] Therefore, "grace alone justifies."[145] In Rom 3:21, however, God still required self-control over carnal weaknesses, "For grace is not given without this self-cultivation."[146]

In 1518, in his *Explanation of the Ninety-Five Theses*, Theses 1 and 2, Luther referred repentant Christians to the priest who pronounces God's forgiveness because Christ gave his followers authority to forgive the repentant.[147] This corresponds to the repeated conversion from sin found in the faithful walk of Christians who are still sinners as well.

In 1519, from his comments and teaching on Galatians, Luther proclaimed that God forgives those who hear the word of Christ, confess their sins in his name, and trust that God forgives them and draws them to himself through Christ (Gal 2:15–16, 21).[148] This completed Luther's "incremental breakthrough." As David saw the futility of his sins and asked for mercy (Ps 51), the Holy Spirit overruled Luther's feelings of unworthiness and redirected his trust to the mercy of God.[149] Through Scripture, the Holy Spirit led him to his breakthrough and guided his later work as pastor, expositor, Reformer, and educator, influencing thousands of students throughout Europe.

Opposition to Scholastic Theology

Through his study and teaching of philosophy and Scripture Luther discovered contradictions between scholastic theology and Scripture, which initiated his rejection of scholasticism. Using Augustine, nominalism, and

---

143. *LW* 25:368; *WA* 56:379, 1–9; Harran, *Conversion*, 88.
144. *LW* 25:151; *WA* 56:171–72.
145. *LW* 25:242; *WA* 56:255–56.
146. *LW* 25:244; *WA* 56:57–58.
147. *LW* 31:83–85, *WA* 1:529–31.
148. Oberman, *Luther*, 165; *LW* 27:220–21, 241–43; *WA* 2:490, 504–5.
149. *LW* 12:314–15; *WA* 40^{II}:333, 23–29, Ps 51:1[3].

Scripture, Luther, being faithfully loyal to Scripture, replaced the priority of the Aristotelian system with his theology of the cross. While lecturing on scholastic philosophy and theology, Luther resisted principles conflicting with Scripture, such as *facere quod in se est*. Even as a *Sententiarius* (1509) he began to question nominalism: "Smoke of the earth has never been known to lighten heaven; rather it blocks the stream of light over the earth. Theology is heaven, yes even the kingdom of heaven; man, however, is earth and his speculations are smoke."[150]

Commenting on Biels's *Collectorium* (1515), and in later disputations (1516-17), Luther criticized Biel's theology and, specifically, rejected all aspects of *facere quod in se est*, demonstrating his independence from this aspect of nominalism, while still belonging to the school of Occam regarding anthropology and epistemology.[151] Responding to his opponents, Luther separated their methods from their content, and, ironically, using scholastic methods along with Scripture, he successfully opposed scholasticism and Catholic theology. Ernest Schweifert comments on the *Disputation against Scholastic Theology* (1517), theses 20-30:

> Luther made a direct attack on Gabriel Biel, by claiming that an . . . act of love without God's grace . . . is impossible for the natural man. . . . [Biel] was also charged with false statements about . . . acquired merits. Luther . . . attacked . . . Biel's claim that when . . . natural man does *facere quod in se est* . . . he then acquires from God . . . merit . . . after which God begins to bestow his "saving grace." This offered an opportunity for . . . discussion against Scotus, Lombard, Occam, and Biel, for it implied that natural man could prepare himself for God's saving grace by his own efforts and natural powers. It was really a contradiction of . . . Romans 1:17 that "the just shall live by faith," . . . [and] to his discovery of *Iustitia Dei*, as revealed in the Bible.[152]

The following selected theses indicate how the *Disputation* ushered Aristotle out of Wittenberg:

> 33. And this is false, that doing all that one is able to do can remove the obstacles to grace. This is in opposition to several authorities (Contr. *Facere quod in se est.* . . .).

---

150. Oberman, *Dawn*, 93-103; citing 94, *Comment on Lombard, I Sent*, D. 12 c. 2; WA 9:65.

151. Oberman, *Dawn*, 101, WA 9:9, 33, 40, 54, 83, 91.

152. Schwiebert, *Luther and His Times*, 455; LW 31:10-11, WA 1:26; Grane, *Contra Gabrielem*, 72.

37. Nature . . . necessarily glories and takes pride in every work that is apparently and outwardly good.

40. We do not become righteous by doing righteous deeds but, having been made righteous, we do righteous deeds. This in opposition to the philosophers.

43. It is an error to say that no man can be a theologian without Aristotle.

44. Indeed, no one can be become a theologian unless he becomes one without Aristotle.[153]

Referring to the writings of Scotus, Occam, and Biel, the *Disputation* portrayed scholasticism's perversion of Augustinian theology by mixing it with Aristotelian philosophy. When *via moderna* teachings were tested by Augustine and Scripture they were proven to be Aristotelian rather than Christian, stridently departing from early Catholicism.[154]

Consequently, Luther expressed his break with *facere quod in se est*:

> If a man receives grace by doing what is in him, it seems impossible that not everyone or at least the majority of men might be saved. . . . When man is proud, sins, etc., does he do such a work by himself, or is it done by another? Of course, he himself does it . . . and by his own strength. Therefore, on the contrary, if he does what is in him, he sins.[155]

This concurs with Luther's theology of the cross. Therefore, using Augustine, nominalism, and Scripture, Luther replaced Aristotle's priority with his theology of the cross.[156]

When Luther met with Cardinal Thomas Cajetan (1518)—a biblical scholar and representative of Rome—"he met . . . theology on a different level, in so far as the cardinal lent it a tinge of authority which he could not ignore, but found it nevertheless impossible to accept."[157] Therefore, Luther pitted the authority of Scripture against the authority claimed by the Pope and his ecclesiastic scholastic establishment and ignited the Reformation.

---

153. *LW* 31:11–12; *WA* 1:27.

154. Schwiebert, *Luther and His Times*, 456; Grane, *Contra Gabrielem*, 476.

155. *LW* 31:68–69 (*Heidelberg Disputation*).

156. Although Luther continued to oppose the primary influence of Aristotle, he later used Aristotle's methods when helpful in his cause of the gospel. This has been suggested, or maintained, to be laying the seeds of continuity from pre-Reformation scholasticism to post-Reformation Protestant scholasticism or orthodoxy. See Bagchi, "*Sic et Non*," 14–15; Muller, "Scholasticism, Reformation, Orthodoxy," 94–96.

157. Grane, *Martinus Noster*, 1.

Education in Germany

Luther's inclusion of the humanities in the communication of his work revolutionized education across Europe from elementary to university. He went beyond dialectics and Aristotelian logic to promote Ciceronian rhetoric, history, poetry, classical and biblical languages, Latin drama, music, and the natural sciences. Luther's humanism replaced scholastic dialectics with rhetoric, because Scripture contains rhetorical statements, not a collection of syllogisms. Rhetoric was important as Luther presented Scripture as the carrier of God's truth. Alongside this, he emphasized the Holy Spirit's working through Scripture to bring about spiritual awakening.[158]

Luther and Melanchthon called for the reconstitution of education in Germany to reform the church's understanding and preaching of the gospel. They abandoned Aristotle and Plato because their ancient pagan philosophy opposed the teaching of Scripture. Preparation in biblical languages was necessary to understand Scripture and Luther's lectures and to appropriate fully his theology of the cross.[159] Luther's treatises, *To the Christian Nobility* (1520) and *To the Councilmen of all Cities in Germany That They Establish and Maintain Christian Schools* (1524) proposed general education (male and female) to promote spiritual growth and good citizenship. It included the best features of humanism alongside Christian training. Luther claimed that this plan would enrich community life by teaching the gospel and founding public libraries. Students would learn the gospel, languages, Scripture, the Fathers, and the history of the church. Beginning in 1524, several German cities adopted these reforms.[160]

Summary of Background and Influences

The above influences contributed to the diverse callings of Martin Luther's life work. He had assimilated the Scriptures and established the Reformation upon them. He was transformed from one who feared God's wrath into a bold protagonist of the powerful God who rescues the faithful.

Luther's capacity for hard work combined his parents' example and their demands of him. In his studies, he mastered the materials. He sought God's favor in relentless monasticism and mercilessly disciplined his body. He mastered the languages and content of the Bible to find peace with God.

---

158. Harran, *Learning*, 169; Spitz, "Luther and Humanism," 71–78; Kittelson, "Luther the Educational Reformer," 95–114.

159. Schwiebert, *Luther and His Times*, 450.

160. *LW* 45:344, "Introduction," *To the Councilmen of Germany* (1524).

His self-discipline released from within his seemingly limitless capacity to maximize his life space in service for his Lord.

Luther's dependence upon the Holy Spirit working through Scriptures was the most significant influence in his life and work. Humanism's work—*ad fontes*, to the sources—provided him an authentic foundation in Scripture and the teachings of true Catholicism in the church Fathers. As he assimilated these resources, he led his attack against the errors of the church and her teachers.

Luther began his Reformation work by rejecting significant elements of scholastic theology, such as the teaching that man's free will can take the initiative to open the door of his heart to receive God's gracious assistance to receive God's gift.[161] Rather, Luther depended upon the Holy Spirit to convolve Christ's cross with the lives of repentant, faithful followers according to the theology of the cross—the "New Wittenberg Theology."

Luther's discipline of study, his understanding of both the usefulness and weaknesses of the tools of humanism and nominalism, his loyalty and submission to the authority of Scripture, and his growing awareness of the work of the Holy Spirit propelled him into his roles of Reformer of the church and Reformer of German education.

When Luther used the methods of nominalism to test, by Scripture, the teaching of the church, he found himself in a battle of authorities. In his *Ninety-Five Theses* he appealed to the authority of the pope to overturn indulgences and lost. At Leipzig, he appealed to the authority of the councils and lost again. He thus declared that God's authority, expressed in Holy Scriptures, ruled over the authorities of pope, or councils or their *magisterium*, saying (1520), "And now farewell, hopeless, blasphemous Rome! The wrath of God has come upon you in the end, as you deserved, and not for the many prayers which are made on your behalf, but because you have chosen to grow more evil from day to day!"[162]

Influences on Martin Luther, beginning with the tough discipline of Hans and Margaretta, followed by rigorous studies in university and monastery, and capped by his dependence upon the powerful work of the Holy Spirit through Scripture, produced a man whose influence subsequently reformed the church and education. His influence still permeates the lives of the faithful in Christ's church today.

---

161. Oberman, *Harvest*, 180.
162. WA 6:329.

Luther's Theology of the Cross

Luther said the essence of true theology is the theology of the cross,[163] as expressed in his commentary on Ps 5:11 [12], "*CRUX sola est nostra Theologia.* (The cross alone is our theology)."[164] "The cross becomes a methodological key to the whole of theology"—*CRUX probat omnia* (The cross is the criterion, or test, of all things)[165]

In *Luther's Theology of the Cross*, Regin Prenter noted that Luther's first use of the term *theologia crucis* is in his Hebrews lectures (1517–18); Heb 12:11, "For the moment all discipline seems painful rather than pleasant, but later it yields the peaceful fruit of righteousness to those who have been trained by it."[166] Luther said, "Here we find the theology of the cross."[167]

Prenter maintained that two crosses make up Luther's theology of the cross: "The deep truth of Luther's theology of the cross is that it views the cross on Golgotha and the cross which is laid upon us as *one* and the same."[168]

The Cross and the Holy Spirit

Luther's conception of the Holy Spirit began with his understanding of the theology of the cross. The Holy Spirit draws us to God to see his love revealed in this mystery of the cross.[169] The life of faith in the theology of the cross is complete submission, taught, led, and empowered by the Holy Spirit. Through obedience in suffering, the Holy Spirit brings believers into union with Christ in his sufferings for their sin. He bears their sin and they share in his righteousness. This is not *Imitatio Christi*, but God's grace working through his gift of the obedience of faith—the cross tests all things.

Luther's theology of the cross influenced and formed his understanding of the person and work of the Holy Spirit. As God's Holy Spirit raised Christ from death so the Holy Spirit gives victory in sufferings and believers find God hidden in Christ's cross of suffering and death.

Luther's conception of the Holy Spirit follows Jesus Christ through his ministry with this understanding of the theology of the cross. Jesus calls

---

163. Althaus, *Theology*, 25.

164. *WA* 5:176, (Ps 5:11 [12], *Op. Ps.*, 1519–21.)

165. Richardson, "Theologia Crucis," 335; "Theologia Crucis," 1603; Bauckham, "Cross, Theology of the," 181–82; *WA* 5:179, 1 Cor 2:2.

166. Prenter, *Theology of the Cross*, 1.

167. See "Hebrews Lectures" in Atkinson, *Luther Early Works*, 233–34.

168. Prenter, *Theology of the Cross*, 18.

169. Prenter, *Church's Faith*, 38–40.

believers to give up everything. They take up their personal crosses to follow Jesus (Matt 16:24–25; Mark 8:34) for the outworking of the will of God. The Holy Spirit is present to enable this sacrificial love among the faithful.[170]

The Cross and the Word

The Reformation principles—*sola fides, sola scriptura*, and the priesthood of believers—are rooted in Luther's theology that links the word and the cross. The theology of the cross is the path to knowing God in a reality that surpasses Old Scholasiticism and Augustinian Neoplatonism, that are based on human rationality and striving.[171] Prenter notes, "Luther's theology of the cross must travel the narrow road between 'a theology of the cross without the word' and a 'theology of the word without the cross.'" The former was common to the "imitation" piety of medieval mysticism and in modern existentialism. The latter is an intellectualism that reinterprets Christian theology without sacrifice or suffering and therefore omits repentance.[172]

The Cross and Knowing God

God can be known only by his revelation in the cross of Christ's sufferings. God is not known by human religious activity reaching up to God, but by God, hidden in the shame of human sin, suffering, and death on the cross, reaching down to sinful humanity.[173]

The theology of the cross expresses the relationship of God to his fallen creation. As Christians experience suffering in the fallen world along with their faith in Christ, they are united with him in his suffering.[174] As he is victorious through his suffering, so they, through their faith in Christ, are victorious.

Luther said the true theologian sees God through suffering and the cross.[175] Luther referred to Jesus' statement about the Jews who would persecute the apostles [John 16:3],

> "These things will they do unto you, because they have not known the Father nor me." But how was it that *they* did not know,

170. *LW* 25:294; *WA* 56:307.
171. Iwand, *Theologia Crucis*, 1.
172. Prenter, *Theology*, 7, 12–13.
173. Bayer, *Theology the Lutheran Way*, 11–12.
174. Prenter, *Church's Faith*, 38–39.
175. *LW* 31:40; *WA* 1:354, 19–20; *Heidelberg Disputation*, Thesis 20.

who had held such great contentions with Christ about God? To know Christ, is to know the cross, and to understand God in the midst of the crucifixion of the flesh: this is the design of God, this is the will of God, yea, this is God. And therefore, their hating and persecuting the cross, and the word of the cross, as being contrary to their affections and opinions, which were vanity and lies, are the cause of their not knowing God, or, (which is the same thing) of their not knowing the will of God.[176]

The Cross and Faith

Luther insisted that faith is the necessary human point of contact with the hidden God. It is also a critical factor in explaining his theology of the Holy Spirit. Faith is the only point of contact with the activity of God who stands contrary to the world.[177] Luther's idea of the hidden God raised questions about faith. Some of these are addressed by saying what faith is <u>not</u> in the theology of the cross.[178]

Faith Is Not Conscience

Before Luther, Scholasticism maintained that there was a point of contact with God which Jerome called the "spark of conscience," or *synteresis*, remaining in Adam after the fall. Others called it ethical consciousness, or the knowledge of good and bad. Aquinas called it the inherent human habit that incites to good and murmurs at evil. Biel called it "an infallible moral ability of knowledge" which tends toward the good. As his theological understanding developed, Luther rejected these explanations as semi-Pelagian. In a December 1514 sermon, Luther said that man wants God's goodness but the sinful "wisdom of the flesh" inhibits the original will toward the good.[179] Though *synteresis* could provide a point of contact for grace, a danger lies in

---

176. WA 5:108, 7-14, *Operationes Psalmos* (Ps 4:3), "*Haec facient vobis, quia non noverunt patrem neque me. Quomodo non noverunt, qui tam multa cum Christo pro deo contenderunt? Sed Christum nosse, est Crucem nosse et deum sub carne crucifixa intelligere. Haec voluntas dei, immo hoc dues est. Ideo quod crucem Crucisque verbum suis affectibus et opinionibus tanquam vanitati et mendacio contrarium odiunt et persequuntur, in causa est, quod ignorant deum, seu (quod idem est) voluntatem dei non noverunt*"; cf. Cole, *Select Works*, 3:147-48.

177. Loewenich, *Luther's Theology*, 50.
178. Loewenich, *Luther's Theology*, 52-76.
179. Loewenich, *Luther's Theology*, 53-58; WA 1:30-37.

the human tendency to consider any inclination toward good as merit for grace. This selfish motivation shows that *synteresis* has no value in Luther's theology of the cross since a longing for the good may oppose the will of God for one to suffer as God works out his salvation within. Therefore, Luther said that conscience is not faith.

Faith Is Not Understanding

Luther said that invisible truth differs from the natural, and only in Christ can one understand the hidden things of God and the invisible truth revealed in his creation (Ps 14:1 [40:1]; Rom 1:20).[180] Without the knowledge of God, philosophy can observe the works of God in creation, but it can only speculate about his invisible truth. In contrast, Luther said faith's spiritual understanding (Ps 74:3 [73:3]) is different from philosophy. Philosophy speaks about deductions from evidence, while faith is not a matter of deductions or evidence, but a revelation from heaven.[181] Therefore, Luther distinguished between philosophical speculation and the revelation to man in the reality of faith. Therefore, understanding is not faith.

Faith Is Not Reason

Luther attacked his contemporaries when they would neglect the word of God, elevate philosophy above theology (Ps 1:1), and "fill the church of Christ with the opinions of the philosophers . . . and the counsel of their own minds and oppress poor souls."[182] As a philosophically trained theologian, Luther felt called to wield the Bible against philosophy. It was time to turn from the church's philosophy, the theology of glory, to the crucified Christ, to the theology of the cross, as the creation turns away from what is now and desires what is still in the future.[183] Syllogistic demonstration of divine truths is impossible. It is contrary to faith and unable to reach theological results. He accepted reason in logic and culture, but rejected it as a worldview principle. Though needing each other, philosophy and theology cannot be mixed, but rather they are bridged by the revelation of Scripture that contains and explains the matters of God. Scripture reaches

---

180. *LW* 10:191; *WA* 3:230, 25–27; *First Psalm Lectures* (1513–15).

181. *LW* 10:452; *WA* 3:508, 1–3.

182. *LW* 14:293; *WA* 5:32, 6–8; "Qui opinionibus philosophorum . . . consiliis capitum suorum replent Ecclesiam Christi opprimuntque miseras animas." Ps 1.

183. *LW* 25:361; *WA* 56:371, 17–19.

human understanding through the humility of faith, i.e. the theology of the cross,[184] and not through syllogisms that are no more helpful in leading to God than the law. Therefore, reason and faith must be separated. Only faith, informed by and committed to the authoritative Scriptures, can receive the revelation of the hidden God. It is impossible for human reason to arrive at this knowledge of God. The pillars of the theology of glory—philosophy and reason—are not faith but are toppled from dominance in the study of God's word by the theology of the cross.[185]

Faith Is Not Experience

Faith is experienced only when the word of promise is realized in the theology of the cross.[186] It must be disconnected from one's natural senses and capacity for knowledge so it may demolish all human glory in the cross of self-denial, confession, and the terror of the remoteness of God.[187] Luther claimed that faith looks beyond sensed evidence to the message of the word perceived only by faith, from the present to eschatological events[188] so that faith and hope are almost synonymous. In his Romans commentary, Luther used Heb 11:1 to identify two difficulties of faith (Rom 4:20). The power of God is required to believe a view contrary to what is known to be true, and there is an anxiety of waiting to see if God is faithful to his word.[189] Therefore, regarding causality and confidence, faith, if it is to remain as faith, cannot depend upon experience for either initiation or continuance.

Faith and experience can be rightly related, however. Luther said faith cannot be humanly determined, nor is it a baseless hope that things will work out; rather it is a confidence of present and future truth. Faith as a human event grasps God's revealed word and believes it although human circumstances and reason may protest. Luther said that experience within the context of the theology of the cross "must be an event following faith rather than establishing it."[190] Therefore, faith is not fostered by experience, but, as

---

184. *LW* 31:12; *WA* 1:226, 24–26; "Against Scholastic Theology (1517)"; cf. Loewenich, *Luther's Theology*, 71–75.

185. Cf. Loewenich, *Luther's Theology*, 76. See Bruce Gerrish's qualification below.

186. *WA* 40^{III}:56, 5–6; cf. Althaus, *Theology*, 55–56.

187. *WA* 3:282, 27–283, 3; *LW* 10:233; *WA* 18:209–10; *LW* 4:103; *WA* 18:480–81; *LW* 14:141; *WA* 1:356, 33–357, 17, 363, 31–32; *LW* 31:44, 55; *WA* 1:123, *Epiphany Sermon* (1517); cf. Loewenich, *Luther's Theology*, 77–79.

188. *LW* 25:416; *WA* 56:425, 3–5 (Rom 10:15).

189. *LW* 25:41; *WA* 56:48, 1–4 (Rom 4:20).

190. Jungkuntz, "Secularization Theology," 20–21.

the "higher realism"[191] of the Christian's life with God, faith is experience, as part of the *sola fide* doctrine of the Reformation principle. Commenting on the *Magnificat*, Luther tells how believers experience peace in suffering. His style of teaching testifies to his own experience of faith:

> It has been hidden, since it is peace in the Spirit, which is revealed only through much tribulation. For who would think that this is the way of peace when he sees Christians persecuted . . . and that their whole life through they do not possess peace but the cross and sufferings? . . . But lying hidden under these sufferings is a peace, which no one knows unless he believes and experiences it.[192]

Through such experiences, the Holy Spirit teaches and produces faith.

> No one can rightly understand God or His word who has not received such understanding directly from the Holy Spirit. But no one can receive it from the Holy Spirit without experiencing, proving, and feeling it. In such experience, the Holy Spirit instructs us as in His own school.[193]
>
> But where there is this experience . . . that he is a God who looks into the depths and helps only the poor . . . and those who are naught, there a hearty love for him is born, the heart o'erflows with gladness . . . for the great pleasure it has found in God. There the Holy Spirit is present and has taught us . . . through this experience.[194]

---

191. WA 4:355, 29–31; cf. Loewenich, *Luther's Theology*, 90.

192. LW 25:232; WA 56:246, 12–18, "Est abscondita, cum sit pax in spiritu et velata multis tribulationibus. Quis enim hanc putet Viam pacis, si Videat Christianos vexari . . . ac tota vita non pacem, Sed crucem et passiones possidere? . . . Sed sub istis latet pax, quam nemo cognoscit, nisi credat et experiatur, illi autem credere noluerunt et potius abhorruerunt experii." (Rom 3:17); Hoffman, *Theology*, 105–28, cites Hering, *Die Mystik Luthers*, 50–55, 257–60, to maintain that Luther used the writings and examples of mystic Tauler and the Frankfurter, and Staupitz in his development of the reality of the faith-life with God through obedience and suffering.

193. PE 3:127; WA 7:546, 24–28; "Denn es mag niemant got noch gottes wort recht vorstehen, er habs denn on mittel von dem heiligen geist. Niemant kansz aber von dem heiligenn geist habenn, er erfaresz, vorsuchs, und empfinds denn, unnd in der selben erfarung, leret der heilig geist alsz inn seiner eigenen schule." "The Magnificat Translated and Explained (1520-21)."

194. (PE 3:129); WA 7:548, 6–11; "Wo aber erfarenn wirt, wie er solcher got ist, der inn die tieffe sihett, und nur hillfft den armen . . . unnd die gar nichts feint, da wirt er szo hertzlich lieb, da geht das hertz uber fur freudenn, hupfft und springet fur grossen wolgefallen, den es inn got empfangen. Unnd da ist den der heilig geist, der hat . . . inn der erfarung geleret."

Luther depended on this inner testimony of the Holy Spirit to know God in experience. Mary's exultationn was not in her circumstances but in the Lord and his regard for her.[195] Mary's experience is perhaps the most astonishing experience recorded in Scripture. Yet the virgin birth appeared to Luther a trivial miracle compared with the Virgin's faith. Mary believed the angel's nearly unbelievable message. Had she not believed, she could not have conceived. Her faith was the basis for the experience that followed.[196]

Faith is fulfilled in a reality outside itself that is hidden in God. It is a trust not motivated by experience but which leads to it. Luther said, "God wants us to have a true, simple faith and firm trust, confidence, and hope."[197] Even in adversity, believers must stand in trust to complete the sacrifice that the Holy Spirit commends to them. Such faith is not psychological but the powerfull work of God.[198]

The Cross and the Law

Commenting on Rom 2:14-15, Luther spoke of the works of the law being written on the gentiles' hearts as being the same as "God's love has been poured into our hearts through the Holy Spirit" (Rom 5:5). Luther described this interplay of the law and the Holy Spirit by pointing out that the Holy Spirit was given to the church at Pentecost, the anniversary of the giving of the law.[199] He explained this relationship by distinguishing between working the law and fulfilling the law to show that the law is spiritual because "the works of the law and fulfilling the law are two very different things":[200]

> The work of the law is everything that one does, or can do, toward keeping the law of his own free will or by his own powers. But since in the midst of all these works and along with them there remains in the heart a dislike of the law and compulsion with respect to it, these works are all wasted and have no value. That is what St. Paul means in chapter 3[:20], when he says, "By works of the law no human will be justified in his sight." . . . How can a man prepare himself for good by means of

---

195. PE 3:139-40, 146; WA 7:556, 13-18, 561, 10-13.

196. Bainton, *Luther's Christmas Book*, "Introduction," 5, and "Annunciation," 15.

197. LW 14:152; WA 18:489, 36-37; "Denn ein rechten einfeltigen glauben und feste vertrauen, zubersicht, hoffnunge will Gott von uns haben," Commentary on Ps 32: 9.

198. WA 40^{II}:464, 1922; LW 12:407; WA 3:542, 34-35; LW 11:28; *First Psalm Lectures*, cf. Loewenich, *Luther's Theology*, 98.

199. LW 35:366-69 (DB 7:3-8), *Preface to Romans*.

200. LW 35:367 (DB 7:4-5), *Preface to Romans*.

works, if he does good works only with aversion and unwillingness in his heart? How shall a work please God if it proceeds from a reluctant and resisting heart?[201]

To fulfil the law, however, is to do its works with pleasure and love, to live a godly and good life of one's own accord, without the compulsion of the law. The Holy Spirit puts this pleasure and love for the law into the heart, as St. Paul says in Romans 5:5. But the Holy Spirit is not given except in, with, and by faith in Jesus Christ . . . through God's word or gospel, which preaches Christ.[202]

Luther clarified how his theology of justification by faith and the theology of the cross involve the law and the Holy Spirit:

Faith alone makes a person righteous and fulfils the law. . . . Out of the merit of Christ, it [faith] brings forth the Spirit. . . . The Spirit makes the heart glad and free, as the law requires that it shall be. . . . Good works emerge from faith itself. That is [with Paul] . . . "We uphold the law by faith."[203]

Thus, the believer's work of the law is the expression of the love God gives through the Holy Spirit. This love is the self-sacrifice of giving up all for the outworking of the will of God through his law.[204] This is the cross Christ calls believers to take up to follow him. Luther commented regarding the love of God poured into believers,

It is called "God's love" because by it we love God alone, where nothing is visible, nothing experiential, either inwardly or outwardly, in which we can trust or which is to be loved or feared but it is carried away beyond all things into the invisible God. . . .

Thus the apostle asserts that this sublime power which is in us is not from ourselves, but must be sought from God. . . . Poured into us, not born in us . . . . this takes place through the Holy Spirit.[205]

The Holy Spirit is present to enable self-sacrificial love in life experience when Christians pour out their lives for God and for others.[206] This is

---

201. LW 35:367-68 (DB 7:4-8) *Preface to Romans*.
202. LW 35:368 (DB 7:7-8) *Preface to Romans*.
203. LW 35:368 (DB 7:7-8) *Preface to Romans*.
204. LW 25:186-87, 292-96; WA 56:203, 306-9.
205. LW 25:294; WA 56:307, 3-18.
206. Kolb, "Luther's Theology of the Cross," 80-81, 82-83; WA 40^{III}:322, 23-26, 334, 27-37.

the intersection of Luther's theology of the cross and his understanding of the Holy Spirit and his work. This expresses Luther's theology of the reality of the presence of the Holy Spirit.

The Theme of the Hidden God

Walter von Loewenich maintained that the concept of hiddeneness expresses the dynamics of the theology of the cross and is central to Luther's theology of justification.[207]

> The theology of the cross rejects speculation as a way to knowledge. Metaphysics does not lead to a knowledge of the true God. For Luther all religious speculation is a theology of glory. He condemns this theology of glory because in it the basic significance of the cross of Christ for all theological thinking is not given its due. The cross of Christ makes plain that there is no direct knowledge of God for man. Christian thinking must come to a halt before the fact of the cross.[208]

Alister McGrath cites Luther's concept of the hidden God: "Man hides his own things, in order to conceal them; God hides his own things, in order to reveal them."[209] Therefore, from Luther's understanding, God is both hidden and revealed at the same time. The ideas comprising Luther's concepts of the revealed God (*Deus revelatus*) and the hidden God (*Deus abscanditus*) pervade his thought and works.

McGrath notes the two kinds of hiddenness of God in Luther's theology: 1.) God's hiddenness under signs that are opposite to God—suffering and death, particulary in the cross of Jesus Christ, and 2.) God's hiddenness in his person outside of his revelation.[210]

First, *Deus absconditus* refers to the God who is hidden under apparent weakness and folly. Thus, this understanding of the "hiddenness" of divine revelation means *Deus absconditus* and *Deus revelatus* are identical.[211] At the same time, faith discerns *Deus revelatus*, while the senses see only *Deus*

---

207. Miller, *Promise*, 9; cf. WA 5:165, 33–37; Bayer, *Theology the Lutheran Way*, 106–14; Westhelle, "Hybridity and Luther's Reading," 249–62.

208. Loewenich, *Luther's Theology*, 27.

209. McGrath, *Theology of the Cross*, 167; WA 1:138, 13–15; see *LW* 51:26, "Sermon on Matt 11: 25–30," February 24, 1517.

210. Miller, *Promise*, 13; cf. McGrath, *Theology of the Cross*, 164–65.

211. McGrath, *Theology of the Cross*, 165, citing Kattenbusch, *Deus absconditus bei Luther*, 170–214.

absconditus. Which is recognized depends upon the observer. An example from McGrath:

> Consider the wrath of God revealed in the cross. To reason, God thus appears wrathful; to faith, God's mercy is revealed in this wrath. There is no question of God's mercy being revealed independently of his wrath, or of an additional and subsequent revelation of God's mercy which contradicts that of his wrath. In the one unitary event of revelation in the cross, God's wrath and mercy are revealed simultaneously, but only faith is able to recognise the *opus proprium* (God's proper work) as it lies hidden under the *opus alienum* (alien work); only faith discerns the merciful intention which underlies the revealed wrath; only faith perceives the real situation which underlies the apparent situation.[212]

This kind of God's hiddenness relates to Luther's theology of the cross, the Heidelberg Disputation, and others of Luther's related theological themes.

Secondly, *Deus absconditus* is the God hidden *behind* or outside his revelation in God's person, as used by Luther in his controversy with Erasmus in *de servo arbitrii* (1525).[213] Luther maintained that beyond the *Deus revelatus* God exists in ways always hidden from us; thus *Deus absconditus* forever remains unknown to us—a mysterious and sinister being with undisclosed intentions.[214]

Joshua Miller crisply describes Luther's dispute with Erasmus:

> Erasmus neglects to distinguish between God preached and God not preached. That is, Erasmus does not distinguish between God as God is proclaimed in the promise of salvation in the gospel of Jesus Christ and God as God is hidden in God's self. It is true, says Luther, that God does not will the death of the sinner as God exists in revelation, as God is revealed in Jesus Christ through the word. Yet, says Luther, God is not bound to exist in revelation alone but also exists above and beyond revelation, hidden in God's self. While God as God is preached and revealed in Christ through the word does not desire the death of the sinner, God unpreached and hidden outside of revelation, does desire the death and damnation of the sinner. There are, thus, two wills of God. There is the will of God revealed in which God wills the life and salvation of the sinner, and there

---

212. McGrath, *Theology of the Cross*, 165.

213. Miller, *Promise*, 14–15; McGrath, *Theology of the Cross*, 165, citing Grislis, "Martin Luther's View," 81–94.

214. McGrath, *Theology of the Cross*, 165–66.

is the will of God hidden in God's self wherein God wills the death and damnation of the sinner. Luther emphasizes that God hidden in God's self and the hidden will of God are not to be speculated about by the sinner. Instead, the sinner has to do only with God revealed in Jesus Christ through the word, who wills and promises the sinner's life and salvation.[215]

Luther's understanding of God's hiddenness in God's self can be discerned from his discussion in four writings: *Bondage of the Will*, the *Lectures on Jonah*, the *Lectures on Isaiah*, and the *Lectures on Genesis*. Luther taught that God hidden in God's self and his hidden work are incomprehensible. God hidden in God's self kills and damns sinners in order that they may be raised to life and saved by God revealed, and that God revealed in Christ through the word is the only way by which one can know God. Luther's explanation of God's hiddenness in God's self in *Bondage of the Will* written against Erasmus in 1525 provided the foundation of this teaching. His lectures on Jonah, Isaiah, and Genesis then serve as further clarifications of this teaching.[216] Thus, assuming there is much more to God than we can ever know from his self-revelation, Luther showed the strong tension between the *Deus revelatus* and the *Deus absconditus*. They may stand in total antithesis. Therefore, he conceded that behind the merciful God, who is revealed in the cross of Christ, there may be a hidden God whose intentions and methods are diametrically opposite.[217] In the discussions concerning Luther's theology of the cross and the Holy Spirit, only the "preached" understanding of *Deus absconditus* is involved.

In his *Luther's Outlaw God* (three volumes), Steven Paulson presents another aspect of the hidden God related to Luther's theology of proclamation. Paulson maintains that Luther separated speculation from evangelical preaching. Luther distinguished between God without the preaching of God's word of rescue in Jesus Christ—the naked God—and God preached with the evangelical content of the preacher's word—the clothed God. God is either without his word (hidden or naked), or God is with his word. Luther's distinction between unpreached word and the preached word finds expression in the liturgy. A sinner finds the direct application of absolution when the preacher preaches the word of redemption and it is heard. Those who do not preach the gospel do not know that God is hiding, because they keep covered over what the preaching of forgiveness uncovers. Luther made

---

215. Miller, *Promises*, 18; *LW* 33:138-40; *WA* 17:676, 680-82; *WA* 18:684-86, *The Bondage of the Will* (1525).

216. Miller, *Promises*, 33.

217. McGrath, *Theology of the Cross*, 165.

all theology a distinction in one's life, between God naked and God clothed. This theology exchanged the transcendence that sought a wholly other God for the way that is incarnate, earthly, and practical.[218]

Gerhard Forde often reiterated, "Theology is for preaching, not understanding, and especially not for self-understanding."[219] Preaching Scripture often puzzles and offends the hearers. The distinction between God preached and not preached offends when hard issues such as predestination and the suffering of the cross of Christ are considered. Preachers and theologians must ask, "Is anything going on between God and those who neither preach nor hear any radical texts of evangelical scripture?"

Luther is fascinating in answering and interpreting the offensive texts of Scripture because

> [Luther] knows where the rabbit holes are when one is missing the theological distinction between the clothed and unclothed God. Luther knew how near to grace and death these questions come, and he felt how tragic . . . life is without a preacher.[220] . . .We preach knowing that both the art and science of the thing depend upon how God marvelously and frighteningly ceases being unpreached and speaks to us. . . .
>
> Theology's basic distinction is not an idea before it is a pronouncement. . . . The vital difference between a naked and clothed God is first heard, then felt. Indeed, no one is born with a preached God. No one can live without suffering evil.[221]

Paulson notes that in Luther's understanding, the release from the suffering and evil produced by the preaching of the clothed God comes through the twin acts of preaching and hearing the word of God.[222]

Paulson summarizes his understanding of hiddenness in Luther's theology:

> Luther is intent upon addressing evil, predestination, and suffering with just . . . an apparently worthless act as preaching. . . .
>
> You will either be left with a speculation or a promise. The difference between these two makes all the difference between knowing or not knowing, patience or impatience, hell or heaven, life or death, law or gospel. Absurd as it sounds, the difference

218. Paulson, *Outlaw God*, 1:ix–x.
219. Forde, *Proclamation*.
220. Paulson, *Outlaw God*, 1:x. Paulson also notes, "He [Luther] also learned how to become a better preacher accordingly and could even impart this skill to others."
221. Paulson, *Outlaw God*, 1:x.
222. Paulson, *Outlaw God*, 1:xi.

between fate and chance, predestination and damnation, joy and despair, death and life depends entirely upon a preacher. God could not be more . . . hidden than that, because it means that God is not the law that everyone assumes and hopes for, and God's freedom comes to a creature through a creature in the simplest form of a word that promises forgiveness. God is an outlaw, and so both dangerous and surprisingly free.[223]

Paulson uses Luther's several "persistent observations" to present Luther's concepts of hiddenness:

1. Divine hiddenness of the Father in the masks of creation. This is presence not absence or emptiness, but God's overpowering, all-present nearness. This opposes the space sinners want.

2. Preaching—rather than silence—of Christ. He is hated by sinners for choosing not the prideful, but the faithful, and for the public horror of his crucifixion.

3. The law, until Christ comes. This hides the Holy Spirit in the preachers of sermons without the cross, until the preaching of the cross and baptism come to bestow faith.[224]

God is present in all situations; but he is hidden and naked when his redemptive word is not proclaimed. However, when the preacher proclaims God's redemptive word, God is clothed and revealed to the hearers as the Holy Spirit works within the hearers the miracle of faith. As Paulson declares, "The proper work of the Holy Spirit is sending a preacher by whom the external word unto eternal life arrives."[225]

Prenter explained how the hiddenness of God is foundational to Luther's theology of the Holy Spirit:

> The thought that God . . . hides himself under his contradiction, that he kills when he makes alive, judges when he acquits, permits us to suffer when he would bless us—all because his creative love must conquer the last opposition of hate and evil—is what Luther calls the "theology of the cross" (*theologia crucis*). This is the most noble triumph of the faith in creation. The love in which God creates and upholds his creation is so divine and unconquerable that he also creates and leads his creation

---

223. Paulson, *Outlaw God*, 1:xii.
224. Paulson, *Outlaw God*, 1:xxxi–xxxii.
225. Paulson, *Outlaw God*, 2:19.

toward the goal of his love, where *we* see nothing but suffering and death.²²⁶

In summary, Luther maintained that God is hidden from human powers of intellect and inquiry. Human beings seek God according to their self-motivated and self-powered realm—the theology of glory. God is hidden from human explorations of suffering and the cross that are outside their realm. Yet, to those trusting in his promises of deliverance, God reveals himself in the humility of human life—born to the virgin, sacrificing himself for his creation. He calls human beings to live through the suffering of repentance and death and to come alive with Christ in newness of life with God in the Holy Spirit. In this way, the Triune God is revealed and received. Those who so see and receive Jesus Christ receive the love of the Father, the obedience of the Son, and by the power of the Holy Spirit believe God and become his children.

Miller notes that the concepts of hiddeness prominent in the theology of Luther and his immediate followers were not as significant in the succeeding generations:

> The generations of Lutheran theologians between Luther and the Enlightenment to greater or lesser extents neglected Luther's doctrine of the hidden God. Neither Melanchthon nor his followers the Philipists acknowledged, interpreted, or developed Luther's understanding of God's hiddenness outside of revelation. Although the Gnesio-Lutherans at least made passing reference to the doctrine, they did not give it the attention due a topic that Luther himself felt was so important to theology. As the doctrine was rejected by the theologians of Lutheran orthodoxy and forgotten by the pietists, it was not to be taken up again until the nineteenth century.²²⁷

The Theme of Atonement

Luther viewed the sinful human race as hopelessly lost and judged to die under the wrath of God. As part of his contribution to *Christian Dogmatics* under the heading of "The Work of Christ," Gerhard Forde discussed

---

226. Prenter, *Church's Faith*, 39–40.

227. Miller, *Promise*, 41. In chapter 3 of *Promise*, "The Reception of Luther's Doctrine of the Hidden God in the Modern German Protestant Theological Tradition," Miller summarizes the views from Luther to Theodosius Harnack (1816–89), and from Harnack to Eberhard Jüngel (1934–2021), in preparation for his treatment of Oswald Bayer's views of the hiddenness of God—the subject of his book, *Hanging by a Promise*.

different atonement theories that attempt to describe the Christian doctrine of how Christ achieved forgiveness and reconciliation for hopeless sinners. Forde began with the Scriptural tradition and then discusses three major traditional descriptions of how the biblical material has been interpreted: 1) The Vicarius Satisfaction of Divine Justice (Anslem of Canterbury, 1033–1109); 2) The Triumph of Divine Love (Abelard, 1079–1121, to nineteenth- and twentieth-century theologians of loving and moral communities); and 3) The Victory over Tyrants (Gustaf Aulén, 1877–1977, and purportedy M. Luther).[228] Forde maintained that Luther's view of the atonement was beyond subscribing to any one of these pre-Reformation theories such that he (Luther) could use their various terms without contradiction and sought to be a theologian of the cross. This involved a great reversal. "A theologian of glory, he said, calls the bad good and the good bad. A theologian of the cross says what a thing is. To be a theologian of the cross, one has to learn to see things as they are."[229] Therefore, first and foremost a theologian of the cross must maintain a "theology of reality"—the "Pigtails on the Pillow" that Luther has portrayed all along.

What is this reality? Forde asked, "If the traditional systems proclaim abstact ideals of release, why are we still terrorized under the wrath of God's law and judgment?" He answered, "Because we cannot fulfill the demands of God's righteous law, the atonement theories are powerless to give relief." "I am still under wrath, actual wrath."[230] Forde summarized Luther's portrayal of God's atoning reversal of direction.

> Atonement occurs when God gives himself in such fashion as to create a people pleasing to God, a people no longer under law or wrath, a people who love and trust God. . . . God is "satisfied." . . God was in Christ reconciling the world unto himself. . . . The question is . . . whether God has acted decisively . . . to save us. For God is not the problem, we are. Can God actually deliver us from wrath, save us from sin and embittered hostility and bring something new? What Luther has to say centers around the question *the way things are*. Can wrath be ended? But that is a question of what God gives and not what God gets, for it is, one should not forget, *God's* wrath, and only God can end it. . . .
>
> But [God's] wrath cannot be placated in the abstract by heavenly transactions between Jesus and God. . . . God's wrath

---

228. Forde, "Work of Christ," 2:11–46.
229. Forde, "Work of Christ," 2:50.
230. Forde, "Work of Christ," 2:50.

against us is placated only when God's self-giving makes us his own, when God succeeds in creating faith, love, and hope.[231]

Preceding the terror of World War II, in 1934, Dietrich Bonhoeffer captured the practicality of this reality—a practicality that he would radically live out in the next eleven years:

> There is no way to peace along the way of safety. For peace must be dared; it is itself the great venture and can never be safe. Peace is the opposite of security. To demand guarantees is to want to protect oneself. Peace means giving oneself completely to God's commandment, wanting no security, but in faith and obedience laying the destiny of the nations in the hand of Almighty God, not trying to direct it for selfish purposes. Battles are won, not with weapons, but with God. They are won where the way leads to the cross.[232]

In Luther's Reformation reversal of direction, his theology proclaimed the good news through word and sacrament, which is the channel of the Holy Spirit to continue in his work of *Spiritus Creator* in us.[233] Forde contended that "A radical Lutheranism would be one that regains the courage and the nerve to preach the gospel unconditionally; simply let the bird of the Spirit fly!"[234]

Luther said, "God has ordered things in such a way that the word of the gospel should be the word of the cross."[235] In the gospel of the cross of Jesus Christ, God's love comes through his word with a double purpose: to bring death to the human system, and to work repentance, faith, forgiveness of sins, and the creative power to live through Christ's substitutionary death. The wisdom of the cross and the work of the Holy Spirit imbue Luther's theology.[236] The theology of the cross glories in Christ's work[237] and shows that in balance the Spirit brings the believer to his own cross to partake in God's destiny for him in the life of Christ. In connection with Christ's work on the cross, Luther says that in times of reverses the Spirit does the hidden

---

231. Forde, "Work of Christ," 2:50–51.
232. Bonhoeffer, "The Church and the World."
233. Forde, "Radical Lutheranism," 16.
234. Forde, "Radical Lutheranism," 16.
235. *LW* 30:241; *WA* 20:647, *Lectures I John* (1527), 1 John 2:7.
236. *LW* 14:305, 309; *WA* 5:42, 45, *Commentary on Psalm 1*; cf. Althaus, *Theology*, 30; Loewenich, *Luther's Theology*, 110.
237. Christenson, *Welcome*, 191.

work of God in those who trust him, that they may have hope in prayer.[238] So, "Just let the bird fly!"[239]

Regin Prenter summarized Luther's understanding of the Trinity in view of the cross:

> God is the trinitarian God. He is the God of life, the Creator; he is the God of the Word, the Savior; he is the God of faith, the Holy Ghost. This Trinity, as Father, in our common experience of life, as Son, in the preached Word, and as Holy Ghost, in our personal convictions, teaches us in the last analysis what these words mean: *Omnia bona in cruce et sub cruce abscondita sunt* ("All good things are hidden in and under the cross"). Therefore they cannot be understood anywhere else except under the cross; "under the cross" means under the cross on which Jesus, our Redeemer, bore our punishment, and under the cross which my Creator has laid upon me in my suffering and in my death. In both places we are talking about the same cross.[240]

Luther's Formulation of the Theology of the Cross

From the late-nineteenth- to the mid-twentieth century, a school of thought maintained that Luther's theology of the cross was the quintessence of the pre-Reformation views of Luther and pointed back to the humility-piety of mysticism. Hans Iwand countered this idea by pointing to the work of Loewenich and to his own work (followed by many others) that show how Luther's theology of the cross was a new understanding of the theme found also in traditional mysticism.[241] For most of Luther's formative years, and all his adult years, the concept of the cross was primary in his life and in his message.

Five documents demonstrate how the theology of the cross pervaded Luther's thinking, his experience, and his work throughout his ministry. Four are from his extremely productive period of theological writing from 1516–21. Of these, three are written by Luther: *The Penitential Psalms* (1517 and 1525), *The Heidelberg Disputation* (1518), and *Operationes Psalmos* (1518–21). A German monk of the Teutonic Order in Frankfurt am Main wrote the fourth work, the above-mentioned *Theologia Germanica*, in

---

238. LW 25:366; WA 56:376, 29–377, 1; *Romans*; cf. Prenter, *Spiritus Creator*, 184–89.

239. Forde, "Radical Lutheranism," 15.

240. Prenter, *Theology*, 18.

241. Iwand, "Theology of the Cross," 1.

German ca. 1350.²⁴² A fifth work, *In XV Psalmos graduum* (1540), includes Luther's lectures on the Song of Assent (Pss 120–34) of 1532–33.²⁴³ Of the three works in the Psalms, Jaroslav Pelikan observed,

> Throughout his career, Luther paid very much attention to the Psalter. . . . His attention to it was personal, devotional, political, exegetical, polemical—all at the same time. Each of these motifs appears somewhere in the commentaries collected here. What unifies the commentaries is the way each of them succeeds in blending Luther's personality with the message of the sacred text.²⁴⁴

In the other document by Luther, *The Heidelberg Disputation* (1518), Luther presented twenty-eight theological and philosophical theses that provided an orderly biblical and theological basis for his theology of the cross and its distinction from the theology of glory.

These five documents are discussed below to show Luther's consistent scriptural and historical development of his theology of the cross and his theology of the Holy Spirit from 1516–33.

Die Sieben Bußpsalmen (The Seven Penitential Psalms) (1517 and 1525)

From early church times, Psalms 6, 32, 38, 51, 102, 130, and 143 have been recited on the Fridays in Lent.²⁴⁵ These *Seven Penitential Psalms* include supplications of penitence over the psalmists' own anguish regarding their failures.²⁴⁶ They acknowledge guilt both of universal unrighteousness and of personal deviant relationships toward God's law. They plead, "that the punitive chastisement of God, as the just God, may . . . be changed into the loving chastisement of God, as the merciful One."²⁴⁷ H. C. Leupold summarized the thrust of these psalms:

> In not every instance in these psalms is there an express confession of sin. A deep sense of being under the wrath of God, however, appears to be common to all. There is also conviction that only God, who has been sinned against, can deliver man from

242. Hoffman, *Theologia Germanica*, xv.
243. See "In XV Psalmos graduum, 1532/33 (1540)" in WA 40^{III}:1–475.
244. Pelikan, "Introduction to Volume 14," ix.
245. Pelikan, "Introduction to Volume 14," ix.
246. Payne, "Psalms, Book of," 4:939.
247. *K&D* 5:78–79.

the serious situation into which he has plunged himself. Each of these has something distinctive about it.... Unique about the group of psalms as a whole is the manner in which sin is seen to bring a man under the wrath of God... a terrible reality.[248]

As Luther prepared his exposition of these seven Psalms, he portrayed this "terrible reality" as the description of the relationship between the holy righteous God and sinful humankind. His printed exposition of *The Seven Penitential Psalms* in 1517 was based on a German translation of the Vulgate Latin Old Testament text. It was the first publication of his own works.[249] In 1523, Luther started the German translation of the Old Testament from Hebrew.[250] As his grasp of the original Hebrew text developed, he felt it proper to revise his German translation and his exposition of *The Seven Penitential Psalms* and published a revision in 1525. In the 1517 edition, he had presented his early conception of his theology of the cross and the 1525 edition demonstrated that his teachings had continued unchanged.[251]

Iwand noted that up to his day (mid-twentieth century) the theological importance of this beginning work of Luther's had not been significantly observed or analyzed.[252] Since Iwand's 1959 lecture, Luther's *theologia crucis* and his statement "*Crux sola est theologia nostra*" have become more prominent in statements of Luther's theology and his understanding of Christian discipleship. However, it seems peculiar that with the renewed interest in Luther's theology of the cross in the past ninety years, or so, few studies of Luther's exposition of the Penitential Psalms have been done.

Fifty-six years later, Jonathan Seiling echoes Iwand's observation: "Scholarly interest in this early publication has been surprisingly low despite the relevance of a comparison of the two texts for either demonstrating or refuting the thesis that Luther's theology changed significantly by the mid–1520s.... Major studies of Luther's development rarely ever mention... Luther's *The Seven Penitential Psalms*."[253] Iwand considered Luther's writing on these Psalms:

> To exemplify the theologian of the cross's understanding of life.... In linguistic respects they belong to the most beautiful writing of his that we possess. These could also be named

248. Leupold, *Exposition of the Psalms*, Ps 25.
249. Leupold, *Exposition of the Psalms*, Ps 25.
250. *LW* 14:45n3.
251. Pelikan, "Introduction to Volume 14," ix.
252. Iwand, "Theology of the Cross," 14.
253. Seiling, "'Radical' Revisions of the Commentary," 31.

the *Vademecum* ("Guidebook") of evangelical pastoral care and comfort.²⁵⁴

Iwand adjudged, in the context of the theology of the cross, that Luther's "Guidebook" demonstrates, "the pastoral character of his [Luther's] theology and will develop into a new concept of reality which resigns itself to the cross in faith." This is an "immense change in the view of Christian existence.... [that] meets God in the reality of an entirely unpredictable, historical life filled with ... unfathomable vicissitudes."²⁵⁵ This is the foundation of Luther's theology of reality. With a pastoral style, Luther wrote the work in German, for "coarse Saxons" to understand.²⁵⁶

If this were his Guidebook of pastoral care, Luther may have introduced the material of these Psalms with his comment on Ps 32:8, "I will instruct you and teach you in the way you should go." This summarizes Luther's theology of the cross as he elaborates on what he senses to be the "pastoral care" of the loving Triune God (Luther paraphrased how he felt God would speak).²⁵⁷

> This is where I want you to be. You ask that I deliver you. Then ... surrender yourself to me. I am competent to be your Master. I will lead you in a way that is pleasing to me. You think it wrong if things do not go as you feel they should. But your thinking harms you and hinders me. . . . Submerge yourself in a lack of understanding, and I will give you My understanding. Lack of understanding is real understanding; not knowing where you are going is really knowing where you are going. Thus, Abraham went out from his homeland and did not know where he was going (Gen 12). He yielded to My knowledge and abandoned his own knowledge; and by the right way he reached the right goal. Behold, that is the way of the cross. You cannot find it, but I must lead you like a blind man. Therefore not you, not a man, not a creature, but I, through My Spirit and the word, will teach you the way you must go. You must not follow the work, which you choose, not the suffering which you devise, but that which comes to you against your choice, thoughts, and desires.²⁵⁸

Not every psalm in the *Bußpsalmen* contains every aspect of the theology of the cross, but the combination of all seven presents the concepts.

---

254. Iwand, "Theology of the Cross," 2.
255. Iwand, "Theology of the Cross," 14.
256. Pelikan, "Introduction to Volume 14," ix.
257. Ps 32:10 in the 1517 edition, and Ps 31:8 in the Vulgate.
258. *LW* 14:152; *WA* 18:489, 10–27; Iwand, "Theology of the Cross," 14.

A key concept in all seven is Luther's theology of reality. The theologian of the cross sees things the way they really are and experiences both the cross of trials and suffering and real-life deliverance by the ministry of the Holy Spirit through the word. To enter into real life in Christ, the potential disciple must yield to Christ's call to take up the cross that is given to each one (Matt 16:24) and to follow Christ into death and the life of resurrection (Rom 6:3–11). This is the heart of his theology.[259]

Luther saw God as the initiator. God says, "I will instruct you and teach you in the way you should go (Ps 32:8)." His call is an invitation to follow him as disciples ("called out ones") and later to be engaged in apostolic ministry ("sent out ones"). The *Bußpsalmen* make it clear, however, that not all who are called will follow. Those who follow we could call the "penitents." The response of the penitent is "Teach me to do your will, for you are my God. Let your good spirit lead me on a level path (Ps 143:10). The penitents are convicted of their sinful Adamic nature and the behavior it provokes: . . . self-love, impure love that seeks to possess God for personal enjoyment, so that man is pious out of fear of hell or hope of heaven and not because of God." Luther noted that "this is difficult to recognize and still more difficult to overcome. Indeed, it is impossible except the grace of the Holy Spirit."[260] The recognition of their sin causes great anguish and fear and causes them to realize their only hope is in the Lord and they cry out for his mercy.

Those who do not follow the call of the Lord are the "wicked" of whom Luther said

> These . . . rule themselves and do not want God's rule. They act only according to their own judgment. And yet they think they respect and honor God in the best possible way, as the most obedient, the most pious, and the most righteous; for they have good intentions and consider right what their good intentions suggest. God always opposes them, for they are of a proud spirit and not obedient to the will of God. Hence, they will suffer much and have many sorrows.[261]

---

259. *LW* 14:175; *WA* 18:507.

260. Iwand, "Theology of the Cross," 17: "*Den nennen die doctores amorem sui, amorem dei concupiscentie, ßo der mensch umb forcht der hellen adder hoffnung des himels, und ni umb willen gottisfrum ist,*" *WA* 1:168, 7–10; "*Das ist aber schere tzurkennen, nach schwerlicher loß zuwerden, und als beyd nit dan durch gnade des heyligen geysts gescheen mag.*" See also *LW* 14:149; *WA* 18:486, 29–31.

261. *LW* 14:153; *WA* 18:489, 1–4.

The wicked refuse to accept God's offer of restoration and therefore fail to see things as they really are. They are sinners needing restoration and the only way to find God's truth is through their crosses, which they reject. Correlating the *Bußpsalmen* to the theology of the cross, the "penitent" and "wicked" correspond to the "theologian of the cross" and the "theologian of glory."

In several places of Luther's exposition, the struggles for the "penitent" refer to their crosses and to the Holy Spirit. Struggles are crosses the saints bear in hope, honoring God's will (Ps 6:5).[262] They are the way of the cross whereby their Master, the Holy Spirit through the word, teaches them the way they must go (Ps 32:8) to learn God's understanding of reality—the way things are.[263]

Struggles for the "wicked" have no resolution because, as Luther interprets Ps 32:9, "These are the people who do not let me rule. Like dumb animals, they obey where they agree; and where they do not agree . . . they do not obey. They do not understand the Spirit."[264] In Ps 38:20, where the psalmist says, "Those who render me evil for good accuse me because I follow after good," Luther interpreted, giving the reason for their opposition:

> Those who think themselves wise and righteous cannot help but repay evil for good. For they persecute and repay with hatred and torture the true doctrine that . . . tells them that which is best and most useful. Besides, they slander and malign all who seek that good thing and follow after it. That is because this very good is not apparent but is under the cross, lowly, and hidden in God. But they refuse to become lowly. . . . They want to be somebody or . . . create havoc, and yet they think they do well. But it is real evil, and they destroy themselves. This the child of God avoids. Therefore, they speak evil against him.[265]

---

262. *LW* 14:143; *WA* 18:482.

263. *LW* 14:152; *WA* 18:489.

264. *LW* 14:153; *WA* 18:489, 1–4; "Das sind die, die mich nicht lassen regiren, sondern gleich wie die sinnliche thiere folgen, so fern fülen, wo sie nicht fülen . . . solgen sie nicht, und verstehen den geist nicht."

265. *LW* 14:162; *WA* 18:497; "Die selbweisen und eigen rechtfertigen künnen nicht anders, denn bös fur gut widder geben, denn die rechte leere, . . . das beste saget und vol dienet, das doch gut ding ist, verfolgen sie und geben hass und marter da fur, dazu versprechen sie und nach reden allen, die das selbe gut suchen und yhm folgen , das macht, dasselbe gut nicht offenbar ist, sondern under dem creutz, und zu nichte werden, verborgen ist ynn Gott, Sie aber wöllen nicht zu nicht werden . . . Sie wöllen auch ettwas sein odder. . .unglück anrichten, und doch ynn dem selben dem guten zu folgen vermeinen. Es ist aber warhafftig das böse und verderben ihr selbs, davon weicht der frome, und wird darumb versprochen von yhm."

In his comments on Ps 51:6, "Behold, you delight in truth in the inward being, and you teach me wisdom in the secret heart," Luther explains how the theology of the cross distinguishes between the theologian of glory and the theologian of the cross. The "proud" or "wicked" theologian of glory holds to outward righteousness and apparent piety. This baseless deception, without truth, merely masks inner sin and is only a facade of real and true righteousness. Such outer falsehood is loved by sinful humans but hated by God. God loves inner truth and describes how the humble or "penitents" correspond to theologians of the cross:

> The wisdom of God is revealed to the proud only in its outward appearance, but it is revealed to the humble in its inner truth and hidden foundation. Now the outward appearance of this wisdom consists in this, that man believes he serves God with many words, thoughts, and works, and measures up to God's standard. It is all an outward show, which is apparent and possible to anyone, as there are many ways and means of doing this. In all this, men seek God, but entirely in reverse and outwardly. Inwardly they know him less than all others, because they seek themselves, and under the pretext of studying and learning about God!
>
> The inner hidden part of this wisdom is nothing else than knowing oneself thoroughly, and therefore hating oneself. It is seeking all righteousness not in self but in God, always dissatisfied with oneself and yearning for God, that is, humbly loving God and looking away from self. This inner, unknown righteousness is revealed in all kinds of outward behavior, manner, words, and works, in which the proud remain and harden themselves. Therefore, God, who loves reality and truth, hates them, because they love the outward appearance and hypocrisy.[266]

---

266. *LW* 14:169; *WA* 18:502, 12–28; "*Die weisheit Gottes wird den hoffertigen nur ym eussern schein offinbart, aber den demütigen wird sie ynn ynwendiger warheit und verborgenem grund erzeigt. Das eusser nu disser weisheit stehet darinne, das der mensch meinet, mit viel worten, tichten, wercken Gott zu deinen und nach zukomen, alles ynn eusserlichem scheine, das eim iglichen menschen offenbar ist und müglich zu thun, als denn der geberden und weisen viel find. Ynn dissem suchet man alles Gott, aber gantz mit dem ruden und eusserlich, ynwendig kennen sie sein weniger denn all ander, darumb das sie sich selbs suchen, auch an Gott mit den selben weisen studiren und Gottes erkennen! ... Das ynnerliche aber und verborgen disser weisheit ist nicht anders, denn sich grundlich, und also sich hassen und alle gerechtikeit nicht bey sich, sondern bey Gott suchen, alzeit sein verdrissen und nach Gotte senen, das ist demütig Gott lieben und lassen sich, disse ynnere unbekante gerechtigkeit wird bedeutet ynn allen eussern zierden, weisen, worten, wercken, ynn wilchen die hoffertigen verbleiben und verharten, darumb Gott, der den grund und warheit lieb hat, hasset sie, das sie lieb haben den schein und heuchel.*"

In this passage from the translation of the 1525 comments on Ps 51:6b, Luther revealed that the elements of his theology of the cross were in place in mid-1517, a few months before the *Ninety-Five Theses* and about a year before the presentation of his theology of the cross at the Heidelberg Disputation (April 25, 1518).[267] The 1525 edition includes the same concepts, with almost identical wording as the 1517 edition.[268] Seiling notes several twentieth-century comparisons made between the 1517 and the 1525 documents. These studies essentially agree that Luther's theological and religious positions remained unchanged from 1517 to 1525.[269]

Describing the cross in the Christian life, Luther maintained that the cross comes to Christians from others and from the Lord himself. Luther's comments on Ps 38:20 speak of persecutors who think themselves wise and righteous. They refuse the lowly way of the penitent and try to make their life difficult.[270]

Luther presented his understanding of the purpose of life under the cross in his comments on Ps 51:2, "Wash me thoroughly from my iniquity, and cleanse me from my sin." In most of the Psalms, David prays that he be washed of his sin. Grace is a continuous process that begins with washing and cleansing so "that Adam must get out and Christ come in, Adam become as nothing, and Christ alone remain and rule."[271] This is the goal of the way of the cross. The penitent's status in sin cannot be resolved on his own (Ps 32:2). His plea to be washed whiter than snow, Luther saw, can only be accomplished by the inward sprinkling of the grace of the Holy Spirit (Ps 51:7).[272]

Concern and hope come in the reality of God's righteousness and judgment, "If you, O LORD, should mark iniquities, O Lord, who could stand? (Ps 130:3)." Luther emphasized the importance of fearing the judgment of the LORD, yet knowing that the old Adam must be crucified, for "As long as the old man lives, the fear, that is, the crucifixion and execution of this old man, must not cease; nor dare not the judgment of God be forgotten. And

---

267. *LW* 14:169–70; 51:7; *WA* 1:188 [1517]; *WA* 18:502–3 [1525].

268. The 1525 edition is a study in how certain archaic spellings and phraseologies were being "modernized" from the 1517 time period as Luther and his associates were "inventing" the "modern" German language that would appear in his editions of the German Bible of the 1530s.

269. Seiling, "'Radical' Revisions of the Commentary," 32–33, cites the bibliographic works of Seiling's resourses.

270. *LW* 14:162; *WA* 18:497.

271. *LW* 14:167; *WA* 18:500, 8–9, "Nu ists mit uns also, das Adam aus mus, und Christus eingehen, Adam zu nicht warden, und Christus alien regiren und sein."

272. *LW* 14:149, 170; *WA* 18:486, 503.

whoever would be without this crucifying and this fear and the judgment of God, does not live aright."[273] However, there is hope in the following verses: "But with you there is forgiveness, that you may be feared. I wait for the LORD, my soul waits, and in his word I hope" (Ps 130:4–5). Luther commented that with God alone there is forgiveness. Good works give no help. In the face of this is the cross of waiting and walking in the fear of God. Luther notes this Psalm describes how walking in fear and hope has two options: fear, the beginning of despair or hope, the beginning of recovery. "The old man must fear, despair, and perish; the new man must hope, be raised up and stand." This trust is in God's grace alone.[274]

In Ps 51:11–12, David pleaded, "Cast me not away from your presence, and take not your Holy Spirit from me. Restore to me the joy of your salvation, and uphold me with a willing spirit." Luther asserted that possession of the Holy Spirit is necessary to be accepted by God. Only the Spirit can make free and willing people from those who opposed God. Those without the Holy Spirit cannot be cleansed in their hearts because they love themselves more than they love God.[275]

Psalm 143, the Seventh Penitential Psalm, concludes the *Bußpsalmen* with several concerns of the penitent:

1. Supplications for judgment to be replaced by mercy,
2. Deliverance from persecutions by God's enemies,
3. Times of spiritual weakness,
4. Remembrance of the LORD's mighty acts,
5. Trust in the love and teaching of the LORD,
6. Refuge in the LORD and his righteousness,
7. Preservation of life,
8. Declaration that he is a servant of the LORD.

Verse 7 depicts the cross of the penitent: "Answer me quickly, O LORD! My spirit fails! Hide not your face from me, lest I be like those who go down to the pit (Ps 143:7)." Luther notes that the penitent's cross comprises the *inner* cross and the *outer* cross. God cherishes the cries for grace from the soul, which finds nothing in itself. Such a cry cannot come from one who

---

273. *LW* 14:190; *WA* 18:517, 39–41. "*Und die weil der alt mensch lebt, soll die furcht, das ist sein creutz und tödten nicht auss hören und das gerichte Gottes nicht vergessen, Und wer on das creutz und on furcht und on Gottes urteil lebet, der lebet nicht recht.*"
274. *LW* 14:191; *WA* 18:518.
275. *LW* 14:172; *WA* 18:504–5.

delights in the good life and does not fear God's judgment. Conversely, the penitent sees his own spiritual inadequacy and suffers internally concerning this, as well as with waiting for God's grace. God's delay is part of the inner cross that refines his desire for God and he becomes the "Christ-formed man"—inwardly disconsolate with a constant longing for God's grace and help. His outward cross comes when those with whom he shares his cross and wants to teach, ungratefully despise and reject his teaching. "Thus he is inwardly and outwardly crucified with Christ. The proud, on the other hand, stand boldly in their presumption that they are like those who are going to heaven. They do not have any fear of hell or thirst for grace."[276]

On Ps 143:10, "Teach me to do your will, for you are my God. Let your good spirit lead me on level ground!" Luther pointed out that God's teacher and guide—the Holy Spirit—"Creates gentle, kind, and good hearts, which walk the right path, on which they seek God in all things and not themselves."[277]

In these texts of the *Bußpsalmen* Luther linked the theology of the cross with the presence of the Holy Spirit—the Master and Teacher of the way of the cross, who works through the word of God to rescue the penitent as they trust the promises and obey the call of the Lord.

The *Theologia Germanica* of Martin Luther (1516 and 1518)

As briefly mentioned above, when Luther's theology of the cross was in its early stages of development (1516–18) he encountered the writing (ca. 1350) of an unknown German monk assumed to be from the Teutonic Order of Sackshausen near Frankfurt am Main.[278] Luther published a short version of the work in 1516 and a full version in June 1518 (shortly after the *Heidelberg Disputation*) under the title *Theologia Germanica* or *Theologia Deutsch* (*A German Theology*), with the following "warning" and endorsement:

> I wish to warn everyone who reads this book not to harm himself and become irritated by its simple German language or its unadorned and unassuming words, for this noble little book, poor and unadorned as it is in words and human wisdom, is the richer and more precious in art and divine wisdom. To boast

---

276. *LW* 14:201; *WA* 18:526, 15–18; "Also auswendig und ynnwendig mit Christo gecreutziget wird, denn die hoffertigen stehen ynn yhrer vermessenheit, das sie gleich sind denen, die gen himel faren, solche furcht der hellen und der gnaben durft haben sei nicht."

277. *LW* 14:203; *WA* 18:527.

278. See Hoffman's Introduction to Hoffman, *Theologia Germanica*, 2.

> with my old fool,²⁷⁹ no book except the Bible and St. Augustine has come to my attention from which I have learned more about God, Christ, man, and all things. I now for the first time become aware of the fact that a few of us highly educated Wittenberg theologians speak disgracefully, as though we want to undertake entirely new things,²⁸⁰ as though there had been no people previously or elsewhere. Indeed, there have been others, but God's wrath, aroused by our sin, has prevented us from being worthy enough to recognize or hear them. It is obvious that such matters as are contained in this book have not been discussed in our universities for a long time, with the result that the holy word of God has not only been laid under the bench but has almost been destroyed by dust and filth.
>
> Let anyone who wishes read this little book, and then let him say whether theology is original with us or ancient, for this book is certainly not new. But some may say, as in the past, that we are German theologians. We shall let that stand. I thank God that I hear and find my God in the German tongue, whereas I, and they with me, previously did not find him either in the Latin, the Greek, or the Hebrew tongue. God grant that this little book will become better known. Then we shall find that German theologians are without a doubt the best theologians. Amen.
>
> Doctor Martin Luther, *Augustinian at Wittenberg*²⁸¹

While Luther may have advanced a work from the period and setting of the Medieval Pietists, the theological message portrays the powerlessness of the human will and rationality and the need for dependence upon God, at the heart of Luther's "breakthrough" theology of true reality about God and man.

In his preface to Bengt Hoffman's English translation of the *German Theology*, Bengt Hägglund noted that the work distinguishes clearly between the world of creation and the eternal spiritual world. Hägglund challenged Christians to live in the present with accommodations to their eternal destination. The standard example of such sacrificial human life is the human life of Jesus Christ. In such a life the Christian experiences the struggles of sin and contrition while following "two roads"—heaven and hell—in their transition of awakening into a new spiritual life.²⁸²

---

279. Faith in Christ, Luther maintained with Paul, makes one a fool with Christ.

280. Luther refers to his new evangelical theology. On numerous other occasions he voices his concern over the question, "Am I the only wise one?"

281. *LW* 31:75–76; *WA* 1:378–79.

282. See Hägglund's Preface to Hoffman, *Theologia Germanica*, xi.

Discussing Luther's preface to the larger *German Theology* [1518], Harold Grimm cautioned that, while Luther expressed theological concerns with late-medieval German mystics, he also emphasized the necessity of a spiritual rebirth of despair in order for one to be united with God.[283] Luther pointed to his experience with the mystics:

> There is a saying of Tauler's, . . . [Luther first thought Tauler to be the author of *The German Theology*] "Man should know that he has done great damage if he does not wait for God's work," namely, when God wants to crucify him, mortify him, and reduce the old man to nothing. This does not come about except through suffering and the cross; for then you are upholding the work of God, who forms you. . . . He cuts down everything that hinders the eternal building.[284]

By 1518, when Luther had established his doctrine of justification by faith, he valued his own despair as the indispensable prerequisite to receive God's grace. God had never deserted him. As he continued his battle with the scholasticism of his opponents, he treasured the mystics' simple evangelical "wisdom of experience" rather than the scholastics' "wisdom of theology."[285]

Luther declared that the "noble little book" provided a link to the past theology of the church, which validated that he and his fellow Wittenbergers were not proclaiming a new theology.[286] They had merely rediscovered the ancient theology of the church.

According to the Frankfurter (Luther's nickname for the German Theologian), sin is turning from obedience to the unchangeable perfect God to following the desires of the imperfect self. The only way for the imperfect to know the perfect God is for the imperfect to abandon selfish creatureliness to its destruction.[287] This correlates with the Wittenberg New Theology, the theology of the cross. The Frankfurter agrees with Luther's concept of the theology of glory. To God alone belongs glory and he gives it to no other. When sinful creatures claim goodness as their own they "usurp

---

283. Grimm, "Introduction to *A German Theology*," 73.

284. LW 7:133; WA 44:397; "*Extat vox Tauleri, quanquam non loquitur in terminis scripturae sanctae, sed alieno et peregrino sermone utitur: Magnum damnum sciat homo se fecisse, qui non expectat opus Domini, videlicet, quando vult eum crucifigere, mortificare et redigere veterem hominem in nihilum, quod non fit nisi passione et cruce, ibi enim sustines opus Domini, qui format te . . . et quidquid est impedimenti ad aedificationem aeternam, praecidit secure*," Gen 41:1–7 (1544).

285. Grimm, "Preface to *A German Theology*," 73.

286. Grimm, "Preface to *A German Theology*," 75.

287. Hoffman, *Theologia Germanica*, 60–61.

merit and honor" and 1) fall away into apostasy and 2) take away God's honor to call it ther own. "Nothing *good* belongs to man."[288] The conclusion sounds like the Wittenberg "New Theology," the theology of the cross.

> For when the illusion and the ignorance turn into a realization of the Truth, the assumption that the Good comes from us will disappear of its own.
>
> Man will then say, "Look, I poor fool imagined that it was I but, in truth, it is and was God!"[289]

The Frankfurter relates the life of turning, submission, contrition, confession, and obedience to the Lord with what he called obsession, or pouring out of the Spirit. It is the same relationship as the theology of the cross with the Holy Spirit. He speaks of the life in the Spirit:

> Let us imagine a person who is obsessed and held by God's spirit to such a degree that he is unaware of the flow and ebb from God and thus does not act in his own power. The power of God then directs at will that person's works, deeds, and leisure. He would be one of those about whom Saint Paul speaks: Those who are guided and led by God's spirit are God's children and are not under law (Rom 8:14, 6:14).
>
> Christ spoke about such a person: "For it is not you who speak, but the Spirit of your Father speaking through you" (Matt 10:20).[290]

The Frankfurter speaks of preparation for the pouring of the Holy Spirit:

> The concerns of the I and the self are the devil's field. That is why he is a devil.
>
> My many words on the subject can be summed up by a few: Cut off your self, cleanly and utterly. . . .
>
> If man is not prepared and will not be prepared, it is his own fault.
>
> If man were, in all his thinking and striving, single-mindedly bent on a preparation,[97] how to become prepared, then God would indeed prepare him.
>
> For God devotes as much zeal and love and earnest resolve to preparing man as He does to the pouring out of the Spirit once man is prepared. . . .

---

288. Hoffman, *Theologia Germanica*, 63–64.
289. Hoffman, *Theologia Germanica*, 65.
290. Hoffman, *Theologia Germanica*, 86.

> Four things are needful:
> Needed in the first place is keen yearning for, diligence in, and steadfast resolve about the way to prepare for the Lord. Let us add that nothing ever happens where such yearning is absent.
> Second, you should have an example to learn from.
> Third, you must constantly and intently look to your Master, and see to it that you believe, obey, and follow him.
> Fourth, you should set about the work and practice it.
> If one of these four breaks down, the art will never be learned and mastered.
> This is precisely the case with the preparation.
> He who has the first, namely diligence and steadfast, determined yearning toward that end, will seek and find all that belongs to, serves, and leads to salvation.
> But he who does not have resolve and love and yearning will not seek. Thus he will not find but will remain unprepared and never attain the end.[291]

The result of the above submission is an authentic Christian life that lives out the life of Christ until the end of bodily life on earth.[292] This teaching, along with Tauler's sermons, provided helpful comfirmation as Luther formulated his theology of the cross. Carter Lindberg points out the distinctions Luther had to make as he valued the confirmation and influences of Tauler and the *German Theology*:

> It should be clear that Luther agreed with various themes in Tauler and the *German Theology*. These mystical writings confirmed Luther's stress on the hidden activity of God, which gives the Christian life "bitterness" to the selfish human nature and reason, which tries to flee suffering. They deepened Luther's understanding of faith in terms of passive resignation and conversion from self-reliance to trust in the incarnate and crucified Lord. On the other hand, their ontological anthropology with its call for the annihilation of "creatureliness" and the soteriological quest for "deification" are rejected by Luther.[293]

---

291. Hoffman, *Theologia Germanica*, 86–87.
292. Hoffman, *Theologia Germanica*, 88.
293. Lindberg, *Third Reformation?*, 29.

The *Heidelberg Disputation* (1518)

In April 1518, about six months after posting his *Ninety-Five Theses,* Luther was asked to introduce his new evangelical theology to his Augustinian brothers at Heidelberg. On April 26, he presented his *Heidelberg Disputation,* comprising twenty-eight theological and twelve philosophical theses, in which he claimed that the essence of true theology is the theology of the cross. This is the context for Luther's understanding of the Holy Spirit's reality in the Christian life.[294]

The theological theses provide an orderly biblical and theological basis for Luther's theology of the cross.[295] Theses 1–12 describe the hopelessness of human works, even under the law. Works may appear good, but they cannot lead to righteousness—only to futility and mortal sin.[296] In contrast, "Although the works of God are always unattractive and appear evil, they are really eternal merits (Thesis 4)."[297]

Theses 13–18 portray the impotency of the human will to obtain grace.[298] Thesis 17 describes the turning point of lostness where the only hope is repentance and turning to Christ, leading to Thesis 18 that describes the believer's cross, "man must utterly despair of his own ability before he is prepared to receive the grace of Christ."[299] Hope comes to those who, at the preaching of sin, confess their hopelessness, empty themselves, die to themselves, and trust in Christ to escape the condemnation of God's law.[300]

Theses 19–24 show that the theologian of the cross sees signs of God "through suffering and the cross"[301] and "calls the thing what it actually is."[302] Luther contrasted the theologian of the cross with the theologian of glory, the fool (Theses 19–21), and said, "True theology and recognition of

---

294. Althaus, *Theology*, 25; Loewenich, *Luther's Theology*, 28–31, Prenter, *Theology of the Cross*, 1–2.

295. LW 31:39–41; WA 1:353–55; *Heidelberg Disputation*. In his *On Being a Theologian of the Cross*, Gerhard Forde provided a helpful framework of how the theology of the cross is imbedded in the theological theses of the disputation.

296. LW 31:42–44.

297. LW 31:39; WA 1:353.

298. LW 31:48–52.

299. LW 31:40; WA 1:354, 13–14; "*Hominem de se penitus oportere desperare, ut aptus fiat and consequendam gratiam Christi.*"

300. LW 31:51–52; WA 1:361, 6–30.

301. LW 31:52; WA 1:362, 210–22; "*per passiones et crucem conspecta inrelligit*"; McGrath, *Theology of the Cross*, 148–50.

302. LW 31:53; WA 1:362, 22; "*dicit id quod res est.*"

God are in the crucified Christ."³⁰³ The fool, by a human theology of glory claims to see God's hidden things (Theses 19, 21a, 22). He mislabels human works good and God's suffering evil. When people do not know the cross, they hate it and love the opposite—wisdom, glory, and power—and become more blinded and hardened (Thesis 22).³⁰⁴ Luther clarified this seeming contradiction by applying the theology of the cross to Thesis 22.

> The remedy for curing desire does not lie in satisfying it, but in extinguishing it. . . . He who wishes to become wise does not seek wisdom . . . but becomes a fool . . . he who wishes to have much power, honor . . . must flee [them] . . . , which is folly to the world.³⁰⁵

Theses 25–28 (along with Thesis 4) show that God's hidden work in Christ leads to eternal merit and creates new beings for him to love (Theses 27–28)—the creative work of the Holy Spirit, *spiritus creator*. The power of the theology of the cross is both passive and active. Though that commanded by the law is never humanly accomplished, Christ is working. What is believed about grace is a work already done and pleasing to God (Theses 26–27). The love of God creates what is pleasing to him, while the love of man comes into being through that which is pleasing to man (Thesis 28).³⁰⁶ Passive faith is commanded to believe what is already accomplished through the creative power of the love of God.

The knowledge of God gained from works and the knowledge of God gained from suffering oppose each other. The theologian of glory claims to see God's invisible things and exchanges good for evil; yet only by the cross "works are dethroned and the old Adam, who is especially edified by works, is crucified."³⁰⁷ Luther contrasted these two:

> A theologian of the cross . . . teaches that . . . [sufferings] . . . are the most precious treasury of all . . . blessed is he who is considered by God to be so worthy that these treasures of Christ be given to him. . . .³⁰⁸

---

303. *LW* 31:53; *WA* 1:362, 18–19; "*ergo in Christo crucifixo est vera theologia et cognitio Dei*," "Explanation to Theses 20."

304. *LW* 31:53; *WA* 1:362, 35–36; "Explanation to Thesis 22."

305. *LW* 31:54; *WA* 1:363, 9–14; "*Restat ergo remedium, ut non explendo curetur, sed extinguendo . . . qui vult fieri sapiens non querat sapientiam . . . sed fiat stultus . . . qui vult fieri potens, glorious . . . fugiat . . . quae mundo est stulticia.*"

306. *LW* 31:41; *WA* 1:354, 35–36.

307. *LW* 31:52–53; *WA* 1:362, 23–33; "Explanations to Theses 20–21." See Althaus, *Theology*, 29.

308. *LW* 31: 225–26; *WA* 1: 613, 23–30; "*Theologus crucis . . . mortem docet*

> A theologian of glory does not recognize ... the crucified and hidden God. He sees and speaks of God's glorious manifestation.... How his invisible nature can be known from the things which are visible ... and how he is present and powerful in all things everywhere. This theologian of glory ... learns from Aristotle ... he defines the treasury of Christ as the removing and remitting of punishments, things which are most evil and worthy of hate.[309]

Contrasting the theology of the cross and the theology of glory, Jungkuntz said the character of the theology of the cross depends on the revelation of the historical Christ in the word of God. It is apprehended in the Spirit by faith through the word and sacraments and it visibly expresses love and obedience in suffering in participation in Christ. The theology of glory depends on autonomous human reason that apprehends understanding by human senses (Thesis 16) in order to express law-oriented egocentric works and rebellion.[310] According to the theology of the cross, because God is hidden in the cross, reason's self-confident speculations about God are silenced.

Bruce Gerrish claimed that Luther rejected reason and philosophy as the dominant or guiding force in interpreting Scripture because they belonged to the natural sphere and should not be allowed to judge matters of faith. However, Luther did find them indispensable for the regenerate since faith comes through hearing and understanding the word.[311]

The cross exposes humanity's defective judgment and the futility of its acts toward God. God's suffering for people is experienced only through Christ on the cross.[312] Luther, with Paul in Romans 1, rejected the natural knowledge of God and endorsed the "folly of our preaching" (1 Cor 1:21).[313]

The "hidden God" (*Deus Absconditus*) is accessed by God's self-revelation in the cross and the work of the Holy Spirit through evangelical

---

thezaurrum esse presiosissimum ... benedictus, qui dignus fuerit deo visus, ut ei donentur hii, thesauri reliquiarum Christi, immo qui intelligat sibi donari." Explanation of the Ninety-Five Theses (1518).

309. LW 31:227; WA 1:614, 17–24; "*Theologus vero gloriae . . .* [*non . . . solum crucifixum et absconditum deum novit, sed gloriosum cum gentibus, ex visibilibus invisibilibus eius, ubique presentem, omninia potentem videt et loquitur*] *discit ex Aristotle . . . diffinit, thesaurum Christi esse relaxationes et solutiones poenarum tanquam rerum pessimarum et odibilissimarum . . .*" Explanation of the Ninety-Five Theses (1518).

310. Jungkuntz, "Secularization Theology," 6.

311. Gerrish, *Grace and Reason*, 26–27.

312. Althaus, *Theology*, 28.

313. Christenson, *Welcome*, 191.

preaching.³¹⁴ He cannot be derived from the works of creation, because he hides himself (Isa 45:15)³¹⁵—it is his peculiar property.³¹⁶ Luther understood that the hidden God reveals himself to faith that trusts in the word of God over and against the obvious. God is not revealed to the speculations of human wisdom and philosophy.³¹⁷ Natural sinful people cannot know God (Rom 1), because "God hides his own things in order to reveal them."³¹⁸ God is concealed to be revealed and to be comprehended. Therefore, God "hides Himself . . . under the curse, a blessing; under the consciousness of sin, righteousness; under death, life; and under affliction, comfort."³¹⁹ By concealing himself, God removed obstructing human pride. When the cross of the Christian disarms pride in repentance, God reveals himself in that which had concealed him. To argue with the theses of the *Heidelberg Disputation*, which say that God is hidden in suffering, is to sit in judgment of God.³²⁰ In *The Bondage of the Will* (1525), Luther said his view of God surpassed Erasmus's intellectualism; for to try to describe God is to put oneself above God and God remains hidden. While he has revealed himself to us in his word, he is still greater than his word, and so is hidden to us.³²¹ Thus, the hidden God of the *Heidelberg Disputation* and the *Bondage of the Will* connect with Luther's idea that faith deals with unseen things (Heb 11:1) and everything to be believed is hidden. A clear fact requires no faith and there is no connection with God. The hidden God is necessary for our redemption and reconciliation because faith itself requires a hidden God.³²² If God's righteousness could be humanly judged, it would be neither divine nor different from human righteousness. However, since

---

314. See "Hiddenness" discussion earlier in this chapter.

315. Loewenich, *Luther's Theology*, 27.

316. *LW* 6:148; *WA* 44:110, 23; Loewenich, *Luther's Theology*, 39.

317. Loewenich, *Luther's Theology*, 45; citing Kattenbusch, *Deus absconditus bei Luther*, 183; Luther's idea of the hidden God is a unique and positive idea of faith.

318. *LW* 25:154, 158; *WA* 56:174, 18–25, 177, 25–30; *WA* 1:138, 13–14 (a 1517 sermon), "*Deus abscondit sua ut revelet . . .*"; Loewenich, *Luther's Theology*, 28, 30.

319. *LW* 1:14; *WA* 42:11, 28–30; Lectures on Genesis 1–5 (1535–36); *LW* 6:148; *WA* 44:110, 23–25; *Lectures on Genesis 1–5* (1535) Lectures on Genesis 31–37 (1544); *LW* 4:7; *WA* 43:140, 28–30; "'Deum absconditum': sub maledictione enim latet benedictio, sub sensu peccati iustitia, sub morte vita, sub afflictione consolatio." Lectures on Genesis 21–25 (between 1536 and 1542); Loewenich, *Luther's Theology*, 39–40.

320. *LW* 31:53; *WA* 1:362, 25–27; *LW* 25:167; *WA* 56:185, 26–32.

321. *LW* 33:139–40; *WA* 18:685, 16–24; *Bondage* (1525).

322. *LW* 33:62–63; *WA* 18:633, 15–17; Loewenich, *Luther's Theology*, 36–37.

he is the one true God—inscrutable and remote—his righteousness is also necessarily inscrutable.[323]

Commenting on Isa 45:15 and Ps 118:4, Luther said that the flesh sees nothing and concludes there is nothing. Nevertheless, faith, convinced by unseen things, sees that God's inscrutable plans work out through his consoling word. The doctrine of the hidden God says that God's realities of grace, salvation, and life, are hidden with him in the cross, and appear to the world as eternal wrath, while the ungodly appear to be God's children. Skill and grace are required to discern God's hidden blessings.[324] Luther warned of speculations about the hidden God that may cause one to side step Christ—the sure way to the Father—and to fall into the consuming fire of the "nude" God, whom natural people cannot endure.[325]

Loewenich and McGrath identify five essentials of Luther's theology of the cross:

1. It is a theology of revelation opposing speculation.
2. God's revelation is indirect and concealed.
3. God's revelation is not comprehended by ethical works, but through suffering and the cross.
4. The hidden God is known only by faith.
5. God is known through suffering and repentance. The believer's cross intersects with the cross of Christ as the creative power of God's love begins its work in the believer.

Further, Luther noted a sixth essential in Theses 26–28, and in his Corollary.

6. In the battle between flesh and Spirit of Rom 7:22–23; Matt 26:41; and Gal 5:17, the Holy Spirit is the active force of God's love—the *Spiritus Creator* forming the believer into Christ.[326] As Forde is quoted above, "Simply let the bird of the Spirit fly!"[327]

---

323. *LW* 33:290; *WA* 18:784, 11–13; *Bondage* (1525).

324. *LW* 17:131–32; *WA* 32^{II}:364, 21–23, *Isaiah 45:15* (1527–30); *LW* 14:58; *WA* 31^{I}:51, 21–24; *Ps 118:4* (1530); cf. Loewenich, *Luther's Theology*, 38–39; and Althaus, *Theology*, 30.

325. *LW* 5:50; *WA* 43:463, 3–5; *Lectures on Genesis 26–30* (1542–44); *LW* 16:54–55; *WA* 31^{II}:38, 21–23; *Commentary on Isaiah 1–39* (1528); *LW* 26:29–30; *WA* 40^{I}:77, 11–13, 79, 20; *Commentary on Galatians* (1535); cf. Loewenich, *Luther's Theology*, 42.

326. Loewenich, *Luther's Theology*, 22; McGrath, *Theology of the Cross*, 149–52; Theses 26–28, and Corollary; *LW* 31:41, 56–57, 60–61; *WA* 1:354, 31–36.

327. Forde, "Radical Lutheranism," 16.

Operationes in Psalmos (1518–21)

In his 1519 dedication of *Operationes in Psalmos* to Elector Frederick the Wise, Luther expressed his appreciation and love for his prince and discussed the importance and the methods of writing such a work. He confessed his own sense of inadequacy and need to consult with associates, but that was not enough—"He rises the highest, who comes nearest to the Holy Spirit."[328] He felt the Psalms were superior to all books of Scripture, teaching and showing how we should follow God's word.

> What else then is the Psalter but praying to, and praising God? that is, a book of hymns?
> Therefore, the most gracious and blessed Spirit of God, the Father of his humble scholars, and the teacher of infants, well knowing that "we know not how to pray as we ought," as Paul saith in Romans 8:26, in order to help our infirmities, like schoolmasters who compose letters or subjects for their pupils to write home to their parents, has prepared for us in this book words and sentiments with which we may converse with our heavenly Father, and pray unto him concerning those things which he has taught us in the other books ... unto his eternal salvation. So great are the care of God over us and his kindness to us![329]

Luther's comment on Ps 5:11, "But let all who take refuge in you rejoice; let them ever sing for joy, and spread your protection over them, that those who love your name may exult in you," expresses the focus for all his work, and the slogan of his theology—The cross alone is our theology (*CRUX sola est nostra Theologia.*).[330] In the commentary material preceding this passage, Luther laid out the issues regarding God and his faithful children that lead up to his "slogan."[331]

Luther contrasted human works and merit with hope in the promises of the hidden God. Human philosophy and works do not merit God's provisions. Faith and hope in God's provision depend upon the word and promise of God, from which works and merit flow. In this life, we continually stretch from hope to hope reaching for God's promised protection of his righteousness and sanctification. As we trust in him passively through trials and suffering—our personal crosses—we receive his promised righteousness, not

---

328. Luther, *Commentary on the First Twenty-Two Psalms*, 1:23.
329. Luther, *Commentary on the First Twenty-Two Psalms*, 1:23–24.
330. Luther, *Commentary on the First Twenty-Two Psalms*, 1:289; WA 5:176, 32–33.
331. Luther, *Commentary on the First Twenty-Two Psalms*, 1:286–89; WA 5:175, 4–176, 31.

through our striving but by his grace through our faith, for faith, hope, and love are perfected inwardly only through passive suffering.[332] Such suffering and the death of our crosses lead to new life, trusting and hoping only in God's promises of life and salvation. Thus, Luther declared, "The cross alone is our theology!"[333]

Hans Iwand points to *Operationes on Psalmos* as the key to Luther's theology:

> He who wants to understand Luther's theology of the cross rightly must read the *Operationes on Psalmos* . . . the genuine interpretation of this theological principal. The Psalms and the theology of the cross—they are one and the same. Here it was lived, confessed, and expounded . . . in scripture.[334]

This process for Luther and for all Christians is the work of the Holy Spirit. The cross Luther bore trying to meet God's commands for righteousness was met by the cross of Christ. The obedient Christian bears the cross appointed by Christ to serve him and to further the work of the gospel. Both aspects of the manifestation of the cross are works of the Holy Spirit. The Spirit brings faith, assurance of salvation, and supernatural abilities to obey the differing calls to varieties of Christians.

Luther not only came to know these truths from Scripture, but he experienced them in his own life. For that reason his theology can be called a theology of reality. Those things that God speaks of and promises in Scripture actually happen now in the lives of believers.

Psalmos Graduum (Song of Ascents) (1532/33 and 1540)

Just as he finished Ps 22 in *Operationes in Psalmos* Luther was called to the Diet of Worms and then was wisked away to his year at Wartburg Castle to begin many new tasks. It appeared that his work on the Psalms and his "new theology"—the theology of the cross—were set aside. Did the theology of the cross continue as the key issue in Luther's theology, or was it merely a passing phase of the "young Luther" as his career matured?

Considering this question Kolb examined Luther's *Lectures on the Psalms* (1532–33) and showed that fifteen years after the *Heidelberg*

---

332. Luther, *Commentary on the First Twenty-Two Psalms*, 1:287–88.
333. Luther, *Commentary on the First Twenty-Two Psalms*, 1:289; WA 5:176, 32–33.
334. Iwand, "Theology of the Cross," 9.

Disputaion, where Luther introduced the theology of the cross to the Augustinian community, he still used the term and maintained its principles.[335]

In 1533 Luther still referred to the theology of the cross as "our theology," stressing the suffering of Christians from Ps 126:5, "Those who sow in tears shall reap with shouts of joy!"; Acts 14:22, "Strengthening the souls of the disciples, encouraging them to continue in the faith, and saying that through many tribulations we must enter the kingdom of God," and 1 Pet 1:11, "Inquiring what person or time the Spirit of Christ in them was indicating when he predicted the sufferings of Christ and the subsequent glories."[336] In these texts Luther linked the suffering of Christians with Christ's suffering, death, resurrection, and ultimate glory.

> You know this teaching very well since our theology is a theology of the cross. It is necessary for Christians to suffer, etc., and after that the glory in Christ. There is no other way for no walk of life is experienced apart from the cross.[337]

Kolb identified a 1540 alteration by Veit Dietrich, "For theology is properly called the profession of the holy cross. So it was fitting for Christ the head of the church and the prophets to suffer through the Holy Spirit."[338]

A key principle from his 1518 works was retained in 1532-33, *per Spiritum sanctum*—through the Holy Spirit. Christians can only survive the testing and proving of the cross as they obediently trust and depend on the Holy Spirit to accomplish that which the Father has promised for the faithful.

Kolb asks, "Does this definition of his [Luther's] *theologia crucis* as focused on human suffering mean that the hermaneutic of trust in God's revelation of himself and the life of faith it creates had disappeared from Luther's way of practicing theology by 1533?"[339] He points to the Dietrich text, "For theology is properly called the profession of the holy cross," and asks what is profession—"the Christian's walk of life or the confession of faith?"[340] Kolb notes that in 1532-33, as in 1518, Luther was struggling with personal issues. In 1518, he struggled in explaining the Wittenberg hermeneutical principles resulting in his criticism of Roman Cathlic scholasticism, biblical interpretation, and ecclesial tradition. In 1532-33, his struggles included

---

335. Kolb, "Luther's Theology of the Cross," 69-85.
336. Kolb, "Luther's Theology of the Cross," 73-74; WA 403:193, 6-8, 19-23.
337. WA 403:193, 6-8.
338. Kolb, "Luther's Theology of the Cross," 74; WA 403:193, 19-21.
339. Kolb, "Luther's Theology of the Cross," 74.
340. Kolb, "Luther's Theology of the Cross," 74.

external threats—Saxon Duke George and the papacy challenged the Wittenberg reforms, and other evangelicals raised theological challenges regarding Reformation interpretations—and he experienced some ongoing personal health challenges, as well.[341] Therefore, Kolb observes the similarities and gives an important summarizing assessment.

> Tribulations of various kinds plagued Luther throughout his career, and these days were no different. His practice of theology in the manner of the cross, *in via Wittenberg*, had established itself and needed no special reinforcement, no fresh formulation or definition.
>
> Nonetheless, although Luther narrowed the focus of the term *theologia crucis* to the suffering of believers in the particular citation treated here, throughout his lectures on the Psalms of ascent there are examples of his observing the hermeneutical guidelines for practicing theology set forth in the *Heidelberg Disputation*.[342]

The presence and work of the Holy Spirit appears in another text Kolb examined from these lectures, Luther's commentary on Ps 129:4, 8, "⁴The LORD is righteous; he has cut the cords of the wicked.... ⁸nor do those who pass by say, 'The blessing of the LORD be upon you! We bless you in the name of the LORD!'" Luther sees (verse 4) that the Holy Spirit is present as teacher to show the faithful how the "righteous" God destroys the wicked and their power in the end. Further (verse 8), Luther noted that the baptized Christian, through this conflict between God and Satan, has the Holy Spirit and the word—the power of God in Christ—to be victors even as their battles are losing, "My grace is sufficient for you, for my power is made perfect in weakness. Therefore, I will boast all the more gladly of my weaknesses, so that the power of Christ may rest upon me (2 Cor 12:9)." This is the blessing in the name of the Triune God in action, demonstrating the presence and work of the Holy Spirit through conflict and suffering.[343]

In these lectures of 1532–33, Luther's approach to biblical texts followed the principles developed in 1518. He proclaimed these elements of his theology of the cross in his lectures on the Song of Ascent.[344]

---

341. Kolb, "Luther's Theology of the Cross," 74–75.

342. Kolb, "Luther's Theology of the Cross," 75.

343. Kolb, "Luther's Theology of the Cross," 80–83; WA 40^{III}:322, 23–26, ... 334, 27–37.

344. Kolb, "Luther's Theology of the Cross," 76–77.

1. Believers are to distinguish the hidden God, lying beyond human comprehension, from the revealed God, who discloses his essence through Christ's death on the cross for the sins of the world.
2. Believers are to rely on faith in God's word over human reason.
3. Believers are to perceive how God acts hidden under opposites that seem contrary to his will and love.
4. Believers are to be encouraged in the midst of their battle against Satan and every form of evil he uses as they live the life of daily dying and rising in repentance.[345]
5. Believers are to have confidence that the Holy Spirit is present and powerful through the word, to bring them to faith in his victory through the reality of daily conflicts and suffering in their personal crosses.

These principles represent hermeneutical guidelines for practicing theology, Luther's theology of reality. Kolb, referring to them, answered his question, "Had the hermeneutic of trust in God's revelation of himself and the life of faith it creates disappeared from Luther's way of practicing theology by 1533?"

> These axioms can be found in the Reformer's expression of his theological agenda and method in 1518 and 1519. They remained the guidelines for his exposition of the Song of Ascent in 1532 and 1533. The *theologia crucis* served the Reformer as a hermeneutic throughout his career.[346]

Luther's Theology of the Holy Spirit

The Person of the Holy Spirit

Luther, following Augustine, affirmed the divinity of the Holy Spirit and his full personal participation in the divine essence (*homoousios*) and majesty,[347] and simply linked the *persona* and the work, or office of the Spirit, in the *Confession Concerning Christ's Supper* (1528):

---

345. Points 1–4 follow Kolb, "Luther's Theology of the Cross," 75–84.
346. Kolb, "Luther's Theology of the Cross," 85.
347. *BSLK*, 414; *BC*, 300, *Smalcald Articles*, Part I, Art. 1; *BSLK*, 653–54, 36; *BC*, *Large Catechism*, "Explanation of the Third Article," 435–36.

> I believe in the Holy Spirit, who with the Father and the Son is one true God and proceeds eternally from Father and the Son, yet is a distinct person in the one divine essence and nature. By this Holy Spirit, as a living, eternal, divine gift and endowment, all believers are adorned with faith and other spiritual gifts, raised from the dead, freed from sin, and made joyful and confident, free and secure in their conscience.[348]

Silcock discusses different interpretations of *filioque* that Luther had used at different times, but notes that he never departed from the *filioque* of the Western tradition.[349] Luther also linked the procession with a distinction in his view of God as both *persona* and *donum* (person and gift). The Father gives himself, along with the whole creation to benefit humankind; the Son gives himself and his righteousness in order to reconcile and restore sinful humankind to the Father; and the Spirit gives himself to humankind. "He teaches us to understand this deed of Christ which has been manifested to us, helps us receive and preserve it, use it to our advantage and impart it to others, increase and extend it."[350] The divinity of the Holy Spirit is imbedded in the orthodox doctrine of the Trinity, that the Old and New Testaments show that there are three Persons and one God.[351]

Prenter showed how Luther moved from Augustine's passive ideas of the Trinity to an orthodox biblical view of the living Triune God who is actively redeeming helpless humanity.[352] Prenter connects the theology of the cross with the doctrine of the Trinity,

> If the divinity of the Son and the Spirit is not preached without limitation, the *humilitas* theology becomes imitation-piety and the most refined form of self-righteousness. . . . it limits the domain of the divine work of the Son and the Spirit and

---

348. LW 37:365-66; WA 26:505, 29-31; *Confession concerning Christ's Supper* (1528).

349. Silcock, "Luther on the Holy Spirit," 306.

350. LW 37:366-67; WA 26:261-509; Lohse, *Theology*, 232-33; Malcolm, "Holy Spirit," 338.

351. WA 39^{II}:305; WA 10^{I}:1, 152-54, 157, 180-82; LW 52:43-44, 49; WA 10^{I}:185-86, 191; WA 39^{II}:287-88 (theses 5, 7), 293, 305, 339-40; WA 46:436; WA 49:238-40; cf. Althaus, *Theology*, 199-200, and Selcock, "Luther on the Holy Spirit," 307. See Kolb, *Martin Luther: Confessor*, 59-63 for a tight integration of Luther's Trinitarian views and a broad range of Luther's sources on the subject.

352. Prenter, *Spiritus*, 174-78, citing WA 1:20, 1-3, *Christmas Sermon* (1514); WA 26:440, 21-23, 34-38; LW 37:297, *Confession*.

thereby also robs them of their divine honor. All piety that is not *theologia crucis* is an attack on the Trinitarian faith in God.[353]

Luther described the dynamic relationship within the Godhead:

> The Father, generating, transfers his substance in the divinity to the Son. Thus the Father and the Son and the Holy Spirit are three distinct persons, and yet in truth one essence. These things can be believed but they will never be capable of being understood by human reason. However, I say that the Father, remaining the same God, transfers his divinity to the Son in such a way that the Son is the complete and perfect image and stamp of the Father.[354]

Luther opposed modalism by stressing the Spirit's distinct personality.[355] The identification of the distinction of each person of the Godhead is necessary for the Spirit to relate believers to the historical resurrected Christ.

In his commentary on Gen 1, Luther saw the mystery of the Trinity set forth in the work of the creation:

> The Father creates heaven and earth out of nothing through the Son, whom Moses calls the Word. Over these [heaven and earth], the Holy Spirit broods. As a hen broods her eggs, keeping them warm in order to hatch her chicks, and, as it were, to bring them to life through heat, so Scripture says that the Holy Spirit brooded, as it were, on the waters to bring to life those substances, which were to be quickened and adorned. For it is the office of the Holy Spirit to make alive.[356]

The Office and Work of the Holy Spirit

The office of the Holy Spirit is defined by different aspects of his work. Bernard Lohse noted that Luther's simple thought of the Holy Spirit's work is that the Holy Spirit continually keeps the central focus on Jesus Christ and

---

353. Prenter, *Spiritus*, 179.

354. *LW* 38:257; *WA* 39^{II}:24, 9–14, "Pater generans transfundit suam substantiam in divinitate in filium. Sic pater et filius et spiritus sanctus sunt tres distinctae personae, et tamen revera una essenntia. Credi haec possunt, sed intelligi a ratione humana haec nunquam poterunt. Sed dico, quod pater manens idem Deus profundit suam divinitatem in filium ita, ut filius sit plena et perfecta imago et character patris." The Disputation on "The Word Made Flesh," Argument 19 (1536).

355. *LW* 52:42–43, 48–49; *WA* 10^{I}:1, 183, 191; cf. Prenter, *Spiritus*, 180.

356. *LW* 1:9; *WA* 42:7–8; *Genesis*, 1:2; cf. *LW* 1:16; *WA* 42:13.

his mission, and therefore, "With this constant reference to Christ the Holy Spirit assumed an extraordinarily important place in Luther's theology."[357]

From eternity, the Holy Spirit continually creates life and works miracles. He proclaims the good news of God's gift in Jesus Christ and creates faith in hearers of this word for their redemption and reconciliation with God through forgiveness of sins. He works to form the redeemed into the image and character of Christ, bearing fruit in communion with the Triune God and fellow believers. He calls and establishes the holy community—the church—who exercises her gifts and ministries to worship the Triune God, to love fellow Christians, and to proclaim and to express God's gospel love to the world.

Lohse summarized the work of the Spirit:

> It is the peculiar office of the Spirit to comfort believers, make them alive, and sanctify them. Of course, ... the Spirit exercises a punitive office; but this is his "alien" work. The Spirit's proper work is precisely a strengthening in faith, as Luther put it in his explanation to the Third Article [SC].[358]

Luther pointed to the work of the Holy Spirit from the beginning to the end of Scripture. His lectures on Genesis demonstrate the concept of the office of the Holy Spirit working in three ways:

1. The Spirit tended over the new creation, as Luther noted, "The Holy Spirit brooded.... on the waters to bring to life those substances that were to be quickened.... For it is the office of the Holy Spirit to make alive."[359] This is his function throughout both the Old and New Testaments. Luther sourced this concept from the Nicene Creed.[360]

2. The persons of the Triune God of creation are referenced somewhat obliquely in the creation story, but are unfolded and named—Father, Son, and Holy Spirit—in some psalms, the prophets and the New Testament.[361]

3. Luther stressed that the complex word of God concerning creation comes to us by the Holy Spirit, "These are difficult matters, and it is unsafe to go beyond the limit to which the Holy Spirit leads us."[362]

---

357. Lohse, *Theology*, 234–39.
358. Lohse, *Theology*, 239.
359. *LW* 1:9n20.
360. *BC*, 23.
361. *LW* 1:18.
362. *LW* 1:17.

Luther compared Gen 1 from the Old Testament with John 1 from the New Testament—"In the beginning was the Word." It is such a powerful word that it makes all things out of nothing. John expressly adds, "This Word is God and yet is a Person distinct from God the Father, just as a word and he who utters a word are separate entities."[363] Luther noted that the Holy Spirit leads us by teaching us these matters.[364] By the Word, God calls things into being, which, to Luther, is evidence of the eternal presence of the omnipotent Word through whom, along with the Holy Spirit, all things are made. For Luther, this binds together the Word and the Spirit in the acts of creation.[365]

Luther opened *The Bondage of the Will* with an attack upon Erasmus's dismissal of assertions that were common among Christians. Luther maintined that if such assertions were removed there remained no Christianity. Assertions, or proclamations, are given by the Holy Spirit to Christians to glorify Christ and perhaps to testify to him even unto death. Through such assertions the Holy Spirit, who is no skeptic, accuses the world of sin (John 16:8) and through Paul encouraged Christians to do the same (2 Tim 4:2).[366]

In the *Large Catechism*, Third Article, Luther described two parts of the work of the Holy Spirit: He brings humankind to *Redemption* and *Sanctification*: "He first leads us into his holy community, placing us in the church's lap, where he preaches to us and brings us to Christ." Secondly, through *Sanctification*, the Holy Spirit makes sinful, but faithful, persons holy. This all happens in the Christian church, "a unique community in the world, which is the mother that begets and bears every Christian through the word of God, which the Holy Spirit reveals and proclaims, through which he illuminates and enflames hearts so that they grasp and accept it, cling to it, and persevere in it." Luther made it clear that where Christ is not preached there is no Holy Spirit to create, to call and to gather the church, apart from which no one can come to Christ.[367]

Lois Malcolm notes that, from the *Large Catechism*, in the Third Article:

> Luther's pneumatology centered on who the Spirit is as Sanctifier and Comforter.... The Spirit gives [him]self by proclaiming and teaching what Christ has done for all.... Without the Holy Spirit, Christ's person and work would remain hidden to human

---

363. *LW* 1:16-17; *WA* 42:13-14.
364. *LW* 1:17; *WA* 42:14.
365. *LW* 1:18-19; *WA* 42:15.
366. *LW* 33:21, 24; *WA* 18:604-6, *Bondage of the Will* (1525).
367. *BC*, 435-36; *Large Catechism*.

beings.... What distinguishes the Holy Spirit from other spirits ... is that only God's Spirit can sanctify and make holy by bringing human beings to Christ to receive what they could not come to by themselves.[368]

Luther saw that in both justification and sanctification the Spirit works to make believers alive in Christ and to enrich and to empower them to walk in what the apostle Paul called the "obedience of faith" (Rom 1:5; 16:26).

In his concept of the Holy Trinity, Luther saw the Holy Spirit as a person of action. Where God is active, there the Spirit is at work. Luther's theology of reality positions the Spirit and his works in the center. Therefore, as we consider Luther's theology of the Holy Spirit we encounter the person and his works together.

The Holy Spirit works daily to bring repentance and forgiveness of sins through the word, the holy sacraments, and absolution in the setting of the unity of the Christian community. He makes believers holy despite the sin that they continue to carry. "Here there is full forgiveness of sins, both in that God forgives us and that we forgive, bear with, and aid one another."[369] Luther summarized this work of the Holy Spirit:

> All this, then, is the office and work of the Holy Spirit, to begin and daily increase holiness on earth through ... the Christian church and the forgiveness of sins. Then, when we pass from this life, in the blink of an eye he will perfect our holiness and will eternally preserve us in it ...
>
> This article [of the Creed] must always remain in force. For creation is now behind us, and redemption has also taken place, but the Holy Spirit continues his work ... until the Last Day.... When his work has been finished and we abide in it, having died to the world and all misfortune, he will finally make us perfectly and eternally holy. Now we wait in faith for this to be accomplished through the word.[370]

This is the beginning and the process of living the new life in the Spirit.

Silcock summarizes the content and character of Luther's view of the Spirit's work:

> Luther's treatment of the work of the Holy Spirit covers all items mentioned in the Third Article of the Apostles' Creed: the holy Catholic Church, the forgiveness of sins, the resurrection of the

---

368. Malcolm, "Holy Spirit," 338; *BC*, 435 (*BSELK*, 1058), *LC*, "Third Article."
369. *BC*, 438, *Large Catechism*.
370. *BC*, 438, *Large Catechism*.

body, and the life everlasting. These are all God's work, carried out by the holy and life-giving Spirit, whom Luther calls the 'sanctifier' because he alone is holy and sanctifies all who have faith in Christ.[371] ... *The Large Catechism* ... is one of the main primary sources for Luther's thought on the person and work of the Spirit.[372] ... The emphasis ... [is] on the word and the Spirit, and the linkage between them, understood from a Trinitarian perspective, for this is the *novum* of Luther's theology, which comes out vividly in his fight against the unbridled enthusiasm [*Schwarmerei*] of the spiritualists or heavenly prophets of his day.

In his treatise *Against the Heavenly Prophets* (1525), Luther made a vital distinction between salvation *won* and salvation *distributed*. Christ won forgiveness for all on the cross, but he did not distribute it on the cross. Rather, he distributes it here and now through the proclaimed gospel and the enacted sacraments. It is Christ's work on the cross that acquired salvation *for* us, and Christ's work through the word and the sacraments that distributes it *to* us, and creates and sustains faith *in* us.[373] Again, in the same vein, the Reformer maintains that Christ on the cross and all his suffering would be useless to us if we did not have the Spirit who announces it through the word and brings it to us as a gift.[374] Although, in the treatise Luther does not expressly name the Spirit as the one who delivers the gift of salvation through the word and the sacraments, he does make this explicit in *The Large Catechism*. There he says that God caused the word to be published and proclaimed, in which he has given the Holy Spirit to offer and apply to us the treasure of Christ's redemptive work on the cross.[375] This "word-event" is central to Luther's hermeneutic of contemporaneity.... "The living Spirit-filled word which both brings God's power and presence into the present as well as draws the reader into the experience of the text."[376]

---

371. *BC*, 435; *BSLK*, 653–54.

372. *BC*, 435–40; *BSLK*, 653–62.

373. *LW* 40:213–14; *WA* 18:203, 27–38.

374. *LW* 40:213; *WA* 18:202, 34–203, 2.

375. *BC*, 436; *BSLK*, 654.

376. Maschke et al., *Ad Fontes Lutheri*, 182; Silcock, "Luther on the Holy Spirit," 295–96.

Two Kinds of Righteousness

Luther viewed the Holy Spirit's work in justification and sanctification through the framework of his concept of righteousness. He distinguished between two kinds of righteousness.

By the time of his Galatians commentary of 1535,[377] Luther's theology had expanded from the theology of the cross, referred to as "The cross is our theology,"[378] to include an encompassing framework of "Two Kinds of Righteousness," also referred to as "our theology."

> This is our theology, by which we teach a precise distinction between these two kinds of righteousness, the active and the passive, so that morality and faith, works and grace, secular society and religion may not be confused. Both are necessary, but both must be kept within their limits.[379]

In a sermon of late 1519, Luther described the two kinds of righteousness of regenerated Christians:

> The first is alien righteousness that is the righteousness of another, instilled from without. This is the righteousness of Christ by which he justifies through faith, as it is written in 1 Corinthians 1:30: "Who became to us wisdom from God, righteousness and sanctification and redemption." This righteousness, then, is given to men in baptism and whenever they are truly repentant. Therefore a man can with confidence boast in Christ and say: "Mine are Christ's living, doing, and speaking, his suffering and dying, mine as much as if I had lived, done, spoken, suffered, and died as he did."[380]

Luther summarized the first kind of righteousness—Christ's righteousness in believers:

> This alien righteousness instilled in us without our works by grace alone—while the Father, to be sure, inwardly draws us to Christ—is set opposite original sin, likewise alien, which we acquire without our works by birth alone. Christ daily drives out

---

377. Pelikan, "Introduction to Volume 26"; *LW* 26:ix, reports that Luther gave twenty-eight lectures on Galatians from July 3, 1531 through November 14, 1531. After careful and thorough editing by George Rörer, Viet Dietrich, and Casper Cruciger, the lectures were published in 1535. Since the current literature denotes the work as *Lectures on Galatians (1535)*, that identification continues in this volume.

378. *WA* 5:176; Ps 5:11 [12]; *Op. Ps.*, 1519–21.

379. Kolb, "Two Kinds of Righteousness," 449, citing *LW* 26:7; *WA* 401:5, 24–27.

380. *LW* 31:297; *WA* 2:145–52; *Two Kinds of Righteousness* (1519).

the old Adam more and more in accordance with the extent to which faith and knowledge of Christ grow. For alien righteousness is not instilled all at once, but it begins, makes progress, and is finally perfected at the end through death.[381]

The second kind of righteousness, our own proper righteousness, lives out the first alien righteousness in a life of good works (Gal 5:24; Titus 2:12), as Luther describes, "In this world let us live soberly (belonging to Christ and crucifying one's own flesh), justly (loving one's neighbor), and devoutly (fearfully loving God)."[382] This righteousness is the fruit of the Holy Spirit working in the lives of Christian disciples (Gal 5 22). The indwelling righteousness of the first kind produces the fruit of the Holy Spirit in the second kind.

> There the flesh is extinguished; and Christ rules with His Holy Spirit, who now sees, hears, speaks, works, suffers, and does simply everything in him, even though the flesh is still reluctant. In short, this life is not the life of the flesh, although it is a life in the flesh; but it is the life of Christ, the Son of God, the life that Christians possess by faith.[383]

The Holy Spirit continues to renew repentant sinners who are "born of the Spirit" (John 3:6), and to energize the second kind of righteousness to live in sacrificial works toward others and towards God.[384] The second kind of righteousness completes the first, doing away with the old Adam and the body of sin. Together they comprise the Holy Spirit's work of sanctification.

Kolb maintains that Luther's concept of the two kinds of human righteousness accurately describes what it means to be human, distinguishing between identity and performance, passive and active righteousness:

> For the distinction of the two dimensions in which we relate to God and his world, the two aspects that constitute our humanity, is "our theology," and it is impossible to understand the Lutheran tradition without recognizing and employing it.[385]

Kolb describes the dynamic new life provided for believers in the working together of Luther's two kinds of righteousness.

---

381. *LW* 31:299; *WA* 2:145–52; *Two Kinds of Righteousness* (1519).
382. *LW* 31:299; *WA* 2:145–52; *Two Kinds of Righteousness* (1519).
383. *LW* 26:172; *WA* 40:292–93; *Lectures on Galatians* (1535) (Gal 2:20).
384. *LW* 31:299–300; *WA* 2:145–52; *Two Kinds of Righteousness* (1519).
385. Kolb, "Two Kinds of Righteousness," 465.

> For fallen sinners the gift of this passive righteousness, which expresses itself first of all in trust toward the loving Father, comes through Christ's obedience to the Father as he took the sinfunness of fallen creatures into death with himself and as he reclaimed life for them in his resurrection. Christ promises forgiveness and life through his death and resurrection, and thus he elicits trust from those sinners whom the Holy Spirit has turned back to himself. That trust, directed toward the Crucified and Risen God, is the righteousness of Eden, restored and revivified, [justification] ready to advertise its identity in the performance of activities suitable for God's children. [sanctification][386]

Justification

In *The Bondage of the Will*, Luther wrote that words and works of God lead to eternal salvation. The words of God in the law require works, and the words of God in the gospel, require faith. Only faith leads to God's grace and eternal salvation since the grace of the Spirit is life itself, to which we are led by God's word and work.

This eternal salvation, however, passes human comprehension. The apostle Paul quotes from Isa 64:4 in 1 Cor 2:9: "What no eye has seen, nor ear heard, nor the heart of man conceived (imagined, ESV), what God has revealed to us (prepared for those, ESV) who love him."[387] Paul shows how this happens in 1 Cor 2:10, "these things God has revealed to us through the Spirit." Unless the Spirit reveals it, no human heart would know it, be able to apply it, or to seek after it. The experienced and distinguished, but unenlightened, human mind cannot fathom the resurrection and the future life. They seem absurd. Luther said that unless one is thoroughly imbued with the Holy Spirit, he cannot enter into eternal salvation. Only faith and trust in the work of the Holy Spirit leads to Christ and his work of justification giving eternal life.[388]

In his comments on Ps 51:2, Luther explained the two parts of justification.

> The first is grace revealed through Christ, that through Christ we have a gracious God, so that sin can no longer accuse us, but our conscience has found peace through trust in the mercy of God.[389]

---

386. Kolb, "Two Kinds of Righteousness," 464.
387. *LW* 33:105; *Bondage*.
388. *LW* 33:106; *Bondage*.
389. *LW* 12:331; Ps 51:2.

The Holy Spirit gives life by the proclamation of the word of the crucified, resurrected, and ascended Christ. Not merely an historical account, it is the present historical experience of the truth of God in Christ. For Luther the Word is Christ, the Father's eternal inward word spoken into the world by the incarnation. The outward word—the gospel—is the only way to God. In the word, the risen Christ is present as God's gift and thereby directs the motion of faith from self-righteousness to Christ as the alien righteousness. The Spirit uses the external word of the gospel, sacramentally, to point the hearer to Christ.[390] According to Prenter, Luther saw the law as a dead writing, but the gospel as another voice manifesting the living Christ.[391] Luther stressed that the gospel is not just a written record but is to be publicly declared in confession and preaching. Under the Spirit's control, this external message comes from the present reality and authority of Christ. Conversely, the reader of the written word who only knows it as a written text and understands it intellectually "continues to be his own master." However, to those who hear the external word in faith, as the living word, the word becomes the Holy Spirit's instrument to bring Christ.[392] Luther emphasized the preached word:

> The Word, the Word, the Word. Listen, lying spirit, the Word avails. Even if Christ were given for us and crucified a thousand times, it would all be in vain if the word of God were absent and were not distributed and given to me with the bidding, this is for you, take what is yours.[393]

Luther taught that the Spirit justifies through the hearing of the word of the gospel.[394] The Holy Spirit bridges the time between God's past works and people living today and brings Christ to all the nations through the word.[395] Luther noticed how the psalmist was comforted through the unity of the word and the Spirit,

> "Who is this? It is the Lord Himself upon whom I called. In my sore distress, He came to me through his eternal word and Spirit.

390. Cf. Prenter, *Spiritus*, 106–13, 122.

391. Prenter, *Spiritus*, 114.

392. Prenter, *Spiritus*, 117–21.

393. LW 40:212–13; WA 18:202, 37–203, 2; "Das wort, das wort, das wort, hörestu du lügen geyst auch, das wort thuts, Denn ob Christus tausentmal fur uns gegeben und gecreutzigt würde, were es alles umb sonst, wenn nicht das wort Gottes keme, und teylets aus und schencket myrs und spreche, das soll beyn seyn, nym hyn und habe dyrs," *Against the Heavenly Prophets* (1525).

394. LW 12:368; WA 40^{II}:410, 17–21; Ps 51:8 [10].

395. WA 10^I1:131; WA 2:203; WA 30^I; 191; cf. Vajta, *Worship*, 70, 72.

I scarcely know that I have been troubled." We must not . . . imagine that God comforts us immediately, without his word. Comfort does not come to us without the word, which the Holy Spirit effectively calls to mind and enkindles in our hearts.[396]

Prenter summarized Luther's idea of the unity of the word and the Spirit:

> No matter how strongly Luther emphasized the instrumental view of the relationship between the Spirit and the word, he never directly identified the work of the outward word with the work of the Spirit, but he always laid down an interval of time between the outward work of the word and the coming of the Spirit. First, the word must be heard, and thereafter the Spirit will come. . . . This interval of time is necessary . . . for the motion of faith away . . . from all self-righteousness to Christ.[397]

From the Commentary on Ps 51:2, Luther explained the second part of justification:

> The second part [of justification] is the conferring of the Holy Spirit with His gifts, who enlightens us against the defilements of spirit and flesh (2 Cor 7:1). Thus we are defended against the opinions with which the devil seduces the whole world. Thus the true knowledge of God grows daily, together with other gifts, like chastity, obedience, and patience. Thus our body and its lusts are broken so that we do not obey them. Those who do not have this gift or do not use it this way, but fall into the uncleanness of either the flesh or the spirit, so that they approve of all doctrines without discrimination—they are dominated by the flesh, and they do not know the bath of the Holy Spirit for which David is asking.[398]

The "bath" here is the initial sacrament of water baptism of repentance for forgiveness of sins that also confers the baptism with the Holy Spirit promised by John and Jesus (Matt 3:11; John 1:33; Acts 1:5). The Spirit remains with the faithful Christian throughout life.

---

396. LW 14:62; WA 31:99, 31–100, 2; "Wer ist der? Ah, Es ist der HERR selber, den ich anreiff, Der füllet mir mein hertz, durch sein ewigs wort und geist, mitten inn der not, das ich sie kaume füle, Denn wir müssen nicht . . . uns für nemen, das uns Gott on mittel und on sein wort im hertzen tröste, Es gehet on eusserlich wort nicht zu, Welches der heilige geist wol weis ym hertzen zu erynnern und aufferblasen." Ps 118:6 [1529-30].

397. Prenter, *Spiritus*, 124–26.

398. LW 12:330; *Commentary on Ps 51:2*.

Sanctification

Jesus and his apostles used the terms "sanctify" and "sanctification" (John 17:17; Rom 15:16; 1 Pet 3:15) to teach and "to establish his strength among babes and infants" to fight against the devil, death, and the world. Here is the beginning and foundation of sanctification.[399]

Commenting on Ps 51:11–13, Luther described sanctification as it fits into the gift and the work of the Holy Spirit in the believer,

> So in these three verses the prophet (David) expounds the gifts which are given to the justified by faith. The first is a sure confidence in the mercy of God [inner testimony of the Holy Spirit]. The second is sanctification, by which the old man is put to death with his passions and the new man arises in new and holy obedience. The third is free confession, so that everything is condemned that refuses to give in to sound doctrine.[400]

Luther called the third commandment a Sabbath Rest in God for forgiveness and sanctification—human passivity and God's activity.[401] God thus confounds the devil and the flesh. Luther linked Christ's rest in the grave with the Christian life. Christ's death is the believers' death. As God raised Christ, so he gives new life to those who have died to their own works. The commandment directs them to God's work and Christ meets them through the means of grace.

The Holy Spirit produces this new life in two ways: 1) Believers are united with Christ in his death and resurrection. Luther pointed to Rom 6:3–11,[402] and in 1:4[403] they are united with Christ when baptized into his death and raised by the power of the Holy Spirit to newness of eternal life. 2) Luther engaged the teachings of Rom 8:1–16 that describe this new life and how the Holy Spirit lives within the faithful to empower them as they live by faith and hope, trusting the call and promises of God.[404] Union with Christ is the natural state of the Christian life. As believers are baptized into Christ's death, they are in him and he and the Holy Spirit dwell in them.

For Luther, the presence or absence of Christ and the Holy Spirit was the key to whether the work of sanctification is accomplished or not. This

---

399. *LW* 12:113; *WA* 45:221; Ps 8:2.

400. *LW* 12:384; Ps 51:12.

401. *WA* 6:248; *LW* 44:78; *WA* 9:663; *WA* 1:436; *WA* 30^1:145; *WA* 42:61–63; *LW* 1:80–83; Vajta, *Worship*, 130–32.

402. *LW* 25:309–16; *WA* 56:321–28; *Lectures on Romans*.

403. *LW* 25:49; *WA* 56:5; *Lectures on Romans*.

404. *LW* 25:67–82; *WA* 56:73–91; *Lectures on Romans*.

is the heart of his 1525 dispute with Erasmus regarding the freedom or the bondage of the will (*De Liber Abitrio/De Servo Arbitrio*). Early in his disputation, under the heading "*Divine Necessity and the Human Will*,"[405] Luther addressed the matter, asserting, "If it is not we, but only God, who works salvation in us, then before he works we can do nothing of saving significance, whether we wish to or not."[406] This is because we cannot restrain our own powers, but we keep on willing and doing the wrong because our inner will remains averse to and resentful toward whatever resists it. Luther called this "the necessity of immutability." The will cannot change itself to a different direction, but is, rather, aroused by resistance into willing the wrong as shown by resentment. People may yield to force or to a greater attraction to something else, but they never yield freely: they simply let strong influences take their course.[407]

When God works, the will is changed by the Holy Spirit to act of its own accord—not from compulsion. It cannot be diverted by any opposing power, even by the gates of hell, but continues to will, to delight in, and to love the good, just as before it sought out evil. This is proven by the invincibility and steadfastness of the holy ones who, tempted by evil, are all the more spurred on to will and do the good, as a fire is fanned into flames by the wind. Luther concluded, "So not even here is there any free choice, or freedom to turn oneself in another direction or will something different, so long as the Spirit and grace of God remain in a man."[408]

Luther viewed faith as an empirical piety, which, while it takes refuge in the alien righteousness of the indwelling Christ, expresses itself in prayer, praise, and service. When empirical piety is considered independent from Christ's alien righteousness, it is "flesh" under the wrath of God. Empirical piety is "Spirit" when it forsakes all visible things and clings to Christ's alien righteousness, which battles the sin of the human nature.[409] Empirical piety is not the new man, but is the fruit of identification with the alien righteousness of Christ. Empirical piety is either the fruit of the "flesh," or the fruit of the "Spirit" of the new man. In the "flesh," nomism replaces the work of the Spirit with an empirical righteousness under the law, and replaces the righteousness of the indwelling Christ with the human free will. Antinomianism replaces the indwelling Christ with a doctrine of forgiveness based on the work of Christ. This message about Christ without the Spirit is a

---

405. *LW* 33:64–70; *WA* 18:634–39; *Bondage*.
406. *LW* 33:64; *WA* 18:634; *Bondage*.
407. *LW* 33:64–65; *WA* 18:634; *Bondage*.
408. *LW* 33:65; *WA* 18:635; *Bondage*.
409. Prenter, *Spiritus*, 66–71.

false Christ.⁴¹⁰ Luther distinguished empirical piety, which is the faithful expression of the new man (prayer, praise, and works of love), from the progress in sanctification, which the Spirit makes as he gains more mastery over the flesh.

Paul Althaus maintained that in the Third Article of the Creed Luther saw sanctification as the Holy Spirit's completion of baptism, which, considering that Luther saw baptism as a completed event, may be better stated as a continuation of baptism.⁴¹¹ The Holy Spirit makes believers holy in the communion of saints. He brings them to Christ through forgiveness, the resurrection of the body, and life everlasting. The Holy Spirit continues to work through the word, granting daily forgiveness and leading the godly to seek God in all things.⁴¹²

Between baptism and resurrection, people constantly take refuge in Christ's alien righteousness, where the new man is Spirit, and the old man is flesh. In the Law and Gospel context, the Spirit wars with the flesh, until, as the resurrection draws near, the old man is being destroyed, and the new man, with Christ's alien righteousness, is the only possibility left. Thus, sanctification is the Spirit's progressive mastery over the flesh. Luther said that the law is a guide for the faithful, even if they cannot perform it.⁴¹³ In his lectures on Rom 5, Luther spoke of God's love in the Holy Spirit working through the law. Through the law, God overcomes sin by progressively completing justification in sanctification. Luther noted how Paul encouraged believers to allow the Holy Spirit to weaken and kill their old nature so his work of justification and perfection, which he began, may be completed (Rom 7:24).⁴¹⁴ Prenter distinguished between *peccatum regnans* (sin ruling) and *peccatum regnatum* (sin defeated). The tyrant *peccatum regnans* governs the conscience, in concert with and under the ruling wrath of God. As empirical piety clings to Christ's alien righteousness, however, sin becomes *peccatum regnatum*—having lost the power of the law, and is *non-imputatum* (not counted against the faithful).⁴¹⁵

Prenter pointed to Luther's portrayal of three aspects in the progress of sanctification. First, is a continual starting anew, turning repeatedly, and constantly taking refuge in Christ's righteousness. Each moment includes

---

410. Prenter, *Spiritus*, 231.

411. Althaus, *Theology*, 355; cf. Lehmann, *Prayer*, 121.

412. BSLK, 654, 659; BC, 435-36, 37-38; 438, 58; *LC*, "Explanation to the Third Article"; *LW* 14:203; *WA* 18:527; Ps 143.

413. *LW* 25:243; *WA* 56:257, 4-6; Rom 3:21, citing Augustines's *Patr. Ser. Lat.* 44.214.

414. *LW* 25:245; *WA* 56:258, 15-20.

415. Prenter, *Spiritus*, 73.

the events from which the next must repent and move on in faith. "Progress may be . . . said to be a constant seeking and praying, not only in words, but also in works."[416] Secondly, a believer is righteous in Christ, but a sinner in himself. Thirdly, the overpowering Holy Spirit is continuously leading people to Christ.[417]

Luther outlined the biblical order of moving from faith in Christ to the outpouring of the Holy Spirit: the preaching of the gospel, faith in Christ, the outpouring or conferring of the Holy Spirit with love and fruit. The promises of God's word strive against natural human priorities to remove any claim of human effort. In these struggles, the gift of the Spirit is given and from the struggles, faith emerges with love, joy, and peace.[418] Luther insisted on this order so that God is the subject in the word, the Spirit, and faith. The ensuing life is brought about by the present reality of Christ and not from one's own empirical piety.

Luther said the Christian's whole being requires faith and love. As the law convicts people of sin and drives them to conviction, confession, and repentance, the gospel holds forth the promise of forgiveness so that by faith they turn from self to God in Christ and are accounted righteous, as their faith becomes the fruit of the Spirit. Love brings God to believers who move in Christ's *agape* (self-sacrificial) love toward others.[419] These movements of faith and love find expression in prayer and work. The Spirit intercedes to God and Christ with groans and cries: "Lord, Help!" Believers are instruments of Christ's love. Therefore, faith and love cannot be separated because they are the reality created by the Spirit when he makes the living Christ truly present. Luther saw a double movement in believers' participation in the death and resurrection of Christ. As the "old Adam" is being killed, he cries out to God for help by the Spirit in faith. God counts all such faithful people righteous. They can then reach out to their neighbors in Christ's resurrection life in love and power.[420]

Kolb notes in the *Freedom of the Christian* (1520), that Luther considered justification and sanctification together:

> Luther presented Christ as the one who substituted himself for sinners and vanquished all that imprisons them or keeps them

---

416. Prenter, *Spiritus*, 74.
417. Prenter, *Spiritus*, 74–80.
418. LW 27:221; WA 2:25–33; Gal 2:15–16; cf. Prenter, *Spiritus*, 84–88.
419. WA 8:355, 20–24.
420. Prenter, *Spiritus*, 92–95.

from practicing their true humanity in trust toward God and the obedience that results from it.[421]

In *The Freedom of a Christian*, Luther listed three powers of faith at work in the inner person (soul), by the Holy Spirit, in bringing people to justification and on through sanctification. These powers are: 1) True faith in Christ (God's Word), alone, "Whoever believes and is baptized will be saved, but whoever does not believe will be condemned (Mark 16:16)."[422] 2.) Honor and trust in the Lord whose promises of salvation and life we have received. If we do not trust God and obey him, then we live in contempt of God and instead of his promised salvation, we receive his condemnation.[423] 3) True faith "unites the soul with Christ as a bride is united with her husband. . . . They hold everything they have in common." Christ will deal with the believing soul's sin and death, and impart his grace, life, and salvation to the believing soul.[424]

Larry Christenson said the believers' union with Christ in justification and sanctification, like the two natures of Christ, cannot be separated, which correlates with Luther's understanding of two kinds of righteousness. In justification Christ's natures are joined in the cross, to accomplish the first kind of righteousness, while in sanctification God's will is done in believers by the Spirit to accomplish the second kind of righteousness. Sanctification is grounded in justification.[425] Thus, justification and sanctification are one inseparable act of God whereby the Spirit tears people out of the kingdom of the devil and leads them into Christ's kingdom.[426]

The Means of the Holy Spirit

Throughout his writing and teaching, Luther emphasized that the Holy Spirit comes to people through the physical means of the word and the sacraments. God indwells the physical, just as Christ comes to humanity as true God and true man. To claim that God comes directly without means misrepresents Christ and his word. Through the physical means of the word

---

421. Kolb, *Martin Luther: Confessor*, 79-80.
422. *LW* 31:347.
423. *LW* 31:350.
424. *LW* 31:351.
425. Christenson, *Welcome*, 184-89, 194; cf. *BSLK*, 511-12, 6 (*BC*, 355-56, 6), *SC*, 3rd Article.
426. Prenter, *Spiritus*, 226.

and the sacraments, the Holy Spirit makes Christ physically present in the world today.

The Word of God

Oswald Bayer cites Luther's foundational principle for the priority of Scripture, "The Holy Scripture is its own interpreter"; and for its application, "The text itself causes one to pay attention."[427] Bayer continues to emphasize that even with all the qualities of academic and philosophical tools and studies, true interpretation "involves the gift of the Spirit over which we have absolutely no control. Luther himself received it as a gift with his Reformational discovery, when "the doors of Paradise" opened to him with the flash of insight concerning the righteousness of God."[428] Here Luther expressed his theology of reality found in his theology of the cross and through the presence and work of the Holy Spirit.

Robert Kolb writes that, "He (Luther) looked upon Scripture less as a source of information than a tool to accomplish the Holy Spirit's work. Luther repeatedly identified passages in Scripture as the Holy Spirit speaking, and the Spirit spoke with specific purposes in mind."[429] Kolb notes Luther's further explantion, "John's gospel and his first epistle, Saint Paul's epistles, especially Romans, Galatians, and Ephesians, Saint Peter's first epistle are the books that show you Christ and teach you all that is necessary and salutary for you to know."[430] In this way, Scripture is God's conversation with those who hear, read, and receive it. Luther held that a central function of the office of the Holy Spirit is his ministry through the word of God.

Luther said of Scripture:[431]

1. "The Scriptures are God's testimony of himself."[432]

2. "The Holy Spirit himself and God, the creator of all things, is the author of this book."[433]

---

427. Bayer, *Theology the Lutheran Way*, 68, *Sacra scriptura "sui ipsuis interpres."*

428. Bayer, *Theology the Lutheran Way*, 68–69, citing LW 34:337; WA 14:47; "Preface to the Latin Writings," 1545.

429. Kolb, *Martin Luther: Confessor*, 48; LW 35:152–53; WA 10^{II}:91–91; *Avoiding the Doctrines of Men* (1522); (LW 41:50–51); WA 50:545–47; *On the Councils and the Church* (1539); Althaus, *Theology*, 35–42, 72–102, 338–41.

430. LW 35:362; WADB 6:20, "Preface to the New Testament."

431. Plass, *Luther Says*, 62.

432. LW 34:227; WA 50:282.

433. WA 43:6.

3. "This book, the Holy Scripture, is the Holy Spirit's book."[434]

4. Referring to David's writing Ps 51, "Where is there a man who could speak about repentance and the forgiveness of sins the way the Holy Spirit speaks in this psalm?[435] . . . In it David, or rather the Holy Spirit in David, instructs us in the knowledge of God and of ourselves. He does both of these gloriously. First he clearly shows sin, then the knowledge of God, without which there is despair."[436] Commenting on Ps 51:4, "The Holy Spirit speaks the same way in Psalm 32:35: 'I said . . .'" Luther saw the Holy Spirit speaking and having the Scriptures written.[437]

5. Referring to John 1 as an explanation of the whole Old Testament, Luther said, "This is the speech of St. John, or rather of the Holy Spirit who quickens all things."[438]

6. Luther notes that both Isaiah and Paul speak God's words to those who faithfully listen: "If only we believed that God is speaking to us and that whatever we read or hear in the Bible is God's word, we would find and feel that it is not read or heard futilely or in vain. But our confounded unbelief and miserable flesh keep us from seeing and noting that God is speaking with us in Scripture or that Scripture is God's word. Rather we think it is the word of Isaiah, Paul, or some other mere man, who has not created heaven and earth. Therefore it is not God's word to us and does not bear its fruit until we recognize it within ourselves as God's word."[439]

The Holy Spirit is the Author and Interpreter of the Word

The Holy Spirit is the writer of Scripture. He inspired the composition of the text and he interprets and teaches it through those called to be prophets, patriarchs, pastors, apostles, preachers, teachers, etc., among God's people.

Concerning the Creation account of Gen 1 and 2, Luther maintained that the Holy Spirit was the composer of the text who worked through Moses

---

434. WA 48:43.
435. LW 12:303–4; WA 40^{II}:316; "Introduction to Ps 51."
436. LW 12:310, Ps 51.
437. LW 12:341.
438. LW 15:299; WA 54:55.
439. WA 48:102.

as his writer. The text is not mystical or allegorical, but is literal, teaching about real creatures in a real world, experiencing real events—all informing Luther's theology of reality. The Holy Spirit also teaches through difficult scriptural passages.[440] Luther illustrated this in his comments on Ps 45:

> I have taken up Psalm 45 . . . in which we shall see how fluent a speaker the Holy Spirit is, who is able to express and picture one and the selfsame thing in various ways. For the subject matter dealt with is the same throughout . . . namely, faith and . . . justification—now with one and then with another ornament of dress. He does this to forestall any excuse . . . that God has not abundantly . . . instructed and exhorted us to righteousness and truth . . .
>
> Our foolishness is apparent. . . . Once we have heard the doctrine of eternal salvation, we think have exhausted all there is of the Holy Spirit; . . . we throw the book from our hands, and we follow instead our fleshly inclinations. . . . It should be . . . different: since we see that to the Holy Spirit it is not wearisome to proclaim . . . the same matter continually, neither should we shrink from the work involved in learning it, particularly since the words of the Holy Spirit are such that they can never be learned sufficiently. So because of such foolishness . . . we shall have to face graver retribution on Judgment Day, since the Holy Spirit will hold up to us the fact that He set down the doctrine of faith so diligently . . . in all possible hues, . . . so that the herbs and flowers do not enjoy such great variety as there is in the Scriptures. Throughout Scripture He has presented such variety in teaching . . . the same thing, in order to keep us from giving up our study and to rouse us against the satiety from which we otherwise suffer.[441]

Luther showed how the Holy Spirit's language relates to his material and to his hearers. The Holy Spirit is a great teacher and teller of God's story.

> One must accustom oneself to the Holy Spirit's way of expression. With the other sciences, too, no one is successful unless he has first duly learned their technical language. Thus lawyers . . . physicians and philosophers—unfamiliar to the other professions. No science should stand in the way of another science, but . . . should continue to have its own mode of procedure and its own terms.

---

440. *LW* 1:5; *WA* 42:5; *LW* 1:30; *WA* 42:23.
441. *LW* 12:197–98; *WA* 40^{II}:472–73; *Commentary on Psalm 45*.

> Thus, we see that the Holy Spirit . . . has His own language and way of expression. . . . God, by speaking, created all things and worked through the word, and . . . all His works are some words of God, created by the uncreated Word. Therefore, just as a philosopher employs his own terms, so the Holy Spirit, too, employs His. Let each . . . speak in his own terminology.[442]

Luther maintained that the certainty and understanding of Creation through Jesus Christ (Col 1:16) "is founded on Holy Scripture, which is the word of the Lord and remains forever (1 Pet 1:25)."[443] Luther also maintained that, as the word of God, the Scriptures are a miracle and without a flaw. Therefore, "We must pay attention to the expression of Holy Scripture and abide by the words of the Holy Spirit."[444]

From the beginning of Creation, the Holy Spirit has made his children alive by speaking through the Holy Scripture and aiding the faithful not only to obey God but also to resist unbelief, envy, and other vices in order to glorify the name of the LORD and His word.[445] Therefore, Luther maintained that since, as the Holy Spirit has written the Scriptures and reveals the LORD and his ways through them, "Nowhere can the Spirit be found more present than in the very holy letters which he wrote."[446] Silcock summarized Luther's view of the closely intertwined relationship of the Spirit and the word:

> He [Luther] consistently stresses this indivisible nexus between word and Spirit. The biblical basis for this is Psalm 33:6 "By the word of the LORD the heavens were made, and by the breath of his mouth all their host." Here clearly word and breath/spirit (*ruah*) are set in parallel. Since God breathes out (his Spirit) to speak, it is impossible to separate the word he speaks from the Spirit by which he speaks. As Luther says . . . anyone who refuses to hear the voice gets nothing out of the breath either.[447]

Luther said that the Holy Spirit is continually present through the word, and Holy Scripture is the Spirit's tool for the ministry of his presence to God's people. His presence in its pages gives authority to the text.[448]

442. WA 42:35–36; LW 1:47–48.
443. WA 46:548; LW 22:14; Kolb, *Enduring Word*, 76.
444. WA 40^{II}:521; LW 12:242; Kolb, *Enduring Word*, 77.
445. WA 42:47–50, LW 1:64–66.
446. WA 7:97; Kolb, *Enduring Word*, 78.
447. WA 9:632; Silcock, "Luther on the Holy Spirit," 298.
448. See Kolb, *Enduring Word*, 79, for a wide range of Luther citations on the Holy Spirit's style, content, and purpose in his details of his presence in the composition and

MARTIN LUTHER'S THEOLOGY OF THE HOLY SPIRIT

The External Word and the Internal Word

Luther's *littera-spiritus* concept distinguished the external word from the internal word. The Scripture, the spoken word, and the sacrament are external words that come from the outside through people. The Spirit speaks the internal word into hearts.[449] The external word is a tool and is nothing until the Spirit speaks the inner word to write living words onto believers' hearts.[450] The internal word gives life to an otherwise dead external word, as Luther noted:

> The spirit is concealed in the letter [of the law], which is a word that is not good, because it is the law of wrath. But the spirit is a good word, because it is a word of grace. Therefore, to draw this out of the letter is to utter the Spirit itself.[451]

Luther emphasized the order of the Spirit's work.

> The outward factors should and must precede. The inward experience follows and is effected by the outward. God has determined to give the inward to no one except through the outward. For he wants to give no one the Spirit or faith outside of the outward word and sign instituted by him.[452]

Prenter summarized Luther's idea of the outward word and the inward word:

> No matter how strongly Luther emphasized the instrumental view of the relationship between the Spirit and the word, he never directly identified the work of the outward word with the work of the Spirit, but he always laid down an interval of time between the outward work of the Word and the coming of the Spirit. First, the word must be heard, and thereafter the Spirit

---

ministry of the text of Scripture.

449. WA 10¹:13; LW 35:121; *A Brief Instruction on What to Look for in the Gospels* (1521); WA 31¹:99, LW 14:62; WA 32:343; LW 21:55; *Commentary on the Sermon on the Mount* (1522); cf. Althaus, *Theology*, 35-37, and Prenter, *Spiritus*, 102.

450. WA 3:255-56, 258-60; *LW* 10:212, 216; Ps 45:1, 3.

451. LW 10:212-16; WA 3:256, 28-30; "*Spiritus enim latet in littera, que est verbum non bonum, quia lex ire. Sed spiritus est verbum bonum, quia verbum gratæ. Et ideo illud educere de litera est ipsumeructare.*" Ps 45:1 [1513-16].

452. LW 40:146; WA 18:136, 14-18; "*Die eusserlichen stucke sollen und müssen vorgehen. Und die ynnerlichen hernach und durch die eusserlichen komen, also das ers beschlossen hat, keinem menschen die ynnerlichen stuck zu geben on durch die eusserlichen stucke. Denn er will niemant den geyst noch glauben geben on das eusserliche wort und zeychen.*" *Against the Heavenly Prophets* (1525).

will come.... This interval of time is necessary... for the motion of faith away... from all self-righteousness to Christ.[453]

Still, Luther said that the word and Spirit are inseparable, and that man, always dependent upon the external word, must keep hearing that word.[454]

The Oral Word and the Written Word

A. Skevington Wood asserted that Martin Luther was primarily a preacher for whom the proclaimed, or oral word of God, was predominate. It is God speaking—"the spearhead of the Reformation."[455] God, by his Spirit, spoke his living word of creation. God's Spirit spoke through the prophets, the apostles, and through Christ himself. The Spirit still speaks through preachers of the word. The Spirit who inspired the word breathes it anew and applies it to the hearers.

Prenter explained Luther's thoughts:

> The spoken word points in a double sense to the living and present Christ and by this reveals itself as the actual instrument of the Spirit.... First, the *living* Word proves by comtemporaneity and by its personal form of address that Christ is a risen Christ who lives and speaks and gives himself in his church... the reality and presence of Christ, which the living Word.... [Secondly] The living Word expresses the fact that Christ is only really present as the Christ of *faith*, as the hidden, as the one who is opposed to all... natural experience.... who can be apprehended only by the fact that the message about him is believed.[456]

Wood noted the existential quality of Luther's preaching: Through preaching "God is speaking directly to his people, and to those who still reject him."[457] Christ is truly present through preaching. This sacramental aspect of his preaching was Luther's theology of reality expressed in the pulpit.

Silcock maintains that Luther clearly gave prority to the oral word over the written word as the *via vox Dei* (the living word of God). Christ commissioned his apostles to preach and proclaim, not to write, though several

---

453. Prenter, *Spiritus*, 124–26.

454. WA 17^{II}:179; cf. Althaus, *Theology*, 40.

455. Wood, *Captive to the Word*, 86. Luther and his interpreters used mixed terminologies for the oral word: the word, *Verbum vocale*, proclamation, spoken word, sermon, revelation, living and present Christ, etc.

456. Prenter, *Spiritus Creator*, 120.

457. Wood, *Captive to the Word*, 90.

did write to teach and to serve the emerging church as well as document the early development of the church. These writings became important parts of what the church received as the New Testament portions of the written word of Scripture. Selcock describes Luther's views of the relationship of the two:

> Luther knows that these two forms of the word cannot be separated, for the proclaimed word is grounded in the written word as a normative criterion to preserve it from error. The *Oral Word* and the *written Word* belong together because in and through both the Holy Spirit communicates and mediates Jesus Christ the saviour, who is the chief content of the Bible.[458]

Selcock notes how Luther assessed the authenticity of the written text of Scripture. Since the Bible is Christ's book, the texts of Scripture first must be "what promotes Christ" (*Was Christum treibet*). This is Luther's main criterion of inspiration and canonicity. Whatever does not promote Christ is not from God's word, oral or written. Since the Holy Spirit inspired the Scriptures to be written, the Scriptures are full of the Holy Spirit. The internal criterion for acceptance of the written word of God is the gospel pointing to Jesus Christ and the inner testimony of the Holy Spirit. Luther considered the written word of God, written in the language and grammar of the Holy Spirit, to be the Spirit's gift to the church.[459]

Luther often entered the pulpit with an unfinished sermon manuscript; his copiers took down what he preached—the word proclaimed (*verbum efficax*)—and prepared it for publication, the written word. Much of the early such "Written Word" documents of the Reformation in Germany were printed versions of what was first preached at Wittenberg and elsewhere. Many of Luther's printed lecture notes began as sermons he had preached at Wittenberg pulpits.[460]

Luther saw Christ and the Spirit working inseparably through the word in the work that includes the historic ministry of the church. Through the preaching of the word the Spirit proclaims God's redemptive history in the work of Christ to the nations of the world.[461]

---

458. Silcock, "Luther on the Holy Spirit," 302.

459. *WADB* 7:384, 25–32; *LW* 35:396; "Luther on the Holy Spirit," 302–3; Sasse, "Luther and the Word of God," 87–88.

460. Wood, *Captive to the Word*, 86.

461. Cf. Vajta, *Worship*, 72.

David Steinmetz stated Luther's position, when different aspects of the word are considered, "There is for Luther, one means of grace. And that one means of grace is the word of God in all its complexity."[462]

Action Words of the Holy Spirit

Erik Heen notes that Luther considered God's word as a performance speech act—a deed-word or *Thette-Wort*—such that things happen when God speaks.[463] Luther explained these special types of deed-words in his lecture concerning God's blessing of Abraham as a blessing to the nations (Gen 22:17–18). Luther calls this a blessing in actuality as distinct from a verbal blessing of words:

> The blessing in actuality is truly divine; for when God blesses, the result is the thing itself or that which is said, in accordance those well-known statements: "For He commanded and they were created" (Ps 148:5b) and "God said: 'Let there be light'; and there was light" (Gen 1:3). He is One who blesses with effect and does all things through what he says, because his word is the thing itself, and his blessing is an abundant blessing, physically as well as spiritually.[464]

David Steinmetz also defined such "actuality," or deed-words:

> A deed word, . . . once uttered, brings into existence a thing that did not exist before and could never have existed apart from that spoken word . . . for Luther, the instrument by which God creates and redeems the world is his *Thettel-Wort* (deed-word, *verbum efficax*).[465]

In his section, "Preaching," of *Melanchthon Neben Luther*, Martin Greschat connected Luther's understanding of oral proclamation of God's word with *verbum Dei efficax*, the power and presence of Christ. Preaching and teaching the word of God are in the foreground of Luther's ministry and practice because of the concrete testimony to God manifest through the working of his word.[466]

---

462. Steinmetz, "Luther, the Reformers," 169, cited in Heen, "Word of God," 799.
463. Heen, "Word of God," 798–99.
464. *LW* 4:154–55; *WA* 43:247.
465. Steinmetz, "Luther, the Reformers," 167–68.
466. See *"Die Predigten"* in Greschat, *Melanchthon Neben Luther*, 185–89.

For Luther, the verbal proclamation of God's word produces a certainty that guards against one-sided conclusions, achieved by the mighty reality of the *verbum Dei efficax*. In this proclamation the Spirit brings about the presence of Christ, through whom God the Creator himself acts. However, when God's word is heard, his divine essence must also be perceived, because the word and the works are not ours, but our Lord God's alone. If the movement of the Triune God comes to humankind, then the statements about God's actions of this person are word statements—active concretizations of the one, ever-active word of God alone.[467]

Oswald Bayer shows the effective result of such "actualities":

> The sentence "I absolve you of your sins!" is not a judgment that merely states what is true already. It does not assume that an inner, divine, proper absolution or justification has already taken place. Rather, the absolution is seen as a speech act that first constitutes and brings about a state of affairs, by creating a relationship between the one in whose name it is spoken and the one to whom it is spoken and believes in the promise (which has been previously given). Such a speech act establishes communication, liberates, and gives certainty. Luther calls it "*verbum efficax*," an active and effective word.[468]

Isaiah 55:11, often quoted by Luther, demonstrates *verbum efficax*:

> So shall my word be that goes out from my mouth;
> It shall not return to me empty,
> But it shall accomplish that which I purpose,
> And shall succeed in the thing for which I sent it.

Luther understood the Trinity to be one divine substance, but with three separate inter-related persons. The will of the Father is spoken by the word as the Spirit moves in power to make it happen—one God, three distinct persons in action. Luther maintained that God especially wants his word to be proclaimed, so that the mouths of Paul, the apostles, and preachers can be called the mouth of God. "God's spoken *Thettel-Wort* always accomplishes its purpose."[469] The proclamation of God's word of action is where the triune God is found in fellowship with his people.

---

467. See "*Die Predigten*" in Greschat, *Melanchthon Neben Luther*, 185–89.
468. Bayer, *Theology the Lutheran Way*, 129–30.
469. Heen, "Word of God," 799; *WA* 44:401; *LW* 7:138; *WA* 31–32:458; *LW* 17:258.

Exclusivity of the Word

The Holy Spirit's multi-functions might appear to express his work through countless means. Luther said, however, that the Holy Spirit is given only through the word of the gospel[470]—that is, only by preaching, hearing, and believing the word—and administration of the sacraments.[471]

Tension can exist between word and Spirit. Emphasis on the authority of the Spirit could depreciate the external word, and the identification of the Spirit with the external word could reduce the Spirit to be just another attribute of the word. Luther maintained that the Holy Spirit resolves this tension through Christ, whom the Spirit makes present in the word. When the living Christ is absent from the word, it is merely a dead book of law. When the Spirit makes Christ personally present in the external word, it is the living gospel word. The external word is separate from the Spirit as promise is separated from fulfillment. By the dynamic of faith, these meet in Christ as the Spirit gives the presence of Christ to the external signs. The Spirit brings the real presence of Christ into the ambiguity of faith, just as he brought him into incarnation (Luke 2:15). Only faith sees him as the divine Son of God, with Scripture as his spiritual body.[472]

Some examples of these principles follow:

> [Luther maintained that the Holy Spirit's] ministry is thoroughly external and completely available to our "senses" . . . we see and hear the Holy Spirit in the dove, in tongues of fire, in baptism, and in a human voice.[473]

> The Holy Spirit is now truly present among us and works in us through the word and sacraments. He has covered himself with veils and clothing so that our weak, sick, and leprous nature might grasp him and know him. If he came to us in his majesty, we would not be able to comprehend him and to bear so bright a light. So it is that he comes to us in his prophets; and he is in

---

470. WA 8:541, 8–9; LW 36:202; *Misuse of the Mass*. Luther was sad that since the pope allowed only the canon law preached the people didn't receive the Spirit of God; cf. Lohse, *Theology*, 237.

471. WADB 11, 409:30–33; LW 35:293; "Prefaces to the Old Testament."

472. Prenter, *Spiritus*, 104.

473. WA 39¹:217; "Ministerium autem est planc externum quiddam et sensible . . . in columba, in linguis ignitis, in baptismo, in voce humana videmus et audimus Spiritum sanctum." *Die Promotionsdisputatio von Palladius und Tilemann* [1537].

truth bodily and substantially present in us through the word and sacraments.[474]

The Spirit cannot be with us except in material and physical things such as the word, water, and Christ's body and in his saints on earth.[475]

Luther stressed the word as the exclusive means of the Holy Spirit:

If you want to obtain grace, then see to it that you hear the word of God attentively or meditate on it diligently. The word, I say, and only the word, is the vehicle of God's grace.... The verdict that the Spirit is received from the hearing of faith stands firm. All those who have received the Spirit have received it in this way.[476]

Luther said, "Reason does not know this teaching, but the Holy Scriptures teach it, as you see in the first verse of this psalm 'Have mercy on me, O God.' (Ps 51) ... They are the words of the Spirit which have life."[477] Therefore, any human words that are claimed to be "canon," compiled without God's Spirit, must yield to the gospel and the Spirit.[478]

The Holy Spirit uses different ways of expressing the word as the *verbum efficax*—the words by which the Spirit comes. Along with the word of the dialectic of law and gospel, these expressions or means are his tools to bring hearers to faith, to new life, and to sanctification—the goal of Christian maturity. Heen notes the distinctions of these ways, or means, and their unity found in Luther's understanding:

---

474. WA 39$^\text{I}$:244; "Nunc revera adest et operatur in nobis per verbum et sacrament Spiritus sanctus, suis involucris tectus et vestibus, ut posit capi ab hac valetudinaria, infirma et leprosa natura ac intelligigi a nobis. Si veniret ad nos in sua maiestate, non possemus eum capere et hanc tantam lucem ferre. Itaque venit ad nos prophetia, adest vere corporaliter seu substantialiter et opratur in nobis per verbum et sacramenta," cf. Althaus, *Theology*, 21n1.

475. LW 37:95; WA 23:193, 31-33; "Der geist bey uns nicht sein kan anders denn ynn leiblichen dingen als ym wort, wasser und Christus leib und ynn seinen heiligen auff erden," *This Is My Body (1527)*.

476. LW 27:249; WA 2:509, 13-15; "Si vis gratiam consequi, id age, ut verbum dei vel audias intente vel recorderis diligenter: verbum, inquam, et solum verbum est vehiculum gratiae dei ... stat fixa sententia, ex auditu fidei accipi spiritum. Hoc modo acceperunt spiritum, quincunque acceperunt." Gal 3:2-3 [1519].

477. LW 12:321; WA 40$^\text{II}$: 342, 24-30; "'Miserere mei, Deus.' Hanc doctriam ratio nescit, sed sacrae literae tradunt, sicut in hoc primo huius Psalmi versu videtis.... sunt verba Spiritus, habentia vitam," Ps 51:1[3] [1538].

478. WA 8:526-28; LW 36:185-87; *Misuse of the Mass*.

Though Luther at times had a tendency to privilege (1) the *proclaimed* word of God over its other forms, one should note that this was not meant to eclipse either (2) the *written* word, which also contains God's clear promises (Matt 28:2) and is fully God's word, or (3) the *sacramental* Word, in which Christ, by the power of the Holy Spirit, is also truly, efficaciously present.[479]

Luther said that the word and Spirit are inseparable, and that man, always dependent upon the external word, must keep hearing that word.[480] This unity of the word and Spirit are what Luther sought to describe in the Smalcald Articles where he insisted that the Spirit and the external word always go together. He was not trying to alienate scriptural revelation from the Spirit's ongoing work and manifestations, but was merely stressing that these all must be rooted in the external word.[481] Regarding this, Althaus commented that God's word in the hand of the Spirit is indispensable for man's soul and spirit.[482] Luther saw Christ and the Spirit working inseparably through the word in the work that includes the historic ministry of the church. Through the preaching of the word, the Spirit proclaims God's redemptive history in the work of Christ to the nations of the world.[483]

Can either the Spirit or the word be present without the other? Luther held that because of the intimate union with the word, the Spirit does not speak without the word; the Spirit speaks through and in the word.[484] Prenter maintained that Luther's contrast of the word as *littera-spiritus*, or Law-Gospel, "goes through the whole of Scripture . . . in such a way that it is really only as gospel that the Scriptures can be called the word of God. . . . The word '*spiritus*' can even be directly identified as God Himself."[485]

---

479. Heen, "Word of God," 799–800; cf. Bayer, *Theology the Lutheran Way*, 129, 131.

480. WA 17^{II}:179; cf. Althaus, *Theology*, 40.

481. Cf. Jungkuntz's chapter, "*Sola Scriptura*—Scripture Alone," in Christenson, *Welcome*, 121, referring to Luther's statement in the Smalcald Articles, *BSLK*, 456, 10; *BC*, 323, 10. This is an important issue regarding contemporary manifestations of the Spirit, particularly regarding guidance, wisdom, and prophecy. Among many charismatic Christians today, there is a strong attitude of "companionship" with God, which disregards both Luther's warning, and Jungkuntz's qualifying explanation.

482. Althaus, *Theology*, 41–42, citing WA 7:22.

483. Vajta, *Worship*, 72.

484. Prenter, *Spiritus*, 101, 122–24; Althaus, *Theology*, 36, 38.

485. Prenter, *Spiritus*, 101–2.

The Holy Spirit Inspires and Teaches the Word

The Spirit and his internal word enliven the external word so that after one has heard it and grasped it in his heart, the teaching Holy Spirit empowers the word so that it takes hold.[486] Without God's Spirit, one is like a deaf person upon hearing the external word of Scripture, and it remains the word of man. Without the Spirit, speakers and hearers toil in vane and sadness, hearing only human words. However, when God speaks by the Spirit evil is put away and good is bestowed.[487] The external word is God's inspired word. It becomes effective as the tool of the Spirit when he speaks the inner word in the heart to give understanding.[488]

Luther depended on the Holy Spirit's counsel and inspiration and teaching in his own ministry[489]—"The Holy Spirit neither lies nor errs nor doubts"[490]—and submitted his work to be evaluated relative to the Scriptures and the fathers. He maintained that the Holy Spirit inspired the Holy Scriptures through his enlightened ones, such as Jacob (Gen 49:10):

> He [Jacob] was enlightened by the Holy Spirit, and he foresaw these things very sharply from afar ... when he said: "To Him [Shiloh, referring to the coming Christ] there shall be a gathering of the obedience of peoples."[491]

Luther insisted on the Holy Spirit's inspiration of Scripture and an interrelation of the Spirit and the word as God draws people to faith.[492] Luther accused Carlstadt of falsely claiming possession of the Spirit without the inner righteousness of the Spirit[493] and ignoring the necessity of preaching the external word in order that the the deeds of the flesh may be put to death by the Spirit. The confusion of Carlstadt's books testified to the devil's inspiration and not the Holy Spirit's. Their lack of forgiveness and peace proved they were inspired by the devil.

Luther gave a three-step approach for the study of theology ("The Three Rules of Theology") guided by the Spirit:

---

486. *WA* 17^{II}:459–60; cf. Althaus, *Theology*, 37.
487. *WA* 3:347–48; *LW* 10:294, Ps 60:6; cf. Prenter, *Spiritus*, 102.
488. *WA* 3:262–63; *LW* 10:220–21, Ps 45:1; *LW* 33:18, 28, 90–91; *Bondage*.
489. *WA* 1:353, 8–11; *LW* 31:39; *Heidelberg Disputation* (1518).
490. *LW* 37:279; *WA* 26:418, 19–20; "*Denn der heilige geist leuget noch feylet noch zweivelt nicht*," *Confession Concerning Christ's Supper* (1528).
491. *LW* 8 244; *WA* 44:758; "Lectures on Genesis," Gen 49:10.
492. *LW* 8:244–45; *WA* 44:759; "Lectures on Genesis," Gen 49:10.
493. *WA* 18:212–13; *LW* 40:221–22; *Against the Heavenly Prophets* (1525).

1) *Oratio*—Ask the Holy Spirit for enlightened discernment of the source of all truth—the Scriptures; 2) *Meditatio*—Pray over the external words and messages of Scripture in order to be internally enlightened by the Holy Spirit; and 3) *Tentatio*—Let trials of personal experience test the learned truths to discover true wisdom.[494] The Spirit teaches about the cross of Christ in the midst of trouble, which requires trust in the Spirit. Difficult circumstances and disappointments call for self-sacrifice—his ultimate teaching.[495]

Oswald Bayer sprinkles his book, *Theology the Lutheran Way*, with references to "The Three Rules of Theology" which find their focus in Part One: Luther's Understandig of Theology.[496] With these "sprinklings" Bayer shows Luther's development of his "theology of reality," in which he (Bayer) presents Luther's theology of the Holy Spirit as a major factor of his theology.[497] This understanding of the work of the Holy Spirit is likewise related to Luther's experience and teaching of the inner testimony of the Holy Spirit.

The Holy Spirit is a sure teacher in whom everything is "Yes, Yes." He illumines darkness with light.[498] Those who would ignore the limits set by God's commands for living in the Spirit[499] and those who set themselves up as teachers to interpret and apply laws beyond God's intention, drive off God's teacher, the Holy Spirit. The Holy Spirit teaches through the Scriptures that confirm the truth of his doctrine, though the content may be presented in different ways to different hearers.[500]

> Unless they (the Scriptures) are taught by the Great Spirit, they cannot enter the heart of man. . . . True knowledge of these doctrines does not depend upon the intelligence and wisdom of human reason. . . . But it is revealed and given from heaven. Where is there a man who could speak about repentance and forgiveness of sins the way the Holy Spirit speaks in this Psalm (Ps 51)?"[501]

---

494. WA 50:659-61; *LW* 34:285-88; *Preface to the Wittenberg Edition of Luther's Writing* (1539); cf. Lehmann, *Prayer*, 136.

495. WA 40^{II}:464, 19-22; *LW* 12:407, Ps 51:18 [20] (1538); cf. Lehmann, *Prayer*, 114.

496. Bayer, *Theology the Lutheran Way*, 10, 12, 22, 84-85, 93, 212.

497. Bayer, *Theology the Lutheran Way*, 33-66.

498. WA 23:215, 31-32; 225, 2-3; *LW* 37:107, 112; *This Is My Body* (1527).

499. WA 18:112, 11-19; *LW* 40:129; *Against the Heavenly Prophets* (1525).

500. WA 6:538, 23-25; *LW* 36:74; *Captivity* (1520); WA 8:496; *LW* 36:152; WA 8:504, 24-28; *LW* 36:160; *Misuse of the Mass* (1521).

501. *LW* 12:303-4; WA 40^{II}:315, 30-32, 316, 20-24; "Qui, nisi magno spiritu doceantur, non est possibile, ut ascendant in cor hominis . . . vera cognitio horum locorum non pendent ex cognitione et sapientia rationis humanae . . . sed de coelo revelantur et

The Holy Spirit teaches spiritual knowledge and confidence in God through the life of faith.[502] Luther opposed Carlstadt's blaspheming "spiritual knowledge" and identified the true spirit and true spiritual knowledge that the Holy Spirit works in us. In contrast, Carlstadt made studies a human, carnal devotion, which the devil and the hypocrites also know, but do not match what Christ had given.[503] Only the Spirit of God, who teaches about God and Christ, can produce spiritual knowledge. While God can be generally known through his creation, he cannot be known personally except through the revelation of Christ through the Holy Spirit.[504] Nature and all natural hearts know there is a God, but only the Holy Spirit teaches who he is and what he is like.[505] No one can learn to understand God and know his word except they experience the realistic teaching of the Spirit in what Luther called "the inner testimony of the Holy Spirit" in "the school of the Holy Spirit."[506]

The Sacraments

Luther taught that what is promised in God's word becomes real when believers receive the work of the Holy Spirit through physical means—the proclamation of the word and the sacraments.

Faith's focus and expectation are on God, and the efficacy of the sacraments rests not on Christians' personal worthiness, but on the work of God.[507] As John Pless notes, "Luther, . . . in *The Babylonian Captivity of the Church* . . . saw sacraments as the external means that God established to promise and deliver the benefits of Christ's redeeming work to sinners. . . . His [Luther's] starting point [was] the words of Jesus, which institute

---

datur. Quis enim hominum sic posset loqui de Poenitentia et Resmissione peccatorum, sicut Spiritus sanctus in hoc Psalmo loquitur?" (Ps 51).

502. *WADB* 7:10, 16–19; *LW* 35:370–71; "Preface to the Epistle of St. Paul to the Romans" (1522); *LW* 1:64, 66; *WA* 1:47–50; Gen 1:26.

503. *WA* 18:198, 7–9; *LW* 40:208; "Against the Heavenly Prophets."

504. *WA* 56:177, 8–18; *LW* 25:157–60. Luther understood the improper knowledge of God to be when people assign the name of "God" to things of their own creation. The proper knowledge of God is disclosed through the word of God and the Holy Spirit as "inside" knowledge of God; *WA* 45:90; *WA* 19:207, 3–8; *LW* 19:55; *Commentary on Jonah* (German text, 1526); Jonah 1:5; *WA* 56:445, 21–27; *LW* 25:437; cf. Althaus, *Theology*, 15–17; Loewenich, *Luther's Theology*, 110.

505. *WA* 19:206–7; cf. Althaus, *Theology*, 7, 16–17.

506. *WA* 7:546, 24–28; *LW* 21:299; *The Magnificat* (1521).

507. *WA* 6:158, 362; *LW* 39:28–29; cf. Vajta, 137.

or establish the sacraments, [as] seen in the Small Catechism ... [and] ... in his longer theological treatises."[508]

Luther described a sacrament by its contents, its benefits, and its receivers.[509] The sacrament's content is Christ's word of promise connected with a physical sign; its benefits are forgiveness, renewal in the Holy Spirit, and the continued washing of regeneration; and its receivers are those who receive the benefits of the sign when they believe the word of promise. In the church God gathers people around the pastor to receive the sacrament. They are sanctified by Christ's blood, anointed by the Holy Spirit, and consecrated in baptism.[510] Luther said, "Where there is a holy, Christian Church, there all the sacraments, Christ himself, and the Holy Spirit must be."[511]

In two treatises, *The Sacrament of Penance*[512] (1519) and *A Discussion on How Confession Should Be Made* (1520), Luther discussed issues related to the Roman Catholic sacrament of penance including confession and absolution of sin. In his discussion of his treatise, *The Sacrament of Penance*, Luther distinguished between what he called the sacrament of penance and penance. The sacrament of penance consists of the word of God in absolution, in the grace of faith that trusts in the absolution, and in the peace that follows the forgiveness which is given through the believers' faith and trust in the word of God. In contrast, what he calls penance includes contrition (sorrow for sin), confession (of sin), and satisfaction (works to right the remaining wrongs caused by the sin).[513]

The content in the sacrament of penance is faith in the promises of Christ found in Scripture through which the Holy Spirit works. Luther noted that faith in the sacrament of penance brings about true forgiveness and peace, while in the Catholic model of the Sacrament of Penance, "Where there is no faith, neither contrition, nor confession, nor satisfaction ... adequate[ly]" results in forgiveness or peace.[514] So Luther saw, as we've noted many times above, that when the Holy Spirit proclaims the word of God to sinners, he bring hearers to faith, conviction of sin, confession, absolution, and forgiveness. Luther saw this gospel action as a display

---

508. Pless, "Sacraments," 653.
509. BSLK, 708; BC, 467; *Large Catechism*, "The Sacrament of the Altar."
510. WA 38:247, 10–23; LW 38:208; *The Private Mass*.
511. LW 38:212; WA 38:252, 30–31; "Wo aber eine heilige Christliche Kirche ist, da müssen alle Sacrament sein, Christus selbs und sein Heiliger geist." *The Private Mass*.
512. LW 35:9–27.
513. LW 35:19, "Sacrament of Penance."
514. LW 35:20, "Sacrament of Penance."

that he labeled The Sacrament of Penance—the common term he used for the "confession/forgiveness" model he was describing.

In his treatise *The Sacrament of Penance* (1519), Luther raised questions about the proper use of the confessional. Is confession driven by fear of God's judgment and wrath or by his mercy and forgiveness? Having become concerned that "faith and trust in God has nearly ceased,"[515] Luther responded in his treatise *A Discussion on How Confession Should Be Made* (1520), addressing his understanding of penance and auricular confession.[516] Luther asserted that the sacrament is not a fearful response to God's wrathful judgment, but rather depends upon the mercy of God in Christ who is ready to forgive the sins of the penitent who believes. Therefore Luther stated, "This sacrament does not depend upon the priest, nor on your own actions, but entirely on your faith; you have as much as you believe."[517] He encouraged those who plan confessions not to put their trust in the confessions they prepare but with faith, to trust in God's merciful promises of forgiveness to those who confess their sins to him. These are the abundant promises found in Scriptures.[518] In this treatise, Luther referred to "the salutary sacrament of confession,"[519] for through it, penitents are forgiven their sins and saved or restored to new life and a trusting fellowship with God.

Later, Luther wrote the *Babylonian Captivity* (1520) where he recognized two sacraments in some places and three sacraments in other places. He finally recognized just two sacraments—baptism and the Lord's Supper—because they included scriptural promises attached to physical signs, but he could see the Holy Spirit working through the word to bring forgiveness of sin in all three.[520] In his later version of the *Small Catechism* (1531),[521] he tucked instructions for confession in between baptism and the Lord's Supper.

While Luther challenged some practices of Roman Catholic traditions, he retained the sacramental understanding of the gospel and the means of grace. He rejected the "spiritualizing" of the enthusiasts by insisting on the real presence of Christ. In his view of the sacraments, the real

---

515. WA 6:158; LW 39:28; "Confession."

516. LW 39:27–46.

517. LW 35:16.

518. LW 39:28–30.

519. LW 39:40.

520. See *The Sacrament of Penance* (1519), LW 35:9–22; WA 2:714–23; *The Holy and Blessed Sacrament of Baptism* (1519), LW 35:23–43; WA 2:727–37; *A Discussion On How a Confession Should Be Made* (1520), LW 39:27–47; WA 6:157–60; *Captivity* (1520), LW 36:3–126; WA 6:497–573.

521. BC, 360–62; BSELK, 884–89; SC (1531).

presence of Christ is manifest through the word, the Spirit, and the physical signs. Since the Holy Spirit is inseparable from the word, then, as the word acts in the sacraments, so the Holy Spirit acts to unite the promises with the signs. His view, that the Holy Spirit brings Christ's real presence in the unity of the physical and the spiritual, was more realistic than either the Roman Catholic's or the enthusiast's views.[522] Luther said when believers receive the elements in faith, linked to the promises of God's word; there the body and blood of Christ and God's Holy Spirit are present.[523] The word calls believers to relinquish physical and logical security, to repent of self-dependence, and to believe the promise of the word that points to Christ. The Holy Spirit assumes their inner conflict, gives them faith, and brings Christ to them as their alien righteousness. The word itself is the physical sacramental representation of a hidden spiritual reality—the gospel of Jesus Christ. The kernel of Luther's understanding of the sacraments is that by virtue of the word of promise, the content of the sacraments is the gospel, Christ himself.[524]

The word and the sacrament are inseparably united, such that the preached word is also a part of the sacrament. The preached message and the sacrament both belong to the same historico-eschatological reality and whole. The preached message with the confession of sins assumes a sacramental quality as it is linked to the sacramental signs. Therefore, because they are both based on God's total work of salvation—promise, incarnation, baptism, preaching, the Supper, and the fulfillment—preaching is integral to the right use of the sacraments. We rightly receive preaching and the sacraments by promise and sign.[525]

Luther insisted on a realistic understanding of the true presence of Christ in the sacrament that required proper discernment of the body and the blood. Luther stressed that the reality of the sacramental promise is linked to the historical promises God made and fulfilled in the saints of old: Adam, Noah, Abraham and Sarah, Moses, and David, that pointed to God's greatest promise revealed in Jesus Christ. Luther's "theocentric" view of God's promise puts the sacraments in the center of the salvation story from creation to consummation.[526] This promise, guaranteed by the hidden

---

522. Cf. Prenter, *Spiritus*, 130–31, 142–60.

523. WA 6:532, 36—533, 1; *LW* 36:66; *Captivity*. Cf. Prenter, *Spiritus*, 132–33; WA 38:214, 27–28; *LW* 38:169, *Consecration*.

524. Cf. Prenter, *Spiritus*, 137–42.

525. Cf. Prenter, *Spiritus*, 158–60.

526. WA 6:513–17; *LW* 36:37–42, *Captivity*; cf. Prenter, *Spiritus*, 139–41.

realities of God, is fulfilled when it is claimed by faith. The promise must be received in faith, or it will fall away unused and useless.[527]

Luther emphasized that the sacraments of baptism and the Lord's Supper are established from the words Christ used to institute them. For Luther the chief thing was that these words of institution are God's word—*verbum efficax*, his word of action. In the *Large Catechism* Luther cited Augustine to explain, "'When the word is added to the element or the natural substance of the sign or the symbol, it becomes a sacrament,' that is, a holy, divine thing and sign," and Silcock concludes that Luther said the sign points to itself and is the divine thing.[528] Luther continued to say that we are to honor the sacraments not merely as physical elements, but because these physical elements are joined to the word of God. "You should give honor and glory to baptism because of the word, for God himself has honored it by both words and deeds and has confirmed it by miracles from heaven." This text also applies to the Lord's Supper.[529] Luther maintained that the word of God and the Holy Spirit are inseparably joined. Through the words of institution the Holy Spirit brings life and forgiveness of sins to those who receive them through faith in Jesus Christ. The physical elements with God's sacramental word function as means of the Holy Spirit.

Baptism

Jonathan Trigg writes, "Luther insists that baptism is the appointed way into the kingdom."[530] God's promise comes true as he imparts new life in Christ through baptism. Luther wrote,

> This is what the sacrament declares . . . he [God] begins to make you a new person. He pours into you his grace and Holy Spirit, who begins to slay nature and sin, and to prepare you for death and the resurrection at the Last Day.[531]

---

527. WA 6:518; LW 36:44–45; *Captivity*; WA 6:363, 11–15; LW 35:91; *Treatise on the Mass*; and WA 1:604 (LW 31:209); *Explanation of the 95 Theses*; cf. Prenter, *Spiritus*, 137–38.

528. BC, 458, 467, LC; Augustine, *Tractate 80*; cf. Silcock, "Luther on the Holy Spirit," 303.

529. BC, 467–68.

530. Trigg, *Baptism*, 64.

531. LW 35:33; WA 2:730, 24–29; "Nach anzeygung des sacraments . . . hebet von stund an dich new zu machen, geust dyr eyn feyn gnad und heyligen geyst, der anfahet die natur und sund zu todten und zu bereyten tzum sterben und auffersteen am jungsten tag." *The Holy Sacrament of Baptism* (1519).

Baptism is the epitome of the cross of suffering that God ordains to form Christ in Christians. Baptism is to be applied daily[532] as Christians' experiences bring them to conviction of sin and repentance, and as God acts according to his covenant promises to drive out all sin in them. Baptism confirms the promise that the believer receives "victory over death and the devil, forgiveness of sin, God's grace, the entire Christ, and the Holy Spirit with His gifts."[533] The *Large Catechism* affirms the purpose of baptism:

> Nor can we better understand this than from the words of Christ. . . . "The one who believes and is baptized will be saved (Mark 16:16)." This is the simplest way to put it: the power, effect, benefit, fruit, and purpose of baptism is that it saves. . . . To be saved, . . . is nothing else than to be delivered from sin, death, and the devil, to enter into Christ's kingdom, and to live with him forever.[534]

The authority in baptism is the Lord's word of command to baptize. When baptizing we should not heed the words said as much as who is saying them because the Holy Spirit points to the water of baptism as God's word and will that reveals God's decision for a person's salvation in Christ. Therefore, people should follow these words of God rather than their own reasoned ideas.[535] Baptism also incorporates the candidates into the eschatological people of God from the Old Testament through to the final Day of the Lord. After baptism, God's Spirit works in Christians until the final resurrection, giving the sacrament an eschatological quality.[536]

Baptism is administered in obedience to the Holy Spirit, "Baptize with water!" We attribute the washing [of regeneration] not to the water but to the Holy Spirit."[537]

> You can see the water of baptism as you can see the dew . . . but you cannot see or hear or understand the Spirit, or what he accomplishes thereby: that a human being is cleansed in baptism and becomes a saint in the hands of the priest so that from a

---

532. *LW* 36:124-25; *WA* 6:572, *Captivity*; cf. Prenter, *Spiritus*, 146.

533. *BC*, 461, 41; *BSLK*, 742; "Überwindung des Teufels und Tods, Vergebung der Sünden, Gottes Gnade, den ganzen Christum und heiligen Geist mit seiner Gaben." LC, "Baptism"; cf. Althaus, *Theology*, 353-54.

534. *BC*, 459 (*BSELK*, 1116 or 1117).

535. *WA* 19:496, 20; *LW* 36:345, *Sacrament of the Body and Blood of Christ* (1526); cf. Elert, *Structure*, 293-94.

536. Prenter, *Spiritus*, 146-47.

537. *LW* 38:18; *WA* 30^{III}:115, 7; "*Aquae non lotionem, sed spiritus tribuimus.*" *The Marburg Colloquy* (1529).

child of hell he is changed into a child of God. Nevertheless, this is truly and actually accomplished. One has to say, in view of the power, which attends it, that the Holy Spirit was present at the event and was making believers by means of water and the word.[538]

Here Luther clearly maintains that through the physical rite of water baptism linked to the aforementioned word commanding it, the Holy Spirit is present and actively regenerating new believers—Luther's theology of baptismal regeneration. Trigg notes that such statements include and presume that faith is included because the Holy Spirit is "making new believers" and they are continuing in their faith.[539]

The Lord's Supper

The Lord's Supper continually recalls the covenant of baptism as a bridge from this life to the life to come. The sign of the Supper is the physical eating and drinking of the true body and blood of Christ that the communicants receive in and under the bread and wine of the sacrament.

The cup, sacramentally united with the blood of Christ, is the New Testament promise that bestows grace, forgiveness of sins, and the Holy Spirit[540] who, through baptism, sustains those who are in union with Christ and his death. The Supper unites Christians with Christ in their struggles against sin, death, and the devil,[541] that was Luther's understanding of Christians' day-to-day battles. As baptism is union with Christ that leads through his death to regeneration and new life, the Lord's Supper is a sacrament of identification with Christ's death.[542] Throughout life, the Supper connects the death of Christ with Christians to sustain them in their processes of dying, and to make them alive in him.

Luther saw the words of Christ as the chief elements of the Lord's Supper, "This is my body," to take and eat and drink.[543] The power of the Lord's Supper is that believers receive the total person of Jesus Christ—physical and spiritual, human and divine. Christ's flesh, born of the Spirit, belongs to the new realm of the Spirit (John 3:6).[544] To feed on Christ's body and

538. *LW* 13:303; *WA* 41:166, 22–30, on Ps 110:3.
539. Trigg, *Baptism*, 77–79.
540. *WA* 26:468, 35–42; *LW* 37:325; *Confession*; cf. Prenter, *Spiritus*, 148–50.
541. *WA* 2:748, 14; *LW* 35:58; *WA* 6:376, 17–24; *LW* 35:109.
542. *WA* 6:572; *LW* 36:124–25, *Captivity*.
543. *WA* 26:415, 29–30; *LW* 37:277; *WA* 26:474, 5–6; *LW* 37:332; *Confession*.
544. *WA* 26:349, 35–36, 350:19; *LW* 37:236; *Confession*.

blood is to feed on his humanity and divinity as God hides his wisdom in the mystery of the Sacrament.[545] Luther saw that this fleshly-spiritual presentation of Christ's person[546] intimately links believers to the Triune God. It also pertains to the Father's begetting of Jesus as true God and true man through the conception in the Virgin Mary by the Holy Spirit.[547] Jesus said, "He who has seen me has seen the Father" (John 14:9). Filled with the Godhead (Col 1:19) he is one with the Father (John 10:30). These Scriptures, with, "This is my body" (Matt 26:26), formed Luther's understanding of how the Holy Spirit brings Christ's real presence to the Lord's Supper. As the Spirit formed Christ's flesh in Mary, so he brings Christ's flesh in the sacrament as spiritual food.[548] As the Spirit brought about Christ's incarnation, human flesh indwelt by the omnipresent God, so also, the bread and wine are united with the body and blood of the omnipresent Christ by the work of the Spirit. The soul and spirit of Christ and the whole Godhead are present in the sacrament.

Luther emphasized that the work of reconciliation and renewal that comes through the sacrament involves the fullness of God—no more, no less.[549] God's omnipresence and omnipotence operate in Christ by the creative power of the Spirit,[550] and that which is "physical" is truly "spiritual" as well, because of the work of the Spirit. Luther related this to the life of faith:

> All that our body does outwardly and physically, if God's word is added to it and it is done through faith, is in reality and in name done spiritually.... "Spiritual" is nothing else than what is done in us and by us through the Spirit and faith, whether the object with which we are dealing is physical or spiritual.[551]

---

545. WA 6:551-52; LW 36:94; *Captivity*; cf. Prenter, *Spiritus*, 150.

546. WA 23:191-203; LW 37:94-99; *This Is My Body*.

547. WA 23:165, 8-7; LW 37; *This Is My Body*. Luther called Christ's conception by the Holy Spirit "The greatest of all God's miracles"; WA 30^{III}:161, 5-10; LW 38:85-86, *Marburg Articles*.

548. WA 23:201-3; LW 37:98-99, *This Is My Body*; WA 19:490, 24-35; 491, 13-16; LW 36:341; *Sacrament of the Body and the Blood of Christ* (1526); cf. Brunner, *Worship*, 304-5.

549. WA 11:450, 8-13; LW 36:297; *Adoration*.

550. WA 23:139; LW 37:60-61; *This Is My Body*.

551. WA 23:189, 9-13; "Alle das ienige, so unser leib euserlich und leiblich thut: wenn Gotts wort dazu kompt und durch den glauben geschicht, so ists und heisst geistlich geschen ... Das geistlich nicht anders ist Denn was durch den geist und glauben ynn und durch uns geschicht, Gott gebe, das ding, da mit wir umb gehen, sey leiblich odder geistlich"; LW 37:92, *This Is My Body*.

The Holy Spirit deals with humanity in the "bodiliness of history" to validate God's revelation. Christ's real presence in the sacrament and in Christian preaching produce faith as the Spirit speaks through the words of institution—for forgiveness of sins, salvation, and life everlasting[552]—to stir hearts to faith and assurance, and to draw them to Christ.[553]

The Holy Spirit in Law and Gospel

Luther explained his emphasis on preaching, the proclaiming aspect of the work of the Holy Spirit, in his *Lectures on Galatians*. There he presented the dynamic of spiritual rescue that involves law, word, gospel, and the Holy Spirit. In *The Bondage of the Will*, he noted that for those who accept the preaching of the kingdom of God and do not spurn grace, "the Spirit that fulfills the law, so splendidly effective are its endeavor and desire."[554] Silcock summarizes,

> Luther maintains . . . that the law's function is not only to disclose sin but also to drive us to Christ. The law, however, cannot do this by itself but only through the power of the Spirit, and then only in conjunction with the gospel.[555] Luther insists that the law, in its accusing role, can never convey the Spirit as gift, for this happens only through the gospel. After the law exposes sin and accuses the conscience, the Spirit, working through the gospel, presses the law into the service of the gospel and makes it lead the penitent to Christ.[556]

Robert Kolb states the importance of the distinction between law and gospel for Luther:

> All who engage Luther are irresistibly drawn into the magnetic field at the heart of his practice of theology, insuring that the distinction of law and gospel will be debated wherever his works are read.[557]

---

552. *LW* 37:338; *Confession*.
553. *WA* 26:474, 5–6; *LW* 37:332, *Confession*; *WA* 6:515, 28–33; *LW* 36:40; *Captivity*; cf. Althaus, *Theology*, 397.
554. *LW* 33:158, *Bondage*.
555. *WA* 40¹:489–90; *LW* 26:315–16.
556. *WA* 40¹:529–32; *LW* 26:345–47; Silcock, "Luther on the Holy Spirit," 301.
557. Kolb, "Luther's Hermeneutics," 175.

Steven Paulson notes that "law" and "gospel" are two contradictory words, or categories of scriptural words that establish the divine office of proclamation to sinners. The law kills and the gospel gives life (2 Cor 3:6).[558]

In his lecture on Gen 21:10–16, Luther joined Paul from Gal 4:21–31, to discern the root of the distinction between law and gospel as portrayed in a story of Ishmael and Isaac, Ishmael being thirteen years older than Isaac. The Genesis text describes events some time after the feast celebrating Isaac's day of weaning (at about three years old). Keil and Delitzsch interpreted Ishmael's laughter as mocking and ridicule at this occasion.

> Isaac, the object of holy laughter, was made the butt of unholy wit or profane sport. [According to the Hebrew Masoretic textual distinction] Ishmael did not laugh but made fun. The little Isaac a father of nations! Unbelief, envy, pride of carnal superiority, were the causes of his [Ishmael's] conduct. . . . It seemed to him absurd to link so great a thing to one so small. Paul calls this the persecution of him who was after the Spirit by him that was begotten after the flesh (Gal 4:29).[559]

Luther interpreted the point of the Hebrew text and his German translation of Gen 21:8–19:

> The circumstances show that these events took place some years after the weaning and that the quarrel went on, not for one day but even for several years. Paul indicates this (Gal 4:29) when he speaks of the time of persecution. . . . Ishmael wanted to have the prerogative of primogeniture, and his mother Hagar was proud in a boastful manner because Abraham became a father through her. These things the brother threw up to the boy Isaac, who now, because of his age, was susceptible to insult and persecution; and perhaps, as is wont to happen, he [Ishmael] brought the greater part of the domestics over to his side, as though he were the sole heir to the promise. For what he had heard about the twelve princes who would be born of him (Gen 17:20), this undoubtedly caused his youthful mind to become puffed up. Therefore he dreamed of a kingdom for himself and despised Isaac in comparison to himself. His mother acted the same way toward Sarah (Gen 16:4). . . . Finally, Sarah became impatient of the contempt and the insults. When she saw that there was no remedy except to expel Hagar and her son from the house, she reported the matter to Abraham. . . . Sarah [had] concealed the insults for a number of years. . . . Hagar appears to have stirred

558. Paulson, "Law and Gospel," 414.
559. K&D, 1:156; Gen 21:8–21.

up her son and to have fomented quarrels in the household. For this reason Sarah attacked her rather severely.[560]

Luther commended Sarah for her firmness to accuse Hagar and Ishmael for their stubborn pride and intention to secure Abraham's inheritance and rule. So Sarah submissively, but abruptly, implored her husband Abraham for help in removing the problem of Hagar and Ishmael.[561] Luther noted that, as Augustine maintained, Sarah is acting as an excitable woman, but she is under the influence of the Holy Spirit as she relies on the sure promise of God's covenant about her son, Isaac.[562] She is not commanding Abraham, but imploring him, as he struggles with the situation concerning his two sons–Ishmael, the son of his flesh through Hagar without the promise of Christ, and Isaac the son of his flesh through Sarah by the promise of the LORD. He dearly loved them both. Sarah wanted the slave woman and her son to be cast out because they ridiculed Isaac, the child of God's promise of a messianic lineage through Abraham. Their ridicule was really a ridicule of the LORD himself, and so Luther interpreted her call to cast them out as the word and call of the Holy Spirit. Therefore, Abraham was tested and torn between two elements: 1) the works of the flesh without the promise, which is under the law, and 2) the working of the promises of the LORD, which is the gospel. The Holy Spirit forced Sarah and Abraham to face these tensions and enabled them to respond with the obedience of faith to trust in the promise of God.[563]

Sarah's response to Ishmael's behavior was, "Cast out this slave woman with her son, for the son of this slave woman shall not be heir with my son Isaac." (Gen 21:10). Therefore, through the impatience, anger, and harshness of Sarah's voice, God cast Hagar and Ishmael out into the desert wilderness.[564] Luther used the casting out and the thirst of Ishmael to demonstrate the killing results of the law. As God heard the cries of Ishmael, suffering under the law for his mockery of Isaac and God's promise, and as good as dead without water, he sent his angel to show them water and relief. Their cries of hopelessness and terror were answered by God's gospel of rescue with a promise to make of Ishmael a great nation.

Luther's thorough treatment of this somewhat obscure passage is an example of how consistently important the distinction between law and

---

560. *LW* 4:17–18; *WA* 43:148.
561. *LW* 4:18; *WA* 43:148.
562. *LW* 4:19, 21; *WA* 43:149, 150.
563. *LW* 4:23–27; *WA* 43:151–54.
564. *LW* 4:35; *WA* 43:160.

gospel was for him throughout his ministry and writing, and how he interleaved this understanding with his view of the work of the Holy Spirit.

The Holy Spirit and the Kingdom of God

God's first promise of the Messiah in Gen 3:15 was passed down to Abraham (Gen 12) and through his family line to his son, Isaac, and his grandson, Jacob (Gen 35:9–12). Just before his death and burial, Jacob gathered his 12 sons to give them his final words (Gen 49:1–28).[565]

> ¹Then Jacob called his sons, and said, "Gather yourselves together, that I may tell you what shall happen to you in days to come. ²Assemble and listen, O sons of Jacob, listen to Israel your father." (Gen 49:1–2)

Jacob prophesied that God's kingdom would proceed through his son Judah, integrated with God's promises and threats. Luther's summary of Jacob's final words described the criteria for those who would enter God's kingdom and dwell there forever, and those who would not enter, be banished, and suffer eternal punishment. Luther explained:

> The main teaching and argument of this chapter is why and to what end God threatens and promises. He does so to keep faith in the word at work. He who wants to deal with God must learn this, so that he does not live by bread alone but by every word which proceeds from the mouth of God (cf. Deut 8:3). If bread is lacking, a strange god should not be called upon on this account. No, then the heart should be strengthened by faith in the word. God has promised that He will be my God and Lord. If He wants to slay me with hunger, let Him do so, by all means. I will hope in Him in spite of this (cf. Job 13:15).[566]
>
> Faith and fear should exist in the hearts of men, because a promise and faith, like a threat and fear, are correlative. There is no promise if faith is not present; and, on the other hand, there is no faith without a promise, just as there is no fear where a threat is lacking. But God defers both in order to test us. And since the world is not willing to endure this trial, it despises

---

565. *LW* 8:ix–x. Luther concluded his ten-year task of *Lectures on Genesis* on November 17, 1545, seven days after his sixty-second birthday and three months and one day before his death in Eisleben, the town of his birth. His composition of his lectures on Gen 49–50 include a comprehensive compendium of his theology—especially that of the Holy Spirit—of his *theology crucis*, and of the Holy Spirit and the kingdom of God.

566. *LW* 8:204; *WA* 44:727.

both and neither fears him who threatens nor believes Him who promises.[567]

According to Luther, "[God] wants us to be people who are patient of delay—people with the certain expectation that He will give abundantly and richly what He has promised."[568] Jacob, the patriarch, learned this when the promise of the future Seed was given to him, and when Joseph was raised to the highest honor and rank in Egypt. The nation Israel learned of God's delayed abundance when Canaan was given to Jacob's descendants.[569]

With these thoughts in mind, Jacob prophesied to his assembled sons what would transpire. They should remember and acknowledge the LORD's promises and threats so that they might have a God in whom they trusted and hoped and whom they feared. Luther interpreted Jacob thusly, as if Jacob could see the future:

> I know that many of you will be evil and obstinate. You will become scoundrels, and there will be a worthless rabble among you. They will be idolaters and despisers of God when he threatens and when he promises, just as Moses, Samuel, David, and many others prophesied concerning their descendants. Nevertheless, among those descendants of mine there will be some who will fear God and have confidence in him.[570]

Jacob's blessings, promises, and threats were expressed for those trusting God. Others, operating in the flesh, hated the God who postponed his help, and worshiped heathen gods, as denounced in the Old Testament books of Judges, Kings, and the Prophets.[571] Therefore, starting with Reuben, Jacob strongly begs his sons to heed his prophecies, so that from God's threats they may learn of God's wrath against sin, and of his mercy from the promises made to his sons.[572]

Jacob's words to his sons contain prophetic blessings to inform and to guide them, and threats and curses on their bad examples to frighten them.

Jacob's word to Reuben is a serious sermon with horrible reproaches and results. Luther noted that he would have cried himself to death under such a fatherly address.[573]

---

567. *LW* 8:204; *WA* 44:727–28.
568. *LW* 8:202; *WA* 44:726.
569. *LW* 8:202; *WA* 44:726.
570. *LW* 8:203; *WA* 44:727.
571. *LW* 8:202–3; *WA* 44:727.
572. *LW* 8:203–4; *WA* 44:727.
573. *LW* 8:204–15; *WA* 44:728–36. The discussion on Rueben's fall from favor is

> ³Reuben, you are my firstborn, my might, and the firstfruits of my strength, preeminent in diginity and preeminent in power. (Gen 49:3)

Jacob reminded Reuben of the entire honor he would have had as the beginning of Jacob's strength, his firstborn. To Reuben would belong the glory of the priesthood and sovereignty of the house of his father that come through God's promise of eternal salvation and the reign of the Messiah. However, Reuben had disqualified himself from the privilege of this position.

> ⁴Unstable as water, you shall not have preeminence because you went up to your father's bed; then you defiled it—he went up to my couch! (Gen 49:4)

Reuben's crime was incest with his father's concubine, Bihal. He had disgraced Jacob's family (Gen 35:22).

Though Reuben was the firstborn, he despised this very important matter, and in a fickle manner wandered about, like water, to rush blindly into his desires and to ignore his marriage. He did not remain within his proper limits. He showed that he had no faith, as a firstborn should.

Since Reuben was denied the primogenital rights and the line of the Messiah, Jacob turned to his secondborn, Simeon, and to his thirdborn, Levi. They, however, were also disqualified because of violence that threatened Jacob's entire family (Gen 34).

> ⁵Simeon and Levi are brothers; weapons of violence are their swords. ⁶Let my soul come not into their council; O my glory, be not joined to their company. For in their anger they killed men, and in their willfulness they hamstrung oxen. ⁷Cursed be their anger, for it is fierce, and their wrath, for it is cruel! I will divide them in Jacob and scatter them in Israel. (Gen 49:5–7)

Jacob's words for Simeon and Levi are no less curses than those for Reuben for, as Luther noted, they are not only brothers by nature with the same mother and father, but also brothers in wickedness and treachery—vessels of iniquity. Lest their descendants use the examples of Simeon and Levi to defend their own carnal crimes, Luther saw that Jacob rejected and cursed Simeon and Levi for being murderers.[574]

Jacob's words to Judah were prophetic reassignments of Judah to the role of firstborn among his brothers, and the precedence of the tribe of

---

summarized from Luther's lecture regarding it.

574. *LW* 8:215; *WA* 44:736.

Judah to be the ruling and messianic tribe of Israel. Verses 9 and 10 include the origin of "the Lion of Judah" and a clear messianic reference.

> [8]Judah, your brothers shall praise you; your hand shall be on the neck of your enemies; your father's sons shall bow down before you. [9]Judah is a lion's cub; from the prey, my son, you have gone up. He stooped down, he couched as a lion, and as a lioness; who dares rouse him? [10]The scepter shall not depart from Judah, nor the ruler's staff from between his feet, until he [Shiloh] comes;[575] and to him shall be the obedience of the peoples. (Gen 49:8–10)

The prophecy declares that the first kings from the tribe of Judah would rule from David to the time of Heord, until the kingdom of Messiah comes.[576] Commenting on Ps 8:1, "O LORD (Yaweh), our Lord (Adonai) . . . ," Luther described the Kingdom of God on earth and in heaven with Jesus Christ as the divine heavenly King (Yaweh) and as Lord and earthly human ruler (Adonai). As both, he is immortal king of all kings and Lord of all lords. This is Israel's promised Messiah, coming through the tribe of Judah.

> In this kingdom Christ, the King of glory, exalted to the right hand of God and established as head over all, rules His Christians in faith through the gospel and the Holy Spirit, amid sin, death, devil, world, and hell. Though physically they are still living upon earth, He sets them in heaven by the power of His kingdom, word, Spirit, and faith. . . .
>
> This is what it really means to live in heaven, not with the body but with the heart and the soul in faith and hope. By faith in the word, our heart has taken hold of life and heaven through the power of the Holy Spirit.[577]

Luther used Jacob's blessing of Judah to show the messianic relationship of the Holy Spirit and the kingdom of God, ruled by the word of God in the power of the Holy Spirit.[578] Luther distinguished between these

---

575. This presentation of the ESV text includes a literal English rendition of the Hebrew found in the ESV footnotes of Gen 49:10. This is how Luther used the text.

576. *LW* 8:244; *WA* 44:756; cf. *LW* 20:29–30; *WA* 13:572 (Zech 2:8, 1526) and *LW* 9:50; *WA* 14:584–85; (Deut 4:2, 1525); *LW* 8:34–44; *WA* 44:750–58. Here Luther describes the coming of Messiah after the kingdom of Judah has fallen from her reign. This demonstrates Luther's consistency over a twenty-year span of his career (1525–45) of teaching the coming of the kingdom of Messiah after approximately one thousand years of various kingdoms of Judah.

577. *LW* 12:104–7; *WA* 45:213–18 (Ps 8:1).

578. *LW* 8:244; *WA* 44:757–58. This is detailed in the discussion below.

kingdoms. The kingdom of Messiah is not a kingdom of worldly power overcoming worldly kings, but a spiritual one of hearing and obeying God's word, "In this word there is divine power and wisdom, and he who believes it will be saved.... The kingdom of Messiah is a kingdom of the word, for He calls and rules the peoples by the word alone, without arms and force, but by the powerful word of the Holy Spirit by which God draws hearts to believe."[579] Luther summarized this comparison:

> For this is what Jacob means: "The kingdom of my son David, which cannot be administered without the sword and arms, will not endure, but the kingdom of Shiloh [Messiah, or Christ] will follow ... and it will be governed by the word alone." Thus, Christ says: "Go into all the world and preach the gospel to the whole creation."[580]

Jacob continues his word to Judah:

> [11]Binding his foal to the vine and his donkey's colt to the choice vine, he has washed his garments in wine and his vesture in the blood of grapes. [12]His eyes are darker than wine, and his teeth whiter than milk. (Gen 49:11–12)

Luther interpreted these words to prophesy the kingdom of Messiah. The donkey is tied to the vine and eats his fill of Messiah's plenty and becomes drunk by the wine. Jacob speaks through the Holy Spirit about the wonderful kingdom of Christ where even the donkeys eat grapes, drink wine, and get drunk. For Luther this represented Christ's godly apostles filled with and drunk with the Holy Spirit.[581] Luther summarized:

> In Christ and in the time of Christ we must become drunk on the abundance of His house (cf Ps 36:8); that is, we are to receive the Holy Spirit from the word and hearing. This causes us to become other [different] men, just as an inebriated man conducts himself far differently from one who is fasting and famished.[582]

However, they were not drunk but filled with the Holy Spirit, and at Pentecost, they fearlessly rushed through Jerusalem preaching the unjust crucifixion of Jesus Christ and the wonderful things of God.[583] Luther maintained that Christ, in his kingdom, has called all believers to be drunk with

---

579. LW 8:244–45; WA 44:759.
580. LW 8:244; WA 44:57–58.
581. LW 8:246–48; WA 44:760.
582. LW 8:249; WA 44:761.
583. LW 8:249; WA 44:761; LW 8:251; WA 44:763.

the Holy Spirit, and filled with his spiritual gifts. "There is a new language in that abundance of the Spirit according to which the godly speak with new tongues."[584]

Luther saw the blessing of Judah culminating from the wounds and the blood of Christ that are brought forth by the Holy Spirit. The hearers of the good news about Christ are sprinkled with Christ's blood by the Spirit in the word, baptism, the Lord's Supper, absolution (remission of sins), and consolation (among the brethren) through the Spirit.[585]

> We become drunk, like the ass [donkey] . . . from the divine promise in the Holy Spirit, which is the vine, the grape, and the wine. . . . What is left in the old man he washes and purges until we rise up in incorruptibility. Then we shall be completely clean. In the meantime, we are sustained by the forgiveness of sins; have the certain hope of eternal life; are full of wine, or the Holy Spirit; and washed in the bath by which the old man is mortified, washed, and renewed from day to day.[586]

Luther said the Holy Spirit brings his kingdom to Christians as they pray the Lord's Prayer together.[587] "Thy kingdom come." In God's kingdom, the Spirit teaches through the word to enlighten and strengthen faith. Believers pray that the Lord will lead them into his kingdom of grace and salvation, and that through the word and the power of the Spirit, his kingdom will prevail over the devil now and in the final battle. The faithful pray and believe the teaching of the word by the Holy Spirit that they will always live godly lives in God's kingdom.[588] The Spirit brings Christ and his kingdom through the word. Christ brings God's love and reconciles the world to the Father by submitting himself to the "guilty" verdict that convicts all humankind. He was then raised from the dead to reign victoriously over the bonds of death in his kingdom. He defeats Satan and kindles victorious faith through the word of truth.[589]

Luther saw the kingdom of God—that is, the kingdom of Christ—issuing out of the fullness of the Holy Spirit. The kingdom is perpetually

---

584. *LW* 8:255; *WA* 44:766.

585. *LW* 8:258-59; *WA* 44:768-69. Luther presented these five items as means of the gospel coming to us, *BC*, 319-23; *BSELK*, 764-73 (*Smalcald Articles*, 1537).

586. *LW* 8:259; *WA* 44:769.

587. *BC*, 446-47; *BSLK*, 673-74; *LC*, "Explanation to the Second Petition of the Lord's Prayer"; cf. Christenson, *Welcome*, 126-27.

588. *BC*, 356-57; *BSLK*, 513; *SC*, "Explanation of the Lord's Prayer," Second Petition.

589. *WA* 29:273; *WA* 17^{II}:132; *LW* 37:92-93; *WA* 23:189; *WA* 26:569-70 (Rörer); *LW* 12:169; *WA* 51:286-87, 3; *Ps* 23; cf. Vajta, *Worship*, 73-75.

fed with the richness and the gifts of the Spirit, according to the promise of the divine wisdom and power of the word.[590] In the *Smalcald Articles* (1537), Luther noted that the Holy Spirit works through the word of God to strengthen true faith and lead his faithful into holiness. Therefore, Luther concluded that the kingdom of God, established by Jesus Christ the Messiah, truly manifests the gifts of the Holy Spirit in the faithful through the word of God. This kingdom of God is also the true church of Jesus Christ.[591]

The Holy Spirit and the Church

In his lecture on Gen 17:21,[592] Luther pointed out that the word מוֹעֵד denotes a definite place "for the tabernacle" where (God) had commanded that his word would be taught and that he would be worshiped."[593] Luther further noted that מוֹעֵד pertains to designated festivals and places for worship and the Levites' teaching of the word.[594] These "places" established Luther's principle and practice that Sabastian Madejski describes:

> Luther states "*ubi est verbum, ibi est ecclesia*"[595]—"where the word is, there is [the] church." The church is present not since Pentecost or the crucifixion but since the beginning of Creation. Therefore, the essence of the church is the gospel, which saves and gives life in Christ—*Ecclesia enim creatura est Evangelli.*[596] . . . Where the gospel is there is the church, is not a place—Wittenberg or Rome. The church is [the] result of God's activity among people.[597]

For Luther, these places are the events of the Spirit's proclamation of God's word—oral, written, sacramental, or liturgical—that produces faith, conviction and confession of sin, forgiveness, redemption, and regeneration of the church. Both Madejski and Jonathan Trigg interpret Luther to say that the church, as the "place of God's word," has continued from Adam onwards.[598] This is verified by Luther's writing and teaching.

590. *LW* 8:259–60; *WA* 44:769.
591. *BC*, 324–35, 1–3.
592. *BHS*, 147; מוֹעֵד.
593. *LW* 3:163; *WA* 42:665.
594. *LW* 3:164; *WA* 42:665–66.
595. *WA* 39^{II}:176, 8–9.
596. *WA* 2:430, 6–7.
597. Madejski, "Apostolicam Ecclesiam," 19.
598. Madejski, "Apostolicam Ecclesiam," 19; Trigg, *Baptism*, 19.

Trigg points out that in his Lectures on Genesis (*Genesisvorlesung*, 1534-45) Luther identified the places or events called מוֹעֵד as the GATE OF GOD into heaven.[599] Trigg also notes,

> In Genesis Luther finds that the record of his dealings with mankind shows God to have chosen a whole variety of external objects, signs, and places in which he is to be encountered. . . . These in their different ways were divinely appointed signs to which a word of promise had been joined, and through which God was to be known.[600]

This is where God's people should be "seeking God where he wills to be found"—the means of grace. Trigg refers to the means of grace "as 'places,' chosen by God for his tryst with mankind."[601] He identifies Luther as "a theologian of the means of grace."[602] Here the realities of the Triune God are hidden under the physical elements of conversations, worship, proclamation of God's word, and the sacraments. This represents God's personal dealings—beyond all angelic appearances—with all of his created humanity as portrayed in both Old and New Testaments.[603] Because the word and Spirit are inseparably bound together, the Holy Spirit is found wherever Christ is present and uses the power of God to minister his love and grace to his people.[604] Luther referred to John 14:23:

> Christ says, "If anyone loves me, he will keep my word." Therefore, those who want to be the people of God or the church must have the word of Christ, that is, the promises of God; and they must keep them, that is, believe them. These are the people whom the Father loves and to whom He comes to make His home in them.[605]

Abraham and Sarah, by the Holy Spirit, received, believed, and obeyed the word of God in both Law and Gospel, and therefore showed that they were people whom the Father loves and in whom he makes his home.[606]

---

599. Trigg, *Baptism*, 20; WA 43:599; LW 5:247.
600. Trigg, *Baptism*, 21.
601. Trigg, *Baptism*, 22-30.
602. Trigg, *Baptism*, 20.
603. Trigg, *Baptism*, 20-22.
604. Trigg, *Baptism*, 63-64.
605. LW 4:31-32; WA 43:158.
606. See LW 4:32-35; WA 43:158-61 for more of Luther's discussion and application of these matters.

Luther described the church as the place where God teaches all who have the Spirit of God. Although the Holy Spirit may inspire diversely, as, for example, the four evangelists arranged their works with different wording,[607] Luther said the Spirit's inspiration is demonstrated by the doctrinal integrity of the ministry. He mentioned two priestly offices, teaching and prayer. In teaching, the Holy Spirit comes to believers in the sermon or absolution and enables them to believe and to perceive God's word. In prayer, which follows the declaration of God's truth, believers speak unto God who hears their prayers.[608]

From the day of Pentecost, in the environment of faith, the Holy Spirit continues to create, renew, deepen, and strengthen faith through the proclaimed word of God and the administration of the sacraments. Believers respond by praising and thanking God for his goodness, mercy, and blessing, and praying for one another.[609]

In the last stanza of his hymn "Lord Keep Us Steadfast in Thy Word," Luther described the Holy Spirit gathering and unifying the church,

> God Holy Ghost, who comfort art,
> Give to thy folk on earth one heart;
> Stand by us breathing our last breath,
> Lead us to life straight out of death.[610]

When there is discord and division in the church, Luther maintained it is caused by the devil. Luther attacked his opponents who interpreted the Spirit's works to suit their own ideas. This misled many. The many disagreements among Luther's opponents show that their ideas could not have come from the Holy Spirit.[611] He contrasts this disunity of his enemies to warn of their lying spirit and to show that the Holy Spirit is a Spirit of unity.[612] In contrast, Luther described God's "flock,"

---

607. *LW* 36:151, 163–65; *WA* 8:497, 507–9; *Misuse of the Mass*.

608. *LW* 5:197; *WA* 43:564, 17–18, *Lectures on Genesis* (1535–45); cf. Lehmann, *Prayer*, 116–17.

609. *LW* 53:11–12; *WA* 12:35, 19–21, 24–25; *WA* 36:12–13; cf. Lehmann, *Prayer*, 95, 105.

610. Lehmann, *Prayer*, 151, citing *WA* 35:468, 5–8; *LW* 53:305.
The German text:

> Gott heilger Geist, du Tröster werd,
> Gib deim Volck ein'rley sinn auff Erd.
> Steh bey uns in der letzten Not,
> Gleit uns ins Leben aus dem Tod.

611. *WA* 26:262, 29–33; *LW* 37:163; *Confession*.

612. *WA* 26:434, 4–9; *LW* 37:289; *Confession*.

> I believe that there is on earth a holy little flock... of pure saints under one head, Christ. It is called together by the Holy Spirit in one faith, mind, and understanding. It possesses a variety of gifts, yet it is united in love without sect or schism.[613]

Luther believed that through the Holy Spirit God guided the history of the church with the gospel, forgiveness, prayers, the sacraments, and the calling of ministry. "Christ has surely been here among his own with his Holy Spirit and preserved the Christian faith in them."[614] Luther believed that the Spirit guided the church's decisions at its councils.[615] The church's ministry has authority because in justification by faith, the Holy Spirit makes the redemptive merit of Christ operative in all members, and by the power of the keys, a third office of the church, Christ's authority dwells in that body.[616]

In the controversies concerning the church of the 1530s and 1540s, Luther portrayed the ancient Christian church described by the early church fathers as the first authentic site of the Holy Spirit's work of forming Christians.[617] Luther saw that the Triune God created the church according to the promise and power of Christ's word.

The church is, "the community... of all Christians in all the world, the one Bride of Christ, and his spiritual body of which he is the only head."[618] "In this Christian Church... is to be found the forgiveness of sins... the gospel, baptism, and the sacrament of the altar, in which the forgiveness of sins is offered, obtained, and received. Moreover, Christ and his Spirit and God are there. Outside this Christian Church there is no salvation or

---

613. BSELK, 1062, 27—1063, 1064, 2; BC, 437–38, 51; "Ich gleube, das da sey ein heiliges Heuflin... auf Erden eiteler Heiligen unter einem heupt, Christo, durch den heiligen Geist zusammen beruffen, in einem Glauben, sinne und Verstand, mit mancherley gaben, doch eintrechtig in der liebe, on Rotten und spaltung." LC, "Explanation to the Third Article of the Creed."

614. WA 38:221, 33–35; LW 38:178; "Drumb ist hie gewislich Christus bey den seinen gewest mit seinem heiligen geist und inn inen den Christlichen glauben erhalten." The Private Mass and the Consecration of Priests (1533).

615. WA 6:561, 13–18; LW 36:108; Captivity; WA 25:34, 13–20; LW 29:40; Lectures on Titus (1521). Luther did not always hold this opinion concerning councils.

616. WA 11:451, 6–17; LW 36:298; Adoration of the Sacrament (1523).

617. Two representative works written in German, that addressed these disputes, are On the Councils and the Church (1539), LW 41:3–178; WA 50:509–653; and Against Hanswurst (1541); LW 41:179–256; WA 51:469–572.

618. WA 26:506, 3133; LW 37:367; "Die gemeyne... aller Christen ynn aller welt, die einige braud Christi und sein geistlicher leib, des er auch das einige heubt ist." Confession.

forgiveness of sins, but everlasting damnation."[619] "He [the Spirit] first leads us into his holy community, placing us in the church's lap, where he preaches to us and brings us to Christ."[620] "Where Christ is not preached, there is no Holy Spirit to create, call, and gather the Christian Church, apart from which no one can come to the Lord Christ."[621] Luther called the assembly where Christ is preached "'a Christian holy people' (*sancta catholica Christiana*) who believe in Christ.... They are called Christian people and have the Holy Spirit, who sanctifies them daily, not only through the forgiveness of sin, acquired ... by Christ, ... but also through the abolition, the purging, and the mortification of sins, on the basis of which they are called holy people."[622] In *The Private Mass* (1533) Luther maintained that these are the true clerics of universal priesthood from the ranks of the church, who are "sanctified by his blood and consecrated by his Holy Spirit," to serve in offices of apostle, preacher, teacher, pastor, on behalf of all.[623] This happens,

> where God's word is pure and certain, there everything else must be: God's kingdom, Christ's kingdom, the Holy Spirit, baptism, the sacrament, the office of the ministry, the office of preaching, faith, love, the cross, life and salvation, and everything the church should have.[624]

God's grace in the Christian's life comes through workings of the Holy Spirit in the processes of salvation (or justification) and sanctification. Luther, seeing these workings of the Spirit as the "holy possessions" (*Heiligthumer* or *Heilthumer*) of the ancient church, asked, "But how will ... a poor confused person tell where such Christian holy people are to be found in this

---

619. WA 26:507, 7–11; LW 37:368, "Ynn dieser Christenheit, ... ist vergebung der sunden ... das Euangelion, die tauffe, das sacrament des altars, darinn vergebunge der sunden angeboten, geholet und empfangen wird. Und ist auch Christus und sein geist und Gott da selbs. Und ausser solcher Christenheit ist kein heyl noch vergebung der sunden, sondern ewiger tod und verdamnis." Confession.

620. BSELK, 1058, 28–29; BC, 435–36, 37, "Das er uns erstlich füret in seine heilige Gemeine und in der Kirchen schos legt, dadurch er uns predigt und zu Christo bringt." "Explanation to the Third Article of the Creed," LC (1529); cf. Lehmann. Prayer, 94.

621. BSELK, 1060, 28–30; BC, 436, 45, "Denn wo man nicht von Christo predigt, da ist kein heiliger Geist, welcher die Christliche Kirche machet, beruffet und zusamen bringet, ausser welcher niemand zu dem Herrn Christo komen kan." "Explanation to the Third Article of the Creed," *Large Catechism* (1529); cf. Lehmann. Prayer, 94.

622. LW 41:143–44; WA 50:624, 29–33; Councils and Church.

623. WA 38:230–33; LW 38:185–88; Private Mass.

624. WA 38:237, 11–14; LW 38:196; "Wo aber Gottes wort rein und gewis ist, da mus es alles sein, Gottes reich, Christus reich, heiliger geist, Tauffe, Sacrament, Pfarrampt, Predigampt, Glaube, Liebe, Creutz, Leben und seligkeit, und alles, was die Kirchen haben sol." The Private Mass and the Consecration of Priests [1533].

world?"⁶²⁵ Luther answered by describing how the works of the Holy Spirit that mark a true church of holy Christian people linked back to the first ancient congregations of faith. He showed that the holy possessions of the ancient church were found, not in the practices of the Papal Roman Catholic Church of his day, but in the churches of the Reformation being formed through the diverse work of the Holy Spirit. In *On the Councils and the Church* (1539) and in *Against Hanswurst* (1541) Luther showed, by the evidence of these "marks" of the ancient church, that he and his fellow Reformers were recovering a true continuity with the authentic ancient "catholic" church through the Holy Spirit's work. Since the Roman Catholic Church of his time rejected or falsified these "marks," it had invalidated claims of being the true continuation of the ancient church. This revealed the urgent need for the Reformation.

Luther listed and described the "holy possessions" in *On the Councils of the Church*. He presented proofs that the Reformers remained faithful to the ancient church in *Against Hanswurst*. While the lists of "possessions" and proofs in these documents are not identical, they contain the same information in describing the Holy Spirit's work in forming, guiding, and empowering the church of the Reformation (see detailed lists in footnote).⁶²⁶ Luther described the significance and importance of the first seven items in *On the Councils and the Church* that are often referred to as "The Seven Marks of the Church."⁶²⁷

> These are the true seven principal parts of the great holy possession whereby the Holy Spirit effects in us a daily sanctification and vivification in Christ, according to the first table of Moses.

625. *LW* 41:148; *WA* 50:628, 19–21; *Councils and Church*; cf. *LW* 41:194; *WA* 51:478, 27—479, 19; *Hanswurst*.

626. "Holy possessions" (*Heiligthumer*) according to *On the Councils of the Church* are 1) Possession of the holy word of God; 2) sacrament of baptism; 3) sacrament of the altar 4) office of the keys—the forgiveness of sins; 5) call of ministers to the office of ministry; 6) prayer, praise, thanksgiving to God; 7) the holy cross of misfortune and persecution. Other signs by Moses' second table: honor parents, serve princes, no anger nor vengeance, forgiveness, no arrogance nor drunkenness, chastity, self control, friendly, gentle, humble, no stealing nor usury, charitable, truthful, not false, trustworthy, Sanctification and growth by the Holy Spirit through the Decalogue; *WA* 50:628, 29—643, 37; *LW* 41:148-66.

The "Holy possessions" or proofs according to *Against Hanswurst*, *LW* 41:194-99; *WA* 51:479, 4—487, 8; are: 1) baptism, 2) sacrament of the altar, 3) keys, 4) preaching office and the word of God, 5) Apostles' Creed, 6) Lord's Prayer, 7) honor the temporal power, 8) honor marriage, 9) suffering, 10) no vengeance.

627. Silcock, "Luther on the Holy Spirit," 294-304; Lohse, *Theology*, 287; *WA* 50:632-33; *LW* 41:154; *WA* 51:481; *LW* 41:196; Kolb, *Enduring Word of God*, 80-94; Heen, "Word of God," 799-800.

By this we obey it, albeit never as perfectly as Christ. But we constantly strive to attain the goal, under his . . . remission of sin, until we too shall one day become perfectly holy and no longer stand in need of forgiveness. Everything is directed toward that goal. I would even call these seven parts the seven sacraments, but since that term has been misused by the papists and is used in a different sense in Scripture, I shall let them stand as the seven principal parts of Christian sanctification or the seven holy possessions of the church.[628]

The lists from *On the Councils and the Church* and *Against Hanswurst* are combined below with summaries of Luther's thoughts of the Holy Spirit's work through them and how they are "marks" indicating the authentic Holy Christian people of God, the Holy Christian church.

The *Word of God*, in its purist form, "is the principal item, and the holiest of holy possessions." Everything the holy word touches is sanctified, or made holy, including his people, because the word is the power of God for salvation for everyone who has faith (Rom 1:16). The Holy Spirit sanctifies the church through God's word and prayer (1 Tim 4:5).[629] The holy word Christ left to his church is a holy link between the ancient church and the faithful ones who proclaim it in every age, and through which the Holy Spirit works miracles to defeat the devils of every age.[630]

In the *holy sacrament of baptism* Christians are washed of sin and death by the Holy Spirit, in the innocent holy blood of the Lamb of God (Titus 3:5), through which we are anointed with his Holy Spirit for authoritative ministry in the holy fellowship of the church. Wherever it is taught, believed, and administered correctly, as Christ has ordained, and which sanctify God's people, you may know that the church must surely be present.[631] The holy Christian church of the Reformers received holy baptism and therefore was called Christian. This is the baptism instituted by Christ, in which the apostles and the ancient church and all Christians have been baptized. Therefore those of the church of the Reformers belong to the same ancient universal church, together with the apostles themselves and all of Christendom in "one baptism" (Eph 4:5), and baptism is therefore the most important sacrament, without which there is nothing.[632]

---

628. *LW* 41:165–66; *WA* 50:642, 32–43, 5; *Councils and Church*.
629. *LW* 41:149; *WA* 50:629, 2–8; *Councils and Church*.
630. *LW* 41:149–50; *WA* 50:629, 16—630, 10; *Councils and Church*.
631. *LW* 41:151; *WA* 50:630, 21—631, 5; *Councils and Church*.
632. *LW* 41:195; *WA* 51:479, 20–34; *Against Hanswurst*.

Regarding the *sacrament of the altar*, Luther wrote, "God's people... are recognized by the holy sacrament of the altar, wherever it is rightly administered, believed, and received, according to Christ's institution."[633] This public sign—"a precious, holy possession left behind by Christ"—sanctifies his people so that they may believe and confess that they are Christians. Where this sacrament is properly administered, there are the people of God, as with the word and baptism.[634] The church of the Reformers has the holy sacrament of the altar, which Christ had instituted among the apostles and which Christendom has since practiced. All believing Christians eat and drink with all of Christendom to receive with them the one ancient sacrament. Consequently, there is one church, as Saint Paul says (1 Cor 10:17), "one body" and "one loaf." Therefore, since all believers eat of one loaf and drink of one cup, believers and the ancient church are one through one sacrament.[635]

By the *call of ministers* to the offices of ministry, God's people are publicly recognized as the church of God. Luther highly valued the call to ministry because the minister is the instrument of the Holy Spirit.[636] The minister's authority is derived solely from his call. He can declare only the forgiveness, which Christ obtained, or else the ministry becomes a sort of tyranny. That which he receives from Christ by virtue of his call he must pass on in cooperation with God. Therefore, his office is essential, for through the medium of human discourse, Christ imparts the word to his people.[637] Luther assigned the Holy Spirit's call to ministry and ordination to the congregation, which is God's instrument for public ministry.[638] Luther stressed that the Holy Spirit calls ministers through the prayers of Christ's body, the holy Christian people.[639] The church calls bishops, pastors, and preachers, to administer the holy possessions on behalf of Christ and his church according to Eph 4:8, "He gave gifts to men—apostles, evangelists, pastors, and teachers." Regular laity do not serve in these offices, but rely on

---

633. *LW* 41:152; *WA* 50:631, 6-9; *Councils and Church*.

634. *LW* 41:152; *WA* 50:631, 6-10; *Councils and Church*.

635. *LW* 41:195; *WA* 51:480, 19-26; *Against Hanswurst*.

636. *WA* 20:350; *WA* 30^{II}:498; *LW* 40:365-66; *WA* 47:451; *WA* 38:239; *LW* 38:194; *WA* 49:140; *WA* 6:564; *LW* 36:113; *WA* 12:190; *LW* 40:37; *WA* 6:543; *LW* 36:82; *WA* 8:428; *WA* 31^{I}:191; cf. Vajta, *Worship*, 112.

637. *WA* 6:530; *LW* 36:62-63; *WA* 1:233, 545; *LW* 31:26, 107-8; *WA* 17^{II}:179; *WA* 44:648; *LW* 8:94; cf. Vajta, *Worship*, 112-13. Paul called apostles co-operators of God who operates alone yet through them.

638. Prenter, *Spiritus*, 235-36; cf. Vajta, *Worship*, 118-21.

639. *WA* 11:411; *LW* 39:308-9; *WA* 12:191; *LW* 40:37; *WA* 38:253; *LW* 38:212; (Matt 18:19).

ordained clergy to preach, to baptize, to absolve, and to administer the sacraments. The assembly consents to this arrangement. Wherever this occurs, the holy Christian people of God are present.[640] Prenter interpreted this as God's call of Christians to be a gathering of the fruit of the Spirit whereby, in union with Christ, God draws them into his purpose and enables them by the Spirit to serve his love to their neighbors.[641] To protect its ministry, the Spirit instructs the church to use only the word of God, and he installs overseers who speak words of correction to care for the flock.[642] Therefore, Luther only recognized the calls of bishops who met the scriptural criteria[643] and were known by their fruits.

The *office of the keys* has both public and private usages. Luther understood Christ's decree in Matt 18:15-20 to say that "if a Christian sins, he should be reproved and if he does not mend his ways, he should be bound in his sin and cast out. If he does mend his ways, he should be absolved." Some, with such grieved consciences, need to be individually absolved in private by the pastor. In contrast are those stubbornly impenitent who will change neither internally to seek forgiveness, nor stop their sinful behavior. Luther concluded, "Where you see sins forgiven or reproved in some persons, be it publicly or privately, you may know that God's people are there."[644] Christ gave the keys as a public sign by which the Holy Spirit renews and sanctifies sinners redeemed by Christ's crucifixion, and by which "Christians confess that they are a holy people in this world under Christ."[645] Those who refuse this ministry of the keys will be cast out from God's holy people. This office of "the church's keys" (*Claves Ecclesiae*)[646] belongs to God's holy people around the world and to the holy people of the Reformers.[647] Regarding those who appoint and administer the office of the keys, Luther explains:[648]

> What he says or does is not his, but Christ, your Lord, and the Holy Spirit say and do everything, as far as he adheres to correct doctrine and practice. The church, of course, cannot and should not tolerate open vices; but you yourself be content and tolerant,

---

640. *LW* 41:154; *WA* 50:632, 35-633, 11; *Councils and Church*.

641. Prenter, *Spiritus*, 235-36; cf. Vajta, *Worship*, 118-21.

642. *WA* 8:534, 21-26; *LW* 36:194-95; *Misuse of the Mass*; *WA* 25:17, 2-6; *LW* 29:17; Titus 1:5 and Acts 20:28.

643. *WA* 8:502, 36-39; *LW* 36:158; *Misuse of the Mass*.

644. *LW* 41:153; *WA* 50:632, 10-11; *Councils and Church*.

645. *LW* 41:153; *WA* 50:632, 15-16; *Councils and Church*.

646. *LW* 41:154; *WA* 50:632, 28-34; *Councils and Church*.

647. *LW* 41:195-96; *WA* 51:480, 31—481, 23; *Against Hanswurst*.

648. *LW* 41:156; *WA* 50:634, 21-28; *Councils and Church*.

since you, an individual, cannot be the whole assembly or the Christian holy people.[649]

Luther claimed that the fellowship of the Reformers maintained the *preaching office* of the word of God true to the ancient church and were faithful to the one true church that teaches and believes the one word of God.[650] The Holy Spirit administers the use of the word in preaching and teaching and with the word anoints the Christian church unto sanctification.[651]

The Lutheran Reformers held to the *Apostles' Creed* (Children's Creed). They believed it, sang it, and confessed in the same way as the ancient church. Therefore, Luther maintained that, "Whoever believes as the ancient church did and holds things in common with it belongs to the ancient church."[652]

Prayer, public praise, and thanksgiving to God link the holy Christian people from the ancient church with the church for all time, including the Reformers. This prayer, praise, and thanksgiving includes faithful teaching and practice of the Lord's Prayer, Psalms or other spiritual songs, Christian confessions, and catechism. Through prayer, everything is sanctified (1 Tim 4:5).[653]

Christ's church is known for *honoring temporal authorities*, for example, parents, teachers, and princes. The Holy Spirit sanctifies his holy people by enabling them to honor their fathers and mothers, to raise Christian children in honorable living, to faithfully obey and be subject to their lords, and to aid the princes to love and to protect their subjects.[654]

The holy Christian people endure *the holy possession of the sacred cross* in misfortune, persecution, trials, and evil from the devil, the world, and the flesh.[655] They experience sadness, fear, poverty, contempt, illness, and weakness to become like Christ. They suffer according to Christ's word (Matt 5:11), "Blessed are you when others revile . . . you falsely on my account." They must be pious, quiet, obedient, and serve everyone with their lives and possessions. No other people must endure such bitter hatred. This is not because they are vile sinners but because they have Christ, and no other

---

649. *LW* 41:156; *WA* 50:634, 28–33; *Councils and Church*.

650. *LW* 41:196; *WA* 51:481. 24–34; *Against Hanswurst*.

651. *LW* 41:149; *WA* 50:628, 7–8; *Councils and Church*.

652. *LW* 41:196; *WA* 51:482, 22–23; *Against Hanswurst*.

653. *LW* 41:164; *WA* 50:641, 20–27; *Councils and Church*; *LW* 41:196; *WA* 51:482, 24–28; *Against Hanswurst*.

654. *LW* 41:166; *WA* 50:643, 7–12; *Councils and Church*. *LW* 41:196–97; *WA* 51:482, 32—483, 8; *Against Hanswurst*.

655. *LW* 41:164; *WA* 50:641, 20–27; *Councils and Church*

God. Thus, it may be known that the holy Christian church is there, and as Christ says (Matt 5:12), "Rejoice and be glad, for your reward is great in heaven..." This is a holy possession whereby the Holy Spirit sanctifies his people and blesses them. Luther related enduring such suffering to the work of the Holy Spirit:

> When you are condemned, cursed, reviled, slandered, and plagued because of Christ, you are sanctified. It mortifies the old Adam and teaches him patience, humility, gentleness, praise and thanks, and good cheer in suffering. That is what it means to be sanctified by the Holy Spirit and to be renewed to a new life in Christ; in that way we learn to believe in God, to trust him, to love him, and to place our hope in him, as Romans 5:1-5 says, "Suffering produces endurance."[656]

Luther related this suffering of the Reformers to that of the ancient church and so the Reformers are the true ancient church—partners with the historical church in the real suffering of the Lord Christ on the cross.[657]

Luther described the Reformers' regard for the ancient office of *marriage* as a mark of the church in place among the Reformers:

> We praise and honor marriage as a divine, blessed, and well-pleasing ordinance of God's creation for the procreation of children and the prevention of carnal unchastity.... Just as God from the beginning instituted it, and Christ confirmed it (Matt 19:4-6), and the apostles and the ancient church honored and taught it, so have we remained in this same ancient rule and ordinance of God. In this, we have been like the ancient church and have indeed been its true and proper members.[658]

Luther maintained that the church of the Reformers practiced *forgiveness* and exercised no envy, grudges, anger, vengeance, or murder against their opposition but instead forgave them and tried to counsel and help them.[659] They portrayed the Christian behavior enjoined by Christ and the apostles. As the ancient church publicly endured, admonished, and prayed for others, so did the Christian fellowships of the Reformers in their litanies and sermons. This followed the example and teaching of Christ the Lord and the ancient church.[660]

---

656. *LW* 41:165; *WA* 50:642, 27-32; *Councils and Church*.
657. *LW* 41:197-98; *WA* 51:484, 17—485, 17; *Against Hanswurst*.
658. *LW* 41:197; *WA* 51:483, 26-34; *Against Hanswurst*
659. *LW* 41:166; *WA* 50:643, 12-14; *Councils and Church*.
660. *LW* 41:198; *WA* 51:485, 18-24; *Against Hanswurst*.

Luther listed several items related to *Christian behavior* that are additional characteristics of the Holy Spirit's sanctification of true Christian fellowship: no arrogance or drunkenness, chastity, self-control, friendliness, gentleness, humility, no stealing nor usury, charitable, truthful, and trustworthy. These demonstrated, in Luther's view, how the Holy Spirit used the Decalogue in sanctification to raise up the holy people of Christ at the time of the Reformation.[661]

Luther's conclusion regarding his critics and the status of the fellowships of the Reformation was that because of the marks of the Holy Spirit shown in the church, his critics can "find nothing in us but what belongs to the ancient church—that we are like it, and are one church with it."[662]

> Now we know for certain what, where, and who the holy Christian church is, that is, the holy Christian people of God; and we are quite certain that it cannot fail us. Everything else may fail and surely does, as we shall hear in part. Men should be selected from this people to form a council; that might be a council ruled by the Holy Spirit. . . . The church is not to be assessed by the high or spiritual vocations in it, but by the people who truly believe.[663]

The Holy Spirit and the Priesthood of All Believers

In the *Babylonian Captivity* (1520) Luther said, "Every Christian is anointed and sanctified both in body and soul with the oil of the Holy Spirit,"[664] and, in *the Lectures on Titus*, "Every minister ought to glory in this, that he is an instrument of God through which God teaches, . . . because he speaks what God has given to him . . . through his Holy Spirit from heaven."[665]

Luther sourced his understanding of the priesthood of all believers in both the Old Testament and the New Testament. In Exod 19:5–6 the LORD spoke to the people of Israel from the covenanting text:

> ⁵Now therefore, if you will indeed obey my voice and keep my covenant, you shall be my treasured possession among all

---

661. *LW* 41:166; *WA* 50:643, 16–20; *Councils and Church*; *LW* 41:218; *WA* 51:469-572; *Against Hanswurst*.

662. *LW* 41:196; *WA* 51:481, 24–34; *Against Hanswurst*.

663. *LW* 41:167; *WA* 50:644, 1–8; *Councils and Church*; cf. *LW* 41:199; *WA* 51:487, 18–20; *Against Hanswurst*.

664. *WA* 6:566, 16–17; *LW* 36:115; *Captivity*.

665. *WA* 25:7, 8–10; *LW* 29:4; *Lectures on Titus* (1527).

peoples, for all the earth is mine; ⁶and you shall be to me a kingdom of priests and a holy nation.

In 1 Peter 2:9, Peter wrote,

> you are a chosen race, a royal priesthood, a holy nation, a people for his own possession, that you may proclaim the excellencies of him who called you out of darkness into his marvelous light.

Norman Nagel defined *priest* in the primary sense as an individual performing a specified ordained service, in the place of, and accountable to, a known person, in a specific place and time. In contrast "kingdom people" is plural, those called as priests to serve in a secondary sense. These priests include those whom the Lord calls his priestly kingdom and his holy people. Priests, both in the primary sense and in the secondary sense, serve only as the Lord has designated them to serve before him (*coram Deo*).[666]

The Old Testament includes both primary and secondary priests. The New Testament includes just one priest of the primary sense—the Messiah-King, Jesus Christ. Priests in the secondary sense comprise the faithful children of Israel and the faithful baptized Christians.[667]

The primary function of Old Testament priests was the sacrifice of animals for the sins of the people. In the New Testament, Jesus Christ—our priest before God—sacrificed himself for our sake, in our place, before God. God forgives our sin by his one sacrifice. No more sacrifices for our sin are required. Nagel explained our position as priests in God's kingdom of priests:

> By his priestly sacrifice we are priested . . . to offer ourselves, no longer forfeited to death by our sins, but alive by the forgiveness that delivers us from the dominion of sin, death, the devil, and the law. We are living sacrifices whose lives are poured out in sacrifice to him where he has put himself to receive the sacrifice of our lives, that is our neighbor in his need.[668]

In his Treatise on the New Testament, Luther condemned the Roman notion of continuing priestly sacrifice, declaring, "We do not offer Christ as a sacrifice, but Christ offers us." The only sacrifice Luther permitted for Christians is the Spirit-worked response of sacrificing themselves for God in service to others. In *The Freedom of a Christian*, he says, "I will give myself as Christ to my neighbor just as Christ offered himself to me."[669]

---

666. Nagel, "Luther and the Priesthood," 279–80.
667. Nagel, "Luther and the Priesthood," 279–80.
668. Nagel, "Luther and the Priesthood," 279–80.
669. Lazareth, "Priesthood," 1966.

Nagel noted the move from Exod 19 to Rom 12. "I appeal to you therefore, brothers, by the mercies of God, to present your bodies as a living sacrifice, holy and acceptable to God, which is your spiritual worship." This is how the Lord is to be worshiped, now that the last bloody sacrifice for sin has been made. In Rom 12: 2–21, Paul showed how Christians give the utmost concern for others in their interrelated lives. He went on to describe the reality of the living sacrifice of Christian daily life. While Jesus is the only priest in the primary sense in the New Testament, priests in the secondary sense are found in the obedience of faith of his followers.[670]

By 1520, Martin Luther's ideas about the priesthood of believers were raising questions among both his Reformation supporters and his Roman Catholic opposition. In response, he wrote *To the Christian Nobility*, in German, to his supporters and leaders. This caused further confusion and misunderstanding and so, two months later, he wrote the *Babylonian Captivity*. It was written more clearly and carefully in Latin for the clergy and the learned.[671] Luther defended his position in *The Babylonian Captivity*:

> How then if they [Luther's Catholic opponents] are forced to admit that we are all equally priests, as many of us as are baptized, and by this way we truly are; while to them is committed only the Ministry (the preaching office) and consented to by us. . . ? If they recognize this they would know that they have no right to exercise power over us except insofar as we may have granted it to them, for thus it says in 1 Peter 2, "You are a chosen race, a royal priesthood, a priestly kingdom." In this way, we are all priests, as many of us as are Christians. There are indeed priests whom we call ministers. They are chosen from among us, and who do everything in our name. That is a priesthood which is nothing else than the Ministry. Thus 1 Corinthians 4:1: "No one should regard us as anything else than ministers of Christ and dispensers of the mysteries of God."[672]

---

670. Nagel, "Luther and the Priesthood," 280–81.

671. Nagel, "Luther and the Priesthood," 283–84. The sequence of Luther's discussions on the (universal) priesthood is the German *To the Christian Nobility*, the Latin *Babylonian Captivity*, and then Luther's defense against their misunderstandings, particularly his *Answer to the Hyperchristian, Hyperspiritual and Hyperlearned Book by Goat Emser* (1521), his *Retractions* (1521), and *Against Henry King of England* (1522). By following Luther he may be his own interpreter.

672. *LW* 36:112–13; *WA* 6:564, 6–14; according to Nagel's translation of the text and Scriptures, "Priesthood," 283–84, *Babylonian Captivity*.

Luther spoke of papal priests, of priests as ministers (as the apostle speaks of them), and of priests as those baptized.[673] He referred to priests, "whom we call ministers." As ministers of Christ, they may not go beyond what has been committed to them. This was precisely how the pope's priests had been going beyond, exercising power that Luther denounced as tyrannical, jeopardizing people's salvation. Use of such power was the way the pope and his priests or ministers neglected the very things committed to them.[674] Luther denounced those who failed to do what the office requires. Instead, they did things invented by men that were useful for their power in tyrannizing the baptized. They did what lies outside their office in the unmandated realm of human decision, when they have nothing more than what the baptized may grant them.[675] Luther held that they were put there to administer the Lord's specific gifts of preaching the gospel, the sacraments, and other duties.[676] If they do not serve these gifts, they have forsaken the office to which the Lord assigned them. If, instead of giving the Lord's gifts they exercise power over the people, Luther declared them guilty of sacerdotalist tyranny (priestly or ecclesiastical power management).[677]

In *To the Christian Nobility*, Luther rejected the concept of higher and lower Christians but maintained only differences of office and work. This appeal, in German, was made to laity who had not been doing what was really theirs to do. His appeal was to the baptized, who, with every member of Christ's body, the church, are gifted with the Holy Spirit.[678] If "spiritual" comes from the Holy Spirit and Holy Baptism, then all the baptized are "Spiritual," and in the same way they are priests. Luther therefore spoke both of the laity and of the clergy as priests. The clergy are there for giving "the word of God and the Sacraments, which is their work and office."[679] The laity are there for receiving the gifts and living them out in their callings. Whatever their calling as laity, that calling makes them neither a lower level of Christian, nor inferior in their service to God below the clergy. Their calling is their priestly service to God as they serve their neighbors in their calling.

---

673. Nagel, "Luther and the Priesthood," 284.
674. WA 6:562, 12; LW 36:109.
675. Nagel, "Luther and the Priesthood," 284–85.
676. WA 7:630, 10—631, 30; LW 39:154–55.
677. Nagel, "Luther and the Priesthood," 285–86.
678. *Tractatus de libertate Christiana*, WA 6:408, 28–35; LW 44:129–30.
679. WA 6:409, 3; LW 44:130; WA 7:58; LW 31:356; *To the German Christian Nobility* and *The Freedom of a Christian*; cf. 1 Cor 4:1 and LW 31:356.

"Just as all members of the body serve one another."[680] What matters is how Christ is related to his body—"There is one head and he has one body."[681]

The Holy Spirit is alive and at work through his gifts in every Christian, who then "offers Spiritual sacrifices acceptable to God through Jesus Christ." Christians are both the temple and the royal priesthood and the sacrifice: all of them, all of their lives (Rom 12). They rejoice in the diversity and in the way the same gifts, which are given by the Spirit as confessed in the Third Article, work out in the particularity of each Christian life. Each is unique.[682] However,

> The universal priesthood expresses not religious individualism but its exact opposite, the reality of the congregation as a community. The individual stands directly before God; he has received the authority of substitution. The priesthood means "the congregation." . . . This characteristic distinguishes Christians from the rest of humanity. They are a priestly generation, a royal priesthood.[683]

As priests, all Christians pray for others, sacrifice themselves to God, and proclaim the word to one another.

Luther quoted Paul in 2 Cor 3:5-6 to say that "God . . . has made us sufficient to be ministers of a new covenant, not of the letter, but of the Spirit." Paul spoke these words to all Christians. Peter also spoke to all Christians: "That you may declare the might [excellencies, ESV] of him who called you out of darkness into his marvelous light (1 Pet 2:9)." "Since all Christians are called out of darkness, each one is bound to declare the might of Him who has called him."[684]

Not only are all Christians commanded to preach the word, they also function as priests in absolution. In his Treatise on the Sacrament of Penance, Luther said, "the ordained clergy have no exclusive monopoly on the declaration of absolution. God alone forgives sin, and in God's name every Christian, even a woman or child, may declare the forgiveness of sin to a repentant brother."[685]

---

680. *WA* 6:409.10; *LW* 44:130.

681. *WA* 6:408.35; *LW* 44:130.

682. Nagel explains: As always we may not stop short of the Christ point; each doctrine is worth what it confesses of him. Only if we stop short of him can we get stuck at the point of "the pope or the papal priest is not the boss here, the priesthood of all believers is."

683. Althaus, *Theology*, 314-15.

684. *LW* 36:149.

685. Lazareth "Priesthood," 1966.

In the latter half of 1522, *Prediger* (Preacher) Luther (he was not the *Pfarrer* (the Pastor)) preached a series of sermons on 1 Peter at St. Mary's Church. He was not writing for the Christian nobility, or for the clergy and the learned, or his opponents; he was preaching to the people. Luther preached to the laity of St. Mary's as priests. The first thing about a priest is that he is that before God. "We are all priests before God." Priests are those who may draw near to God. Talk of priests begins best with Christ. Luther explained:

> Now Christ is the high priest, none higher than he, anointed by God himself. What is more he sacrificed his own his body for us; there is no higher priest's office than that. Along with that, he on the cross prayed for us. Thirdly, he has proclaimed the gospel and taught all men to know God and himself. These three offices he has also given to us all. So then, since he is a priest and we are his brothers, all Christians have the power and command, which they must do, to preach, to draw near to God, pray for one another and offer themselves as sacrifice to God.[686]

Christians as priests are the Spirit's temple, offering Spirit prompted sacrifices. They are called holy priesthood, chosen race, royal priesthood, and holy nation. All the terms are collective. Such priests are not inward by themselves. They, born again, offer God their praises together. They pray both with and for one another. What is theirs before God, what is given them there cannot be held to one's individual self without destruction. Its vitality flows on and out into each one's calling, where in serving one's neighbor one is offering God the unbloody, the living sacrifice of his life. Liturgy into living: the priesthood of the baptized. So, Luther priested the people of St. Mary's Church. Faith receives from the Lord; love gives to the neighbor.

Luther drew his teaching regarding the priesthood of all believers from Scripture, solidly based on the self-sacrifice of Jesus Christ, the high priest. Christians, then, perform their self-sacrificing role as priests through the word of God under the direction of the Holy Spirit.

New Life in the Holy Spirit

Luther personally experienced new life in the Holy Spirit. Like the reality of Katie's pigtails on the pillow, the Holy Spirit, working through Luther's study of Scripture, evoked a theology of reality. Not merely ideas, or

---

[686]. *WA* 12:307, 27; 308, 8; *LW* 30:53–54. *Zusagen* refers to Sacraments for which it is constitutive. *WA* 6:572, 10–12; *LW* 36:124; Lohse, "Von Luther," 2:27.

experiences or remembrances of past events, the matters proclaimed and the actions taken portray events that were real present-day happenings. Luther expressed the prominence of the Holy Spirit who does what people cannot do for themselves in their daily lives.[687] This is the dynamic action of the Holy Spirit who dominates Luther's theology in matters of conviction of sin and forgiveness, justification by faith, assurance of salvation through Christ's rescue, the authority of Scripture, the priesthood of believers and in the public office of ministry through preaching, the sacraments, and the administration of the office of the keys.

The Holy Spirit Is *Spiritus Creator*

Walter von Loewenich noted in Luther's concept of the Christian faith, that the Holy Spirit creates a new life that experiences faith out of the despair of the Christian's personal cross.[688] Vilmos Vajta described this as "in the midst of hell it hears a voice inspiring hope in the Creator, who can create the new man out of nothing."[689]

In *The Bondage of the Will* Luther gave an example of the breadth of the new creation in a believer in the life and ministry of the apostle Paul:

> Paul cooperates with God in teaching the Corinthians (1 Cor 3:9) inasmuch as he preaches outwardly while God teaches inwardly, each doing a different work. He also cooperates with God when he speaks by the Spirit of God (1 Cor 12:3), and both do the same work. . . . when God operates without regard to the grace of the Spirit, he works all in all, even in the ungodly, inasmuch as he alone moves, actuates, and carries along by the motion of his omnipotence all things, even as he alone has created them, and this motion the creatures can neither avoid nor alter, but they necessarily follow and obey it, each according to its capacity as given it by God; and thus all things, including the ungodly, cooperate with God. Then, when he acts by the Spirit of grace in those whom he has justified, that is, in his Kingdom, he actuates and moves them in a similar way, and they inasmuch as they are his *new* [italics added] creation, follow and cooperate, or rather, as Paul says, they are led by the Spirit (Rom 8:14). . . .

---

687. Prenter, *Spiritus*, ix; BSLK, 511–13; BC, 355–56.
688. Loewenich, *Luther's Theology*, 110.
689. Vajta, *Worship*, 137.

> What [can] we do ... to prepare ourselves for the new creation of the Spirit? ... [1] Before man is created and is a man, he neither does nor attempts to do anything toward becoming a creature, and after he is created he neither does nor attempts to do anything toward remaining a creature, but both of these things are done by the sole will of the omnipotent power and goodness of God, who creates and preserves us without our help; but he does not work in us without us, because it is for this he has created and preserved us, that he might work in us and we might cooperate with him, whether outside his Kingdom through his general omnipotence, or inside his Kingdom by the special virtue of his Spirit, [2] In just the same way, before man is changed into a new creature of the Kingdom of the Spirit, he does nothing and attempts nothing to prepare himself for this renewal and this Kingdom, and when he has been recreated he does nothing and attempts nothing toward remaining in this Kingdom, but the Spirit alone does both of these things in us, recreating us without us and preserving us without our help in our recreated state, as also James says: "Of his own will he brought us forth by the word of his power, that we might be a beginning of his creature" (James 1:18)—speaking of the renewed creature. But he does not work without us, because it is for this very thing he has recreated and preserves us, that he might work in us and we might cooperate with him. Thus it is through us he preaches, shows mercy to the poor, comforts the afflicted. But what is attributed to free choice in all this? ... Nothing![690]

Luther said that grace is given at justification so sin can no longer accuse and so the conscience finds peace in God's mercy. The Holy Spirit begins to battle sin in the flesh as soon as one begins to believe. In this struggle, the opinions and lusts of the flesh are broken and overcome.[691] The Spirit thus initiates his work of creation and formation at justification as he leads believers from concupiscence to the character of Jesus Christ.

Prenter summarized Luther's view of the Spirit as *Spiritus Creator*:

> In inner conflict man is completely in the power of death. Nothing of his own righteousness is effective. The groaning of the *Spirit* toward God is a real raising from death, a new creation. When the gospel says that no one can enter the kingdom of God without the new birth of water and the Spirit it simply means that the old man must be destroyed totally ... so that God the

---

690. *LW* 33:242-43; *Bondage*.

691. *WA* 40^{II}:357, 35-38; 358, 19-23; *LW* 12:331; Ps 51:2 [4] (1538); cf Hägglund, *History of Theology*, 231.

Holy Spirit can create the new man out of nothing. . . . There is . . . no difference between the first and second creation because in both cases it is actually a creation out of nothing.[692]

The annihilation of the old man—the theology of the cross—thus describes how the *Spiritus Creator* provides escape from the traumatic universal human entrapment in sin.

The Spirit and the Flesh

Luther described life in the Holy Spirit as a distinction between living according to the flesh and according to the Spirit. He cited Paul in the *Bondage of the Will*:

> Paul . . . divides the human race into two types, namely, flesh and spirit (just as Christ does in John 3[:6]), he says: "Those who live according to the flesh set their minds on the things of the flesh, but those who live according to the Spirit set their minds on the things of the Spirit." That Paul here calls carnal all who are not spiritual is evident both from this very partition and from opposition between spirit and flesh, and from his own subsequent statement: "You are not in the flesh but in the Spirit if the Spirit of God really dwells in you. Anyone who does not have the Spirit of Christ does not belong to him" (Rom 8:9). . . And if anyone does not belong to Christ, to whom else does he belong but Satan? . . . Hence, the loftiest virtues of the best of men are in the flesh, that is to say, they are dead, hostile to God, not submissive to the law of God and not capable of submitting to it, and not pleasing to God. For Paul says not only that they do not submit, but that they cannot. So also Christ says in Matthew 7[:18]: "A bad tree cannot bear good fruit," and in Matthew 12[:34]: "How can you speak good when you are evil?" You see here not only that we speak evil, but that we cannot speak good.[693]

Luther described this renewal work of the Spirit in the redeemed person:

> Man has a twofold nature, a spiritual and a bodily one. According to the spiritual nature, which men refer to as the soul, he is called a spiritual, inner or new man. According to the bodily

---

692. Prenter, *Spiritus*, 198-99, referring to Rom 8:26; Gen 1:1.
693. *LW* 33:274-75; *WA* 18:7; *Bondage*.

nature, which men refer to as flesh, he is called a carnal, outward, or old man, of whom the Apostle writes in 2 Corinthians 4 [:16] "Though our outer nature is wasting away, our inner nature is being renewed every day." Because of this diversity of nature the Scriptures assert contradictory things concerning the same man, since these two men in the same man contradict each other, "for the desires of the flesh are against the Spirit, and the desires of the Spirit are against the flesh," according to Galatians 5[:17].[694]

The Inner Testimony of the Holy Spirit

The inner testimony of the Holy Spirit gave Luther confidence that he was rescued through faith in Christ, his sins were forgiven, and he had a home in heaven.

The subject of Luther's theology and personal experience was the dynamic God who initiates salvation and sanctification. Larry Christenson called Luther's explanation of the Third Article of the Apostle's Creed the "Lutheran Magna Carta of church renewal" because it brings Christians to radical dependence on the Holy Spirit under Christ.[695] This radical experience brought Luther to personal peace and empowered his work.

In his treatise *Against the Heavenly Prophets* Luther explained how the Holy Spirit and the word work together to apply the pure gospel to form faith and pure consciences in the inner person. This is promised in Isa 55:1, that his word will not go forth in vain, but will be activated, as reported in Rom 10:17, faith comes through preaching.[696]

> Now when God sends forth his holy gospel he deals with us in a twofold manner, first outwardly, then inwardly. Outwardly, he deals with us through the oral word of the gospel and through material signs, that is, baptism and the sacrament of the altar. Inwardly he deals with us through the Holy Spirit, faith, and other gifts. But whatever their order the outward factors should and must precede. The inward experience follows and is effected by the outward. God has determined to give the inward to no one except through the outward. For he wants to give no one the Spirit or faith outside of the outward word and sign instituted by him, as he says, "Let them hear Moses and the prophets" (Luke

---

694. *WA* 7:49; *LW* 31:344.
695. Christenson, *Welcome*, 173.
696. *LW* 40:146; *WA* 18:135.

16:29). Accordingly, Paul can call baptism a washing of regeneration wherein God richly poured out the Holy Spirit (Titus 3:5-6). And the oral gospel "is the power of God for salvation to every one who believes [has faith]" (Rom 1:16).[697]

The outward work of the Holy Spirit includes the material signs of the power of the oral gospel for salvation, the Spirit's conviction of the world of sin through the preaching of the word, the washing of regeneration in baptism, and the Lord's Supper. The inward work of the Holy Spirit includes faith and other gifts. If knowledge of God, his Son, and faith come by the Spirit through the outer word, Luther asked, "Then how can this outer word, through which the Holy Spirit is given with all his gifts, be of no avail?"[698] He comes to give faith to whomever acknowledges their sin and wherever he wills, from which follows mortification, the cross, and works of love. Any other order is of the devil.[699]

As the divine Logos was hidden in the man Jesus Christ, the Spirit hides himself in the means of the external word as his instrument, which he enlivens with his inner word.[700] The inner word has the divine power to convince the heart of God's truth, which Luther called the "inner testimony of the Holy Spirit."[701] Luther explained, "We should, therefore, not believe the gospel because the church has approved it, but rather because we feel that it is the word of God.[702] ... Everyone may be certain of the gospel when he has the testimony of the Holy Spirit in his own person that this is the gospel."[703]

The Spirit speaks through the word by inspiring its writers, and forbidding changes to what is written, since faith comes only through the work of the Holy Spirit through the external word.[704]

> God gives no one his Spirit or grace apart from the external word which goes before. We say this to protect ourselves from the enthusiasts ... who boast that they have the Spirit apart

---

697. *LW* 40:146; *WA* 18:135-36.

698. *LW* 37:137; *WA* 23:263, 31-33, "Denn sie habens ja durchs leibliche eusserliche wort und schrifft, Wie sol denn nu solch eusserlich wort kein nütz sein, durch welchs der heilige geist gegeben wird mit all seinen gaben?" (1527).

699. *WA* 18:139, 22-26; *LW* 40:149; *Against the Heavenly Prophets* (1525).

700. *WA* 3:262-63; *LW* 10:220-21; Ps 45:1.

701. *WA* 9:632-33; *WA* 10$^{I.1}$: 130; cf. Althaus, *Theology*, 37-38.

702. *WA* 30^{II}:687, 32-33; "Non enim ideo creditur, quia Ecclesia approbat, sed quia verbum Dei esse sentitur" (Acts 17:11; 1 Thess 1:5). See Althaus, *Theology*, 37-39n.

703. *WA* 30^{II}:688, 2-4; "Certus erit de Euangelio unusquisque in semetipso testimonium habens spiritus sancti, hoc esse Euangelion (Acts 2:32)" [1530].

704. *WADB* 10^{I}: 99, 27—100, 2; *LW* 35:254; *Prefaces to the Old Testament* (1545 [1523]); *WA* 8:489, 31-37; *LW* 36:142; *Misuse of the Mass*; *WA* 17^{II}:459-60.

from and before contact with the word. On this basis, they judge, interpret, and twist the Scripture or oral word according to their pleasure.[705]

Although Luther attacked the enthusiasts for an unmediated spiritualism, he stressed the Spirit's inner work of holiness. His understanding of the Spirit started with Romans 8:26, "Likewise the Spirit helps us in our weakness. For we do not know what to pray for as we ought, but the Spirit himself intercedes for us with groanings too deep for words."

Believers experience the Spirit in overcoming their inner conflicts because he fulfills the promises of the external word and internally brings believers from the domain of the law into that of the gospel. The Holy Spirit uses the experiences of daily discipleship in Christ's suffering[706] and inner conflicts as his school. Luther maintained that daily the Spirit calls and proclaims the gospel. In his explanation to the third article of the Creed in the *Small Catechism*, he declared the reality of this work of the Holy Spirit, "He daily and richly forgives all my sins and the sins of all believers."[707]

Luther's theology of reality expressed his own experience of inner conflict, faith, and deliverance by Christ. All Christians, likewise, experience Christ in trials as well as in deliverance. When one experiences the Spirit's intercession, he knows that Christ is real and not a dream, and holiness becomes his real possession.

After baptism, the Holy Spirit reveals to Christians the reality of their new life in Christ. Luther agreed with Tauler and other pre-Reformation awakenings who considered the church to be a life experiencing God, not a doctrinal system.[708] In the theology of the cross Luther saw that personal adversities are the "School of the Holy Spirit" to teach faith in the God who is present to overcome trouble.[709] The Holy Spirit gives reality and confidence in Christ to the life of faith by the inner testimony of the Holy Spirit, that assures believers of the forgiveness of their sins,[710] "and because you

---

705. BC, 322, 3; BSLK, 453, 17-454; "Gott niemand seinen Geist oder Gnabe gibt ohn durch oder mit dem vorgehend äußerlichen Wort, damit wir uns bewahren vor der Enthusiasten ... so sich rühmen, ohn und vor dem Wort den Geist zu haben, und danach die Schrift oder mündlich Wort richten, deuten und dehnen ihres Gefallens." Smalcald Articles, Part III, Art. VIII [1537].

706. WA 5:639, 20-21; 18:489, 15-17; LW 14:152; WA 2:106, 26-28; LW 42:44-45; cf. Loewenich, *Luther's Theology*, 118-19; Prenter, *Spiritus*, 205-8.

707. Luther, *Small Catechism (Enchridion)*, 8.

708. Christenson, *Welcome*, 236, citing WA 9:98-100.

709. LW 21:299; WA 7:546, 24-28; *The Magnificat*; cf. Loewenich, *Luther's Theology*, 109.

710. LW 29:171; WA 57^{III}:169, 15-20; Heb 5:1.

are sons, God has sent the Spirit of his Son into our hearts, crying, 'Abba! Father!' So you are no longer a slave, but a son, and if a son, then an heir through God" (Gal 4:6–7).[711]

Christians experience faith by living under the leading of the Spirit, (Gal 3:5–6).[712] The Spirit creates the confident reality of living and trusting the external testimony to Christ in the gospel and the inner witness of the Spirit.[713] Since this experience is supernatural and distinct from empirical sense or reason, Luther often put the experience of the Spirit in opposition to reason.[714] The word of God—Law and Gospel—brings experience to the school of the Holy Spirit. The word without the Spirit is *littera*—letter—the law to judge human performance, yet the Spirit brings the gospel through the word. The message about Christ may become a law if the Spirit does not change its content, so it becomes an experienced reality of the new life.[715] Without this personal internal experience of the testimony of the Holy Spirit, Luther's theology of the cross would be a meaningless terrorization. Luther said of the Lord's Supper, "This is our assurance if we feel this witness of the Spirit in our hearts, that God wishes to be our Father, forgive our sin, and bestow everlasting life on us." (See footnote 348)

Regen Prenter maintained that, while Luther had no "systematic doctrine" of the Holy Spirit," he experienced a powerful living testimony of the Spirit.[716]

The Holy Spirit and Holiness

Luther called *holiness* practical living unto God. This is living in the faith, hope, and power developed by the Spirit through sanctification. Luther said holiness is the passive Godward attitude of faith, which the Holy Spirit works in pardoned sinners. The church and its members are holy because they possess the call to the ministry of the gospel and the sacraments.[717] Believers are the church because of the work of the Holy Spirit through the

---

711. *LW* 25:359; *WA* 56:369, 22–24; commentary on Rom 8:15, citing Gal 4:6–7.

712. *WA* 40^I:359, 18–24; *LW* 26:226; cf. *WA* 7:546, 24–26; *LW* 21:299.

713. *WA* 11:453, 24–29; *LW* 36:301–2; *Adoration of the Sacrament* (1523).

714. *WA* 9:189, 32–34; *WA* 18:605, 32–34; *LW* 33:24; *WA* 56:185, 26–28; 186, 1–3; *LW* 25:167; *WA* 18:489, 15–17; *LW* 14:152; *WA* 31^{II}:500, 9–11; *LW* 17:311; cf. Loewenich, *Luther's Theology*, 109–10.

715. Prenter, *Spiritus*, 59.

716. Prenter, *Spiritus*, 201–2.

717. *WA* 40^I:41–42, 70; *LW* 26:4–5, 25; cf. Christenson, *Welcome*, 237; Vajta, *Worship*, 128–29.

word and the sacraments—not because of their efforts. Through the word and sacraments, God sanctifies them, as Christ lives his life in their empirical piety.[718]

Outwardly, the church is composed of sinners. Its holiness depends upon the Spirit's hidden internal work of forgiveness and protection from evil. Luther said that believers in Christ are not sinners sentenced to death, but are holy and righteous lords over sin and death who live forever. This is because Christ is the Savior and cleanser of the church, and so it is holy.[719]

> The Holy Spirit is given to believers in order to battle against the masks of wisdom in our hearts, which exalt themselves against the righteousness of God; and in order to arouse us to prayer and to the performance of the duties of humanity to all men, expecially to the brethren, so that thus both mind and body might be exercised and we might become more holy day by day.[720]

Holiness is the practical, experiential aspect of sanctification, which works through believers' bodies and minds to express themselves toward God and people. Luther was influenced by Tauler's emphasis that one could not simply think about God, but by the Spirit, must hear and obey God's voice.[721] Holiness includes being set apart for the work of God's Spirit; it is listening to the Spirit through the word, sacraments, preaching, and life experiences. It is obedience to the Lord's call to faithful listeners.

New Life in the Holy Spirit Is Hidden

Luther described the hidden aspects of the new life in the Holy Spirit:

> "The kingdom of heaven is like a treasure hidden in a field" (Matt 13:44). . . . So also our wisdom and righteousness are not at all apparent to us, but are hidden with Christ in God. But what does appear is that which is contrary to these things, namely, sin and foolishness (1 Cor 3:18).[722]

As faith clings to the God hidden in opposites, so the Christian life is hidden in opposites. The Christian life may not outwardly exhibit its

---

718. *WA* 56:280, 8; *LW* 25:267; Rom 4:7; cf. Vajta, *Worship*, 130; Prenter, *Spiritus*, 67–68.

719. *BSLK*, 653–59; *BC*, 435–39, 34–60; Vajta, *Worship*, 130; *WA* 40^I:444, 34–36, 445, 16–18; *LW* 26:285; *Lectures on Galatians* (1535).

720. *WA* 40^{II}:356, 19–23; *LW* 12:330; Ps 51:2 [4].

721. Christenson, *Welcome*, 236.

722. *WA* 56:393, 7–9; *LW* 25:383.

imputed righteousness. The believer buried with Christ understands the hidden reality of the Spirit, which the world does not.[723]

Luther called this a life of opposites,

> For he who loves himself not in himself but in God, that is, in accord with the will of God, who hates, damns, and wills evil to all sinners, that is, to all of us. For what is good for us is hidden, and that so deeply that it is hidden under its opposite. Thus our life is hidden under death, love for ourselves under hate for ourselves, glory under ignominy, salvation under damnation, our kingship under exile, heaven under hell, wisdom under foolishness, righteousness under sin, power under weakness.[724]

Luther said that those who honor God's word and serve him must suffer as did Paul (2 Tim 3:12) and Christ (Luke 9:23).[725]

The Holy Spirit and Suffering

Luther's theology of the cross led him to observe that faith's finest art is to have sure confidence in God when suffering appears, especially under his wrath against sin. Spiritual struggles test but also display faith at this highest stage.[726] If righteousness in God's sight consists of God's gift of that righteousness in Christ and trusting his promise of that righteousness, then works are clearly the result of that faith, which constitutes the believer's walk in Christ his Savior.

The joy and victory of forgiven Christians are hidden as they obediently follow Christ into his sufferings (Mark 8:34b) and as Paul willingly (Gal 6:14) entered into what the world calls foolishness, sinfulness, and shame. These are destroyed on Christ's cross as the Christian dies in order to experience the joy and glory of Christ living within.[727] Jesus calls Chris-

---

723. WA 56:324, 4-6; LW 25:311-12; WA 31^{II}:445; LW 17:238; WA 56:346; LW 25:334; cf. Loewenich, *Luther's Theology*, 116.

724. LW 25:382-83; WA 56:392, 25-32; "Qui sic seipsum diligit, vere seipsum diligit. Quia non in seipso, Sed in Deo se diligit, i. e. qualiter est in voluntate Dei, qui odit, damnat, malum optat omnibus peccatoribus i. e. omnibus nobis. Bonum enim nostrum absconditum est et ita profunde, Vt sub contrario absconditum sit. Sic Vita nostra sub morte, dilectio nostri sub odio nostri, gloria sub ignominia, salus sub perditione, regnum sub exilio, celum sub inferno, Sapientia sub stultitia, Iustitia sub peccato, virtus sub infirmitate." Rom 9:3.

725. WA 31^{I}:90, 12-91, 2; LW 14:58; Ps 118; cf. Loewenich, *Luther's Theology*, 108, 113; and Althaus, *Theology*, 30.

726. WA 6:208-9, 24; LW 44:28-29.

727. WA 2:614; LW 27:404-5; Gal 6:1; Ps 31:9.

tians to follow him in lowliness and disgrace, to repeat his sufferings in this life.[728] Faith unfolds in suffering, and excels in tribulation.[729] The Spirit crucifies Christians' flesh to form Christ in them, and they become offensive to the world because of the offense of the gospel of the cross.[730] Therefore, the Christians' purpose is to follow Christ, and to be conformed to him in his sufferings. Luther said that God "has decided that all men should conform to the image of his Son, that is, to the cross (Rom 8:29)."[731] Luther pointed to Paul's linking such suffering to the gift of the Holy Spirit in Rom 5:3-5,

> [3]Not only that, but we rejoice in our sufferings, knowing that suffering produces endurance, [4]and endurance produces character, and character produces hope, [5]and hope does not put us to shame, because God's love has been poured into our hearts through the Holy Spirit who has been given to us.

Luther sagely observed that, "Of whatever quality suffering finds characteristics and people to be, such it makes them even more," if carnal then more wicked; if spiritual then more spiritual. "For suffering does not make a person impatient but merely shows that he has been and is still impatient. Thus a person learns in suffering what kind of a man he is."[732] Therefore Luther warned, "Whoever is unwilling to suffer tribulation should never think that he is a Christian, but rather . . . an enemy of Christ."[733] For that person robs Christ of his saving power for those who reject him.[734] For those who endure the tests of suffering, God pours out his Holy Spirit and his gifts to persevere and to reach out sacrificially to love God and to love others.[735]

The Spirit teaches an eschatological knowledge of Christ so that by faith Christians are certain of Christ's coming and are willing to suffer until his work is completed.[736] Through suffering and weakness, Luther said, the Spirit teaches the believer perceptions and understandings about Christ not

---

728. *WA* 18:511; *LW* 14:181; Ps 102:7-9; *WA* 3:167, 24-23; *LW* 10:139; Ps 31:9.

729. *WA* 56:50, 16-17; *LW* 25:44; Rom 5:3.

730. *WA* 2:548, 25-29; *LW* 27:308; Gal 4:19; *WA* 18:626-27; *LW* 33:52-53; *Bondage*.

731. *LW* 31:153; *WA* 1:571, 34-36; "*Licet enim posset deus . . . ad imaginem filii sui, id est crucem, omnes conformare* (Rom 8:29)." Explanation of the Ninety-Five Theses (1518).

732. *LW* 25:288; *WA* 56:300-301; Rom 5:3.

733. *LW* 25:289; *WA* 56:301-2; Rom 5:3.

734. *LW* 25:290; *WA* 56:302. But for those who endure the tests, Rom 5:3.

735. *LW* 25:290-96; *WA* 56:302-6; Rom 5:3-5.

736. *WA* 30^{III}:133, 14-17; *LW* 38:46; the Marburg Colloquy and the Marburg Articles (1529).

otherwise possible to know, "that he may perceive in the Spirit how Christ precisely through his suffering and death has attained true life and glory."[737]

Luther reminded Christians of the secret peace where they stand before the gracious presence of God with joy, in the Spirit's hidden safety, which is known only by faith or experience, and not in any worldly ways.[738] Therefore, the new life in the Holy Spirit cannot circumvent the dying of the cross, which is the only access to Christ's resurrection power in the Spirit.[739] Christians' hidden righteousness will be revealed when the hidden God is finally revealed. They will no longer be on alien soil but will be living their true righteous character in their true home in heaven.[740]

Infusion of Love into the Heart

Luther taught that the love the Holy Spirit plants in believers turns them from themselves toward God. From conception, people do nothing but sin and fall deeper into the wrath of God. When they hear and believe that Christ is their Savior from sin and wrath, God's Spirit brings grace and love to their hearts so they love and praise God and let him work through them.[741] Then the Spirit begins his internal work to fulfill the law written on their hearts through acts of love (Rom 2:15; 5:5).[742] For to love is to hate oneself, to condemn oneself, and to wish the worst, in accord with the statement of Christ: "Whoever hates his life in this world will keep it for eternal life (John 12:25)."[743] Prenter commented,

> The paradoxical "love of self" about which Luther speaks, hates, condemns and wishes the self every possible evil because it agrees with the judgment of God . . . upon all sinners . . . The rightly understood "love of self" which can become love to God is for Luther identical with an unconditional hatred of

---

737. WA 26:312, 29-30; LW 37:202; "Das er ym geist erkenne, wie Christus eben durch sien leiden und sterben recht lebendig und herlich wird." *Confession*; cf. WA 7:546, 24-28; LW 21:299; Christenson, *Welcome*, 117-18.

738. WA 2:456, 33-36; LW 27:170; Gal 1:3; WA 3:57, 36-37; LW 10:69; *Lectures on the Psalms (4:7)* (1513-15); cf. Rom 14:17; WA 5:36, 15-16; LW 14:298.

739. Jungkuntz, "Secularization Theology," 23.

740. WA 50¹:197; LW 26:109; Gal 2:11; cf. Loewenich, *Luther's Theology*, 116.

741. WA 8:552, 36-553, 1; LW 36:217; *Misuse of the Mass* (1521); cf. Prenter, *Spiritus*, 198-99.

742. LW 25:187; WA 56:203, 8-10; Rom 2:15.

743. WA 56:392, 20-22; LW 25:382; "Est enim diligere seipsum odisse, damnare, malum optare, secundum illud Christi: 'Qui odit animam suam in hoc mundo, in vitam eternam custodit eam.' (John 12: 25)" Rom 9:3.

oneself ... which agrees with and accepts the judgment of God upon all sinners and therefore also upon oneself.[744]

This love of self is a love of God that hates everything God hates, even one's self (*odium sui*). This is not one's own work, but the gift of the Holy Spirit. Luther opposed Augustine's idealistic concept of self-love, which strives toward God's will.[745] Luther denied self-worth and ability and relied on God's Spirit to deal with sin and to enable true love of God, of self, and of others. Prenter said the Holy Spirit is the subject of the self-condemnatory act. *Odium sui* is a unity with God in his judgment of sin and the sinner. The Holy Spirit, present in the believer as the judging God, is the power of God's love, which causes believers to accept God's judgment as their own.[746]

Conformity to Christ

The restoration of a person's first love relationship with God, which Prenter called an infused love, is a conformity of the believer's will to the will of God by the Holy Spirit, as Christ was conformed to the Father's will. According to Romans, "the flesh" is the person living in service of the present temporal life, while "the spirit" is the person living in the service of the Spirit and the future life. The preacher should rebuke and convict those not living according to the Spirit that they may know their wretchedness and be led to help.[747] Help comes when the Spirit leads believers to willingly follow and put "the flesh" to death (Rom 8:13-14). When the Spirit slays the "old man" of sin, consciences, which were bound to the law under that "old man," are freed to lay hold of Christ. They gladly renounce all that is not of God, even themselves, and they fear death no more, because the Spirit is at work.[748] This conformity to the will of God, by the crucifixion of the "old man," is conformity to Christ, who is sacrificially conformed to God's will. This is to be distinguished from the fleshly imitation piety of medieval mystics. God conforms believers to Christ and to his will, not by the struggling of the human will, but by his Spirit. They are God's work by his grace in justification

---

744. Prenter, *Spiritus*, 5.

745. Prenter, *Spiritus*, 4-7, notes, on self-hatred, Anders Nygren, Adolf Hamel, Junge Luther, and differences with Augustine.

746. WA 56:228; LW 25:212-13; Rom 3:7, and WA 57^{III}:109, 15-17; 186, 13-15; LW 29:119, 186-87; *Lectures on Hebrews* (Heb 1:9; 6:13); cf. Prenter, *Spiritus*, 7-8.

747. WADB 7:12, 5-15; LW 35:372; *Preface to Romans* (1522); cf. Prenter, *Spiritus*, 8.

748. WADB 7:4, 31-33; LW 35: 367; WA 56:366, 14-19; LW 25:356; Rom 8:14; cf Prenter, *Spiritus*, 9-11.

and regeneration, as the Spirit works to make them his children. Luther described how the Spirit gives assurance in this struggle:

> Christ has given us his Holy Spirit; he makes us spiritual and subdues the flesh, and assures us that we are still God's children, however hard sin may be raging within us, so long as we follow the Spirit and resist sin to slay it. Since, however, nothing else is so good for the mortifying of the flesh as the cross and suffering, he comforts us in suffering with the support of the Spirit of love, and of the whole creation, namely, that [both] the Spirit sighs within us and the creation longs with us that we may be rid of the flesh and of sin.[749]

This is the inner testimony of the Holy Spirit that Luther taught. He said that in conformity to Christ, the Spirit gives a new heart that issues forth in love and pleasure for God's will and law with new desires to live a godly life.[750] Prenter described the joy and assurance of this conformity to Christ:

> They who have the wisdom of the Spirit love the will of God and rejoice in being conformed to it. . . . The one who is conformed to the will of God does not fear the last day with its wrath but rejoices because then the will of God will be fulfilled. If only the will of God comes to pass he will yield himself to it even though it means he must go to hell and eternal death.[751]

The Spirit works what Prenter has called *resignatio ad infernum* in the one conformed to God's will. He climaxes conformity to Christ with unity with God, which would prevent anyone from going to hell. Its historical reality is in Christ's descent into hell.[752]

Luther observed that, because of concupiscence, people naturally fear punishment under the law, suffering, and loss of goods. In conforming believers to Christ, God gives his Spirit, who appearing as an enemy, makes it possible to agree with him with no more fear. The believer knows him as a friend and Father who leads through paths of fear to eliminate fear. No

---

749. *LW* 35:377; *WADB* 7:23, 16–23; "*Uns seinen heiligen Geist gegeben hat, der uns geistlich machet, und das Fleisch dempffet. Und uns sichert, das wir dennoch Gottes Kinder sind, wie hart auch die Sünde in uns wütet. So lange wir dem Geiste folgen, und der Sünde widerstreben sie zu tödten. Weil aber nichts so gut ist, das Fleisch zu teuben, als Creutz und leiden, tröstet er uns im leiden, durch beystand des Geistes, der liebe, und aller Creaturen, nemlich, das beide der Geist in uns seuffzet, und die Creatur sich mit uns sehnet, das wir des Fleisches und der Sünde los werden.*" Preface to Romans (1522).

750. *WADB* 7:5, 32–35; *LW* 35:367–68.

751. Prenter, *Spiritus*, 11.

752. Prenter, *Spiritus*, 12.

longer slaves (Gal 4:6-7), they love and hate the same things God loves and hates because they are his children, led by his Spirit.[753]

Luther said that due to human sin and God's hiddenness, even a committed one cannot obey God, but the Spirit makes it possible to understand God's invisible will.[754] This dynamic work of the Spirit to conform believers to the crucified Christ is the *operatio* of God, as in their inner conflict believers experience the theology of the cross. God uses this inner conflict to reveal the potential danger of committing the unpardonable sin. Good works do not help. Agreeing with the angry God, man stands guilty before him, enduring the hell of God's wrath. There is no escape from the temptations and terror, which, by being conformed to the will of God in Christ, train believers to love God and hate self. God hides this work under the attacks of Satan who tries to provoke blasphemous sins as God takes away everything until the believer sees that God's mercy is the only hope. Luther said this is the work of the word of Christ, that brings salvation and peace by killing what remains of the life of the flesh in order "that the spirit and its desires may come to life" in the believer.[755]

God works the cross in the lives of the saints who, in faith, hope, and love follow his word into darkness, suffering, and weakness. Sinners gladly follow Christ in God's way, so as God permits them to suffer, and the Savior judges them, the Holy Spirit conforms them to Christ. Luther said only the Holy Spirit's intercession makes it possible to endure this work of God.

> Romans 8:26 is the basic testimony about the work of the Holy Spirit as the source of the true love to God. When the sinner groans ... in the midst of the excruciating experience of the wrath of God ... this greatest love to God ... is not possible for man. It is not man himself who calls ... in a final religious effort, but it is God himself who, as the subject of this greatest act of love, is truly present in us, it is the Holy Spirit himself who, as our helper and comforter, groans in us and for us.[756]

Luther broke from Augustine and the scholastics who saw the Holy Spirit as God prodding people's latent Godwardness to enable them to live God-pleasing lives. Luther's idea of the Holy Spirit began with the death of the old man and new life in the Spirit, which collapsed the foundation of the Augustinian system. Prenter concluded that Luther no longer thought

---

753. WA 56:366-70; LW 25:356-59; *Commentary on Romans*.
754. WA 57^{III}:185, 27-186, 1; 186, 25-27; LW 29:186-87; Heb 6:13.
755. WA 5:64, 2-5; LW 14:335; "*Ut vivificet spiritum et concupiscentias eius*"; Ps 2:9; Prenter, *Spiritus*, 13-16.
756. Prenter, *Spiritus*, 17.

of the Spirit as a transcendent cause of a supernatural nature in man with infused grace, but rather as God's presence in the anxious groanings of the tempted soul held in the grip of death and hell. The core of Luther's theology is the real personal presence of God the Holy Spirit. Through baptism, he conforms believers into the image of Jesus Christ and in sanctification he conforms their works to Christ through their sharing in his Godward suffering and self-denial.[757]

The Real Presence of Christ

Luther said God is remote. In his wrath, God left humanity alone to suffer inner conflicts, temptation, death, and hell. People cannot reach him—only he can span the separation. In the person of the Holy Spirit, he approaches believers in Christ's cross. As intercessor and comforter, the Spirit brings the presence of God to their place of damnation to struggle for grace and salvation for them (Rom 8:26). The Holy Spirit conquers accusations in the depths of human spiritual paralyzation, condemnation, and anguish in the realism of biblical revelation.

Prenter described Luther's view of fallen humanity:

> In the inner conflict every religious force is dead. In this inner conflict it is not just a matter of perfecting man's inner nature and sublimating his idealistic struggle, but he must himself be completely raised from the dead. Luther therefore does not recognize any idealistic division into two parts of man, a higher and a lower nature. The contrast between flesh and spirit is to Luther a contrast between the whole of man without the real presence of God and the whole of man within and under this real presence of God. There is therefore no real affinity between the spiritual nature of man and the Spirit of God.[758]

Augustine said the infused love of God was an imitation piety following the ideal of Christ. In contrast, Luther said true love is a passive conformity to Christ in his death and resurrection, in which the indwelling Holy Spirit mediates the "real relationship to the truly present crucified and risen Christ."[759]

Christians experience the reality of God when the Spirit brings the real presence of Christ into inner conflicts through the cries and moaning of a

---

757. Cf. Prenter, *Spiritus*, 19.
758. Prenter, *Spiritus*, 26.
759. Prenter, *Spiritus*, 28.

loving child to the Father. This is not an imitation of Christ, but the reality of Christ. The inner testimony of the Holy Spirit fulfills the biblical expectations that God quickens new life in believers. Through trust and reliance given by the Spirit, he mediates the presence of Christ, and the believer's faith in Christ. The distinct persons of the Spirit and Christ are inseparable in the life of God as the Spirit mediates the true presence of Christ.[760]

The Gifts of the Holy Spirit

In 1525 Luther cited Paul's admonition (1 Cor 14:27–28) that, when there is an interpreter, speaking in tongues should not be prevented. However, the supernatural aspect the gift of the Spirit is missing when, soon after, he interprets a "tongue" as Latin.[761] Later, Luther maintained that, as the second part of justification, the Holy Spirit and his gifts are conferred to each of the normal Christians throughout the church—those drunk with the wine of the Holy Spirit and living in the kingdom of Christ,[762] with whom the Triune God makes his dwelling (John 14:23). This is the "continuing rule, conversation and growth of spiritual action in the faithful heart."[763] Luther explained his understanding of spiritual gifts in this context and related it to grace:

> The true Spirit dwells in the believers, not merely according to His gifts, but according to His own substance. He does not give His gifts in such a way that He is somewhere else or asleep, but He is present with His gifts and creatures by preserving, ruling and strengthening them.[764]

Luther understood spiritual gifts as the action of the present person of the Holy Spirit himself. Commenting on Ps 51:10, Luther further described the Christian life, indwelt by the Holy Spirit:

> We teach and believe . . . that grace is the continuous and perpetual operation or action through which we are grasped and

---

760. Prenter, *Spiritus*, 60–62, 237–38.

761. WA 18:122–24; LW 40:141–43; *Against the Heavenly Prophets* (1525). Luther's hermeneutical principle of the plain reading of the text would be not to limit the work of the Spirit here any more than for any other miraculous events—some of which he personally experienced (i.e., healing, prophecy, teaching, etc.).

762. LW 8:249; WA 44:761; see above under "The Holy Spirit and the Kingdom of God."

763. LW 12:254; WA 40^{II}:472–610; Ps 45:8–9; LW 12:376–78; WA 40^{II}:472–610; Ps 51:10–13; John 14:16–25.

764. LW 12:377; WA 40^{II}:470–610; Ps 51:10.

moved by the Spirit of God so that we do not disbelieve His promises and that we think and do whatever is favorable and pleasing to God. The Spirit is something living, not dead. Just as life is never idle, but as long as it is present, it [the Holy Spirit] is doing something.... So the Holy Spirit is never idle in the pious, but is always doing something that pertains to the kingdom of God. I am warning you to get used to understanding these theological terms properly so that when you hear the word "create" you do not think of one momentary work, but of the continuing, rule, conservation and growth of spiritual actions in the faithful heart.[765]

This includes the spiritual gifts that are endowed to faithful individuals—"To *each* is given the manifestion of the Spirit for the common good" (1 Cor 12:7); and to the communion of faithful individuals (1 Cor 12:4-7), the church. These diverse provisions also include the different estates of the faithful apostles, prophets, etc.—the gifts of ministry given to the church (Eph 4-11).[766] Luther noted that the gifts of the Holy Spirit (*charismata*) follow the forgiveness of sins.

Luther said the word of God is the church's test of truth, while prophecy and the witness of the Spirit and miraculous signs confirm Scripture as God's word.[767] However, the word of God always precedes—signs apart from the word of God are from the devil.[768] God permits our faith to be tempted by signs,[769] as the devil opposes and counterfeits God's effective ministry. Yet Luther acknowledged signs, miracles, and portents (Mark

---

765. *LW* 12:377–78; *WA* 40^{II}:470–610.

766. *LW* 4:122; *WA* 43:223–34; *LW* 8:269–70; *WA* 44:777; *LW* 11:423; *WA* 4:311.

767. *WA* 8:492, 5–9; *LW* 36:145; *WA* 8:532, 17–18; *LW* 36:192; *Misuse of the Mass* (1521); *WA* 16:363–64; *LW* 35:161–62; *How Christians Should Regard Moses* (1525). Luther maintained there were only two powerful sermons when God spoke with great signs and languages: the revelation to Moses and Pentecost. This does not indicate that he was against the ongoing manifestation of the Spirit. If it did, he would be found denying Biblical as well as contemporary events. Rather, Luther isolated the outward manifestations and direct preaching of God, which he saw nowhere else in Scripture or the history of the church. In other preaching and prophecy, he noted the internal inspiration of the Spirit and outward physical speaking.

768. *WA* 8:492, 5–9; *LW* 36:145; *WA* 8:532, 17–18; *LW* 36:192; *BSLK*, 456:3–5; *BC*, 323, 10; *Smalcald Articles*, 8.10; *WA* 8:532, 19–21; *LW* 36:192; cf. *WA* 8:492; *LW* 36:145; addressing the relationship of the word and the church.

769. *WA* 8:532; *LW* 36:192.

16:17–18),[770] as the normal exercise of spiritual gifts in the Christian life (1 Cor 12–14) which he himself experienced.[771]

In his *Romans Preface* Luther distinguished the gifts of the Spirit from the grace of God. This helps to understand spiritual gifts in the setting of his theology of reality in the context of *simul iustus et peccator*. Grace is the favor of God's good will toward his faithful children by which he gives them Christ and the Holy Spirit with his gifts (Rom 5:12, "the grace and gift in Christ"). In sanctification, while daily the gifts and the Spirit increase in his children, they are still accompanied by evil desire and sin battling the Spirit (Rom 7:5–6; and Gal 5:17). The Lord predicted this in Gen 3:15. Through the reality of the Holy Spirit in the Christian life, God's children experience *simul iustus et peccator*. Therefore, Luther maintained that it is by the grace of God and not according to spiritual gifts that the faithful are made righteous and restored before God.[772]

Nevertheless, in the midst of the struggles of life, God, by his grace, faithfully and consistently applies Christ's righteousness to the faithful so that they are accounted righteous before him. He gives spiritual gifts for occasions of specific ministry, worship and devotion. Therefore, his grace is not divided or parceled out, as are the gifts, but it brings the faithful thoroughly into God's favor through the mediational intercession of Christ the Savior. Because of this expansive grace, the Spirit and his gifts are poured out upon restored believers.[773]

Luther believed in prayer for healing. He said we must pray to God to overcome the devil's attacks on our bodies.[774] Luther experienced spiritual powers, of both wickedness and of God. His dependence upon the activity of the Holy Spirit through the word frames his view that the Holy Spirit ministers his miraculous gifts through people of faith to defeat the power of their enemy, the devil.

---

770. *WA* 57^{III}:115; *LW* 29:124–25; Heb 2:4.

771. *WADB* 7:87; *LW* 35:383; "Preface to the First Epistle to the Corinthians" (1530), Jungkuntz, "Secularization Theology," 24.

772. *LW* 35:369; "Romans Preface."

773. *LW* 35:369–70.

774. *BSLK*, 689, 15–90, 10; *BC*, 455–56, 114–18; *LC*, "Explanation to the Seventh Petition of the Lord's Prayer"; cf. Christenson, *Welcome*, 107.

The Holy Spirit and Faith

For Luther, faith's content is the word of God and Christ. In trouble, faith clings to God's word and grace, knowing that God will hear and help.[775] Faith endures as it depends upon the content of the promises of God's word in difficult times.

In his discussion of Abraham's sacrifice of Isaac, Luther attributed faith to Abraham and Isaac under the idea that "God the Creator, who makes all things out of nothing, can raise the dead."[776] Therefore, Luther maintained that Abraham and Isaac trusted God to fulfill his promise of a multitude of blessed progeny to Abraham through this command to sacrifice Isaac.

Luther stressed that access to God depends upon faith in Christ. Christians' lives are linked to the protective righteousness of Christ.[777] Therefore, the object of faith is Jesus Christ—the Son of God put to death for the sins of the world for forgiveness of sins and eternal life—"faith and Christ cannot be torn apart."[778] Christ makes faith possible. As faith takes hold of Christ, he is the One who is present in the faith itself to direct it, to adorn it, and to inform it with sure trust and firm acceptance in the heart.[779] The righteous ones do not live to themselves, but, in union with Christ, who lives in them through faith, pours his grace into them, and gives them his governing Spirit. Because of Christ they believe, they are righteous, they are dead to the law, and they put their lusts to death.[780] Luther said that, as part of the baptismal process (Rom 6 and Col 2), believers as sinners must be destroyed for Christ to be formed in them.[781] Repentance and confession join Christians with Christ in his death. Thus, the Holy Spirit makes God's demands true in their lives. Repentance, confession, and union with Christ loose the power of the Holy Spirit to flow as described in the theology of the cross.[782]

The Spirit creates and gives faith through the preaching of the word (Rom 10:14–17).[783] The Spirit brings awareness of Christ, faith, and confi-

---

775. *WA* 18:495, 36–40; *LW* 14:160; "Commentary on Psalm 38."
776. *LW* 4:120; *WA* 43:221–22; *Genesis Lectures*, Gen 22:11.
777. *WA* 56:299, 20–27; *LW* 25:286–87.
778. *WA* 40¹:164, 22–24; *LW* 26:88; Loewenich, *Luther's Theology*, 103–4.
779. *WA* 40¹:228, 29–30; *LW* 26:129.
780. *WA* 2:502, 12–17; *LW* 27:238; *Galatians* (1519), Gal 2:20.
781. *WA* 2:548, 25–29; *LW* 27:308; *Galatians* (1519), Gal 2:19.
782. *WA* 40¹:649–50; *LW* 26:430–31; *Galatians* (1535), Gal 4:19.
783. *WADB* 7:7; *LW* 35:368; *Preface to Romans* (1546); cf. Althaus, *Theology*, 47–48; *WA* 8:106–7; *LW* 32:227–28; *Against Latomus* (1521); cf. Prenter, *Spiritus*, 32–35.

dence to those who believe, and bestows on them the merit of Christ.[784] This faith from the Holy Spirit through the word is a gift of God that cannot be earned or achieved by human effort. Werner Elert called faith a pact of the intellect with the word of the gospel enacted by the Holy Spirit.[785] Martin Lehmann asserted that unless the Holy Spirit brings people to faith through the word, as Luther explained in the Third Article of the Creed, we could not trust in God's revelation in Christ.[786] Faith is not a humanistic set of ideas or dreams but is an internal power of God's word, which kills the old Adam. The Spirit makes faith a living confidence in God's grace on which believers stake their lives.[787] This union with Christ links believers with Christ's righteousness. Prenter said that as Christ's righteousness is reckoned to sinners they are delivered from God's judgment and their sin is reckoned to Christ. These divine actions lead to fellowship with God and the real presence of Christ. Luther said all this comes through faith in Christ (*per fidem Christi*) that the Spirit brings while he works to destroy sin in the flesh.[788] Therefore, faith in Christ is the substance of Christ's righteousness and the life that issues from it.[789] The Christian's union with Christ means that his faith possesses the direct reality of Christ's redemption and his saving victory.[790]

Luther spoke of the *totus homo*—while the believer is justified through faith in Christ, his personal union with Christ does not change his sin nature. This unites *justus* (righteousness) with *peccator* (sin), to give the totality, *simul justus et peccator*. Faith in Christ, then, results from putting the flesh to death by the Spirit while clinging to Christ. Luther stressed the necessity of faith when partaking of the Lord's Supper, because God and the Holy Spirit are poison and death if received without faith.[791]

Abiding sin does not mean that grace is lost, but that Christ's righteousness is opposing the sinful nature.[792] Luther saw the raging battle as God's almighty word, faith, and the Spirit, always active and engaged in combat. They battle against the most powerful foes: the flesh, the world, death, and the devil. Therefore, Christ is called the Lord Sabaoth, a God of

---

784. WA 11:453, 24–29; LW 36:301–2; *Adoration of the Sacrament* (1523).

785. Elert, *Structure*, 84.

786. Lehmann, *Luther and Prayer*, 45, citing LC, BSLK, 661; BC, 439, 62; cf. Vajta, *Worship*, 132–33.

787. WADB 7:10, 16–19; LW 35:370–71.

788. WA 56:306, 2–4; LW 25:349; Rom 8:3.

789. WA 57^{III}:114, 2; LW 29:123; Heb 2:3.

790. WA 2:458, 24–26; LW 27:172; Gal 1:4; WA 2:502, 12–14; LW 27:238; Gal 2:20; WA 56:280, 3–5; LW 25:267; Rom 4:7; cf. Prenter, *Spiritus*, 29.

791. WA 26:353, 27–31; LW 37:238; *Confession Concerning Christ's Supper* (1528).

792. WA 30^{II}:426, 131; LW 38:131; *Admonition Concerning the Sacrament* (1530).

hosts, who always is engaged in combat within us. During the attack, the Holy Spirit encourages faith not to fear.[793] Faith recognizes sin and trusts in the presence of the crucified and risen Christ as its only hope.

Luther said that faith constitutes a passive righteousness, which God imputes through Christ for nothing rendered to God.[794] More than just a passive acknowledgment of Christ, faith actively clings to Christ. Faith in Christ is expressed in a life of penitence, prayer, praise, and work. God's gifts of grace and faith form the redeeming reality of Christ. When Christ is received, God gives faith that Christ maintains by his real presence. As Christ is really present, faith is really present. Therefore, the substance of faith is Christ's real and redeeming presence. Faith is a hidden reality opposing all other reality. The Spirit makes Christ and his righteousness real, not through sense experience—*theologia gloriae*—but when the word is received and believed—*theologia crucis*. Luther saw the new person in this reality as both righteous and sinful. One's righteousness is Christ that forces the new believer to recognize the old fleshly person, as completely condemned by the presence of Christ—his alien or outside righteousness (*justia aliena*), which is his only righteousness. Only Christ is the vicarious atoning righteousness, which protects against the wrath of God. Grace and faith as living power in the heart are not righteousness before God, but only Christ, comprehended by faith.[795]

Luther believed that *per fidem Christi* (through faith in Christ) the Holy Spirit brings Christ to believers and conforms them to him. Thus, faith in Christ brings the redeeming reality of the real presence of Christ to believers, and conformity is simply another expression for faith in Christ.[796] As faith conforms one to Christ the believer becomes obedient to God's will, as Christ was obedient to his father in suffering, death, and resurrection. The condemnation of the "old man" is the content of "faith in Christ," while conformity with Christ in his resurrection is the reality of the "new man." The Spirit does his primary work in believers—God himself struggles in believers in their troubles—to join conformation to the crucified and resurrected Christ with the living reality of his redeeming presence. Prenter summarized,

---

793. WA 38:14, 15–17; LW 35:218; *Defense in Translation of the Psalms* (1531); also WA 40^{II}:418, 19–20; LW 12:374; *Commentary on Ps 51* (1538); cf. Prenter, *Spiritus*, 40–41.

794. WA 40:41; LW 26:4–5, *Galatians* (1535).

795. WA 40:41; LW 26:4–5, *Galatians* (1535).

796. Cf. Prenter, *Spiritus*, 50.

> Without the work of the Spirit Christ is not a redeeming reality. . . . Christ remains an example and faith a historical faith. Without the work of the Spirit with our faith, without Christ, and without the new life we remain under the law . . . under the wrath of God.[797]

The real presence of Christ, experienced through faith and conformity to Christ, is fundamental in Luther's theology and determines many differences with his opponents. It permeates his understanding of faith, conversion, the word of God, the Lord's Supper, the church, and the Christian life.

Responses to the Holy Spirit

Prenter described Luther's ideas of the Christian life as double motions of response wrought by the Spirit, which relate to his two kinds of righteousness. One motion is faith to God, according to the first table of the law. The second motion is love to neighbors and service to the creation with the fruit of the spirit, according to the second table of the law. These responses are in the context of empirical piety.[798] The Holy Spirit stirs up responses in believers that include prayer, worship, and good works.

Prayer

Regarding Gen 6:3, Luther noted the ever-growing human wickedness on earth at the time of Noah. These people were not the "sheath" in which the Holy Spirit would dwell. Since all teaching of such wicked people was in vain, the LORD would neither care for nor direct them by his Spirit. Therefore, since Satan had obstructed the word of God from them and they refused to listen to God, God withdrew the Holy Spirit who is the Spirit of doctrine, the Spirit of grace, and the Spirit of prayer. The Spirit of doctrine teaches the word of God, the Spirit of grace convinces of sin and the forgiveness of sin, and the Spirit of prayer leads to fellowship with God. "When the Spirit of doctrine is taken away, the Spirit of prayer will also be taken away," for no one can pray who does not have the Spirit who brings God's word of repentance and forgiveness.[799]

---

797. Prenter, *Spiritus*, 54.

798. *LW* 30:238–39; *WA* 20:641–42; *LW* 26:255; *WA* 40^1:401, 4–5; *WA* 6:186, 15–17; cf. Prenter, *Spiritus*, 233–38.

799. *LW* 2:18–19; *WA* 42:274–75; Gen 6:3.

MARTIN LUTHER'S THEOLOGY OF THE HOLY SPIRIT

Romans 8:26 is a key to Luther's understanding of the Holy Spirit's ministry of calling and enabling Christians to pray.[800] Luther said, "A Christian without prayer is just as impossible as a living person without a pulse."[801] Referring to David in Ps 5:11, Luther noted that without the Spirit, David could not pray as he did.[802] Luther gave prayer high priority because God speaks in prayer.[803] Prayer is the particular work of Christians, but is not possible without the gift of the Holy Spirit and the faith he works in believers. As the Spirit keeps renewing and confirming faith, believers continue to pray to the Heavenly Father, as they should.[804] The Holy Spirit, the counselor, supports their prayers. With this support, prayers express trust in God.[805] Luther said that the Holy Spirit enables believers to call God "Father" in the Lord's Prayer. He rouses them to believe that God is their true Father in heaven and brings them to him. Luther said that God commanded prayer as an external ministry in which believers may share in the Holy Spirit's work of the gospel.[806] Luther taught that prayer formats should be adapted to the circumstances so the Holy Spirit is free to preach his sermon to believers. In his own meditations and prayers, Luther depended upon the Spirit's power, preaching, and enlightenment to lead him to follow God in obedient faith.[807]

Luther related prayer to justification by faith,[808] whereby the Holy Spirit brings believers to God through forgiveness in Christ.[809] Through grace, the Holy Spirit moves Christians to come before God in prayer and to rely only upon the unmerited love of God in Christ.[810]

---

800. *WA* 56:376, 4–8; *LW* 25:365; cf. Lehmann, *Prayer*, 107; Prenter, *Spiritus*, 18; cf. Rom 6:3–11.

801. *LW* 24:89; *WA* 45:541, 34; "Das man keinen Christen kan finden so beten so wenig als ein lebenigen menschen on den puls." Sermons on the Gospel of John; cf. Lehmann, *Prayer*, 91.

802. *LW* 12:380; *WA* 40^{II}:472–74; Ps 51.

803. *WA* 44:574, 35–575, 1; *LW* 7:369; *Lectures on Genesis* (1545); cf. Lehmann, *Prayer*, 152.

804. *WA* 2:83, 34—84, 2; *LW* 42:23; *WA* 10^{II}:393, 18–22; *LW* 43:28; *Personal Prayer Book* (1522); cf. Lehmann, *Prayer*, 81–82.

805. *WA* 32:414, 24–25; *LW* 21:138; *WA* 40^{III}:503, 21–22; *LW* 13:87–88; cf. Lehmann, *Prayer*, 15, 94.

806. *WA* 43:81, 26–31; *LW* 3:288; cf. Lehmann, *Prayer*, 21–22.

807. *WA* 38:363, 6–16; 366, 11–15; *LW* 43:198, 201–2; *A Simple Way To Pray* (1535); cf. Lehmann, *Prayer*, 92–93.

808. *WA* 7:571, 5–7, 11–23, 16–18; *LW* 21:324–25; *WA* 40^{II}:427, 20–21; 428, 18–20; *LW* 12:380–81; cf. Lehmann, *Prayer*, 43 and 67.

809. *BSLK*, 660, 62; *BC*, 439, 62; *Large Catechism*; cf. Lehmann, *Prayer*, 45.

810. *WA* 45:540, 21–25; *LW* 24:88; cf. Lehmann, *Prayer*, 47.

Christians sometimes feel unworthy, which blocks prayer. The Holy Spirit comes to discouraged Christians with hope and comfort and reminds them that prayers commanded by God do not depend upon their worthiness.[811] Prayer drives away the devil and brings in the Holy Spirit.[812] When the devil fires his darts, the Holy Spirit reminds the faithful of the word of God that is already in their hearts, and directs them to pray for forgiveness.[813] When the devil reminds them of sin, his attack thus becomes the instrument of his own defeat.[814] The Holy Spirit turns such feelings as weapons back at the enemy, because their fears prompt calls for mercy from God.[815] The Spirit works perseverance against doubts in believers' prayers as he encourages them to believe that God continues to forgive mercifully and graciously.[816] Luther said that God gives his Spirit in prayer to gain victory over the weakness of the flesh.[817]

Ernest Schwiebert noted the report of Urbanus Rhegius who, in Coburg in 1530, overheard Luther's prayer, talking with God as to another human being in the room. Luther was speaking to the Lord pleading for strength for Melanchthon and his supporters at the Diet of Augsburg.[818]

Luther experienced God's answers to prayer for healing. His wife Katie was rescued from severe illness. Once when Melanchthon was severely ill, Luther "literally snatched his ill colleague from the jaws of death." He reported,

> In that instance, our Lord God had to listen to me, for I threw the whole burden at his feet and kept dinning into his ears all his promises which I was able to enumerate from Scripture, insisting that he had to answer my prayer if indeed I were to trust his promises.[819]

Melanchthon was healed! Luther claimed that his own recovery from a gallstone attack at Smalcald was due to the intercessory prayer of the local

---

811. WA 40^{II}:333, 32–34; LW 12:315; *Commentary on Ps 51* (1538); WA 2:697, 31–34; LW 42:115; cf. Lehmann, 78.

812. WA 56:466, 6–10; LW 25:459; *Romans*; cf. Lehmann, *Prayer*, 6.

813. WA 40^{II}:386, 25–28; 395, 33–36; LW 12:352, 358; cf. Lehmann, *Prayer*, 54–56.

814. WA 38:205, 10–31; LW 38:157–58; *The Private Mass and the Consecration of Priests* (1533).

815. WA 40^{II}:337, 35–39; LW 12:318.

816. WA 40^{II}:417, 33–36; 418:16–20; 427:14–15; LW 12:374; cf. Lehmann, *Prayer*, 87.

817. WA 56:376, 2–6; LW 25:364, *Romans*; WA 40^{II}:355–56, 452, 33–34; LW 12:330, 397, *Psalms*; cf. Lehmann, *Prayer*, 107–8.

818. Schwiebert, *Luther and His Times*, 439.

819. Lehmann, *Prayer*, 130–31, quoting Ludolphy, "Luther als Beter."

congregation.[820] Jungkuntz cited a 1545 letter in which Luther instructed a pastor how to pray for a man with an affliction which Luther called the work of Satan. Luther's prayer was one of authority, according to the word of Mark 16, and of release from the power of Satan.[821]

Luther linked the priestly offices of teaching and prayer. He called Christian ministers to combine word and Spirit in their prayers. Because the church always faces trials, Luther urged continual prayer that God would give his grace and his Spirit to make the doctrine powerful and efficacious among his people. Such prayer includes the petition for the gift of the Holy Spirit who uses the word to accomplish a renewing and saving work in human hearts.[822]

Luther said the Holy Spirit groups Christians together for prayer in the church.[823] Prayer is a distinctive mark of the church. God sanctifies his people when the true church prays and moves from the firstfruits of the Spirit to sanctification: the Lord's Prayer unifies Christians; prayer is the true work of Christians; and the Holy Spirit focuses the prayers of God's people through the means of the word and the sacraments.[824]

---

820. *WATR* 5:96-97, no. 5368; cf. Lehmann, *Prayer*, 131.

821. Jungkuntz, "Secularization Theology," 23-24, citing a letter to Ernst Schulze, Pastor in Belgern, *WA BR* 11:112; translation by Bernard Martin in *Healing for You*, 185-86.

822. *LW* 42:61; *WA* 2:115, 19-26; "Exposition of the Lord's Prayer for Simple Laymen" (1519), *Triglot*, 711-12; *BC*, 427, *Large Catechism* (1529).

823. *BSLK*, 654: 37-39; *BC*, 435-36, 37-39, *LW* 53:11-12; *WA* 12:35, 19-21, 24-25; 36, 12-13; cf. Lehmann, *Prayer*, 94-95.

824. *LW* 41:164; *WA* 50:641, *On the Councils and the Church* (1539); *LW* 13:89; *WA* 40^{III}:506, 18-19; *WATR* 3:261, no. 3303; *LW* 24:88; *WA* 45:540, 19-20, *Sermon on St. John*, Chapter 14 (1537); *LW* 53:103; *WA* 12:48, 11-12; *Order of Baptism* (1523) regarding the importance of the prayers of the church for the one being baptized. *LW* 38:133; *WA* 30^{II}:622:33, *Admonition Concerning the Sacrament of the Body and the Blood* (1530); cf. Lehmann, *Prayer*, 96-102 and Brunner, *Worship*, 298-99. Brunner maintains that Luther's doctrines of the Trinity and the two natures of Christ relate to the Holy Spirit's activity in the Supper as requested in the *epiclesis*, which invokes the Holy Spirit to bring a spiritual-physical unity in the bread and wine as there is in Christ. The *epiclesis* includes a request for the descent of the Holy Spirit to consecrate the elements of bread and wine as the body and blood of Christ, and a request for reception of the meal's gifts of grace. It is an invocation of the authority and power of Christ's words of institution to unite the bread and wine with the body and blood of Christ, while avoiding the extremes of the miracle service of transubstantiation, and the memorial service where the physical presence of Christ is excluded; cf. Luther, "An Order of Mass and Communion," in *LW* 53:20-22, 25-17, and Olson, *Reclaiming*, 74-76, who have refuted and rejected such invocations as Brunner describes as Godward works contrary to Lutheran theology.

Luther's theology of the cross links prayer and the Holy Spirit. In prayer, believers must not look to their own works but trust in God's promises and in the Holy Spirit. As they are conformed to Christ through suffering, they pray to God and the Spirit prays for them and helps them. God commands them to pray humbly and contritely while he ministers his saving word in Jesus Christ. The Spirit helps, comforts,[825] and intercedes for believers in their weaknesses. Therefore, at all times, believers must cling to Christ who gives the Holy Spirit to help them in their prayers.[826]

Worship

Vajta relates the Holy Spirit to worship and notes that Luther's "newly found theological convictions led to a complete liturgical reorientation" that, influenced by his theology of the cross and his doctrine of the Holy Spirit, "points to the very center of his whole thought."[827] Luther said the chief and foremost thing in the sacrament is the word of Christ, that is, the word of life and salvation that Christ established as the word of ministry.[828] When he found that the human words of the prescribed worship canon hindered the gospel and true worship in the Spirit,[829] Luther turned from the traditions of the church and gave priority to the Holy Spirit, who brings the word to Christian worship. Luther focused worship on the gospel words of institution, and the Spirit's gathering of the church.[830] In worship, the Holy Spirit expresses his power through the faith of the devout. While the human work in worship can be unbelief and idolatry, in the Spirit—transcending rational analysis—God brings Christ to believers in the word and sacrament, enmeshing faith, grace, and forgiveness.[831] Luther's explanation of the Third Article of the Creed demonstrated his view that the Spirit comes through God's grace and not by human control. The Holy Spirit teaches the faithful to rest and wait

---

825. *LW* 25:367; *WA* 56:378, 12; Rom 8:26; *LW* 14:96; *WA* 31^I:171, 31–33; cf. Lehmann, *Prayer*, 111–14.

826. *LW* 26:384–85; *WA* 40^I:585, 23–31—586, 20–28; Gal 4:6; cf. Lehmann, *Prayer*, 92.

827. Vajta, *Worship*, x.

828. *WA* 11:432–33; *LW* 36:277–78; *The Adoration of the Sacrament* (1523); cf. *WA* 6:355; *LW* 35:81–82; *WA* 8:431–34; Vajta, *Worship*, 67; *WA* 6:543–44; *LW* 36:82–83; *Captivity*.

829. *WA* 6:524; *LW* 36:53–54; *WA* 8:448; cf. Vajta, 62.

830. *BSLK*, 511–12; *BC*, 355, 6; *Small Catechism*, "Explanation to the Third Article of the Creed."

831. *WA* 6:301; *LW* 6:76; *On the Papacy in Rome* (1520); *WA* 8:448; cf. Vajta, *Worship*, 144–45.

for him in worship in order to produce the new man out of the submission of the old, and leads in the sacrifice of thanksgiving and praise.[832]

Luther's theology of the Spirit portrays God bringing faith through physical signs. He offers the word and sacrament in worship in the "intersection of worship and faith." Faith is the separation between true and false worship. Believers trust God and thank him for his gifts in Christ, while unbelievers circumnavigate God's activity to trust in their own works.[833] Through worship, God comes sovereignly to the faithful and the unfaithful to inspire faith. The Holy Spirit either inspires faith in those who will believe or brings eternal condemnation upon those who do not.[834] Luther pointed to Abraham's obedience in faith to show how faith in God is the supreme worship and the supreme sacrifice.[835]

Luther said that in praise believers return gratitude to God by acknowledging him as Creator.[836] They renounce any claims based on their own works to praise and acknowledge his work.[837] This links praise with the theology of the cross. Vajta lists four ways the Spirit teaches praise. First, God's love leads from the confession of sin, admitting God's justice, to the confession of praise. Secondly, the Holy Spirit is present in repentance to teach the art of praising God. Thirdly, the Holy Spirit, the firstfruit of the new creation, is received by faith and teaches how to sing praises to God. Fourthly, the Holy Spirit inspires faith in God in those who are killed by the law and raised to life through the gospel.[838] Vajta notes that in the hymns of the church Luther credited the Holy Spirit as the greatest poet who praises the Lord. The Spirit of God comes to those who faithfully bow down in repentance, according to the theology of the cross, to help them praise the Lord.

Luther said the Spirit works in the church, not in legal canons, but frees Christians to live with God's continued help. He rejected the Roman Church's binding ceremonial laws where the pope played the devil by requiring obedience for fear of death, obscuring the need of Christ as savior.

---

832. *BSLK*, 511–12; *BC*, 355, 6; cf. Vajta, *Worship*, 148.
833. Cf. Vajta, *Worship*, 127.
834. *WA* 56:38; *LW* 25:32–33; cf. Vajta, *Worship*, 142–43.
835. *WA* 40^{II}:359, 25–33; 360, 12–28; *LW* 26:226–27; Gal 3:6.
836. *WA* 8:378; *WA* 7:553–55; *LW* 21:306; *WA* 30^{II}:603; *LW* 38:107, Vajta, *Worship*, 155–57.
837. *WA* 56:356; *LW* 25:346; Vajta, *Worship*, 157.
838. Vajta, *Worship*, 158, 161, citing: *WA* 56:214–15, 268, 290; *LW* 25:199–201, 256–57, 277–78; *WA* 3:173, 191, 512; *LW* 10:145, 162–63, 456; *WA* 30^{II}:406; *WA* 7:546; *LW* 21:299; *WA* 18:633; *LW* 33:62–63; *WA* 40^{II}:458; *LW* 26:294–95.

He also rejected the anti-liturgical biblicism of the enthusiasts that was as legalistic as Rome.[839]

Luther followed a middle-road principle in liturgy, using what was necessary to express the spirit of Christian worship, with sensitivity for those who needed structure. He warned pastors about changes and strictness while also encouraging freedom. In consideration for others, Luther always stayed with his own tradition, keeping the portions of the mass, which did not speak of sacrifice. While not standardizing worship,[840] his revisions retained the same basic form as he adapted the mass for diverse situations. He followed this principle regarding the Sabbath, the church year, communion, buildings, and church ministry. Free faith and orderly love guided all worship, the hymnody, and the fine arts. Luther held that worship was not bound to rites, or forms, or buildings, or art, but to the sovereign God who decides when his Spirit will grip the human heart to experience Christ in worship. Worship forms, and other outward forms, must give way to God's will so that the Spirit, unhindered by human efforts, is free to bring the word as the true outward sign.

God calls and ordains priests to impart the Spirit by preaching the gospel of Christ to renew people through faith in the word of Christ.[841] To equip these ministers, God commands that they put to death the deeds of the body by the Holy Spirit.[842] Luther said that priestly service correlates with the theology of the cross. The priests sacrifice their own sinful natures so that, in their deaths, they are conformed to Christ, the high priest, in his death. They then minister out of lives raised from the dead, alive in the Spirit. These issue from their baptisms in which their sacrifices are hidden with their fellowship with Christ. It may be expressed by externals, but never deduced from them.[843] Because he is divine, Christ is present everywhere, but he is known to be present only where his word, faith, Spirit, and worship are found.[844] The sacraments, then, are an intersection of grace, worship, and faith. By grace,

839. Vajta, *Worship*, 178–79, citing *WA* 10^I:2, 175; *WA* 26:573, 581.

840. *WA* 18:122; *LW* 40:141; *WA* 6:686; *WA* 26:562; *WA* 10^I:2, 67, 79; *WA* 18:419; *PE* 6:147; *WA* 12:214; *PE* 6:92; *WA* 19:72–73; *LW* 53:61–62; cf Vajta, *Worship*, 178–82, 187.

841. *WA* 8:539, 26–31; *LW* 36:200–201; *Misuse of the Mass* (1521); cf Vajta, *Worship*, 67.

842. *WA* 8:492, 24–34; *LW* 36:146; *Misuse of the Mass*.

843. *WA* 17^{II}:9; *WA* 12:185; *LW* 40:28–29; *WA* 2:147–49; *LW* 31:300–303; *WA* 12:370–71; *LW* 30:115–16; *WA* 31^I:419, 249; *LW* 13:379; *LW* 14:30–31; *WA* 57^{III}:221; *LW* 29:223–24; *WA* 30^I:220–21, 382–83; *LW* 53:119; cf. Vajta, *Worship*, 152–54.

844. *WA* 19:197; which links Luther's Trinitarian concept where each person (of the Godhead) shares and partakes of the complete divine nature; cf. Vajta, *Worship*, 85–86, 126–27.

faith grows daily in the school of worship, passively receiving God's gracious gifts—the essence of worship—through word and sacrament.

Good Works

According to Luther, the Christian life is a creation of the Holy Spirit, which responds in good works of love.[845] The only good works are those God has commanded, the greatest being faith in Christ (John 6:28–29).[846] Because life and faith in Christ are the work of the Holy Spirit, good works in obedience to God are the normal outflow of the Christian life.

Luther viewed all good works from the aspect of faith, that the Spirit frees believers to work.[847] "Faith, through the working of the Holy Spirit ... performs good works through us, namely, love toward the neighbor, prayer to God, and the suffering of persecution of every kind."[848] Luther listed different degrees of faith, including responsible work, sufferings, and torments of conscience.[849] His theology of the cross provides understanding of the practical Christian life in the Spirit, where good works are the outward fruits of penance.[850]

Adam and Eve freely performed God's will in paradise, not to win God's favor but because they had confidence that he loved them. Believers distinguish performance of good works to gain favor with God from what they do for God's sake out of trust and delight in him. The former kind is not truly good, for those who perform them worship their own efforts, not God.[851] Faith's works aim simply at serving and benefiting others, meeting their needs, promoting their advantage, and following Christ's example (Phil 1:1–11), for Christ lives in them (Gal 2:20).

The Holy Spirit fills believers' hearts with love that renders them free, joyful, almighty performers of good, who overcome all afflictions, serve their neighbors, and nevertheless remain lords of all things.[852] In such service, those bound to their neighbors in love find true Christian freedom.

---

845. *WA* 11:453, 24–29; *LW* 36:301; *Adoration of the Sacrament* (1523).

846. *WA* 6:204, 13–25, 25–26; *PE* 1:187; *Treatise on Good Works* (1520).

847. *WA* 6:206–7; *PE* 1:190.

848. *WA* 30^III:166, 4; *LW* 38 87; "Glaube durch wirckung des heiligen geistes ... gute wercke durch uns ubet, Nemlich die liebe iegen dem nyesten, beteb zu got und leyden allerley verfolgung," *The Marburg Colloquy* and *the Marburg Articles* (1529).

849. *WA* 6:207–8; *PE* 1:191–92.

850. *WA* 1:532, 30–32; *LW* 31:87; *Explanation of the Ninety-Five Theses*.

851. *LW* 31:360.

852. *WA* 7:64, 13–66; *LW* 31:365–69.

Luther concluded that Christians live not in themselves but in Christ and in their neighbors, or they are not Christian: in Christ through faith, in the neighbor through love. This love expresses itself in the context of their callings or walks of life. Through faith, they move above into God; through love, they move down into the neighbor.[853] Therefore, reliance on works, including the ceremonial works of ritualistic religion, has no place in the Christian's life; those ceremonies serve only to teach and guide, not as ways to earn God's favor.[854] Faith recognizes God as the loving Lord and throws itself completely into his hands. This faith forms the orienting core of the human being as God originally created humanity. It is passive in receiving the identity God gives his people as his own, and expresses itself inevitably in works of love. Luther made that point in *On Good Works*, a commentary on the Decalog in the medieval catechetical tradition.[855] Positing that only what God has commanded can be a good work—not those "religious" works which humans invent—Luther stated, "the first, highest, and most noble good work of all is faith in Christ," as Christ said in John 6(:29), "That is God's good work, that you believe in him whom he has sent."[856]

Summary and Conclusions

Luther's theology of the Holy Spirit developed from his background of pious parents, scholastic education, his immersion in the Bible, and his personal experience. He stated his positions on the Holy Spirit early in his career and seldom changed his opinions. For Luther, the work of the Holy Spirit was his personal daily reality, not merely a theological position. Throughout his writings he presented the three emphases noted in the first chapter: 1) The Holy Spirit is the heart of his theology as expressed in his theology of the cross; 2) The means of the Holy Spirit are the word of God and the sacraments; 3) His theology expressed his own experience of release, emphasizing the inner testimony of the Holy Spirit, assurance of forgiveness of sins, and adoption as a child of God with an eternal home in heaven.

Essential to Luther's theology is the theology of the cross, through which the Holy Spirit links believers to Jesus Christ. The Holy Spirit uses God's word to call sinful people to repentance, faith, and life. God hides himself, so that the Holy Spirit may reveal him to those who by faith hear the word of God and trust in him. God reveals himself and his truth by his

---

853. WA 7:69, 12–18; LW 31:371.
854. WA 7:72, 1–36; LW 31:375–76.
855. Estes, *Secular Authority and the Church*, 9–13.
856. WA 6:204, 13–26; PE 1:187; *Treatise on Good Works* (1520).

Spirit through the Scriptures. He opposes human logic by revealing himself in opposites.

As God and his truths are hidden, so is the Christian life. Through the lowliness and suffering of their crosses, the Holy Spirit brings Christians into union and conformity with Christ in his cross. As God raised Jesus from the dead so he raises the faithful ones to newness of life through the work of his Spirit.

The reality of the Holy Spirit in every aspect of Luther's theology infused his work with vigorous and overwhelming power. No aspect of the Christian's experience, from birth to death, escapes the Spirit's ever-present determination to accomplish the will of God. Luther did not deal with ideas or philosophies that cannot change lives for eternity. His struggle was with the powers of the world, death and the devil. He laid out in volume after volume of Scripture commentary and theological formulation the truth of Christ's righteousness and sacrifice—the only hope for humankind. He clearly delineated the life of the Spirit and the life of the flesh and demonstrated the utter helplessness of the human race. With countless literary devices and sometimes jarring bluntness ("Everything is condemned that refuses to give in to sound doctrine"[857]) he made his appeal and stated the case for yielding to the call of the Holy Spirit. And, like Moses of old, he would say, "Choose Life!" (Deut 30:2)

Luther's co-reformers picked up his urgency to raise up a new generation of pastors, teachers, and theologians who would understand the theology of the cross that undergirded his theology of the Holy Spirit. Together the Reformers challenged the theology and practices of the Roman Catholic Church that was leading Christendom astray. Years of struggle, both within Lutheran circles and without, rocked the Lutheran boat, but throughout, Luther's grip on the reality and theology of the Holy Spirit held fast and anchored the church of the Reformation in the Truth.

---

857. *LW* 12:384; Ps 51:12.

3

Philip Melanchthon's Theology of the Holy Spirit

"The Dynamic Will of God"

Introduction

Philip Melanchthon's theology of the Holy Spirit is pivotal for the Reformation since he influenced the formulation of Lutheran theology, he educated the next generation of pastors and theologians, and his theological system guided the formation of Lutheranism for 100 years after his death.

Melanchthon followed patristic Trinitarian doctrine and perceived the Spirit as a person of the divine substance and the dynamic power, who proceeds from the Father and the Son,[1] as he described in the 1521 *Loci*:

> Christianity is freedom, because those who do not have the Spirit of Christ cannot in any way perform the law; they are rather subject to the curse of the law. Those who have been renewed by the Spirit now conform voluntarily even without the law to what the law used to command. The law is the will of God; the Holy Spirit is nothing else than the living (*dynamic*) will of God and its being in action (*agitatio*). Therefore, when we have been regenerated by the Spirit of God, who is the living (*dynamic*) will of God, we now will do spontaneously that very thing which the law used to demand. It was to express this idea that Paul wrote in 1 Timothy 1:9: "The law is not laid down for

---

1. CR 21, 354; 1535 *Loci*; Rogness, *Reformer*, 78–79.

the just." Romans 8:2 is also relevant: "the law of the spirit of life (that is, the law as the activity of the life-giving Spirit) in Christ Jesus has set me free from the law of sin and death."[2]

David Rogness said, from the 1555 *Loci*, that Melanchthon saw the Holy Spirit as an enlightening counselor who dwells within: "When we receive God's word, he produces joy and love to God and to our Lord Jesus Christ . . . Thus the term 'Counselor' should be understood."[3]

Historical evaluations of Melanchthon range from accusations of diverging from Luther,[4] reintroducing philosophy, and causing controversies,[5] to his being Luther's most loyal disciple. Bengt Hägglund's helpful middle position disagrees with the extremes of either total divergence or total agreement. Though they worked closely together, both Luther and Melanchthon made significant contributions to the Reformation, while they sometimes differed at points in content and presentation.[6]

Melanchthon was a complicated personality, often misunderstood during his lifetime and evoking swirling contradictory positions after his death. Historians have examined his life and his work and have sometimes arrived at stereotypes that overlook important elements that produced this towering Reformation figure.[7] Research continues, but the mystery of Philip Melanchthon is likely to remain.

---

2. Pauck, *MLC21*, 123; "*Quare ubi spiritu dei, qui viva voluntas dei est, regenerati sumus, iam id ipsum volumus sponte, quod exigebat lex.*"

3. CR 22, 93; *MLC55*, 24; "*So wir Gottes wort annemen, und wircket frewde an Gott, und liebe zu Gott, und zum Herrn Jhesu Christo, . . . und andere tugenden. Also soltu den namen Tröster hie verstehen,*" 1558 *Loci Communes*.

4. Lund, "Luther's Third Use," 63–85. Lund particularly mentions the biases of Karl Holl, Gerhard Forde, and G. Frederick Bente, as well as the constructive work by Manschreck, Maurer, Rogness, and Stupperich, and notes the warning of Lowell Green, "Good scholars should beware of following prejudices against Melanchthon that have been handed down," Green, *Formula of Concord*, 10–11.

5. E.g., Bente, Dorner and Seeberg. Bente's and Dorner's views are discussed in chapter 1. R. Seeberg comments, e.g., "The 'timidity' and 'philosophy' of Melanchthon, and his attempts to moderate and compromise, do not belong in the History of Doctrines." Seeberg, *History of Doctrines*, 2:334.

6. Hägglund, *History of Theology*, 248.

7. Wengert, "Beyond Stereotypes."

Background and Influence

Personal Background

Philip (Schwartzerd) Melanchthon's childhood was influenced by a strict adherence to the church, scholasticism, and the *Devotio Moderna*.[8] Timothy Wengert describes Philip's beginnings with connections:

> His maternal grandfather, Johann Reuter, was an influential merchant in Bretten, the Palatine city where Philip was born. His father Georg Schwartzerd was armorer of princes—especially of the elector of the Palatinate. Born in Heidelberg to a father who was a blacksmith, Georg learned his trade in Nuremberg, a center for armor-making..... Small wonder, then, that Georg named his first son Philip, after his employer, the Palatine elector, Philip the Upright—an appropriate gesture for the father who held, for a commoner, one of the most respected positions at court.[9]

Philip's father died in 1508, when Philip was eleven years old. His patron was the great humanist and Hebraist, Johannes Reuchlin, a relative of Philip's by marriage. Philip and his brother George stayed with Reuchlin's sister during their years of study at the Latin school of George Simler. Reuchlin made sure that Philip obtained an excellent education in Latin, Greek, and philosophy[10] and Hellenized Philip's German name, Schwartzerd (Black Earth), to its Greek equivalent, *melan-chthon*.[11] Melanchthon received a Bachelor of Arts from the University of Heidelberg where he encountered the humanism of Rudolf Agricola.[12]

---

8. Stupperich, *Melanchthon* (1965), 12, 20-26.

9. Wengert, "Melanthchon Christian Politics," 32.

10. Manschreck, *Quiet Reformer*, 31; Stupperich, *Melanchthon* (1965), 13-15, 28-29; Reuchlin sent books to Melanchthon to stimulate his study in humanists and the Latin Bible. Manschreck, *Quiet Reformer*, 41-42. Reuchlin recommended Melanchthon to Frederick the Wise and advised Melanchthon to go to Wittenberg. Stupperich, *Melanchthon* (1965), 34-35. When Reuchlin became uneasy with the development of the Reformation at Wittenberg, he invited Philip to join him and John Eck at Ingolstadt.

11. Wengert, *Human Freedom*, 6.

12. Stupperich, *Melanchthon* (1965), 12, 20-26; Manschreck, *Quiet Reformer*, 33-34; Holm, "Humanism," 1058; Pauck, "Introduction," 12; Lueker, "Humanism, 16th Century," 396. At Heidelberg Melanchthon worked in philosophy and read Rudolf Agricola, the guiding light of German humanism, who taught at Heidelberg twenty-four years earlier. Oecolampadius gave Melanchthon a three-volume set of Agricola's Dialectics. Agricola's works influenced Melanchthon to rely on the methods of the ancient rhetoricians and dialecticians. Agricola promoted gathering of material around loci, which was the pattern for Melanchthon's *Loci theologici*, and which became the

Melanchthon received the Master of Arts at Tübingen where he focused on the writings and philosophy of Erasmus.[13] Melanchthon immersed himself in the Latin classics, the ancient languages, philosophy, Scripture,[14] humanism, history, Aristotle, Ockham, and John Wessel. The latter, who had influenced Luther, taught that the church was the invisible communion of those united in Christ. Melanchthon hoped to rediscover the primitive church by shedding the additions of the centuries.[15] He published several works, including *Rudiments of the Greek Language*, and strongly criticized the education system of his day for its neglect of the intellect and lack of true heavenly wisdom. He turned his humanism from an elitist pursuit of the classics into a popular movement which redesigned public education.[16] His widespread reputation included the praise of Erasmus. He left Tübingen for Wittenberg where, through Luther's Reformation theology, he reordered his philosophical and theological perspectives. His orientation toward humanistic philosophy, however, tended to shape his forensic Reformation theology. He recognized that people have responsibilities related to their positions in society, but also for their sin before God, while God is responsible for their justification through his re-creating word.[17]

Without losing his allegiance to academics Melanchthon was quickly won over to Reformation theology by Luther and soon had integrated Scripture, Reformation theology, humanistic study, and philosophy into his work.[18]

When Melanchthon first appeared at Wittenberg in 1518, at age twenty-one, Luther wrote that despite his frail appearance he was the "David destined to battle the Goliath of scholasticism," and unreservedly supported Melanchthon's efforts to bring improved knowledge and moral development to their university. In 1519 Melanchthon's scriptural studies and the Leipzig Debate led him to brand philosophical ethics as the enemy

---

foundation for Reformation dogmatics. Agricola's position between the old and the new influenced Melanchthon as he adapted Agricola's methods into his work.

13. Stupperich, *Melanchthon* (1965), 27. Pauck, "Introduction," 13; Klotsche, *History*, 204. Melanchthon followed Erasmus's ideas that philosophical studies improve life, but rejected his universalistic tendency.

14. Manschreck, *Quiet Reformer*, viii–ix.

15. Manschreck, *Quiet Reformer*, 38–40; Stupperich, *Melanchthon* (1965), 29–30.

16. Green, *Melanchthon Helped Luther*, 108.

17. Green, *Melanchthon Helped Luther*, 109.

18. Manschreck, *Quiet Reformer*, 44; Rogness, *Reformer*, vi–viii; Hill, *Loci Communes*, 23; Wengert, *Melanchthon's* Annotationes in Johannem, 210–12, a discussion of Melanchthon's integration of his humanist background and dialectical exegetics with Luther's Reformation theology, which finds knowledge of God through the Scriptural Law/Gospel mechanism.

of grace.[19] He opposed Aristotle and turned to Paul, as the one who gave the true understanding of Christ, and his "benefits," and whose teaching would lead to a right "order of life." In his first *Loci* he opposed philosophy as the kingdom of Satan and advocated the clear authority of Scripture.[20] Sixteenth-century Lutheran theologians considered the *Loci*, Luther's writings of the 1520s, and the Augsburg Confession, as the three foundation pillars of the Reformation.[21] By 1523 Melanchthon began to enhance theology with the incomparable educational value of ancient philosophy. They must break through to the original languages and sources of Scripture and philosophy—*ad fontes*. He used Aristotle's dialectics as the foundation for his system. Its strength is its moral philosophy which trains responsible citizens. God's Holy Spirit overcomes philosophy's deficiencies, lack of fear of God, and ignorance of original sin.[22]

Melanchthon, remaining an Erasmean humanist, was the well-tempered scholar and diplomatic spokesman for Wittenberg.[23] Humanism—the disciplines of language, literature, philosophy, rhetoric, etc.—remained more important to Melanchthon than the church's tradition, and so philosophical presuppositions put their stamp on his theology. *Ad fontes* influenced his methodology throughout his career.[24] He introduced Wittenberg to a new education in classical and biblical languages, believing that God uses the natural law with reason and the divine law as he deals with redeemed humanity in his creation.[25] In his academic works Melanchthon integrated all elements of truth as "handmaids" of theology.[26] A pious humanist, he derived the method of his "theology of definitions," or *loci*, from R. Agricola, but never forsook the authority of the Scriptures and

---

19. Stupperich, *Melanthchon* (1965), 32–37. Melanchthon's important works of this period are: *A Theological Introduction to Paul's Epistle to the Romans* (1519); *CR* 15:797-1052; *Paul and the Scholastics* (1520); translated in Hill, *Loci Communes* 31-56n3, 187-88, and which mentions 4 editions not in *CR*; Lectures on the Gospel of Matthew (1519-20); *CR* 14:529, 1042; and "Oration against Thomas Rhadimus (1520)"; *CR* 1:212-62.

20. *CR* 21, 228; *MLC21*, 152; Pauck, "Introduction," 9.

21. Manschreck, *Quiet Reformer*, 88–89.

22. Hildebrandt, *Alien or Ally?*, 1–9.

23. Hildebrandt, *Alien or Ally?*, ix–xi; Pauck, *Luther to Tillich*, 43–44.

24. Hägglund, *History of Theology*, 253.

25. Manschreck, *Quiet Reformer*, 43–44; Hall, "Protestantism," 296.

26. Seeberg, *History of Doctrines*. 2:353; Manschreck, *Quiet Reformer*, 44.

the importance of studying them.²⁷ He pictured Christian humanism with church, state, and university working together.²⁸

Melanchthon's views of historical theology and Scripture's authority over the Fathers' rationalism influenced Luther against Eck at Leipzig.²⁹ Luther and Melanchthon shared the work of teaching, writing, and editing and they supported one another throughout their twenty-eight-year relationship. Luther was a prophet and Melanchthon was a teacher who combined theology and scientific humanistic education.³⁰

Oswald Bayer, in Gunter Frank's *Der Theologe Melanchthon*, notes Melanchthon's parallel of science with theology.³¹ The understanding of natural sciences is determined by empirical and rational-deductive procedures. Melanchthon, in teaching Christian theology, replaced scientific procedures with God's revelation. He thus handed down his teaching to the human race through certain and plausible testimonies. The main factor is the certainty that overcomes doubt that Melanchthon derived from the exactness of mathematics in natural sciences. These are just as certain as the articles of faith, such as God's threats of judgment and promises of mercy. If certainty is the same in both mathematics and theology, it happens in completely diverse manners. The certainty of mathematics results from natural human judgments. The certainty of faith results from revelation that is confirmed by the sure and certain testimonies of God, such as by the resurrection from the dead and other miracles. Melanchthon maintained that the certainty or the assent of faith and biblical authority was brought about by virtue of the Holy Spirit.³²

Wengert, in the conclusion of his work on Melanchthon's *Annotationes in Johannem*, summarizes the stature and complexity of Melanchthon's work interrelated with Luther's Wittenberg theology:

> We have . . . come to attack the notion that Melanchthon's career at Wittenberg must be seen as a series of crises and breaks, as if the young teacher of Greek was torn between the humanism of Erasmus and the theology of Luther. At the heart of this misinterpretation is an incorrect understanding of humanism and a

---

27. Pauck, "Introduction," 11, Manschreck, *Quiet Reformer*, 56–58. On the use of the locus method in sixteenth-century Lutheranism, see Kolb, "Teaching the Text," 571–85; and Wengert, *Human Freedom*, 59–60, addresses challenges of the claims that Melanchthon depended upon Rudolf Agricola for the *loci* method.

28. Fraenkel, *Testimonia Patrum*, 143.

29. Stupperich, *Melanthchon* (1965), 35–36; Manschreck, *Quiet Reformer*, 48.

30. Rogness, *Reformer*, v–vi; Hägglund, *History of Theology*, 248–49.

31. Bayer, "Melanchthons Theologiebegriff," 40–41.

32. Bayer, "Melanchthons Theologiebegriff," 41–42.

failure to recognize that divergence from Luther did not necessarily prevent Melanchthon from sharing the same theological platform. In our investigation of the *Annotationes in Johannem* we have discovered Wittenberg's theology and humanist methodology coexisting. Melanchthon's dialectical and rhetorical methods, which he developed prior to his acceptance of Luther's theological position and which owed a great deal to humanists such as Agricola and Erasmus, find a prominent place in the *Annotationes*. Melanchthon's dialectics even helped him define his positions on important issues such as the certain knowledge of God and the distinction of Law and Gospel. The *Annotationes in Johannem* shows Melanchthon as a humanist, a "Martinian," and an independent theologian and exegete, who is struggling to unlock the message of John's gospel for a world obsessed with uncertainty and affliction, with true knowledge of God in a false age, with the effects of the Word upon the mystery of the individual's salvation.[33]

Wengert reminds us of the humanistic context of the early Reformation, as humanism swept down over the Alps in the late fifteenth and early sixteenth centuries, early taught by Erasmus, Rudolph Agricola, Johannes Reuchlin, and Martin Luther and Philip Melanchthon themselves. They were soon joined by the next half to a full generation of reformers that included the diversity of John Oecolampadius (Basil reformed), John Cochlaeus (Roman Catholic), Conrad Grebel (Anabaptist), Martin Bucer (eventually Anglican reformed), Johannes Brenz (Schwäbisch Hall Lutheran), and many others.[34] Wengert notes:

> None of the first-generation Reformers . . . Martin Bucer in Strasbourg, John Brenz in Schwäbisch Hall, Oecolampadius, or Martin Luther himself—were immune from the influences of this movement [humanism], so they may all be considered both humanists and Reformers. This also means that Erasmus, as the prince of humanists, played a critical role in the intellectual development of all these figures—only rarely as theologian and philosopher, but always as linguist and rhetorician: that is, as humanist. Thus, many of these scholars could praise Erasmus's philogy and blame his philosophy in almost the same breath.[35]

---

33. Wengert, *Melanchthon's* Annotationes in Johannem, 233.
34. Wenger, *Human Freedom*, 10, 59.
35. Wengert, *Human Freedom*, 10.

In this balance Melanchthon used the methods of humanism to explicate the theology of Luther while at times sharply criticizing Erasmus, whose work he used, but who, Melanchthon felt, had departed from the theology of his church.[36] Melanchthon and Luther supported one another in the twenty-eight years of their joint efforts. Melanchthon systematized and defended Luther's ideas, and made them the basis of a religious education. Throughout his life Luther endorsed Melanchthon's *Loci communes* through their various editions and set them next to the canon of Scripture![37]

Melanchthon's Influence on Emerging Lutheran Theology

Melanchthon, as Luther's closest theological associate, holds a crucial position in the history of Lutheran theology. As the scribe and teacher of the Reformation, he systematized Luther's theology in his *Loci communes*, the first systematic theology of the Reformation, and wrote documents included in the *Book of Concord* that Lutherans consider theologically foundational. His *locus* method of doing theology persisted until the analytic method of Georg Calixtus (1586–1656) was broadly adopted.[38] Carl Maxcey, in opposition to Bente, Dorner, and Seeberg, emphasized Melanchthon's importance, "Since Melanchthon is recognized as the first systematizer of Evangelical doctrine, it is not surprising that Lutheranism has taken its form from Melanchthon rather than Luther. There are even some who claim that Lutheranism might readily be referred to as 'Melanchthonianism.'"[39] Quirinius Breen claimed that Agricola and Erasmus used the *locus* method more along the lines of Cicero than Aristotle.[40] Melanchthon, their most illustrious pupil, surpassed his masters. Although Melanchthon, more than Luther, approved of the use of Aristotle, he could not have foreseen the increased Aristotelianism and scholasticism of later generations. Wilhelm Maurer traced Melanchthon's development from his appearance at Wittenberg to the production of the 1521 *Loci*. During that time, as he moved from Erasmus to Luther, Melanchthon integrated his studies in Paul's Epistle to the Romans with his background in rhetoric and reason to form his theology.[41] Starting with the

36. Wengert, *Human Freedom*, 64; 110–36, presents the current discussions among scholars concerning the influences of Erasmus and Luther on Melanchthon, which support the above assertions.
37. Richard, *Melanchthon*, 247–49; Green, *Melanchthon Helped Luther*, 121–22.
38. Tschackert, "Georg Calixtus," 349.
39. Maxcey, *Bona Opera*, 3–4.
40. Breen, "'Loci Communes,'" 199–209.
41. Maurer, *Der Junge Melanchthon*, 2:139–40.

books of Lombard, he left them for the message of sin and Law and Gospel he found in the Scripture.[42]

More important for the Reformation was the emphasis on original sin and justification found in the 1521 *Loci* which Melanchthon derived from his work in Romans.[43] He highlighted the powerlessness of human reason and will that succumbs to natural wicked desires, the works of the law that lead to damnation, and the sweetness of God's grace by which Christ's atoning work merited forgiveness for sinners. With the forensic understanding, though not explicitly mentioning it, Melanchthon also pointed to the gift of the Holy Spirit who works new "affections" in believers as the disposition of changed hearts. Hence, in his early work, Melanchthon already included a subjective aspect of justification with the forensic.[44]

At Augsburg (1530) Melanchthon consulted with princes, theologians, and Luther to prepare a document for the Imperial Diet called by Charles V. Coincidentally, at that time, John Eck's "404 Articles" appeared. Melanchthon was able to address Eck's "404 Articles" while restoring the ancient teachings of the true "catholic" church, and showing that the Roman church had departed from the scriptural faith. The resulting *Augsburg Confession*, written by Melanchthon from several documents by Melanchthon and Luther,[45] has remained as the symbol of true Lutheran belief. In it Melanchthon publicly expressed his own theology as he was becoming an important spokesman for the Reformation. His later mature theology flowed from the *Confession*.

In 1531 Melanchthon replied to the "Roman Confutation"—a Catholic response to the *Augsburg Confession*—with the *Apology to the Augsburg Confession*, also his own creation. The *Augsburg Confession* and the *Apology* have become recognized as official confessions of the Reformation faith.

Melanchthon was the theological professor for most of the major theologians of the period following the initial Reformation era. He had particular influence through three of his students: Martin Chemnitz, David Chytræus, and Nicholas Selnecker. They, with Jacob Andreae, and others, wrote the Formula of Concord (1577), to resolve the controversies which arose after Luther's death and whose theology was foundational for several generations of Lutherans, including seventeenth-century Lutheran

---

42. Maurer, *Der Junge Melanchthon*, 2:142–46.
43. Green, *Melanchthon Helped Luther*, 129–32.
44. Green, *Melanchthon Helped Luther*, 214, 133.
45. Maurer, *Historical Commentary*, and Reu, *Augsburg Confession*, describe the documents and the genesis of the preparation of the Augsburg Confession.

orthodoxy and Pietism.[46] Melanchthon's brilliance and unique love for the church combined with his work as theologian, spokesman, and teacher of the Reformation as he became a powerful influence in the church.

Melanchthon's Theological Framework

Melanchthon drew conclusions from Scripture rather than from human ideas, a strength Luther recognized as a mighty enemy of the devil and of scholastic theology.[47] Melanchthon based his work on the principles of Scripture alone and justification by faith derived from Law and Gospel themes of the Bible. His major theological ideas, the church of pure doctrine and justification by faith,[48] are expressed in the evangelical teaching of grace, freedom, and the sacraments.[49]

The Church of the Pure Doctrine

Melanchthon saw the church as the community that embraces Holy Scripture as the source and standard of Christian truth and salvation,[50] and regulates its life and worship by it. In this church God accomplishes his divine purposes for the world through the work of Christ.[51]

Melanchthon's theology started with Matthew and Romans,[52] giving priority to Paul's writings and his doctrines of Law and Gospel and justification by faith.[53] Holding that the church is the speaking instrument of the Scripture, he opposed those who held the Catholic system above Scripture, and attacked its sacramental and ecclesiastical practices.[54] Melanchthon wanted people to understand Christ from the Scriptures in order to slough off the old Adam and follow Christ's commands.[55] Church history and the

---

46. Andreae, Chemnitz, and Chytræus are discussed in chapter 5.
47. Stupperich, *Melanchthon*, 39–41.
48. Seeberg, *History of Doctrines*, 2:351–56.
49. Herrlinger, *Theologie Melanchthons*, iv.
50. Fraenkel, *Testimonia Patrum*, 206.
51. Seeberg, *History of Doctrines*, 2:351–52, 354–55.
52. Stupperich, *Melanchthon*, 46–48.
53. See "Melanchthon, Paul and the Scholastics" in Melanchthon, *Selected Writings*, 33.
54. Fraenkel, *Testimonia Patrum*, 223–24. See "Letter to Dr. Hess" in Melanchthon, *Selected Writings*, 46–56; Manschreck, *Quiet Reformer*, 52.
55. Stupperich, *Melanchthon*, 33.

creeds provided an important connection to the apostolic deposit and conciliar teaching of Holy Scripture's testimony to God.[56]

Melanchthon saw the church as a school to provide the academic foundation necessary to perform its functions as keeper, interpreter teacher, and practitioner of the Holy Scriptures, where theology maintains truth in its purity and simplicity. He established schools of the Holy Scriptures, trained teachers and prepared textbooks.[57] Thus, as the "Praeceptor of Germany," Melanchthon trained preachers of the word of God.

Melanchthon taught that the church is the people who hold to the true belief in the knowledge of Christ,[58] and it is the communion of saints where the gospel is rightly taught and the sacraments rightly administered.[59] He saw the two sacraments (baptism and the Lord's Supper) as visualizations of God's word and seals of his promises.[60]

Faith accepts what it sees.[61] New Testament worship is a spiritual exhibition of the righteousness of faith in the heart that shows fruits of faith[62] and issues forth in forgiveness and thankfulness. In the first *Loci* he saw baptism as a sign of repentance and God's work of forgiveness and regeneration. In the Lord's Supper, Melanchthon stressed the redemptive work of Christ as the "benefits of Christ" where Christ's body and blood signify the forgiveness of sins.[63] He emphasized the "ubiquity" of the whole Christ, maintaining that Christ's true presence was "with" the bread.[64] Melanchthon later adapted his language concerning the Lord's Supper, including that of later editions of the *Augsburg Confession*, to approach some of Calvin's reformed views, which eventually brought down on him the anger of some other Lutherans.[65]

---

56. Fraenkel, *Testimonia Patrum*, 162–64, 187–93, 228, 149–50.

57. CR 11:280–81, Declamat. (No. 38) de Philosophia (1536); CR 11:355, Declamat. (No. 48) de Ineriio et Bartola (1537); CR 11:934, Declamat. (No. 119) de doctrina physica (1550); Seeberg, *History of Doctrines*, 2:353; Manschreck, *Quiet Reformer*, 133.

58. Seeberg, *History of Doctrines*, 2:356.

59. BSLK, 62; BC, 42–43; Augsburg Confession, Art. 7, "Church."

60. CR 21, 208, 9–16; MLC21, 133.

61. BSLK, 369, 70, 408; BC, 271, 70.

62. BSLK, 356, 25–26; BC, 262, 25–263, 27.

63. CR21, 220–22; MLC21, 145–46; CR21, 208; MLC21, 133; Melanchthon defines signs as promises which testify that we will receive what God has promised.

64. Rogness, *Reformer*, 73–74.

65. See "Historical Introduction," in Bente, *Concordia Triglotta*, 177–78.

Justification by Faith

The doctrine of justification is, for Melanchthon, the chief article of faith, which he derived from the Law and the Gospel. The law speaks of God's punishment on evildoers, and the gospel teaches about Christ and his benefits of forgiveness.[66] God the creator is both provider and judge who is satisfied by Christ the Redeemer whose presence restores those people who otherwise could not come to God.[67]

Melanchthon said people are bound by original sin,[68] by the human will, and by the will of Satan who tempts their reason, the seat of sin.[69] God opposes sinners and removes his Holy Spirit from leading them (Rom 8:5).[70] Through baptism and the Holy Spirit[71] believers are forgiven their original sin and committed sins, while the sinful flesh still remains.[72] God's election is grounded in his mercy toward those who hear the promises of the gospel and respond in faith.[73]

Wengert says that, for Melanchthon, true repentance, confession, faith, and forgiveness become realities when "The Holy Spirit convicts the world of sin, righteousness, and judgment.... Therefore, this is *poenitentia* (repentance), so to acknowledge sins that we truly sense the wrath and judgment of God against sin and are truly terrified."[74] This conviction by the Holy Spirit and repentance come through the preaching of the word. Melanchthon viewed justification as a forensic act of God that includes: Jesus Christ the God-man, his substitutionary sacrifice, the forgiveness of sins, the imputation of Christ's righteousness, and the giving of the Holy Spirit.[75] Faith, produced by preaching God's word and the Spirit's illumination, is the constant assent to God's word and trust in his mercy promised in

---

66. CR 12:605, 614, *Disputat. LXVI* (1554); 605; CR 12:658–59, *Disputat. LXX* (1560); CR 21, 421, 1535–41 *Loci*; CR21, 685, 741, 885; MLC43, 57, 85, 157–58; CR21, 139; MLC21, 70–71; Seeberg, *History of Doctrines*, 1:358.

67. Rogness, *Reformer*, 30–32; Hill, *Loci Communes*, 45.

68. CR 21, 207, 4–8; *MLC21*, 132.

69. BSLK, 75; BC, 52; *Augsburg Confession*, Art. 19, "Concerning the Cause of Sin."

70. CR 21, 208, 23–25; MLC21 132; CR21, 97–101; MLC21, 30–35.

71. BSLK, 53, 2; BC, 38, 2; *Augsburg Confession*, Art. 2, "Concerning Original Sin."

72. CR 21, 206–7; MLC21, 130–32.

73. CR 15:680, *Commentary on Romans* (1532); Richard, *Melanchthon*, 236.

74. Wengert, *Law and Gospel*, 159, *Scholia*, 1528, 40r-v.

75. CR 21, 159; MLC21, 88–89; Seeberg, *History of Doctrines*, 2:358–58.

Christ.[76] Therefore, faith is imputed as righteousness, people can love God and others, and they can hope in God's promises in his word.[77]

The Two Kingdoms

In addition to the theological framework of the church and of justification, Melanchthon used the concept of two kingdoms. In his essay, "Philip Melanchthon and a Christian Politics,"[78] Wengert presents Melanchthon's concept of the Holy Spirit's involvement in the teaching about the two kingdoms.

> Melanchthon argued that Paul's condemnation of "human commands and teachings" pertained specifically to righteousness in Christ, that is, to a person's standing before God. This means that the text (Col 2:22) applies best to ecclesiastical traditions that claim to merit forgiveness of sin. However, Paul's comments do not apply to the proper realm for human regulation, namely the body politic. Thus, at the beginning of his exposition, Melanchthon divided his comments into two parts: civil traditions and ecclesiastical ones. Underneath his entire discourse ran Wittenberg's commitment to discerning God's two ways of working among human beings, what Melanchthon here calls the two kingdoms.[79]

Then, Wengert lets Melanchthon speak for himself to describe the work of the Holy Spirit:

> Therefore let us carefully discern these two kingdoms: the kingdom of this world and the kingdom of Christ. The kingdom of Christ is found in the hearts of the saints who according to the gospel believe that they have been received into grace on account of Christ, who are renewed and made holy by the Holy Spirit and taste eternal life, who show forth their faith in good works and, on account of God's glory, do good to all, so that they invite many to knowledge of the gospel. They tolerate all things . . . [and do not] . . . allow themselves to take up arms in a desire for vengeance against those who have injured them. They obey the magistrates with great care, they hold public offices (if such are entrusted to them) with vigilance and courage. If duty demands, they punish the guilty and fight in battle. However,

---

76. CR 21, 162–63; *MLC21*, 91–93.
77. CR 21, 183–84; *MLC21*, 111.
78. Wengert, "Melanchthon and a Christian Politics," 49–50.
79. Wengert, "Melanchthon and a Christian Politics," 50.

they do not rush in to seize public offices of their own accord, but, if forced by their calling, they take them up. Furthermore, the kingdom of this world, as I have often said, is a legitimate order that defends public peace with the authority of magistrates, with laws, judgments, punishments and war.[80]

Similar to Luther's doctrine of two kingdoms, Melanchthon said the Holy Spirit guides Christian magistrates. In the unrest following the Peasants' Revolt Melanchthon, in the *Scholia* of 1528, attacked those who would undermine civil authority. Let the leaders consult Scripture. Wengert notes,

> Melanchthon argued that knowing the Holy Spirit's word on the subject would lead many to godliness and that knowing God was pleased with such work and defended such officeholders, would console the Christian magistrate.[81]

Melanchthon's Theology of the Holy Spirit

Theology of the Cross

While not explicitly addressing Luther's theology of the cross in his writings, Melanchthon understood that Law and Gospel bring a person to conviction of sin, to the struggles of faith, and to the gift and encouragement of the Holy Spirit. These contain the elements of the theology of the cross.[82] Melanchthon taught the third use of the law for Christian living as the tool of the Holy Spirit to put to death the sin remaining in believers. Though free from the law's condemnation, "We openly confess, therefore, that the keeping of the law must begin in us and then increase more and more."[83]

---

80. Melanchthon, *Scholia*–1528, 69–70; in "Melanchthon and a Christian Politics," 50.

81. Wengert, *Human Freedom*, 124–25; See also, Estes's *Peace, Order, and the Glory of God* in which he discusses fully the essential agreement of Luther and Melanchthon regarding the foundations of the relationship of secular authority and the church from 1518 to Luther's death and beyond.

82. *BSLK*, 345, 59; *BC*, 268–69, 59; *Apology*, Art. 24, "Mass."

83. *BSLK*, 187, 136; *BC*, 142, 136; "*Darum sagen wir auch, daß man muß das Gesetz halten, und ein jeder Glaübiger sähet es zu halten, und nimmt je länger, je mehr zu in Liebe und Furcht Gottes*" (Note: Following Charles Arand, in his translation of the *Apology* in *BC*, the most recent German text of *BSLK* is used as the textual baseline, *BC*, 109), *Apology*, Art. 4, "Justification"; *CR*21, 205–6; *MLC*21, 130; Lund, "Luther's Third Use," 86–88.

Melanchthon interrelates the power of Christ's divinity and the weakness of his humanity, demonstrating his understanding of the theology of the cross. Wengert discusses this:

> This juxtaposition excludes speculation into the naked divinity of Christ. Instead this divinity must be experienced in the foolishness of the cross, which puts our blind and vain reason to the test and brings us to a certain knowledge of God. The theology of the cross becomes for Melanchthon the mechanism whereby the suffering individual is moved from speculation, curiosity, and doubt concerning the Deity to a true and salutary knowledge of God.
>
> Melanchthon and Luther also move the conflict between faith and reason into a discussion of justification by faith. Whereas the theology of the cross views the relation between God and the believer in terms of God's humble descent and self-emptying incarnation and of His identity with the suffering and afflictions of humanity, the doctrine of justification concentrates upon God's action in bringing the individual to himself in the face of the individual's total inability and unwillingness to save himself.[84]

Melanchthon used the elements of the theology of the cross as he discussed the Holy Spirit's function in the New Testament priesthood:

> The priesthood of the New Testament is a ministry of the Spirit. . . . It presents the gospel and sacraments to others so that they may thereby receive faith and the Holy Spirit, be put to death, and be made alive. . . . The Holy Spirit works in our hearts. Therefore his ministry benefits others when he works in them and gives them new birth and life.[85]

This speaks of repentance, conversion, and ongoing renewal.

Luther, in his theology of the cross, denied reason and rational theology as a means of God's revelation, because, as Bruce Gerrish explained, reason and philosophy belong to the natural sphere and can not be allowed to judge matters of faith. However, Luther did find them indispensable for

---

84. Wengert, *Melanchthon's* Annotationes in Johannem, 162–63, referring to *CR* 14:1048–49, *Annotationes Johannem* (John 14:4).

85. *BSLK*, 366, 59; *BC*, 268–69, 59, "Das Priestertum des neuen Testaments ein Amt ist, dadurch der heilige Geist wirkt." Here Arand's translation follows the Latin of *BSLK*, "Sacerdotium novi testamenti est ministerium spiritus . . . Exihibet aliis evangelium et sacramenta, ut per haec concipiant fidem et spiritum sanctum, et mortificentur et vivificentur. . . . Spiritus sanctus efficax est in cordibus . . . ita prodest aliis, cum in eis efficax est, cum regenerast et vivificat eos." Apology, Art. 24, "Mass."

the regenerate since faith comes through hearing and understanding the word.[86] Nonetheless, Melanchthon's humanistic background was more open to include them in the context of his grasp of the theology of the cross:

> No one learns this without many severe struggles. How often our aroused conscience tempts us to despair when it shows our old or new sins or the uncleanness of our nature! This handwriting is not erased without a great conflict in which experience testifies how difficult a thing faith is.
> While we are receiving encouragement and comfort in the midst of our terrors, other spiritual impulses increase, such as knowledge, fear of God, and hope.[87]

These are the experiential symptoms which Luther delineates as the work of the Holy Spirit in his theology of the cross. Many of these elements can be derived from Melanchthon's theology of Law and Gospel. Melanchthon centers on Christ as the revelation of God who comes in humility,[88] and combines the theological concerns of justification by faith alone, the theology of the cross, and the relation of Law and Gospel.[89] Therefore, to accept Christ is to accept one's own humility as well, similar to Luther's *simul iustus et peccator*.[90] The true knowledge of God, then, is revealed in the cross of Christ. People can know God only by turning from their own false ideas, within the framework of Law and Gospel. This is evident in the earliest writings of both Luther and Melanchthon and is basic to all subsequent Lutheran theology.[91] With emphasis on the humiliation of the incarnation and its fulfillment in the cross, the Christian life is a following of Jesus in the way of humiliation as adopted sons of God. Melanchthon's ideas on Law

---

86. Gerrish, *Grace and Reason*, 26–27.

87. *Triglota*, 216; Tappert, 161, 350–51), "*Haec non discuntur sine magnis et multis certaminibus. Quoties recurrit conscientia, quoties sollicitat ad desperationem, quum ostendit aut vetera peccata aut immunditiem naturae! Hoc chirographum non deletur sine magnoagone, ubi testatur experientia, quam difficilis res sit fides. Et dum inter terrores erigimur et consolationem concipimus, simul crescunt alii motus spirituales, notitia Dei, timor Dei, spes, dilectio Dei*," Apology, Article IV, Justification. BC follows the octavo edition (September 1531) and omits para. 344–55 of the quarto edition (May 1531).

88. CR 14:1066, 1170–72, 1188, 1199, *Annotations* (1522–1523) (John 14:9); Rogness, *Reformer*, 31.

89. Wengert, *Melanchthon's* Annotationes in Johannem, 191.

90. Wengert, *Human Freedom*, 55.

91. Rogness, *Reformer*, 18–19. Though the *Annotations* appeared two years before Luther's *De servo arbito*, they contain the same stress on the servitude of the will. Wengert, *Melanchthon's* Annotationes in Johannem, 188, where Wengert links Melanchthon's theology of the cross and its scandal with patience in suffering (John 9 and 11).

and Gospel and the theology of the cross intersect here,[92] though his theology does not emphasize the dynamic work of the Holy Spirit so prevalent in Luther's work.

The Person and Work of the Holy Spirit

Melanchthon stated that the Reformers subscribed to the Council of Nicea's definition of God: one divine essence, three persons: Father, Son, and Holy Spirit. He held to a tightly bound Trinity. To receive one person is to receive all persons. The persons are co-eternal and equal in power, yet each exists in and of himself, not as a property of the others.[93] This is seen in the Father speaking through his Spirit (Matt 10:19-20) and enabling God's care for the sparrows through the Son and the Spirit (Matt 10:29-33).[94] Wengert, in his assessment of Melanchthon's *Annotationes in Johannem*, shows how Melanchthon uses Hillary's *De Trinitate* to express his understanding of the Trinity with regard to action and relationship:

> The one from whom all action arises (Father), the counsel of the one acting (Son) and the action itself (Holy Spirit). Melanchthon . . . describes the relation between the persons of the Trinity as the one from whom all (Father), through whom all (Son) and the gift (*donum*) in all (Holy Spirit) and as one Power, the one Offspring and the one Gift (*munus*) of perfect hope.[95]

Melanchthon stated that Christ, after his ascension, ministers in the church today, so that

> through the Holy Spirit he [Christ] may make holy, purify, strengthen, and comfort all who believe in him, also distribute to them life and various gifts and benefits, and shield and protect them against the devil and sin.[96]

---

92. Rogness, *Reformer*, 46-49.

93. *Triglota*, 42, 102; *BC*, 27-28, 100; *Augsburg Confession, Apology*, Article I, God.

94. *CR* 14:837, Matthew.

95. Wengert, *Melanchthon's* Annotationes in Johannem, 80, referring to *CR* 14:1050 and Hilary, *De Trinitate* II. 1.

96. *BSLK*, 44; *BC*, 38; "Durch den Heiligen Geist heilge, reinige, stärke und troste, ihnen auch Leben und allerlei Gaben und Güter austeile und wider den Teufle und wider die Sunde schutze und beschirme," *Augsburg Confession*, Article III, [Concerning the Son of God]; Wengert, *Human Freedom*, 97, which summarizes Melanchthon's understanding of the work of the Holy Spirit: "The Spirit renewed hearts; brought forth in believers new movement, life, light, and knowledge; and through the Word worked fear and faith in their hearts."

The Spirit clarifies the gospel, "Because of Christ's glory we defend it [the gospel] and we ask Christ for the help of his Holy Spirit to make it clear and distinct."[97] The Holy Spirit is received by faith to enable Christians to keep the law "so that we are now able to think rightly about God, to fear God, and to believe him,"[98] and thus the Holy Spirit governs and defends Christians from deception and error.

Reception of the Holy Spirit

Melanchthon said the Holy Spirit is received by faith at justification.[99] "The benefits of Christ are forgiveness of sins by grace, freedom from eternal death, imputed justification, the gift of the Holy Spirit, and eternal life."[100] Herrlinger traced Melanchthon in several documents in the 1540-46 period that consistently say the Holy Spirit is given at the time of justification, remission of sins, and reconciliation. This gift of the Spirit works new attributes and motives in the heart.[101] In the *Annotationes in Johannem* Melanchthon clearly distinguished Law and Gospel: "The Law is that which commands what must be done [and] the Gospel [is] the remission of sins and the gift of the Holy Spirit through Christ."[102] Elsewhere in his *Scholia* Melanchthon noted that the reception of the Holy Spirit is God's testimony to his new covenant with believers.[103] In the 1528 *Scholia*, Melanchthon de-

---

97. Tappert, 139; BSLK, 204; "*Id propter gloriam Christi defendimus et rogamus Christum, ut spiritu sancto suo adiuvet nos, ut id illustrare ac patefacere possimus.*" Apology, Art. 4, "Justification."

98. BC, 141-42, 135; BSLK, 187, 135; "*Daß wir denn recht von Gott halten, ihnen fürchten, ihme glaüben,*" Apology, Art. 4, "Justification"; Wengert, *Melanchthon's Annotationes in Johannem*, 85; CR 14:1067 (John 14:15).

99. BSLK, 185, 126-27 (BC, 140, 126-27).

100. CR 15:495, "*Beneficia Christi, remissionem peccatorum gratuitam, liberationem a morte aeterna, imputationem iusticiae, donationem Spiritus sancti et vitae aeterna.*" The Argument of the Epistle of Paul to the Romans, *Commentary on Romans* (1532). Several places Wengert notes Melanchthon's position that the Holy Spirit is received from Christ along with remission of sins, e.g., *Annotationes*, 156.

101. Herrlinger, *Theologie*, 24-25; CR 21, 421 (1535 *Loci*); *Romerbrief von 1540*, 184; *Loci von 1546*, 15, 82; CR 14:852. The commentary on Mt 12:28, indicates that Melanchthon saw the Holy Spirit given after the work of God and not as an active participant in the process.

102. CR 14:1047, "*Legem esse quae praecipit facienda, Evangelium esse remissionem peccatorum et donationem Spiritus sancti per Christum*"; Wengert, *Melanchthon's Annotationes in Johannem*, 156.

103. CR 14:1180-81; Wengert, *Melanchthon's* Annotationes in Johannem, 206.

clared that Christ was not merely another lawgiver like Moses but came to obtain forgiveness of sins, to give the Holy Spirit, and eternal life.[104]

Conversion and the Synergistic Dispute

In his 1555 *Loci*, Melanchthon maintained that human enmity against God includes all human work, intent, wisdom, and virtue that are without the Holy Spirit.[105] He saw God's Spirit converting people in a "knowing" framework, in which God speaks to them in the word and directs their knowledge, will, and action back to God.[106] The preparation for conversion is therefore, in the intellectual domain,

> God is not received where the Holy Spirit has not first enlightened and kindled the understanding, will, and heart. Without the Holy Spirit man cannot of his own powers perform virtuous works, such as true faith, love of God, and true fear of God.[107]

Melanchthon explained to Landgrave Philip of Hesse that when the Holy Spirit counsels to salvation, he reveals sin in the heart, convicts of judgment, moves the heart to respond, and brings forth faith.[108]

There are distinctions between Luther and Melanchthon in their understanding of the Holy Spirit's work in conversion. First, Luther saw conversion as the work of the Holy Spirit through the word which causes faith to accept the claims of Christ declared in the "shouted word."[109] Melanchthon said there are three causes of conversion: the word, the Spirit, and the human will,[110] which elicited accusations of "synergism" from his critics. Hans Engelland disagreed with the critics and said Melanchthon was speaking of the will of one who is already reborn.[111] Agreeing that Melanchthon said

---

104. Melanchthon, *Scholia*, 48–49; Wengert, *Human Freedom*, 45, 96, 130.
105. *CR* 22, 248; *MLC55*, 121.
106. Engelland, "Introduction," xxxvi.
107. *CR* 22, 147–48n35 (*MLC55*, 52), "Denn Gött wird nicht angenomen, wo nicht der Heilige Geist, verstand, willen und hertzen erleuchtet und anzündet, Und können die Menschen aus eigen krefften, dise tugenden und werck one den heiligen Geist nicht wircken, nemlich rechten glauben, Gottes leibe, vertrawen uff Gott, und rechte Gottes forcht."
108. *CR* 1:703–12, *Epistola* (No. 313) *Philippo Landgravio Hassiae*, "Epitome renovatae ecclesiasticae, doctrinae" (1524); Melanchthon, *Selected Writings*, 94–98; Wengert, *Melanchthon's Annotationes in Johannem*, 90 (John 16:9).
109. Althaus, *Theology*, 35.
110. *CR* 21, 334–35; 1535 *Loci*.
111. Engelland, "Introduction," xxxvii–xxxviii.

the will accepts or rejects the offer of salvation, James Richard also stressed that Melanchthon said the will can have no self-moved activity in spiritual things of righteousness, salvation, and faith. He explained Melanchthon's Spirit-dependent view:

> Faith occurs when man hears the word of God, and when God moves and inclines him to believe. Without the word there is no contact of the Spirit. Thus free will is simply the power to resist the will's own infirmity and to accept the offer of grace ... assisted by the higher powers.
>
> Of the three concurring causes, the will is placed third ... quickened into activity by the other two.[112]

Richard said Melanchthon portrayed a human responsibility not included in Luther's one-sided emphasis of grace, and that Lutheran theology didn't require a moral personality which is "responsible for the use of the means of grace, for the appropriation of salvation, and for righteous living." While Richard's view of Melanchthon's position regarding the will seems to be accurate, Luther's emphases on the place of good works and the responsible action of faith dependent upon the Holy Spirit contradicts Richard's indictment of "one-sided" Lutheranism.

Hägglund noted that Luther said in regeneration man is renewed by the legal judgment and imputation of Christ's righteousness, as God's life-giving word effects the new birth. Luther considered the law as God's created tool, while Melanchthon saw the role of the law as an eternal guide to which God corresponds. Melanchthon divided imputation—Christ's fulfilling of the holy law before the heavenly tribunal—from the regenerating infusion of the Holy Spirit in the believer. In Melanchthon's theology the action of the word and the Spirit comes before; the will is able to act only when it is called through the word and influenced by the Holy Spirit.[113]

About one hundred years ago G. Friedrich Bente picked up the issue of Melanchthon and the three causes of conversion, or the synergistic dispute, again. Bente maintained that Luther, by his "monergism"—"Justification, conversion, perseverance in faith, and final salvation, obtained not by any effort of our own, but in every respect received as a free gift of God alone"— is faithful to the Reformation doctrine.[114] Referring to the later editions of Melanchthon's *Loci communes* Bente charged Melanchthon with being "the Father of Synergism," because Melanchthon held to "three concurring

---

112. Richard, *Philip Melanchthon*, 237.
113. Hägglund, *History of Theology*, 250–51.
114. See "Historical Introduction," in Bente, *Concordia Triglotta*, 125–28.

causes of conversion." Bente claimed this was contrary to the Augsburg Confession.[115]

Joining others who challenged the charges of synergism, Norman Lund maintained that "Melanchthon never embraced or tolerated synergism,"[116] and noted recent work to claim that such anti-Melanchthon opinions need review regarding Luther and justification.

From the late 1550s through the completion of the Formula of Concord in 1577, the synergistic controversy continued among Lutherans seeking to clarify contradictions between Luther's views and the apparent differences between some of Melanchthon's "synergistic" Philipist followers and Gnesio-Lutherans—each claiming to be the true followers of Luther, starting with his 1516 commitment that "By his own understanding or strength he could not believe in Jesus Christ or come to him." Robert Kolb stated Luther's understanding of the relationship between God and human beings:

> In 1516 Luther had asserted that apart from the gift of God's grace there can be no freedom for human beings, while at the same time he insisted that grace does coerce the will. Already at this point he was making every effort to hold God's total responsibility for the salvation of sinners, to present God as the only agent of human salvation, and at the same time to preserve the integrity of human beings as creatures of God by insisting that they must be obedient creatures, exercising full responsibility for those tasks God entrusts to them.[117]

Here, Luther was beginning to establish the foundation upon which he based his later (1525) disputes with Erasmus concerning freedom of the will and bound choice. Upon these the synergistic controversy has been based.

In recent years, Lutheran scholars have studied the disputes over the Lutheran understanding of the Holy Spirit and human will in the causes of conversion. They have laid out the issues, the disputes, and the final action in the Formula of Concord, Article II, but have found it difficult to present a final agreement between sixteenth-century parties, because many of the combatants of that period could not seem to agree on basic items, such as

---

115. See "Historical Introduction," in Bente, *Concordia Triglotta*, 128–29, refers to the *Commentary on Romans* (1532), *Loci* (1533, 1535, 1543), and the *Variata* (1540).

116. Lund, "Luther's Third Use," 75, citing Stupperich, "Melanchthon's Theological–Philosophical World View," 177. Scholars have been divided on the question of Melanchthon's synergism; Warth, "Justification," 107–11; Drickamer, "Synergist?"; Manschreck, *Quiet Reformer*, 121, 293–302; Engelland, *Christian Doctrine*, xxxvii–xxxviii.

117. Kolb, *Bound Choice*, 11–12; BC, 355; WA 1:147; Luther, *Small Catechism*, Creed, Third Article.

presuppositions and definitions, but primarily, because they just did not trust one another.[118]

Lowell Green researched the recurring problem in Christian theology regarding the work of the Holy Spirit and the human work in salvation. While the apostle Paul emphasized that believers are saved by the working of God's grace alone, others have feared that may endanger human responsibility and lead to moral irresponsibility. Historically, there has been shifting back and forth between divine grace and human works which raised disputes, such as Pelagius (who denied original sin) versus Augustine, among Medieval churchmen, and Martin Luther (*de servo arbitrio*) and Erasmus. Luther proclaimed *sola gratia* contra Erasmus's attention to human responsibility. Green noted that in initial conversion of unbelievers or unregenerate,

> In the language of the "Formula of Concord," "synergism" was the teaching that the unregenerate needed to . . . contribute some action to the working of divine grace. Such a teaching was decisively renounced in Article II of the "Formula of Concord." [Green asks] "Now, how was it possible that Melanchthon, the great teacher of a forensic justification which excluded all works . . . might have fallen into synergism?" It has often been said that Melanchthon taught that in "conversion" three causes concur, namely, the word of God, the Holy Ghost, and the human will. No such statement is to be found in the second or third editions of the "*Loci commune rerum theolocarum.*" Except that these three causes concur in a "good action." (Nicene Creed, ca. 1547–50)[119]

Green explained that for Melanchthon, the Holy Spirit moves hearts to consent to the voice of the gospel in the Creed. Elsewhere, 1554–59, the human will does not oppose the word of God and God's Holy Spirit whom he sends to cause conversion.[120] Green cited scholars up to the mid-twentieth century who have inaccurately applied Melanchthon's teaching of conversion and employed two words that can cause confusions—confusions his opponents have used for their purposes. These words are *conversio* and *causa*.

Conversio, conversion, or "*Bekehrung*" can apply to nonbelievers and initiates whom the Holy Spirit, working through the preaching of Holy

---

118. See E.g., Green, "Three Causes"; Kolb, *Bound Choice*; Bode, "Synergistic Controversy"; Wengert, *Law and Gospel*, and *Human Freedom*.

119. Green, "Three Causes," 90.

120. Green, "Three Causes," 91.

Scriptures, has brought to new faith and regeneration. They are born again through two working *causes*—the Holy Spirit and the Holy Scriptures.

Conversio and *causa* can also apply to regenerated Christians as the Holy Spirit works through Holy Scriptures through the process of sanctification in cooperation with the wills of the ones already reborn who are living Christian lives of continual repentance. Such a life of conversion and renewal includes three *causes*: God's Holy Spirit working through his holy word, along with the believer's cooperating renewed human will.[121] Green noted that Melanchthon was often accused of teaching three causes in conversion to pertain to the initial rebirth of unbelievers, and cites four writings where Melanchthon gives three causes of redemption whereby the will assents or accepts or agrees to the redemptive work of the Spirit through the word.[122] Green seems to agree with an Aristotelian line of thought that Melanchthon's understanding of the causes of the Christian life can be posited as:

causa efficiens (the agent that acts) = the Holy Spirit

causa instrumentalis (the means used) = the word of God

causa materialis (that which is acted upon) = the human will[123]

Green's conclusion, then, is this:

> We see that when the Aristolian term of "cause" is applied to the will, this does not imply that the unregenerate person is expected to cooperate toward his salvation, but rather that the will is the "material" upon which the first two "causes" operate, namely the Spirit and the word.[124]

This conclusion of the three causes applies to those already regenerated in their process of being renewed, or "converted," by the Holy Spirit in sanctification and not to the conversion of the unregenerated. Unfortunately, as Green explained in his article, Melanchthon's critics presumed that Melanchthon taught the three cause concept of conversion applied for all. Melanchthon could thus be rightly adjudged to be a teacher of synergism.[125]

Towards the end of the development of the Formula, Green reported that David Chytraeus, a devoted student of Melanchthon, and a member of the group tasked with writing the Formula, attempted to redeem his

---

121. Green, "Three Causes," 92–93.
122. Green, "Three Causes," 90–91.
123. Green, "Three Causes," 97.
124. Green, "Three Causes," 97.
125. Green, "Three Causes," 95. Green cites Chemnitz agreeing that the three causes only apply to the regenerate, 100.

Preceptor against the rising criticism of his supposed synergistic "three cause" teaching. Green summarized:

> Chytraeus wrote the new article on "Freedom of the Will" . . . distinguishing between the two kinds of conversion: 1. In man before his first regeneration, the will is completely impotent—there are only two causes of the first conversion the word and the Spirit; 2. after his rebirth, man must lead the life of sanctification which God wills to give him, and here three causes or forces concur—the Spirit, the word, and the cooperation of the newly-regenerated will of the believer.[126]

Chytraeus attempted to record for approval a statement he felt included all that had been said in the discussions concerning "Free Will." However this content was finally replaced and rewritten by Jacob Andreae for inclusion in the final version of *The Formula of Concord*, Art. 2. Though the content entered into the Formula seemed to cover the concerns of Chytraeus and his supporters, Chytraeus felt that his contributions regarding "Free Will" and, indirectly, that of his teacher, Melanchthon, had been ignored, and thus rejected, in the version of the final document of the Formula.[127]

While the Formula settled many issues of contention among Lutheran Reformers, it seemed only to exacerbate the disagreements regarding Melanchthon's teaching of the place of the human will in conversion, and so the synergistic dispute continued.

Faith and Hope

In the first *Loci*, under the heading of "Justification and Faith," Melanchthon said the enlightenment of the Holy Spirit brings conviction of things unseen.[128] In the *Commentary on Romans* he maintained that, in conjunction with the word, the Holy Spirit brings faith which apprehends hope.

> Hope therefore does not throw into disorder, because God surely loves us; and this love we lay hold of by our half-dead faith which is effective by the Holy Spirit (Romans Commentary, 1532).[129]

126. Green, "Three Causes," 105–6.

127. Green, "Three Causes," 108–9. For information on the inner controversies among four of the formulator (Andreae, Chemnitz, Chytraeus, and Selnecker) see Jungkuntz, *Formulators*, 110–14, 146–54.

128. CR 21, 168–69; *MLC21*, 96.

129. CR 15:618, "*Spes ideo non confundit, quia Deus certo diligit nos. Et hanc dilectionem apprehendimus ipso mortu fidei, quo Spiritus sanctus est efficax.*" Romans 5,

> In other ways it may be added, hope does not cause distress, because we have the earnest pledge of the Holy Spirit. It does not disturb me in a logical connection, and is in the place of the line of progression of the promise, and of the cause of assistance, just as may be said: Already we have the establishment and first-fruits of eternal life, namely the Holy Spirit, who even consoles and helps us, and is the assurance of future glorification.
>
> This consolation, although it may not be examined by our nature, but is being sought out, is known in the comfort in the word. For the Holy Spirit is effective through the word, it does not precede the word. And so the Holy Spirit is at hand in this way, he helps us, in order that we may lay hold of the love of God, and thus with the word we endure.... But it is plainly able to add that hope does not confuse because God loves us and you have already taken hold of this through the Holy Spirit, you are surely deciding the fact that God loves you, because hope in him results in good for you. And this point is that because we know that he loves, it causes hope.[130]

This hope is the guarantee of God's love. Melanchthon saw the work of the Spirit bound to the word. The Spirit does not precede the word.

Melanchthon maintained that the Holy Spirit relates faith, reason, and certainty through the word.[131] God wants people to believe the word of his Son and not to seek after other teachings or miraculous signs. One must wait patiently on the word and its promise. Knowledge comes through the light of the word's revelation of truth while faith comes through its promise. Melanchthon approached pure doctrine with both enlightened reason and careful repetition of the biblical doctrines.[132]

Romans Commentary (1532).

130. CR 15:619, "*Caeterum si quis sic attexat, Spes non confundit, quia habemus arrabonem Spiritum sanctum. Non displicet mihi connexio, estque locus ab ordine effectum promissionis, et a causa adiuvante, quasi dicat: Iam habemus incoationem et primitias vitae aeternae, scilicet Spiritum sanctum, qui nos etiam consolatur et adiuvat, et est pignus futurae glorificationis.*

Sed hic sciendum est, quod tamen non sit inspicienda nostra qualitas, sed quaerenda est consolatio in verbo. Nam Spiritus sanctus ita demum est efficax per verbum, non praecurrit verbum. Itaque sic adest, sic adiuvat nos, ut apprehendamus dilectionem Dei, cum verbo nos sustentamus. Sed planius potest sic attexi, Spes non confundit, quia Deus diligit nos, et hoc iam apprehendistis per Spiritum sanctum, vos certo statuitis quod diligat vos, ergo sperate eum vobis benefacturum esse. Et est locus ex causis, quia scire quod diligit, est causa sperandi." Romans 5, *Romans Commentary* (1532).

131. CR 15:339; CR 14:384; CR 15:106; Hildebrandt, *Melanchthon*, 29.

132. BC, 120–73.

Justification

Melanchthon defined justification as regeneration, as born again, and as being made alive. In the first *Loci* Melanchthon presented justification as "regeneration under the living power of the Holy Spirit."[133] Later in the Apology he said that the one who is freed by the Son is born again through the Holy Spirit.[134] Melanchthon understood that in conversion the Holy Spirit offers the gospel through the word and sacraments and works in the hearts of believers to make them alive.

Repentance was discussed in Melanchthon's commentary on Matthew. He described the Spirit's work in the two parts of repentance: contrition and consolation. In contrition the Holy Spirit dwells in the cross and accuses the world. In consolation, the Holy Spirit fulfills the promise that the seed of the woman will crush the head of the serpent. This is fulfilled when the arrival of the king of heaven brings forgiveness of sins, justice of the Holy Spirit, and eternal life according to Christ.[135] In his dispute with John Agricola, Melanchthon defined two parts of the Holy Spirit's work of *poenitentia* as contrition and justification. The first comes from the Spirit's preaching of the condemnation of the law and the second from his preaching of the promises of forgiveness in the gospel.[136] Lowell Green argued that Melanchthon said the presence of the indwelling God must be acknowledged in the context of forensic justification.[137]

Sanctification

Melanchthon said that at justification the Holy Spirit immediately begins sanctification by his rule in the believer's life, "our sanctification begins as an act of the Spirit of God, and we are in the process of being sanctified until the flesh is utterly killed off."[138] Wengert notes how Melanchthon relates the Spirit's work of justification and sanctification:

---

133. Pauck, "Introduction," 15.

134. See "Apology" in Bente, *Concordia Triglotta*, 128; *BC*, 111, Apology, Art. 4, "Justification."

135. CR 14:564, *Matthew* (1519–20).

136. Wengert, *Law and Gospel*, 162–63, citing *Scholia* 1528, 43v, 43r.

137. Green, *Melanchthon Helped Luther*, 230–34.

138. CR 21, 206; MLC21, 130, "Quod et sanctificatio nondum in nobis consummata sit. Coepimus enim spiritu dei sanctificari, sanctificamurque dum caro illa prorsus enecetur." "The Old Man and the New"; Wengert, *Law and Gospel*, 98–99, citing CR 26:10–18, *Visitation Articles*.

> Those are brought to perfection... who believe in Christ and are sanctified by Christ through the Holy Spirit. This second phase forced Melanchthon to discuss the role of the Holy Spirit in mortifying the flesh and making us new creatures. Reason and free will cannot change the heart in this way. Melanchthon did not distinguish clearly between Christ's satisfaction of the Father and the renewal of the Holy Spirit. They were two aspects of the same thing.[139]

Thus the Spirit transforms believers to hate sin.[140] He gives the virtuous life, teaches the things of God, and takes over impure hearts to transform and rule in them.[141] Wengert summarizes Melanchthon's view of sanctification, which included the word of God and the Holy Spirit in the theology of the cross:

> He subsumed the scandal of the cross under the Holy Spirit's work of sanctification. The cross was for him the sign of the Christian experiencing the death of the old creature and the birth of faith.... Theology of the cross for him described the life of the believer moving through the various parts of the Christian existence, from repentance to faith in the midst of affliction.[142]

Though Christians are free from the entire law, the Spirit uses the Decalogue to put to death every remnant of sin in their flesh. Melanchthon maintained that,

> For believers, laws are prescribed through which the Spirit mortifies the flesh. For freedom has not yet been consummated in us, but it is being appropriated, both while the Spirit is increasing and while the flesh is being slain.[143]

Franz Hildebrandt noted that in such texts Melanchthon's view of the law as a tool in sanctification opposes the antinomians who saw no use for the law. In addition, Melanchthon said all people who are without the Spirit of God are sinners. God uses the Law and Gospel to show and forgive sin so the Spirit can inflame the heart to obey the law.[144]

---

139. Wengert, *Law and Gospel*, 182; StA 4:244, 30–31.

140. Wengert, *Law and Gospel*, 183.

141. Wengert, *Human Freedom*, 84–85.

142. Wengert, *Human Freedom*, 108.

143. CR 21, 206; MLC21, 130, "*Et leges praescribuntur fidelibus per quas spiritus mortificet carnem. Nondum enim consummata in nobis libertas est, sed vindicatur dum et augescit spiritus, et necatur caro*"; Hildebrandt, *Melanchthon*, 37.

144. CR 21, 208, 15–23; MLC21, 133.

Melanchthon opposed Erasmus's claims that by the freedom of the will people could learn about God and obey him. Melanchthon agreed that by natural creation humans are free to eat, to drink, to come and to go, but only by the rebirth and the power of the Holy Spirit promised by Christ can people fear and believe God and love the cross.[145] In the *Loci* of 1522 Melanchthon declared human reason incapable of understanding the problems of the world. Through the word, the Holy Spirit overcomes this blindness to comfort troubled souls.[146] Melanchthon defined this as Christian freedom, where God through forgiveness of sins and the gift of the Holy Spirit frees Christians from sin and the devil.[147]

Commenting on Rom 8, Melanchthon said that the Holy Spirit helps believers walk according to the law of the Spirit of life in Christ Jesus as he rules, motivates anew, and makes faith possible. The Spirit enables people to see God's wrath and judgment.[148] Christ works through the Holy Spirit to establish believers in God, to free them from death, and to make them alive. Melanchthon saw the Spirit as Christ's adjunct given at conversion to do Christ's work through a spiritualized word. This differed from Luther who saw the Spirit working through the real concrete word to bring union with Christ.

Melanchthon asserted that before the fall, humans could fulfill God's law but that after the fall this freedom was undermined by human weakness. After the fall they could not obey God without the enlightenment and work of the Holy Spirit.[149]

According to Melanchthon's framework of the two kingdoms, he clearly distinguished the kingdom of Christ as the working of the Holy Spirit in sanctification:

> The kingdom of Christ is found in the hearts of the saints who according to the gospel believe that they have been received into grace on account of Christ, who are renewed and sanctified by the Holy Spirit and taste eternal life, who show forth their faith in good works and on account of God's glory do good to all, so that they invite many to knowledge of the gospel.[150]

---

145. Wengert, *Law and Gospel*, 89–92 referring to *StA* 4:222–41.

146. Wengert, *Human Freedom*, 104–5.

147. Wengert, *Law and Gospel*, 92, *referring to StA* 4:287–91 and 196.

148. CR 15:655, 660–61.

149. Wengert, *Human Freedom*, 143.

150. Melanchthon, *Scholia* 1528, 69rf, "*Regnum Christi versatur in cordibus sanctorum, qui credunt uixta Evangelium se a Deo propter Christum in gratiam receptos esse, qui renovantur & sanctificantur a spititu sancto, & vitam aethernam degustant, qui bonus operibus foris ostendunt suam fidem & propter gloriam Dei, omnibus benefaciunt, ut*

Teaching

Melanchthon taught that Jesus gives the Holy Spirit as the teacher for people who are alone in their darkness of sin. "The Spirit of Christ is light, and he alone teaches all truth."[151] "The merciful Spirit of God has designed that Scripture be understood by all of the faithful with as little difficulty as possible."[152] In his first *Loci* Melanchthon described the Holy Spirit as the teacher of the Scriptures who gives assurance of renewal in Christ.[153]

> The Holy Spirit is the one and only teacher, the most simple and the most definite, who expresses himself most accurately and most simply in the Holy Scriptures. . . . Those who depend not on the Spirit, but on the judgment and opinion of men, do not see things as they are, but only some vague shadows of things.[154]

The interpretation of Scripture is a gift of the Holy Spirit but not identical with Scripture. Melanchthon opposed those whose faith depends on the claim that God has given and upholds the gift of interpretation in the church.[155] Against the philosophers he maintained that spiritual things can not be understood except the Holy Spirit move our hearts.[156] He held that this important gift of teaching of the Holy Spirit is the means God employs to keep Christian faith alive through all ages and in many aspects: faith, knowledge, orthodoxy, piety, study of Scripture. This is "represented by the

---

ad agnitionen [sic] *Evangelii plurimos invitent.* Wengert, *Human Freedom*, 131. See the "Two Kingdoms" section on p. ##[x-ref].

151. CR 21, 113; MLC21, 47; "*Lux est Christi spiritus, is solus docet omnem veritatem.*" CR 21, 84; MLC21, 20. Therefore, the Holy Spirit cannot teach anything false. Wengert, *Melanchthon's* Annotationes in Johannem, 113, referring to CR 14:1160–63, 1137, and 1178 relative to comments on John 14:15.

152. StA 1:47, 37–38, "*Immo hoc benignus dei spiritus agebat, ut ab omnibus piis quanto minimo negotio intelligeretur,*" *Epistola ad Johannem Hessum Theologum* (1520). See "Letter to Dr. Hess" in Melanchthon, *Selected Writings*, 51–54; Wengert, *Melanchthon's* Annotationes in Johannem, 89; the Holy Spirit works through faith to bring understanding (John 16:7).

153. CR 21, 157; MLC21, 87; Pauck, "Introduction," in *Melanchthon and Bucer*, 14–16.

154. CR 21, 112; MLC21, 46, "*Unus est idemque ut simplicissimus, ita certissimus doctor, divinus spiritus, qui sese et proxime et simplicissime in sacrris literis expressit, . . . Qui pendent non a spiritus sed hominum iudicio aestimationeque non res ipsa, sed vix tenues quasdam rerum umbras cernunt.*" Wengert, *Human Freedom*, 48–49, citing the *Scholia* of 1528, 28v, that the Holy Spirit teaches through the language of Scriptures.

155. CR 5:532, *Lecture Announcement on Romans*, Nov. 1544; CR 11:645, *Declamatio de Dono Interpretationis*; Fraenkel, *Testimonia Patrum*, 225.

156. Wengert, *Human Freedom*, 99.

Fathers of the Church and the succession of true teachers," and to quote the interpretation of the Fathers is merely a prolongation of Scripture and leads back to it.[157]

The Means of the Holy Spirit

Melanchthon said that when the gospel is heard, people obtain the saving faith of justification and God gives them the Holy Spirit through the office of the gospel and the sacraments. The Lutheran churches opposed Anabaptists and others who said that the Holy Spirit comes through their own preparations without the external word.[158] Melanchthon portrayed the sacraments as extensions God's word that picture him working through his promises.[159]

The Word of God

The Bible is described by Melanchthon in his preface of the 1555 *Loci*. It is the story of God's church from beginning to end and the story clearly lays out all the doctrines God wants his people to understand. The church started with Adam and Eve and when they fell away, God demonstrated the twofold doctrine of the law and of the future Savior to take away sin. He gave his church a particular land so that it would always be known, like a castle on a mountain visible from afar.

There are stories about how mankind always has two parts, God's people and a larger company who despise God, reject his word, and persecute his church. Throughout all time, Christ abides in his true church and watches over the small company where his word shines. He disperses the devils and does not allow tyrants completely to devour his church.

Stories of how God preserved his church through the Old Testament time are found in the books of the prophets; even the time of the year is given, and the countries and peoples are named so that we may know when, where, and how God with marvelous signs revealed himself.

In the New Testament, the apostles wrote the story of the promised Savior, telling the details of his birth, his life and work, and finally of his death, glorious resurrection, and visible ascension into heaven. The story

---

157. CR 7:396, *Preface to Luther's Works*, Vol. 3 (1549); CR 11:238, *Oration on the Study of Languages* (1533) on the "gift of tongues"; CR 10:733 "*Question on the Postesta Interpretationis* (1541)"; Fraenkel, *Testimonia Patrum*, 225–27.

158. BSLK, 58; BC, 40; *Augsburg Confession*, Art. 5, "Concerning the Office of Preaching."

159. BSLK, 369–70, 69–70; BC, 270–71, 69–70; *Apology*, Art. 24, "Mass."

continues with the visible sending of the Holy Spirit and the great work of the apostles and their teaching. The story concludes with Christ gathering his church to himself forever and the final judgment where he casts the godless, with the devils into eternal punishment.

Thus the books of the prophets and apostles constitute a beautiful story, a story that sets forth all the doctrines of God's being, human weakness, law, sin and punishment, and the promise of the Savior. Melanchthon is careful to point out the distinctions in various doctrines, especially the difference between Law and Gospel. He explains that Christian doctrine is not dubious. On the contrary, we are obliged to believe firmly, as the divine voice from heaven commanded, "This is my Son, in whom I have delight and joy; to him you must listen!" (Matt 3:17).[160]

Melanchthon explains his concept of the Spirit and Scripture:

> If prophecy, inspiration, and the knowledge of things sacred are worth anything at all, why do we not embrace this kind of literature through which the Spirit flows? Or does not God accomplish all things by means of his word? For the Spirit . . . will teach many things by the use of the Scriptures.[161]

The design of the Holy Spirit's sweet instruction in Scripture is only that people be saved.[162] Regarding the Holy Spirit and free will, Melanchthon emphasized the work of the Spirit through the word,

> When human minds hear the word of God and do not repudiate it, at the same time the Holy Spirit moves them so that they are both terrified and again raised up and believe the promises and truly hold that God forgives, is present for, hears, helps, defends, and governs us, and that he helps human minds in bringing about true virtues.[163]

---

160. *MLC55*, xlvi–xlviii.

161. CR 21, 84; *MLC21*, 20; "*si omnino prophetia et adflatus quidam est, cognitio sacrarum rerum, cur non hoc literarum genus amplectimur, per quod illabitur spiritus? An non omnia sui sermonis opera deus efficit? Multa enim docebit scripturarum usu spiritus.*"

162. CR 21, 142; *MLC21*, 73.

163. Scholia 1534, hXlv, "*Sed cum humanae mentes audiunt verbum Dei & non repudiant, Spiritus sanctus simul movet eas, ut et perterrefiant et rursus erigantur & credant promißionibus & vere statuant Deum nobis ignoscere, adesse, nos exaudired, iuvare, defendere, gubernare, Et adiuvat humanas mentes in efficiendis veris viritutibus.*" Wengert, *Human Freedom*, 142.

Wengert quotes Melanchthon, "The human will does not obey God without the Holy Spirit."[164]

Manschreck says Melanchthon believed the Holy Spirit brings revelation in the Scriptures. Without the Spirit in the heart and mind as one reads, revelation remains hidden, so that one has eyes and sees not, ears but hears not.[165]

Against Thomas Rhadinus (who is believed to be Hieronymus Emser, who wrote to flatter the Elector and to condemn Luther and thus to divide them) Melanchthon said the Christians' authority is the Scripture written by the Holy Spirit, which teaches that polluted humanity can be cleansed only by the Spirit of God.[166] Melanchthon closed his *Loci* of 1521 saying, "the teaching of the Spirit cannot be drunk in purity except from the Scripture itself. For who has expressed the Spirit of God more appropriately than he [the Spirit] himself?"[167]

The Sacraments

Melanchthon said the Sacraments are means of the Holy Spirit, faith, and teaching.[168] As the word of God is the Holy Spirit's efficacious instrument, so are the sacraments, when they are received in faith.[169]

> The sacrament is a ceremony added to the promise, in which God ... may testify that in the gospel he indeed gives forgiveness of sins and justification on account of Christ. ...
>
> This spectacle is placed before the eyes and the mind so that ... faith is stirred up in us. For Christ testifies to us that his benefits belong to us when he imparts his body to us and joins us to himself as members; and no other union will be efficacious in us because he himself is life; he gives us his blood so that he may cleanse us.[170]

---

164. Wengert, *Human Freedom*, 143; CR21, 376.

165. Manschreck, *Quiet Reformer*, 310.

166. CR 1:212–62, *Oration against Thomas Rhadinus*; Manschreck, *Quiet Reformer*, 64.

167. CR 21, 228; MLC21, 152; "Quod doctrina spiritus pure, nisi e scripturis hauriri non possit. Quis enim spiritum dei propius expresserit, quam ipse sese?"

168. BSLK, 58, 4–6; BC, 40, 2; *Augsburg Confession*, Art. 5, "Concerning the Office of Preaching."

169. CR 21, 468, 1535 *Loci*; Quere, *Melanchthon's Christum Cognoscere*, 350, 112; StA 4:177, 26, 178, 26, 179, 15–17.

170. CR 21, 477, *Sacramentum ceremoniam esse additam promissioni, in qua Deus ... testetur nobis exhiberi in Evangelio promissas, scilicet remissionem peccatorum*

Ralph Quere says that Melanchthon did not confine Christ's presence in the sacraments to be merely efficacious, but maintained that Christ is personally present in the sacraments to perform that which is promised in them by faith.[171]

BAPTISM

Melanchthon taught that in Jesus' baptism (Matt 3:17) God testified to himself through the Holy Spirit, that the complete Trinity might be known and believed. Melanchthon noted that John's baptism, though different from that of the apostles, began an ongoing ministry for God's people. In the latter the sacrament was instituted, faith was required, and the forgiveness of sins and the Holy Spirit were given. Melanchthon did not say the Spirit worked through the word and sacrament to bring faith, but faith received the Holy Spirit with forgiveness of sins and grace.[172]

THE LORD'S SUPPER

Melanchthon understood that the Holy Spirit brings the real presence of Christ in the Supper, though he said *with* the bread and not *in* the bread.[173] At the time of the Marburg Colloquy (1529) he said forgiveness and the Holy Spirit are given as God works through the Sacrament.[174]

> The Holy Spirit is given when God, either through word or through sign thoroughly terrifies and consoles and vivifies our hearts. For both the word and the sign are applied so that God through them may move hearts, thoroughly terrify and raise

---

et iustificationem propter Christum.

Et hoc spectaculum oculis atque animo obiicitur, ut . . . fides in nobis exuscitetur. Christus enim testatur ad nos pertinere beneficium suum, cum nobis impertit suum corpus, et nos sibi adiungit tanquam membra; qua non potest alia coniunctio cogitari propior; Quere, *Melanchthon's Christum Cognoscere*, 376, 380.

171. Quere, *Melanchthon's Christum Cognoscere*, 371–72. See also Johannes Hund, *Das Wort ward Fleisch* for discussions among Lutheran theologians from 1567–74 whose theological terminologies varied according to their localities while they essentially agreed on their understandings, teachings, and applications.

172. CR 14:553–54.

173. CR 2:222, 315; CR 9:276; Rogness, *Reformer*, 72, 132–33; Quere, *Melanchthon's Christum Cognoscere*, 371–72.

174. StA 4:285, 24–27, 249, 12–14; *Commentary on Colossians* (1527); Quere, *Melanchthon's Christum Cognoscere*, 247–49.

through faith when our hearts contemplate either the word or the sign.[175]

Melanchthon saw that God himself baptizes, forgives sins, and brings the real presence of his Son in the sacrament.[176]

The Holy Spirit in Law and Gospel

Before his first *Loci*, according to Maurer, the young Melanchthon agreed entirely with Erasmus in his opinion of the performance of the law as a life standard which one must fulfill to achieve bliss. In the Erasmus structure, Jesus Christ demonstrated this foundation of life, and his Spirit showed believers the right way. The Old Testament was information for the apostle Paul whose writings aimed toward the proper purpose of the law. The New Testament established the Spirit of virtue, conveyed Christ, and brought about the "kingdom of grace and peace." The law was the binding strength of human life, not due to the claims of godly wills, but to the Spirit's blessed impulses.[177] In early 1520, through Paul's writings, Melanchthon remarkably changed from Erasmus's "Christian philosophy" to Pauline philosophy.[178] He recommended "Pauline Philosophy" to young Christian students as that knowledge by which the Holy Spirit leads to a reality beyond human powers. It is not speculative knowledge, but practical Christian truth which leads to the comfort and well-being of the soul. Melanchthon stressed what has been called Luther's theology of reality.[179] Erasmus taught that ancient thought and Christian morality were "seamless with each other" and that Christianity was only a gradual degree from the other. Maurer describes Melanchthon's radical break-off from Erasmus that was more than a "gradual degree:"

---

175. StA 1:281, 10–15: "*Datur . . . Spiritus sanctus, quando Deus vel per verbum, vel per signum perterrefacit et consolatur ac vivificat corda. Nam et verbum et signum adhibentur, ut per ea Deus moveat corda, perterrefaciat ac rursus erigat per fidem, cum intuentur vel verbum vel signum.*" *Adversus anabaptists iudicium* (1528); Melanchthon, *Selected Writings*, 110, "Answer to the Anabaptists"; Quere, *Melanchthon's Christum Cognoscere*, 254.

176. See Jammerthal, *Melanchthons Abendmahlstheologie*.

177. Maurer, *Studien*, 108–11.

178. Maurer, *Studien*, 41n, 109–10. Maurer cites two speeches in StA 1:26–29, *Declamatiuncula in Divi Pauli doctrinam. Epistollla ad Johannem Hessum Theologum* (Feb. 1520) (translated in "Declamation on St. Paul's Doctrines," Melanchthon, *Selected Writings*, 31–34), and CR 11:34–37, *De studio doctrinae Pauli*, in May, 1520.

179. See chapter 2.

For Melanchthon, however, it is not a question of improvement, but of a breaking off. The Christian [now he means Pauline] philosophy is quite capable, alone, to rouse a real moral movement. It alone points the way to well-being. All other is death, falsehood, darkness, and error. The Christian philosophy [Pauline] is queen; the ancient only a monkey in a red robe. It is not enough to know what is proper and what is not, while at the same time not to live in a "good and beautiful way"; that is all the shadow of a fulfilled way of life. . . . The secular sciences are not able to rouse the love for the moral law; it requires a strength with which the producing Spirit sweeps in and inflames. Christ informs, pouring out from His wounds the Spirit of moral strength.[180]

While Melanchthon continued to be a Christian humanist, his spirit was different from Erasmus's and his entire conception of the law of the Spirit began to change. He said man is destroyed by the dominant will of God in his law so he can be saved through the gospel. This classical Reformation Law-Gospel motif radically departed from Erasmus's understanding of the freedom of the will.

Wengert reports that Luther presented his thesis of the distinction between Law and Gospel in 1518 in Heidelberg. This became the hallmark of Lutheran theology and a common key to the work of both Luther and Melanchthon.[181] In 1523 Melanchthon wrote in his *Annotations on Matthew*:

> The law says: "Do what you owe." The Gospel: "Believe in Christ and what you owe has been forgiven." The law commands what you cannot do. The gospel places Christ before you. If you—thirsting for righteousness—call upon him, you have the cleansing Spirit who gives you new affections. Therefore this is nothing other than grace. . . . The law says, "You are a sinner, despair, you will be damned!" The gospel says, "Trust in, flee to

---

180. Maurer, *Studien*, 110–11, "Für Melanchthon aber handelt es sich nicht um einen Fortschritt, sondern um einen Bruch. Die christliche Philosophie ist allein imstande, ein echtes sittliches Streben zu erwecken, zeigt allein den Weg zum Heil; alles andere ist Tod, Lüge, Finsternis und Irrtum. Die christliche Philosophie ist Königin, die antike nur ein Affe in Purpurgewand. Zu wissen, was sich ziemt und was nicht, genügt nicht, auch nicht äußerlich >>bene beautique<< zu leben; das alles ist der Schatten einer erfüllen Lebensform . . . Die Liebe zum sittlichen Gestez vermögen die profanen Wissenschaften nicht zu erwecken; es bedarf einer Kraft, die trägen Geister mit fortreißt und entflammt. Christus teilt sie mit, aus seinen Wunden strömt der Geist der Tugendkräfte (spiritus virtutum). (Decl. 37, 10–11)."

181. Wengert, "Beyond Stereotypes," 19.

Christ, and believe that through him every sin is forgiven, you will be saved."[182]

This understanding of the distinction between Law and Gospel continued at the heart of Melanchthon's entire theological enterprise.[183] In 1552, nearly thirty years later, he insisted that this distinction was one of the chief doctrines of the church "and where it is allowed to be extinguished . . . there follows terrible blindness."[184]

As he moved away from Erasmus during his work in 1520, Melanchthon saw how the law of the Spirit stands against the law of the flesh in a struggle between the godly and God's demonic enemies.[185] In this position Melanchthon maintained that the love of God required by both the godly and natural laws is impossible and causes hatred and a slavish fear of God. The root of this, self-love or sin, resists the law's command to love God, and creates wrong attitudes. His Romans studies produced the awareness that while the law of God is holy, man is carnal. Therefore the law stimulates anger against God, not love. However, Melanchthon began to see the soteriological value of the law to expose unholiness and to lead the way to salvation. This dialectic of Law and Gospel goes beyond Augustine to a message of freedom Luther drew from his Galatians lectures. Luther made the distinction between Law and Gospel foundational for Reformation theology. As a humanist, Melanchthon saw the demands of natural reason, in agreement with the law, and in conflict with man's true existence. Cheerful intention for good is merely a reminder of human depravity before God, that causes one to strike out in anger against God and his commandment, while the conscience burns weakly within, longing for forgiveness.

In this sad state, the law, along with the conscience, exposes sin and causes enmity between God and man. The law of the Spirit reverses the direction of the self-controlled will, as the Spirit of God leads the believer into new affections to obey God.[186] Central for Melanchthon is that the spiritual character of the law intends to bind the will of man to the love of God. It strikes out at self-love which is the root of all sin.

---

182. *MSA* 4:136.

183. Wengert, "Beyond Stereotypes," 19.

184. *MSA* 6:186.

185. *StA* 1:24, 4-6; *Baccalaureatsthesen* (1519), Theses 1-8; CR 21, 11-14, 23, 52, 56-57; *Lubcubratincula* (1520); *StA* 1:55, 21-30; *Themata Circularia*, Thesis 17; Maurer, *Studien*, 111-14.

186. Maurer, *Studien*, 113-14.

Melanchthon believed that one cannot correctly keep the law unless by faith he has received the Holy Spirit.[187] Melanchthon tied his doctrine of the Holy Spirit closely to the law and Christian freedom.

> Those who have been renewed by the Spirit of Christ now conform voluntarily even without the law to what the law used to command. The law is the will of God; the Holy Spirit is nothing else than the living will of God and its being in action. . . .[188]
>
> The beginning of repentance consists of that work of the law by which the Spirit of God terrifies and confounds consciences. . . . For the putting to death, the judgment, and the confounding of the sinner, wrought by the Spirit of God through the law, begin the justification and moreover the genuine baptism of man.[189]
>
> Those in whom Christ's Spirit dwells are entirely free from all law. . . . The Spirit is actually the righteousness of the heart. . . . The Decalogue cannot help being fulfilled now that the Spirit has been poured out into the hearts of the saints.[190]

People can love God when the mercy of God's forgiveness is grasped by faith. While outward works of the law may be possible, the Holy Spirit enables one to love according to the divine law. He emphasized that, in justification, believers receive the power of God's Holy Spirit to keep his law in love and good works.[191] Therefore, the keeping of the law is a work of the Holy Spirit who enables believers to obey God's law and mortify human lust: to love him, to fear him, to be sure that he hears, and to obey him in all afflictions.[192] "Do we then overthrow the law by this faith? By no means! On the contrary, we uphold the law," and the Holy Spirit works to lay the law on the heart so that "we ought to begin to keep the law and then keep it more

---

187. BSLK, 187, 24–25; BC, 142, 135; Apology, Art. 4, "Justification."

188. CR 21, 195; MLC21, 123, "Qui spiritu Christi innovati sunt, ii iam sua sponte, etiam non praeeunte lege, feruntur ad ea quae lex iubebat. Voluntas dei lex est. Nec aliud spiritus sanctus est, nisi viva voluntas, et agitatio, quare ubi spiritu dei, qui viva voluntas dei est, regenerati sumus, iam id ipsum volumus sponte, quod exigebat lex."

189. CR 21, 153; MLC21, 83, "Hic satis sit monuisse hoc opus legis initium esse poenitentiae, quo spiritus dei terrere ac confundere conscientias solet. . . . Nam iustificationem hominis, adeoque verum baptismum auspicatur mortificatio, iudicium, confusio, quae fit a spiritu dei per legem."

190. CR 21, 199; MLC21, 126, "Adeoque in quibus spiritus Christi est. hi prosus ab omni lege liberi sunt." "Spiritus ipsa cordis iustificatio sit. . . . Ita non potest non praestari decalogus effuso in corda sanctorum spiritu."

191. BSLK, 186, 135; BC, 141–42, 135; Apology, Art. 4, "Justification."

192. BSLK, 168–69, 45, 185–86; BC, 127, 45, and 140–41; Apology, Art. 4, "Justification."

and more.... These things cannot happen until after we have by faith been justified, reborn, and received the Holy Spirit.... [I]t is impossible to keep the law without Christ... without the Holy Spirit."[193]

Melanchthon used Luther's gospel freedom in terms of the Augustinian idea of Law and Gospel that showed the relationship of the two covenants to temporal and earthly promises. The Old Testament relates the requirements of the law to the promise of temporal goods, while the New Testament relates to the promises of unconditional spiritual goods.[194] In his 1521 *Loci* Melanchthon said that the New Covenant was more than a supernatural blessing but a word of mercy and comfort for the soul wounded by the wrath of God. It is not a humanly energized attribute but is the grace of the good news of God offered in the gospel.[195] The law commands God's will to be done, but the Holy Spirit, God's living will in those born again, powerfully meets the law's demands in them. He not only frees believers from the law's condemnation but enables them to fulfill the law.[196]

In summary, Melanchthon argued that "the distinction between Law and Gospel applied in practical terms to the shape of the Christian life. God's word moves a person from repentance to faith and from terror to comfort, that is, from law to gospel."[197]

New Life in the Holy Spirit

Melanchthon said faith brings the Holy Spirit who produces new life and new spiritual impulses in believers' hearts.[198] He believed the Holy Spirit is sent by Christ into the hearts of the faithful to sanctify them, and to kindle joy and the love of God,[199] which is similar to Luther's inner testimony of the

---

193. BSLK, 185, 123–26; BC, 140, 123–26, "Wir heben das Gesetz nicht auf durch den Glauben." "Wir das Gesetz halten sollen, ..und also je länger je mehr.... Dieses alles kann nicht geschehen, ehe wir durch den glauben gerecht werden, ehe wir neu geboren werden durch den heiligen Geist... So kann auch niemands das Gesetz erfüllen ohne den heilegen Geist." Jer 31:33; Rom 2:13; 3:33; Matt 19:17; 1 Cor 13:2; *Apology*, Art. 4, "Justification."

194. Maurer, *Studien*, 96–98.

195. CR 21, 82–87; *MLC21*, 18–24; Maurer, *Studien*, 96.

196. CR 21, 195; *MLC21*, 123; Maurer, *Studien*, 97, and Wengert, *Philip Melanchthon's Annotationes in Johannem*, 102 (John 14:15).

197. Wengert, "Beyond Stereotypes," 19.

198. BSLK, 185, 125; BC, 140, 124–25; *Apology*, Art. 4, "Justification."

199. CR 22, 79; *MLC55*, 13. At CR 22, 335–36 and *MLC55*, 162, Melanchthon summarized the relationship of justification, the gift of the Holy Spirit, and the ensuing life of love and joy to God.

Holy Spirit. As a humanist, Melanchthon said the purpose of justification is the fulfillment of the law. In justification Christ gives the Spirit to transform believers and to enable them to turn from lust to obey the law.[200] The Holy Spirit changes believers' hearts and gives them a new capacity for obedience and frees them to want to obey God.[201] In the 1521 *Loci* Melanchthon said God's Spirit gives faith as he leads believers to do his will and to perform the commands of the law. This is freedom from the law, because the Christians' renewal by the Holy Spirit frees them from their sinful inabilities to obey the law's demands.[202]

Renewal

Melanchthon explained that after repentance and mortification of the flesh the believer is renewed by the Holy Spirit to overcome the powers of sin and to live to God.[203] "Those on whom the Holy Spirit has been poured out have in them a sense of God, a trust in God, and the love of God."[204] He tied his idea of renewal directly to satisfying the law:

> Paul says that the righteousness of the law is not fulfilled except in those who live according to the Spirit. Therefore, those who are not filled with the Holy Spirit do not satisfy the law. But not to do the law, what else is that than to sin? For, indeed, every motion and impulse of the mind against the law is sin.[205]

Melanchthon said that the Holy Spirit enables justified believers to follow the way of the Spirit in penitence. Those whose terrified hearts have fled from sin to receive forgiveness cannot continue in lustful living. The Holy Spirit gives new spiritual impulses to lead the believers' battle to

---

200. *StA* 4:196, 17–18 and 190, 5–6; *Matthew* (1519–20); Rogness, *Reformer*, 36–38.

201. *CR* 22, 373–74; *MLC55 Loci*, 177; almost forty years later, Melanchthon's treatment on good works is in substantial agreement with his earlier work.

202. Rogness, *Reformer*, 43–44, citing 1521 *Loci*; *CR* 21, 128, 26 and 130, 25–26.

203. *CR* 21, 215–17 (*MLC21* 140–41); *CR* 21, 103–6 (*MLC21* 37–39); Maxcey, *Bona Opera*, 127, explains Melanchthon in the 1535 *Loci*, "Once the Holy Spirit is received a new life, a whole new attitude is begun, and this *renovatio* is called regeneration. Consequently, 'a new obedience ought to follow,'" citing *CR* 21, 428.

204. *CR* 21, 106, 21–22 (*MLC21* 39), "in quos spiritus sanctus effusus est, in iis est sensus dei, fiducia in deum, amor dei." Rom 8:5, *Romans Commentary* (1532).

205. *CR* 21, 106, b19–21 (*MLC21*, 39), "Paulus non impleri iustificationem legis, nisi in iis qui secundum spiritum sunt. Ergo qui non sunt perfusi spiritu sancto, non satisfaciunt legi. At legem non facere, quid aliud est quam peccare? Siquidem peccatum est omnis motus et impulsus animi adversus legem."

suppress and destroy feelings of distrust in God and trust in the temporal.[206] Thus the Holy Spirit releases people from the law to motivate the new life in the Spirit. Melanchthon emphasized Paul's teaching in Rom 7 that the Holy Spirit is necessary to provide discernment and faith, to console fearful hearts, to inspire true prayer, and to work true fear of God. Without true faith in Christ and without the Holy Spirit, religious activity is merely imitation spirituality. The Holy Spirit brings believers to true spirituality:

> The Spirit shows . . . the true fear of God and true faith, which are received in true consolation with, of course, hearts in terror which edify themselves by the promise of the gospel and take hold of mercy according to the promise of Christ: at that time when they know mercy they begin to truly entreat God, and truly to expect help from him, to truly love, etc. These emotions are true religion and the new obedience, about which he speaks. And they are motivated by the Holy Spirit who is received by this consolation. Accordingly, Paul says in Galatians 3, so that we may receive the promised Spirit through faith. Therefore the Spirit and the letter are discerned. "The Spirit" indicates lively emotional activity from the Holy Spirit. The letter signifies true understanding, propositions, and imitations without the true emotions of the heart: and so the letter pertains to discipline.[207]

Melanchthon understood that the Holy Spirit works in the intellects of believers to motivate them to turn from fleshly desires to the life of trust, faith, and prayer to be released from their terrors.

Assurance and the Inner Testimony of the Holy Spirit

Drawing from Rom 8:15–16, Melanchthon said the Spirit works confidence in believers to trust in God.

---

206. *BSLK*, 187–95, 136–71; *Tappert*, 126:30, 136:71; *Apology*, Article. IV, Justification.

207. *CR* 15:646, "*Spiritus significat . . . verum timorem Dei et veram fiduciam, quae concipiuntur in vera consolatione, cum scilicet corda in terroribus erigunt se promissione Evangelii, et apprehendunt misericordiam, propter Christum promissam: Ibi cum agnoscunt misericordiam, incipiunt vere invocare Deum, et vere expectare ab eo auxilium, vere diligere etc. Hi motus sunt veri cultus et nova obedientia, de qua hic loquitur. Et sunt excitati a Spiritu sancto, qui in illa consolatione, cum fide erigimur, concipitur. Sicut inquit Paulu Gal. 3: Ut promissionem spiritus accipiamus per fidem. Sic igitur discernuntur Spiritus et Litera. Spiritus significat vivos motus excitatos a Spiritus sancto. Litera vero cogitationes, intentiones, proposita et imitationes sine vero motu cordis: et tamen litera ad disciplinam pertinet,*" Rom 6, Romans Commentary (1532).

> So long as the conscience is without faith, in panic-stricken hopelessness, it flees God, it doubts, or it may listen clearly, or it may look for help, etc. It does not call upon God. Therefore Paul joins comfort and prayer together, and features only these which already have been established through the gospel by faith. For of these he says: We cry aloud Abba Father, this shows that already we know God to be father and to truly listen to us, and by this faith we receive comfort and call upon God. Regarding this faith and knowledge of the merciful heart of God he makes proper distinction between the Christians and the godless, because the godless maintain doubt and indignant opposition to God. But in believing faith is a new awareness of the merciful heart of God, and it repudiates unbelief and positions us to be heard according to Christ. This faith itself is comfort and life-giving and the testimony of the Holy Spirit in the heart, about which he said: The Spirit gives testimony to our spirits, that is, through the word of the gospel, the Holy Spirit gives comfort in true hopelessness.[208]

Melanchthon equated the testimony of the Holy Spirit with faith. While not explicitly saying it is the assurance of being a child of God, it is the believer's experience of comfort and assurance which the Holy Spirit gives a child of the heavenly Father in the midst of hopelessness. The certitude of salvation is found not merely in trusting, but in the object of one's trust—the promises of the word of God.[209] This can be equated to Luther's understanding of the inner testimony of the Holy Spirit.

The Spirit and the Flesh

Melanchthon viewed the Christian life as an internal struggle between the flesh and the indwelling Holy Spirit. After the fall, the Holy Spirit was no

---

208. CR 15:667, "*Donec conscientia sine fide est, in pavoribus desperabunda, fugit Deum, dubitat, an exaudiat, an respiciat etc. Non invocat Deum. Ideo Paulus consolationem et invocationem coniungit, et tantum his tribuit, qui iam per Evangelium fide eriguntur. Nam cum ait: Clamamus Abba Pater, hoc significat, Iam agnoscimus Deum esse patrem, et vere nos exaudire, et hac fide concipimus consolationem, et invocamus Deum.*""*Haec fides et agnitio misericordiae Dei facit proprie discrimen inter Christianos et impios, quia in impiis manent dubitatio et indignatio adversus Deum. Sed in credentibus fides est nova agnitio misericordiae Dei, et repugnat dubitationi, et statuit nos vere propter Christum exaudiri, Haec ipsa fides est consolatio et vivificatio, et testimonium Spiritus sancti in cordibus, de quo hic loquitur: Spiritus dat testimonium spiritui nostro, id est, Spiritus sanctus per verbum Evangelii efficit consolationem in veris pavoribus,*" Romans 8:15–16, *Commentary on Romans* (1532); cf. MLC43, "Holy Spirit," 28–32.

209. Wengert, *Melanchthon's* Annotationes in Johannem, 152–53 (John 15:7–9).

longer the ever-present guide within man,²¹⁰ but deep-seated "affections" tyrannically controlled the human will and reason with a strong self-love opposed to God. As a humanist, Melanchthon looked at man as a free agent regarding external acts, but as a Christian, he understood that in God's view of his inward "affections" man was not free at all,²¹¹ and could not contribute to his own justification. The Holy Spirit alters these "affections" when one comes to faith by a struggle between the flesh (human will, reason, and affections) and the Spirit. Melanchthon described his view of this struggle:

> As long as we do not will to follow . . . evil tendencies with action, but painfully strive against them and believe that these sins are forgiven for the sake of *Christ* . . . we remain holy; and the Holy Spirit is in us, ruling us, and giving light and strength to our hearts, to strive against the sins, as Joseph through the Holy Spirit strove against adultery.
>
> Significantly, St. Paul says that we are to slay the activities of the flesh through the Holy Spirit.²¹²

Melanchthon maintained that the Holy Spirit does not remain in a person who has committed a mortal sin but guards the "choices" of believers against such failings.²¹³

Melanchthon told the Saxon churches how God uses Law and Gospel to bring people through fear of judgment, repentance, justification, and fruit of the Spirit. The indwelling Holy Spirit overcomes their "affections" to release believers and to enable them to obey the law and to produce the fruit of the Spirit.²¹⁴

---

210. *StA* 2:9-11, 13, 17-18, 21, 38, 1521 *Loci*; Rogness, *Reformer*, 12-14.

211. Hägglund, *History of Theology*, 249.

212. CR 22, 383-84, MLC55, 184, "Aber dieweil die Heiligen Geist . . . bösen neigungen nicht volgen mit williger that, sondern haben schmerßen und widerstreben inen, und gleuben, das inen die sünde verben sind, umb des Herrn Christi willen . . . bleiben sie heilig, und ist in inen der Heilige Geist, der herrchet und gibet dem hertzen liecht und stercke, den sünden zu widerstreben, wie Joseph durch den heiligen Geist dem Chebruch widerstrebet.

Und spricht S. Paulus deutlich, Wir sollen die wirckungen des fleisches tödten durch den Heiligen Geist."

213. Wengert, *Law and Gospel*, 203, citing CR 2:749-50.

214. CR 26:7-8, 49; Melanchthon, *Visitation Articles* (1527-28); Rogness, *Reformer*, 57.

Responses to the Holy Spirit

Prayer

After years of opposition and struggle Melanchthon acknowledged the strength of evil in the world to undermine the work of the Reformation. He finally rejected "any attempts to enter into the labyrinths of disputations where one becomes prey for the devil's machinations." Instead he instructed believers to turn to God in prayer.[215]

Melanchthon often prayed to be formed by God into a "vessel of mercy" (Rom 9:23). Fearing the future, his prayers and letters revealed doubts about human possibilities, including his own. However, his prayers had strong connections to the Bible, containing quotes from Scripture invoking biblical promises, and making comparisons with situations reported in the Bible.[216]

While Melanchthon's prayers often repeated certain forms, he also freely addressed specific situations requiring prayer. Martin Jung noted that, throughout Melanchthon's ministry, "The words of prayer in the letters were addressed to the first or second person of the Godhead, while the Holy Spirit was not directly worshiped. . . . A revealing breakdown can be observed. When prayer concerned preservation and guidance in general, Melanchthon usually turned to God the Father. But when it concerned averting specific dangers, Jesus Christ was invoked as mediator and advocate because, from Melanchthon's point of view, it was God the Father himself who, as the omnipotent ruler of history, also caused dangers and disasters. In praying to the *Deus revelatus*, Melanchthon sought protection from the *Deus absconditus*."[217]

Melanchthon taught that the Holy Spirit is necessary to strengthen the weaknesses of the heart. God helps us in our afflictions so our faith and hope will not fail:

> Seek and you will receive, in a great measure your Father will give the Holy Spirit to those asking: Come to me all who labor: I will not leave you orphans: I will ask the Father and he will give you another Counselor, so that he may remain forever. However, how is the Holy Spirit given and in what manner is he put into effect? I answer: When we persevere by the word in the times of opposition, and we call out to God. . . . When I cried out, the God of my righteousness listened to me. And

---

215. CR 15:997-98.
216. Jung, *Frömmigkeit*, 108.
217. Jung, *Frömmigkeit*, 108.

Christ said concerning prayer: He will give the Holy Spirit to those asking. . . .

In danger, persecution, death, and other afflictions, and also physical or spiritual hardships, the natural disposition hardly submits, or steadfastly desires to drive them away. For that reason Paul says: We do not know what we should speak, namely, when with natural weakness we entreat steadfastly to be freed, and bear the cross impatiently. Meanwhile, nevertheless, the Holy Spirit makes it possible that to some extent we may obey and pray. Paul calls this obedience and prayer inexpressible sighs. For by the Spirit we subject ourselves under God, and in like manner we petition the will of God for freedom, not according to fleshly desire.

"Now Paul speaks of true and intense struggle, not of cold and idle thoughts, therefore these things cannot be understood with human capabilities, but each in his own way, in his own temptations, ought in some measure to experience the power of God's consolation when praying for it. For nothing greater can be promised than the presence and efficacy of God; for this is promised when it is promised by the Holy Spirit."[218]

Melanchthon portrayed how the Spirit helps believers call out to God from their hopeless human weaknesses. God answers with the motivating power of the present and active Holy Spirit. Manschreck shows Melanchthon's attitude about prayer and the Holy Spirit in the prayer he spoke on the day he died:

---

218. CR 15:673–74, "*Petite, et accipietis, quanto magis pater vester daturus est Spiritum sanctum petentibus: Venite ad me omnes qui laboratis: Non relinquam vos orphanos: Rogabo patrem, et alium paracletum dabit vobis, ut maneat vobiscum in aeternum.*""*Quomodo autem datur Spiritus Sanctus, et quomodo est efficax? Respondeo: Cum sustentamus nos verbo in ipsis certaminibus, et invocamus Deum. . . . Cum invocarem, exaudivit me Deus iusticiae meae. Et Christus inquit de invocatione: Dabit Spiritum sanctum petentibus.*""*In periculis, persecutione, morte, et quibuscunque afflictionibus, ac aerumnis corporalibus aut spiritualibus, natura aegre obtemperat, ac statim eas excutere cupit. Ideo Paulus inquit: Nescimus quid oremus, scilicet, cum naturali imbecillitate petimus nos statim liberari, et impatienter ferimus crucem. Interea tamen Spiritus Sanctus efficit, ut aliqua ex parte obediamus et invocemus. Hanc obedientiam et invocationem vocat Paulus gemitus inenarrabiles. Spiritu enim subiicimus nos Deo, et iuxta voluntatem Dei petimus liberationem, non iuxta carnale desiderium.*""*Loquitur autem Paulus de vera et ingenti lucta in believers, non de frigidis et otiosis cogitationibus Ideo haec a securis non possunt intelligi, sed singuli pro suo modo in suis tentationibus, aliqua ex parte experiri debebant in invocatione vim huius consolationis. Nihil enim maius promitti potest, quam praesentia et efficacia Dei: haec enim promittitur, cum promittitur Spiritus Sanctus.*" Rom 8:26, Romans Commentary (1532).

> Sanctify me with thy holy, living Spirit of purity and truth that through thy Spirit I may truly know thee as the only God, the omnipotent Creator of heaven and earth and men, the Father of our Lord Jesus Christ; that I may know thy beloved Son, thy Word and Image; that I may know thy Holy Spirit of truth and purity, my living Comforter; that I may firmly believe in thee.... Purify and unite us with thy Holy Spirit that we may be one in thee.... Through thy Holy Spirit increase in me the light of faith, help me to overcome my weakness....
>
> Almighty, Holy Spirit of truth and purity, our living Comforter, enlighten me, direct me, and sanctify me. Strengthen the faith in my soul and heart, and grant me a sincere trust. Sustain and guide me that I may dwell in the house of the Lord all the days of my life, that I may see the will of the Lord, that I may forever be in God's holy temple, and with a joyous heart give thanks unto him and in the assembly of his eternal church and praise him forever. Amen.[219]

In his last prayer to the Triune God, Melanchthon modeled his understanding of the Holy Spirit and of prayer and demonstrated his trust in the Holy Spirit for sanctification, enlightenment, and comfort.

Worship

Melanchthon addressed worship in his discussion of The Mass in the Apology. He used the term "ceremonies" to represent the living aspect of the service whereby people may learn the Scriptures, be admonished by the word, experience faith, and, as a result, enter into prayer.[220] This is similar to Luther's concept of the theology of reality.

Sacraments are elements of the mass, as Melanchthon defined and described:

> A sacrament is a ceremony or work in which God presents to us what the promise joined to the ceremony offers. Thus baptism is not a work that we offer to God, but one in which God, through a minister who functions in his place, baptizes us and offers and presents the forgiveness of sin, etc., according to the promise (Mark 16:6), "The one who believes and is baptized will be saved."[221]

---

219. Manschreck, *Quiet Reformer*, 317.
220. BC, 258.
221. BC, 260–61.

Melanchthon explained that this ministry is the work of the Holy Spirit, who works in people's hearts through the gospel and the sacraments to give them faith, new birth, and life.[222] This work of the Spirit brings about inner peace among the faithful that results in what Peter called sacrifices of praise and thanksgiving (1 Pet 2: 5) and Paul called "a living sacrifice" and "spiritual worship (Rom 12:1)." This "refers to the work of the Holy Spirit within us," when we "worship where God is recognized and grasped by the mind, as happens when it fears and trusts God."[223] Melanchthon called these sacrifices of praise, or "eucharistic sacrifices." They included preaching of the gospel, faith, prayer, thanksgiving, confession, afflictions of the saints, and all the good works of the saints. These are the sacrifices of praise performed by those already reconciled.[224]

Melanchthon considered Old Testament worship analogous to the proclamation of the gospel with the different elements depicting Christ's New Testament sacrifice and worship. For example:

> The drink offering signifies the sprinkling (that is, the sanctifying) of believers throughout the world with the blood of the lamb through the proclamation of the gospel, just as Peter says (1 Pet 1:2), "... sanctified by the Spirit to be obedient to Jesus Christ and to be sprinkled with his blood."[225]
>
> Although the ceremony (the rite of the Mass) is a memorial of Christ's death, nevertheless in itself it is not a daily sacrifice. Instead, the ... real daily sacrifice, that is, proclamation and faith that truly believes God is reconciled by the death of Christ. A drink offering is required, namely, the effect of the proclamation, that through the gospel as we are sanctified by the blood of Christ having been put to death and made alive. Offerings are also required, that is, thanksgiving, confession, and affliction....
>
> Let us understand that spiritual worship and the daily sacrifice of the heart are signified here, because in the New Testament we must consider "the body" of good things (cf. Co. 2:17), that is, the Holy Spirit, being put to death, and being made alive.[226]

222. *BC*, 269.
223. *BC*, 262.
224. *BC*, 262.
225. *BC*, 265.
226. *BC*, 266, 38–39; *BSLK*, 361, 38–39. (Here, Arand's translation follows the Latin of *BSLK*.) *Quare etiamsi ceremonia est memoriale mortis Christi, tamen sola non est iuge sacrificium, sed ipsa memoria est iuge sacrificium ... ut per evangelium aspersi*

Through the gospel in worship, the Holy Spirit brings believers to the death of repentance and the life of forgiveness and renewal. This role of the gospel in worship is another glimpse of the theology of the cross in Melanchthon's theology.

Melanchthon's personal practice of worship was mentioned in his funeral eulogy,

> Jacob Herrbrand [a student of Melanchthon] noted that Melanchthon was anxious to frequent public worship, not only to set a good example, but because he knew that the Holy Spirit exercised his power through the Word of God and that the Son of God was present.[227]

Good Works

Melanchthon said the Holy Spirit renews people at justification for good works,[228] which flow out of them in sanctification.

> Good works are necessary . . . We are justified for this purpose, that . . . we might . . . do good works and obey God's law. For this purpose we are reborn and receive the Holy Spirit, that this new life might have new works and new impulses, the fear and love of God, hatred of lust, etc.[229]

Melanchthon relates good works, faith, and the power of the Holy Spirit.[230] Good works cannot be done without faith, but "good works should

---

sanguine Christi sanctificemur, mortificati. Requiruntur et oblationes, hoc est, gratiarum actiones, confessiones et afflictiones. . . significari cultum spiritualem et iuge sacrificium cordis, quia in novo testamento corpus bonorum, hoc est, Spiritus Sanctus, mortificatio et vivificatio requiri debent. Apology, Art. 24, "Mass."

227. Manschreck, *Quiet Reformer*, 310.

228. CR 21, 429, 762, 775–76; Maxcey, *Bona Opera*, 31, 53. Melanchthon saw good works as the natural response of one reborn to love, fear, please and entreat God, and to want to care for the neighbor, CR 27:447–48, *Apology*. This happens because the Holy Spirit has been received and has put new spiritual and holy inclinations in newborn hearts. When honest works are done without the Holy Spirit they are an affront against God. CR 27:433–34, *Apology*. Maxcey's major theme is the motivational enabling of the Holy Spirit.

229. Tappert, 160, 348; BSLK, 227, 348, "*Vero necesse est bene operari. . . . At nec fidem nec iustificatiam retinent illi, qui ambulant secundum carnem. Ideo iustificamur, ut iusti bene operari et obedire legi Dei incipiamus. Ideo regeneramur et spiritum sanctum accipimus, ut nova vita habeat nova opera, novos affectus, timorem, dilectionem Dei, odium concupiscentiae etc.*" *Apology*, Art. 4, "Justification."

230. BSLK, 81, 27–29; BC, 56, 27–39; *Augsburg Confession*, Art. 10, "Concerning

and must be done... for God's sake and to God's praise."²³¹ The Holy Spirit is given through faith; the heart is also moved to do good works.²³² The Holy Spirit gives God's power to do good works in his love.²³³ Works show the righteousness of the heart and faith, and their fruit.²³⁴

There is a progression of Melanchthon's thoughts on good works. The Holy Spirit enables Christians to speak the necessary words.²³⁵ "I understand work as accomplished by the Holy Spirit in us."²³⁶ "When 'the Holy Spirit is given' a new spiritual and moral life is begun."²³⁷ The Holy Spirit becomes a good conscience by which renewed people do good works.²³⁸ "Man's righteousness is that new obedience which the Holy Spirit affects in us through charity and other virtues."²³⁹

In the *Apology* Melanchthon said God commanded good works to exercise faith. Though the partly unregenerate flesh may foul the works motivated by the Spirit, since they are done in faith, they are holy and divine sacrifices through which Christ reigns and shows his rule before the world. By "these works he sanctifies hearts and suppresses the devil.... that the knowledge of God might not perish utterly from the earth."²⁴⁰ The sacrificial ministry of biblical saints and the fathers are God's defense of his people against the devil. Melanchthon saw this as Christian vocation. The work of the Holy Spirit accomplishes obedience to the command of God,

---

Faith and Good Works."

231. BC, 56, 27; BSLK, 80, 27, "Gute Werke sollen und müssen geschehen... sondern um Gottes willen und Gott zu Lob"; (note: Following Eric Gritsch in BC, the German text of the *Augsburg Confession*, the 1531 *editio princeps*, is considered the more official one, BC, 24) *Augsburg Confession*, Art. 10, "Concerning Faith and Good Works."

232. BSLK, 80, 29; BC, 56, 29, "Durch den Glauben der heilige Geist geben wird, so wird auch das gherz geschickt, gute Werk zu tun," *Augsburg Confession*, Article XX, Faith.

233. BSLK, 187, 136; BC, 142, 136.

234. BSLK, 230, 375; Tappert, 164, 375, *Augsburg Confession*, Article IV, Justification.

235. CR 14:837, *Commentary on Matthew*.

236. CR 2:502, "Intellego opus factum a Spiritu Sancto in nobis," *Epist.* No. 935, I, Brentius (May 1531); Maxcey, *Bona Opera*, 69.

237. CR 21, 290, 36b, "Praeterea cum datur spiritus sanctus concipimus novos et pios motus," *Loci* (1533); Maxcey, *Bona Opera*, 102.

238. CR 21, 775-76; MLC43, 103-4; Maxcey, *Bona Opera*, 200; Wengert, *Law and Gospel*, 201, citing CR 2:723.

239. CR 8:195, "Hominem esse iustum novitiate, id est, illa obedientia, quam efficit spiritus sanctus in hominibus dilectione et omnibus virtutibus," *Epistolarum* No. 5520, *Iudicum*, (1553); Maxcey, *Bona Opera*, 189.

240. Tappert, 133, 189, 191; BSLK, 197-98, 189, 191, "His enim sanctificat corda et reprimit diabolum... ne penitus extingueretur notitia Dei in terries"; *Apology*, Art. 4, "Justification."

sanctification, and defeat of the devil. Melanchthon added that these works earn rewards in this life and the next. Faith and the works of love issuing from it are the Spirit's works as he frees us from death and gives us comfort.

Summary and Conclusions

The Holy Spirit is the living, dynamic will of God in Philip Melanchthon's theology. The law takes a central position in Melanchthon's theology because he defines the law as the will of God. This will of God cannot be fulfilled by any human enterprise. Only with the Holy Spirit's power can the law be fulfilled. In the context of many different issues Melanchthon emphasized this role of the Holy Spirit, repeating that "when we have been regenerated by the Spirit of God, . . . we now will do spontaneously that very thing which the law used to demand."[241]

His humanistic educational background permeated the framework of his thinking, but Melanchthon rejected the tenants of scholasticism. His contribution to Lutheran theology and German education was greatly enhanced by his emphasis on thoroughly mastering languages and classic learning. "*Knowledge*" is a key word in his writings. (A word count of this chapter is convincing.) This could suggest that Melanchthon was always studious, objective, and serious-minded. Although he was a respected intellectual, he wrote with passion, often describing the Holy Spirit in emotional terms such as the "Spirit can inflame the heart."[242]

Luther's theology of the cross is not specifically featured by Melanchthon using this title, but the elements of dying and coming alive by the work of the Holy Spirit are found throughout his writings, including the same terror of the miserable sinner that Luther experienced and described. The Spirit, through the law, terrorizes unbelievers and puts them to death so that through the gospel they may experience new life through faith in Christ. Melanchthon saw the believer coming through the sufferings of the cross to the joy on the other side manifested by a new relationship with the law and with God.

Melanchthon stood with Luther in linking the giving of the Holy Spirit with justification, which comes through the word of Law and Gospel in preaching the Scriptures and in forgiveness through Baptism and the Lord's Supper. For Melanchthon, then, the Holy Spirit is experienced through the means of the word and sacraments consistent with Luther's theology.

---

241. Pauck, *MLC21*, 123.
242. *CR* 21, 208, 15–23; *MLC21*, 133.

PHILIP MELANCHTHON'S THEOLOGY OF THE HOLY SPIRIT

While Melanchthon defended Reformation theology with brilliant logic and argument, he did not view theology as sterile or lifeless. His theology was not limited to ideas but embraced everyday reality. He saw the dynamic work of the Holy Spirit making truth come alive. "The Holy Spirit penetrates the inner being... for ascertaining truth."[243] He said the Holy Spirit is necessary to provide discernment and faith, to console fearful hearts, to inspire true prayer, and to work true fear of God. Without true faith in Christ and without the Holy Spirit, religious activity is merely imitation spirituality. The Holy Spirit brings believers to true spirituality. These emotions are true religion.[244]

Melanchthon said true spirituality is life-giving and described it as awareness of the merciful heart of God and as comfort. "Each in his own way, in his own temptations, ought in some measure to experience the power of God's consolation."[245] He said this is the testimony of the Holy Spirit in the heart. The Spirit gives testimony to our spirits through the word of the gospel of comfort in hopelessness.[246] Luther called this the inner testimony of the Holy Spirit.

Luther and Melanchthon developed the Wittenberg theology in the midst of controversies between the Catholic Church and the Reformers and also among various groups of Reformers. They defended each other from false accusations and countless misrepresentations. Other Reformers, contemporary with Luther and Melanchthon, endorsed and adopted the Wittenberg theology and labored to spread and establish it in other German-speaking areas. Together, against opposition from princes and popes, in danger and in sacrifice, the Reformers struggled on, relying on the power of the Holy Spirit, to proclaim and defend Reformation truth.

---

243. *StA* 1:7 (translated in "Letter on the Leipzig Debate, 1519" in Hill, *Selected Writings*, 24).
244. *CR* 15:646.
245. *CR* 15:673–74.
246. *CR* 15:667.

4

The Early Reformers' Theology of the Holy Spirit

Johannes Brenz, Urbanus Rhegius, Johann Spangenberg

"Co-Workers in the Vineyard of the Lord"[1]

Introduction

Johannes Brenz, Urbanus Rhegius, and Johann Spangenberg were Lutheran pastors and theologians contemporary with Martin Luther and Philip Melanchthon. Luther and Melanchthon were centered in the University at Wittenberg. Brenz, Urbanus and Spangenberg represented other German–speaking regions with various cultural and linguistic differences and local clerical and civic challenges. Their theologies of the Holy Spirit are examined here and compared with the theologies of Luther and Melanchthon.

Background and Influences

Reformation theology was being formed primarily in Wittenberg, but the process of spreading its understanding and adoption was chaotic and

---

1. A well-known painting by Lucas Cranach the younger (1556) portrays the Roman Catholic hierarchy devastating the Lord's vineyard on one side of the picture and in contrast, the Reformers watering and cultivating the vineyard on the other side.

strongly opposed. The state of the Reformation in Germany was fragmented. The following Reformers labored to form Lutheran/evangelical unity in the face of Catholic power and pressure, theological confusion and confrontation, and regional wars.

Johannes Brenz (1499–1570)

Johannes Brenz was the Reformer of the imperial city of Schwäbisch Hall (1522–48). He was the chief architect who reorganized the Lutheran territorial church in the duchy of Württemberg, a church whose polity became the model for Protestant German-speaking regions and thus profoundly affected the history of the territorial church in that country until recent times.[2]

Brenz was born June 24, 1499, in the small imperial city of Weil der Stadt near Stuttgart, the capital city of Württemberg. As he matured, Brenz observed the management of a small municipality in touch with the business of the empire, and this influenced his career work of reorganizing the territorial church of Württemberg in its society and culture.[3] After Latin schools in Weil der Stadt, Heidelberg, and Vaihingen, Brenz completed his BA (1516) and MA (1518) at Heidelberg in preparation for theological studies in the arts faculty at Heidelberg. Brenz, with fellow student Martin Bucer, was strongly influenced by the Erasmian humanist faculty, especially Johannes Husschin (Oecolampadius), who had assisted Erasmus in preparation of his Greek New Testament.[4] As part of his humanist studies with Oecolampadius, Brenz became a *vir trilinguis* ("man of three languages"), competent in Latin, Greek and Hebrew, and earned the praises of Oecolampadius to Erasmus, "A young man ... who is as industrious as he is enthusiastic in all kinds of studies, and is your great admirer."[5] However, in April 1518, Brenz heard Luther, already famous for his *95 Theses*, at the Heidelberg Disputation. Though he was strongly affected by the influences of his humanist education, when, with Bucer and many other young scholars, he heard Luther at the Disputation his commitment was significantly changed. After the conference, Brenz spoke at length with Luther and

2. Estes, "Brenz, Johannes," 105; Estes, *Territorial*, 18.
3. Estes, *Territorial*, 21.
4. Burnett, "Oecolampadius," 559; Estes, "Brenz, Johannes," 105. Later, Bucer joined Oecolampadius with Zwingli against the team of Martin Luther, Philip Melanchthon, and Brenz. Even later, Bucer married Wibrandis (nee Rosenblatt), the widow of Ludwig Cellarius, Johannes Oecolampadius (married, 1528–31), and Wolfgang Capito (married, 1532–41)—Bucer being her fourth husband.
5. Estes, *Territorial*, 21, citing *Collected Works of Erasmus* 4:306, 46–48 (Oecolampadius to Erasmus, March 27, 1517).

became a lifelong advocate of Luther's position.[6] After receiving his MA, Brenz continued his studies in the theology faculty, and in 1520 was called as vicar of the Church of the Holy Spirit in Heidelberg, while still lecturing on the New Testament at the university.[7]

In 1522 the city council of the imperial city Schwäbisch Hall (Franconia)—following the recommendation of Johann Isenmann, a native of Hall and associated with Brenz at Heidelberg—appointed Brenz city preacher at St. Michael's Church.[8] Brenz abruptly left his doctoral studies in Heidelberg to assume the duties of this appointment.[9] In 1523, the city council appointed Isenmann pastor of St. Michael's, thus becoming Brenz's superior, though from the beginning Brenz clearly and smoothly assumed the greater role.[10]

Though larger than Weil der Stadt, Hall (about 5,000) was significantly smaller and less important than other imperial cities, e.g., Augsburg, Strassburg, or Nürnberg. It had a prosperous salt industry, a responsible city council, and the tradition of a town preachership at St. Michael's, the principal church. The preacher was to provide scholarly leadership to the clergy of the town.[11] Because there had been no Lutheran preaching in Hall before Brenz's appointment, the townspeople were accustomed to traditional Catholic usages. In the years 1522 to 1528 Brenz and Isenmann slowly combined Lutheran preaching and other practices with the older traditions while eliminating Catholic elements that conflicted with Lutheran teaching and practice. Since the city fathers grew in their support of Brenz's work, he proceeded to take holy orders to become a priest and celebrated his first mass at his home church in Weil der Stadt (1523). Later that year he celebrated a traditional mass in Hall without reference to it as a sacrifice. Brenz's exceptional preaching and his ability to influence public opinion enabled him to address issues of the old religion, e.g., the cult of the saints, and introduce new aspects, e.g., the Lutheran Reformation view of the church. In these ways Brenz and Isenmann won over the Hall city council to Lutheranism, and began to initiate the Reformation in the territory under Hall's

---

6. CR 3:22; Bossert, "Johann Brenz," 260; Estes, *Territorial*, 22; Merle d'Aubigné, *History of the Reformation*, 119–20.
7. Estes, *Territorial*, 22.
8. Estes, "Brenz, Johannes," 105.
9. Estes, *Territorial*, 22.
10. Estes, *Territorial*, 23.
11. Estes, *Territorial*, 23–24.

THE EARLY REFORMERS' THEOLOGY OF THE HOLY SPIRIT

jurisdiction.[12] About that time (≈ 1523) Brenz married Margaretha Graeter, who bore him three children.[13]

Until his final departure from Hall in 1548, Brenz developed his theological and ecclesial ministry with Reformation support from the council of Hall, the dukes of Württemberg in Stuttgart-Ulrich and Christian in Stuttgart-and George, the Franconian Margrave of Brandenburg-Ansbach-Kulmbach. The geographical location of Hall in western Franconia, in the midst of these above mentioned principalities, facilitated the productivity of Brenz's establishment of the Reformation in the regions where he broadly and loyally served until his death.

In 1524 the Reformation broke through in Hall. Brenz defeated the local Franciscans, his strongest opposition, in a disputation arranged by the city council. Soon, the friars relinquished their cloister, which became a school. Brenz and Isenmann convinced their congregation to abolish the popular feast of Corpus Christi, because it was inconsistent with Lutheran sacramental doctrine. Most importantly, the council legislated against practices that violated Reformation principles. They abolished clergy privileges and required priests and pastors to live as ordinary citizens: paying taxes, bearing normal responsibilities of property ownership, permitted to marry, and forbidden to keep concubines. The council banished from Hall a priest who opposed Brenz, denounced his teaching, and started a brawl at the church.[14]

In the spring and summer of 1525 Brenz opposed the Peasants' Revolt in his commentary on the Twelve Articles of the Peasants, written for the Elector Ludwig of the Palatinate. Brenz was sympathetic with many of the peasants' demands, while condemning as unchristian their use of rebellion against legitimate authority. After the peasants' defeat, Brenz urged the victorious governments to be lenient with them.[15] By the end of 1526 after the Peasants' Revolt subsided, the first phase of the Reformation in Hall was completed. Brenz led the Reformation to Swabia and the surrounding area. At that time Brenz officiated at the first fully Lutheran celebration of the Lord's Supper at St. Michael's. By then the doctrines, ceremonies, catechisms, church organization, and staff at Hall's main churches were also thoroughly Lutheran. Mass continued to be celebrated in St. John's Church and in St. Mary's Chapel because they were not under the patronage of the city council.[16]

12. Estes, *Territorial*, 23.
13. Google Genealogy.
14. Estes, *Territorial*, 24; *CRR3*, 22; Bossert, "Brenz," 260.
15. Estes, *Territorial*, 29.
16. Estes, *Territorial*, 24–25.

In early 1527 Brenz presented a plan to the city council to address the remaining problems in Schwäbisch Hall and its rural territory. He requested the replacement of the mass in the territory by the ceremonies already adopted at St. Michael's. He proposed qualified clergymen for the rural parishes, an ecclesiastical court for moral discipline, support for the poor, and changes in marriage law. Regarding schools, Brenz followed Luther's ideas of free public schools to provide instruction in German to boys for manual trades, and advanced instruction in Latin for subsequent university study and professional careers. Also, from Luther he proposed that girls be taught reading and writing, "For Scripture belongs not to men alone, but to women as well."[17] The church order in rural areas and for the entire region was completed by 1543. Brenz supported the Wittenberg Lutherans at conferences between Protestants and Catholics, most notably on the Lord's Supper. He also prepared catechism materials, postils, and Bible commentaries.[18]

James Estes noted that the above well-thought-out plan for reformation lacked two functions. 1.) A detailed plan for the agency or office of church government. 2.) A plan for meeting the church's financial needs, such as Brenz's idea, two years earlier, that requested church income be gathered into a central church treasury and used strictly for ecclesiastical and charitable purposes. More detailed proposals would come a few years later, but Brenz had requested more than he was able to get. The controversial morals court proposal had to be dropped. The city council finally ended Mass at St. John's and St. Mary's in 1534. The reform of the rural parishes had to be postponed, partially because some were under the control of local nobles who opposed the Reformation. The city council did not feel strong enough to enforce its will on the rural pastors over the opposition of the Catholic patrons and the emperor. Brenz, familiar with the village politics of Weil, deferred to the judgment of the city fathers in such matters.[19] In dealing with patrons supporting priests in local or rural churches, Brenz scrupulously regarded the legal rights of the patrons and the priests appointed by them, even if Catholic. Brenz recommended that the city council bear the expense for a special Reformation-oriented pastor should the peasant congregation request the sacrament in the evangelical manner.[20] From 1529 the city council tried unsuccessfully to force the rural clergy to follow the Hall church order. When Hall entered the League of Smalcalden in 1540

---

17. Estes, *Territorial*, 23–25; See also Luther, "To the Councilmen of all Cities in Germany" (1524); *WA* 15:27–53; *LW* 45:347–78.
18. Estes, "Brenz, Johannes," 105.
19. Estes, *Territorial*, 26.
20. Estes, *Territorial*, 27.

the council was free to order all pastors to conform to the ceremonies used in the city churches. Church vacancies were filled with Lutheran pastors. By the fall of 1542 the Hall city council finished its last parish acquisition and appointed a new pastor and the old rural organization became a central church government. Estes summarized the results: "In 1543 a new church order for the city and territory was published. These measures brought to long-postponed fruition Brenz's efforts to give the Hall territory a uniform ecclesiastical constitution."[21]

As early as 1525, Brenz was already responding to requests of advice and assistance to address problems beyond Schwäbisch Hall. In September of 1525, Johannes Oecolampadius, now a professor in Basel, tried to draw the pastors near Schwäbisch Hall to the Zwinglian view of the sacrament—most of whom he had known at Heidelberg. Brenz, unequivocally on Luther's side, opposed his revered mentor with his *Syngramma Suevicum*, called the "Book of the Swabians," as reported Estes.[22] In October 1525, the *Syngramma* was signed in Hall by thirteen Swäbian/Franconian region pastors. Widely circulated in Latin and German translations, hailed by Luther and deplored by Zwingli, the *Syngramma* opened Brenz's campaign to keep the southwest German reform movement Lutheran. Brenz was recognized as the leader of the Reformation in the area, and in 1529 was appointed to be the principal counsel regarding theology and church order by Margrave George of Brandenburg, Margrave of Brandenburg-Ansbach-Kulmbach.[23] George was born in 1484 and died in 1543 at Onolzbach (Ansbach) in Middle Franconia, near Nuremburg.[24]

The controversy over the Lord's Supper was theological *and* political, since it threatened to weaken the united evangelical front against the powerful Catholics. In summer 1529, when Philip of Hesse, trying to reconcile the evangelical factions, planned the Marburg Colloquy (October 1529), Margrave George recommended Brenz—admirable, learned, and irenic—to be among the Lutherans invited. Although Brenz was not in the debate, his careful notes are the principal record of what happened.[25] Brenz's presence

---

21. Estes, *Territorial*, 28–29.

22. Estes, *Territorial*, 29–30. In an email to F. Hall on October 21, 2022, Robert Kolb comments "I think that "Syngramma"—something "together-written" literally—was a term for a summary statement or a treatise that pulls together a topic, and "Suevicum" is "Swabian." So it is the Swabian declaration of faith in regard to the Lord's Supper above all against the "Swiss" confession of Oecolampadius and Zwingli. It is really a very important document."

23. Estes, "Brenz, Johannes," 105; Estes, *Territorial*, 30.

24. Erdmann, "George of Brandenburg," 457a.

25. Estes, "Brenz, Johannes," 105. At Marburg, in October 1529, Brenz and

at Marburg underlined his role in Margrave George's ecclesiastical politics. In this role from 1529–33 Brenz provided the margrave advice on such items as armed resistance to the emperor and the treatment of Anabaptists. In 1530 Margrave George, Brenz, and Andreas Osiander attended the Diet of Augsburg for important behind-the-scenes negotiations with the Catholics. In 1531–32, they assisted in the preparation of the Brandenburg-Nürnberg Common Church Order, along with Brenz's memoranda for ecclesiastical administration (1533).[26]

In 1534, Duke Ulrich of Württemberg sought to introduce the Reformation into Württemberg.[27] The task was complex because the existing clergy contained a mix of loyalties to the Augsburg Confession (Lutheran), Zwingli, and Roman Catholic traditions. Ulrich, under his patron, Landgrave Philip of Hesse, "attempted to reconcile the confessions at the Marburg Colloquy (1529) and continued to tolerate the adherents of various theological tendencies in his own lands... [an] experiment in confessional coexistence."[28] The attempt proved to be unhappy and unsuccessful. Clearly the institution of uniform theology, ceremonies, and institutions was needed for the new territorial church that the existing divided and disagreeing clergy could not produce. So, considering Brenz's established reputation in matters of ecclesiastical organization, Ulrich requested him to assist in finishing the work. At completion (Summer 1535) it included Catholic traditions (Latin, and priestly garments), adoption of the Augsburg Confession as the official confession of the Württemberg Church, and the use of Brenz's catechism, giving the Church a solid Lutheran basis. The new Württemberg church order was inaugurated in 1536.[29] Next, Ulrich, with the recommendation of Philip Melanchthon, enlisted Brenz to complete the reorganization of the University of Tübingen along the lines of the Reformation. From April 1537 to April 1538, Brenz with his friend Joachim Camerarius, produced a new set of statutes, enlisted an evangelical faculty, and provided his lectures, which Estes called "a treasury of conservative Lutheran views on all issues in dispute with the Zwinglian-Swiss branch of

---

Melanchthon, while refusing to associate with the Zwinglians, tried to work out agreements which concurred with the ancient faith.

26. Estes, "Brenz, Johannes," 105; Estes, *Territorial*, 30.

27. Estes, *Territorial*, 31–32. In 1524–25, after a wayward life of early youth, Ulrich had adopted the evangelical faith and was a faithful supporter of the Reformation thereafter. Estes briefly summarizes the theo-political skullduggery of Ulrich's development and the reacquisition of his lost duchy of Württemberg.

28. Estes, *Territorial*, 33.

29. Estes, *Territorial*, 34.

the Reformation."[30] Regardless of the successful work by Brenz and his team in Württemberg and at Tübingen, however, Ulrich's experiment with "confessional harmony" was disintegrating with ongoing differences of opinions between Lutherans and Zwinglians. So, in 1538, Ulrich released the Zwinglians, and, as Estes reported, "Brenz's quiet persuasive advocacy of Lutheranism probably counted for something as well," as "Württemberg became an unequivocally Lutheran principality."[31] During these times of serving the Reformation in Württemberg and for several years following (until 1548) Brenz continued to loyally serve the congregation in Schwäbisch Hall. In 1543 the city council generously made him town preacher for life. That same year Brenz declined attractive calls from the universities of Leipzig, Tübingen, and Strasbourg.[32] Gustaf Bossert noted, "He devoted himself with great zeal to his pastoral duties, and side by side with his sermons was evolved a valuable series of expositions of Biblical writings."[33]

During those years Brenz was involved with many Reformation activities in the region. With Andreas Osiander, Brenz attended conferences at Smalcald (with Luther) (1537), Urach (1537), Hagenau (1540), Worms (1540), and Regensburg (1546).[34] The Smalcaldic alliance of Evangelical (Lutheran) princes, cities, and territories intended to defend themselves against Emperor Charles V, the imperial organization, and other Catholic princes of the empire.[35] From that time until the Smalcald War (July 1546–April 1547), Brenz became ever more wary of the hostilities of Charles V and the Catholics, and ever more committed to the Lutheran theology of his city and parish at Schwäbisch Hall.[36] Brenz opposed the soldiers of Charles when they captured the city, December 16, 1546, and fled while they captured and destroyed his papers, letters, and sermons. He returned to the city and his pulpit January 4, 1547,[37] and remained until the end of the war. In late 1547–48 Benz received additional attractive offers: a renewal from the University of Leipzig, a canonry in Feuchtwangen, and a call to join Bucer in Stassburg. He declined them all to care for his dear parish in Hall.[38] Soon, the imperial diet at Augs-

---

30. Estes, *Territorial*, 35.
31. Estes, *Territorial*, 35.
32. Estes, *Territorial*, 37; Bossert, "Brenz," 260.
33. Estes, *Territorial*, 37.
34. Estes, *Territorial*, 37.
35. Halvorson, "Smalcald War," 690.
36. Bossert, "Brenz," 260.
37. Bossert, "Brenz," 261; Estes, *Territorial*, 36.
38. Estes, *Territorial*, 36.

burg, menaced by Charles, approved the Augsburg Interim. Estes described the impact upon Johannes Brenz, his city, and his parish:

> [The Interim] . . . provided for the reimposition of Catholicism in all Protestant territories . . . valid until a general religious settlement at a church council. The Hall city council had no choice but to accept . . . and to endure . . . enforcement by the emperor's troops. But Brenz formally refused to abide by the provisions of what he called, punning on *Interim*, the *Interitus Germaniae*, the "ruination of Germany." On June 24, 1548, his 49th birthday, Brenz, given only a few minutes, . . . had to flee Schwäbische Hall, never to return.[39]

Brenz hastened to Ulrich, who also was endangered by Charles and his Interim and in danger of potential charges of being Lutheran under the Catholic Hapsburgers. Ulrich courageously hid Brenz in local ducal fortresses where he proceeded to write expositions on Pss 93 and 130. Ulrich soon whisked him away via Strassburg to Basel's friendly freedom, where he wrote an exposition on Isaiah.[40]

Ulrich's son and heir was Duke Christopher (1515–68), who for a period of his youth was raised in the court Charles V where he learned the ways of the Hapsburger Catholics. He had grown up in a Catholic environment and was heir to a Lutheran duchy. His father later appointed him to be regent where the leading theologian was Zwinglian. He had to decide among these diverse religious claims: Catholic, Lutheran, and Zwinglian. He studied representative works of each group. Estes described the result:

> Christopher emerged a convinced Lutheran with an unusually thorough and independent grasp of theological issues and a deep sense of his responsibility to foster the true faith among his subjects. He was, in brief, the perfect embodiment of Brenz's ideal of a Christian prince.[41]

When Brenz learned of his wife's death, he dared a risky rescue of his children, and Ulrich protected them for eighteen months in the castle Hornberg near Gutach, where Brenz went by the name of Huldrich Engster. He was active in the parish while theologically advising Ulrich. During this period (1548–51) Brenz, from loyalty to Ulrich and Christopher, declined calls from Magdeburg (high church office), Prussia (bishop), Denmark, and

---

39. Estes, *Territorial*, 36.
40. Bossert, "Brenz," 261; Estes, *Territorial*, 36.
41. Estes, *Territorial*, 38.

England (the deceased Bucer's chair at Cambridge) to remain serving the House of Württemberg.[42]

In August 1549, Brenz visited his friend, Isenmann, now pastoring in Urach, to counsel with Ulrich and his advisors concerning reestablishing Lutheran divine services. In the fall of 1550 Brenz married his second wife, Catherine, Isenmann's oldest daughter, who bore a daughter (1554).[43]

During the Interim in Württemberg Ulrich and his officials proceeded to introduce the required Catholic doctrines and services. Three to four hundred clergy were dismissed when they refused to abide by these requirements. There were not enough qualified replacement priests for the population, that was mainly loyal to the Reformation, and so Ulrich, advised by Brenz, rehired many of the dismissed as catechists or preachers to minister to the people without interfering with the Interim requirements. Brenz produced strategies to exploit the vague requirements of the Interim to defend their Reformation faith. As Estes assessed the situation, "It was a confused, unstable, and unhappy situation but not a hopeless one. Any serious weakening of the authority . . . imposed by the Interim would produce the better times . . . Brenz hoped for."[44]

During this confusion, Duke Ulrich died (November 1550) and Duke Christopher, ready to start evangelical restoration, quickly summoned Brenz. Since the Interim was still in effect, and Christopher was slowed in regaining Württemberg, Brenz continued to serve cautiously in ecclesiastical matters without public office. In March 1552, Brenz prepared the *Confessio Wirtembergica* which, with other Wittenberg and Strasburg Lutheran theologians, he defended at the Council of Trent.[45] Maurice of Saxony's victory over Charles V in the spring of 1552 abolished the Interim in Württemberg (June), secured recognition of Christopher's succession (August), and freed Brenz to proceed openly with the work of ecclesiastical reorganization.

In January 1553 Christopher named Brenz chief councilor in ecclesiastical matters for life, and in September 1554, appointed him provost (*probst*) at Collegiate Church (*Stiftskirche*) in Stuttgart, the highest ecclesiastical post in the duchy[46]—"the right hand of the duke in the organization of ecclesiastical and educational affairs in Württemberg."[47] These appointments justified Brenz's loyalty in refusing the opportunities mentioned

---

42. Estes, *Territorial*, 36.
43. Bossert, "Brenz," 261; Google Genealogy.
44. Estes, *Territorial*, 39.
45. Bossert, "Brenz," 261; *CRR3*, 20.
46. Estes, *Territorial*, 39.
47. Estes, *Territorial*, 39; *CRR3*, 20.

above in other regions. He would be serving as the highest ranking cleric in the system he had designed along with Dukes Ulrich and Christopher with a ranking equal to or higher than the other offers, and with his Christian friend Duke Christopher in his beloved home territory.

The work of ecclesiastical reorganization, begun quietly in 1551 was completed with publication of the very comprehensive, The Great Church Order of 1559. This included ecclesiastical legislation from 1551, Brenz's *Confessio Virtembergica* (for the Council of Trent, 1551, the official confession of the Württemberg church), Marriage Court Order, Welfare Ordnance, School System Ordinance, and church government. Estes gave an overall assessment of The Great Church Order of 1559:

> All the basic features of this system had their origin in various proposals that Brenz had made in the 1520s and 1530s but had only partially achieved in practice. The elaboration of these ideas into a coherent, effective, durable ecclesiastical polity, soon to be imitated all over Protestant Germany, was Brenz's greatest accomplishment as a Reformer.[48]

In 1568 Duke Christopher died, a great sorrow for Brenz, and, in 1569, Brenz had a disabling stroke, from which he died on September 11, 1570. He was buried beneath the pulpit of Collegiate Church, Stuttgart—a simple flagstone remains.[49] In the last years of his life, as throughout his ministry, Brenz continued to blend his firm, yet humane, demeanor to help organize the territorial Reformation church, to write commentaries, expositions, theological works, and catechism, and to contact different groups of the Reformation in attempts to reconcile differences.[50] These reflect the breadth of his work defending the Lutheran views of Württemberg and surrounding territories.[51] Bossert noted the manner of Brenz's work, "The great church order of 1553–1559 . . . is distinguished by clearness, mildness, and consideration. In like manner, his *Catechismus* (Frankfort, 1551) became a rich source of instruction for many generations and countries."[52]

Because the Reformation was a powerful, complicated, and turbulent movement, imposing order upon it was a long and difficult process. Brenz brought exceptional talents to bear on that process, and his success entitles him to recognition as one of the major figures in the history of the German

---

48. Estes, *Territorial*, 41.
49. Bossert, "Brenz," 260–61; Estes, *Territorial*, 41–42.
50. Bossert, "Brenz," 261.
51. CRR3, ib. 22.
52. Bossert, "Brenz," 261.

Reformation.⁵³ The political and theological maelstrom through which Brenz labored was in the same period in which Urbanus Rhegius and Johannes Spangenberg worked. Summaries of their Reformation work follow.

Urbanus Rhegius (1489–1541)

Urbanus Rhegius was born on Bodensee, near Constance.⁵⁴ He did his university work under Dr. John Maier of Eck at Freiburg-im-Breisgau, and was influenced by the humanism of Erasmus, Faber, and Zwingli. He received the doctor of divinity degree at Basel⁵⁵ and followed Eck to Ingolstadt in 1510. In 1518 he published the orthodox Roman Catholic *De dignitate sacerdotum*, and in 1519 he sided with Eck against Luther. Ordained as a priest at Constance in 1519, Rhegius replaced Oecolampadius as cathedral preacher of Augsburg in 1520. In 1521, when he adopted Luther's views, he had to leave that position. Later, in 1524 he returned as Pastor of St. Anne's where he administered the Lord's Supper in both kinds. A critical issue for Rhegius was the Lord's Supper controversy in which he attempted to mediate between the views of Zwingli and Luther. Philip Schaff observed that Rhegius's moderate opinion sympathized most with Bucer. However, he aligned with Luther against the radical Anabaptists, and worked hard alongside the Wittenberg theologians.⁵⁶

When the emperor prohibited evangelical preaching in June 1530, Rhegius's career in Augsburg was ended. During the Augsburg Diet he accepted the appointment by the duke of Lüneburg as pastor at Celle. Schaff tells of his only meeting with Luther.

> On his way from Augsburg to Celle, [Rhegius] called on Luther... at Coburg. It was "the happiest day" of his life and made a lasting impression on him, which he thus expressed in a letter: "I judge, no one can hate Luther who knows him. His books reveal his genius; but if you would see him face to face, and hear him speak on divine things with apostolic spirit, you would say, the living reality surpasses the fame. Luther is too great to be judged by every wiseacre. I, too, have written books, but compared with him I am a mere pupil. He is an elect instrument of the Holy Ghost... for the whole world."⁵⁷

53. Estes, *Territories*, 221.
54. Tschackert, "Rhegius, Urbanus," 22.
55. Schaff, 7:576.
56. Tschackert, "Rhegius, Urbanus," 22.
57. Schaff, 7:728–29.

Rhegius's early admiration of Zwingli, from 1519, ultimately shifted to Luther, after they met. From that time, "Rhegius belonged to the party of theologians who produced the Augsburg Confession."[58] Rhegius had high praise for Luther, asserting that Luther and his theology had strong worldwide implications. Still, Rhegius did not reduce the Reformation to Luther and his theology, resisting the tendency in Luther to restrict the Reformation possession and authority to himself.[59]

Though highly educated, Rhegius considered himself a pastor aiming only for practical pastoral ministry and never holding a university chair. As Scott Hendrix explains, "Seen through the eyes of Rhegius, the Reformation seemed much more practical than academic and more similar to the day-to-day work of clergy than to the ruminations of scholars."[60] In 1531, as general superintendent of the duchy of Braunsweig,[61] Rhegius began the important task of leading the Reformation of Celle, Soest, Hanover, Minden, Lemgo, and other regions in the duchy.[62] He addressed the moral and spiritual states of the territory with several church orders, catechisms, *loci*, and comparisons of Catholic and Reformation beliefs. Rhegius's church order, written for Hanover in 1536, was still in effect at the end of the nineteenth entury. He opposed the Anabaptists in northern Germany, and as Duke Ernest's advisor, he influenced the acceptance of the Wittenberg Concord in Lüneberg. Urbanus Rhegius died at Celle in 1541.[63]

Rhegius demonstrated Christianity through ministry to those suffering and dying, which he called Christianization. Ronald Rittgers noted the degree of Rhegius's commitment:

> Rhegius was one of the sixteenth century's most important spiritual guides for the sick, the suffering, and the dying, as well as for those who attended to them. This ministry of instruction and consolation, especially through the written word, may be seen as a deliberate attempt at Christianization on the part of Rhegius; he was a missionary who sought to make Christendom more authentically Christian through the development and promotion of an evangelical ministry of consolation—he sought to Christianize through consolation.[64]

58. Rittgers, "Christianization," 327; see Hendrix, "Urbanus Rhegius and the Augsburg Confession."
59. Rittgers, "Christianization," 327.
60. Rittgers, "Christianization," 327, citing Hendrix, *Preaching*, 5.
61. Tschackert, "Rhegius, Urbanus," 22.
62. Schaff, 7:576.
63. Tschackert, "Rhegius, Urbanus," 23.
64. Rittgers, "Christianization," 322.

Picking up from Luther, Rhegius emphasized that such suffering can be a testing of faith to show how dear one may be to God and how dearly one loves and trusts in God. This happens when Christians turn in confession and repentance to God to receive forgiveness and the Holy Spirit.[65] Rittgers notes that Rhegius was among those theologians with strong convictions regarding justification and the primacy of Scripture, but were flexible regarding different emphases and practices in such issues as the Lord's Supper and private confession. However, Rhegius opposed doctrines of believer's baptism and emphases on unmediated inspiration and visions from the Holy Spirit.[66]

Johann Spangenberg (1484–1550)

Johann Spangenberg, German Lutheran theologian, educator, and musician, was born near Göttingen. He was educated at Göttingen and Einbeck and began studies at the University of Erfurt in 1508 (BA 1511)[67] where he was influenced by humanist circles (e.g., Conrad Mutianus, Eobanus Hessus).[68] Later, Botho, Count of Stolberg (Harz), called Spangenberg as rector at the Latin school and midday preacher, where he served until 1520 when he also became preacher at St. Martin's Church in Stolberg. After accepting Luther's theology in 1524 he was called to St. Blasius's Church in Nordhausen and entered upon a twenty-two-year ministry where he introduced a new church order and greatly improved the school system. Recommended by Luther, Spangenberg was called in 1546 as general inspector (superintendent) of the Mansfeld churches and schools. He served there until his death on June 13, 1550 at Eisleben.[69] Except for his first position at Stolberg, Spangenberg worked primarily in the Nordhausen and Mansfeld districts in the Harz region in which he was reared. Although he did not travel far from his home, his influence spread throughout Germany and as far as England. His parish work and his extensive writing were a valuable contribution to the Reformation cause.

---

65. Rittgers, "Christianization," 334.

66. Rittgers, "Christianization," 327; Hampton, "Urbanus Rhegius," 178–203; Zschoch, *Reformatorische Existenz*, 218—95.

67. Kawerau, "Spangenberg," 35a.

68. Schwiebert, *Luther and His Times*, 307. See Schwiebert, *Luther and His Times*, chapter 19, for a concise summary of the influence of Humanism on the German Universities during the Reformation.

69. Kawerau, "Spangenberg," 35a.

At Nordhausen, beginning in 1527, Spangenberg cultivated a Wittenberg-style reform and promoted the education of children. It is noteworthy that he introduced music courses into the curriculum. He established the Lutheran evangelical doctrine and furthered higher education, in addition to his pastoral practice.[70] When the cathedral and municipal schools were destroyed in the Peasants' War, Spangenberg opened a private school in his home. In 1525, at his request, the council established a new Latin school in the Dominican monastery and Spangenberg wrote the school text books.

His literary efforts provided key support for the integration of Luther's thought and bear the marks of pastoral theology and practice found among Luther's followers. Besides school textbooks, Spangenberg wrote music books for all ages, a handbook for music theory to use in the Nordhausen schools, catechisms, conservative church orders, systematic theology, and biblical commentaries. His writings include *Margarita Theologica* (Theological Pearls): an introduction to biblical teaching for advanced students formatted as questions and answers and shaped by Melanchthon's *Loci communes*, as well as numerous aids to preaching and devotional literature. His postil was second only to the two prepared by Luther with regard to the number published. His works include *Postilla, Das ist: Auslegung der Episteln und Evangelien, Auf alle Sontage und vornehmsten Feste durch das ganze Jahr, für die einfältigen Christen in Frag-Stucke verfassset: Canitiones ecclesiasssticae Latinae.*[71] The several English translations of The *Summe of Divinitie* (ET of *Margarita Theologica*), London, 1548–61, may indicate Spangenberg's influence in mid-sixteenth-century English Protestantism.

Spangenberg introduced new types of devotional literature, viz., edifying interpretations of church hymns. His large set of musical publications includes hymns of his own with accompaniment. A well-known bilingual work, *Cantiones Ecclesiasticae*, relates to Luther's *Formula Missae* of 1522 and Spangenberg's *Deutsche Messe* of 1526. This is the most significant liturgical-musical work of the early Lutheran Church for its liturgical year.[72]

Luther was also an enthusiastic advocate for music in the church. He said it was as important as theology and a powerful weapon against the enemy of the Holy Spirit.

> We know that music is hateful and intolerable to devils. I firmly believe, nor am I ashamed to assert, that next to theology no art is equal to music; for it is the only one, except theology, which is able to give a quiet and happy mind. This is manifestly

---

70. Kawerau, "Spangenberg," 35a.
71. *LC*, "Spangenberg," 729b.
72. Ludolphy, "Spangenberg," 2245.

proved by the fact that the devil, the author of depressing care and distressing disturbances, almost flees from the sound of music as he does from the word of theology. This is the reason why the prophets practiced music more than any art and did not put their theology into geometry, into arithmetic, or into astronomy, but into music, intimately uniting theology and music, telling the truth in psalms and songs.[73]

Spangenberg's extensive theological writing and publication of song books and music theory served the early Lutheran Reformation "telling the truth" in theology and music.[74]

The Early Reformers' Theology of the Holy Spirit

In their ministries and theology Brenz, Rhegius, and Spangenberg reflect what they had been taught from their Wittenberg leaders—Luther, Melanchthon, and the rest. The following examination of their writing demonstrates a solid continuity of position from Luther throughout his contemporary German theologians.

The Theology of the Cross

In Luther's theology the Holy Spirit was formulated and taught primarily within the framework of his theology of the cross. While the Holy Spirit was also instrumental for other early Reformers, the theology of the cross was not commonly mentioned among them. However, the essence, characteristics, and practical implications were prominent in their teaching and ministry. Their work may not fit into a "Theology of the Cross" template, but their teaching and ministry in their diverse regions demonstrate the footprint of the teachings and practices of Luther in Wittenberg during the same time period.

Brenz, in his commentary on Jeremiah, often described a *Schema mortificatio-vivicatio* with regard to justification.[75] In this model Brenz linked the life and resurrection of the Righteous One, who obtains justification for the unrighteous, as he kills and makes alive again unto holiness. This is an act of God, while the Spirit fulfills and proves the truth of the promises of

---

73. Plass, *Luther Says*, 983; LW 49:428; WABr 5:639; LS 21a, 1575.
74. Ludolphy, "Spangenberg," 2245.
75. Brecht, *Theologie*, 142.

God.⁷⁶ Here the theology of the cross and the distinction of law and gospel are woven into each other. Therefore, discussing Brenz's commentary on Job, Martin Brecht said: "The Theology of the Cross is a central element of Brenz's theology. The gospel is laid in the Theology of the Cross,"⁷⁷ because Brenz's theology was of the "School of Luther." This probably stems from Brenz's introduction to Reformation theology at Luther's presentation of his theology of the cross at the Heidelberg Disputation of 1518.

In his Job commentary, Brenz described the controversy between Job and his friends to show how the punishment of the just is not understood by reason but only by faith. While being justified and being tempted go together, reason is blinded from seeing that punishment alone does not conclude the matter. The wisdom of God, hidden in the cross, is accessible only to faith.⁷⁸

Brenz's early sermons relate his theology of the cross to the earthly and spiritual nature of the church. He highly regarded the church as the community of the saints living in Christ and the Spirit. Its reality is hidden in Christ and in the opposites of his cross. The eye of faith sees that God gives life and glory only through death and the cross.⁷⁹ "The earthly Church shares the lowness of the incarnate Christ. The chosen have not yet overcome death and they look at the glory of God first in faith."⁸⁰ Thus he saw the life of faith tightly tied to the life, death, and Spirit of Christ. The trials of the Christian life belong to the earthly domain. To believe in Christ means to take the cross and follow him.⁸¹ Brenz notes in his commentary on John that Christ was glorified by the cross and death because true victory and true glory stand together with the suffering and shame of the cross, not with action and human praise.⁸²

---

76. Brecht, *Theologie*, 142, citing *Jeremiakommentar* S.920, 31, 10; S.924, 32, 28.

77. Brecht, *Theologie*, 160; "Die Theologie crucis ist ein Kernstück von Brenzens Theologie. Was mit dieser Theologie crucis laut wird, ist Evangelium." Also, 144, "Die Theologie des Kruezes ist ein wesentliches Moment in Brenzens Theologie überhaupt."

78. Brecht, *Theologie*, 153–54, citing *Der Hiobkommentar von 1526*, S.84–85, 9.1; S.190, 21, 23; S.223b, 28, 1; S.47, 5, 8.

79. Brecht, *Theologie*, 27, citing *Sermon von der Kirches*, A1b, A2; *Sermon von Heiligen*, S.2–3, 7–8.

80. Brecht, *Theologie*, 27; "Die irdische Kirche teilt die Neidrigkeit des menschgewordenen Christus. Die Erwählten haben den Tod noch nicht überwunden und schauen die Herrlichkeit Gottes erst im Glauben," citing *Sermon von Heiligen*, S.5.

81. Brecht, *Theologie*, 28, citing *Sermon von den Heiligen*, S.10.

82. Brecht, *Theologie*, 188, citing *Johanneskommentar*, S.929, 13, 31.

Person of the Holy Spirit

Brenz presented an intimate relationship among the persons in the Godhead: "Is not the Holy Spirit related to Christ so that they are inseparable?"[83] and "Christ is able to send the Spirit since he is inseparably allied with him."[84] Spangenberg, describing the Godhead, noted that the Father will send the Holy Spirit in the Son's name, or from the Father and the Son.[85] Brenz said that the persons of the Trinity each exist in the presence of the others in all goodness with eternal self-sufficiency and majesty.[86]

Spangenberg held a standard "homoousian" Trinitarian doctrine, which was related to the Great Commission (Matt 28:19), Jesus' Baptism (Matt 3:16), the Johannine Comma (1 John 5:7), and the ancient creeds.[87] Biblical evidences of the distinct persons are at Jesus' Baptism, Christ saying he will send the Spirit from the Father, and Christ's promise that the Spirit will bear witness to him. He stressed that if one does not have the Spirit of Christ, he does not belong to Christ. He said the Spirit's preexistence before the incarnation, calling the Spirit the Spirit of Christ, and the texts of Joel and Acts 2 witness to the Holy Spirit's existence as a person distinct from the Father and the Son.[88]

These early Lutheran Reformers related their teaching of the indwelling of the Holy Spirit in Christ to the Trinity. Rhegius said God's power acted through the Spirit in the incarnation as the "work master" to conceive and form the human body of Christ in the body of the Virgin Mary.[89] Although Christ's human flesh is from a woman, he is free of human sin since the seed of conception was not from sinful man but from the Holy Spirit himself. For this, Mary should be highly regarded since, in the 16th century words of Rhegius,

> She is praised, and called blessed, as the noble undefiled lodge or Tabernacle, wherein the eternal wisdom of the Heavenly Father has rested, and the Holy Ghost wonderfully has wrought the great work of the blessed humanity of God. Her immaculate,

---

83. Brenz, *Frühschriften*, 275, "Nonne spiritus sancto Christo agnatissimus adeoque ab ipso inseparabilis?"

84. Brecht, *Theologie*, 84–85, "Den Geist kann Christus senden, obwohl er untrennbar mit ihm verbunden ist," referring to S.194 (Singr.).

85. Spangenberg, *Summe*, "Of God."

86. Brenz, *Operum* (1576), 4–5.

87. Spangenberg, *Margarita Theologia* (1561), under "Of God."

88. Spangenberg, *Summe*, "Of God."

89. Rhegius, *Twelve Articles*, Art. 3.

pure, virginal flesh of her body was coupled in unity of persons of the inestimable high blessed Godhead, that by reason of such inexplicable union, of both natures in her person, she is called the mother of God.[90]

This description features the work of the Holy Spirit while carefully honoring Mary's person and immaculate purity. Rhegius called this the proper way to honor saints—to remember the work of God through them with praise and love.

Brenz cited Christ's own claim that the Spirit of the Lord was upon him as his ministry went forth.[91] By the Spirit, Christ is the Lord and King over sin, death, and hell. He is the priest offering for the sin of the others and "the Spirit is the indelible character of this priesthood."[92]

Rhegius concentrated on the knowledge of God who is known through the orderliness of the creation. Knowledge of God's salvation comes only through his Son, the Christ, whom he has sent to us.[93] In the first of his Twelve Articles, Rhegius saw the whole Trinity at work in the creation.[94] To trust in the actions of the Holy Spirit is to trust in God himself, e.g., the creation, David in Ps 34, the Holy Spirit descending as a dove (John 1), Christian baptism in the name of the Trinity (Matt 28), Jesus sending a Comforter (John 14), and Peter praying that they receive the gift of the Holy Spirit (Acts 2). To confess him as God is to trust in his majesty as the third person in the Godhead who mysteriously proceeds from the Father and the Son.[95] Although the views of the person of the Holy Spirit were not identical among these early Reformers they all held to the Trinitarian concept, along with Luther and Melanchthon.

The Means of the Holy Spirit

Brenz closely related faith with the Holy Spirit's means to bring the new birth, the sacraments, and the word.[96] He spoke of not depending upon signs but upon the word which adds the reality of the person of God to the sign. For example, the Holy Spirit is not designated by fiery tongues, or

---

90. Rhegius, *Common Places*, "xxiii. Honouring of Saynctes."
91. Brenz, *Syngramma*, 275.
92. Brecht, *Theologie*, 29, "Der Geist ist der character indelebilis deises Priesterdums."
93. Rhegius, *Common Places*, "ii. God."
94. Rhegius, *Twelve Articles*, Art. 1.
95. Rhegius, *Twelve Articles*, Art. 8.
96. Brecht, *Theologie*, 34, *Epheserkommentar* S.33, 3, 17.

doves, the breath of Christ, or the bread and the wine unless accompanied with an added appropriate word, e.g., "as in the supper it is said: receive [no doubt the bread], this is my body (*hoc est corpus meum*)."[97]

The Word of God

Brenz held that the inspired Old Testament Scriptures, are the "oracle of the Holy Spirit"[98] with present-day Christian applications. The Holy Spirit caused them to be written so every God-fearing ruler might be led by their example. His nation will be blessed if he establishes divine worship, but judgment and punishment will come upon it if he promotes or tolerates worship contrary to God's word.[99] Rhegius agreed with Luther that the books of Holy Scripture came from the Holy Spirit, they cannot lie or fail, and they contain whatever is necessary for salvation. To rule consciences in the kingdom of faith, nothing is necessary except the Bible—the Old and New Testaments. The same Holy Spirit promised the coming of Christ through the prophets and has ruled the hearts and pens of the prophets, apostles, and evangelists, as Peter said. Therefore it is not man's doctrine but God's own word, written by men. As Christ said, my doctrine is not mine, but his that has sent me.[100] Rhegius stressed the divine authorship and authority given to Scripture by its own witness and that of Jesus. It has the doctrines of God himself, written by the Holy Spirit. He identified the authority of the Scriptures as the instrument of the unwavering Holy Spirit in contrast with the authority of the declarations of the popes who have erred many times. He was sure that the Scripture of the gospel comes from the Holy Spirit. If individuals or the institutions of the popes and councils conform to the Bible, then their conclusions should be kept. If they are contrary to the Bible, then they err. The Holy Spirit is consistent, and that which he spoke through the evangelists for salvation is still true, for he does not speak against himself. Agreement with the Bible comes from the Spirit of God; disagreement is from the devil.[101]

Following the apostle Paul, Rhegius called the word of God the "sword of the Spirit" (Eph 6:17),[102] and said the Holy Spirit comes through the preaching of the gospel, which teaches how one shall be saved and truly

97. Brenz, *Syngramma*, 257–58.
98. Brenz, *Operum*, 3.
99. Estes, *State Church*, 38, citing Richter, *Evangelischen Kirchenmordungen*.
100. Rhegius, *Common Places*, "i. Holy Scriptures."
101. Rhegius, *Common Places*, "xxv. Difference of meats."
102. Rhegius, *Old Learnyng*, G.viiia.

serve God. Therefore, we turn to the gospel to learn of God himself and how to serve him in holiness.[103] The result is, "The Holy Ghost has gathered this church through the word of God, kept and governed it."[104]

Important to the relationship of the Holy Spirit and the word of God is the understanding that not only does the Holy Spirit speak through the word but that the word is the means of mediating the person of the Holy Spirit himself. Brenz said Christ gives the Holy Spirit through the word, e.g., in Acts 10, as Peter was preaching the word of the gospel, the Holy Spirit fell upon all the hearers. The mediation of the Spirit occurs through the word, yet the Lord reserves for himself the right to reveal to whom and when he wills.[105] With this understanding Brenz opposed the "false meaning" which would maintain that the Spirit is "first from above without a mediator." He said, rather, that the Spirit is communicated through the word and preaching.[106]

Brenz understood that the word is the means of the Holy Spirit, who portrays the promises of the Father fulfilled in Christ,[107] and as the instrument of the Holy Spirit, the external teaching of the word enables faith. Through preaching, the Spirit mediates the word and brings the presence of God.[108] Brenz established that the external word mediates God's word. When people believe what they hear, they are given the renewing Spirit. The Spirit shows the gravity of sin and then makes alive, consoles, and directly brings about chastity and love.[109]

Rhegius felt strongly that the word of God is the means of God's Spirit. He said whatever is given against it or in addition to it to bind consciences in the name of the Holy Spirit, is accursed. It must be refuted. "The Holy Ghost titles human traditions as the deceivers of minds which bind consciences where God biddeth not."[110] Rhegius saw the Reformation strife as evidence that the Spirit was wielding his two-edged sword to divide and bring dissention. Christians should not marvel but strive for the inward peace which comes through God's word.[111]

---

103. Rhegius, *Lytle Treatice*, A.viib.
104. Rhegius, *Twelve Articles*, Art. 9.
105. Brenz, *Syngramma*, 275; cf. Brecht, *Theologie*, 85.
106. Brecht, *Theologie*, 90–91.
107. Brecht, *Theologie*, 134.
108. Brecht, *Theologie*, 134.
109. Brecht, *Theologie*, 134–36.
110. Rhegius, *Old Learnyng*, D.via–b.
111. Rhegius, *Common Places*, "xliii. Peace."

The Sacraments

Spangenberg defined the sacraments as "visible tokens of the will of God toward us" that speak forth the gospel promises that take effect when they are received in faith.[112]

Brenz taught that through baptism believers become God's children with Christ as their brother, and they possess the Holy Spirit. God established the priesthood to work externally with water while Christ lives and works internally through the Spirit to bring the new believer into the pure newly-created heavenly kingdom. The Spirit is received by faith as baptism is received through faith.[113]

Brenz said the purpose of the incarnation was to include believers into God's lineage. They are baptized into Christ, enter into his cross and resurrection, and possess all the gifts of the goodness of God including the Holy Spirit.[114] At baptism the Spirit gives life and sanctifies.

Though not always specifically addressing baptism in these sections, the early Reformers related baptism to grace; as grace is linked to the Holy Spirit, so is baptism. Spangenberg defined *Gratia* as the remission of sins and reconciliation that he connected with the gift of the Holy Spirit at baptism.[115]

Brenz discussed the Lord's Supper in his *Syngramma*, against Oecolampadius. Using several Old Testament and New Testament texts Brenz stressed the real physical aspects of the means of the Holy Spirit and their sole dependence upon the words of Christ.[116] Likewise, the Spirit reveals himself through the cup, not because it is the sign of the New Testament, but because it has the real physical blood of the New Testament.[117] The distribution of the bread is the communication of the real resurrection body of Christ and the Holy Spirit of holiness and of sanctification.[118] Because of the close relationship of the persons of the Trinity, Brenz maintained that by the word, the means of the Holy Spirit, Christ's body and blood are really present in the Lord's Supper.

> If the Holy Spirit is brought to us by the carrying of the word, while at the same time remaining most intimately connected

---

112. Spangenberg, *Summe*, discussing "Of Sacraments."
113. Brecht, *Theologie*, 114.
114. Brecht, *Theologie*, 181.
115. Spangenberg, *Summe*, "Grace."
116. Brenz, *Syngramma*, 248; Isa 50:6; Luke 24:23; 1 Cor 15:44; Eph 4:4.
117. Brenz, *Syngramma*, 251.
118. Brenz, *Syngramma*, 263; Rom 1:4.

with Christ sitting at the right hand of the Father, is it not possible at the same time for the body and blood of Christ to be brought to us by the transporting word? How can we say that the Holy Spirit may be more closely joined to Christ than his body and blood to us?[119]

Brenz thus stressed that the Holy Spirit brings the presence of Christ's body and blood through the mediation of the bread and the wine. He believed in the real physical presence of Christ and the real spiritual presence of the Holy Spirit.

Spangenberg did not tie Christ's gifts outwardly to the means, but said faith cannot be confirmed by the Lord's Supper outwardly but only by the work of the Holy Spirit who uses the outward signs to internally stir up believers' faith.[120]

Brenz opposed Casper Schwenckfeld who maintained that God's gifts, such as the new birth, were given by the Spirit without external mediation through the Scriptures or sacraments. Brenz insisted that God gives the Spirit internally through the external means of word and sacrament and that Schwenckfeld had made the gospel into law.[121] A conference between Schwenckfeld and Luther in 1525 revealed several issues of disagreement regarding the Lord's Supper, the church, and Christology.[122] Schwenckfeld's attempts to reconcile things by finding a middle road between Lutherans, Zwinglians, and Catholics only served to antagonize all concerned. H. K. Carroll assessed the exchange, "In successive Interviews with Jonas, Bugenhagen, and Luther, both sides [Schwenkfelders and Lutherans] stood firm on this and other questions; and henceforth Luther and the Wittenberg theologians regarded Schwenckfeld as a dangerous heretic."[123] Luka Ilić concludes, "By offering original views on Word and Spirit, the church, baptism, and the Lord's Supper, Schwenckfeld was preaching a middle way, in which he attempted to bring together the Lutherans and Roman Catholics [and Zwinglians]. [However] He rejected the stances of the Augsburg Confession on predestination, free will, and infant baptism."[124] In 1540 Melanchthon and other early Lutheran theologians condemned and rejected

---

119. Brenz, *Syngramma*, 275, "*si spiritus sancto vehiculo verbi nobis advenitur, manens interim Christo in dextra patris sedenti coniunctissimis cui eodem verbi vehiculo non posset ad nos advehi corpus et sanguis Christi, quando, ut ita loquamur, spiritus sanctus Christo multo coniunctior sit corpore et sanguine eius?*"

120. Spangenberg, *Summe*, "Of the Supper of the Lord."

121. Brecht, *Theologie*, 108.

122. Brecht, *Theologie*, 108.

123. Brecht, *Theologie*, 108.

124. Ilić, "Schwenckfeld," 672b.

Schwenckfeld's Christology because, in their opinion, Schwenckfeld denied the true humanity of Christ."[125] The early Reformers' rejection of Schwenckfeld held and eventually, the *Formula of Concord* specifically stated the Lutheran rejection and condemnation of the beliefs and teachings of the Schwenckfelders.[126]

Reception of the Holy Spirit

The early Reformers held that the Holy Spirit is received at baptism with remission of sins.[127] Spangenberg viewed Christ's baptism as God's action giving the Holy Spirit and everlasting life. In comparison, he said John's baptism only gave the outward sign and preached the word.[128] Spangenberg reaffirmed the biblical testimony of John 10 and 15, that Christ will send the Holy Spirit, the Comforter, to the disciples,[129] and that the Holy Spirit is given with remission of sins and the acceptance of eternal life.[130] Rhegius and Spangenberg said the Holy Spirit is received with eternal salvation when believers are received by God as his forgiven children.[131] Though the law has made it clear that no one can stand before God on his own, without Christ, the mediator has obtained for God's children grace, remission of sins, the Holy Spirit with his gifts, and new hearts with God's law written on them (Jer 31).[132]

Spangenberg recalled that Paul called the Holy Spirit the reward which is received with the grace of remission of sins or the undeserved accepting for Christ's sake unto everlasting life.[133] Therefore when Christians are baptized into the death of the incarnated Christ they possess the Spirit

---

125. Ilić, "Schwenckfeld," 673a.
126. *BC*, 658–59.
127. Brenz, *Clavibus*, 163a.
128. See "Of Baptism" in Spangenberg, *Summe*.
129. See "Of God" in Spangenberg, *Summe*.
130. See "Justification" in Spangenberg, *Summe*.
131. Rhegius, *Instruccyon*, 26–28, 75; Spangenberg, *Summe*, "Justification," relates justification and the Holy Spirit. He said "God promiseth that he will forgive sins for Christ his son's sake, and pronounceth us justified, that is to say acceptable, and giveth us the Holy Ghost and everlasting life.... the natural cause, that is the very affection and corruption of nature, remaineth as yet in nature, and yet when the Holy Ghost is given unto them which have faith, they conceive new and godly motions whereby the evil is something mitigate."
132. Rhegius, *Instruccyon*, 43–45.
133. See "Grace" in Spangenberg, *Summe*.

as a gift of the goodness of God in Christ and the Spirit seals them unto the promise of God.[134]

The Work of the Holy Spirit

Repentance

Rhegius said that by illumination through the word of God, the Holy Spirit brings faith, which leads to repentance.[135] The Spirit brings repentance to the humble through illumination of the infinite mercy of God promised through Christ.[136] Spangenberg said that sorrows and fears in the repentant are evoked by the word of God and the Holy Spirit which rebuke the world of sin and declare the wrath of God upon all ungodliness.[137] Brenz said that the Holy Spirit brings repentance through the word as Law and Gospel, as Brecht describes: "The Holy Spirit's appeals to repentance are both 'part of the Law in which to reveal sins,' and 'part of the Gospel, because they manifest the favor of God by which restoration is completed.'"[138] Thus the early Reformers agree that the Holy Spirit works repentance in sinners through Law and Gospel.

Faith

Rhegius called the many natural human attempts to quench sin and obtain righteousness "erroneous bypaths" that do nothing for salvation but lead away from God to hell, because they are blind and unable to do anything that is good. Their hearts must be illumined by the Holy Spirit with God's gift of faith that Christ has earned for them. Though one's outward works may be good, the inner heart is unclean. The Holy Spirit cleanses and purifies hearts by bringing people to true faith in Christ,[139] which the Holy Spirit stirs up so they may follow Christ's example and his commands in patient

---

134. Rhegius, *Instruccyon*, 61.
135. Rhegius, *Lytle Treatice*, B.v [B].
136. Rhegius, *Lytle Treatice*, B.v [B].
137. Spangenberg, *Summe*, "Repentance."
138. Brecht, *Theologie*, 131, "*Die Bußmahnungen des Geistes sind sowohl pars legis, indem sie die Sünde zeigen, als auch "pars Evangelii, quia favorem Dei, quo resipiscentes complectitur, manifestant,"*" lectures on Jeremiah, S.937, 43,2.
139. Rhegius, *Lytle Treatice*, A.vii [A]–B.ii [B].

lives of love.[140] Faith comes by the work and illumination of the Holy Spirit through hearing the gospel.[141] Faith, springing from repentance, takes up the cross to follow Jesus as his disciple. Without the fruit of repentance and good works, there can be no tree of faith.[142] Faith is evidence of "a new Christian" who walks not after flesh, but after the Spirit (Rom 8)."[143] Faith and works are closely linked through the Holy Spirit who informs faith of justification in Christ. God chooses people beforehand and comes by grace through his Spirit who produces faith through the word. Such faith cannot be idle, said Rhegius, but with gratefulness and obedience enabled by the Spirit, believers use the gifts of the Spirit "to proceed from virtue to virtue" to approach the Father's kingdom nearer and nearer.[144]

According to Spangenberg, the Holy Spirit moves hearts by the gospel to teach the forgiveness of sins and cause an unshakeable faith that one is accepted before God for the sake of Christ the mediator.[145] The Spirit brings the effects of God's grace, which are faith and trust in God to be merciful, to overcome fears, and to grant everlasting life.[146] This faith learns how the Holy Spirit is received and how the Spirit stirs up new abilities to obey the law.[147] Spangenberg described this work of the Holy Spirit to build faith and trust:

> The Holy Ghost moves our hearts by the gospel, which teacheth that sin is forgiven us for Christ, which was made an offering for us. So then standeth this when we hear this promise, and behold Christ our mediator, we believe for his sake that we be forgiven and acceptable before God, and to be heard, nor we suffer not this trust to be shaken of us.[148]

Brecht says that Brenz saw a struggle between the Holy Spirit and sin. God can be known only through faith, over and above reason. God's works are seen in his word and he works faith in the one who hears his promises in that word. Brenz pictured the Christian life as God's new creation of faith where his Spirit is given to obedient believers.[149]

---

140. Rhegius, *Instruccyon*, 21–22.
141. Rhegius, *Lytle Treatice*, B.ii [B].
142. Rhegius, *Instruccyon*, 22.
143. Rhegius, *Instruccyon*, 23.
144. Rhegius, *Old Learnyng*.
145. Spangenberg, *Summe*, "Repentance."
146. Spangenberg, *Summe*, "Of Grace."
147. Spangenberg, *Summe*, "Justification."
148. Spangenberg, *Summe*, "Fayth."
149. Brecht, *Theologie*, 144–50.

These early Reformers understood faith to be the work of the Holy Spirit who moves through the gospel to change the hearers inwardly and bring them to faith. It is not an appeal to reason, but a transformation of ability to see the truth of God in Christ as mediator, and to rely totally upon him. Reason can neither do this, nor apprehend it, but God's power changes people.

Justification

Spangenberg said the three causes of justification are the Holy Spirit, the word, and the human will moved by the Spirit through the word not to resist but to consent and hear his voice through the word.[150] This is similar to both the three causes of justification discussed in chapter 3, and to the *Formula of Concord's* (SD 11) statement on election.[151]

Rhegius claimed it is necessary for the Spirit to make it possible for the person to be born again and to understand godly things.[152] Being born again is a firstfruit of the Spirit and includes being born of the water and of the Spirit.[153] The Holy Spirit fulfills what Christ has earned and bestows Christ on believers that they may be partners with him in his life and passion. Unless the Spirit draws people to Christ they will continue in death.[154] These early Reformers saw justification as a renewing work of the Holy Spirit in those who otherwise are incapable of seeing, understanding, or apprehending the gospel of Christ.

Sanctification

According to Brecht, Brenz described sanctification as the Holy Spirit working to give faith in Christ, to put to death and to make alive, and to cleanse the flesh.[155] Rhegius viewed God's works of justification and sanctification as linked together. As they are called to faith, God offers his new children the life justified in Christ that mortifies the flesh as his gift in the sanctifying Spirit. This is not accomplished by the human spirit but only by the Spirit of God, who distributes his gifts among those being sanctified.[156] Rhegius said

---

150. Spangenberg, *Summe*, "Justification."
151. *BSLK*, 107; *BC*, 647.
152. Rhegius, *Common Places*, "xi. Flesh."
153. Rhegius, *Common Places*, "xii. Spirit"; "xxviii. Vowe."
154. Rhegius, *Twelve Articles*, Art. 8.
155. Brecht, *Theologie*, 122, lectures on Jeremiah [1525], S. 901-2, 17, 21.
156. Rhegius, *Instruccyon*, 71-73.

the Holy Spirit leads the spiritual battles in believers by commanding them "to cast away the works of darkness (e.g., gluttony and drunkenness), and to put on the armour of light."[157]

Teaching

Brenz said the Scriptures contain the teachings of the prophets and apostles. The Holy Spirit teaches the truths of God in Christ through them, including the Ten Commandments and the apostolic witness of the church.[158] Rhegius said the Holy Spirit was uniquely given at Pentecost to begin a new era of teaching and work.[159] The Holy Spirit used Paul as his instrument through whom he taught the message of the Scriptures to the church.[160] He said the Spirit continued to teach through the church's tradition after the New Testament time.[161] Brenz agreed, but added that the Holy Spirit is the author of true doctrine. This was challenged at the Council of Trent.[162]

Rhegius said the apostles were taught by the Spirit and not by "heathen masters," nor were they university doctors, but simple people. Along with Luther and Melanchthon, Rhegius overthrew the priority of scholastic philosophy in the work of evangelical Christianity. If the Spirit could teach evangelical truth "without the help of heathen philosophy, Scotistry, and other men's books," could he not also teach the Scripture to simple laity who can expound Scripture better than some great doctors? In contrast with worldly wisdom, the Holy Spirit is God's true teacher of the faithful, if they set aside their own interpretations and let their understanding be captive to the glory of Christ. The Spirit helps break down the armor of worldly wisdom which assaults the wisdom of God. People, in their own wisdom and strength, cannot find the way to God, nor be made righteous by natural strength. God himself must teach the right way by the Holy Spirit through his word and faith in Christ.[163] Human nature is corrupt and cannot independently come to the knowledge of sin and true righteousness or know the way to the kingdom of God and salvation; otherwise human philosophers could do so. They failed because they lacked the gospel. Therefore, Rhegius

157. Rhegius, *Lytle Treatice*, D.viii [A].
158. Brenz. *De Clavibus*, 161B.
159. Rhegius, *Old Learnyng*, G.iii[b]–iv.
160. Rhegius, *Handbook*, 91.
161. Rhegius, *Old Learnyng*, G.ii [A].
162. Brenz, *Syntagma*, G viiAf (not to be confused with *Syngramma* by Brenz of 1525).
163. See "Conclusion" in Rhegius, *Common Places*.

depended upon the Spirit of God over and against human philosophy, to work through the word of God as his means of revealing his doctrine of justification by faith.[164] Rhegius joined Brenz and Spangenberg in a Luther-like denunciation of teaching philosophy and reason without the Holy Spirit.

The Holy Spirit and the Church

Brenz conceived of the church as the community of believing saints in whom the Holy Spirit works holiness through faith. Together, believers inherit the Father's heavenly goodnesses.[165]

Brenz said that in the ideal church the Spirit is the life of the body of Christ (Rom 8). He dwells uniformly in all faithful members, who are called saints. He rejected the Roman Catholic opinion that the church exists where the hierarchy resides, but said that the church is made up of those who are assembled in the Spirit and in truth. He saw no practical distinction between the religious and the laity.[166] This view of equality of clergy and laity is consistent with Luther's understanding of the priesthood of believers. Brenz thanked God for his kindness in the ministry of the Holy Spirit received through the apostles and the church.[167] In his *Syntagma*, Brenz, referring to "the convention of the fathers in synod,"[168] said that such consecrated assemblages can be legitimate in their deliberations and propositions while listening to the Spirit.[169] In the congregation Brenz saw the integration of the ministry of the Holy Spirit in the church with the Sacraments, preaching, etc.

According to Spangenberg the true church is the congregation of the righteous who truly believe in Christ and are sanctified by Christ's Spirit. Speaking against praying to and worshiping saints, he said of the fellowship of the saints, "The father does acknowledge them [as] his children. The Son calls them brethren and fellow heirs. The Holy Ghost calls them his temple."[170] Spangenberg said that hypocrites have the same gospel and

---

164. Rhegius, *Treatice*, A iiii[b], v[a]; cf. *Old Learnyng*, D.vii[b]–viii.

165. Brecht, *Theologie*, 32–33.

166. Brecht, *Theologie*, 26–27, citing *Sermon von der Kirche* A12.

167. Brenz. *Clavibus* (1555), 166B: "*Agamus igniter, quas possumus gratias Deo patri Domini nostri Iesu Christi, pro beneficio huius Apostolici ministerii, ac utamur eo summa diligentia, et conseramus ad conseruationem eius in Ecclesia omnem operam nostram, ut coelestem fructum eius, per Spiritum sanctum capiamus.*"

168. Brenz, *Syntagma*, C vi[a]: "*Aiunt enim quadraplex esse genus conuentus patrum in synodo.*"

169. Brenz, *Syntagma*, D iiii[a], and I iv[a]–v[a].

170. See "Of Invocation of Saintes" in Spangenberg, *Summe*.

sacraments in the church, but not their content. They equate their traditions with the gospel, and pray without true faith. Their false doctrine scatters and troubles consciences, unlike the Holy Spirit, which gathers and comforts consciences.[171]

Rhegius, the pastor, teacher, and church superintendent had a dynamic, broad, and efficacious view of the Holy Spirit's ministry in the church, "The whole universal Church has the Holy Ghost by her, by whom she is governed, and cannot err."[172] This was true as long as the church had the word of God and was obedient to it, as the bride to the bridegroom. Thus all believers have the power of the Spirit and the commission to preach the gospel.[173]

In the matter of councils, Rhegius believed that John 4 teaches that spirits should be tested whether they are of God or not. Therefore it is right for Christians to judge the spirit of councils by the word of God. If the Holy Spirit, who taught the apostles the truth in Scripture, rules the councils, then the constitutions and the councils must agree with the learning of Christ and his apostles in the Holy Scripture. But since the councils openly have decrees contrary to Scripture and the Holy Spirit, then their constitutions should be tested.[174] Rhegius concludes that God is above the councils. An example of a proper council was the Jerusalem Council (Acts 15) which decreed according to Scripture and celebrated the Holy Spirit.[175] He noted that the council recognized the Holy Spirit's authority in accord with the Old Testament and with the gospel of salvation through faith in Jesus Christ.

For these early Reformers, the true church is not dependent upon human tradition but upon God's Spirit and his dynamic of word and sacrament. This was consistent with the Wittenberg Reformers.

The Office of the Keys

Brenz held that God gives the ministry of the service of word and sacrament to those who possess the Spirit so God himself can be the mediating priest, and they can be servants of the true priest by preaching the word and serving the sacraments.[176] Spangenberg believed the Holy Spirit is linked to

---

171. See "Of Invocation of Saintes" in Spangenberg, *Summe.*
172. Rhegius, *Common Places,* "xxxvi. The churche."
173. Rhegius, *Instruccyon,* 67.
174. Rhegius, *Instruccyon.*
175. Rhegius, *Old Learnyng,* G.vi f, G.viii .
176. Brecht, *Theologie,* 29, citing *Sermon von der Kirche* A3–A4.

the office of forgiving sins.¹⁷⁷ Rhegius saw that when Christ breathed on his disciples (John 20), he gave them the Holy Spirit and his authority to retain and forgive sins.¹⁷⁸ This power of the Spirit was given to all believers who were also commissioned to preach the gospel.

Brenz portrayed the Spirit's activity in the office of keys among believers:

> The word of the gospel, which by the Spirit is the strengthening key of the kingdom of heaven, that you may scatter forgiveness throughout the universal world of sinners, as it follows after the promise, John 20 [20-21]: Receive the Holy Spirit, if you forgive the sins of any, they are forgiven them. Whereas before, he said, I will give, now he says you receive, whereas before he said key, now he says Holy Spirit. For the Holy Spirit is the image and guarantee of the word, by which word sins are both forgiven and retained.¹⁷⁹

The Spirit ministers the office of the keys through preaching because he is the author of preaching in the name of Christ. Such preaching has the power to bring repentance, faith, forgiveness of sins, the gift of the Holy Spirit, and victory over evil spirits.¹⁸⁰

The Kingdom

Rhegius identified the gift of the Holy Spirit to the church for preaching the gospel as the beginning of Christ's kingdom.¹⁸¹ Brenz said the Holy Spirit enables the proclamation of the message of God's kingdom,¹⁸² and links the giving of the Holy Spirit in John 20 with the preaching of the gospel and

---

177. See "Of Ecclesiastical Power" in Spangenberg, *Summe*.

178. Rhegius, *Old Learnyng*, F.v[b].

179. Brenz, *Syngramma*, 261, "*Verbum euangelii, quod spiritu confirmantis regni caelorum clavis est, ut peruniversum orbem peccatorum remissionem spargatis, quam promissionem post exequitur Ioan. 20 [22-23]: Accipite spiritum sanctum, quorum remiseritis peccata, remittuntur eis. Quod ante, dixit dabo, nunc ait accipite, quod ante dixit dabo, nunc ait accipite, quod ante dixit claves, nunc ait spiritum sanctum. Nam spiritus sanctus verbi sigillum et arrabo est, quo verbo et remittuntur et tetinentur peccata; quod enim hoc loco remitti peccata dicitur.*"

180. Brenz, *Clavibus*, 163B, 165A-B, John 16, 165A; Rom 10; John 17; 1 Thess 2; 1 Cor 3, 5; 1 Pet 1.

181. Rhegius, *Instruccyon*, 67.

182. Brenz, *Clavibus*, 161a.

the keys of the kingdom.[183] On Pentecost the Holy Spirit was a publicly manifested message of the many aspects of the work of Christ.[184]

Spangenberg explained the second petition of the Lord's Prayer as praying for the governance of the gospel that God would begin his kingdom among us through the Holy Spirit.[185] Brenz saw the kingdom in the activity of the Holy Spirit in the exercise of the office of keys among believers.[186]

Magistrates

A major part of Brenz's Reformation work dealt with the relationship of the church and the state, especially stressing that the state was the instrument of the Holy Spirit to accomplish the Reformation. Spangenberg agreed, saying, "The gospel doth not abolish the rules or the Magistrates, but rather confirms them."[187] Estes noted that Brenz approved a greater role for magistrates in the life of the church than they had before the Reformation. He said the bishops should have abolished the godless service of the mass and dismissed the priests who obstinately adhered to it. Instead, they opposed the gospel, so the Holy Spirit called the secular authorities to the Reformation task. One of Brenz's major accomplishments was persuading the magistrates to do this.[188]

The Gifts of the Holy Spirit

From their usage, it appears that these early Reformers considered the gifts of the Holy Spirit to be the enabling of the Christian life and ministry. Rhegius said the gifts of the Holy Spirit are a normal aspect of salvation obtained by Christ in his kingdom.[189] He saw the gifts operating in those

---

183. Brenz, *Clavibus*, 160b. On 162a he contrasts Peter's confession, followed by the manifestation of Satan in Matt 16. Brenz said the authority was not given according to Peter's person but his confession of the truth of the gospel of Jesus Christ. In John 20 all the apostles received the Holy Spirit from the resurrected Christ with the authority of the keys of the kingdom and the ability to loose (*Soluere*) and to bind (*Ligare*) sins.

184. Brenz, *Clavibus*, 162b.

185. See "Of the Lordes Prayer" in Spangenberg, *Summe*.

186. Brenz, *Syngramma*, 261.

187. See "Of reuenging" in Spangenberg, *Summe*.

188. Estes, *State Church*, 34.

189. Rhegius, *Lytle Treatice*, B.iii[b]. Rhegius lists the salvation works of Christ, including sin, the devil, death, the incarnation, atoning death of Christ, reconciliation, the resurrection, the Holy Spirit and his gifts, and the call for the apostles to declare the news of salvation to all who have faith and trust in Christ, B iii[b]–B iiii[a].

who are justified and sanctified as God had said believers would be able to do. They will do what he has commanded them to do, based on no merit of their own but on his word.[190] The Holy Spirit is active through the miracle ministry of Jesus Christ, as at the wedding at Cana.[191] After Christ obtained satisfaction for our sins, he "deserved for us [counted us worthy to receive] the Holy Ghost with his gifts."[192]

Estes said that Brenz's view of the gifts of miracles contrasts with that of Rhegius. Brenz limited gifts to validating the ministry of the biblical apostles. He said God's call to the prophets and apostles was proven by their performing miracles. Leaders of new sects must provide such evidence to justify their breach of the established order. Pastors who have been properly called by the community do not need such justification.[193] Among Lutherans, the tension between these two views of spiritual gifts has continued from Luther himself to the present.[194]

New Life in the Holy Spirit

Renewal

Renewal is the Spirit's work of stirring up within people a new life that is alive to God and is shown by actions caused by the Spirit. As they awaken to everlasting life, they begin to understand the will and law of God and want to follow them. Spangenberg said the Spirit will not remain in unholy vessels who submit to sinfulness provoked by the devil.[195]

Spangenberg discussed Paul's distinguishing the letter, the Spirit, and the gospel. The *letter* is all ideas, observings, good intentions of reason, and even law and gospel, without the Holy Spirit, true fear, or true faith in Christ. The *Spirit* is the spiritual motions which the Holy Spirit stirs within. The *gospel* is the means of the Spirit as it promises free remission of sins.[196]

---

190. Rhegius, *Instruccyon*, 73–74.
191. Rhegius, *Old Learnyng*, F.iiib.
192. Rhegius, *Lytle Treatice*, B.iiib.
193. Estes, *State Church*, 46.
194. Note: Taking the position of Brenz is Martin Chemnitz whose early Lutheran systematization has had a significant impact on the Lutheran Church of the twentieth century at the advent of Charismatic renewal among Lutherans.
195. See "Good Workes" in Spangenberg, *Summe*.
196. See "Of the Difference between the New and Old Testament" in Spangenberg, *Summe*.

Rhegius's picture of the work of the Spirit is modeled by Paul's experience in Rom 7 and 8. Before baptism, sin reigns through lust; but after the washing of regeneration, it is overcome and subdued. While human nature is evil, a regenerate person, not walking after the flesh, represses sin with the Spirit of grace so there is no condemnation for those grafted into Christ (Rom 8).[197]

Rhegius and Spangenberg said the Holy Spirit works renewal in the context of the law. Spangenberg used a paradigm similar to seventeenth century Lutheran orthodoxy of *ordo salutis* that relates the gift of the Holy Spirit to "Grace." The Spirit moves hearts from repentance to faith, a new obedience to the law, prayer, fear of God, love, and patience.[198] Rhegius said that Saint Paul found at his conversion that while the law of God was still in effect, he was given a new amiability for the law and a willingness to do it.[199] With a view which may be closer to Calvin than to Luther, Rhegius's picture of the work of the Spirit makes the law a positive force in the life of the Christian. The purpose of the law and its achievement by the work of the Spirit demonstrates the spiritual power available for renewal which goes beyond secular philosophy and ethics without the Holy Spirit.

Rhegius maintained that Christ has freed believers from sin and its punishment, from the eternal curse, and from the power of Satan and has given them the Holy Spirit who renews and frees their hearts from sin, death, and hell, so they may walk in the commandments of God.[200] He also saw the Holy Spirit giving faith and pouring love into their hearts to fulfill the law (Rom 8:10).[201]

Spangenberg emphasized that the Holy Spirit has a governing role in the life of believers in which the Spirit succeeds where the law has failed. The law is ordained for the faithless, those not yet under grace, who have not received Christ with faith, and are not governed by the Spirit. The gospel brings eternal spiritual life to keep the part of the law that teaches about the new life. Those who are justified and have received the Holy Spirit enter a new life of spiritual obedience required in the Ten Commandments or moral law.[202] When the Holy Spirit is received believing hearts are com-

---

197. Rhegius, *Old Learnyng*, C.iiii. Rhegius tells how Augustine had early thought Rom 7 referred to an unregenerate man, but later, against Julian, he reversed his position to say that it referred to the Christian person after baptism.

198. See "Synne" in Spangenberg, *Summe*.

199. Rhegius, *Common Places*: "xxxv. Christian lybeerte."

200. Rhegius, *Common Places*: "xxxv. Christian lybeerte." 69.

201. Rhegius, *Treatise* (1548), B. vii [B].

202. See "Of Abrogation of the Law" in Spangenberg, *Summe*.

forted in repentance. New desires for the law of God are created, followed by a new obedience toward God in prayer, fear, love, patience, etc.[203]

Rhegius used Saint Paul's conversion to show how the Holy Spirit changes one's relationship with the law. The Ten Commandments did not change, but Paul changed. He became another man. Before his conversion the law of God was bitter and contrary to his will. When by faith he was purified and the Holy Spirit poured love into his heart, the law became amiable and he was willing and empowered to follow it.[204] This concept, that the Holy Spirit makes the law a positive force in the Christian life, pertains to a comparison where Rhegius said legalism would "play . . . the Jews . . . against the doctrine of the Holy Ghost."[205] However, the view of Paul's freedom and willingness to follow the law seems to assume that Rom 7 reflects Paul's pre-conversion struggles with the law, while Rom 8 depicts his post-conversion victory. That model opposes Luther's Reformation *simul iustis et peccator* theology found in much of the rest of Romans, the New Testament, and conflicts with the continuing day-to-day struggles and trials of the Christian life. The Holy Spirit bridles the flesh to protect it so that it may ask God for help to prepare for the Lord's Supper with thanksgiving, fasting, and living moderately.[206] Christians in the church should honor one another since they are the temple of the Holy Spirit[207] and God intends the Christian life to include trust, faith, sonship, and prayer.[208]

Brecht gives Brenz's idea of how the forgiveness of sins ends the struggle of temptation and brings the peace of salvation. This is the new life caused by the indwelling Spirit in which he removes the remains of the old Adam.[209] The Holy Spirit was present in the apostles before Christ's death and resurrection when they confessed Christ (Matt 16:16–17) and were drawn to him by the Spirit.[210] After Pentecost the ascended Christ sent the Holy Spirit to believers, according to his promise, as proof of forgiveness of sins, sanctification, and that he dwells in their hearts.[211]

---

203. See "Synne" in Spangenberg, *Summe*.
204. Rhegius, *Common Places*, "xxxv. Christian lybeerte."
205. Rhegius, *Old Learnyng*, E.ii [B].
206. Rhegius, *Old Learnyng*, 85.
207. Rhegius, *Old Learnyng*, 93.
208. Rhegius, *Instruccyon*, unnmb. 60–61.
209. Brecht, *Theologie*, 151.
210. Brenz, *Syngramma*, 267–68.
211. Brenz, *Syngramma*, 275.

Spangenberg agreed with Brenz that the new life in the Holy Spirit results from an indwelling of the Holy Spirit.[212] Spangenberg described the weakness of the human will which, without the Holy Spirit, cannot do that which God requires, that is, fear God, trust in mercy, suffer adversity, and love God. The children of God are those who are empowered by the Holy Spirit, have the Spirit of Christ, and enter the kingdom of God. Though their human judgment wanders, when their infirmity is revealed by the Holy Spirit, they are stilled. The gospel should provoke, stir up, and inflame them to call upon God for help. The Holy Spirit helps this infirmity to avoid outward faults and to sharpen human diligence. So Paul commands them to beware of receiving God's grace and the Holy Spirit in vain, and not to be idle or to despise the gift, but to pray for it. Spangenberg said that God left people in the counsel of their own wills and they should be diligent in godly actions. To be truly free and effective, however, their wills need to be helped by the Holy Spirit. He said that there is corruption in the human will after the fall which is judged by the law, and still continues in believers. The Spirit helps them to obey the law in outward things, though otherwise they may have been hindered by the devil.[213] His view included Luther's *simul iustus et peccator*, and Melanchthon's "affections" to obey the law. Spangenberg said that through the Lord's Supper the Holy Spirit confirms faith with outward signs as instruments of his testimony and seals, to stir up believers to faith and trust.[214] He held a dynamic sense of the Christian's continual need and the Holy Spirit's consistent meeting of that need. The Spirit acts in those in whom he dwells to raise them up in their mortal bodies on the last day as firstfruits of God's election.[215]

The early Reformers declared in unity with Luther and Melanchthon that the Christian life is continually sustained, made fruitful, and empowered by the Holy Spirit.

Holiness and Christian Liberty

Spangenberg taught freedom from accusation of the law through remission of sins and "imputing" of justice. In addition, the Holy Spirit will be given to govern and to defend them against the tyranny of the devil.[216] Brenz

---

212. See "Synne" and "Of the Difference between the New and Old Testament" in Spangenberg, *Summe*.

213. See "Free Wyll" in Spangenberg, *Summe*.

214. Spangenberg, *Summe*, "Of the Supper of the Lord."

215. See "Of the Rysing Again of the Dead" in Spangenberg, *Summe*.

216. See "Of the Abrogation of the Law" in Spangenberg, *Summe*.

pictured the Spirit working to defeat the fundamental root of sin. Reason, meanwhile, works with the appearances of the natural, physical opportunities at hand. Spirit and reason stand in double contrast. Accordingly, the Spirit goes to the foundation, to the root, while reason remains stuck in the branches.[217] Spangenberg and Brenz saw the Holy Spirit freeing believers from the grips of rationality and the devil to live in true godliness and Christ-likeness.

Inner Testimony of the Holy Spirit

Rhegius believed that the Holy Spirit is given as an act of God alone, whose testimony cries out in the hearts of his children.[218] God gives the Holy Spirit so that believers may be received as sons, live the new life in Christ, trust him, have faith, and pray. This pertains to what Luther called the Inner Testimony of the Holy Spirit, as well as to Melanchthon's "affections" to do the law. Rhegius said Paul's personal experience in Rom 7 and 8 demonstrated the victory over the sinful plagues of the flesh. This is described as the testimony of the Spirit in the Christian's life after baptism.[219] This act of God's Spirit bears inner testimony in the lives of believers:

> Saint Paul says we receive the Holy Ghost not by our working but by hearing of the gospel, this Holy Ghost will not suffer us to doubt..., but with a bold trust cries in our hearts to God Abba father, and witnesses with our spirit that we be the children and the heirs with Christ.[220]

Spangenberg observed that with remission of sins, the Holy Spirit is the Spirit of grace, whereby we know that God in his mercy has forgiven our sins. As the Spirit of prayer he continues all worship, invocation, and faith. He brings comfort as we believe that we have remission of sins for Christ's sake,[221]

---

217. Brecht, *Theologie*, 44.
218. Rhegius, *Instruccyon*, 60–61.
219. Rhegius, *Old Learnyng*, C.iiii.
220. Rhegius, *Instruccyon*, 60–61.
221. See "Grace" in Spangenberg, *Summe*.

Responses to the Holy Spirit

Prayer and Worship

Rhegius and Spangenberg said the Holy Spirit gives believers a new spiritual dimension of experience and communication with God in prayer and worship. According to Rhegius, prayer is the place where the Holy Spirit speaks in the economy of the Holy Trinity, whereby faith comes to believe the commands of the Father given through his Son.[222] Speaking of the uses of prayer in the Christian Church, he said that the devil probably is not afraid of things such as holy water but should be "afraid at the sight of a Christian man, whom the ointment of the Holy Ghost has made holy, and is the temple of the Holy Ghost."[223] He said that prayer occurs, not just in temples or in church structures, but widely everywhere because God is found everywhere and the Holy Spirit is given to those desiring him in prayer.[224]

Good Works

In his *Handbook for Preaching*, Rhegius includes practical instructions for pastors to tell their flocks about the ministry of the Holy Spirit. While Christ has won our forgiveness through God's grace in Christ, we can not obey his commandments except that "He alone gives us his Spirit through his word, so that we also receive the understanding, will, and ability to keep God's commandments."[225] We are naturally children of wrath—slaves to sin incapable of doing good until Christ regenerates us, gives us faith and the Holy Spirit. This frees us to do good things through the Holy Spirit. Otherwise we are only free to ponder and do evil as the evil one intends. This is our fault. God forbids evildoing and rewards it with temporal and eternal punishment. The causes of all sin are the devil and our perverted wills.[226]

Spangenberg said the Holy Spirit motivates what he inwardly accomplishes through the work of the gospel in the lives of believers. Good works are given by the Holy Spirit to enable Christians to please and glorify God. This is part of their Christian vocation in the holy priesthood, to offer spiritual sacrifices unto the Father. The Holy Spirit helps in good works, lest the devil entice believers into dangerous errors and ungracious mischiefs.

222. Rhegius, *Old Learnyng*, E.v[a].
223. Rhegius, *Old Learnyng*, E.vii[a].
224. See "Of Prayer" in Spangenberg, *Summe*.
225. Rhegius, *Handbook*, 61.
226. Rhegius, *Handbook*, 63.

Spangenberg saw works as different uses of the law, similar to the *Formula of Concord*'s three uses of the law. The law prescribes outward works in civil living and justice for the ungodly without the Holy Spirit. He also requires inward spiritual works of the heart: fear of God, trust, prayer, love, and patience, according to his law written in their hearts.[227]

The Sin against the Holy Spirit

Spangenberg discussed Christ's distinction between sins which can be forgiven and the sin against the Holy Spirit, which is a sin unto death that shall be forgiven neither now nor in the world to come. Spangenberg noted Augustine's understanding of the sin against the Holy Spirit to be either in them who never repent or in them who do not receive the gospel. They are those who speak against the Holy Spirit by forsaking the preached word of grace.[228] The judgment of God would not let them trust their own works, but required them to believe in Christ. Let them not make the Holy Spirit of God sorry and cast away the benefits of Christ to perish.[229]

Brecht notes Brenz's thoughts:

> Brenz said the sin against the Holy Spirit occurs when sin is called no sin and unrighteousness is called righteousness, for then it is impossible to come to repentance and forgiveness.[230] "Unbelief as naked stubborn contempt for the word is the sin against the Holy Spirit."[231] Unbelievers are blinded by the word which brings the forgiving God and the cross.[232] The stand against the word of truth is the sin against the Holy Spirit, who inspired its truth, and calls it the word of Christ.[233]

Brenz means here that rejection of the Spirit's work of proclaiming God's word of truth demonstrates a faithless rejection of the Spirit himself—the only way mankind can know about sin and eternal judgment—the sin against the Holy Spirit.

---

227. See "Justification" in Spangenberg, *Summe*.
228. See "Absolution" in Spangenberg, *Summe*.
229. See "Gospel" in Spangenberg, *Summe*.
230. Brecht, *Theologie*, 54–55.
231. Brecht, *Theologie*, 128: "Der Unglaube als obstinatus contemptus aperti verbi ist die Sünde wider den Heiligen Geist. Denn das Wort ist Wahrheit, und der Geist ist der Geist der Wahrheit," citing the Jeremiah lectures, S.900, 17,1.
232. Brecht, *Theologie*, 146, citing S.883, 7, 25.
233. Brecht, *Theologie*, 146, citing the Jeremiah lectures, S.900, 17, 1, 128, citing S.937, 43, 2.

Summary and Conclusions

It is clear that Brenz, Rhegius, and Spangenberg stood with Luther to declare the futility of any attempts by philosophical systems or reason to achieve salvation or the gifts of God apart from the working of the Holy Spirit in the gospel. With Luther, they featured the priority of the Holy Spirit's work in their theologies and emphasized the inner testimony of the Holy Spirit that believers' sins are forgiven and that they are the children of God. They stressed that the Holy Spirit works only through the physical means of the word and sacraments as they are received in faith.

The Wittenburg theology regarding the Holy Spirit was faithfully spread to other territories of Germany by the early Reformers. Each of these Reformers had a specific locale of responsibility and authority. Brenz worked primarily in the city of Schwäbisch Hall in the duchy of Württemberg. Rhegius was general superintendent of the duchy of Braunsweig, where he led the Reformation of Celle, Soest, Hanover, Minden, Lemgo, and other regions in the duchy. Spangenberg was born and worked in the Nordhausen and Mansfeld districts in the Harz region.

Although these three Reformers were pastors and wrote extensively, their impact on the Reformation was distinct. Brenz's work focused primarily on the relationship of the church and the state. He moved in the company of dukes and princes and strongly influenced both church leaders and magistrates with his clear, mild, and considerate manner of writing and speaking. He established a church polity that became the model for Protestant German-speaking regions and thus profoundly affected the history of the church. Rhegius saw the Reformation of the church in practical day-to-day work of the clergy. His theology of compassion for the sick, suffering, and dying sought to make Christendom more authentically Christian through the development and promotion of an evangelical ministry of consolation. He also wrote extensively, including church orders for Hanover in 1536 that were still in effect at the end of the nineteenth century. Spangenberg, like Luther and Melanchthon, made education, both secular and Christian, an important focus of his work. Along with new church orders he generated new educational programs and text books for all ages from children to advanced university studies. He introduced music and wrote music theory, teacher handbooks, and original hymns. He is credited with writing the most significant liturgical/musical work of the early Lutheran Church.

Although these Reformers made distinct contributions to the Reformation, their extensive writing was not distinct. They wrote theology, church orders, catechisms, textbooks, and biblical commentaries and in most cases their personal insights parallel the work of Luther. They all insisted that the work of the Holy Spirit is absolutely the key to every aspect of Lutheran theology and to the Christian life. The vast body of consistent theological writing produced by these Reformers provided continuity following Luther and set the stage for those who subsequently authored the *Formula of Concord*.

5

The *Formula of Concord* Writers' Theology of the Holy Spirit

Jakob Andreae, Martin Chemnitz, David Chytraeus
"The Late Lutheran Reformation"

Introduction

Jakob Andreae, Martin Chemnitz, and David Chytraeus were prominent Reformers whose work on the *Formula of Concord* helped to resolve disputes that arose among Lutherans after the deaths of Martin Luther in 1546 and of Philip Melanchthon in 1560. As Protestant theologians, along with Matthias Flacius Illyricus, Theodore Beza, and many others of the second half of the sixteenth century, the three Reformers examined in this chapter comprise what Peter F. Barton has named the "Late Reformation"—a transition spanning the momentous changes of the early Reformation movement to the orthodox developments of the seventeenth century.[1] The theologies of the Holy Spirit of these Reformers in the period of the *Formula of Concord* are presented here in relation to Luther's theology of the Holy Spirit.

---

1. Barton, *Um Luthers Erbe*, 9; Mahlmann, "Martin Chemnitz," 317.

Background and Influences

Upon the deaths of Luther and Melanchthon, Reformation theology became more and more fractured due to the Smalcaldic War, two Interims during which Reformation teaching and preaching were illegal, and contentions among the followers of various Reformation leaders. Drawing beliefs and districts into unity was a dizzying task. The need for standard definitions and agreements among Lutherans was desperate and the "Confessional" Reformers discussed in this chapter worked tirelessly to achieve those ends. In her article, "The Culture of Conflict in the Controversies Leading to the *Formula of Concord* (1548–1580)," Irene Dingel discusses the period of the controversies that characterized the Lutheran theologians in the latter half of the sixteenth century under the topic of "The Culture of Controversy."[2] In her introduction, Professor Dingel notes "The decisive, crucial role of the controversies that systemized and synthesized the teachings of the Wittenberg theologians, conducted first in personal exchanges and then in print, has been largely neglected, these controversies dismissed as unnecessary squabbles among theologians. Only recently have researchers begun to study the . . . controversies . . . and [to] take seriously this culture of controversy as the decisive motor for the refinement of reformational teaching."[3]

Jakob Andreae (1528–90)

Jakob Andreae was born to the family of a smithy of Waiblingen, in the duchy of Württemberg. His humble origins were often the source of derision by his opponents. He received ducal scholarships for secondary and university work at Tübingen where he earned the masters degree at age seventeen.[4] At eighteen, in 1546, Andreae was called into the pastoral ministry, ordained as a deacon, and married twenty-year-old Anna Entringer of Tübingen, who subsequently bore him eighteen children. In 1548 he lost his job under pressure imposed by imperial forces under the Augsburg Interim. While he earned his doctorate at Tübingen, Andreae continued to work against the Interim in the Swäbian province of Württemberg under the leadership and support of Duke Christopher. They shared a desire for

---

2. Dingel, "Culture of Conflict," 15. Professor Dingel's article presents a collection of the types and information about the controversies and their documents. A website benefiting present and future research has been constructed including bibliographical material of 1500 publications as well as biographies of the authors. The target of the project has been an eight-volume set of texts.

3. Dingel, "Culture of Conflict," 15.

4. Kolb, *Six Sermons*, 9–10.

German political and theological unity.[5] From that time, throughout his career, Andreae resolved disputes and provided theological leadership following his notion that conflicts are settled by working through problems. At age twenty-five (1553) Andreae was appointed to the ecclesiastical superintendency in Göppingen by which time the Interim was no longer in effect.[6] This post provided an effective position for his work of representing the Duke to the university faculty and students, and to the community in a broad ministry of teaching and preaching. He became one of Lutheranism's most active and productive leaders.[7]

Andreae attended the 1557 Colloquy at Worms, where his and Württemberg's leading churchman, Johannes Brenz's mediating position on Andreas Osiander's doctrine of justification earned the animosity of the Gnesio-Lutherans. Though Andreae was unsuccessful in formulating a decentralized church polity with Theodore Beza's Genevan position on the Lord's Supper, this action strengthened his relationship with Brenz, and "ended with Andreae's being won over to Brenz's positions and to ducal service as an ecclesiastical diplomat outside the duchy."[8]

As Duke Christopher's court preacher, Andreae preached—and immediately published—two sermons on justification and the Lord's Supper at the Diet of Augsburg (1559) to demonstrate his theological agreement with Luther over Catholic opponents, and to present a position to end disputes among other members of the Wittenberg group.[9] His acceptance of the Württemberg Confession of 1559 against Calvinist views of the Lord's Supper and Christology became his usual style for defense of Lutheran doctrines.[10] It also confirmed that Andreae shared some significant theological tendencies of the Gnesio-Lutherans, though his work seeking unity often disturbed them.[11] His Christological emphasis carried through in his understanding of the divinity of Christ, Christ's presence at the Lord's Supper, and the ubiquity of Christ's total person. He maintained that the words of institution demonstrated the real presence of Christ against claims of his immobilized position at the right hand of God.[12]

---

5. Jungkuntz, *Formulators*, 22–30.
6. Kolb, "Andreae," 18.
7. Jungkuntz, *Formulators*, 22–30.
8. Jungkuntz, *Formulators*, 22–30.
9. Kolb, "Andreae Preaching—1559," 10–14.
10. Jungkuntz, *Formulators*, 22–30; Kolb. "Andreae Preaching—1559," 10.
11. Jungkuntz *Formulators*, 28–29.
12. Kolb, "Andreae Preaching—1559," 25.

In the two sermons, Andreae demonstrated his developing theological leadership to a large audience as he addressed topics that troubled both Catholics and Evangelicals—Lutherans of several groups, Calvinists, Zwinglians, and Baptists—and clearly aligned with Luther. As Kolb notes, "In addressing these questions in this manner he [Andreae] served the interests of his prince's [Christopher] ecclesiastical policy both in his unremitting critique of Roman Catholic teaching ... and also in his attempt to bring concord among opposing interpretations of the Wittenberg legacy."[13]

In 1561, Duke Christopher called Andreae to Tübingen to strengthen its theological faculty[14] as professor of theology, chancellor of the University of Tübingen, and as diocesan provost—positions he held the remainder of his life, during which he continued to advise the duke's efforts to achieve agreement within Lutheran churches. Kolb notes how Andreae traveled among Lutherans attempting—though not always successful—to unify them under Luther's theology through the time of the *Book of Concord*. His travels included the Erfurt presentation of a common German Evangelical front at the Council of Trent, the Colloquy of Poissy where his delegation arrived late and missed participation in the confrontation of Roman Catholic and Calvinist parties, and Ducal Saxony where he offended Gnesio-Lutherans by compromising with Victorin Strigel's freedom of the human will.[15]

Andreae's aggressive style with Roman Catholics, Zwinglians, Anabaptists, and Schwenckfelders, shown by his series of thirty-three sermons preached in Esslingen in 1568, still did not fully ease some earlier concerns about his apparent compromising theology. In 1568, Christopher dispatched Andreae to his cousin Duke Julius, of Braunschweig-Wolfenbüttel to introduce the Reformation in Julius's lands, while launching a new effort of unity there. Andreae used his "Five Articles":—justification, good works, freedom of the will, adiaphora, and the Lord's Supper—to express Wittenberg teaching in very broad terms. As Andreae journeyed among the towns he convinced his Gnesio-Lutheran critics that he was conforming his positions to theirs. In 1570, Duke Julius and representatives of several Evangelical princes approved the final form of these five articles but theologians of Electoral Saxony in Wittenberg rejected his Christology.[16]

In 1573 Andreae again offered a proposal for settling differences among Lutheran theologians with his *Six Christian Sermons on the Divisions*

---

13. Kolb, "Andreae Preaching—1559," 29.
14. Kolb, "Andreae," 20.
15. Kolb, "Andreae," 18.
16. Kolb, "Andreae," 19.

That Have Continued to Surface among the Theologians of the Augsburg Confession. Written in the homiletical form he had used earlier to acquaint laity with significant theological issues on the basis of the text of Luther's Catechism (so that even illiterate laypeople could defend their beliefs), it set forth solutions to six areas of dispute: justification, good works, original sin and freedom of the will, law and gospel, adiaphora, and Christology. His form now included much more detailed discussion of the issues, with explicit condemnations of false teachings and false teachers (by name), and it sought agreement among theologians apart from princely supervision. Colleagues whom he approached, especially Martin Chemnitz and David Chytraeus, believed that a more substantial argument than one based on the Catechism was necessary. They suggested that the Tübingen faculty compose such a proposal. Andreae persisted, writing the Swabian Concord in 1574, which Chemnitz and Chytraeus revised into the Swabian-Saxon Concord of 1575. The independently compiled Maulbronn Formula of 1576 served as the basis for the *Formula of Concord's* Solid Declaration. To keep this effort alive, Elector August of Saxony, when it was opposed by some of his trusted crypto-Philipist advisers, called on Andreae to assist in applying Luther's insights more broadly to promote a larger Evangelical settlement of disputes within his domains (1576).[17]

August enlisted a committee of his own theological advisers headed by Andreae and Nikolaus Selnecker, to which he added Chemnitz, Chytraeus, and two representatives of the Elector of Brandenburg, Andreas Musculus and Christoph Korner. They hammered out the agreement reached in the *Formula of Concord*. At the same time, Andreae was enlisted to write a digest of the now-lengthy Solid Declaration, which became the Epitome. Andreae tirelessly promoted acceptance of the *Formula* and won adherence from two-thirds of the Evangelical *ministeria* in Germany by 1580. He fashioned a preface for the *Book of Concord* that combined other Lutheran confessions with the *Formula*.

In 1586 Andrea represented his duke, now Ulrich, and Lutheran theology in Mömpelgard (Montbéliard) with Theodore Beza and a team of Calvinists. Andrea spent his last decade teaching and defending the theology of the *Formula of Concord* against Roman Catholics and reformed.[18]

As Andreae concentrated on enduring Lutheran beliefs he strove to achieve lasting German theological unity.[19] Because his writing was so thor-

---

17. Kolb, "Andreae," 19.
18. Kolb, "Andreae," 20.
19. Jungkuntz, *Formulators*, 34.

oughly prepared, much of his original material became part of the *Formula of Concord*.

Martin Chemnitz (1522–86)

Martin Chemnitz was the leading Lutheran theologian of the "Late Reformation" period. He studied at Wittenberg, served as librarian and professor at Königsberg, and was pastor and churchman at Braunschweig.[20] He successfully united Lutherans doctrinally, while bolstering fellow theologians Andreae and Selnecker. His leadership in the writing of the *Formula of Concord* helped settle debates and issues that arose after Luther's death.[21] His mediating position agreed with Melanchthon's on many points while strongly advocating Lutheran biblical methodology. His work, representing the character of the Reformation time, was an important bridge of content and method between Luther and the seventeenth-century dogmaticians.[22]

Chemnitz was born in 1522 at Treuenbritzen in Electoral (Kurfürstentum) Brandenburg. Though Chemnitz's father died when Martin was a child, several men helped him at crucial times to achieve his potential in his service of the church. Balthasar Schüler, mayor of Brandenburg became Martin's guardian. One of Schüler's sons, George, became his educational mentor, assisting him several times in obtaining his education through 1553 at Wittenberg.[23] Chemnitz studied in Wittenberg (Trivialschule), Madgeburg, and Frankfort an der Oder.

At age fourteen Chemnitz heard Luther preach at Wittenberg. Later, Melanchthon influenced him as a university student (1552–54).[24] Ordained at Braunschweig in 1554, he served as pastor (1554–67) and superintendent (1567–86). He was affiliated later with the universities at Königsberg and Wittenberg. In 1555, he married Anna Jaeger, who bore him three sons and seven daughters.[25] He was involved with theological issues at Wittenberg during his ministry at Braunschweig until his death there in 1586, which was a setback for German Protestantism.[26]

---

20. Preus, *Post-Reformation Lutheranism*, 1:47; Schmid, *Doctrinal Theology*, 665.

21. Preus, *Post-Reformation Lutheranism*, 1:48.

22. Klug, *Luther to Chemnitz*, 115; Hägglund, *History of Theology*, 273.

23. Preus, *Second Martin*, 87–88, 90, 91, 94, 96.

24. Kunze, "Chemnitz," 24; Preus, *Post-Reformation Lutheranism*, 1:47.

25. Preus, *Post-Reformation Lutheranism*, 1:47; Schmid, *Doctrinal Theology*, 665; Jungkuntz, *Formulators*, 31; Mahlmann, "Chemnitz," 316.

26. Kunze, "Chemnitz," 24–25.

Joachim Mörlin (1514–71) studied at Wittenberg under Luther and Melanchthon (1532–36). Not one to avoid a debate, he was a faithful, lifelong follower and defender of Luther's doctrines vis-à-vis the Philippists during the struggles from 1543–71, which thrice led to his exile.[27] By 1554, when Chemnitz was leaving Wittenberg, Mörlin was a leader among the Gnesio-Lutherans. Chemnitz followed Mörlin's strong orthodox interpretation of Luther—a relationship that continued the rest of their lives. Mörlin paved the way for Chemnitz to be called, ordained, and installed into service as pastor and coadjutor at Braunschweig, where he worked closely with Mörlin until Mörlin's death.

As early as 1556, Chemnitz and Mörlin had been successful in mediating roles in inter-Lutheran disputes. In 1567, Duke Albrecht of Prussia invited Mörlin to help resolve a doctrinal issue at Königsberg. He was joined by Chemnitz. As theologians and pastors, Chemnitz and Mörlin—the head of the effort—produced their *Corpus doctrinæ Prutenicum* (1567) to reorganize the Prussian church. In his article, "The Braunschweig Resolution: The *Corpus Doctrinae Prutenicum* of Joachim Mörlin and Martin Chemnitz as an Interpretation of Wittenberg Theology," Robert Kolb discusses how well Chemnitz and Mörlin worked together as a team, which was a main characteristic of the collegium in Wittenberg—"they formed a partnership as they led, directed, and modeled the development of Lutheran teaching and ecclesiastical practice, introducing Wittenberg thought, method, and procedures throughout Germany and beyond."[28]

Mörlin modeled churchmanship for Chemnitz by gathering early Gnesio-Lutherans to challenge Melanchthon to define his stand on the Lord's Supper vis-à-vis Calvin's position, and, at Worms, to debate Georg Major's theology of justification and works.[29] In 1561 Mörlin and Chemnitz jointly raised questions about justification and Christology in the Osiander debates, which they addressed again in one of their last joint efforts in Prussia (1568).[30] Many of Chemnitz's early major theological works and church orders were encouraged by Mörlin and written in conjunction and agreement with Mörlin's adherence to Luther's teachings.[31] Mörlin's foundational writings were expressed several years later after his death, in the work leading to the *Formula*

---

27. Lezius, "Mörlin, Joachim," 432; Preus, *Second Martin*, 94.
28. Kolb, "Prutenicum," 67.
29. Mahlmann, "Chemnitz," 316–17.
30. Mahlmann, "Chemnitz," 318; Preus, *Second Martin*, 126.
31. Mahlmann, "Chemnitz," 315–16; Preus, *Second Martin*, 98–100, 104, 108, 111–13, 128, 150, 157.

of Concord (1577).³² Jacob Preus provided citations from a sixteenth-century Chemnitz contemporary and friend, J. Gasmer, who describes the genuine Chemnitz-Mörlin Christian relationship. He observed:

> There was between these two men genuine and mutual love, whereby both having the same love were one in thinking and speaking. They sought nothing through strife or vainglory, but each out of modesty considered the other better than himself and had consideration for the public benefit of the church rather than his own. What shall I say about the smooth and pleasant combination of the gifts of these two men?³³

Their zeal and gentleness complemented each other as they sought to serve and unite the church under Luther's Reformation truth.

Gerhard Bode summarizes Mörlin's significance:

> His efforts to address controversy and achieve doctrinal unity helped to consolidate Lutheranism in the generation after Luther's death. His work with Chemnitz in Braunschweig highlighted the need for agreement and introduced the means to achieve it.³⁴

Philip Melanchthon was an early and noteworthy influence on Martin Chemnitz, especially in his education and career direction. Philip gave Martin a place to stay at Wittenberg, an early foundation in classical languages, the framework relating philosophy with theology, and encouragement to pursue theological studies as pastor and professor. This ultimately led to Chemnitz being a Father of the "Late Reformation" that resulted in the *Formula of Concord* (1577) and *The Book of Concord* (1580).

Working with Mörlin and appreciating his emphasis on Luther's theology, along with his suspicion of the perils of philosophy, Chemnitz understood the importance of Mörlin's caution regarding Melanchthon's compromises with political interims and his allowing the philosophical content of human participation to interfere with his methods of doing theology. Chemnitz developed a somewhat congenial conflation of Luther's content—through Mörlin—with Melanchthon's methods. Melanchthon's *Loci Communes* (1543) provided the outline for Chemnitz's *Loci Theologici*. Although Melanchthon's *Loci Communes* appears in the Chemnitz work, it is obvious that Chemnitz pays absolutely no attention to it and in some cases, such as conversion and the Supper, totally disagrees with Melanchthon,

---

32. Preus, *Second Martin*, 160–66.
33. Preus, *Second Martin*, 128–29, citing Gasmer, *De Vita*, 24.
34. Bode, "Mörlin," 517.

without publicly opposing him.[35] Robert Preus summarized Chemnitz's successful use of Luther's and Melanchthon's influence by pointing out that it was Martin Luther's work and his principles in establishing the Reformation church that dominated Chemnitz's work in documenting theological bases and drawing together those who shared this "Luther" emphasis. Chemnitz worked against the extreme effects of Melanchthonianism through his writings, contacts with fellow theologians (Gnesio-Lutherans), and the *Formula of Concord*.[36]

While librarian at Königsberg, Chemnitz read the church fathers, dogmatics, and biblical theology, and these influenced his examination of the Council of Trent. Following Melanchthon's orderly approach, he started with the church fathers, and initiated the conflation of church history with the history of doctrine by carefully documenting the development of dogma through the various councils, disputes, and pronouncements.

Chemnitz shared Luther's disdain for philosophy, noting that Luther brought theology back to the Scriptures. He emphasized biblical languages and their thought patterns as the bases for theology. In his *Loci* Chemnitz addressed issues using the Law-Gospel motif with the inner unity of Christian theology, assuming that each element of doctrine can be independently treated without any higher structure to hold them together.[37]

Chemnitz was renowned as a pastor, a preacher, and a strong and effective theologian in controversies.[38] Conflicts with Gnesio-Lutherans, Philippists, and the Council of Trent drove him toward Lutheran unity. With the encouragement of concerned Protestant princes, he sought to employ the testimony of Scripture, the Fathers, the history of the church, and of dogma to bring peace through the formulation of orthodox Christian doctrine. His use of Melanchthon's method and Luther's theology produced an effective system that united Lutherans by thoroughly presenting Luther's Reformation position.[39]

These diverse influences on Chemnitz, enriched by his tireless devotion to Scripture and the history of Christ's church, produced the one who provoked the observation of the Catholics: "If the second Martin had not come, the first would not have prevailed."[40]

---

35. See the "Translator's Preface" in Preus, *Second Martin, Loci* 1.5.

36. Preus, *Post-Reformation Lutheranism*, 1:48.

37. Preus, *Post-Reformation Lutheranism*, 1:92, 97.

38. Kunze, "Chemnitz," 24.

39. Preus, *Post-Reformation Lutheranism*, 1:48, 1:92–93; Schmid, *Doctrinal Theology*, 666–67.

40. Kolb, "Chemnitz, Martin," 138.

As a developing theological churchman of the Lutherans of the "Late Reformation" it was necessary that Chemnitz have a cooperative relationship with the secular leadership of his region—Duke Julius of Braunschweig—who used Chemnitz and Andreae to introduce the Reformation to his duchy.[41] Robert Kolb contrasts the relationships with governmental support of Philippists and Gnesio-Lutherans:

> Both Philippists and Gnesio-Lutherans welcomed governmental support for their ecclesiastical programs. However, the Philippists tended to be ready to compromise with their princes and to try not to irritate them while the Gnesio-Lutherans, though willing to use the prince's aid in executing their own reform plans, resisted encroachment into the affairs of the church from friendly princes as well as inimical ones.[42]

Kolb's statement describes Chemnitz's relationship with Duke Julius. Initially they enjoyed fruitful and almost affectionate mutual support through the early establishment of the Reformation in Braunschweig; however, that relationship was ultimately transformed into bitter antagonism over theological differences and ducal practices.

Chemnitz established Protestantism in Braunschweig-Wolfenbüttel with his *Corpus doctrinæ Julium* and *Corpus Wilhelminum* (1568), and initiated the founding of the Julian University at Helmstädt (1576). Chemnitz wrote several of his major works as he dealt with disputes and polemics. He addressed adiaphora and the Zwinglian question of the Lord's Supper in *Repitio sanæ doctrinæ de vera praesentia* (1561). He explained the incarnation in *De duabus naturis* (1570). Using the doctrine of the words of institution as an explanation of the real presence he opposed the Crypto-Calvinists (Philippists) and the *Wittenberg Catechism*. As a result, the Wittenberg faculty was replaced by conservative Lutherans (1570).[43]

To form the *Formula of Concord* he combined the *Six Christian Sermons* of Andreae with some of his own theological work, approved May 17, 1570. During the preparation of this work he maintained that Melanchthon must be interpreted in light of Luther, both are subject to the Confessions, and true unity presupposes pure doctrine. Chemnitz tamed the product of Andreae by providing the orthodox doctrinal tone of the *Formula*. He was disappointed when his own Duke Julius blocked the acceptance of the

---

41. Preus, *Second Martin*, 34, 62.
42. Preus, *Second Martin*, 63, citing Kolb, "Dynamics of Party Conflict," D1299.
43. Kunze, "Chemnitz," 24–25; Hägglund, *History of Theology*, 278.

Formula in Chemnitz's home duchy of Braunschweig and at his own Helmstädt University.[44]

Martin Chemnitz made a significant impact[45] through his evaluation of the Council of Trent, through his pulling together the factions of Lutheranism that produced the *Formula of Concord*, and through his clear, and thorough theological writing which laid the foundation of Lutheran Orthodoxy for the next 150 years.

David Chytraeus (1531–1600)

David Chytraeus was born in Württemberg. He received a master's degree at Tübingen at age fourteen and proceeded to Wittenberg to study under Philip Melanchthon. After the Smalcald War he became a popular teacher at Wittenberg.[46] In 1551 he was called to teach philosophy and theology at the University of Rostock. There he married Margaretha Smedes, who bore him seven children, of which two daughters survived to adulthood. After Margaretha's death in 1571, he married Margaretha Pegel and they had two sons who reached adulthood. Theodore Jungkuntz noted that the frequency of death and illness in Chytraeus's household might explain why the cross was central in his theology. His firm grasp of faith, similar to Luther's theology of the cross, was grounded in the power of the gospel. He saw God at work in the daily cross of living, purifying, cleansing, and perfecting through faith in Christ.[47]

With humanist education and interests, Chytraeus had restrained and cautious respect for Melanchthon,[48] yet he, along with Chemnitz, identified with the theologians who resolved the Lutheran debates with the *Formula of Concord*. Combining his skills as historian, exegete, and systematic theologian, Chytraeus prepared a history of the Augsburg Confession in order to link its Lutheran theological position and the transformation of the Western church with the "bold proclamation of the gospel that occurred when it was first read."[49] In recognition of his thorough and brilliant work, he received a doctor's degree in 1561, and was often asked to teach, mediate, and establish the work of the church. Chytraeus produced works in exegetics, dogmatics, polemics, philosophy, and history.

44. Jungkuntz, *Formulators*, 61–66.
45. Preus, *Post-Reformation Lutheranism*, 1:48.
46. Jungkuntz, *Formulaters*, 69–71.
47. Jungkuntz, *Formulaters*, 72–73.
48. Jungkuntz, *Formulaters*, 74–75.
49. Kolb, *Confessing*, 51.

In 1569 Emperor Maximilian II selected Chytraeus to establish the Evangelical Church in Austria. Chytraeus proposed a conservative church organized under the Emperor with its theology drawn from the Augsburg Confession. This approach was rejected. However, he used it successfully later (1574) in southeast Austria in response to the pleading requests of the estates of Styria. Jungkuntz noted Chytraeus's ability to absorb disappointment and move on to fruitful labor.[50]

By 1569 Chytraeus and Andreae had discussed concordant materials. Chytraeus's Austrian experience caused him to be wary of the "top-down" approach. Rather he encouraged people to seek God's help and guidance in writing their beliefs without external prescription.[51] In 1576 he joined a committee to work out an authoritative history of the Augsburg Confession. By then the works of Chemnitz and Andreae influenced him. At the Torgau conference, he conflated the "Swabian-Saxon Concord" and the "Malbronn Formula" into the "Torgau Book." He was very disappointed at subsequent changes made to obtain the *Formula of Concord*, and later said that his signature was not that of an author but merely of a subscriber.[52] Jungkuntz noted that he was torn by the legalistic orthodox spirit of the meetings. While the final document may have pleased those who agreed, it only heightened the differences with those who did not.[53]

Jungkuntz noted that although Chytraeus studied under Melanchthon, he distinguished between Melanchthon and Luther and stood in the Lutheran camp.[54] This seems to indicate that Chytraeus believed the later Melanchthon and his followers were not as "Lutheran" as the Augustana.[55]

The *Formula* Writers' Theology of the Holy Spirit

The Theology of the Cross

Luther's theology of the cross describes the role of the Holy Spirit in the necessity of death to personal effort and pride and then making one alive by faith in Christ. Through the ministry and comfort of the Holy Spirit one endures the death and by the power of the Holy Spirit, comes alive to joy and

50. Jungkuntz, *Formulators*, 76–79.
51. Jungkuntz, *Formulaters*, 81.
52. Jungkuntz, *Formulaters*, 82–84.
53. Jungkuntz, *Formulaters*, 84.
54. Jungkuntz, *Formulaters*, 84.
55. Loesche, "Chytraeus," 423.

peace in Christ. Chytraeus's view of patience describes Luther's theology of the cross. Patience results from yielding to God in one's own cross and affliction and reverently submitting to the will of God to mercifully mitigate sorrow. Human reason views such miseries as unprofitable, but the Holy Spirit shows in God's word that the calamities of the cross are good and profitable for the godly (Pss 116, 119; Rom 8).[56] Patience under the cross induces one to acknowledge Christ, to see the dangers of sin and judgment, and to repent and believe God for salvation. Adversity changes believers into the image of the Son with whom they share affliction and so, raised with him, they can better hear the word and proclaim its truths in their testimonies. Hardships remove the remnants of sin in the saints and change pride to humility, modesty, temperance, and self-control. Difficulties simplify lives and prepare disciples to care for others, to witness to Christian virtues, and to help people long for the joyous glory promised for all who endure this life's miseries. Chytraeus said the Holy Spirit causes martyrdom by comforting and strengthening Christians to obey God in affliction with Christ, who links them to God—e.g., John Hus and others.[57] He kindles faithfulness to God's call above life and all worldly things, which anticipates the promises of the coming life and glory. He bolsters wills and hearts to endure punishments, reproach, and death.[58] Chytraeus prayed that, as God armed the apostles and Luther, he would support the faith of his persecuted ones today[59] that his Spirit's presence would assure them that nothing can remove his love in his Son the Lord Jesus Christ from them.[60]

The Person of the Holy Spirit

Luther and Melanchthon held to the ancient Christian Trinitarian view of God, as did the *Formula* writers. Andreae said there is one God and three persons, not three gods or three spirits, but one Holy Spirit of the Father and the Son.[61] True doctrine is that the Word of God, the Redeemer, is one with the Father and the Spirit.[62]

---

56. Chytraeus, *Soueraigne Salue*, Av. Chytraeus gives twenty-two results which come through patiently bearing the cross.
57. Chytraeus, *Soueraigne Salue*, Avb-bd, Cii.
58. Chytraeus, *Postil*, 32.
59. Chytraeus, *Postil*, 340, Eph 3:13-21, on the sixteenth Sunday after Trinity.
60. Chytraeus, *Postil*, 456, Rom 8:28-39, on the Feast of St. James.
61. Andreae, *Drey und dreissig Predigten*, I-53; cf. I-15.
62. Chytraeus, *Studio*, 1-2.

Referring to the historical Trinitarian discussions, Chemnitz said the individual persons (*hypostases*) share in the same essence (*homoousia*) of the Godhead,[63] by which there is a communion of the persons of the Godhead. This divine essence "is communicable, common to three persons, the Father, the Son, and the Holy Spirit, and is complete in each of them,"[64] and "Each subsists as an undivided and single entity in the same essence."[65] Therefore there is an eternal unity in the Deity, which we worship in the Trinity, and in which the Holy Spirit shares all the divine attributes with the other persons of the Godhead—coeternal, coequal, consubstantial essence (*homoousios*), will,[66] power, majesty, and glory. Where the Holy Spirit is there are the Son and the Father, which proves the deity of the Holy Spirit.[67] Chytraeus affirmed that Christian theology is grounded in the one true God: Father, Son, and Holy Spirit. Scripture equates the Spirit with the divine Lord, including power, creation, redemption, and omnipresence (1 Cor 12:6; 2 Cor 3:18; Acts 5; Isa 6).[68] Testimonies to this were given at Jesus' baptism (Matt 3:16–17), the Great Commission of Matt 28 and Mark 16, and the words of Christ, "I will call upon the Father, and he will give you another Comforter, the Spirit of truth" (John 14:16–17).[69]

Citing Basil and others, Chytraeus linked the unity of the persons in the Godhead with the baptismal invocation, and several Scriptures in which

---

63. *CLT53*, 1:34, 37; *CLTP*, 69–72; Chytraeus, *Studio*, 12b; Andreae, "Confessions," 58.

64. *CLT53*, 1:37; *CLTP*, 72, "*Communicabilis est, & communis tribus personis, Patri, Filio, & Spiritui S. & est tota in singulis*"; Andreae, *Six Sermons*, 113.

65. *CLT53*, 1:42; *CLTP*, 78, "*Etiam individuum singulare in eadem essentia per se subsistens.*" Cf. *CLT53*, 1:23; *CLTP*, 55; *DNC*, 120, 103; *TNC*, 305, 269–70. In *DNC*, 106 and *TNC*, 276, Chemnitz discusses the ancients' views of the integrity of the hypostatic union: "The ancients ... established and corroborated the homoousian—that there is one and the same substance of the Father, Son, and Holy Spirit" ["*Et Veteres, probant & confirmant homoousias hoc est, unam eandem esse substantiam Patris, Filii, & Spiritus sancti*"].

66. *CLT53*, 1:29, 43, 26; *CLTP*, 65, 79, 58, citing John of Damascus, *De Fide Orthodoxa*, 1.2.

67. *CLT53*, 1:89; *CLTP*, 13, citing Cyril, *Dial. de Trin.* 7.

68. Chytraeus, *Catechesis*, 4, 20.

69. *CLT53*, 1:32; *CLTP*, 66; also Chytraeus, *Catechesis*, 16; cf. Sweete, *Holy Spirit in the Ancient Church*, 319, 321–22, 324. In his *De Spiritu Sancto* Ambrose used similar arguments concerning the divinity of the Holy Spirit. The Spirit's divinity is demonstrated by his actions, his power, and his attributes. He participated in creation, he raises from the dead, he forgives sins, he is without sin, and he is worshiped. Sweete notes that while Ambrose wasn't original he did the Western church the service of introducing the Greek theologians, which his follower Augustine used with some developments of his own. Chytraeus's idea of basing the divinity of the Spirit on his actions is the same as the early fathers.

the Holy Spirit is the Lord God.⁷⁰ Before creation, the Holy Spirit was eternally with God the Father and the Son.⁷¹

Numerous other Scriptures that define the Holy Spirit as a person are quoted in these theologians' writings. His person (*hypostasis*) was demonstrated in union with the dove, in the fiery tongues, in the sevenfold gifts, and in the fire kindled in believers' hearts.⁷² Jesus spoke of the abiding Holy Spirit, (John 14:23, 1 John 3:24), gave the Holy Spirit (1 John 4:13), and promised the Comforter from the Father (John 14:16).⁷³ The Spirit's presence during the pregnancies bearing John and Jesus showed that God was with them personally, even in the womb (Luke 1:41).⁷⁴ The Holy Spirit, consubstantial with the Father and the Son, worked as the third person of the Godhead casting out demons (Matt 12:28; Luke 11:20).⁷⁵ Christ commissioned the church to baptize in the name of the three persons (Matt 28:19). The Holy Spirit was called the Lord (2 Cor 3:17) and led Israel in the desert (Isa 63:14). There are separate witnesses of the three persons, including God's promises to pour out his Spirit on all flesh.⁷⁶ The Father referred to the Spirit's person as wind and as a bird fluttering over the waters at creation (Gen 1:2). Partakers of the divine nature have fellowship with God through the Holy Spirit (2 Pet 1:4). The Spirit of the Lord is in all places and cannot be hidden (Ps 139:7; Wis 1:7) as he searches the deep things of God (1 Cor 2:10). The Spirit of Christ spoke by the prophets (1 Pet 1:11). Jesus spoke by the Spirit only what He heard (John 16:13).⁷⁷

Chemnitz distinguished the Spirit's person from human attributes (1 Cor 12:4–11; Rom 8:5–11; 2 Cor 3:6, 17) and new emotions which stem from the infilling of the Spirit.⁷⁸ When Christ spoke of the Spirit (*to pneuma*, neuter) he used "He" (*ekeinos*, masculine), referring to a person (John 15:26; Matt 28:19). In John 20:22 and 7:39 the evangelist referred to the gifts of the Holy Spirit at Pentecost, not to his person. Chemnitz claimed that those in Acts 19:2 had obviously heard of the Holy Spirit from John's preaching but were not aware of the Spirit's visible gifts of speaking in

---

70. Chytraeus, *Postil*, 218–19.

71. Chytraeus, *Postil*, 216–20.

72. *FSD*, 11, 14-10, 8, 85; *LS*, 54, 61–64, 243 in John 1:32; Acts 2:3; *CLT53*, 1:29; *CLTP*, 62, citing Augustine's *De Essentia Divinitas*, in "A Confession of the Church."

73. *FSD*, 93; *LS*, 264.

74. *CLT53*, 1:73; *CLTP*, 115; Andreae, *33 Sermons*, I-86.

75. *CLT53*, 1:90; *CLTP*, 137, citing Gregory of Nazianzus, *Theol.* 5; *Or. Bas.* 31.29; *MPG* 36.168.

76. *CLT53*, 1:89; *CLTP*, 136, 1 John 5:7, recognizing the textual problems.

77. *CLT53*, 1:9; *CLTP*, 136, from Cyril, *Dial. de Trin.* 7; *CLT53*, 1:2, 94; *CLTP*, 140.

78. *CLT53*, 1:1; *CLTP*, 138; *CLT53*, 1:90-98; *CLTP*, 137-47.

tongues which the early church had received. Their faith in Jesus showed they had received the Holy Spirit (2 Cor 3:5).[79]

To the question "Why are there fewer clear testimonies of the Holy Spirit, as compared to those of the Father and the Son?" Chemnitz answered that it was not fitting for the Holy Spirit, who speaks through the prophets (Zech 7:12) and apostles (Matt 10:20), to testify to himself. When the persons of the Father and the Son are revealed in the Old Testament, then the person of the Holy Spirit is revealed at the same time to speak through the prophets.[80] Chytraeus said, "Through the prophets he foretold Christ's passion and his pouring forth upon the Apostles."[81]

Chytraeus said the Holy Spirit participates in the majesty, might, and substance of the Godhead, and is the Lord God doing the works of God (1 Cor 12:4-6, 11).[82]

Chemnitz said the Father established the worlds (1 Cor 8:6; Heb 1:2), speaking through the Son (Ps 33:6; Col 1:16; Gen 1; Heb 1:3), while the Spirit hovered over the waters (Gen 1:2; Ps 104:30). "All things have been created by the eternal Father through the Son with the help of the Holy Spirit."[83] The Holy Spirit is not created, but, according to the Scriptures and the fathers, is the third person of the Godhead,[84] and with the Son and the Father sustains that which they have created. He was sent by the Father through the Son in visible form to the apostles. The Father has also sent him invisibly through the Son into the hearts of believers throughout the history of the church.

Names and Titles of the Holy Spirit

Chemnitz said the third person does not have a proper name as the first and second persons do.[85] The third person of the Godhead is called the Holy Spirit, because he is a common link of substantial love and joy between the Father and the Son. Chemnitz noted various ways the term "spirit" is used

---

79. *CLT53*, 1:3; *CLTP*, 140–41.
80. *CLT53*, 1:4; *CLTP*, 142, citing Gregory of Nazianzus, *Theol.*; *Or. Bas.* 31.27.
81. Chytraeus, *Postil*, 216–20.
82. Chytraeus, *Postil*, 218–19.
83. *CLT53*, 1:7; *CLTP*, 157, "Ab æternal Patre, per Filium, sovente Spiritu sancto, creata sint omnia"; cf. Chytraeus, *Catechesis*, 32.
84. Chemnitz, *Examen*, 78, 80; Chemnitz, *Examination*, 1:249, 255. Chemnitz cites Gregory of Nazianzen and Basil, who derive dogma and tradition, such as the doctrine of the divinity of the Holy Spirit, from Scripture.
85. *CLT53*, 1:6; *CLTP*, 133; Augustine, *Trin.* 15.

in Scripture: moving nature or power, winds, the human life or soul, angels or messengers, man's created emotions or impulses, "God is a spirit," the name for the third person of the Godhead, and reference to the gifts of the Spirit. Therefore, it is important to distinguish usage when describing the third person. Usually the ancients used "holy" or the article "the" to indicate the person of the Holy Spirit; otherwise, "spirit" referred to the gifts of the Holy Spirit. The Holy Spirit's names in Scripture include Spirit, Comforter (Paraclete, Advocate), pledge, anointing (charisma), "rivers of living water," fire (baptism and cloven tongues), breath and wind, and the finger of God (Luke 11:20). Titles include Spirit of God, Spirit of the Lord, Spirit of the Father, Spirit of Christ the Son, the breath of his mouth, a good Spirit, a right Spirit, Spirit of understanding, Holy Spirit, eternal Spirit, Spirit of sanctification, Spirit of truth, Spirit of life, Spirit of gentleness, Spirit of faith, Spirit of prophecy, Spirit of wisdom and revelation, Spirit of wisdom and understanding, Spirit of counsel and strength, Spirit of knowledge and the fear of the Lord, Spirit of supplications, Spirit of adoption, Holy Spirit of promise, the Spirit which gives and works through gifts, Spirit of grace, and Spirit of power and love and discipline.[86]

Chytraeus connected names and offices of the Holy Spirit with the benefits of the Holy Spirit. As the Spirit of Truth[87] he authors true doctrine and leads people to all truth (John 14:26; 1 John 2:27). As the Holy Spirit of adoption, he stirs up the invocation to cry out, "Abba, Father" (Rom 8:15). As the Comforter, the Holy Spirit takes the believer's place in times of trial, such as Steven's "joyful and confident mind" in his martyrdom. Chytraeus noted that the Spirit comforts believers in the confusion of doubt, grief, perils, poverty, contempt, hatred, and torments when it would be otherwise impossible for hope, faith, and godliness to stand.[88]

Procession of the Holy Spirit

Chytraeus said in the divine Trinity the Holy Spirit proceeds everlastingly from the Father and the Son with unique outward manifestations, such as the form of a dove in the baptism of Christ and in the likeness of fiery tongues at Pentecost.[89] Chytraeus described the relationship of the divine

---

86. *CLT*53, 1:6–70; *CLTP*, 133–37; Didymus, *Bk.* 1.3 (*MPL* 23.111).

87. Chytraeus, *Postil*, 221–24, on Isa 11:1–4 at Pentecost; Andreae, *33 Sermons*, I-33.

88. Chytraeus, *Postil*, 221–24, on Isa 11:1–9 at Pentecost; Andreae, *33 Sermons*, I-56.

89. Chytraeus, *Postil*, 216–20.

persons: the Father begets the Son from eternity; in unity with the Son and the Spirit he has created all things out of nothing and preserves them.[90]

In his *Loci*, Chemnitz's discussion of the procession of the Holy Spirit shows that in the theology of the early Fathers the Greek and the Latin churches agreed that the Spirit is of the Son and of the Father. However, the Greeks said the Spirit is from the Father through the Son, and the Latins said from the Father and the Son (*filioque*).[91]

The Means of the Holy Spirit

Although their writings varied in style and emphases, the *Formula writers* held the same firm view regarding the means of the Holy Spirit as did Luther and Melanchthon. Chemnitz wrote that through the word and the sacraments the Holy Spirit conveys the benefits of the new covenant in Christ. As the physical elements are received by faith, no matter how weak, the merits of the total person of Christ are appropriated through the power of the Spirit.[92] He also said the gospel teaches that the benefits of the Mediator are offered through the Spirit's instruments, the word and the sacraments, to illumine and console hearts, work faith, raise up, and sustain life, and seal God's promises.[93] God wants to use the Spirit's power through the appointed means of the word and the sacraments, to give life, growth, and preservation. Thus New Testament ministry is from the life-giving Spirit. Through this ministry the Spirit transforms believers into the image of the Lord (2 Cor 3:6, 8, 18).[94] Chemnitz used a metaphor to say that God established the word of the gospel and the sacraments as his hands by which he offers the merits and benefits of his Son for salvation (Rom 10:17; 2 Cor 5:19–20; Titus 3:5).[95] God gives the Holy Spirit through these means as the "ministration of the Spirit" (2 Cor 3:3) to guide Christians, to set forth his prohibitions, instructions, and promises, and to bring punishments and rewards that he might mortify and crucify the old sinful flesh.[96] This opposes those whom Luther called the "heavenly prophets," the Anabaptists, and

---

90. Chytraeus, *Postil*, 228, Acts 2:14–38, on Whitsun Monday.
91. *CLT53*, 1:4, 95; *CLTP*, 142–45.
92. Chemnitz, *Examen*, 242–45; Chemnitz, *Examination*, 2:61–65; cf. Chemnitz, *Examen*, 246–47; Chemnitz, *Examination*, 2:71–74.
93. *CLT53*, 2:6–7, 251; Chemnitz, *Justification*, 25–26, 103.
94. Chemnitz, *Ministry, Word and Sacraments*, 43.
95. Chemnitz, *Ministry, Word and Sacraments*, 75.
96. *CLT53*, 3:7; *CLTP*, 604.

Münzer with their claims that the Holy Spirit inspired people apart from the means of the word of God.

Chytraeus said the Holy Spirit works new birth by means of the word of the gospel and baptism.[97] He explained that the Holy Spirit imparts himself and his gifts by the means he has ordained: the word of the gospel, heard, read, or thought upon (suggesting Luther's external word "heard, read" and internal word "thought upon") and by the sacraments of baptism and the Lord's Supper. The Holy Spirit fell upon the hearers of the word in Acts 2:10. When Peter's hearers asked him, how they might obtain the Holy Spirit (Chytraeus's view), Peter answered, "Repent, and be baptized every one of you in the name of Jesus Christ . . . and you will receive the gift of the Holy Spirit" (Acts 2:38). Not by human power—repentance is not a human work—but by the Spirit's power and infinite goodness can we received the word of the gospel. Only the Spirit kindles true knowledge of God and faith to regenerate and renew minds and wills.[98]

The Holy Scriptures

Chemnitz said the preaching, teaching, exhorting, and correcting of the Holy Spirit through the word precedes the human will.[99] He, like Luther and Melanchthon, opposed ideas of mediation of the Holy Spirit through dreams, visions, or any ways violating the principle that the Holy Spirit works only through the voice of the gospel.[100] This links the proclamation of the gospel with the power of the Spirit.[101] Chytraeus agreed that the Holy Spirit comes only as God causes the gospel to be preached,[102] though, as Andreae said, the Spirit could have come without means, but he chose to come through preaching and the sacraments. Conversely, preaching or sacraments without the Holy Spirit are useless.[103] Against the Papists, Andreae said Christ protects against false claims of revelation; the Spirit brings nothing contrary to the teaching of Christ.[104]

The Holy Spirit, the efficient cause of Scripture, inspired the words of the prophets and apostles, and authenticated them with miracles, to present

---

97. Chytraeus, *Postil*, 17, Titus 3.
98. Chytraeus, *Postil*, 225-28, at Pentecost.
99. *CLT53*, 1:86; *CLTP*, 251; cf. Andreae, *33 Sermons*, VI-177.
100. *CLT53*, 1:87; *CLTP*, 252.
101. *CLT53*, 2:243, 44; Chemnitz, *Justification*, 98.
102. Chytraeus, *Postil*, 307, on 1 Cor 15:1-11, on the eleventh Sunday after Trinity.
103. Andreae, *33 Sermons*, III-2-36.
104. Andreae, *33 Sermons*, I-63.

proper doctrine in anticipation of theological disputes.[105] Chemnitz emphasized that the Spirit's authorship was necessary for accurate documentation with proper word selection[106] and unique idiomatic phraseology. Luther said one must accustom oneself to the Holy Spirit's way of expression because the Holy Spirit has his own language and terms.[107] Interpretations based on common speech can be dangerously corrupted.[108] Andreae noted that since Scripture does not witness against itself, so the Holy Spirit must also be consistent with himself. Satan, however, tries to turn the words of Scripture around to false meanings.[109] The Holy Spirit recalls Christ's teachings to the church through the apostles' record so that it is authoritative and factual.[110] Though Scripture does not include everything Christ did and said during his earthly ministry, the Spirit included enough heavenly doctrine for believers to obtain eternal life (John 20:31).[111] The Holy Spirit used the correct words, e.g., justification in the forensic sense, clearly and simply to represent the reconciliation of sinners with God.[112]

Chemnitz revered the relationship of word and Spirit. Because the Spirit is the author he has the doctrine and authority of God behind him.[113] It is safe and correct to use Scripture to imitate the language of the Spirit, to know his pleasure, and to be guided by his light on the way of truth.[114] It is the only means whereby the Spirit gathers and keeps a true and ever growing Christian church on earth. Richly indwelt by the word of God, the church graciously puts away false doctrine.[115]

The power of the Holy Spirit does not make the word of God a magic book, but without the power of the Spirit, it is only a dead letter (2 Cor 3:6).[116] God works through the appointed and efficacious ministry of the word and

---

105. *CLT53*, 1:4; *CLTP*, 69; Chemnitz, *Ministry, Word and Sacraments*, 40, citing Heb 1:1-2; 2:3; 2 Pet 1:21; 1 Tim 3:16; Luke 1:17; Chytraeus, *Postil*, 391-92, on 2 Pet 1:13-21, on the twenty-fifth Sunday after Trinity; Chemnitz, *Examen*, 10 (Chemnitz, *Examination*, 1:54); *FSD*, 35 (*LS*, 120).

106. *CLT53*, 2:1, 229; Chemnitz, *Justification*, 20, 61; Chemnitz, *Examen*, 10, 24-25, 28, 39; Chemnitz, *Examination*, 1:4, 93-96, 105, 135.

107. *WA* 42:35-36; *LW* 1:47-48.

108. *CLT53*, 1:5, 16; *CLTP*, 46; *CLT53*, 2:266, Chemnitz, *Justification*, 136.

109. Andreae, *33 Sermons*, I-4.

110. Chemnitz, *Examen*, 26-27, 39; Chemnitz, *Examination*, 1:100-101, 135-36.

111. Chemnitz, *Ministry, Word and Sacraments*, 41.

112. Chemnitz, *Ministry, Word and Sacraments*, 73.

113. Chemnitz, *Examen*, 44-45; Chemnitz, *Examination*, 1:50, 54.

114. *CLT53*, 2:12; Chemnitz, *Justification*, 38; *DNC*, 161, 174; *TNC*, 395, 425.

115. Chemnitz, *Ministry, Word and Sacraments*, 15-17.

116. Andreae, *33 Sermons*, III-2, 40, 47, 55, IV-208.

of the sacraments—Lutheran theology maintains that there is power in the word—to give increase and preserve the Christian life. The Holy Spirit makes the ministry of the New Testament life-giving as he makes the hearers alive. He writes the (external) word into their hearts (internal), and so they are transformed into the image of the Lord.[117]

Baptism

Chemnitz said that in baptism the Holy Spirit is poured out to overcome original sin, complete the washing of regeneration, begin renewal, and seal believers as the children of God with the true essence of the Godhead. As the chief part of baptism the Spirit makes the water efficacious by the words of institution.[118] Chytraeus, too, said baptism makes one a child of God.[119] He said the Holy Spirit, the forgiveness of sins, and the imputation of righteousness are given in Christian baptism.[120] In baptism, Andreae saw the Holy Spirit working forgiveness of sins and defeating demonic powers.[121]

Chemnitz explained the meaning of Baptism in the name of the Father, Son, and Holy Spirit. The minister is not the active agent but the Triune God is present to minister to the one being baptized. God the Father, through the merit of the Son, receives the believer into grace to sanctify him by the Holy Spirit unto righteousness and life eternal. Those born again of water and the Spirit enter the kingdom of God (John 3:5; Titus 3:5–7).[122] Chemnitz taught that as believers persevere from their baptisms to their resurrections in Christ, they stand with clear consciences before God.[123]

Andreae saw baptism as a sign of God's covenant promises to give rebirth and renewal in the Holy Spirit.[124] He called the Holy Spirit the pledge of baptism that the blood of Jesus is poured over believers so that they are born again as when they were born into the world.[125] Chemnitz combined

---

117. Chemnitz, *Ministry, Word and Sacraments*, 43.

118. *FSD*, 91 (*LS*, 258); Chemnitz, *Examen*, 37, 96, 105, 194, 270; Chemnitz, *Examination*, 1:28, 298, 327, 597–98; 2:137.

119. Chytraeus, *Postil*, 173, Tit 3:5.

120. Chytraeus, *Catechesis*, 130; *Postil*, 283, Rom 6:19–23.

121. Andreae, *33 Sermons*, I–413.

122. Chemnitz, *Ministry, Word and Sacraments*, 113; cf. *CLT53*, 3:148; *CLTP*, 729; cf. Andreae, *33 Sermons*, III–41. On I–94 Andrea said despite the piety of the minister, if the service is according to the Word, the Lord works through the Holy Spirit.

123. Chemnitz, *Examen*, 287, 291; Chemnitz, *Examination*, 2:187, 88, 197.

124. Andreae, *33 Sermons*, IV–46.

125. Andreae, *33 Sermons*, I–175, 76.

Christ's reception of infants, and the seal of righteousness of faith given to infants in circumcision to claim that Christ's promises in baptism apply to infants. Though we cannot understand it, in baptism the Holy Spirit is given to infants so that they receive the kingdom of God. It is a washing of regeneration and the renewal of the Holy Spirit, who is poured out on the baptized (Titus 3:5–7). John the Baptist in his mother's womb demonstrated that the Holy Spirit works in infants before they can use reason (Luke 1:41).[126]

The Lord's Supper

Chemnitz believed the Holy Spirit participates in the opening consecration for the Lord's Supper.[127] By Christ's words of institution, "This is my body," the bread was the same true substantial body that was conceived by the Holy Spirit and born of the Virgin Mary.[128] As believers orally receive the body and blood of Christ, faith is linked with the total human and divine person of Christ, present through the elements, and the Holy Spirit brings them into union with Christ. Through the savior's two natures sinful people are united with God the Father of all life.[129] The real presence of Christ's two natures in the holy supper is why Andreae opposed the Zwinglian position that the flesh is worth nothing and only the Spirit mattered.[130]

Chemnitz claimed the Spirit is present through the words of institution.[131] He said the minister's proclamation of forgiveness to repentant sinners, according to the word of God, absolves them of their sins in Christ's name (John 20:22–23). The Holy Spirit strengthens and preserves faith through the word, while Christ, through this means applies and seals forgiveness of sins to troubled consciences (2 Cor 2:10; Matt 16:19).[132] By the food of the Supper the Spirit restores believers' earthly bodies to immortality to be raised at the last day.[133]

---

126. Chemnitz, *Ministry, Word and Sacraments*, 118–19; cf. Chemnitz, *Examen*, 280, 281–85; Chemnitz, *Examination*, 2:166, 170–74.

127. Chemnitz, *Examen*, 410–11; Chemnitz, *Examination*, 2:513.

128. Chemnitz, *Ministry, Word and Sacraments*, 124.

129. *FSD*, 52–54; *LS*, 162–67.

130. Andreae, *33 Sermons*, V–90.

131. Chemnitz, *Examen*, 320–21; Chemnitz, *Examination*, 2:278–79.

132. Chemnitz, *Ministry, Word and Sacraments*, 134–35; cf. Chemnitz, *Examen*, 184; Chemnitz, *Examination*, 1:569–70; *CLT*53, 3:31; *CLTP*, 597.

133. Chemnitz, *Examen*, 303; Chemnitz, *Examination*, 2:233.

The Work of the Holy Spirit

Chemnitz related the Spirit's work to the *external* and *internal* work of the Trinity. In the *external work* (*opera ad extra*) the three persons work in God's creation.[134] Chemnitz said the Son powerfully worked with the Father and the Spirit, as he said, "My Father works hitherto, and I work" (John 5:17).[135] The *internal work* of the Trinity (*opera ad intra*) is the work God does outside of all created things, within himself, and is peculiar to only one person, e.g., the Father begets. Each person has his own order and characteristic.[136]

From this background of the work of the Trinity, Chytraeus summarized the *external work* of the Holy Spirit, according to Christ, as reproving the world of sin and bearing witness to Christ and his benefits through the ministry of the gospel.[137] Chytraeus demonstrated how the Spirit bears witness to the person of Jesus as the Christ, the Son of God, and as the promised redeemer. He showed John that Jesus was the Son of God by the dove (John 1). He showed Paul that Jesus was the Son of God by the resurrection (Rom 1). In Jesus' public ministry the Spirit used miracles to confirm the divine doctrines concerning Christ's person and his benefits. Jesus promised the Comforter, the Spirit of truth from the Father, who would witness to him. Through the Spirit believers know God in truth, faith, and righteousness (John 15:26).[138]

Remembering that the Father worked through the Holy Spirit in creation (Ps 33:6; Gen 1:26), and sent him through the Son to bolster believers (Eph 3:16-17), Chemnitz called the Spirit's work Benefits and Activities. This work includes the creation and preservation of the universe, the church, and individuals. The Holy Spirit preserves the church through the word and sacraments, touching individuals in soul and body.[139] By the gospel he kindles in people's hearts a true confession of the Triune God, and true righteousness and life, so he may comfort and strengthen them.[140]

Chemnitz noted that opposition to the work of the Spirit includes opinions of the world, human reason and its folly, and the devil, the spirit

---

134. *CLT53*, 1:38; *CLTP*, 74, citing Luther's *Last Words of David* in *LW*, 15:302, where he said that to divide the works of the Godhead is to divide the Godhead itself.

135. *DNC*, 204; *TNC*, 490.

136. *CLT53*, 1:38; *CLTP*, 74.

137. Chytraeus, *Postil*, 176.

138. Chytraeus, *Postil*, 174-75.

139. *CLT53*, 1:39, 98, 101; *CLTP*, 74-76, 147-50.

140. Chytraeus, *Postil*, 242-44, commenting on Rom 11:33-36 on Trinity Sunday.

of error.[141] However, the Spirit overcomes these to sanctify and give life by working in souls, enlightening minds, bending wills, and kindling new desires in hearts and bodies.[142]

The Incarnation

The chief work of the Holy Spirit is to bear witness to Christ. This originates in the incarnation. Chemnitz summarized the work of the Holy Spirit in the incarnation, or hypostatic union of the Son: Jesus was conceived by the Holy Spirit in the Virgin without human seed, to be born a perfect sinless human (2 Cor 5:21).[143] The substance of Christ's body, the seed of Abraham, was produced by the activity of the entire Godhead and the body and blood of Mary and made holy by the Holy Spirit.[144] Chytraeus said the Holy Spirit conceived Jesus' body in the body of the Virgin Mary and sanctified it[145] so that his human nature would be consubstantial with human beings in every way, except without sin.[146] Chemnitz noted that while Jesus was true God and true man, growing as a boy, the Holy Spirit strengthened him, without detracting from his divine nature.[147] The Messiah was anointed by the Spirit in his body of flesh, and was indwelt by the Spirit without measure. In the flesh he breathed out the Holy Spirit.[148]

The following topics describe some of the work the Holy Spirit does in the process of bearing witness to Christ and drawing humankind to faith in him.

---

141. Chemnitz, *Examen*, 8; Chemnitz, *Examination*, 1:47.

142. Chemnitz, *Examen*, 17–21; Chemnitz, *Examination*, 1:76–80.

143. *CLT53*, 1:26; *CLTP*, 58, John of Damascus, *De Fide Orthodoxa*, 1.2; *MPG* 94.792–94; also discussed in *Locus II*, "The Person of the Son of God"; *CLT53*, 1:51, 52, 65–67; *CLTP*, 92, 107–9.

144. Chemnitz, *Ministry, Word and Sacraments*, 61. Also see Chemnitz, *Ministry, Word and Sacraments*, 124 on the nature of the Body present at the Lord's Supper; *DNC*, 78; *TNC*, 210; cf. *DNC*, 11, 13, 19, 21–22; *TNC*, 52–53, 56–57, 70, 74–75.

145. Chytraeus, *Postil*, 6; 430–31 on Isa 7, the Annunciation.

146. *CLT53*, 1:244; *CLTP*, 320.

147. *DNC*, 203; *TNC*, 489.

148. *DNC*, 26, 95; *TNC*, 83–84, 250; John 3:34; Andreae, *33 Sermons*, II-67.

Justification

Justification is in the context of the law. Chemnitz said the Holy Spirit wrote the law.[149] Chytraeus said people cannot stand before God without the Holy Spirit, but the rebirth through faith in Christ causes the imputation of justice (justification) before God and the doing of each of his laws.[150] The Holy Spirit shines through the word within believers to give life to the law, to give righteousness to them, to make them acceptable to God, to free them from the law, from sin, and from God's wrath. Chemnitz said God repeatedly speaks through the law by the Spirit so that the Holy Spirit may convict the world of sin,[151] and bring people to contrition, repentance, and fear of God.

Repentance

Chemnitz said the Spirit brings sinners to repentance by showing them their sin, so they may walk in Christian faith. Opposing the Catholic canon on Penance, he said that God uses repentance positively as a testimony to his goodness and mercy. By his Spirit through the word, he enables the weak flesh to obey.[152] The Holy Spirit opposes concupiscence, natural reason, and philosophy with Scripture's message that works performed without faith apart from Christ are sin.[153] Because of the ongoing need for repentance the Holy Spirit is always needed[154] to lead to a "beginning obedience." God accepts repentance and adorns it with the name "righteousness."[155] Chytraeus said the Holy Spirit causes repentance by preaching the law to kindle the awareness of sin and the wrath of God and to move minds and wills to the admission of sin.[156] The ultimate fruit of repentance is the Holy Spirit enabling believers to approach the Holy of Holies in prayer through the human nature of the saving mediator Jesus Christ.[157] Chytraeus and Chemnitz

---

149. *CLT53*, 2:36, 62; *CLTP*, 371–72, 399.

150. Chytraeus, *Studio*, 12b, Augustine and Ambrose; cf. Andreae, *33 Sermons*, III–84.

151. *CLT53*, 2:21; *CLTP*, 354; Chemnitz, *Ministry, Word and Sacraments*, 68; *CLT53*, 2:29; *CLTP*, 363.

152. *CLT53*, 1:98, 101; *CLTP*, 147–50; Chemnitz, *Examen*, 425; Chemnitz, *Examination*, 2:552

153. *CLT53*, 1:225, 234; *CLTP*, 298, 309; cf. *CLT53*, 1:232; *CLTP*, 307, "lawlessness"; *CLT53*, 1:197; *CLTP*, 265.

154. *CLT53*, 1:236; *CLTP*, 309.

155. *CLT53*, 3:76–77; *CLTP*, 646.

156. Chytraeus, *Catechesis*, 139.

157. Chytraeus, *Catechesis*, 25.

described the struggle between flesh and the Holy Spirit.[158] The flesh, at enmity against God, follows its lusts and marches like an enraged soldier against the Spirit's commands (Rom 7; Gal 5). Andreae opposed those who claim there is something good in people and the will just needs a little help from the Spirit to turn to good from wrong. He stressed that only by the work of the Holy Spirit, as described by Luther in the Explanation to the Third Article of the Creed, can one come to repentance and faith.[159]

Faith

The *Formula* writers applied Luther's Law and Gospel format to explain the formation of faith. The Spirit convinces believers that the law of God judges sin, and his gospel promises life, care, joy, and the hope of eternal acceptance by the loving Father.[160] When the Holy Spirit gives faith, a person knows God through Jesus Christ his savior, through Christ's true doctrines, and through God's will. This knowledge of God is not by human wisdom about the law and civil factors, for people cannot of themselves believe. But the Triune God, by the grace and power of the Holy Spirit through the preaching of the word of God, kindles faith to turn hearers to him.[161]

Chemnitz warned that mortal sins and their actions of serving fleshly lusts block faith and the presence of the Spirit. Faith does not serve sin, but hungers and thirsts after righteousness that releases and frees from sin. Where there is no repentance and faith, there is neither Christ, nor the Holy Spirit, nor the grace of God, nor forgiveness of sins, nor any salvation.[162]

Chytraeus said faith must renounce continuation in sin and cling to God's promises offered in the word and sacraments. Even in death, the

---

158. Chytraeus, *Postil*, 210, 1 Pet 4:7-11; *CLT53*, 2:208-9; Chemnitz, *Justification*, 28-29; *CLT53*, 3:26; *CLTP*, 591, citing Luther's *Smalcald Articles*, 3.43-44; *CLT53*, 1:140-41; *CLTP*, 196-97.

159. Andreae, *33 Sermons*, IV-34-37.

160. Chytraeus, *Postil*, 381-83, Col 1:9-14, on the twenty-fourth Sunday after Trinity; Andreae, *33 Sermons*, I-54; Chemnitz, *Examen*, 186; Chemnitz, *Examination*, 1:577; Andreae, *33 Sermons*, I-66.

161. Chytraeus, *Postil*, 381-83, Col 1:9-14, on the twenty-fourth Sunday after Trinity; 164, commenting on the Resurrection in 1 Cor 15; Andreae, *33 Sermons*, I-54, Andreae, *33 Sermons*, I-178, II-24; cf. Chemnitz, *Ministry, Word and Sacraments*, 134-35; *CLT53*, 1:40; *CLTP*, 76; Chemnitz, *Ministry, Word and Sacraments*, 77; *CLT53*, 2:251-53; Chemnitz, *Justification*, 102, 106-7; Chemnitz, *Examen*, 124; Chemnitz, *Examination*, 1:392.

162. Chemnitz, *Ministry, Word and Sacraments*, 104-6.

Spirit aids the will and heart to hold fast to God's promise of eternal life in the Law and Gospel[163] and to courageously confess the truth of the gospel.[164]

Conversion

Andreae dramatically stated that in conversion, the Triune God through the Holy Spirit grasps a person's heart in the preaching of the gospel to demand obedience from him and to create a new spirit in him. Neither the preacher nor the hearer, but the implanted Holy Spirit, changes one's heart to enable his will and spirit to accept the preached word.[165]

Chemnitz said the Holy Spirit accomplishes conversion through the word.[166] Humanity, fallen in original sin, has lost the Holy Spirit and their relationship with God through the image of God, and stands under the wrath of God in what Luther called *Urerlebnis* (original sinful condition). In conversion, original sin is forgiven, the Holy Spirit returns, and the image of God is restored.[167]

Andreae said the human free will may be active in hearing the gospel, desiring or not to go to church, or to open ears or to stop them, but still people cannot come to faith except through the Holy Spirit's preaching through the word that demands repentance and obedience, and converts hearts to faith. If they resist this ministry of the Spirit, they have obstructed their conversion and salvation.[168] Chemnitz stressed that natural people can only resist the gospel unless the Spirit changes their abilities to understand, obey, and trust in the gospel promises. The Spirit speaks the voice of the gospel through preaching and meditation on the word to bring the Law and Gospel message of justification. He reveals the seriousness of sin and the wrath of God to lead human wills to seek the benefits promised in the

---

163. Chytraeus, *Postil*, 33.

164. Andreae, *Six Sermons*, 96.

165. Andreae, *33 Sermons*, V-42.

166. Chemnitz, *Examen*, 425; Chemnitz, *Examination*, 2:552; cf. Andreae, *33 Sermons*, V-46.

167. Chemnitz, *Examen*, 103–6; Chemnitz, *Examination*, 1:323–26.

168. Andreae, *Six Sermons*, 87; cf. Chemnitz, *Examen*; Chemnitz, *Examination*, 1:425–26; cf. Kolb, *Nikolaus von Amsdorf*, 220. Kolb notes that Amsdorf agreed, saying people cannot assent to the gospel promises without the regenerating power of the Holy Spirit. They have only a capacity to receive the Spirit's action through word and sacrament, not to act. Like a child at birth, the sinner contributes nothing to his rebirth. God justifies the impious whom he has chosen while they still oppose him, hate Christ and the word, and resist the gospel.

gospel.[169] He enlightens hearts, turns their opposition to God into repentance, and kindles, heightens, and preserves their faith through hearing the gospel (Rom 10:17).[170] The Spirit opposes evil influences and heresies, and turns hearers to obedience.[171]

Chemnitz said God wants to justify all who in repentance and faith embrace Christ, but they drive out the Holy Spirit, who reject his word (Acts 13:45–46) with hard hearts (Heb 4:7), who resist the Holy Spirit (Acts 7:51), who unrepentantly persevere in sins (Luke 14:18), who do not seek Christ (Mark 16:16), who choose ways outside of Christ to be justified and saved (Rom 9:31–32), or who are hypocrites (Matt 7:15).[172] He has given them to eternal damnation, since they refused repentance and loved darkness rather than light (John 3:19).[173] People in whom the Holy Spirit works resist him until, through the word, he arouses and begins willingness toward repentance. Chemnitz appealed to people not to allow the Old Adam to hinder the Spirit's work in them (Rom 6:12; 8:13; Gal 5:24).[174] If they hear Christ calling but continue unrepentant in sin, and do not seek to be reconciled with God through faith in Christ but resist the Holy Spirit, they are not among the elect (John 8:47; 10:26). Chemnitz said Christians should never give up on them but should give them the word in the hope that perhaps God will give them repentance.[175]

Election

Chemnitz declared that God does not want any to reject his call to salvation. Some whom the Holy Spirit has called are unwilling to accept the grace he offers to work in them, and so, are not chosen.[176] Those who do not hear or follow Christ's voice but resist the Holy Spirit remain in wickedness and are not among the elect minority of those called, who receive and follow the word. That the disobedient turn away from God is not by divine

---

169. *CLT53*, 2:252, 288–89; *Justification*, 105, 177; cf. Chemnitz, *Examen*, 133–38; Chemnitz, *Examination*, 1:422–35; Andreae, *33 Sermons*, III–101.

170. Chemnitz, *Ministry, Word and Sacraments*, 88; *CLT53*, 2:288–89; *Justification*, 177; *CLT53*, 1:185–86; *CLTP*, 250.

171. *CLT53*, 1:155, 150; *CLTP*, 213, 208.

172. Chemnitz, *Examen*, 197; Chemnitz, *Examination*, 1:607.

173. Chemnitz, *Ministry, Word and Sacraments*, 88.

174. Chemnitz, *Ministry, Word and Sacraments*, 67.

175. Chemnitz, *Ministry, Word and Sacraments*, 91.

176. Chemnitz, *Ministry, Word and Sacraments*, 92; Matt 23:37; Acts 7:51; 13:46.

predestination but because of their obstinate perverse human will.[177] Andreae used Jerusalem as an example of a people who rejected God's prophets and hindered their own salvation. When people are not saved they cannot blame God, but rather they must blame themselves for disregarding God's Holy Spirit.[178] It is a comfort for believers to know that God wills their salvation and that they are not tempted by him.[179] Many who began in grace will defect and fall away, not because God denies them grace and perseverance, but their own wills insult the Spirit of grace (Heb 10:29) when they turn from his holy commandments (2 Pet 2). Chemnitz concluded this rejection grieves the Holy Spirit, so that they adorn themselves for Satan in a final state of deserved condemnation.[180] Predestination is God's execution of free justification by faith in creatures otherwise incapable of such faith. Without this working of God and left to themselves, with all the powers of their natural wills, they are only enmity against God. But God, in his eternal counsel, decreed that he wanted, through his Spirit, to convert humankind.[181]

The *Formula* writers described how God brings the elect to faith. Chemnitz said the unregenerate ones lack the renewal of the Holy Spirit and in spiritual darkness do not trust God to answer their prayers or to forgive their sins.[182] Andreae said the Holy Spirit brings hearers to faith and life through the gospel.[183] Chytraeus said the Holy Spirit is poured out on believers to renew human nature through justification. Little by little he abolishes the remaining sin and kindles true knowledge of God in their minds. He works a new obedience of God's commandments which, hoping for perfection, bears the fruit of the renewed life of the Holy Spirit.[184] Chemnitz related this being "reborn of the Spirit of God" to Jeremiah's promise that the Spirit will write the law into believers' hearts (Jer 31:33),[185] so that, as his work in Christ Jesus, they may walk in good works.[186] Still, in this life those born of God are led by his Spirit only partly, for though their

---

177. Chemnitz, *Ministry, Word and Sacraments*, 92.
178. Andreae, *33 Sermons*, V-39.
179. Andreae, *33 Sermons*, V-45.
180. Chemnitz, *Ministry, Word and Sacraments*, 92.
181. Chemnitz, *Ministry, Word and Sacraments*, 93; Rom 8:7; Gen 6:5.
182. *CLT53*, 1:170, 174; *CLTP*, 232, 237.
183. Andreae, *33 Sermons*, I-62.
184. Chytraeus, *Postil*, 18, Titus 3.
185. Chemnitz, *Ministry, Word and Sacraments*, 55–57, 66.
186. *CLT53*, 2:207; Chemnitz, *Justification*, 26.

minds are led by the Spirit of God in fellowship (*konoinia*) with him, they still serve sin with their flesh.[187]

Regeneration

Chemnitz said the Holy Spirit is given through the gospel and baptism. Believers are born again and renewed by the washing of regeneration; sin and death are abolished, and he restores the righteous life of joy.[188] Through the gospel the Holy Spirit calls and enlightens their minds, converts their hearts, renews their wills and produces new desires.[189]

Chemnitz warned Christians not to confuse justification and renewal in the Holy Spirit. In justification the law is forensically satisfied in God's righteousness, Jesus Christ. Justification is not an infusion of righteousness.[190] Chemnitz agreed with Augustine that after objective justification comes the subjective renewal of life in the Holy Spirit. This includes the gift of the Spirit, spiritual gifts, renewal, reconciliation, mortification, newness of life, good works, and fruits. Thus, Abraham was justified by faith and renewed in the Spirit with many gifts.[191]

Chytraeus taught that, by regeneration through the word of God and baptism, the Holy Spirit makes a child of wrath and death into a God-pleasing child of God and an adopted heir of eternal life. After justification, regeneration is the rebuilding of sinners who are taken from their natural lives of pollution, sin, and wrath and made anew through forgiveness. The Spirit gradually eradicates remaining sin, and extends new light, justice, and life into believers' hearts.[192] The adoption as an heir of God corresponds to Luther's two kinds of righteousness. The first kind is the righteous of Jesus that is instilled into the believer's heart from the outside. It is passive. The second kind is "our own" as the believer lives out Jesus' righteousness. "The

---

187. DNC, 175; TNC, 429; Rom 7:25; 2 Cor 13:14.

188. Chytraeus, *Postil*, 14–15, 17, Titus 3; FSD, 10; LS, 53; Chemnitz, *Examen*, 247–48; Chemnitz, *Examination*, 2:75–76.

189. CLT53, 2:252, 53; Chemnitz, *Justification*, 106–7; CLT53, 1:176; CLTP, 240.

190. CLT53, 2:232, 237; Chemnitz, *Justification*, 66–77.

191. CLT53, 2:268, 69, 274, 279; Chemnitz, *Justification*, 139, 148, 160; Chemnitz, *Examen*, 147; Chemnitz, *Examination*, 1:465; cf. Chemnitz, *Examen*, 187–88; Chemnitz, *Examination*, I:580, where he connected renewal as the outflow of remission of sins and the gift of the Spirit. Chemnitz seems to equate renewal and sanctification here.

192. Chytraeus, *Catechesis*, 117–18; cf. Chemnitz, *Examen*, 134; Chemnitz, *Examination*, 1:424, where Chemnitz presents the gradual work of the Holy Spirit in renewal similar to Chytraeus's description of regeneration.

instilled righteousness of the first kind produces the fruit of the Holy Spirit in the second kind.[193] It is active. Internal renewal and rebuilding enables believers to live in obedience to God

Sanctification

Reaching back to the original definition of the Holy Spirit, David Chytraeus described the origin of sanctification to "quicken all things."

> The Holy Spirit is the third person of the Godhead proceeding from the Father and the Son of one substance and of one everlastingness with the Father and the Son, which in the first creation together with the Father and the Son did cherish and quicken all things that breathe, and afterward at all times is sent into the hearts of those that believe the gospel, to kindle in them light to the true knowing of God, and to be their Advocate, cherishing, comforting, and quickening their hearts with spiritual righteousness and everlasting life.[194]

Chemnitz stressed the ongoing role of the Holy Spirit in sanctification, the battle against original sin, which moves from justification to new obedience.[195] In sanctification God washes away sin through forgiveness, regeneration, and renewal, so the Holy Spirit may apply the merit of Christ's righteousness by the washing of the word.[196] Chytraeus stressed forgiveness for those in Christ Jesus who walk according to the Spirit and not the flesh.[197] The cleansing work is necessary because sin still dwells in the believer's flesh in forms of concupiscence that take him captive.[198] The Spirit uses the Decalogue and the New Testament to expose sin, to oppose efforts to hide it, and to kill it so it may be covered by the obedience of the Son of God.[199] As unleavened bread needs continual cleansing, Chytraeus said the Spirit needs to cleanse believers of the remnants of sin so Christ's imputed righteousness may be completed in them. Faith, fear, love of God, and other virtues are

---

193. *LW* 26:177.
194. Chytraeus, *Postil*, 218.
195. Chemnitz, *Ministry, Word and Sacraments*, 88.
196. Chemnitz, *Ministry, Word and Sacraments*, 61–62; John 3:6; Eph 5:25–26; Titus 3:5.
197. Chytraeus, *Catechesis*, 101, discussing venial sins.
198. Chemnitz, *Ministry, Word and Sacraments*, 62–63; cf. *CLT53*, 1:229; *CLTP*, 303; Rom 7:8, 18, 23–24; Gal 5:17.
199. *CLT53*, 2:74, 76, 92; 3:99; *CLTP*, 412–15, 431, 674, discussing the sixth, ninth, and tenth commandments.

faint in the will, while many sinful inclinations and vehement tendencies to carelessness, distrust, and pride remain. In sanctification, those regenerated by the Spirit strive against these things.[200] Chemnitz stressed the victory of the Spirit through the defeat of concupiscence, which begins at baptism and continues until the death of the mortal body.[201] Andreae taught that enlightenment and sanctification occur in the church gathered together in true faith in Jesus Christ.[202] Chytraeus said that Paul's post-conversion battle (as described in Rom 7) showed the need to kill the deeds of the flesh.[203] Andreae said the Holy Spirit uses the teaching and admonition of God's law to guide the believer's unregenerate parts so they can live in obedience to God.[204]

The above writings demonstrate that the *Formula* writers were fully convinced of Luther's concept of *simul justus et peccator*. Luther believed that in sanctification, although the gifts of the Holy Spirit increase in God's children, they are still accompanied by evil desire and sin.[205] The believer's personal union with Christ does not change his sin nature.[206] This truth is echoed in the following statements that were written above by the *Formula* writers: "sin still dwells in the believer's flesh in forms of concupiscence that take him captive" (Chemnitz); "sinful inclinations and vehement tendencies to carelessness, distrust, and pride remain" (Chytraeus); "the Holy Spirit uses the teaching and admonition of God's law to guide the believer's unregenerate parts" (Andreae).

Believers are still held to a high standard of godliness regardless of their natural spiritual weakness. Chytraeus reminded Christians that, as the Spirit's dwelling place, they should keep themselves clean and pure.[207] Chemnitz said Christians must yield to the control of the bridle of the Holy Spirit and not be drawn into mortal sins and the danger of losing salvation.[208] Scripture warns that some of the reconciled fall and lose life eternal, unless they turn again in faith to be reconciled to God.[209] Chemnitz said

---

200. Chytraeus, *Postil*, 142, 1 Cor 5:7-8; Andreae, *33 Sermons*, III-65.

201. Chemnitz, *Examen*, 111, 116; Chemnitz, *Examination*, 1:348, 364.

202. Andreae, *33 Sermons*, V-37.

203. Chytraeus, *Postil*, 142, 1 Cor 5:7-8; Andreae, *33 Sermons*, III-65.

204. Andreae, *Six Sermons*, 103.

205. *LW* 35:369.

206. *LW* 37:238.

207. Chytraeus, *Postil*, 106, 1 Thess 4:1-8.

208. *CLT53*, 2:681; Chytraeus, *Postil*, 285-90.

209. Chemnitz, *Ministry, Word and Sacraments*, 103, Rom 8:13; 1 Cor 6:10; Gal 5:21; Eph 5:5, Col 3:6; 1 John 3:6, 8; 1 Titus 1:19; 2 Pet 1:9.

that the Holy Spirit must govern the regenerate so they do not sin against conscience and grieve the Holy Spirit, or "neglect repentance, or lose faith, grace, and salvation, or give place to the devil, or run into any of his traps."[210]

According to Andreae, only the Holy Spirit can guide believers into righteousness and holiness.[211] Chemnitz said, to accomplish the call to the new obedience of holiness, Christ gives his Holy Spirit to believers so they may obey the Ten Commandments, which, without faith and the Holy Spirit, is an impossible task.[212] Chytraeus said the new obedience is the result and evidence of regeneration and renewal wherein the Holy Spirit enables believers to delight in God's law and do good works.[213] In the new life in the Spirit, the Holy Spirit delivers obedient believers out of the darkness of sin.[214] He gives them a new light, a confident compliance, gladness, and a burning love for God that desires to obey all his commandments.[215] Andreae said the reborn should not attempt to obey God's law in their own power, but by grace with the Holy Spirit's helping power.[216] The Holy Spirit is not a spirit of bondage to sin and death, but for the adoption of God's children to prayer, virtue, love, and wisdom. All born of the Spirit can turn from displeasing the Father to obeying him, as children born to love and obedience,[217] with inward and outward acts that honor God.[218]

Chemnitz applied Augustine's anti-Pelagian view of the Holy Spirit and faith. Where Pelagius "imagined" that justified man could fulfill the law without any help from the Holy Spirit, "Augustine describes 'righteous' as the new obedience, 'grace' as the aid of the Holy Spirit, and 'to justify' as making an unrighteous man righteous."[219] According to what Augustine called "co-operating grace," the renewed person agrees with God's law and will and by continuous grace and support of the Holy Spirit, walks in weakness into the

---

210. *CLT53*, 3:104; *CLTP*, 681, "*poenitentiam conclucari, fidem, gratiam, & salutem amitti: dari locum diabolo, & incurri in laqueos ipsius*"; cf. Andreae, *33 Sermons*, III-81.

211. Andreae, *Six Sermons*, 103.

212. *CLT53*, 2:93; 3:32; *CLTP*, 431, 598; Chemnitz, *Ministry, Word and Sacraments*, 51.

213. Chytraeus, *Catechesis*, 118; *CLT53*, 3:40; *CLTP*, 607.

214. Chytraeus, *Postil*, 333, Gal 5:25—6:8, on the fifteenth Sunday after Trinity.

215. Chytraeus, *Postil*, 68, Rom 12:8-10; Chytraeus, *Postil*, 360, commenting on Eph 5:15-21, on the twentieth Sunday after Trinity.

216. Andreae, *33 Sermons*, I-241-44.

217. Chytraeus, *Postil*, 285-90, commenting on Rom 8:12-17, on the eighth Sunday after Trinity.

218. Chytraeus, *Catechesis*, 119.

219. *CLT53*, 1:6; *CLTP*, 33, "*Ideo Augustin, justitiam vocat novam obedientiam, gratiam, auxilium Spiritus S. & justificare, ex injusto justum facere.*"

new obedience.²²⁰ Luther, in contrast, saw that the Holy Spirit enables faithful obedience in good works apart from any human ability at all.

According to Chemnitz the Holy Spirit works salvation and renewal in believers by his grace, and creates a new people for good works and turns their hearts to follow him with new obedience. They celebrate their remission of sins and the reception of the Holy Spirit with willingness to delight in the law of God and to obey God.²²¹ They have confidence that it is not the weak flesh but the Spirit who succeeds. When they are sluggish or undo the work of the Spirit, they confess their sins, plead for mercy, and move on in obedience.²²² Though lapses occur in the regenerate because concupiscence prevents them from obeying God's law perfectly,²²³ they know that the law's requirements are fulfilled, because, by faith they are justified and have good consciences.²²⁴ By faith they know the Spirit is present to lead them in new obedience and bear fruit in their sinful bodies.²²⁵ Therefore, they do not waste the Spirit's gifts, but live in new obedience with faith, fear, and worship of God.²²⁶ Chytraeus emphasized that the reborn walks in the Spirit by new obedience. He sows not to the tyrant flesh, but to the Spirit and obeys the Spirit.²²⁷

Teaching

The leaders of the Reformation believed the Holy Spirit was the author and therefore, the interpreter of Scripture.²²⁸ They looked to the Holy Spirit as Christ's teaching instrument to guide and enlighten the minds of teachers and learners in the language of the Spirit,²²⁹ and to give a love for sound doctrine and truth.²³⁰ They said the Spirit works in teachers to propagate the truth of his word in his church.²³¹ Chytraeus prayed for the governing

---

220. *CLT53*, 1:182–83; *CLTP*, 246–47.
221. *CLT53*, 2:8, 9; *CLTP*, 339, 341.
222. *CLT53*, 2:29; *CLTP*, 364.
223. *CLT53*, 2:93, 44; *CLTP*, 432, 611.
224. *CLT53*, 2:10, 93; *CLTP*, 342, 431.
225. *CLT53*, 2:93, 9; *CLTP*, 432, 341.
226. *CLT53*, 1:183; *CLTP*, 247.
227. Chytraeus, *Postil*, 337, Gal 5:25—6:8, on the fifteenth Sunday after Trinity.
228. DNC, 126; TNC, 319.
229. *CLT53*, 1:200; *CLTP*, 268; also Chytraeus, *Catechesis*, 1.
230. *CLT53*, 2:201; Chemnitz, *Justification*, 13.
231. *CLT53*, 3:132; *CLTP*, 711.

advice of the Holy Spirit of God to teach in fruitful study.[232] He and Andreae claimed the Holy Spirit makes it possible to interpret the sacred writings.[233] Chytraeus and Chemnitz said the Holy Spirit delivers true doctrine to the church through the word and kindles the light of knowledge in the minds of believers through Scripture and its teachers.[234] The Spirit uses the Decalogue and Old Testament stories for Christian doctrine, he interprets the Old Testament prophets in the New Testament,[235] and he often explains doctrine by repeating the message in different places.[236] Andreae added that the Spirit also uses the principles of the Decalogue to lay the foundation for teaching the gospel.

By nature, people do not know who the Holy Spirit is, so even if they can read German and Latin, they cannot understand the spiritual truths of God and salvation without the Spirit's interpretation. Believers, however, enlightened from the divine word by God's Spirit, can discern all things, even though the devil may try to use Scripture to confuse them.[237]

Chemnitz stressed the deficiency of scholastic teaching and philosophy and said it must be carefully weighed.[238] The "learned" are spiritually blind without the Spirit and lead people astray.[239] Pure doctrine could not be found if the Holy Spirit had not kindled the light of the word,[240] and captured reason by the obedience of faith. By faith, learners hold firmly to Scripture's message, even when it is not understood.[241] Using Scripture

---

232. Chytraeus, *Catechesis*, 8.

233. Andreae, *Confession*, 59; Kolb, *Andreae*, 54–57; Chytraeus, *Studio*, 2b, 21b.

234. Chytraeus, *Postil*, 345–48, Eph 4:1–6, on the seventeenth Sunday after Trinity; 392–93 on 2 Pet 1:13–21, on the twenty-fifth Sunday after Trinity; *CLT53*, 2:34; 3:14, 58; *CLTP*, 369, 578–81, 627; *FSD*, 16; *LS*, 67.

235. *CLT53*, 2:68–71, 89–90; *CLTP*, 406–9, 427–28.

236. *FSD*, 25; *LS*, 92–93; cf. *FSD*, 23, 29, 30, 41–42, 46, 65; *LS*, 88, 103, 105, 136–37, 148, 195.

237. Andreae, *33 Sermons*, I-44–45; Chemnitz, *Ministry, Word and Sacraments*, 53; *DNC*, iii, iv (unnumb.), 5; *TNC*, 17–18, 38–39. God reveals his mysteries by the teaching of the Spirit through the word of God. The Son through the Holy Spirit has stirred "many men of proven and outstanding learning and true piety, who have clearly and accurately shown from the true and apostolic meaning of the statements of Scripture"; *DNC*, 97, 128; *TNC*, 257, 323; *CLT53*, 2:99, 100, 25–26; *CLTP*, 440, 591; Chytraeus, *Studio*, 3.

238. *CLT53*, 1:120; *CLTP*, 172; *CLT53*, 2:266; Chemnitz, *Justification*, 136.

239. Chytraeus, *Studio*, 2b, 21b; Kolb, *Andreae*, 54–57; Andreae, *Confession*, 59.

240. *CLT53*, 2:201; Chemnitz, *Justification*, 12.

241. *DNC*, 91; *TNC*, 241.

directly and indirectly, the Holy Spirit teaches, structures, and interprets theology for the church.[242]

The Holy Spirit and the Church

Chemnitz said of the catholic (universal) church, "The Father through the Son has redeemed the church and through the Holy Spirit he governs, rules, and gives it life."[243] According to Chytraeus the church includes those who, filled and governed by the Holy Spirit, are heirs of eternal life. Hypocrites who practice their religion without faith and trust, or are openly wicked, maintain error and idolatry.[244] There are living members of the church to whom the Holy Spirit brings true knowledge of God, true faith, and the true life. There are also dead members who are double-minded, stress external piety, but are not reborn, are without the Holy Spirit, and are without true fear of God and faith.[245] Andreae called the Christian congregation a gathering of sinners covered by Christ's blood, who are sealed by the Holy Spirit, and who receive God's word and the sacraments.[246] It is the kingdom of Christ in which Christ rules through the scepter of his word and his Holy Spirit in the peoples' hearts so they can know God and call upon him.[247]

Against the Catholic scholar, Andrada, Chemnitz said proof of the Holy Spirit leading the church is that he governs according to the word of God.[248] The visible church embraces Christ's gospel and properly uses the sacraments. Christ gave the church his word and the anointing of his Holy Spirit for growth and to fight against the devil and tyrants.[249] Andreae said the Spirit continues to bring the gospel to the church to teach, to comfort, to bring hearts to obedience to the word, and to overcome trials and the devil with patience and peace.[250] This relationship of the Spirit and the word was in opposition to the papists who maintained that the church with the Holy

---

242. *CLT53*, 1:213; 2:3; *CLTP*, 284, 333–34; also Andreae, *Six Sermons*, 87.

243. *CLT53*, 1:26; *CLTP*, 59; Albertus Novicampanus, a preceptor of the king of Poland, "*Pater per Filium redemit Ecclesiam, per Spiritum sanctum gubernat, regit, vivificat eandem*"; *CLT53*, 1:156; *CLTP*, 214; cf. *CLT53*, 3:31, 16; *CLTP*, 597, 695.

244. Chytraeus, *Postil*, 471–74, Rev 7:9–17, All Saints' Day.

245. Chytraeus, *Catechesis*, 150–51.

246. Andreae, *33 Sermons*, IV–70, 54; V–42.

247. Chytraeus, *Catechesis*, 155–56; Andreae, *33 Sermons*, IV–106.

248. Chemnitz, *Examen*, 205–6; Chemnitz, *Examination*, 1:633–35.

249. *CLT53*, 3:119; *CLTP*, 697; cf. Chytraeus, *Catechesis*, 25–27, 150; *CLT53*, 3:129; *CLTP*, 707.

250. Andreae, *33 Sermons*, IV–185.

Spirit cannot err and that Christ's Spirit rules synods without regard to the word. Chemnitz and Andreae opposed this because the word of God, which is kindled in the churches by the Holy Spirit, can not oppose the Spirit.[251] The Jerusalem council (Acts 15:6–29) showed the Lord ruling the church by the Holy Spirit through the word.[252] Chemnitz prayed that Christ, by his Spirit, would rule the church of his day.[253] Andreae saw his life work of establishing church order and doctrine a calling inspired by the Holy Spirit.[254]

Chemnitz claimed a spiritual union among believers in whom the Holy Spirit dwells.[255] In this fellowship (*koinonia*) Christians participate in the indwelling Holy Spirit (Heb 6:4, 1 Cor 3:16), and thus are partakers of the flesh and blood of Christ as children partake of milk.[256] As Christ's human and divine natures are hypostatically united in a fellowship without commingling, so the Holy Spirit and the saints in the church fellowship are united in a non-hypostatic union without equating or commingling their substances.[257] Chemnitz said through the Holy Spirit the entire Trinity dwells in the saints (2 Cor 6:16; John 14:23). The Spirit ministers through the word as he converts, regenerates, renews, preserves, and governs the saints, bestowing gifts upon them, kindling light, wisdom, justice, happiness, and sanctifying them by arousing new desires in them. However, in this life the Holy Spirit can be lost, his gifts cut off, and the indwelling in this life can be destroyed.[258] "Therefore, the hypostatic union in Christ differs from all other modes of union, presence, or indwelling,"[259] because it gives believers access to the whole Trinity. By access to the assumed nature of Christ through the consubstantial relationship and faith, believers can approach the deity of the Logos, which dwells in the assumed nature, and are finally brought into fellowship not only with the Son but also with the Father and the Holy Spirit because of the consubstantiality (*homoousia*) of the Trinity.[260]

---

251. Chemnitz, *Examen*, 216, 366–67; Chemnitz, *Examination*, 1:663; 2:398; Andreae, *33 Sermons*, IV–106.

252. *CLT53*, 2:10; 3:16; *CLTP*, 348, 580.

253. *CLT53*, 3:62; *CLTP*, 630.

254. Andreae, *Six Sermons*, 61–120.

255. *DNC*, 36; *TNC*, 107.

256. *DNC*, 39–40; *TNC*, 116.

257. *DNC*, 57; *TNC*, 158. Chemnitz also addresses this subject while discussing the Trinity and the hypostatic union of the two natures in Christ at *DNC*, 122; *TNC*, 309.

258. *DNC*, 37; *TNC*, 108.

259. *TNC*, 110; *DNC*, 38; "*Ita ergo Hypostatica unio in Christo differt ab omnibus aliis modis unionis, præsentiæ, & inhabitationis.*"

260. *DNC*, 124; *TNC*, 316.

The Call to Christian Ministry

The church of the Reformation was caught between two extremes, the ultra-hierarchical Roman Catholic Church and spiritualist groups called enthusiasts. The Reformers rejected the complicated and corrupt Catholic process of designating priests, cardinals, etc. They also opposed enthusiasts, Anabaptists, and spiritualist, Winkelprediger, who claimed direct calls from God by the Spirit apart from the mediation of the body of believers.

Martin Chemnitz serves as spokesman here for the Reformation position on the call to ministry. He stressed that no one is a legitimate minister of the word and the sacraments unless he has been sent by a legitimate call (Jer 23:21; Rom 10:15).[261] There must be a call and it must be legitimate, neither the Catholic position nor the enthusiast position. Chemnitz turned to the gospel to cite Christ's prayer to the Father for laborers in the harvest field (Matt 9:38), and the gifts of ministry given after he ascended (Eph 4:8, 11–12). He insisted that God extends his call through established ministers and does not recognize as pastors those who have not been sent by him.[262] As such, the minister is the special possession of the Lord of the Harvest.

Chemnitz said God called the patriarchs, prophets, and apostles directly without any intervening human means. They had the testimony of the Spirit and of miracles proving they did not err in doctrine,[263] protecting against enthusiasts and fanatics. God endowed those called without means with either the gift of miracles or with other testimonies of the Spirit to prove and to confirm their calls. Thus Moses established his call before Pharaoh with the gift of miracles (Exod 4:1–3). Paul also called signs, wonders, and mighty deeds proofs of the apostolate (2 Cor 12:12).[264]

Chemnitz said we should no longer expect immediate calls with proofs of signs and miracles. The New Testament does not promise that after the apostles, God will send laborers through immediate calls, nor is there a command to wait until ministers are appointed by immediate calls, as were the apostles. Since that time God calls and sends ministers to his church through mediate calls or regular means, such as in Ephesus.[265]

> Timothy, bishop at Ephesus, was not called immediately, but through Paul and the presbytery, 1 Tim 4:14, 2 Tim 1:6, and he had a mandate similarly also to appoint other ministers of

---

261. Chemnitz, *Examen*, 484; Chemnitz, *Examination*, 2:705.
262. Chemnitz, *Ministry, Word and Sacraments*, 30.
263. Chemnitz, *Ministry, Word and Sacraments*, 30.
264. Chemnitz, *Ministry, Word and Sacraments*, 31; cf. *CLT53*, 2:121; *CLTP*, 699.
265. Chemnitz, *Ministry, Word and Sacraments*, 31; *CLT53*, 3:122; *CLTP*, 700–701.

the church, 2 Tim 2:2. And yet Paul says to the elders of the church at Ephesus, Acts 20:28: "The Holy Spirit has made you overseers, to rule the church of God."[266]

Chemnitz concluded there are no longer immediate calls accompanied and verified by signs and miracles but only mediate calls through human instrumentalities in the church. This is consistent with his personal view that miracles no longer happen, maintaining the only reason for miracles was to validate the authority of ministry.

The mediate call is issued through the human means of the church, which is a royal priesthood (1 Pet 2:9).[267] Through the rite of ordination the whole church by common and earnest prayers, commits to God the ministry of him who is called, so that God by his Holy Spirit, divine grace, and blessing might be with his ministry. Through the laying on of hands the minister is presented to the Lord and the church reminds God of his promises. They ask that he would graciously empower the minister with his Spirit, grace, blessing, efficacy, working, governance, and direction. Thus public ordination declares the doctrine of the call of ministers.[268]

Chemnitz prayed for the Spirit to unify the church through its claim to the doctrines of the word[269] and to inspire its legitimately called preachers to right doctrine and proper ministry. In this proper ministry Chemnitz said the Holy Spirit prescribes and informs the minister's sermons and works to direct his doctrine. He flows through the minister's life and ministry to comfort, give patience, and direct.[270] Chemnitz desired ministers of the church to be faithful pastors, with the Holy Spirit governing and assisting them, so they might minister faithfulness to God knowing that their labor would not be in vain in the Lord.[271]

The Office of the Keys

Jesus established the church with the authority of the keys to forgive or bind sins when he breathed the Holy Spirit upon his disciples (John 20:22).[272] Chytraeus said the office of the keys ministers the voice of the gospel,

266. Chemnitz, *Ministry, Word and Sacraments*, 32.

267. Chemnitz, *Ministry, Word and Sacraments*, 30.

268. Chemnitz, *Ministry, Word and Sacraments*, 36–37; Chemnitz, *Examen*, 234; Chemnitz, *Examination*, 2:40.

269. Chemnitz, *Ministry, Word and Sacraments*, 18.

270. Chemnitz, *Ministry, Word and Sacraments*, 46.

271. Chemnitz, *Ministry, Word and Sacraments*, 47.

272. *CLT*53, 3:133; *CLTP*, 712.

pronounces forgiveness of sins or excommunication, and bestows the gifts of the Holy Spirit.[273]

Chemnitz related the office of the "keys of the kingdom of heaven" to the preaching of the word of God through which the Holy Spirit ministers to unlock the kingdom of heaven, so many may be brought into it. Therefore, ministers of the word should speak the doctrines of sin, repentance, faith, forgiveness, and obedience, and faithfully and diligently apply them to their hearers and to themselves. Ministers should be confident that the Spirit kindles these doctrines in the hearts of the hearers, as they depend on the Holy Spirit to supply and kindle them in themselves through the means of the word and sacraments. When the law convicts, let them know that its warnings cannot be shaken off but that what this office binds on earth is bound in heaven, "because it is done through the keys of the kingdom of heaven." When they hear the promises of the gospel let them believe that the word of God is the voice of the Holy Spirit himself, bringing comfort through this means.[274]

By including the minister as needing the ministry of the law and the gospel himself, Chemnitz clearly and practically linked the priesthood of believers to the office of the keys. He saw that God's presence through his Holy Spirit accomplishes the church's ministry with his grace and gifts. He assists the planting and nurturing of those legitimately called to set forth doctrine and ministry faithfully and guilelessly (1 Cor 3:6; 15:58).[275]

Gifts of the Holy Spirit

The *Formula* writers viewed the gifts of the Holy Spirit with a broad perspective. Chytraeus named the principle gift of the Spirit as the acknowledgement of Jesus Christ as Lord and Savior. He also noted three Scriptural lists of gifts: Isa 11,[276] Eph 4,[277] and 1 Cor 12.[278] He said the Ephesians gifts (apostles, prophets, shepherds, and teachers) were to establish and equip the ministry of the gospel. The 1 Corinthians gifts[279] were to benefit the

---

273. Chytraeus, *Catechesis*, 143; Andreae, 33 *Sermons*, I-58.

274. Chemnitz, *Ministry, Word and Sacraments*, 132-33.

275. Chemnitz, *Ministry, Word and Sacraments*, 29-30; cf. *CLT53*, 3:120, 21; *CLTP*, 699; Chemnitz, *Examen*, 479; Chemnitz, *Examination*, 2:692, 93.

276. Chytraeus, *Postil*, 221-24, on Isa 11:1-3 at Pentecost.

277. Chytraeus, *Postil*, 200-201, Acts 1:1-11; cf. *CLT53*, 3:119; *CLTP*, 698.

278. Chytraeus, *Postil*, 297-303, 1 Cor 12, on the tenth Sunday after Trinity.

279. Chytraeus, *Postil*, 202-5, Acts 1:1-11.

common good of the whole church.[280] The Isaiah gifts were wisdom, understanding, counsel, strength, knowledge, godliness, and fear of God.[281]

The following paragraph is Chytraeus's explanation of the 1 Corinthians list. Wisdom uses Christian doctrine to tell truth from falsehood to inform faith, worship, and behavior. Knowledge understands what to do. Faith courageously trusts God to do great things, e.g., the apostles and Luther spread the gospel against world opposition. Through healing, the apostles and saints after them touched people. Miracles deliver from danger and perform the duties of one's calling in God's power. Prophecy foretells things to come or expounds Scripture's prophecies, as did Luther.[282] The discernment of spirits, e.g., exposed the false doctrines of Arius. Speaking several languages is being skillful in a diversity of tongues, e.g., Jerome.[283] Through the interpretation of tongues Luther translated Scripture's foreign languages into German.[284] It is worth noting that Chytraeus with Luther considered tongues and interpretation as natural language skills and not glossalia and its interpretation. The Holy Spirit is the efficient cause of the gifts and, to prevent human pride, he distributes them according to his will, not according to human ability.

Chemnitz wrote that through the fall Adam lost the Holy Spirit and the gifts. Christ was anointed with the Holy Spirit so that the Spirit exercises all of his divine powers in Christ's human nature. Thus, the Spirit, with his gifts, is poured out upon the apostles and all flesh (Acts 2:4–6), because Christ as the firstborn received gifts from his Father according to his human assumed nature (Ps 68:18) and shares them with his human brothers and sisters.[285] Chytraeus wrote that the gifts of the Spirit testify to the presence of the Godhead, the Father, Son, and Spirit.[286] Chemnitz said the Spirit produces actions in believers that are characteristic of himself. Through the indwelling of the saints, which the Scripture calls the fellowship *(koinonia)* of the Holy Spirit (2 Cor 13:14), believers partake of the divine nature (2 Pet 1:4). The gifts conferred on the saints through the gracious indwelling[287] are

---

280. Chytraeus, *Postil*, 298–99, 1 Cor 12, on the tenth Sunday after Trinity.

281. Chytraeus, *Postil*, 224, on Isa 11:1–3 at Pentecost.

282. Andreae, *Six Sermons*, 87. Andreae agreed, saying such ability is not given to all, but is available in interpretive works like the catechism.

283. Chytraeus, *Postil*, 299, Chytraeus says Jerome knew Latin, Greek, Hebrew, Slavonish, and Chaldean.

284. Chytraeus, *Postil*, 299–302, 1 Cor 12, on the tenth Sunday after Trinity.

285. DNC, 131; TNC, 329, Heb 2:11–15.

286. Chytraeus, *Postil*, 302–3, 1 Cor 12, on the tenth Sunday after Trinity.

287. DNC, 26; TNC, 83.

not themselves essential attributes of the Deity, but are finite gifts, the effects of the Deity, which reside and function in the saints.

Chemnitz and Chytraeus agreed that there are two manners of gifts of the Holy Spirit. One is common to all believers: faith, joy, peace, and love, etc (Gal 5). The other is the peculiar privilege of some persons, e.g., the sudden knowledge of diverse tongues, courage to declare one's faith, spreading abroad the gospel, the gifts of healing, and other miracles. They are distributed among the saints by God's goodness, so that not all are given to all, but expediently by God's grace (1 Cor 12:11).[288] At Pentecost he poured out upon the apostles both the common and ordinary gifts and also the special gifts of the Spirit. The Spirit's gifts were given visibly to show that he is always present with the preaching of the gospel. He kindles true prayer, joy, and hope in believers, while he transforms them into the image of God.[289] Thus God ministers his gracious gifts to the church through his presence in the Holy Spirit.[290] Chytraeus and Chemnitz saw the special gifts of the Spirit limited to particular times to witness to his reality, rather than available for all members of the church at all times.

Chemnitz said the enduring gifts are teaching, interpretation, management, etc. For them the "difference" of gifts was more of degree—some are better teachers than others—than of variety of gifts—tongues, interpretation of tongues, healing, prophecy, etc.[291] Chemnitz and Andreae said the visible gifts of miracles—healings, tongues, prophecy, etc.—were given temporarily to validate the ministry and doctrine of the biblical ministers, and so only appeared for the brief time recorded in Scripture.[292] Chytraeus, while not specifically mentioning the limitation of the gifts, also said the purpose was the proof of the divine authority of the prophets and apostles.[293]

Chemnitz saw that by means of controversy over the gifts Satan sought to deprive the historic church of the fruit of the loveliest promises concerning the Comforter, which Christ had willed to be given to all believers as our great consolation. This confirmed his idea that the spectacular gifts of the Spirit had ceased.[294]

---

288. *DNC*, 93; *TNC*, 247.
289. Chytraeus, *Postil*, 217, on Pentecost.
290. Chemnitz, *Ministry, Word and Sacraments*, 29.
291. Chemnitz, *Ministry, Word and Sacraments*, 30.
292. *CLT53*, 1:180, 181; *CLTP*, 244; Andreae, *33 Sermons*, I-414.
293. Chytraeus, *Catechesis*, 1.
294. *CLT53*, 1:92, 93; *CLTP*, 140.

New Life in the Holy Spirit

New Life in the Holy Spirit was described variously by the *Formula* writers. Chemnitz called the Christian life a fellowship (*koinonia*) of the indwelling Holy Spirit because Christians partake of the divine nature in this fellowship.[295] He said believers receive the indwelling person of the Spirit and not just a bestowal of his gifts.[296] The divine essence dwells within the believers as his temple.[297] He gives his gifts and powers through a divine "*koinonia*" which Chemnitz called God's "special action" that is necessary for the new life in the Holy Spirit.[298] The indwelling Spirit leads believers to look away from their hopeless sinful flesh to Christ and his promises of grace and hope.[299] The Holy Spirit defends believers as they live their new life by his commandments in their appointed ways of faith.[300]

Andreae encouraged Christians to pray for the Holy Spirit of truth, who enables all aspects of this new life: faith, prayer, love, forgiveness, obedience to God, and the strength to stand in joy.[301] He said that after sinners receive the grace of forgiveness, Christ, the Father, and the Holy Spirit dwell in them to help struggle against sin, to make them more godly, and to bring them to eternal life.[302]

Chytraeus said the apostles are the best examples of new life in the Spirit. They received salvation and the Holy Spirit, who helped them live for the sake of Jesus Christ as they quietly obeyed God and exercised the gifts of the Spirit.[303]

---

295. *DNC*, 58; *TNC*, 160; 2 Cor 13:14; 2 Pet 1:4.

296. *CLT53*, 1:96, 97; *CLTP*, 145–46; Gal 4:6; Rom 8:11; 5:5; Joel 2:28; 1 John 4:13; 2 Pet 1:4; Phil 1:6; Eph 4:30; Luther, *WA* 40^{II}, 422; *LW* 12, 377, in *Commentary on Ps. 51* Luther refers to John 14:23 as evidence that the Spirit dwells with believers according to his substance as well as his gifts. Chemnitz says others, e.g., Lombard and Osiander, do not distinguish between the person of the Holy Spirit and his gifts.

297. *FSD*, 95; *LS*, 268; *CLT53*, 1:124; *CLTP*, 176; Rom 8:9; 1 Cor 6:19; 2 Cor 13:14.

298. *FSD*, 42; *LS*, 138; *CLT53*, 1:145; *CLTP*, 201.

299. *CLT53*, 2:260; Chemnitz, *Justification*, 120.

300. *CLT53*, 3:78, 87; *CLTP*, 648, 660; Chemnitz, *Ministry, Word and Sacraments*, 88.

301. Andreae, *33 Sermons*, I-33, 62, 58.

302. Andreae, *Six Sermons*, 76.

303. Chytraeus, *Postil*, 270–71, Rom 8:17–27, on the fourth Sunday after Trinity.

Receiving the Holy Spirit

Chytraeus tied the reception of the Holy Spirit to God's promise of life in Christ Jesus[304] and to faith to call on God. When faith has been kindled by the Holy Spirit in believers, they also receive the Holy Spirit (Gal 3:14), since God gives eternal salvation, remission of sins, righteousness, and the Holy Spirit to those who call on him in faith (Acts 2:1–4).[305]

Chytraeus linked the gift of the Holy Spirit given at Pentecost to the law because the feast of Pentecost was the celebration of the giving of the law.[306] The international aspect of Pentecost showed that God's Spirit and his gifts are available to all nations.[307] He also said those who are justified by God's mercy for Christ's sake have received the Holy Spirit.[308] He encouraged Christians to seek the Spirit, whom God wants to give (Luke 11:13), to intercede for them. They are to seek his governance and gifts in their lives, as they try to live so as not to grieve the Spirit or to drive him out (Ps 51).[309]

Chemnitz said the Spirit ministers through gospel preaching, so by faith we receive him when we hear the gospel and meditate on it.[310] This differs from the prophets of Israel who received the Spirit by dreams and visions. Chytraeus and Andreae said that God does not give the Spirit secretly by "fanatical and accursed" dreams and visions,[311] but through the preaching of the word.[312] Thus, Chemnitz said, Scripture gives no command to follow the apostles' example or a divine promise that God wants to send, give, and confer the Holy Spirit by the laying on of hands.[313] Chytraeus said the Spirit is given along with the fruit of the Spirit (Gal 5), and with the spiritual gifts of knowledge, tongues, courage, spreading the gospel, healing, and others.[314] Jesus promised that the Father gives the Spirit to those

---

304. *CLT53*, 2:212; Chemnitz, *Justification*, 39; Chytraeus, *Catechesis*, 103, 105.

305. Chytraeus, *Postil*, 234, Acts 2:14–38, on Whitsun Monday.

306. Chytraeus, *Postil*, 213–26, on Pentecost.

307. Chytraeus, *Postil*, 230, Acts 2:14–38, on Whitsun Monday.

308. Chytraeus, *Postil*, 68, Rom 12:8–10; also 438, Luke 1:68–79, on the Feast of John the Baptist; *Catechesis*, 101.

309. Chytraeus, *Postil*, 225–26, on Pentecost.

310. *CLT53*, 1:181; *CLTP*, 244.

311. Chytraeus, *Postil*, 232, Acts 2:14–38, on Whitsun Monday.

312. Andreae, *Six Sermons*, 87.

313. Chemnitz, *Ministry, Word and Sacraments*, 110–11.

314. Chytraeus, *Postil*, 216–20, on Pentecost.

who ask him.³¹⁵ Jesus gave the Holy Spirit when he breathed on his disciples as God breathed the breath of life at creation.³¹⁶

Evidence of the presence of the Holy Spirit, according to Chemnitz, is not spiritual feelings but is when believers desire him and groan while contending with God. The Lord prepares them not to reject the Holy Spirit but to assent to him.³¹⁷

The Human Will

Chemnitz taught that the human will without the Holy Spirit can neither initiate spiritual desires nor obey God, but can only hinder the work of the Spirit by wicked carnal desires.³¹⁸ He said the natural person, a slave of sin without the Spirit, is free only to do evil.³¹⁹ The Spirit of God fills renewed persons which causes them to obey him.³²⁰ Andreae agreed that the Lord causes them to will and to work through the Holy Spirit, so that honor belongs to God alone.³²¹

Chytraeus taught that through the Spirit's testimony in believers, he reveals God's truths that people can not naturally perceive.³²² His teaching of divine Christian truth is confirmed through the miracles of God, e.g., raising from the dead, and the universal experience of all who live in prayer and repentance. These come by impulses from the Holy Spirit and not from the human will.³²³

Chytraeus said those reborn by water and the Spirit are freed from serving sin and are helped by the Holy Spirit to live a life of inward and outward morality. They have true knowledge of God and resist the indulgences of worldly inclinations.³²⁴ Chemnitz wrote that the Holy Spirit leads the will

315. *CLT53*, 1:180, 81; *CLTP*, 244; Chytraeus, *Postil*, 13, Luke 11:13. Chytraeus noted that Jesus anointed his followers in the church with the Holy Spirit, but not the angels.

316. *CLT53*, 1:113; *CLTP*, 164–65.

317. *CLT53*, 1:182–83; *CLTP*, 245–46.

318. *CLT53*, 1:175; *CLTP*, 238.

319. *CLT53*, 1:167; *CLTP*, 228.

320. *CLT53*, 1:182; *CLTP*, 246, Ezek 36:26–27; Kolb, *Nikolaus von Amsdorf*, 194. In comparison, Kolb notes that Luther's contemporary Amsdorf said the human will is a depraved and corrupt captive of Satan. The *Formula* writers have a more dynamic dependence upon the power of God to overcome human weakness than Amsdorf.

321. Andreae, *Confession*, 59; cf. Andreae, *33 Sermons*, I–241, 44.

322. Chytraeus, *Catechesis*, 99.

323. Chytraeus, *Catechesis*, 6.

324. Chytraeus, *Catechesis*, 38.

through the word to correct the will and arouse it to reach out for God's renewal.[325] The will, still engaged in the battle between the flesh and the Spirit, begins to move and operate with the aid of the indwelling Holy Spirit.[326] Through the voice of the gospel the Holy Spirit points the will of the regenerate to good desires and right intentions so it can make free choices.[327]

Chemnitz followed Melanchthon to say there are three causes for good action: the word of God, the Holy Spirit, and the human will, because "the sons of God are led by the Holy Spirit" and "grace makes unwilling men willing."[328] Senses and experience do not precede faith, but are directed by the word. When believers hear the word, they do not resist but are strengthened. Although they struggle they are certain that the Holy Spirit is powerful to aid their wills.[329] When Jesus assumed human nature, he restored believers back to life in the image of God, so they no longer doubted concerning the salvation of their human nature through Christ.[330]

Renewal

In renewal, Chytraeus and Chemnitz saw the Spirit working in those who are justified, but are still clouded by doubts, fears, and crooked inclinations. The Spirit purges the effects of depravity and restores them to God's image. He gives their minds the light of God and puts new obedience in their wills and hearts to praise God by following his law,[331] as his instruments for righteousness.[332]

Chemnitz reminded believers that in renewal they have not reached perfection, since the work of renewal is not complete in this life. A battle is still being waged between minds and hearts that are renewed and the flesh that continues to lust against the Spirit:[333]

> The very wrestling of the flesh and of the Spirit, of the old and of the new man, in the regenerate, clearly shows the difference

---

325. *CLT53*, 1:192; *CLTP*, 258.
326. *CLT53*, 1:184–85; *CLTP*, 249.
327. *CLT53*, 3:29; 1:180; *CLTP*, 595, 243.
328. *CLT53*, 1:186; *CLTP*, 250, "Nam filii Dei aguntur Spiritu sancto" and "gratia facit ex nolentibus volentes."
329. *CLT53*, 1:185; *CLTP*, 250.
330. *FSD*, 62; *LS*, 188–89.
331. Chytraeus, *Catechesis*, 117–18.
332. Chemnitz, *Examen*, 210; Chemnitz, *Examination*, 1:647–48.
333. *CLT53*, 1:181, 82; 2:8, 94; *CLTP*, 245, 340, 433; cf. Chemnitz, *Examen*, 209, 211; Chemnitz, *Examination*, 1:643–44, 651.

between the actions which have the Holy Spirit for their Author and Giver and those which arise or are born of the natural powers of the free will.[334]

Because of *simul justus et peccator* continual renewal is essential for believers.

The Inner Testimony of the Holy Spirit

Andreae said the Holy Spirit received at baptism personally encourages believers. He guarantees that God wills their forgiveness of sins and they are securely children of God and the heirs of his kingdom.[335] Chemnitz said the Holy Spirit seals this with the sacraments.[336] Through the Lord's Supper, the Spirit assures fearful believers' faith of their covenant of adoption as God's children through baptism and the blood of his Son.[337] Chytraeus said the Holy Spirit testifies that he transfers believers into his likeness to govern their thoughts and actions according to his will (2 Cor 3:18). He confirms to them that the Father has adopted them as children and made them heirs because of his Son, Jesus Christ. He helps them in their weakness to stand against the devil and the enticements of pleasures, to shun sin, and to exercise virtue.[338] He kindles faith and prayer so they may approach God as a caring father, not as an angry judge. Fear of wrath is turned to godly fear that obeys God and calls upon him in faith, trust, and love.[339] Chytraeus noted that not only does the Spirit kindle the call to God, but he also puts a witness of trust in God into believers so they thank him for acceptance into his favor as a kind father.[340]

Chemnitz encouraged piety and daily fellowship with the Holy Spirit. Through faith, prayer, confession, and patience in the struggle between the flesh and the Spirit, the Holy Spirit is known as the present God who

---

334. Chemnitz, *Examen*, 138; Chemnitz, *Examination*, 1:436, "*Et ipsa lucta carnis et spiritus, veteris et novi hominis in renatis, illustre ostendit discremen actionum, quæ autorem et donatorum habent Spiritum sanctum, et quæ oriuntur seu nascuntur ex naturalibus liberi arbitrii viribus.*"

335. Andreae, *33 Sermons*, I-57, 175–76; Chytraeus, *Postil*, 381–83.

336. Chemnitz, *Ministry, Word and Sacraments*, 83.

337. *FSD*, 64; *LS*, 192.

338. Chytraeus, *Postil*, 288, on Rom 8:12–17, on the eighth Sunday after Trinity; cf. CLT53, 2:257, 58; Chemnitz, *Justification*, 116.

339. Chytraeus, *Postil*, 289–90, on Rom 8:12–17, on the eighth Sunday after Trinity.

340. Chytraeus, *Postil*, 39, Gal 4.

intercedes for believers even when they feel contrary.[341] This is the Spirit's guarantee which strengthens believers against doubts, and gives them confidence, joy, and hope by which they feel the new life in God and happily rest in his promised grace under the cross.[342] These new emotions harmonize with and delight in the law of God (Rom 7:22).[343]

Chemnitz linked Luther's doctrine of election with the assurance and the testimony of the Spirit. According to God's hidden counsel (Rom 8:29-30) he wants to minister through the word by the Spirit (2 Cor 3:8) in those whom he has foreknown or predestined. That word by which the Spirit calls is the power of God to salvation to everyone that believes (Rom 1:16). This is the highest comfort for pious minds and troubled consciences, that God, as he calls by the word, makes his will known, that he wants to save the hearer and confer the Spirit. Thus the Spirit of God bears witness that the elect are his children, he intercedes for them, and he assures them that God is faithful to confirm and complete the work begun in them.[344]

The Holy Spirit and the Kingdom

At Jesus' ascension, his disciples asked him when he would restore the kingdom to Israel. Jesus answered that they would receive power and the Holy Spirit (Acts 1:6-9). Chytraeus said the ascension showed Christ's kingdom and God's government. God maintains and preserves his creation through the preaching of the gospel while he calls a church to himself. This believing company depends upon the power of God's gospel word and the Holy Spirit for deliverance from the power of evil in a spiritual kingdom not governed by human laws and might. It fulfills Christ's ascension promise of giving the Holy Spirit. The disciples were not to be captains and warriors, but powerful witnesses and preachers of the gospel to the ends of the earth.[345] Chytraeus said the Lord's Prayer declares God's gift of the Holy Spirit to lead the church away from the control of the devil and sin, to sanctify the church, and to guide the church to eternal life and glory.[346]

---

341. *CLT53*, 1:186; *CLTP*, 250-51.

342. *CLT53*, 2:248, 257-58, 252; Chemnitz, *Justification*, 99, 115-16, 105; also Andreae, *33 Sermons*, I-187.

343. *CLT53*, 3:16, 17, 31; *CLTP*, 581, 597.

344. Chemnitz, *Ministry, Word and Sacraments*, 90-91, 1 Cor 1:8; Phil 1:6; 1 Pet 5:10.

345. Chytraeus, *Postil*, 204.

346. Chytraeus, *Catechesis*, 174, 176.

Andreae stressed that the Holy Spirit fights the attack of Satan.[347] He encouraged Christians to pray that in this present life God, by his Holy Spirit, would work through leaders and princes to reign and lead truthfully, since their examples lead either to eternal goodness or evil.[348]

Chemnitz said that at the Parousia believers' bodies and souls will be united, sustained, preserved, and directed by the Holy Spirit. In the resurrection both the body and soul will be perfectly obedient to the Spirit for whatever purposes he wishes. The bodies and souls of the saints in glory will use the power of the Spirit for all things, which he wishes them to do, and they will possess faculties that are spiritual and perfect.[349] Andreae said in God's future kingdom the Holy Spirit will give a new ability to follow the Lord in all eternity no longer needing to be guided through the word.[350]

Responses to the Holy Spirit

Chemnitz said "simple faith" in Christ obeys the Holy Spirit lest believers be drawn away from the voice of the Son of God.[351] This obedient response is expressed in prayer, worship, good works, and the fruit of the Spirit.

Prayer

Chemnitz and Chytraeus said prayer should be directed to the one, true, and eternal God—Father, Son, and Holy Spirit.[352] Chemnitz also said prayer does not spring from natural human powers, but is from the power and work of the Holy Spirit (Gal 4:6; Zech 12:10). Christians should pray zealously, pursuing God's promise to give his Spirit to those who ask him (Luke 11:13). They may expect God's Spirit to kindle zeal for prayer and devotion, so they may cry with his intercession, "Abba, Father" (Rom 8:26; Gal 4:6).[353]

---

347. Andreae, *33 Sermons*, I-43.
348. Andreae, *33 Sermons*, I-25.
349. DNC, 175; TNC, 429.
350. Andreae, *33 Sermons*, V-86.
351. FSD, 37; LS, 126.
352. Chemnitz, *Ministry, Word and Sacraments*, 139. See also 143, commenting on the heathens who do not pray to the triune God, but to their fabricated idols or the God whom they do not know. Chytraeus, *Catechesis*, 28, says true prayer is directed to the Triune God, and honors the Father by honoring the Son.
353. Chemnitz, *Ministry, Word and Sacraments*, 140-42.

Chytraeus said the Spirit of prayer accepts human ignorance and kindles in believers sighs from the heart which groan for release from miseries.[354]

Andreae explained that as one cannot separate the shine from the fire, so persistent prayer is linked with persistent faith, which is maintained by the believer's dependence upon the Holy Spirit of prayer.[355] Prayer honors God by trusting Christ's call to pray, while the Spirit instructs and provides the motivation to ask the Father.[356] The Holy Spirit uses practical prayer for training, nourishment, and preservation in Christian piety, e.g., repentance, faith, patience, comfort, hope, etc., which, without prayer, would gradually diminish and disappear altogether. Therefore, Christians should pray that they are ruled and guided by the Holy Spirit, the Spirit of renewal, and not grieve the Spirit of prayer by giving prayer a low priority.[357]

Worship

Chemnitz said true worship is a believer's faithful response to God's command. The indwelling Holy Spirit motivates worship of God according to the word.[358] Chemnitz regarded the worship of the Spirit as confession of the Holy Spirit's consubstantiality in the divine essence with the Father and the Son. Worship must include the adoration of the Holy Spirit or it is denied that he is the third person of the Godhead. The baptismal formula (Matt 28:19) is the basis for the adoration of the Spirit for in baptism we call upon the one Name of God the Father, the Son, and the Holy Spirit. Worship of the Trinity without separation is directed to the person of the Father, to the person of the Son, and to the person of the Holy Spirit. When we pray, "Come, Holy Spirit" we declare that the Spirit is consubstantial and coequal with the Father and the Son.[359] The church at different times prays to the Father, to the Son, and to the Holy Spirit, for it believes not only that

---

354. Chytraeus, *Postil*, 271, Rom 8:17–27, on the fourth Sunday after Trinity.
355. Andreae, *33 Sermons*, I–180.
356. Chytraeus, *Postil*, 194, Jas 1:22–27.
357. Chemnitz, *Ministry, Word and Sacraments*, 140, 142; *CLT53*, 2:93; *CLTP*, 432.
358. *CLT53*, 3:15; *CLTP*, 579.
359. *CLT53*, 1:97; *CLTP*, 146 citing Gregory of Nazianzus, Bk. 5; *Orat.* 31.12: "who has worshiped the Holy Spirit in either the Old or the New Testament, or where is it written that the Holy Spirit is to be adored, whereas there are clear examples and precepts concerning the adoration of the Father and the Son?" "*Quis vel in Vetere, vel in Novo Testamento Spiritum sanctum adoravit, aut ubi scriptum est, Spiritum S. adorandum: sunt extant exampla & pracepta de adorando Patre & Filio*" (MPG 36.145). He also cites Basil, Chrysostom, and Gregory of Nazianzus.

the three persons are the one true God, but that each person is the entire divine essence, the one true God, with no inequalities among the persons.[360]

Chytraeus said the Holy Spirit hallows the gifts of offerings and enlightens the service,[361] and in the Psalms the Spirit gave the gift of music for worship.[362] Chytraeus also said the indwelling Spirit brings true worship in good works, good fruit, and spiritual sacrifices commanded by God through the word.[363]

Good Works and the Fruit of the Spirit

Chytraeus and Andreae claimed that the purpose for Christians who are born again and filled by the Holy Spirit is to please God with good works as they walk in the light of the gospel.[364] Chemnitz said the Holy Spirit wills to work in them.[365] True faith works through love by the Holy Spirit, who is renewing the heart. He referred to Luther's idea that faith alone fulfills the law by producing good works without the law. Thus faith alone receives forgiveness of sins and through love willingly does good works.[366] Chemnitz concluded that good works spontaneously follow justification, without the law. The Holy Spirit of reconciliation renews minds by the hearing of faith to arouse new desires to agree with God's law. Believers begin to love God and delight in his law, as the Holy Spirit writes it into their hearts. Good works begin to occur, just as a good tree bears good fruit (Matt 12:33).[367] Chytraeus said good works, the labor of God, are commanded of the believer's total being and are actions of faith and the Holy Spirit that honor God.[368] Chemnitz noted that in reconciliation the Spirit does his work of renewal[369] and uses the faithful good works of obedience to the law of God as his instruments to mortify the flesh. God's power comes to the obedient Christian through preaching and meditation on the word.[370] An-

---

360. *CLT53*, 1:39, 40; *CLTP*, 75.

361. Chytraeus, *Postil*, 330, Gal 5:16–26, on the fourteenth Sunday after Trinity.

362. Chytraeus, *Postil*, 364, Eph 5:15–21, on the twentieth Sunday after Trinity.

363. Chytraeus, *Postil*, 373, Phil 1:3–11, on the twenty-second Sunday after Trinity.

364. Chytraeus, *Postil*, 111–14, Eph 5; Andreae, *33 Sermons*, V–70.

365. *CLT53*, 3:58; *CLTP*, 627.

366. *CLT53*, 3:49; *CLTP*, 617, citing Luther, *WA* 391, 354, *Disputatio 4 Contra Antinomos*.

367. *CLT53*, 3:16–17, 29; *CLTP*, 581, 595.

368. Chytraeus, *Catechesis*, 120.

369. *CLT53*, 3:40; *CLTP*, 607.

370. Chemnitz, *Ministry, Word and Sacraments*, 101.

dreae agreed that regenerated believers freely perform good works. In the unregenerate and unwilling, hostile powers make their good works merely coercive obedience of Christ.[371] Chemnitz said the word of God animated by the Holy Spirit is the standard for good works.[372] With the Holy Spirit and pure hearts believers can do all that the law requires.[373] Overcoming sin and good works are the necessary results of the Spirit's renewal in justification.[374] God gives the Holy Spirit to justified sinners as he renews them, though sin may remain. He desires to purify them to be his holy particular people who deny ungodliness and follow him in the good works he himself has prepared.[375] Good works, as fruits of faith, come from love given and worked by the Holy Spirit in renewed Christian liberty.[376]

The *Formula* writers agree with Luther and Melanchthon that if good works are not done, faith may be lost, the Holy Spirit may be grieved and driven out, and salvation may be lost.[377] Believers' good works are necessary so they might be sanctified by the word of God in which they are prescribed, and by the Holy Spirit, by whom they are prepared.[378] Chemnitz, referring generally to Luther, said, it is faith's nature, as part of the Spirit's regeneration or renewal, that of necessity it produce good works. So, good works are the fruit of the Holy Spirit.[379] They are the regenerate's necessary response to the Spirit of liberty, not for salvation, but as an obligation for the sake of the will and command of God.[380] This stance concurs with Article 4 of the *Formula of Concord*, which resolved the controversy in which Georg Major claimed the necessity of good works for salvation. The *Formula* said good works are not necessary for salvation, which is freely given through the work of Christ, yet because they are commanded by God, good works are not free options for believers but are the means by which the Spirit works the obedience of faith in Christians.[381] Good works cannot be mistaken for means of attaining any degree of perfection in this life. Chemnitz noted that

371. Andreae, *Six Sermons*, 105–6.
372. *CLT53*, 3:37; *CLTP*, 604.
373. *CLT53*, 3:33, 34; *CLTP*, 599–600.
374. *CLT53*, 3:18, 19; *CLTP*, 583.
375. Chemnitz, *Ministry, Word and Sacraments*, 96.
376. *CLT53*, 3:41, 28–29, 60–61; *CLTP*, 608, 595, 629.
377. Chemnitz, *Ministry, Word and Sacraments*, 98–99; *CLT53*, 3:22–23; *CLTP*, 587–88; Andreae, *Six Sermons*, 80.
378. Chemnitz, *Ministry, Word and Sacraments*, 101.
379. *CLT53*, 3:59, 61; *CLTP*, 628–29.
380. *CLT53*, 3:49; *CLTP*, 617.
381. *BSLK*, 941; *BC*, 576, 11, 12; *Formula of Concord*, Art. 4, "Good Works."

all the saints, in the midst of their obedience in the Holy Spirit, experience sin clinging to the flesh, which hinders a walk in perfection.[382]

Christians must always differentiate the good works done by the Spirit and the works of the flesh without the Holy Spirit, which is sin.[383] Chytraeus distinguished the good works of the world [*bona opera Ethnicorum*] from those of Christians [*bona opera Christianorum*].

> The good works of the reborn are not only done by man according to the free will, as with the world, but Christians are reached and kindled by the Spirit through the word.
>
> The good works of Christians are of a true and continuous motion in the heart kindled by the Holy Spirit, by which true knowledge of Christ and faith light the way. Without this knowledge it is impossible to please God. The good works that are the excellence of the worldly are all external gestures, that is, controlled actions without spiritual motivation in the heart and without faith.[384]

The word teaches Christians to please God by faith in Christ. Through the word the Spirit kindles true Christian good works, which are to know God, to believe in Christ, to bear fruit, to not resist the Holy Spirit, and to yield members to the will of God.[385] Chytraeus said the Holy Spirit links believers with God by producing in them the fruit of the Spirit, which fulfills the law through the love of God and neighbor.[386]

The Sin against the Holy Spirit

Christians must not allow the world's pollutions to expel the Spirit and his gifts. Chemnitz stressed that the Holy Spirit is driven out by sin and unwillingness to receive him, which is a repudiation of the Spirit.[387] Therefore the

---

382. Chemnitz, *Ministry, Word and Sacraments*, 102; cf. *CLT53*, 3:32; *CLTP*, 598, Rom 7:18, 21; Isa 64:6; Ps 143:2; Luke 17:10.

383. *CLT53*, 3:31, 18; *CLTP*, 597, 582.

384. Chytraeus, *Catechesis*, 124.[*Deinde causiæ efficientibus differunt.*] *Nam virtutes renatorum, non solis humanism seu liberi arbitrii viribus efficiuntur, ut Ethnicæ: sed a Spiritu Dei Sancto per verbum accenduntur & consummantur.*

Bona opera Christianorum sunt veri & serii motus cordis per Spiritum Sanctum accensi, quibus vera agnitio Christi & Fides, sine qua impossibile est Deo placere, prelucet. Bona opera seu virtutes Ethnicæ, sunt tantum externi gestus seu gubernatio locomotiva, sine spirituali motu cordis & sine fide.

385. Chytraeus, *Catechesis*, 125.

386. Chytraeus, *Postil*, 54, Rom 12:1–5.

387. Chemnitz, *Examen*, 143, 211, 277; Chemnitz, *Examination*, 1:450, 649; 2:158.

Holy Spirit charges the world with the sin of unbelief and fights against sin's control. If people continue to resist, God gives them over to their worldly lusts to receive the reward for their errors. The Spirit no longer strives with them or opposes them with the teaching of the law and allows their hearts to harden and their minds to become stupid. Without the Holy Spirit people cannot resist the devil's deceptions and their depravity reveals itself in outward sins.[388] The natural person, regenerate or not, who hears the word of God and faithlessly rejects it, is lost,[389] for "where there is no repentance there is no faith, and no grace. When a person refuses to repent, at the same time the Holy Spirit is driven out and faith is lost."[390] Chemnitz warned that sins against the renewed conscience, e.g., unchecked anger and undermining the gospel promises, grieve the Holy Spirit because the reborn who do such things oppose the Holy Spirit and risk losing their inheritance in God's kingdom.[391] He cited Augustine to say that the sin against the Holy Spirit is the rejection of the Holy Spirit and his works and gifts. Augustine said this cannot be forgiven because in final impenitence a person perseveres to death in sin without repentance.[392] Andreae said one who curses the name of God loses his faith, the Holy Spirit, and eternal life.[393] Therefore we can judge *a posteriori* correctly the sin against the Holy Spirit is not forgiven because God makes known his righteous judgment against those who go astray and die without repentance.[394]

Chemnitz said the ancients taught that not all sins committed against the ministry and operations of the Holy Spirit are unforgivable, yet the sins by which one resists the ministry and work of the Holy Spirit are much more serious and dangerous than other sins. People can be set free from other sins by the power of the Holy Spirit when he arouses and kindles true repentance and faith in their hearts and leads to forgiveness of sins. There is no forgiveness of sins for those who resist the ministry of the Holy Spirit and persist in stubbornness. The ancients warned about specific sins that

---

388. *CLT53*, 1:186; *CLTP*, 214.

389. *CLT53*, 1:176, 77, 215–16; *CLTP*, 240, 287–88; cf. *CLT53*, 3:54; *CLTP*, 623.

390. *CLT53*, 3:100–101; *CLTP*, 676, "*Ubi enim non est poenitentia, ibi nec fides, nec gratia est. Et quando poentitentia abjicitur, simul & Spiritus Sanctus excutitur, & fides amittitur.*"

391. *CLT53*, 2:26, 68–69; *CLTP*, 359–60, 406; Chemnitz, *Examen*, 178; Chemnitz, *Examination*, 1:553; Chemnitz, *Ministry, Word and Sacraments*, 105.

392. Chemnitz, *Ministry, Word and Sacraments*, 106–8, 153–54, citing Augustine Bk 1, *Retract.* ch 19; *Serm.* 1133 on the Words of the Lord, in *Ministry, Word and Sacraments*, ch 83 and *Epist.* 50.

393. Andreae, *33 Sermons*, V–26.

394. Chemnitz, *Ministry, Word and Sacraments*, 106.

oppose the Holy Spirit: 1) presumption regarding the mercy of God; 2) obstinacy that rejects exhortations to repentance; 3) attacks on acknowledged truth that ascribe the Spirit's work to the devil; 4) despair of the grace of God and his salvation, no matter how often it is offered through the word; 5) wicked envy of God's grace to a neighbor; and 6) final impenitence, when one dies without conversion and repentance.

Chemnitz emphasized the importance of continual repentance and renewal of God's grace.[395] Though God's grace often leads rebels back to faith, there is danger in the sin against the Holy Spirit. If one is

> unmoved by repentance and dies thus, the sentence of divine judgment revealed in the word declares that it was a sin or affront against the Holy Spirit, and that of such a kind that it is forgiven neither in this world nor in that which is to come.... For those who, after they once have been enlightened and made partakers of the Holy Spirit, knowingly and in obstinate wickedness again deny the acknowledged truth and completely fall away from Christ, and so persevere ... that ... they crucify Christ anew, regard [Him] as a joke, and tread [Him] underfoot and insult the Spirit of grace—for this, I say there remains no remission of sins, but the prospect of the judgment of God and of eternal fire.[396]

Judas typifies one whose continual denial of the faith grieved the Holy Spirit until his final loss of faith and eternal life.[397]

Summary and Conclusions

In the mid-1500s the Reformation movement was in turmoil. The stress was about to pull the Reformation apart. The Catholic Church was pulling back to its traditions. The Reform movement was pulling ahead into Calvinism. The enthusiasts were pulling outside to heresies. Various Lutheran factions were cementing their loyalties and issues with accusations and defenses. A unifying document was desperately needed. The three Reformers examined in this chapter were instrumental in writing clear statements that helped calm the storm and steady the Reformation. They reached back to Luther's original work and using literary methods learned from Melanchthon, they wrote theology that many of the various Lutheran groups could endorse and the *Formula of Concord* was finally published in 1577.

395. Chemnitz, *Ministry, Word and Sacraments*, 107–8; cf. Chemnitz, *Examen*, 425; Chemnitz, *Examination*, 2:553.
396. Chemnitz, *Ministry, Word and Sacraments*, 108.
397. *CLT53*, 3:102; *CLTP*, 678.

Many of the writings that helped to ease the turmoil were basic Christian teaching. All three *Formula* writers held to the Trinitarian concept of God and the total depravity of mankind. They joined Luther and Melanchthon to declare the futility of attempts by natural human philosophy and reason to achieve salvation apart from the work of God in Christ and his Holy Spirit. In their sermons, postils, catechisms, etc., they consistently insisted that the Holy Spirit is the active ingredient in every part of salvation from repentance and faith to conversion. All aspects of the new life that follows are also infused with the power of the Holy Spirit. Justification and sanctification are clearly the work of the Holy Spirit.

The *Formula* writers featured the work of the Holy Spirit exclusively through the means of the word and sacraments. They emphasized that the inner testimony of the Holy Spirit is the assurance that believers' sins are forgiven and they, as the children of God, are assured an inheritance in his eternal kingdom.

The only gift of the Holy Spirit they all agreed on is that the gift of faith in Christ is the primary gift of the Spirit. Other gifts listed in Scripture were ignored or variously interpreted, as were miracles. Throughout the writing, the unmediated stance of the enthusiasts was rejected and scorned.

The central position of the Holy Spirit in their theology, the means of word and sacrament, and the importance of the inner testimony of the Holy Spirit are evident in these writings and demonstrate continuity of the theology of the Holy Spirit from Luther to the *Formula of Concord*.

6

Comparisons—Contrasts—Conclusions

Introduction

This research has shown that the Holy Spirit is central in the life and theology of Martin Luther and in his contemporaries and in his followers to the *Formula of Concord*. Even as Lutheran theology in this period became more systematized and amenable to philosophical methods, it continued to stress the importance of the Holy Spirit consonant with Luther's theology.

The references in this chapter include Martin Luther, Reformation baseline; Philip Melanchthon; their contemporaries Johannes Brenz, Johann Spangenberg, and Urbanus Rhegius; and later *Formula of Concord* writers Jacob Andreae, Martin Chemnitz, and David Chytraeus. The statements in this chapter are based solely on the research documented in chapters 2–5 of this volume.

Principle Topics

Prenter argued that the Holy Spirit was dominant in Luther's theology and that the cross was fundamental. The Spirit uses the cross of Christ to slay sinful people and he brings the power of Christ's resurrection to make them alive. All a person can do is confess his hopeless, total depravity before God and cling to the promises of God that the Spirit reveals through the word. The spark of faith created by the Holy Spirit is God's most significant miracle. This is the work of *Spiritus Creator*, the creating Spirit of God.[1]

Melanchthon set different accents in his teaching of the Holy Spirit. He saw the Holy Spirit breaking into the human domain to free people from sin. Working in the intellectual domain, the Spirit enables them to obey the law,. The other early Reformers and the *Formula* writers saw the Holy Spirit activating the power of the gospel for salvation and renovation through the means of the word and sacraments, much as Luther did.

The Theology of the Cross

The rediscovered concepts of Luther's theology of the cross portrayed by von Loewenich, Prenter, Althaus, Bayer et al. highlighted the sinner's helplessness and the distinctive character of God's work of restoration. Luther's theology of the cross stressed the centrality of Christ's death on the cross and the cross born by the believer in the struggle of faith. The Christian life begins with personal death in repentance and forgiveness of sins. The Holy Spirit does this through adversities that force believers to throw themselves upon the promises of God. The power of the Spirit links believers to Jesus through the cross. The cross includes a twofold death: the death of human self-dependence and reliance upon the death of Christ.

God chooses to hide himself, and so he is not known by human effort, but the Holy Spirit reveals him to the faithful ones who hear the word of God and trust in that word. Luther called this faith the "higher realism."[2] In anguish the Christian experiences the presence of Christ as the Holy Spirit turns faith into reliance on the promises in Christ. Luther called this process of learning peace through bitter experience, "the school of the Holy Spirit."[3] Just as God and his truths are hidden, so also is the Christian life. In the lowliness and suffering of their crosses Christians follow Christ as the Holy Spirit leads them into spiritual union and conformity with Christ in his cross.

Melanchthon emphasized the work of the Spirit in his theology of repentance, justification, and conversion,[4] but did not emphasize the dynamic union with Christ achieved by the Spirit as perceived in Luther's theology of the Cross. A major distinction between them was that Luther intertwined faith with experience in spiritual union with Christ, and Melanchthon

---

1. Prenter, *Spiritus Creator*, ix.
2. WA 4:355, 29-33; cf. Loewenich, *Luther's Theology*, 90.
3. WA 7:546, 24-28; LW 21:299, *The Magnificat* (1521).
4. MLC21, 15; BSLK, 166, 31-33; BC, 125, 31-33; *Apology*, Art. 4, "Justification."

concentrated on the comfort brought about by the counselor Spirit through the appropriation of the forensic aspect of justification. In Luther's understanding the Holy Spirit assures believers that they are children of God and enables them to live as his obedient children. He develops trust, faith, and obedience in them through their own crosses. In Melanchthon's understanding, believers are equipped to obey the Spirit themselves without featuring the cross as Luther did. Though theologians after Luther did not use the term *theologia crucis*, the elements of death to self and life in the cross are not absent from their thought.

The Person and Reception of the Holy Spirit

Luther, Melanchthon, the three early Reformers, and the three *Formula* writers held to a traditional, "homoousian" Trinitarian doctrine based on Scripture and the creeds that emphasized the unity of the Godhead while distinguishing the persons and their specific functions. The Holy Spirit's person and work are those of God himself. Opposing the Calvinists and Crypto-Calvinists of their day the *Formula* writers emphasized the hypostatic union of Christ's human and divine natures as a basis for the distinct personhood of the Spirit. The common divine essence in the Trinity, which they espoused, simultaneously expressed the unity of God and the *filioque* relationship of the Spirit with the Father and the Son.

According to Luther the Spirit always speaks and is received through hearing the word in faith. The external word—the physical elements of preaching and the sacraments—comes first, followed by the internal word—the inner speaking of the Spirit who gives life to the external word.[5] According to Melanchthon, the Holy Spirit works through the word and the sacraments as pictures of God's promises that the Holy Spirit uses to inform and to lead people to faith and knowledge of God. In contrast, Luther saw the Spirit working through the preaching of the word and the sacraments to bring justification in an active sense. The difference is that Luther saw the Holy Spirit working internally to bring repentance, faith, and justification. Melanchthon saw him working alongside, enabling, informing, assisting, and relating to the cognitive nature of man.

The Reformers shared the dynamic view that the Spirit comes actively to believers through the means of the word and the sacraments. Lutheran theology, neither in its origins nor in its developments, distinguishes between the reception of the Holy Spirit at the new birth of baptism and the baptism with the Holy Spirit.

---

5. Althaus, *Theology*, 36; Bente, *Concordia Triglotta*, 494; *BC*, 312.

All agree that the Scripture is the word of God, because the Holy Spirit is its author, interpreter, and theologian. Chemnitz said the Holy Spirit works through people as his means in the regular call to ministry. The extension of the word in the sacraments is not seen in the *Formula* writers except in the words of institution.

The Work of the Holy Spirit

Luther, the early Reformers, and the *Formula* writers saw the work of the Spirit in much the same way, to bring sinful people to God through faith in Christ. Repentance and faith are totally the work of the Spirit to turn people to God through the infusion of love, by which he brings them to conformity to the will of the Father through union and conformity to Christ. Justification and faith are, thus, practically synonymous.[6]

Melanchthon said the purpose of justification is the fulfillment of the law. In justification Christ gives the Spirit to transform believers and to enable them to turn from lust to obey the law. The Holy Spirit changes believers' hearts and gives them a new capacity for obedience and frees them to want to obey God. The Holy Spirit brings faith through the word and he brings hope as the guarantee of God's love. Consonant with his humanist background, Melanchthon said the Spirit appeals to the human intellect to know that God loves them, to be comforted, and to respond with good deeds.

Melanchthon has been criticized for emphasizing the forensic aspects of justification while ignoring the dynamic, such as Luther's idea of the infusion of love by the Holy Spirit to do battle with the believer's flesh.[7] The criticisms of Melanchthon may not be valid. He saw the Holy Spirit functioning dynamically in justification and sanctification through the Law-Gospel motif of the word and sacrament to release people from the power of sin. The Holy Spirit is imparted at justification and the believer's life, or sanctification, begins immediately. The Spirit releases believers from the law, motivates the new life, provides discernment and faith,[8] consoles fearful hearts, inspires true prayer, and works true fear of God. Melanchthon saw the Holy Spirit working true religious motivation in believers in the cognitive domain to turn them away from the desires of the fleshly heart to the life promised in Christ.[9]

---

6. Christenson, *Welcome*, 184; Prenter, *Spiritus*, 226.
7. Cf. Hildebrandt, *Alien or Ally?*, 53–54.
8. *CR* 15:655, 660.
9. *CR* 15:645–46; *CR* 21:205–6; *MLC21*, 130.

A key idea for Melanchthon is that the Spirit enables regenerated people to walk in penitence and spontaneously to obey the law's demands.[10] However, his work concerning faith and the Spirit does not treat Luther's idea of the Spirit's work to bring union with Christ through faith in Christ which gives meaning to Luther's *simul iustus et peccator* doctrine. Melanchthon did say that the Spirit gives life to the believer's half-dead faith through the word,[11] and that the word and the Spirit are inseparably bound together. Yet while Luther saw the indwelling Spirit of Christ present, Melanchthon spoke of the present Spirit enabling believers to obey the law.

In agreement with Luther, the other early Reformers and the *Formula* writers combined the objective and internal work of the Spirit in justification.[12] Brenz, similar to Luther, characterized the entire Christian life as faith. Brenz, Rhegius, and Spangenberg equated justification with the new birth as works of the Spirit, and firstfruits of the Spirit. The human will is passive in justification—to be subdued by and not to resist the work of the Spirit.

Brenz comprehended sanctification as the Holy Spirit's work in the community of Christians who are joint heirs of God. The Spirit cleanses the flesh by putting to death and making alive (the theology of the cross). Rhegius linked sanctification, justification, and faith. The work of God must be received in faith so that the Spirit may mortify the flesh and make it alive to receive the gifts brought by the life-giving Spirit. According to Rhegius and Spangenberg, in renewal the indwelling Holy Spirit makes it possible to understand the word and enables the will to follow the law. In comparison, Luther linked renewal to the personal union with and conformity to Christ wrought by the Holy Spirit, while Melanchthon internalized the work of the Spirit in renewal necessary to overcome the powers of sin.

It is clear that, though there are some differences, Luther, Melanchthon, the early Reformers and the *Formula* writers see the primary work of the Holy Spirit to be the application of God's salvation in Jesus Christ through justification and sanctification.

Melanchthon saw the Spirit working as an adjunct of Christ and not through the word in the same way as the others. Luther and the other reformers saw the Spirit bringing the word of the Law and the Gospel through the word. Melanchthon said the Spirit is given at the time of conversion to do the work of Christ. In contrast with Luther's idea that the Spirit brings

---

10. CR 21:103–6; MLC21, 37–39.

11. CR 15:618.

12. While the term *ordo salutis* comes up later in Lutheran and Reformed Orthodoxy, the early Reformers have much of this idea in their doctrine of the Holy Spirit. It is picked up later in Lutheran pneumatology as in Weidner, *Pneumatology*, a volume of his systematics devoted to the *ordo salutis* as the work of the Holy Spirit.

conformity to Christ, Melanchthon said that the Holy Spirit enables weak believers to perform the demands of the law. At baseline, all agreed that the primary work of the Holy Spirit is to glorify Christ.

New Life in the Holy Spirit

Luther called the life of faith a reliance on Christ given by the Spirit. This includes the "inner testimony of the Holy Spirit" by which believers in Christ feel the Holy Spirit in themselves and experience the certainty of their forgiveness.[13]

According to Melanchthon, the testimony of the Holy Spirit occurs when he replaces terror and hopelessness with faith. He gives life, comfort, prayer, awareness, and knowledge of the merciful God, trust, and confidence. Melanchthon agreed with Luther, that the key is in the promise of Rom 8 that the Holy Spirit intercedes for believers in their weakness and in the midst of their despair, gives comfort and assurance.[14]

The early Reformers said that when the Spirit is given at justification he testifies that they are God's children, that he will minister in their Christian lives, and that they are sealed into the promises of God. The Holy Spirit stirs up new desires to love God and obey his law, and dwells within believers to subdue their wills as he manifests himself in their experiences. The Spirit testifies internally that as believers they are children of God and joint heirs with Christ. Similarly, the *Formula* writers taught that when believers are indwelt by the divine essence of God—the Holy Spirit—their wills are subdued by the Spirit, who manifests himself in their experience and leads them to follow the commands of God in the new obedience. This is accomplished as believers' wills are bent from following themselves to following God. In this process they experience the presence of the Spirit, the assurance and joy of being heirs of God, and the confidence to call upon him. The apostles are the best examples.

The Holy Spirit and the Church

Luther understood the church to be the community of the Triune God born of the word of Christ's promise. It is maintained and sanctified by the Spirit

---

13. WA 56:324, 4–6; LW 25:311–12; WA 31^{II}:445, 23–28; LW 17:238; WA 56:346, 18–21; LW 25:334; cf. Loewenich, *Theology of the Cross*, 116; WA 57^{III}:169, 15–20; LW 29:171; WA 56:370; LW 25:359.

14. CR 15:667.

through the word and sacrament.[15] He insisted that there is salvation only in this church which has forgiveness, the gospel, baptism, and the sacrament of the altar.[16] The Holy Spirit brings his people to unity and ministers his fruit and gifts only where Christ is preached with worship and prayer.[17]

The basis for ministry in the church is the doctrine of justification by faith, for through Christ's redemption the Holy Spirit makes the merit of Christ operative in the church, and Christ's authority—the power of keys— dwells in that body.[18] Luther said that the Spirit calls those designated and enabled for ministry as his instruments.[19] The Spirit anoints each Christian to his place to serve the love of God to his neighbor according to the doctrine of the priesthood of believers.[20] Luther identified God's word as the primary criteria of truth for the church and calls prophecy and the witness of the Spirit marks of the true church.[21] Luther acknowledged the various signs, miracles, and portents, linking them to Mark 16:17-18 and sees them as the normal exercise of the Christian life relative to 1 Cor 12-14.[22] His personal experience of healing, prophecy, and teaching indicates his perception of the gifts of the Spirit operating through and with the word.[23]

Similarly, Melanchthon saw the church to be the Holy Spirit's instrument as the custodian of pure doctrine, teacher, and minister of word and sacrament. While he understood that the Holy Spirit works through the word and sacraments, as did Luther,[24] Melanchthon's idea of the real presence of Christ in the means of word and sacrament was not as thoroughly developed as Luther's. According to Melanchthon, the gifts of the Holy Spirit are given at justification, but he did not stress them.

The early Reformers perceived the church as the universal body or bride of Christ that is dependent upon the dynamic word and sacrament and full of the Holy Spirit. Rhegius considered the gift of the Holy Spirit to the church as the beginning of Christ's reign or kingdom. Therefore, these

15. Elert, *Structure*, 264.

16. WA 26:507; LW 37:368-69.

17. BSLK, 653-54, 35-58; BC, 435-38, 35-458; *Large Catechism*, "Explanation to the Third Article of the Creed"; WA 12:35, 19-21, 24-25; 36, 12-13; LW 53:11-12.

18. WA 11:451, 6-17; LW 36:298.

19. WA 11:411; LW 39:308-9.

20. WA 6:566, 16-17; LW 36:115; WA 38:230-32; LW 38:185-88.

21. WA 8:493-94; LW 36:144-45; *The Misuse of the Mass* (1521).

22. WA 57^{III}:115; LW 29:124-25; commenting on Heb 2:4; WADB 7:87; WA 5: 383, *Preface to the First Epistle to the Corinthians* (1530).

23. BSLK, 689, 115-16; BC, 455-56, 115-16, *Large Catechism*, The Lord's Prayer, Last Petition.

24. See chapter 3 above.

reformers had high regard for councils as instruments of the Holy Spirit, subject to and enlightened by the Spirit through the Holy Scriptures. Brenz understood that God uses Christian leaders in church and government.

The *Formula* writers said that Jesus established the church when he gave his disciples his Holy Spirit. The Spirit fills the universal church of the redeemed—heirs of eternal life—and guides and governs its members through the visible church. Ministers of the church are called by God through human means by the authority given to the church. The office of ministry includes the power to retain or to forgive sins, to preach and to teach the word, and to administer the sacraments. The Holy Spirit is present in the office of ministry and his gifts are given to equip the ministers. The *Formula* writers agreed that the miraculous gifts were only intended to bear witness to the authority of the prophets and apostles and were not needed afterwards, since their testimony is in the word of God.

Responses to the Holy Spirit

Luther believed the life of faith responds to the Holy Spirit with prayer, worship, and good works. He said faith was the highest good work of all.[25] Prayer, important to the practical Christian life, drives away the devil and brings the Holy Spirit. In his theology of the cross he taught from Rom 8:26 that the Holy Spirit overcomes fleshly weakness and enables believers to take hold of the promises of God for all of life in prayer. The Holy Spirit reminds believers that their basis for prayer is their standing in Christ before the Father. The Spirit leads them to persevere in prayer through the turmoil of inner conflicts and doubts.

The Holy Spirit motivates the faithful to respond in worship by turning away from self-centeredness to God in sacrificial praise, confession, repentance, and faith. Luther allowed freedom in worship and taught that since the Spirit is not bound by the church's canons and laws, he adapted worship to the people's needs.

According to Melanchthon, the importance of the worship service is the presence of the Holy Spirit and his work of putting to death and making alive.[26] He saw the worship service as oral and visible proclamation of the gospel through preaching and participation in the sacraments. In these the worshipers are included into the message of faith, sacrifice, forgiveness, and reconciliation. While the "helper beside" idea may be apparent

---

25. WA 6:204, 13–15, 25–25; *PE* 1:187.

26. *BSLK*, 361–62, 39–40; *BC*, 266, 39–40, *Apology*, Art. 24, "The Mass"; cf. Manschreck, *Quiet Reformer*, 310.

in Melanchthon and Luther believed in the "inner helper," he and Melanchthon were very close in their teaching on the Holy Spirit and prayer: "Stir them up, and build their faith and hope so they can pray."[27]

The early Reformers and *Formula* writers were all involved with practical pastoral ministry. They perceived the Christian life as a continual struggle in which the Holy Spirit uses the experience of faith to produce victory. The responses of this life in the Spirit include prayer, good works, and the caution not to sin against the Holy Spirit by unrepentant unbelief. They said true worship is the faithful response of believers to God. The indwelling Spirit causes worship, sanctifies offerings, and enlightens service. At the time of the *Formula* writers the subject of good works was controversial. In the face of the dispute, they said good works were willed by God for believers, not as necessary for salvation but as a result of their new life in Christ by the Holy Spirit. If the Christian does not obey the Spirit with good works, the Spirit is grieved and driven away, and faith may be lost. Luther, Melanchthon, and the others agreed that the Holy Spirit assists the weakness of believers in prayer, worship, and good works through the word and the sacraments. The Holy Spirit links prayer and worship to all parts of the Christian life.[28]

The *Formula of Concord*

In 1517 Martin Luther presented his well-known *Ninety-Five Theses* in Wittenberg. For the next thirty years he wrote volumes of theology, much of which stirred up controversy and spawned both Reformers and anti-Reformers. By 1577, when The *Formula of Concord* was published, many of his positions had been attacked, defended, ignored, contorted, and revised with distortions, additions, and deletions. This volume is an examination of Luther's theology of the Holy Spirit and how this theology survived among his associates, his contemporaries, and theologians who followed. How did Luther's theology fair in the *Formula of Concord*, which was an effort to corral the conflicts and theological disputes that were tearing up the Reformation? One clue to the regard in which Luther was held is the first footnote on the first page of the "Solid Declaration" of the *Formula*: "The authors of the *Formula of Concord* reflected the widespread belief among Lutherans of their day that Luther had been a special instrument in God's hands for the restoration of the gospel in the church . . . their high regard for his insight,

---

27. Manschreck, *Quiet Reformer*, 317.
28. WA 1:532, 30–32; *LW* 31:87.

wisdom, and historical role reveals itself often in the *Formula*."[29] Dr. Luther's *Small* and *Large Catechisms*, Smalcald Articles, and other writings are liberally referenced. His teaching on the Holy Spirit is quoted on many pages, at least thirty specific citations.

The following quotations from the *Formula of Concordia* indicate that Luther's theology of the Holy Spirit reached the document largely unscathed:

Original Sin—"Only the new birth and renewal of the Holy Spirit can and must heal this deranged, corrupted human nature."[30]

Free Will—"Human beings were so corrupted through the fall of our first parents that ... they are and remain God's enemy until by his grace alone, without any contribution of their own, they are converted, made believers, reborn, and renewed by the power of the Holy Spirit through the Word as it is preached and heard."[31]

Free Will—"The Holy Scripture ascribes conversion, faith in Christ, rebirth, renewal, and everything that belongs to the actual beginning and completion of these things, not to the human powers of the natural free will–neither totally, halfway, somewhat, nor in the slightest and smallest bit–but rather ascribes all this in *solidum* (that is, completely and totally) to divine activity and to the Holy Spirit alone ...

"Reason and free will are capable of 'living honorably to a certain extent externally,' but only the Holy Spirit effects new birth and the inner reception of another heart, mind, and disposition. He opens the mind and the heart so that they understand Scripture and are attentive to the Word."[32]

Free Will and Good Works—"The Smalcald Articles [III, 1,5,10] rejects the following errors regarding the free will: 'That the human being has a free will either to do good and reject evil, etc.' Soon thereafter, it rejects the following error when it is taught 'that there is no basis in Scripture that the Holy Spirit with his grace is necessary for performing good works.'"[33]

The Holy Christian Community—"In the Large Catechism ["Creed" 51–53], Luther wrote, 'Of this community I also am a part and member, a participant and co-partner in all the blessings it possesses. I was brought into it by the Holy Spirit and incorporated into it through the fact that I have heard and still hear God's Word, which is the beginning power for entering it. Before we had come into this community, we were entirely of the

---

29. *BC*, 534n1, SD.
30. *BC*, 534, 14, *Formula*, SD 1, "Original Sin."
31. *BC*, 544, 5, *Formula*, SD 2, "Free Will."
32. *BC*, 549, 25, 26, *Formula*, SD 2, "Free Will."
33. *BC*, 550, 33, Formula, SD 2, "Free Will."

devil, knowing nothing of God and of Christ. The Holy Spirit will remain with the holy community or Christian people until the Last Day."[34]

The Word and Conversion—"Through the preaching of the holy gospel of the gracious forgiveness of sins in Christ and through meditating upon it, a spark of faith is ignited in them, and they accept the forgiveness of sins for Christ's sake and receive the comfort of the promise of the gospel. In this way the Holy Spirit, who effects all of this, is sent into their hearts. It is indeed true that both the planting and watering of the preacher and the activity and desire of the hearer would be in vain, and no conversion would result from these efforts, if the power and action of the Holy Spirit were not added to them. For the Spirit enlightens and converts hearts through the Word that is proclaimed and heard."[35]

The Word of God—"We should be certain, on the basis of and according to the promise that the Word of God, when preached and heard, is a function and work of the Holy Spirit, through which he is certainly present in our hearts and exercises his power there."[36]

Conversion—"Luther holds that human beings in and of themselves or on the basis of their own natural powers are not capable of anything and cannot help with their own conversion. He holds that conversion is not just in part, but totally and completely a product, gift, present, and activity of the Holy Spirit alone, who accomplishes and effects what is done through his own power and might, working through the Word in the mind, will and heart of the human being."[37]

Justification, Sanctification, Good Works—"Good works do not precede faith, nor does sanctification precede justification. Instead, first of all, in conversion, the Holy Spirit kindles faith in us through the hearing of the gospel. This faith lays hold of God's grace in Christ, and through it a person is justified. Thereafter, once people are justified, the Holy Spirit also renews and sanctifies them. From this renewal and sanctification the fruits of good works follow."[38]

Faith and Good Works—"Faith is a living, daring, confidence in God's grace, so sure and certain that the believer would stake life itself on it a thousand times. This knowledge of and confidence in God's grace makes people glad and bold and happy in dealing with God and with all creatures. And this is the work which the Holy Spirit performs in faith. Because of it,

---

34. *BC*, 551, 36, 37, *Formula*, SD 2, "Free Will."
35. *BC*, 554, 54–55, *Formula*, SD 2, "Free Will."
36. *BC*, 554, 56, *Formula*, SD 2, "Free Will."
37. *BC*, 561, 89, *Formula*, SD 2, "Free Will."
38. *BC*, 569, 41, *Formula*, SD 3, "Righteousness."

without compulsion, a person is ready and glad to do good to everyone, to serve everyone, to suffer everything, out of love and praise to God, who has shown this grace. Thus, it is impossible to separate works from faith, quite as impossible as to separate heat and light from fire."[39]

Good Works—"It is God's will and express command that the faithful should do good works, which the Holy Spirit effects in the faithful, so God allows these works to please him for Christ's sake and promises a glorious reward for them in this life and in the life to come."[40]

Law and Gospel—"Everything that proclaims something about our sin and God's wrath is the proclamation of the law, however and whenever it may take place. On the other hand, the gospel is the kind of proclamation that points to and bestows nothing else than grace and forgiveness in Christ.... The Spirit of Christ must not only comfort but through the function of the law must also 'convict the world of sin' [John 6:8]. Thus, in the New Testament the Holy Spirit must perform ... alien work–which is to convict–until he comes to his proper work—which is to comfort and to proclaim grace. For this reason Christ obtained the Spirit for us and sent him to us."[41]

Free from the Law—"When people are born again through the Spirit of God and set free from the law ... they live according to the unchanging will of God, as comprehended in the law, and do everything, insofar as they are reborn, from a free and merry spirit. Works of this kind are not, properly speaking, works of the law but work and fruits of the Spirit."[42]

These statements, and many more, demonstrate the continuity of Luther's theology of the Holy Spirit to the *Formula of Concord*. The *Formula* did not, however, settle all Lutheran disputes. Issues remained with the *Formula*, *Augustana*, and *Apoligia* in the cardinal doctrines dealing with justification and sanctification, conversion, good works, free will and others.[43] The primary issues regarding the Holy Spirit, however, were settled. Luther's theology of the Holy Spirit was clearly recognized and explained.

Conclusion

The Holy Spirit, his means of word and sacraments, and the experience of the inner testimony of the Holy Spirit were important in the theology of

39. *BC*, 576, 11–12, *Formula*, SD 4, "Good Works."
40. *BC*, 580–81, 38, *Formula*, SD 4, "Good Works."
41. *BC*, 583, 11–12, *Formula*, SD 5, "Law and Gospel."
42. *BC*, 590, 17, *Formula*, SD 6, "Third Use of the Law."
43. Jungkuntz, *Formulators*, 76–79.

Martin Luther and in the theologies of prominent theologians leading to the *Formula of Concord*.

Strong areas of agreement with Luther's theology of the Holy Spirit among the theologians considered in this research include:

- The Holy Spirit is part of their Trinitarian theology.
- The Holy Spirit rescues a lost humanity through faith in Christ.
- The Holy Spirit is present in the lives of faithful Christians through the physical means of the word and sacraments.
- The Holy Spirit gives his inner testimony assuring the justified that their sins are forgiven, that they are children of God, and that they have an eternal inheritance in heaven with God.

The theologians shared Luther's dynamic inner working of the Holy Spirit in justification and sanctification in agreement with his view of God's recreating work of restoration through the gospel of Christ in the power of the Holy Spirit.

It is notable that Philip Melanchthon, who worked with Luther and who educated those who followed, is the one whose theology of the Spirit was least like Luther's. The one whose doctrine and life experience most resembled Luther's theology of the cross, David Chytræus, is the one who was probably closest to Melanchthon personally, having lived in his home while a student of philosophy and theology at Wittenberg.

In 1529 Martin Luther presented his *Small Catechism* that included a study of the Apostles Creed. His explanation to the third article of the creed is probably the most succinct statement of his theology of the Holy Spirit. "The Third Article," as it is often called, is quoted in the *Formula of Concord*, 1577.

"I believe that by my own understanding or strength I cannot believe in Jesus Christ my Lord or come to him, but instead the Holy Spirit has called me through the gospel, enlightened me with his gifts, made me holy, and kept me in the true faith, just as he calls, gathers, enlightens, and makes holy the whole Christian church on earth and keeps it with Jesus Christ in the one common true faith."[44]

Luther's original formulation held for over fifty years after he wrote it and it has continued in the Lutheran church as the basis for understanding the Holy Spirit for over five hundred years. As thousands of children have memorized these words in Catechism classes and were confirmed, perhaps not entirely understanding them, the Holy Spirit has continued to do his

---

44. *BC*, 551, 40, *Formula*, SD 2, "Free Will."

good work of maintaining the faith and, as Luther said, "Keeping holy the whole Christian church on earth."

Bibliography

Achelis, E. C. "Andreas Hyperius." In *ERK* 5:432–33.
Althaus, Paul. *The Theology of Martin Luther*. Translated by Robert C. Schultz. Philadelphia: Fortress, 1966.
Anderson, Paul, and Larry Christenson. "Lutheran Charismatics." In *IDPC* 847–51.
Andreae, Jakob. "Confessions." Translated by Robert Kolb. In *Andreae and the Formula of Concord: Six Sermons on the Way to Lutheran Unity*, 58–60. St. Louis: Concordia, 1977.

———. *Drey und dreissig Predigten von den fürnemsten Spaltungen in der christlichen Religion, so sich zwischen den Bäptischen, Lutherischen, Schwenckfeldern, Zwinglischen, und Widerteuffern halten*. Tübingen, Germ.: Morhart, 1580.

———. *Six Christian Sermons on the Divisions Which Have Continued to Surface among the Theologians of the Augsburg Confession from 1548 until This Year 1573, etc.* Translated by Robert Kolb. In *Andreae and the Formula of Concord: Six Sermons on the Way to Lutheran Unity*, 61–120. St. Louis: Concordia, 1977.

Atkinson, James, ed. and trans. *Luther: Early Theological Works*. Philadelphia: Westminster, 1981.

———. *Martin Luther and the Birth of Protestantism*. Atlanta: John Knox, 1981.
Bagchi, D. V. N. "Sic et Non." In *Protestant Scholasticism: Essays in Reassessment*, edited by R. Trueman and R. Scott Clark, 14–15. Carlisle: Paternoster, 1999.
Bainton, Roland H. *Here I Stand*. New York: Abingdon-Cokesbury, 1950.

———, ed. *Martin Luther's Christmas Book*. Distributed through Lutheran Brotherhood. Minneapolis: Augsburg, 1997.

Barton, Peter F. *Um Luthers Erbe: Studien und Texte zur Spätreformation. Tilemann Heshusius (1527–1559)*. Wittenberg, Germ.: Luther-Verlag, 1972.
Bauckham, R. J. "Cross, Theology of the." In *New Dictionary of Theology*, edited by Sinclair B. Ferguson and David F. Wright, 181–82. Downer's Grove: InterVarsity, 1988.
Bayer, Oswald. *Martin Luther's Theology: A Contemporary Interpretation*. Translated by Thomas H. Trapp. Grand Rapids: Eerdmans, 2008.

———. "Melanchthons Theologiebegriff." In *Der Theologie Melanchthon*, edited by Günter Frank, 40–41. Stuttgart, Germ.: Thorbecke, 2000.

BIBLIOGRAPHY

———. *Promissio: Geschcichte der reformatorischen Wende in Luthers Theologie*. Göttingen, Germ.: Vandenhoeck & Ruprecht, 1971.
———. *Theology the Lutheran Way*. Translated and edited by Jeffrey G. Silcock and Mark C. Mattes. Lutheran Quarterly Books. Grand Rapids: Eerdmans, 2007.
Bente, E. F., ed. *Concordia Triglotta: Historical Introductions to the Symbolical Books of the Evangelical Lutheran Church*. St. Louis: Concordia, 1921.
Bergendoff, Conrad. *The Church of the Lutheran Reformation*. St. Louis: Concordia, 1967.
Bode, Gerhard. "Chytraeus, David." In *DLLT* 150–51.
———. "Mörlin, Joachm." In *DLLT* 516–17.
Boehmer, Heinrich. *Road to Reformation*. Translated and edited by John W. Doberstein and Theodore G. Tappert. Philadelphia: Muhlenberg, 1946.
Bonhoeffer, Dietrich. "The Church and the World." Lecture, August 1934.
Bossert, G. "Johann Brenz." In *ERK* 2:260–62.
Braaten, Carl, and Robert Jenson, eds. *Christian Dogmatics*. 2 vols. 1984. Reprint, Philadelphia: Fortress, 1986.
———. *Union with Christ: The New Finnish Interpretation of Luther*. Grand Rapid: Eerdmans, 1998.
Brecht, Martin. *Die frühe Theologie des Johannes Brenz*. Tübingen, Germ.: Mohr, 1966.
———. *Martin Luther: His Road to Reformation, 1483–1521*. Translated by James L. Schaaf. Philadelphia: Fortress, 1985.
Breen, Quirinius. "The Terms 'Loci Communes' and 'Loci' in Melanchthon." *Church History* 16 (1947) 197–209.
Brenz, Johannes. *Confessio V (or W)irtembergia: 1552*.
———. *De Clavibus Regni Coelorum, explicatio*. Strassburg, Fr.: Wendelinus Rihelius, 1555.
———. *De personali unione duarum naturam in Christo* . . . Tübingae, Germ.: Ulrich Morhardi, 1561.
———. *Operum Reverendi et Clarissimi Theologi, D. Ioannis Brentii, Praepositi Stutgardiani*, Tübingae, Germ.: Excudebat Georgius Gruppenbachius, 1576.
———. *Syntagma eorum, quae nomine illustrissimi Principi ac Domini, D. Christophori . . . in Synodo Tridentina per legatos eius, acta sunt . . .* 1553.
———. *Syngramma clarissimorum qui Halae Suevorum, 21 October 1525, Swäbisch Hall*. Teil 1 of *Frühschriften*, vol. 1. Edited by Martin Brecht et al. Tübingen, 1970.
Brown, Dale. *Understanding Pietism*. Grand Rapids: Eerdmans, 1978.
Brunner, Peter. *Worship in the Name of Jesus*. Translated by M. H. Bertram. St. Louis: Concordia, 1968.
Burnett, Amy Nelson. "Oecolampadius." In *DLLT* 559–61.
Caemmerer, Richard R. "Sixteenth-Century German Humanism." In *Lutheran Cyclopedia. A Concise In–Home Reference for the Christian Family*, edited by Erwin L. Luecker, 396. St. Louis, MO: Concordia, 1954.
Chemnitz, Martin. *De duabus naturis in Christo de Hypostatica earum unione: de communicatione idiomatum, et aliis questionibus inde dependentibus* . . . Frankfort & Wittenberg, Germ.: Maevii & Schumacher, 1653.
———. *Examen Concilii Tridentini*. Edited by Eduard Preuss. Berlin: Schlawitz, 1861.
———. *Examination of the Council of Trent*. 4 vols. Translated by Fred Kramer. St. Louis: Concordia, 1971–86.

BIBLIOGRAPHY

———. *Fundamenta Sanae Doctrinae de Vera et Substantiali Praesentia, Exhibitione et Sumptione Corporis & Sanguinis Domini in Coena.* Frankfort & Wittenberg, Germ.: Maevii & Schumacher, 1653.

———. *Justification: The Chief Article of Christian Doctrine as Expounded in Loci Theologici.* Translated by J. A. O. Preus. St. Louis: Concordia, 1985.

———. *Loci Theologici, quibus et loci communes D. Philippi Melanchthons Perspicue Explicantur, & quasi integrum Christianae doctrinae corpus, Ecclesiae Dei sincere proponitur.* Editi opera & studio, Polycarpi Leyser D. Wittenberg, Germ.: Maevii & Schumacheri, 1653.

———. *Loci Theologici.* 2 vols. Translated by J. A. O. Preus. St. Louis: Concordia, 1989.

———. *The Lord's Supper.* Translated by J. A. O. Preus. St. Louis: Concordia, 1979.

———. *Ministry, Word and Sacraments: An Enchiridion.* Translated by Luther Poellot. St. Louis: Concordia, 1981.

———. *The Two Natures in Christ.* Translated by J. A. O. Preus. St. Louis: Concordia, 1971.

Christenson, Larry. *The Charismatic Renewal among Lutherans: A Pastoral and Theological Perspective.* Minneapolis: Lutheran Charismatic Renewal Services, 1976.

———. *Ride the River.* Minneapolis: Bethany, 2000.

———, ed. *Welcome, Holy Spirit.* Minneapolis: Augsburg, 1987.

Chytraeus, David. *Catechesis.* Leipsig, Germ.: Defnerys, 1582.

———. *De Studio Theologiae Recte Inchoando: De Rational Studii Theologii Recte Instituendi.* Wittenberg, Germ.: Schleich & Schöne, 1570.

———. *A Postil or Orderly Disposition of Certeine Epistles Usually Rred in the Church of God, uppon the Sundayes and Holydays throughout the Whole Yeare.* Translated by Arthur Golding (from Latin to English). London: Bynneman, 1570.

———. *A Soueraigne Salue for a Sick Soule.* Translated by F. W. London: Field, 1590.

Cole, Henry, trans. and ed. *Select Works of Martin Luther.* 4 vols. London: Bensly, 1826.

Colinson, Patrick. *The Reformation: A History.* New York: Modern Library, 2004.

Deitz, Reginald W. *Luther and the Reformation.* Philadelphia: Muhlenberg, 1953.

Dingel, Irene. "The Culture of Conflict in the Controversies Leading to the Formula of Concord (1548-1580)." In *Lutheran Ecclesiastical Culture 1550-1675,* by Robert Kolb, 15-64. Leiden, The Neth.: Brill, 2008.

Dingel, Irene, et al. *Philip Melanchthon: Theologian in Classroom, Confession, and Controversy.* Göttingen, Germ.: Vandenhoeck & Ruprecht, 2012.

Dorner, J. A. *History of Protestant Theology.* 2 vols. Translated by George Robson and Sophia Taylor. Edinburgh: T. & T. Clark, 1871.

Drickamer, John M. "Did Melanchthon Become a Synergist?" *Springfelder* 40 (1976) 95-101.

Ebeling, Gerhard. *Luther: An Introduction to His Thought.* Translated by R. A. Wilson. Philadelphia: Fortress, 1970.

Elert, Werner. *The Structure of Lutheranism: The Theology and Philosophy of Life of Lutheranism Especially in the Sixteenth and Seventeenth Centuries.* Translated by Walter A. Hanson. Foreword by Jaroslav Pelikan. St. Louis: Concordia, 1962.

Engelland, Hans. "Introduction." In *Melanchthon on Christian Doctrine, Loci communes 1555,* translated and edited by Clyde L. Manschreck, xxv-xlii. Grand Rapids: Baker, 1982.

Erb, Peter C. "Introduction." In *Pietists: Selected Writings,* 1-25. Classics of Western Spirituality. New York: Paulist, 1983.

BIBLIOGRAPHY

Erdmann, David. "George of Brandenburg." In *ERK* 4:457a–58a.
Estes, James Martin. "Brenz, Johannes." In *DLLT* 105–6.
———. *Christian Magistrate and State Church: The Reforming Career of Johannes Brenz*. Toronto: University of Toronto Press, 1982.
———. *Christian Magistrate and Territorial Church: Johannes Brenz and the German Reformation*. Toronto: Centre for Reformation and Renaissance Studies, 2007.
———. *Peace, Order and the Glory of God: Secular Authority and the Church in the Thought of Luther and Melanchthon 1518–1559*. Leiden, The Neth.: Brill, 2005.
Fischer, Robert H. "Introduction to *Confession concerning Christ's Supper*." LW 37:151–59.
———. "Introduction to *That These Words of Christ, 'This Is My Body,' Still Stand Firm against the Fanatics*." LW 37:3–11.
Fleischer, Manfred P. ed. *The Harvest of Humanism in Central Europe* St. Louis: Concordia, 1992.
Flew, Anthony, ed. *A Dictionary of Philosophy*. 2nd ed. New York: St. Martin's, 1984.
Folkener, Carl W. "Introduction to *Explanation of the Ninety-Five Theses*." LW 31:17–23.
Forde, Gerhard. "Lutheranism." In *BEMCT* 354–58.
———. *On Being a Theologian of the Cross: Reflections on Luther's Heidelberg Disputation, 1519*. Grand Rapids: Eerdmans, 1997.
———. "Radical Lutheranism." *LQ* 1 (1987) 5–18.
———. *Theology Is for Proclamation*. Minneapolis: Augsburg Fortress, 1990.
———. "The Work of Christ." In *Christian Dogmatics*, edited by Carl Braaten and Robert Jenson, 2:11–46. 2 vols. Philadelphia: Fortress, 1984.
Fraenkel, Peter. *Testimonia Patrum: The Function of the Patristic Argument in the Theology of Philip Melanchthon*. Geneva, Switz.: Librarie E. Droz, 1961.
Frank, Gunter. *Der Theologe Melanchthon*. Stuttgart, Germ.: Thorbecke, 2000.
Garcia, Alberto L. García. "Spiritual Gifts and the Work of the Kingdom." *CTQ* 49 (1985) 149–60.
Gaß, Frederich Wilhelm J. H. *Geschicte der Protestantischen Dogmatik*. 5 vols. Berlin: Reimer, 1854–56.
Gasmer, J. *De Vita, Studii, et Obitu Reverendi, et Clarissimie Viri D. Martini Chemnitii* . . . Braunschweig, Germ.: N.p., 1588.
Gerrish, B. A. *Grace and Reason: A Study in the Theology of Luther*. Oxford: Clarendon, 1962.
Grane, Leif. *Contra Gabrielem: Luthers Auseinandersetzung mit Gabriel Biel in der Disputatio contra Scholasticam Theologiam*. Acta Theologica Danica 4. Gyldendal, Den.: N.p., 1962.
———. "Luther and Scholasticism." In *Luther and Learning*, edited by Marilyn J. Harran, 52–68. Selinsgrove, PA: Susquehanna University Press, 1985.
———. *Martinus Noster*. Mainz, Germ.: von Zabern, 1994.
Green, Lowell. *The Formula of Concord: A Historiographical and Bibliographical Guide*. Sixteenth Century Bibliography 11. St. Louis: Center for Reformation Research, 1977.
———. *How Melanchthon Helped Luther Discover the Gospel: The Doctrine of Justification in the Reformation*. Greenwood, SC: Attic, 1980.
———. "The Three Causes of Conversion in Philipp Melanchthon Martin Chemnitz, David Chytraeus, and the Formula of Concord." *Lu J*. 47 (1980) 89–114.
Greschat, Martin. *Melanchthon Neben Luther: Studien zur Gestalt der Rechtferungslehre zwischen 1528 und 1537*. Witten, Germ.: Luther-Verlag, 1965.

Grislis, Egil. "Martin Luther's View of the Hidden God: The Problem of the *Deus Absconditus* in Luther's Treatise *De servo arbitrio*." *McCormick Quarterly* 21 (1967) 81–94.
Grimm, Harold J. "Preface to *A German Theology*," *LW* 31:73–74.
———. "Introduction to *Disputation against Scholastic Theology*." *LW* 31:5–7.
———. "Introduction to *Heidelberg Disputation*." *LW* 31:35–38.
———. "Introduction to *Ninety-Five Theses*." *LW* 31:17–23.
———. *The Reformation Era*. New York: Macmillan, 1966.
Gritsch, Eric W., ed. *Luther's Works*. Vol. 39, *Church and Ministry I*. Philadelphia: Fortress, 1970.
Hägglund, Bengt. *History of Theology*. Translated by Gene Lund. St. Louis: Concordia, 1968.
Hall, Arthur C. A. "Protestantism." In *ERK* 9:290–302.
Hall, Fred P. "Influences in Luther's Reforms." In *Church and School in Early Modern Protestantism. Studies in Honor of Richard A. Muller on the Maturation of a Theological Tradition*, edited by Jordan J. Ballor et al., 49–66. Boston: Brill, 2013.
Halvorson, Michael J. "Smalcald War." In *LDDT* 690.
Hamel, Adolf. *Der junge Luther und Augustine*. 2 vols. Gütersloh, Germ.: Bertelsmann, 1934.
Harris, H. "Hegel, Georg Wilhelm Friedrich (1770–831)." In *NDT* 288–89.
Harran, Marilyn, ed. *Luther and Learning: The Wittenberg University Luther Symposium*. Selinsgrove, PA: Susquehanna University Press, 1985.
———. *Luther on Conversion: The Early Years*. Ithaca, NY: Cornell, 1983.
———. *Martin Luther: Learning for Life*. St. Louis: Concordia, 1997.
Heen, Erik M. "Word of God." In *DLLT* 798–801.
Hegler, A. J. *Brenz und die Reformatum im Herzogtum Wirtumberg, Freiburg, 1899*.
Hendrix, Scott. *Preaching the Reformation: The Homiletical Handbook of Urbanus Rhegius*. Reformation Texts with Translation (1350–1650) 2. Milwaukee: Marquette University, 2003.
———. *Recultivating the Vineyard: The Reformation Agenda as of Christianization*. Louisville: Westminster John Knox, 2004.
Heppe, Heinrich. *Geschichte des deutschen Protestantismus in den Jahren 1555–1581, II* Marburg, Germ.: Elwert, 1853.
Hering, Hermann. *Die Mystik Luthers*. Leipzig: Heinrich, 1879.
Hermann, Willibald. *The Communion of the Christian with God: A Discussion in Agreement with the View of Luther*. London: Williams & Norgate, 1895.
Herrlinger, A. *Die Theologie Melanchthons in ihrer geschichtlichen Entwicklung*. Gotha, Germ.: Fredrich Andreas Berthes, 1879.
Heubach, Joachim. *Der Heilege Geist: Ökumenische und reformatorische Unterschungen*. Erlangen: Luther-Verlag, 1996.
Hildebrandt, Franz. *Melanchthon: Alien or Ally?* Cambridge: Cambridge University Press, 1946.
Hill, Charles Leander. *The Loci Communes of Philip Melanchthon*. Boston: Meador, 1944.
Hoffman, Bengt. *Luther and the Mystics*. Minneapolis: Augsburg, 1976.
———, trans. *The Theologia Germanica of Martin Luther*. New York: Paulist, 1980.
———. *The Theology of the Heart: The Role of Mysticism in the Theology of Martin Luther*. Minneapolis: Kirk, 1998.

BIBLIOGRAPHY

Holl, Karl. *The Reconstruction of Morality.* Edited by James Luther Adams and Walter F. Bense. Translated by Fred W. Meuser and Walter R. Wietzke. Minneapolis: Augsburg, 1979.

Holm, Bernard J. "Humanism (Renaissance)." In *ELC* 2:1058.

———. "The Work of the Spirit: The Reformation to the Present." In *The Holy Spirit in the Life of the Church*, edited by Paul D. Opsdahl, 99–135. Minneapolis: Augsburg, 1978.

Hund, Johannes. *Das Wort ward Fleisch: eine systematisch-theologische Untersuchung zur Debatte um die Wittenberger Christologie und Abendmahlslehre in den Jahren 1567 und 1574.* Göttingen: Vandenhoeck & Ruprecht, 2006.

Ilić, Luka. "Schwenckfeld." In *DLLT* 672a–73a.

Iwand, Hans Jaochim. "The Theology of the Cross." Prepared for presentation to the Beinroder Konvent, Herbst, 1959. Translated by Aaron Moldenhauer, Reformation, 2004. https://www.doxology.us/wp-content/uploads/2015/03/33_cross-iwand.pdf.

Jammerthal, Tobias. *Philipp Melanchthons Abendmahlstheologie im Spiegel seiner Bibelauslegung 1520–548.* Tübingen, Germ.: Mohr/Siebeck, 2018.

Janz, Denis. *Luther and Late Medieval Thomism: A Study in Theological Anthropology.* Waterloo, Ontario: Wilfred Laurier University Press, 1983.

Johnson, Anna Marie, and John A. Maxfield, eds. *The Reformation as Christianization: Essays on Scott Hendrix's Christianization Thesis.* Tübingen, Germ.: Mohr Siebeck, 2112.

Jung, Martin H. *Frömmigkeit und Theologie bei Philipp Melanchthon: Das Gebet im Leben und in der Lehre des Reformators.* Tübingen, Germ.: Mohr Seibeck, 1998.

Jungkuntz, Theodore. *Confirmation and the Charismata.* Lanham, MD: University Press, 1983.

———. *Formulators of the Formula of Concord: Four Architects of Lutheran Unity.* St. Louis: Concordia, 1977.

———. "Secularization Theology, Charismatic Theology, and Luther's Theology of the Cross." *Concordia Theological Monthly* 42 (1971) 5–24.

Kähler, M. "Gewissen." *RE* 6:646–54.

Kärkkäinen, Pekka. *Luthers Trinitarische Theologie des Heiligen Geistes.* Mainz, Germ.: von Zabern, 2005.

Kattenbusch, Ferdinand. *Deus absconditus bei Luther: Festgabe für Julius Kaftan.* Tübingen, Germ.: Mohr-Siebeck, 1920.

Kawerau, Peter G. "Johann Spangenberg." In *ERK* 11:35.

Kittelson, James M. "Luther the Educational Reformer." In *Luther and Learning. The Wittenberg University Luther Symposium*, edited by Marilyn Harran, 95–114. Selinsgrove, PA: Susquehanna University Press, 1985.

Klotsche, E. H. *The History of Christian Doctrine.* Additional chapters by J. Theodore Mueller and David S. Scaer. Grand Rapids: Baker, 1977.

Klug, Eugene F. *From Luther to Chemnitz: On Scripture and the Word.* Grand Rapids: Eerdmans, 1971.

Kolb, Robert. *Andreae and the Formula of Concord: Six Sermons on the Way to Lutheran Unity.* St. Louis: Concordia, 1973.

———. "Andreae, Jacob." In *DLLT* 18–20.

———. *Bound Choice, Election, and Wittenberg Theological Method: From Martin Luther to the Formula of Concord.* Lutheran Quarterly Books. Grand Rapids: Eerdmans, 2005.

———. "Chemnitz, Martin." In *DLLT* 137–38.

———. *Confessing the Faith: Reformers Define the Church*. St. Louis: Concordia, 1991.

———. "Did Luther's Students Hide the Hidden God?" In *Churrasco: A Theological Feast in Honor of Vitor Westhelle*, edited Mary Philip et al., 7–16. Eugene, OR: Pickwick, 2013.

———. "The Doctrine of Ministry in Martin Luther and the Lutheran Confessions." In *Called and Ordained*, edited by Todd Nichol and Marc Kolden. Minneapolis: Fortress, 1990.

———. "Dynamics of Party Conflict in the Saxon Late Reformation: Gnesio-Lutherans vs. Philippists." *The Journal of Modern History Supplement* 49 (1977), D1299.

———. "Historical Background of the Formula of Concord." In *A Contemporary Look at the Formula of Concord*, edited by Robert D. Preus and Wilbert H. Rosin, 12–87. St. Louis: Concordia, 1978.

———. *Lutheran Ecclesiastical Culture 1550–1675*. Leiden, The Neth.: Brill, 2008.

———. "Luther on the Theology of the Cross." *LQ* 16 (2002) 443–66.

———. "Luther on the Two Kinds of Righteousness; Reflections on His Two-Dimensional Definition of Humanity at the Heart of His Theology." *LQ* 13 (1999) 449–66.

———. "Luther's Hermeneutics of Distinctions." In *OHMLT* 168–84.

———. "Luther's Theology of the Cross Fifteen Years after Heidelberg: *Lectures on the Psalms of Ascent*." *JEH* 61 (2010) 69–85.

———. *Martin Luther and the Enduring Word of God: The Wittenberg School and Its Scripture-Centered Proclamation*. Grand Rapids: Baker, 2016.

———. *Martin Luther as Prophet, Teacher, and Hero*. Grand Rapids: Baker, 1999.

———. *Martin Luther: Confessor of the Faith*. Christian Theology in Context. Oxford: Oxford University Press, 2009.

———. *Nikolaus von Amsdorf (1483–1565)*. Nieuwkoop, The Neth.: de Graaf, 1978.

———. "Teaching the Text: The Commonplace Method in Sixteenth Century Lutheran Biblical Commentary." *Bibliothèque d'Humanisme et Renaissance* 49 (1987) 571–85.

Kolb, Robert, and Charles P. Arand. *The Genius of Luther's Theology: A Wittenberg Way of Thinking for the Contemporary Church*. Grand Rapids: Baker Academic, 2008.

Kolde, Theodor. "Arnoldi, Bartholomaeus." In *ERK* 1:304.

———. "Thomas Muenzer." In *ERK* 8:47–50.

Köstlin, Julius. "Martin Luther." In *ERK* 7:69–79.

———. *Life of Luther*. Translated from the German. London: Longmans, Green, 1900.

———. *The Theology of Luther in Its Historical Development and Inner Harmony*. 2 vols. Translated by C. E. Hay. 2nd ed. Philadelphia: Lutheran Publication Society, 1897.

Koyama, Kosuke. *What Does It Mean to Have a God? According to Luther's Second Commentary on the First Twenty-Two Psalms (Operationes Psalmos: 1519–21)*. PhD diss., Princeton Theological Seminary, 1959.

Kunze, Johannes. "Chemnitz (Kemnitz), Martin." In *ERK* 2:24–26.

Lau, Franz. *Luther*. Philadelphia: Westminster, 1963.

Lazareth, William H. "Priest and Priesthood." In *The Encyclopedia of the Lutheran Church*, edited by Julius Bodensieck, 3:1964–66. 3 vols. For the Lutheran World Federation. Minneapolis: Augsburg, 1965.

Lederle, H. I. *Treasures Old and New*. Peabody, MA: Hendrickson, 1988.

Lehmann, Martin E. *Luther and Prayer*. Milwaukee: Northwestern, 1985.
Leupold, H. C. *Exposition of the Psalms*. 1969. Reprint, Grand Rapids: Baker, 1989.
Lezius, F. "Mörlin, Joachim." In *ERK* 7:432.
Lindberg, Carter. *The Third Reformation? Charismatic Movements and the Lutheran Tradition*. Macon, GA: Mercer University Press, 1983.
Linker, James Nicholas, ed., *Luther's Commentary on the First Twenty-Two Psalms (Operationes in Psalmos 1519-1210)*. Sunbury, PA: Lutherans in All Lands, 1903.
Loesche, Georg. "David Chytraeus." In *ERK* 3:116-17.
Loewenich, Walter von. *Luther's Theology of the Cross*. Translated by Herbert J. A. Bouman. Minneapolis: Augsburg, 1976.
———. *Martin Luther: The Man and His Work*. Translated by Lawrence W. Denf. Minneapolis: Augsburg, 1986.
Lohse, Bernard. *Martin Luther: An Introduction to His Life and Work*. Translated by Robert C. Schultz. Philadelphia: Fortress, 1986.
———. *Martin Luther's Theology: Its Historical and Systematic Development*. Translated by Roy A. Harrisville. Minneapolis: Fortress, 1999.
———. "Von Luther bis zum Konkordienbuch." In *Handbuch der Dogmen- und Theologiegeschichte*, edited by C. Andresen, 2:1-164. Göttingen, Germ.: Vandenhoeck & Ruprecht, 1980.
Ludolphy, Ingetraut. "Luther als Beter." *Luther* 33 (1962) 130-31.
———. "Spangenberg, Father and Son." In *ELC* 3:2245.
Lueker, Edwin. "Humanism." In *LCy* 396.
———, ed. *Lutheran Cyclopedia: A Concise In-Home Reference for the Christian Family*. St. Louis: Concordia, 1954.
Lund, Norman J. "Luther's Third Use of the Law and Melanchthon's Tertius Usus Legis in the Antinomian Controversy with Agricola (1537–1540)." Unpublished Doctoral Dissertation, University of St. Michael's College, University of Toronto, 1985.
Luther, Martin. *A Commentarie vpon the Fifteen Psalmes, Called Psalmi graduum, That Is, Psalmes of Degrees: Faithfully Copied Out of the Lectures of D. Martin Luther; Very Frutefull and Comfortable for All Christian Afflicted Consciences to Reade (1577)*. Translated by Henry Bull. Foreword to the Christian Reader by John Foxe. London: Vautroullier, 1577.
———. "Lectures on the Epistle to the Hebrews (1517–18)." In *Luther: Early Theological Works*, translated and edited by James Atkinson, 19–250. Philadelphia: Westminster, 1962.
———. *Luther's Commentary on the First Twenty-Two Psalms*. Translated by John Nicholas Lenker. 2 vols. Sunberry, PA: Lutherans in All Lands, 1903.
———. *Luther's Small Catechism (Enchiridion)*. St. Louis: Concordia, 1991.
———. *Three Treatises*. Philadelphia: Muhlenberg, 1943.
LWF Commission on Liturgy. "Worship Service: Basic Principles for the Ordering of the Main Worship Service." In *ELC* 2524a–53a.
Madejski, Sebastian Ryszard. "Apostolicam Ecclesiam: Socio-Liturgical Interpretation of the Mission of the Church in the Perspective of Friedrich Nietzsche's "Antichrist."" Masters thesis, Luther Seminary, 2019.
Mahlmann, Theodor. "Martin Chemnitz." In *Gestalten der Kirchengeschichte: Die Reformationszeit II*, edited by Martin Greschat, 6:315-31. Stuttgart, Germ.: W. Kohlhammer, 1981.

Malcolm, Lois. "Holy Spirit." In *DLLT* 338–40.
Manschreck, Clyde L. *Melanchthon, the Quiet Reformer.* New York: Abington, 1958.
Martin, Bernard. *Healing for You.* Richmond: John Knox, 1965.
Maschke, Timothy, et al., eds. *Ad Fontes Lutheri: Towards the Recovery of the Real Luther. Essays in Honor of Kenneth Hagen's Sixty-Fifth Birthday.* Milwaukee: Marquette University Press, 2001.
Maurer, Wilhelm. *Der Junge Melanchthon.* 2 vols. Göttingen, Germ.: Vanderhoeck & Ruprecht, 1969.
———. *Historical Commentary on the Augsburg Confession.* Translated by H. George Anderson. Philadelphia: Fortress, 1986.
———. *Melanchthon = Studien.* Gütersloh, Germ.: Gütersloher Veragshaus Gud Mohn, 1964.
Maxcey, Carl E. *Bona Opera: A Study in the Development of the Doctrine in Philip Melanchthon.* Nieuwkoop: de Graaf, 1980.
McGrath, Alister. *Luther's Theology of the Cross: Martin Luther's Theological Breakthrough.* Oxford: Basil Blackwell, 1985.
McSorley, Harry J. *Luther: Right or Wrong?* Minneapolis: Augsburg, 1969.
Meinhold, Peter. *Luthers Sprachphilosophie.* Berlin: Lutherisches Verlaghaus, 1958.
———. *Philipp Melanchthon: Der Lehrer der Kirche.* Berlin: Lutherisches Verlagshaus, 1960.
Melanchthon, Philipp. *Scholia in Epistolam Pauli ad Colossenses recognita ab autore.* Wittenberg, Germ.: Klug, 1528.
———. *Selected Writings.* Translated by Charles Leander Hill. Edited by Flack Elmer Ellsworth and Lowell J. Satre. Minneapolis: Augsburg, 1962.
Merle d'Aubigné, Jean Henri. *History of the Reformation of the Sixteenth Century.* Translated by H. White and the author. London, 1846. (Second reprint, Grand Rapids: Baker, 1987.)
Methuen, Charlotte. "Luther's Life." In *OHMLT* 5–27.
Mildenberger, Friedrich. *Theology of the Lutheran Confessions.* Translated by Erwin L. Lueker. Edited by Robert C. Schultz. Philadelphia: Fortress, 1986.
Miller, Joshua. *Hanging by a Promise: The Hidden God in the Theology of Oswald Bayer.* Forward by Stephen Paulson. Eugene, OR, Pickwick, 2015.
Moltmann, J. *Der gekreuzigte Gott: Das Kreuz Christi als Grund und Kritik christlicher Theologie.* 4th ed. München: Kaiser, 1981.
Muller, Richard A. *Dictionary of Latin and Greek Theological Terms.* Grand Rapids: Baker, 1985.
———. *Post-Reformation Reformed Dogmatics.* Vol. 1, *Prolegomena to Theology.* Grand Rapids: Baker, 1987.
———. "Scholasticism, Reformation, Orthodoxy, and the Persistence of Christian Aristotelianism." *Trinity Journal* 19, no. 1 (Spr 1998) 81–96.
Nagel, Norman. "Luther and the Priesthood of All Believers." *Concordia Theological Quarterly* 61 (1997) 277–98.
Nelson, E. Clifford, ed. *The Lutherans in North America.* Rev. ed. Philadelphia: Fortress, 1980.
Neuser, Wilhelm H. *Der Ansatz der Theologie Philipp Melanchthons.* Neukirchen, Germ.: Buchhandlung der Erziehungsverwins, 1957
Nygren, Anders. *Den Kristna Kärlekstanken genom tiderna, II.* Stockholm, 1936.
Oberman, Heiko. *The Dawn of the Reformation: Essays in Late Medieval and Early Reformation Thought.* Edinburgh: T. & T. Clark, 1986.

———. *Forerunners of the Reformation*. Translated by Paul Nyhus. Philadelphia: Fortress, 1966.
———. *The Harvest of Medieval Theology*. Grand Rapids: Baker, 2000.
———. *Luther: Man between God and the Devil*. Translated by Eileen Walliser-Schwarzbart. New Haven: Yale, 1989.
Olson, Oliver K. *Reclaiming the Lutheran Liturgical Heritage*. Minneapolis: Bronze Bow, 2007.
Opsahl, Paul D., ed. *The Holy Spirit in the Life of the Church*. Minneapolis: Augsburg, 1978.
Otto, Rudolf. *Dei Anschauung vom Heiligen Geiste bei Luther*. Göttingen, Germ.: Vandenhoeck & Ruprecht, 1898.
Pauck, Wilhelm, "Editor's Introduction." In *Melanchthon and Bucer*, edited by Wilhelm Pauck, 3–17. Library of Christian Classics (Philadelphia, Pa.) 19. Philadelphia: Westminster, 1969.
———. *From Luther to Tillich*. Edited by Marion Pauck. San Francisco: Harper & Row, 1984.
Paulson, Steven D. "Law and Gospel." In *DLLT* 414–18.
———. *Luther's Outlaw God*. 3 vols. Lutheran Quarterly Books. Minneapolis, MN: Fortress, 2018.
Payne, J. B. "Psalms, Book of." In *ZPEB* 4:39.
Pelikan, Jaroslav. *From Luther to Kierkegaard*. St. Louis: Concordia, 1950.
———. "Introduction to Volume 14." In *Luther's Works: Selected Psalms III*, edited by Jaroslav Pelikan, 14:ix–xii. St. Louis: Concordia, 1958.
Pelikan, Jaroslav, et al. *More about Luther*. Martin Luther Lectures 2. Decorah, IA: Luther College, 1958.
Philip, Mary, et al., eds. *Churrasco: A Theological Feast in Honor of Vitor Westhelle*. Eugene, OR: Pickwick, 2013.
Pieper, Francis. *Christian Dogmatics*. Translated by Theodore Engelder et al. 4 vols. St. Louis: Concordia, 1957.
Plass, Ewald M. *What Luther Says: A Practical In-Home Anthology for the Active Christian*. St. Louis: Concordia, 1994.
Pless, John T. "Sacraments." In *DLLT* 653–56.
Precht, Fred, ed. *Lutheran Worship: History and Practice*. St. Louis: Concordia, 1993.
Prenter, Regin. *The Church's Faith: A Primer of Christian Faith*. Translated by Theodore I. Jensen. Philadelphia: Fortress, 1968.
———. *Luther's Theology of the Cross*. Philadelphia: Fortress, 1971.
———. *Spiritus Creator*. Translated by John M. Jensen. Philadelphia: Muhlenberg, 1953.
———. *The Word and the Spirit: Essays on the Inspiration of the Scriptures*. Translated by Harris E. Kaasa. Minneapolis: Augsburg, 1965.
Preus, J. A. O. *The Second Martin: The Life and Theology of Martin Chemnitz*. St. Louis: Concordia, 1994.
Preus, Robert D. *Inspiration of Scripture*. 2nd ed. Edinburgh: Oliver & Boyd, 1957.
———. *The Theology of Post-Reformation Lutheranism*. 2 vols. St. Louis: Concordia, 1970.
Quere, Ralph Walter. *Melanchthon's Christum Cognoscere: Christ's Efficacious Presence in the Eucharistic Theology of Melanchthon*. Nieuwkoop: B. de Graaf, 1977.
Reu, Johann Michael. *The Augsburg Confession: A Collection of Sources with An Historical Introduction*. 1930. Reprint, Chicago: Wartburg, 1980.

———. *Luther and the Scriptures*. 1944. Reprint, Columbus: Wartburg, 1980.
Rhegius, Urbanus. *Common Places of the Holy Scripture*. Translated by Walter Lynne. London: Jugge, 1548.
———. *A Declaration of the Twelve Articles of the Christen Faythe with Annotations of the Holy Scripture*. London: Richard Jugge, 1548.
———. *A Lytle Treatice after the Manner of an Epistle*. London: Mierdman, 1548.
———. *An Instruccyon of Christian Fayth Howe to Be*. Translated by J. Foxe. N.p.: N.p.: 1548.
———. *The Old Learnyng and the New, Compared Together*. Translated by Wyllyam Turner. London: Stoughton, 1548.
———. *Preaching the Reformation: The Homiletical Handbook of Urbanus Rhegius*. Translated, edited, and introduced by Scott Hendrix. Milwaukee: Marquette University Press, 2003.
Richard, James William. *Philip Melanchthon, the Protestant Preceptor of Germany, 1497–1560*. New York: Putnam's, 1898.
Richardson, Alan. "Theologia Crucis; Theologia Gloriae." In *DCT* 395.
Richter, Aemilius, ed. *Die evangelischen Kirchenmordungen des sechzehnten Jahrhunderts*. 2 vols. 1846. Reprint, Nieuwkoop, The Neth.: N.p., 1967.
Ritschl, Otto. *Dogmengeschichte des Protestantismus* I/1. Leipzig, Germ.: Hinrichs, 1912.
Rittgers, Roland K. "Christianization through Consolation: Urbanus Rhegus's Soul-Medicine for the Healthy and the Sick in These Dangerous Times (1529)." In *The Reformation as Christianization: Essays on Scott Hendrix's Christianization Thesis*, edited by Anna Johnson Marie and John Maxfield, 321–45. Tübingen, Germ.: Mohr Siebeck, 2012.
———. "Penance, Penitence, Repentance." In *DLLT* 585–88.
Rogness, Michael. *Reformer without Honor*. Minneapolis: Augsburg, 1969.
Sasse, Hermann. "Luther and the Word of God." In *Accents in Luther's Theology: Essays in Commemoration of the 450th Anniversary of the Reformation*, edited by Heino O. Kadai. St. Louis: Concordia, 1967.
Satre, Lowell J. *All Christians Are Charismatic*. Philadelphia: Fortress, 1988.
Schaff, Philip, and David Schaff. "Isaak August Dorner." In *ERK* 3:492.
Scharlemann, Robert P. *Thomas Aquinas and John Gerhard*. New Haven: Yale University. Press, 1964.
Schlinck, Edmund. *Der Kampf der lutheranische Kirche um Luthers Lehre vom Abenmahl im Reformation Zeitalter*. Leipzic, Germ.: N.p., 1868.
———. *The Doctrine of Baptism*. Translated by Herbert J. A. Bouman. St. Louis: Concordia, 1972.
———. *The Theology of the Lutheran Confessions*. Translated by Paul F. Koehneke and Herbert J. A. Bouman. Philadelphia: Fortress, 1961.
Schmid, Heinrich. *Doctrinal Theology of the Evangelical Lutheran Church*. Translated by C. H. Hay and H. E. Jacobs. 1875. Reprint, Minneapolis: Augsburg, 1961.
Schwarzwäller, Klaus. *Theologia Crucis: Luthers Lehre von Prdestination nach De servo arbitrio 1525*. München, Germ.: Kaiser, 1970.
Seeberg, Reinhold. *Grundzüge der Theologie Luthers*. Stuttgart, Germ.: Kohlhammer, 1940.
———. *The History of Doctrines*. Translated by Charles E. Hay. 2 vols. 1895. Reprint, Grand Rapids: Baker, 1977.

Seiling, Jonathan R. "The 'Radical' Revisions of the Commentary on the Seven Penitentary Psalms: Luther and His Enemies (1517-1525)." *Reformation and Renaissance Review* 8 (2006) 28-47.

Selderhuis, Herman. *Martin Luther. A Spiritual Biography.* Wheaton, IL: Crossway, 2017.

Schwiebert, E. G. *Luther and His Times: The Reformation from a New Perspective.* St. Louis, MO: Concordia, 1950.

Silcock, Jeffrey. "Luther on the Holy Spirit and His Use of God's Word." In *OHMLT*, 294-310.

Spangenberg, Johann. *Explicationes evangelorum et epistolarum, quae dominicis diebus more usitato proponi in ecclesia populo, in tabulos . . . redactae.* Edited by his son Cyriakus Spangenberg. Basil: N.p., 1564.

———. *Kommentar zur Apostelgeschichte.* Frankfort, Germ.: N.p., 1546.

———. *Margarita theologica, 1540.* English translation of *The Summe of Divinitie.* London: N.p., 1548.

Spitz, Lewis W., Jr. *Luther and German Humanism.* Aldershot, UK: Variorium, 1996.

———. "Luther and Humanism." In *Luther and Learning. The Wittenberg University Luther Symposium*, edited by Marilyn Harran, 69-72. Selinsgrove, PA: Susquehanna University Press, 1985.

———. *The Protestant Reformation.* New York: Harper & Row, 1985.

Spitz, Lewis W., Sr. "Lutheran Theology after 1580." In *Lutheran Cyclopedia*, 505-6. St. Louis: Concordia, 1954.

Steinmetz, David. *Luther and Staupitz.* Durham: Duke University Press, 1980.

———. *Luther in Context.* Bloomington, IN: Indiana University, 1986.

———. "Luther, the Reformers, and the Bible." In *Living Tradition of the Bible: Scripture in Jewish, Christian, and Muslim Practice*, edited by J. E. Bowley, 163-76. St. Louis: Chalice, 1999.

———. *Misericordia Dei.* Leiden, The Neth.: Brill, 1968.

Stoeffler, F. Ernest. *German Pietism During the Eighteenth Century.* Leiden, The Neth.: Brill, 1973.

———. *The Rise of Evangelical Pietism.* Leiden, The Neth.: Brill, 1965.

Strodach, P. Z. "Introduction to *The Order of Baptism*." In *PE* 6:193-96.

Stupperich, Robert. "The Development of Melanchthon's Theological-Philosophical World View." *Lutheran World* 7 (1960) 168-80.

———. *Der Unbekanntnis Melanchthon, Wirken und Denken des Praeptor Germanie in neuer Sicht.* Stuttgart, Germ.: Kohlhammer, 1961.

———. *Melanchthon.* Berlin: de Gruyter, 1960.

———. *Melanchthon.* Translated by Robert H. Fischer. Philadelphia: Westminster, 1965.

Suelflow, August R., and E. Clifford Nelson. "1840-1875—Following the Frontier." In *The Lutherans in North America*, edited by E. Clifford Nelson, 145-251. Rev. ed. Philadelphia: Fortress, 1980.

Sweete, Henry Barclay. *The Holy Spirit in the Ancient Church: A Study of the Christian Teaching in the Age of the Fathers.* London: Macmillan, 1912.

Tappert, T. G. "Orthodoxism, Pietism, and Rationalism: 1580-1830." In *Christian Social Responsibility*, edited by Harold C. Letts, 36-88. 3 vols. Philadelphia: Muhlenberg, 1957.

Teigen, Bjarne Wollan. *The Lord's Supper in the Theology of Martin Chemnitz.* Brewster, MA: Trinity Lutheran, 1986.

"*Theologia Crucis.*" In *ODCC* 1603.
Trigg, Jonathan D. *Baptism in the Theology of Martin Luther.* Leiden, The Neth.: Brill, 1994.
Troeltsch, Ernst. *Vernunft und Offenbarung bei Johann Gerhard und Melanchthon.* Göttingen, Germ.: N.p., 1891.
Trueman, Carl R., and R. Scott Clark, eds. *Protestant Scholasticism: Essays in Reassessment.* Carlisle, UK: Paternoster, 1999.
Tschackert, Paul. "Georg Calixtus." In *ERK* 2:348–49.
———. "Rhegius, Urbanus." In *ERK* 10:22–23.
Vajta, Vilmos. *Luther on Worship.* Translated by U. S. Leupold. Philadelphia: Muhlenberg, 1958.
Warth, Martin C. "Justification through Faith in Article Four of the Apology." *CTQ* 46 (April–July 1892) 107–10.
Warth, Martin C., and John M. Drickamer. "Did Melanchthon Become a Synergist?" *Springfielder*, (Sept. 1976) XL.
Weber, Hans Emil. *Der Einfluss der protestantischen Schulphilosophie auf die orthodox-lutherische Dogmatik.* 1908. Reprint, Darmstadt: Weissenschaftliche Buchgesellschaft, 1965.
Weber, Otto. *Foundations of Dogmatics.* 2 vols. Translated and annotated by Darrell L. Guder. Grand Rapids: Eerdmans, 1981.
Webster, J. B. "Schleiermacher, Friedrich Daniel Ernst (1768–1834)." In *NDT* 619–20.
Weidner, Franklin. *Pneumatology or The Doctrine of the Holy Spirit.* Chicago: Wartburg, 1915.
Wengert, Timothy J. "Beyond Stereotypes: The Real Philip Melanchthon." In *Philip Melanchthon Then and Now (1497–1997)*, edited by Scott Hendricks and Timothy Wengert, 9–32. Columbia, SC: Lutheran Southern, 1999.
———. *Human Freedom, Christian Righteousness: Philip Melanchthon's Exegetical Dispute with Erasmus of Rotterdam.* New York: Oxford, 1998.
———. *Law and Gospel: Philip Melanchthon's Debate with John Agricola of Eisleben over Peonitentia.* Grand Rapids: Baker, 1997.
———. "Philip Melanchthon and a Christian Politics." *LQ* 17 (2003) 29–62.
———. *Philip Melanchthon's* Annotationes in Johannem *in Relation to Its Predecessors and Contemporaries.* Genève: Librairie Droz, 1987.
———. *Philip Melanchthon, Speaker of the Reformation: Wittenberg's Other Reformer.* Farnham, UK: Ashgate Variorum, 2009.
Westhelle, Vitor. "Hybridity and Luther's Reading of Chalcedon." In *Gudstankens aktualitet. Bidrag om teologiens opgave og indhold og protestantismens indre spaending: Festskrift tu Peter Widmann*, edited by Eise Marie Wiberg Pedersen et al., 233–54. Copenhagen: ANIS, 2010.
———. "Luther's *Theologis Crucis.*" In *OHMLT* 156–67.
Wisloff, Fredrik. *I Believe in the Holy Spirit.* Translated by Ingvald Daehlin. Minneapolis: Augsburg, 1949.
Wolf, Ernst. "Die Christusverkündigung bei Luther." In *Jesus Christus im Zeugnis der Heiligen Schrift und der Kircke.* Munich, Germ.: Chr. Kaiser, 1936.
Wood, Arthur Skevington. *Captive to the Word: Martin Luther: Doctor of Sacred Scripture.* Grand Rapids: Eerdmans, 1969.
Zschoch, Hellmut. *Reformatiorsche Existenz und konfessionelle Identit Existenz und konfessionelle Identität.* Tübingen, Germ.: Mohr (Siebeck), 1995.

Name and Subject Index

Abraham, 112, 128–29, 137, 171, 179, 298, 304
absolution, 59, 93, 113, 120, 135, 138, 151
action words of the Holy Spirit, 112–13
active righteousness, 96–97
ad fontes, 48, 188
adiaphora, 278–79, 284
affections, 192, 218–19, 225, 269, 270
afflictions, 220, 226–27
Against Hanswurst (Luther), 141–42
Against the Heavenly Prophets (Luther), 94, 156–57
Agricola, John, 209
Agricola, Rudolf, 186–90, 191
Albrecht of Prussia (Duke), 281
alien righteousness, 95–96, 98, 101–2, 122
Althaus, Paul, 4, 102, 116, 332
Anabaptists, 213, 240, 245–46, 292–93, 312
ancient Christian church, 139–47
Andreae, Jakob, 1–2, 275, 276–80
   baptism, 295–96
   and Chytraeus, 286
   conversion, 207, 301–2
   election, 303
   gifts of the Holy Spirit, 316
   good works and the fruit of the Spirit, 325–26
   Holy Scriptures, 293-94

   Holy Spirit and the church, 310–11
   Holy Spirit and the kingdom, 323
   human will, 319
   inner testimony of the Holy Spirit, 321
   Julius of Braunschweig, 284
   Lord's Supper, 296
   and Melanchthon, 192–93
   new life in the Holy Spirit, 317
   person of the Holy Spirit, 287
   prayer, 324
   receiving the Holy Spirit, 318
   repentance, 300
   sanctification, 306–7
   sin against the Holy Spirit, 328
   synergistic dispute, 207
   teaching, 309
Anfechtungen, 29, 40, 42
Annotationes in Johannem (Melanchthon), 189–90, 200, 201
Annotations on Matthew (Melanchthon), 218–19
anthropology, 29, 45
Apology to the Augsburg Confession (Melanchthon), 192, 209, 231
apostles, 50–51, 100, 110–11, 134, 142–43, 146, 213–14, 261, 262–63, 266, 268, 290, 293–94, 312, 314–16, 317, 318, 336, 338
Apostles' Creed, 20–22, 102, 145, 156, 158, 172, 178, 205, 300

NAME AND SUBJECT INDEX

Arand, Charles, 3
Aristotle, 27, 36, 42, 45–46, 47, 187–88, 191
assertions, 92
assurance of the Holy Spirit, 165, 212, 223–24, 322, 336
atonement, 62–65
Augsburg Confession, 1, 3, 188, 192, 194, 204, 240, 285–86
Augsburg Diet, 241–42, 245, 277
Augsburg Interim, 242, 276
Augustine, 32
    breakthrough and conversion, 40–42
    conformity to Christ, 166
    disputes, 205
    infusion of love into the heart, 164
    Johann von Staupitz, 31–32
    Law and Gospel, 129
    opposition to scholastic theology, 44–46
    person of the Holy Spirit, 88–89
    real presence of Christ, 167
    regeneration, 304
    sacraments, 123
    sanctification, 307–8
    sin against the Holy Spirit, 272, 328
Augustinians, 30–31
auricular confession, 121
authority, 32, 37–38, 46, 48, 98, 108, 114, 124, 139, 145, 188–89, 197, 215, 253, 263–64, 313, 316, 337–38

The Babylonian Captivity of the Church, 119–21, 147, 149
baptism, 3–5, 20, 123–25, 216
    church of the pure doctrine, 194
    conformity to Christ, 167
    Holy Spirit and the church, 142–43
    inner testimony of the Holy Spirit, 157–58, 270, 321
    justification, 99, 195
    means of the Holy Spirit, 255–57, 293, 295–96
    person of the Holy Spirit, 288, 333
    reception of the Holy Spirit, 257–58, 333
    regeneration, 304
    sacraments, 120–23
    sanctification, 102
    worship, 324
Baptists, 278
Barton, Peter F., 275
Basil, 288–89
Bayer, Oswald, 5, 16, 33–34, 34–35, 105, 113, 118, 189, 332
Benedict's Rule, 41
benefits and activities, 9, 297
Bente, G. Friedrich, 191, 203–4
Bernard of Clairvaux, 41
Beza, Theodore, 275, 277, 279
Bible, 31, 37–38, 111, 193, 213, 226, 253
biblical languages, 283
Biel, Gabriel, 27–28, 33, 42, 45–46, 51
blessing of Judah, 133–35
Bode, Gerhard, 282
The Bondage of the Will (Luther), 28, 59, 82, 92, 97, 127, 153–54, 155
Bonhoeffer, Dietrich, 64
The Book of Concord, 1–2, 191, 278–79, 282
books of the prophets, 213–14
Bora, Katherine von "Katie", 19–21, 152, 176
Bossert, Gustaf, 241, 244
Brandenburg-Nürnberg Common Church Order, 240
Braun, Johannes, 25
Braunschweig, Germany, 280–85
"The Braunschweig Resolution" (Kolb), 281
Brecht, Martin, 250, 258, 259, 260, 268, 272
Breen, Quirinius, 191
Brenz, Johannes, 1–2, 190, 234, 235–45
    and Andreae, 277
    Christian leaders in church and government, 338
    faith, 258–59
    gifts of the Holy Spirit, 266
    holiness and Christian liberty, 270
    Holy Spirit and the church, 262
    the kingdom, 265
    means of the Holy Spirit, 252–57
    office of the keys, 263–64
    person of the Holy Spirit, 251–52
    renewal, 268–69

NAME AND SUBJECT INDEX

repentance, 258
sanctification, 260
sin against the Holy Spirit, 272
teaching, 261–62
theology of the cross, 249–50
work of the Holy Spirit, 258–62, 335
Brethren of the Common Life, 24, 27
Bucer, Martin, 190, 235, 241, 243, 245

Cajetan, Cardinal Thomas, 46
Calixtus, Georg, 191
call to Christian ministry, 143–44, 159–60, 312–13
Calvinists, 277–79, 333
Camerarius, Joachim, 240
Cantiones Ecclesiasticae, 248
Carroll, H. K., 256
Catechism, Luther's, 279
Catechismus (Brenz), 244
Catholicism/Catholics, 24, 37, 45–46, 193, 236–43, 256, 278, 283. See also true Catholic tradition
ceremonies, 182, 228–29
Charles V, 192, 241–43
Chemnitz, Martin, 1–2, 6–7, 9, 275, 280–85
  and Andreae, 279
  baptism, 295–96
  call to Christian ministry, 312–13
  and Chytraeus, 285–86
  conversion, 301–2
  election, 302–4
  faith, 300
  gifts of the Holy Spirit, 315–16
  good works and fruit of the Spirit, 325–27
  Holy Scriptures, 293–94
  Holy Spirit and the church, 310–11
  human will, 319–20
  incarnation, 298
  inner testimony of the Holy Spirit, 321–22
  justification, 299
  Lord's Supper, 296
  means of the Holy Spirit, 292–93
  and Melanchthon, 192

names and titles of the Holy Spirit, 290–91
new life in the Holy Spirit, 317
office of the keys, 314
person of the Holy Spirit, 288–90, 334
prayer, 323
procession of the Holy Spirit, 292
receiving the Holy Spirit, 318–19
reception of the Holy Spirit, 334
regeneration, 304
repentance, 299–300
sanctification, 305–8
sin against the Holy Spirit, 327–29
teaching, 309
work of the Holy Spirit, 297–98
worship, 324–25
Christenson, Larry, 22, 104, 156
Christian behavior, 146–47
Christian conversion, 40–44, 202–7, 209, 211, 267–68, 282, 301–2, 329, 332, 335, 341
Christian discipleship, 67, 96, 158
Christian doctrines, 208, 213–14, 294, 308–9, 312–13, 315
Christian Dogmatics (Pieper), 62–63
Christian freedom, 181, 211, 220
Christianization, 246
Christian liberty, 269–70, 326
Christian life
  causes of, 206
  cross in, 72
  faith, 259
  gifts of the Holy Spirit, 168–70, 265
  good works, 181
  hidden reality of the Spirit, 160–61
  Holy Spirit and the church, 337
  Holy Spirit and the flesh, 224–25
  Holy Spirit and the priesthood of all believers, 151
  new life in the Holy Spirit, 336
  renewal, 268–69
  responses to the Holy Spirit, 338–39
  theology of the cross, 78, 332
  See also Holy Scriptures
Christian piety, 321, 324

NAME AND SUBJECT INDEX

Christians
  authority, 215
  fruit of the Spirit, 325–27
  good works, 182, 231, 325–27
  Holy Spirit and the kingdom, 323
  indwelling Holy Spirit, 311
  new life in the Holy Spirit, 222, 317
  person and work of the Holy Spirit, 201
  prayer, 175–77
  receiving the Holy Spirit, 318
  regeneration, 304
  sanctification, 306, 335
  theology of the cross, 332
Christian vocation, 231. *See also* priesthood
Christology, 256–57, 277–79, 281
church
  call to Christian ministry, 312–13
  and Chemnitz, 280–84
  gifts of the Holy Spirit, 315–16
  and the Holy Spirit, 136–47, 310–11, 336–38
  Holy Spirit and holiness, 159–60
  Holy Spirit and the kingdom, 322
  inner testimony of the Holy Spirit, 157–58
  and Melanchthon, 186–91
  music in, 248–49
  oral and written word, 111
  prayer, 177
  of pure doctrine, 193–94
  sacraments, 256
  and the state, 265
  teaching, 212–13
  theology of the cross, 250
  word of God, 213–14
  worship, 178–80
churchmanship, 281–82
church of the Reformers, 142–43, 146
Chytraeus, David, 1–2, 275, 285–86
  and Andreae, 279
  baptism, 295
  conversion and synergistic dispute, 206–7
  election, 303
  faith, 300–301
  gifts of the Holy Spirit, 314–16
  good works and fruit of the Spirit, 327
  Holy Spirit and the church, 310
  Holy Spirit and the kingdom, 322
  human will, 319–20
  incarnation, 298
  inner testimony of the Holy Spirit, 321
  justification, 299
  means of the Holy Spirit, 293
  and Melanchthon, 192
  names and titles of the Holy Spirit, 291
  new life in the Holy Spirit, 317
  office of the keys, 313–14
  person of the Holy Spirit, 288–90
  prayer, 323–24
  procession of the Holy Spirit, 291–92
  receiving the Holy Spirit, 318
  regeneration, 304–5
  renewal, 320
  sanctification, 305–8
  teaching, 308–10
  theology of the cross, 287
  work of the Holy Spirit, 297
  worship, 325
classics, 29–30, 187
clothed God, 59–61
Cochlaeus, John, 190
Collectorium (Biel), 45
Collegiate Church, Stuttgart, 244
Colloquy at Worms, 277
Colloquy of Poissy, 278
Commentary on Romans (Melanchthon), 207–8
communion of saints, 102, 194
concupiscence, 42, 154, 165, 299, 305–6, 308
confession, 42, 120–22, 171
Confession Concerning Christ's Supper (Luther), 88–89
Confessio Wirtembergica, 243–44
conformity to Christ, 164–67, 173–74, 334–36, 336
conscience, faith is not, 51–52
consciences, 3, 144, 156, 164, 253–54, 263, 295–96, 308, 322

NAME AND SUBJECT INDEX

consubstantiality, 288–89, 298, 311, 324–25
continual repentance, 40, 206, 329
conversion. *See* Christian conversion
Corinthians gifts, 314–15
Corpus doctrinæ Julium, 284
Corpus doctrinæ Prutenicum, 281
Corpus Wilhelminum, 284
Council of Nicea, 200
Council of Trent, 243–44, 261, 278, 283, 285
councils, 263, 338
creation, 38, 50, 75, 90, 91–92, 106–8, 153–55, 252, 297, 319, 322
creative word, 37–38
cross, 49–57, 62–65, 331
cross alone is our theology *(crux sola est nostra Theologia)*, 10–11, 67, 84–85
cross story, 13–14
Crypto-Calvinists, 284, 333
"The Culture of Conflict in the Controversies Leading to the *Formula of Concord* (1548–1580)" (Dingel), 276

David, 44, 72–73, 175, 252
Decalogue, 147, 182, 210, 305, 309
De dignitate sacerdotum, 245
De duabus naturis (Chemnitz), 284
deed-words *(Thette-Wort)*, 112–13
Delitzsch, Franz, 128
Der Theologe Melanchthon (Frank), 189
de servo arbitrii (Luther), 58
De Theologo, seu de Ratione Studii Theologici Libris IIII (Hyperius), 6
De Trinitate (Hillary), 200
Deutsche Messe (Spangenberg), 248
devil, 323, 338
  gifts of the Holy Spirit, 169–70
  good works, 231–32
  holiness and Christian liberty, 270
  Holy Spirit and the church, 138, 310
  inner testimony of the Holy Spirit, 157
  prayer, 176
  renewal, 266, 269
  responses to the Holy Spirit, 271
  sin against the Holy Spirit, 328–29
Devotio Moderna, 186
devotional literature, 248
Dictata super Psalterium (Luther), 41–42
Die Auschauung vom heiligen Geiste bei Luther (Luther's View of the Holy Spirit) (Otto), 21
Diet of Augsburg, 176, 240, 277
Diet of Worms, 39, 85
Dietrich, Veit, 86
Dingel, Irene, 276
discernment of spirits, 315
disciples, 322, 338
discipline, 30–31
A Discussion on How Confession Should Be Made (Luther), 120–21
Disputation against Scholastic Theology (Luther), 45–46
divinity of the Holy Spirit, 88–89
doctrine of the Trinity, 89–90
Ducal Saxony, 278
Duke Christopher of Wurttemberg, 243–44, 276–78
Duke Ulrich of Württemberg, 240–44, 279

early Reformers, 190, 234–74, 332
  background and influences, 234–49
  call to Christian ministry, 312
  Holy Spirit and the church, 141–46, 337–38
  new life in the Holy Spirit, 336
  person and reception of the Holy Spirit, 333–34
  person and work of the Holy Spirit, 200, 251–52
  practical pastoral ministry, 339
  theology of the Holy Spirit, 249–66
  work of the Holy Spirit, 334–35
ecclesiastical reorganization, 243–44
Eck, John, 189, 192, 245
education, 47, 187, 248
Eisenach, 24–25
election, 260, 302–4, 322
Electoral Saxony, 278
Elector August of Saxony, 279
Elector Ludwig of the Palatinate, 237

Elector of Brandenburg, 279
Elert, Werner, 172
emotions, 322
empirical piety, 101–3, 160, 174
Engelland, Hans, 202
English Protestantism, 248
Engster, Huldrich. *See* Brenz, Johannes
Ephesians gifts, 314
Ephesus, 312–13
Erasmus, Desiderius, 28, 29, 58–59, 82, 92, 101, 187, 189–91, 204–5, 211, 217–19, 235
Erfurt Augustinian monastery, 30
Estes, James, 238–45, 265, 266
eternal salvation, 97, 132, 257, 318
ethical consciousness, 51
eucharistic sacrifices, 229
evangelical Christianity, 81–82, 245, 261, 278
events, 20–21, 53, 102–3, 107, 128, 136–37, 153
evil, 160, 226, 271, 319, 322–23
exclusivity of the word, 114–16
experience, 53–55
Explanation of the Ninety-Five Theses (Luther), 44
external and internal word, 4–5, 98, 109–10, 114–16, 117, 157–58, 254, 295, 333
external work of the Trinity (*opera ad extra*), 297

facere quod in se est (to those who do what is in them), 28, 42, 45–46
faith
    baptism, 125, 216, 296
    church of the pure doctrine, 193–94
    conscience, 51–52
    conversion, 301–2
    and the cross, 51, 56
    election, 303
    exclusivity of the word, 114–15
    experience, 53–55
    Formula of Concord, 341–42
    gifts of the Holy Spirit, 315–16
    good works, 181–82, 230–32, 325–27
    The Heidelberg Disputation (Luther), 80–83
    hidden reality of the Spirit, 61, 160–61
    and the Holy Spirit, 171–74
    Holy Spirit and suffering, 161–63
    Holy Spirit and the church, 136–45, 262–63
    Holy Spirit in Law and Gospel, 220–21
    hope, 207–8
    inner testimony of the Holy Spirit, 156–59, 224, 321–22
    justification, 97–99, 195–96, 201, 299
    Lord's Supper, 126–27, 127–28, 296
    means of the Holy Spirit, 216, 255–56, 292–93
    and Melanchthon, 189
    new life in the Holy Spirit, 221–22, 336
    reason, 52–53
    receiving the Holy Spirit, 318
    reception of the Holy Spirit, 201
    renewal, 223, 266–69
    repentance, 299–300
    responses to the Holy Spirit, 226–28, 271, 338–39
    sacraments, 119–23, 215–16
    sanctification, 101–4, 305–8
    sin against the Holy Spirit, 328–29
    teaching, 261–62
    theology of the cross, 250, 286–87, 332–33
    work of the Holy Spirit, 258–60, 300–301, 334–35
    worship, 178–81
faith in Christ (*per fidem Christi*), 171–73
fallen humanity, 167
false doctrine, 294
fellowship (*koinonia*), 311, 315, 317
filioque, 9, 89, 292, 333
five articles, Andreae, 278
flesh
    conformity to Christ, 164–66
    gifts of the Holy Spirit, 315
    good works, 231, 325–27
    The Heidelberg Disputation (Luther), 83
    and the Holy Spirit, 155–56, 224–25
    Holy Spirit and faith, 172

Holy Spirit and suffering, 162
human will, 320
inner testimony of the Holy Spirit, 270
justification, 260
Lord's Supper, 125–26, 296
renewal, 222–23, 320–21
repentance, 299–300
sanctification, 100–102, 209–10, 305–8
work of the Holy Spirit, 334–35
fool, 79–80
Forde, Gerhard, 10, 11–12, 13, 60, 62–64, 83
forensic justification, 192, 195, 209, 333, 334
forgiveness, 44, 73, 100–103, 120–21, 146, 160, 174–76, 218–20, 230
forgiveness of sins, 93, 99, 139–44, 194, 195, 201–2, 216–17, 259, 268, 295, 296, 300, 304, 305, 313–14, 317, 321, 325, 328, 332, 341
Formula Missae (Luther), 248
Formula of Concord, 1–2, 192–93, 275, 331, 339–42
   background and influences, 276–86
   conversion and synergistic dispute, 207
   good works and the fruit of the Spirit, 326
   justification, 260
   prominent themes, 17
   Schwenckfelders, 257
   synergistic dispute, 204–7
   three uses of the law, 272
Formula writers, 332
   background and influences, 276–86
   and the church, 338
   election, 303
   faith, 300–301
   gifts of the Holy Spirit, 314–15
   good works and the fruit of the Spirit, 326
   means of the Holy Spirit, 292
   new life in the Holy Spirit, 317, 336
   person and reception of the Holy Spirit, 333–34
   practical pastoral ministry, 339
   sanctification, 306
   theology of the Holy Spirit, 286–310
   work of the Holy Spirit, 334–35
"404 Articles" (Eck), 192
Frank, Gunter, 189
Frederick the Wise, 33, 84
freedom, 219–21
The Freedom of a Christian (Luther), 103–4, 148
freedom of the will, 204, 211, 218, 278–79
free from the law, 269, 342
free will, 101, 207, 214, 301, 340
fruit of the Spirit, 96, 225, 305, 318, 325–27
fulfillment of the law. *See* justification

Gasmer, J., 282
Geldennupf, Wiegand, 25
George of Brandenburg, 239–40
George (Saxon Duke), 87
A German Theology (Theologia Deutsch) (Luther), 35
Gerrish, Bruce, 81, 198–99
gifts of the Holy Spirit, 100, 150–51, 157, 162–63, 164, 168–70, 175, 177, 192, 201, 212, 260, 265–66, 289–90, 291, 293, 304, 306, 314–16, 317, 318, 325, 327–28, 337–38
Gnesio-Lutherans, 204, 277–78, 281–84
God, 331–32
   action words of the Holy Spirit, 112–13
   baptism, 216, 295
   breakthrough and conversion, 40–44
   call to Christian ministry, 312–13
   church of the pure doctrine, 193–94
   and Chytraeus, 285–86
   conformity to Christ, 164–67
   conversion, 202–7, 301–2
   and the cross, 50–51, 55–57
   election, 302–4
   faith, 53–55, 258–60, 300–301
   gifts of the Holy Spirit, 168–70, 266
   good works, 181–82, 230–32, 325–27
The Heidelberg Disputation (Luther), 79–83

NAME AND SUBJECT INDEX

God (*cont.*)
   hidden God (*Deus absconditus*), 16,
      51, 53, 57–62, 80–83, 84, 163,
      166, 226
   Holy Scripture, 293–95
   Holy Spirit and faith, 171–74
   Holy Spirit and suffering, 161–63
   Holy Spirit and the church, 136–47,
      262–63
   Holy Spirit and the kingdom,
      322–23
   Holy Spirit and the priesthood of all
      believers, 147–52
   Holy Spirit in Law and Gospel,
      217–21
   Holy Spirit inspires and teaches the
      word, 117–19
   human will, 319–20
   infusion of love into the heart,
      163–64
   inner testimony of the Holy Spirit,
      270, 321–22
   justification by faith, 195–96
   kingdom of God, 127, 130–36, 269,
      295–96
   Law and Gospel, 129
   life in the Spirit under the cross, 15
   locus of the person of the Holy
      Spirit, 7–9
   Lord's Supper, 126–27, 216–17
   love of God, 55–56, 64, 80, 102, 164,
      167, 175, 219, 221, 222, 305–6,
      327, 337
   Luther's background and influences,
      47–48
   means of the Holy Spirit, 213–17
   ministry in the church, 337–38
   office and work of the Holy Spirit,
      91–94
   Operationes in Psalmos (Luther),
      84–85
   person of the Holy Spirit, 200–201,
      251–52, 287–90
   post-Reformation issues regarding
      the theology of the cross, 16–17
   prayer, 174–78, 226–28, 323–24
   receiving the Holy Spirit, 318–19
   reception of the Holy Spirit, 257–58
   Reformation theology, 187–88
   renewal, 222–23, 266–69
   and Rhegius, 247
   sacraments, 255–56
   sanctification, 100–104, 209–11,
      260–61, 305–8
   Seven Penitential Psalms, 66–74
   sin against the Holy Spirit, 328–29
   Sola Scriptura, 37–38
   synergistic dispute, 202–7
   teaching, 38–40, 261–62, 309
   Theologia Germanica, 75–78
   theology of the cross, 249–50, 287,
      332–33
   theology of glory, 13
   will of, 70, 164–66, 180, 218, 266,
      287, 300
   work of the Holy Spirit, 3–4, 87,
      200–201, 258–62, 297, 334–35
   worship, 178–81
   See also word of God
Godhead, 90, 126, 251–52, 288–90, 295,
   315, 324, 333
Goerdeler, Karl, 16
good and evil, 51–52
good works
   conformity to Christ, 166
   election, 303
   faith, 258–59
   Formula of Concord, 340–42
   fruit of the Spirit, 96, 325–27
   Luther's emphases on, 203
   responses to the Holy Spirit, 181–
      82, 230–32, 271–72, 338–39
   sanctification, 307–8
gospel freedom, 221
grace, 51–52, 72–74, 79–80
   baptism, 216, 255
   breakthrough and conversion, 41–44
   election, 302–3
   gifts of the Holy Spirit, 168–70
   of God, 76, 97, 137, 140, 178, 259,
      269, 316, 329, 341–42
   Holy Spirit and faith, 171–73
   inner testimony of the Holy Spirit,
      270
   justification, 97–98
   Luther's emphases on, 203

NAME AND SUBJECT INDEX

prayer, 174–75
renewal, 267
sanctification, 100, 307–8
sin against the Holy Spirit, 272, 328–29
Spirit as *Spiritus Creator*, 153–54
worship, 180–81
Graeter, Margaretha, 237
Great Church Order of 1559, 244
Grebel, Conrad, 190
Green, Lowell, 205–7, 209
Greschat, Martin, 112
Grimm, Harold, 76

Hägglund, Bengt, 75, 185, 203
Handbook for Preaching (Rhegius), 271
Harran, Marilyn, 40–42
healing, 170, 176–77, 315–16
hearing the word of God, 60, 81, 98, 110, 116, 117, 134, 199, 259, 301–2, 333, 341
heavenly prophets, 292–93
Hebrews lectures (Luther), 49
Heen, Erik, 112, 115–16
Hegel, G. W. F., 16
The Heidelberg Disputation (Luther), 11–12, 14, 58, 65–66, 72, 79–83, 85–86, 235, 250
Hendrix, Scott, 246
Herrbrand, Jacob, 230
Herrlinger, A., 201
hidden aspects of the new life in the Holy Spirit, 160–61
hidden God *(Deus absconditus)*, 16, 51, 53, 57–62, 80–83, 84, 163, 166, 226
hidden work, 59, 64–65, 80
Hildebrandt, Franz, 210
Hoffman, Bengt, 34, 75
holiness, 158, 159–60, 269–70, 307
holy Christian community, 141–47, 340–41
holy possessions *(Heiligthumer* or *Heilthumer)*, 140–46
Holy Scriptures, 1–2, 31
  authority, 197
  breakthrough and conversion, 42, 44
  church of the pure doctrine, 193–94
  conversio and *causa*, 205–6
  education in Germany, 47
  external and internal word, 109
  faith and reason, 52–53
  Holy Spirit and the church, 263
  Holy Spirit as writer of, 106–8
  Holy Spirit inspires and teaches the word, 117–19
  Holy Spirit's names in, 291
  humanism, 29–30
  Luther's background and influences, 47–48
  Luther's doctoral studies and early teaching, 33
  means of the Holy Spirit, 253–54, 293–95
  and Melanchthon, 187–89, 193–94
  offensive texts of, 60
  opposition to scholastic theology, 44–46
  oral and written word, 111
  person and reception of the Holy Spirit, 333–34
  person of the Holy Spirit, 288–90
  and Rhegius, 247
  sacraments, 120–21, 256
  scholasticism, 27–28
  Sola Scriptura, 37–38
  teaching, 38–40, 212–13, 261, 308–10
  word and the Holy Spirit, 3–5
  word of God, 105–6, 213–15
  worship, 228–30
Holy Spirit, 1–2, 331–32
  action words of the, 112–13
  assurance of the, 165, 212, 223–24, 322, 336
  as the author and interpreter of the word, 106–8
  baptism, 123–25, 295–96
  breakthrough and conversion, 40–44
  call to Christian ministry, 313
  and the church, 136–47, 262–63, 262–66, 310–11, 336–38
  conformity to Christ, 164–67
  consubstantiality, 288–89, 298, 311, 324–25
  conversion, 202–7, 301–2

367

NAME AND SUBJECT INDEX

Holy Spirit (cont.)
   and the cross, 49–50, 55–57
   cross story, 14
   divinity of the, 88–89
   election, 302–4
   exclusivity of the word, 114–16
   external and internal word, 109–10
   faith, 54–55, 171–74, 207–8, 258–60, 300–301
   flesh, 155–56, 224–25
   Formula of Concord, 339–42
   gifts of the, 100, 150–51, 157, 162–63, 164, 168–70, 175, 177, 192, 201, 212, 260, 265–66, 289–90, 291, 293, 304, 306, 314–16, 317, 318, 325, 327–28, 337–38
   good works, 230–32, 271–72, 325–27
   The Heidelberg Disputation (Luther), 79–83
   hidden God *(Deus absconditus)*, 59–62
   holiness, 158, 159–60, 269–70
   Holy Scriptures, 213–15, 293–95
   human will, 319–20
   incarnation, 298
   indwelling, 336, 339
   inner testimony of the, 118–19, 156–59, 165, 168, 223–24, 270, 321–22, 336
   inspires and teaches the word, 117–27
   justification, 195–96, 209, 260, 299
   and the kingdom, 130–36, 264–65, 322–23
   Law and Gospel, 127–30, 217–21
   life in the Spirit under the cross, 15
   Locus of the person of the, 7–9
   Lord's Supper, 125–27, 296
   Luther's background and influences, 48
   Luther's theology of reality, 20–22
   magistrates, 197, 265
   means of the, 104–27, 213–17, 252–57, 292–96
   mediation of the, 254, 293
   and Melanchthon, 188–89
   ministry of the, 271
   music, 248–49
   mysticism, 34–35
   names and titles of the, 290–91
   new life in the, 93, 152–74, 221–25, 266–70, 317, 336
   office of the, 90–94
   office of the keys, 263–64, 313–14
   Operationes in Psalmos (Luther), 84–85
   person of the, 88–90, 200–201, 200–213, 251–52, 287–90, 333–34
   power of the, 264, 286–87, 292, 294–95
   prayer, 174–78, 226–28, 271, 323–24
   presence of the, 87, 338–39
   priesthood of all believers, 147–52
   priesthood of the New Testament, 198
   procession of the, 291–92
   real presence of Christ, 167–68
   reception of the, 201–2, 257–58, 308, 318–19, 333–34
   regeneration, 304–5
   renewal, 120, 222–23, 266–69
   repentance, 299–300
   responses to the, 174–82, 226–32, 271–72, 323–29, 338–39
   and Rhegius, 247
   sacraments, 119–23, 215–16
   sanctification, 96, 209–11, 260–61, 305–8
   school of the, 332
   Seven Penitential Psalms, 69–74
   and sin, 259
   sin against the, 272, 327–29, 339
   Sola Scriptura, 38
   as *Spiritus Creator*, 153–55
   suffering, 161–63
   synergistic dispute, 202–7
   teaching, 39–40, 261–62, 308–10
   theology of the cross, 197–200, 286–87, 332–33
   two kingdoms, 196–97
   unity of the word and the Spirit, 98–99
   and the word, 3–5
   work of the, 9, 17, 18, 20–21, 35, 48, 61, 64, 80, 81–82, 85, 87,

NAME AND SUBJECT INDEX

90–104, 100–101, 105, 118, 119, 127–30, 146, 155–56, 157–58, 159–60, 181, 196–97, 199–200, 200–213, 220, 229, 231–32, 252, 256, 258–62, 297–310, 323–24, 328, 334–36
worship, 178–81, 271, 324–25
homoousia, 7, 288, 311
honoring temporal authorities, 145
hope, 79, 84–85, 207–8
human intellect, 334
humanism, 29–30, 36, 47, 48, 186–91
human nature, 261, 267, 303, 320
human responsibility, 203, 205
human will, 13, 79, 164, 202–7, 225, 260, 269, 278, 293, 303, 319–20, 335
humility, 41, 199
Hus, John, 287
Husschin, Johannes, 235
Hyperius, 6
hypocrites, 262–63, 310
hypostatic union, 311, 333

ideal church, 262
Ilić, Luka, 256
illumination, 258–59
Illyricus, Matthias Flacius, 275
image of God, 301, 320
imitation piety, 50, 164, 167
incarnation, 98, 114, 199, 251, 255, 284, 298
indwelling Christ, 101–2
indwelling God, 209
indwelling Holy Spirit, 224–25, 251, 268–69, 311, 317, 320, 324–25, 335, 336, 339
indwelling of the saints, 315
infants, 296
infusion of love into the heart, 163–64
inner conflicts, 122, 154, 158, 166, 167, 338
inner testimony of the Holy Spirit, 118–19, 156–59, 165, 168, 223–24, 270, 321–22, 336
institution, 178, 296, 334
Interim, 276–77
inter-Lutheran disputes, 281–82

internal word. *See* external and internal word
internal work of the Trinity *(opera ad intra)*, 297
interpretation of tongues, 315
In XV Psalmos graduum (Luther), 66
Isaiah gifts, 315
Isenmann, Johann, 236–37, 243
Ishmael and Isaac, 128–30
Iwand, Hans, 34, 65, 67–68, 85

Jacob, 117, 130–34
Jeremiah, 249–50, 303
Jerome, 315
Jerusalem, 303
Jerusalem Council, 263, 311
Jesus Christ, 331–32
  ascension, 322
  atonement, 62–65
  baptism, 216, 295–96
  breakthrough and conversion, 41
  and the church, 336–38
  church of the pure doctrine, 193–94
  conformity to, 164–65
  cross and knowing God, 50–51
  cross and the Holy Spirit, 49–50
  distinction between sins, 272
  faith, 300
  gifts of the Holy Spirit, 314–16
  good works, 181–82
  hidden God *(Deus absconditus)*, 57–62
  Holy Spirit and faith, 171–74
  Holy Spirit and suffering, 161–63
  Holy Spirit and the church, 262–63
  Holy Spirit and the kingdom of God, 133–37
  Holy Spirit and the priesthood of all believers, 148–52
  Holy Spirit as the author and interpreter of the word, 108
  Holy Spirit in Law and Gospel, 217–21
  inner testimony of the Holy Spirit, 156–59
  justification, 97–99, 195–96
  Lord's Supper, 125–27, 216–17, 296

NAME AND SUBJECT INDEX

Jesus Christ (*cont.*)
  new life in the Holy Spirit, 221–22, 317, 336
  office and work of the Holy Spirit, 90–94
  office of the keys, 313–14
  oral and written word, 110–12
  person of the Holy Spirit, 251–52, 288–90
  prayer, 226–28
  real presence of, 121–22, 167–68, 172–74, 296
  reception of the Holy Spirit, 200–201, 201–2, 318–19
  regeneration, 304–5
  renewal, 266–69
  repentance, 299
  sacraments, 119–23, 215–16, 255–57
  sacrificial human life, 75
  sanctification, 100–104, 211, 305–6, 305–7
  Spirit as *Spiritus Creator*, 154
  teaching, 212–13
  theology of the cross, 198–99, 287, 332–33
  total person of, 125, 292
  two kinds of righteousness, 95–96
  word of God, 3–4, 253–54
  work of the Holy Spirit, 297, 334–36
  worship, 178–81
  See also Christology
judgment of God, 42, 72–74, 121, 272
Julian University, Helmstädt, 284
Julius (Duke), 278, 284–85
Julius of Braunschweig (Duke), 284
Jung, Martin, 226
Jungkuntz, Theodore, 81, 177, 285–86
justification
  and Andreae, 277, 278–79
  breakthrough and conversion, 41–42
  conformity to Christ, 164–65
  conversion, 301–2
  by faith, 20, 40, 56, 76, 139, 193, 195–96, 213, 259, 262, 303, 337
  Formula of Concord, 341
  gifts of the Holy Spirit, 168, 266
  good works, 230, 325–26
  hidden God (*Deus absconditus*), 57

Holy Scriptures, 294
Holy Spirit and the flesh, 225
Holy Spirit in Law and Gospel, 220
inter-Lutheran disputes, 281
and Melanchthon, 192
new life in the Holy Spirit, 222, 336
office and work of the Holy Spirit, 93
person and reception of the Holy Spirit, 201, 333
person and work of the Holy Spirit, 209
prayer, 175
regeneration, 304
and Rhegius, 247
sanctification, 102–4, 209–10
Spirit as *Spiritus Creator*, 154
synergistic dispute, 203–4
theology of the cross, 199, 249–50, 332–33
work of the Holy Spirit, 97–99, 260, 299, 334–35

Karlstadt, Andreas Bodenstein von, 33, 117–19
Keil, C. F., 128
kingdom, 104, 211, 264–65, 322–23, 328
kingdom of God, 127, 130–36, 269, 295–96
kingdom of Messiah, 133–34
kingdom people, 148
knowledge of God, 50–51, 53, 80–82, 157, 199, 252, 300, 303, 333, 336, 341
koinonia (fellowship), 311, 315, 317
Kolb, Robert
  and Andreae, 278
  and Chemnitz, 284
  inter-Lutheran disputes, 281
  Law and Gospel, 127
  life in the Spirit under the cross, 15
  and Luther, 10, 85–88
  sanctification, 103–4
  Sola Scriptura, 37–38
  synergistic dispute, 204
  two kinds of righteousness, 96–97
  word of God, 3, 105
Königsberg, 280–83
Korner, Christoph, 279

NAME AND SUBJECT INDEX

Koyama, Kosuke, 39

laity, 143–44, 150–52, 262, 279
Large Catechism (Luther), 92–94, 123, 124, 340
Late Reformation, 275, 280–84
Latin Vulgate Bible, 24, 31
Lau, Franz, 22–23
law, 332
   and the cross, 55–57
   gift of the Holy Spirit given at Pentecost, 318
   of God, 66, 79, 211, 220, 257, 306–8, 322, 325
   good works, 272, 325–27
   justification, 97–98, 299
   ministry of the, 314
   renewal, 222–23, 266–69
   sanctification, 210–11
   synergistic dispute, 203
   work of the Holy Spirit, 334–36
   worship, 179
Law and Gospel, 127–30, 217–21, 279
   and Chemnitz, 283
   church of the pure doctrine, 193
   exclusivity of the word, 114–16
   faith, 300–301
   Formula of Concord, 342
   Holy Spirit and the church, 137
   Holy Spirit and the flesh, 225
   inner testimony of the Holy Spirit, 159
   justification by faith, 195
   and Melanchthon, 192
   reception of the Holy Spirit, 201
   repentance, 258
   sanctification, 102–3, 210
   theology of the cross, 197–200
   word of God, 214
   work of the Holy Spirit, 334
League of Smalcalden, 238–39
Lectura in Biblia, 36
Lectures on Galatians (Luther), 44, 95, 127, 219
Lectures on Genesis (Luther), 59, 91–92, 137
Lectures on Isaiah (Luther), 59
Lectures on Jonah (Luther), 59
Lectures on the Psalms (Luther), 85–86
Lectures on Titus (Luther), 147
legalism, 4, 268
Lehmann, Martin, 172
Leipzig Debate, 29, 187–88
letter, 266, 294
Leupold, H. C., 66–67
Lex imitationis, 28
Lindberg, Carter, 36, 78
liturgical, Spirit's proclamation of God's word, 136
lives of the saints, 166
Loci (Chemnitz), 283, 292
Loci (Melanchthon), 184–85, 188, 191–92, 194, 202, 207, 209, 211, 212, 213, 215, 221, 222
Loci communes (Melanchthon), 191, 203–4, 248, 282
loci communes method, 5–6
Loci Theologici (Chemnitz), 6–7, 9, 282
Locus I (Melanchthon), 8
Locus III (Chemnitz), 9
locus method, 5–9, 191
Loewenich, Walter von, 11, 17, 34, 57, 65, 83, 153, 332
Logos, 311
Lohse, Bernard, 5, 19, 22, 39, 90–91
Lombard, Peter, 33, 192
"Lord Keep Us Steadfast in Thy Word" (Luther), 138
Lord's Prayer, 135, 175, 177, 265, 322
Lord's Supper, 125–27, 216–17, 296, 321
   and Andreae, 277
   and Brenz, 237–40
   church of the pure doctrine, 194
   faith, 172
   inner testimony of the Holy Spirit, 157, 159
   inter-Lutheran disputes, 281–82
   means of the Holy Spirit, 255–56, 293
   renewal, 268–69
   and Rhegius, 245–47
   sacraments, 121–23
   Zwinglian question of, 284
love, 13, 80–81, 101–3, 163–64, 181–82, 208, 219–20, 230–32, 325–27

NAME AND SUBJECT INDEX

love of God, 55–56, 64, 80, 102, 164,
  167, 175, 219, 221, 222, 305–6,
  327, 337
Lund, Norman, 204
Luther, Martin, 1–2, 9, 234, 275, 331–32
  and Andreae, 277–79
  atonement, 62–65
  Augustine, 32
  background and influences, 22–23,
    36–37, 47–48
  breakthrough and conversion, 40–44
  and Brenz, 235–45
  Catechism of, 279
  and Chemnitz, 280–85
  and Chytraeus, 285–86
  conversion and the synergistic
    dispute, 202–7
  cross alone is our theology *(crux
    sola est nostra Theologia)*, 10–11
  cross and faith, 51
  cross and knowing God, 50–51
  cross and the law, 55–57
  discipline, 30–31
  doctoral studies and early teaching,
    33–34
  early education, 24–25
  education in Germany, 47
  election, 322
  faith and conscience, 51–52
  faith and experience, 53–55
  faith and reason, 52–53
  fallen humanity, 167
  Formula of Concord, 339–42
  formulation of the theology of the
    cross, 65–88
  gifts of the Holy Spirit, 315
  good works and the fruit of the
    Spirit, 325–26
  hidden God *(Deus absconditus)*,
    57–62
  Holy Scripture, 293
  Holy Spirit and the church, 336–38
  Holy Spirit in Law and Gospel,
    217–21
  home, 23–24
  humanism, 29–30
  inner testimony of the Holy Spirit,
    270
  Law and Gospel, 300–301
  Locus method, 6–7
  means of the Holy Spirit, 292–93
  and Melanchthon, 185, 186–93,
    187–91
  monastery, 30
  mysticism, 34–36
  new life in the Holy Spirit, 152–74,
    336
  opposition to scholastic theology,
    44–46
  ordination, 33
  person and reception of the Holy
    Spirit, 333–34
  post-Reformation issues regarding
    the theology of the cross, 16–17
  research method, 18
  responses to the Holy Spirit, 174–
    82, 338–39
  and Rhegius, 245–47
  sanctification, 306, 308
  scholasticism, 27–29
  and Schwenckfeld, 256
  Seven Penitential Psalms, 66–74
  simul justus et peccator, 170, 172,
    199, 268–69, 306, 321, 335
  Sola Scriptura, 37–38
  and Spangenberg, 247–49
  Staupitz, Johann von, 31–32
  teaching, 38–40, 261–62
  Theologia Germanica, 74–78
  theology of reality, 19–22, 34, 57,
    68–69, 85, 88, 93, 105, 107, 110,
    152, 158–59, 170, 217, 228
  theology of the cross, 49–88, 197–
    200, 249–50, 286–87, 332–33
  theology of the Holy Spirit, 88–183,
    339–42
  two kinds of theology, 11–15
  university, 25–26
  word and the Holy Spirit, 3–5
  work of the Holy Spirit, 334–36
Luther and Staupitz (Steinmetz), 36–37
Luther on Conversion (Harran), 40–41
"Luther on the Holy Spirit and His Use
  of God's Word" (Silcock), 21
Luther's Outlaw God (Paulson), 59–61

NAME AND SUBJECT INDEX

Luther's Theology of the Cross (Loewenich), 34
Luther's Theology of the Cross (Prenter), 49

Madejski, Sabastian, 136
Magdeburg, 24–25
magistrates, 197, 265
Magnificat, 54–55
Major, Georg, 281, 326
Malcolm, Lois, 92–93
Manschreck, Clyde L., 215, 227–28
Marburg Colloquy, 216–17, 239–40
Margarita Theologica (Spangenberg), 248
marks of the church *(notae ecclesiae)*, 5, 141–42, 177
Martin Luther and the Enduring Word of God (Kolb), 37
The Mass in the Apology, 228
mathematics and theology, 189
Mattes, Mark, 16–17
Matthew, 193, 209
Maulbronn Formula of 1576, 279, 286
Maurer, Wilhelm, 191, 217–18
Maurice of Saxony, 243
Maxcey, Carl, 191
Maximilian II (Emperor), 286
McGrath, Alister, 10, 11, 16, 57–58, 83
means of the Holy Spirit, 104–27, 213–17, 252–57, 292–96
mediation of the Holy Spirit, 254, 293
Medieval Catholicism, 24
Medieval Pietists, 75
A Meditation on Christ's Passion (Luther), 13
Melanchthon, Philip (Schwartzerd), 1–2, 36, 184–233, 234, 275, 331–32, 332
 affections, 269, 270
 and Chemnitz, 280–85
 and Chytraeus, 285–86
 education in Germany, 47
 Holy Scriptures, 293
 Holy Spirit and the church, 337
 humanism, 29
 human will, 202–7, 320
 influence on emerging Lutheran theology, 191–93
 inner testimony of the Holy Spirit, 270
 Locus method, 5–7
 Locus of the person of the Holy Spirit, 7–9
 means of the Holy Spirit, 292
 new life in the Holy Spirit, 336
 personal background, 186–91
 person of the Holy Spirit, 287, 333
 prayer, 176–77, 226–28
 responses to the Holy Spirit, 338–39
 and Schwenckfeld, 256–57
 and Spangenberg, 248
 theological framework, 193–97
 theology of the cross, 332–33
 theology of the Holy Spirit, 197–233
 work of the Holy Spirit, 334–36
Melanchthon Neben Luther (Greschat), 112
Miller, Joshua, 58–59, 62
ministry, 117, 138–44, 175, 178, 262–63, 265–66, 271, 294–95, 314, 328, 334, 337–38
miracles, 266, 293–94, 312–13, 315–16, 319
Moltmann, Jürgen, 16
monastery, 30–31
morality, 319
Mörlin, Joachim, 281–82
Moses, 312
Münzer, 293
Musculus, Andreas, 279
music in the church, 248–49
mysticism, 34–36, 50, 65, 76

Nagel, Norman, 148–49
naked God, 59–61, 83
names and titles of the Holy Spirit, 290–91
natural sciences, 28, 47, 189
new covenant, 292
new life in Christ, 123, 158, 270, 339
new life in the Holy Spirit, 93, 152–74, 221–25, 266–70, 317, 336. *See also* sanctification
new obedience, 305–8

373

New Testament, 13, 89, 92, 111, 125, 137, 147–49, 194, 198, 213–14, 217, 221, 229, 253, 255, 268, 292, 295, 305, 309, 312, 342
New Theology, 29–30, 36, 48, 76–77
Ninety-Five Theses (Luther), 26, 48, 72, 79, 339
nominalism, 27–29, 44–46, 48
non-hypostatic union, 311

obedience, 76–77, 124–25, 173, 179, 181, 222, 231–32, 267–68, 301–2, 305–8, 310, 320, 325–27, 333, 334, 336
obedience of faith, 40, 49, 93, 129, 149, 309, 326
Oberman, Heiko, 35
Ockhamism. See *via moderna*
Oecolampadius, Johannes, 190, 235, 239, 245, 255
offensive texts of Scripture, 60
office of the Holy Spirit, 90–94
office of the keys, 144–45, 263–64, 313–14
old Adam, 14, 72, 80, 96, 103, 146, 172, 193, 268, 302
old man, 166, 173
Old Testament, 89, 92, 124, 131, 137, 147–48, 213, 217, 221, 229, 253, 255, 263, 290, 309
On Good Works (Luther), 182
On the Councils and the Church (Luther), 141–42
Operationes in Psalmos (Luther), 10, 14–15, 65–66, 84–85
oral, Spirit's proclamation of God's word, 3, 136
oral word, 110–12, 157
ordination, 30, 31, 33, 143, 313
original sin, 192, 195, 279, 301, 305, 340
Osiander, Andreas, 240, 241, 277
Osiander debates, 281
Otto, Rudolf, 21–22

Parousia, 323
passive righteousness, 96–97, 173
pastoral care, 68
patience, 287

Paul (apostle), 43, 81, 92–93, 97, 102, 128, 143, 151, 153–54, 155, 161–62, 168, 188, 193, 205, 217–18, 222–23, 253–54, 257–58, 261, 266–69, 270, 306, 312–13
Paulson, Steven, 59–61, 128
Peasants' Revolt, 197, 237, 248
peculiar privilege of some persons, 316
Pelagius, 205, 307
Pelikan, Jaroslav, 66
penance, 120–21, 181, 299
The Penitential Psalms (Luther), 65–66
penitents, 69–74
Pentecost, 261, 265, 268, 289, 316, 318
perfection, 41, 102, 303, 320, 326–27
person of the Holy Spirit, 7–9, 88–90, 200–213, 251–52, 287–90, 333–34
Peter (apostle), 148, 229, 253–54, 293
"Philip Melanchthon and a Christian Politics" (Wengert), 196–97
Philip of Hesse, 202, 239–40
Philippists, 281, 283–84
philosophy, 26, 42, 52–53, 81, 198–99, 261–62, 282–83
Pless, John, 119–20
pneumatic realism, Luther's, 21
poenitentia. See repentance
power of the Holy Spirit, 264, 286–87, 292, 294–95
practical pastoral ministry, 339
practical prayer, 324
praise, 179
prayer, 101–3, 138, 142, 145, 170, 174–78, 226–28, 271, 321–22, 323–24, 338–39
preaching, 3–5, 58–61, 110–11, 112, 116, 117, 122, 127, 145, 148–52, 156–57, 171, 180, 195–96, 209, 229, 236, 253–54, 263–65, 277–78, 293, 301, 314, 318, 322, 325, 333, 338, 341
Prediger (Luther), 152
Prenter, Regin, 331–32
  call to Christian ministry, 144
  conformity to Christ, 164–67
  cross and the word, 50
  exclusivity of the word, 116

NAME AND SUBJECT INDEX

external and internal word, 109–10
hidden God *(Deus absconditus)*,
   61–62
Holy Spirit and faith, 172–74
infusion of love into the heart,
   163–64
inner testimony of the Holy Spirit,
   159
justification, 98–99
Luther's ideas of the Christian life,
   174
Luther's theology of the Holy Spirit,
   21–22
Luther's understanding of the
   Trinity, 65
oral and written word, 110
real presence of Christ, 167
sanctification, 102–3
Spirit as *Spiritus Creator*, 154–55
theology of the cross, 49, 332
word and the Holy Spirit, 4
presence of the Holy Spirit, 87, 336,
   338–39
Preus, Jacob, 282
Preus, Robert, 6, 283
priesthood, 148–52, 180, 198, 255, 271
priesthood of all believers, 147–52, 262,
   314
private confession, 247
The Private Mass (Luther), 140
procession of the Holy Spirit, 291–92
proclamation of God's word, 112–13, 136
proper ministry, 313
prophecy, 315–16, 337
prophets, 261, 266, 289–90, 293–94,
   303, 316, 318, 338
Protestantism, 284
Psalmos Graduum (Song of Ascents),
   85–88
Psalms, 39–40, 66–68, 325
public ordination, 313

Quere, Ralph, 216
Questiones (Occam), 33

real presence of Christ, 121–22, 167–68,
   172–74, 296

reason, 52–53, 81, 115, 159, 198–99,
   211, 225, 250, 259–60, 262, 270,
   287, 296
reception of the Holy Spirit, 201–2,
   257–58, 308, 318–19, 333–34
reconciliation, 37–38, 126, 325
redeemed person, 155–56
Reformation, 1, 5, 34, 184–85, 234–35,
   254, 265, 268, 275, 276, 278, 331
   breakthrough, 40
   and Brenz, 235–45
   call to Christian ministry, 312
   and Chemnitz, 280–85
   churches of the, 141
   evil, 226
   Law and Gospel, 218–19
   Luther's background and influences,
      48
   and Melanchthon, 187–88, 191–93
   opposition to scholastic theology, 46
   and Rhegius, 246
   and Spangenberg, 247–49
   synergistic dispute, 203
   teaching, 308
   true Christian fellowship, 147
Reformation principles, 20, 50, 54, 237
regeneration, 165, 203, 209, 295–96,
   304–5, 305–7
remission of sins, 257, 266, 269, 270, 318
renewal, 120, 126, 155–56, 222–23, 230,
   266–69, 295–96, 303, 304–5,
   307–8, 320–21, 325–26, 329,
   335
renewed conscience, 328
repentance, 50, 62, 79, 82–83, 93, 99,
   171, 174, 179, 209, 230, 258,
   259, 267–68, 293, 299–300,
   301–2, 328–29, 332, 334
Repitio sanæ doctrinæ de vera praesentia
   (Chemnitz), 284
responses to the Holy Spirit, 174–82,
   226–32, 271–72, 323–29, 338–39
restoration, 70, 164, 243, 258, 332, 339,
   343
Reuchlin, Johannes, 186, 190
revealed God *(Deus revelatus)*, 57–59,
   226

revelation of God, 11, 83, 86, 88, 127, 172, 198
reversal of direction, 63–64
Rhadinus, Thomas, 215
Rhegius, Urbanus, 1–2, 234, 245–47
    gifts of the Holy Spirit, 264–66, 337
    inner testimony of the Holy Spirit, 270
    person of the Holy Spirit, 251–52
    prayer, 176
    reception of the Holy Spirit, 257
    renewal, 267–68
    responses to the Holy Spirit, 271
    word of God, 253–54
    work of the Holy Spirit, 258–66, 335
Richard, James, 203
righteousness, 71–73
    baptism, 295–96
    breakthrough and conversion, 44
    faith, 258
    gifts of the Holy Spirit, 170
    The Heidelberg Disputations (Luther), 82–83
    hidden reality of the Spirit, 161
    Holy Spirit and faith, 171–73
    Holy Spirit and suffering, 161
    justification, 299
    New Testament worship, 194
    Operationes in Psalmos (Luther), 84–85
    regeneration, 304–5
    renewal, 320
    responses to the Holy Spirit, 174
    sanctification, 101–4, 104, 305–7
    synergistic dispute, 203
    teaching, 38–39
    two kinds of, 95–97
    work of the Holy Spirit, 297
Rittgers, Ronald, 246–47
Rogness, David, 185
Roman Catholic Church, 120–22, 141, 240, 262, 278–79, 312
Roman Confutation, 192
Romans Lectures (Luther), 36, 38–40, 42–44, 53
Romans Preface (Luther), 170
Romans studies of Melanchthon, 191–92, 193, 219

sacramental, Spirit's proclamation of God's word, 3, 136
The Sacrament of Penance (Luther), 120–21
sacrament of the altar, 139, 143
sacraments, 3, 5, 81, 119–23, 332
    call to Christian ministry, 312
    church of the pure doctrine, 194
    exclusivity of the word, 114–16
    external and internal word, 109
    faith, 300
    Holy Scriptures, 293–95
    Holy Spirit and holiness, 159–60
    Holy Spirit and the church, 138–43, 142–43, 262–63, 310, 337–38
    inner testimony of the Holy Spirit, 321
    justification, 209
    Lord's Supper, 216–17
    means of the Holy Spirit, 104–5, 213, 215–16, 255–57, 292–93
    person and reception of the Holy Spirit, 333–34
    prayer, 177
    worship, 178–81, 228–29
saints, 252, 262, 311, 315–16, 323, 327
salvation, 4–5, 28, 38, 40, 52, 122, 124, 139–40, 142, 150, 156–57, 193, 202–5, 224, 252, 253, 263, 265, 268, 287, 292, 300, 301, 302–3, 308, 309, 317, 320, 322, 326, 332, 337
sanctification
    conformity to Christ, 167
    conversio and *causa*, 206
    exclusivity of the word, 115
    Formula of Concord, 341
    gifts of the Holy Spirit, 170
    good works, 230–32
    Holy Spirit and holiness, 159–60
    Holy Spirit and the church, 140–47
    inner testimony of the Holy Spirit, 156
    office and work of the Holy Spirit, 92–93
    Operationes in Psalmos (Luther), 84
    person and work of the Holy Spirit, 209–11

NAME AND SUBJECT INDEX

sacraments, 255
two kinds of righteousness, 95–97
work of the Holy Spirit, 100–104, 260–61, 305–8, 334, 334–35
Sasse, Hermann, 3–4
Satan. *See* devil
Saul of Tarsus, 41
Saxon churches, 225
Schaff, Philip, 245
Schalbe, Heinrich, 25
Schema mortificatio-vivicatio, 249
scholasticism, 26, 27–29, 27–30, 44–46, 51, 76, 86, 186
scholastic theology, 39, 44–46, 48, 193
Scholia (Melanchthon), 197, 201–2
school of the Holy Spirit, 332
Schüler, Balthasar, 280
Schwäbisch Hall, 235–39, 241
Schweifert, Ernest, 45
Schwenckfeld, Casper, 256–57
Schwenckfelders, 278
Schwiebert, Ernest, 176
science and theology, 189
Scotus, Duns, 27, 46
Scriptural lists of gifts, 314–15
Seeburg, Erich, 21
Seiling, Jonathan, 67, 72
self-discipline, 47–48
self-love, 164, 219, 225
Selnecker, Nicholas, 192, 279, 280
Sentences (Collectorium) (Lombard), 33
The Seven Penitential Psalms (Die Sieben Bußpsalmen), 66–74
shouted word, 202
signs, 313–14
Silcock, Jeffrey, 21, 89, 93–94, 108, 110–11, 123, 127
simple faith, 323
simul justus et peccator, 170, 172, 199, 268–69, 306, 321, 335
sin, 75–77
   baptism, 295–96
   conformity to Christ, 166
   conversion, 301–2
   faith, 300–301
   good works and the fruit of the Spirit, 325–27
   holiness and Christian liberty, 269–70
   against the Holy Spirit, 272, 327–29, 339
   Holy Spirit and the church, 144
   Holy Spirit and the flesh, 225
   Holy Spirit in Law and Gospel, 219
   incarnation, 298
   inner testimony of the Holy Spirit, 156–59
   Lord's Supper, 296
   office and work of the Holy Spirit, 93
   office of the keys, 313–14
   person of the Holy Spirit, 251–52
   power of, 334–35
   reception of the Holy Spirit, 201–2
   regeneration, 304
   remission of, 257, 266, 269, 270, 318
   renewal, 266–68
   responses to the Holy Spirit, 271
   sanctification, 210–11, 305–8
   Spirit as *Spiritus Creator*, 154–55
   theology of the cross, 197
sin against the Holy Spirit, 272, 327–29, 339
sinners, 12, 38, 40, 41, 44, 58–59, 63, 70, 96–97, 120–21, 159–60, 166, 171–72, 192, 195, 258, 299, 304, 317, 326, 331–32
Six Christian Sermons (Andreae), 284
Six Christian Sermons on the Divisions (Andreae), 278–79
Smalcald Articles (Luther), 4, 116, 136, 340
Smalcald War, 241, 276, 285
Small Catechism (Luther), 121, 158, 340
Sola Scriptura, 37–38
Solid Declaration, 279, 339–40
Song of Assent, 66
Spangenberg, Johann, 1–2, 234, 247–49
   and Brenz, 245
   faith, 259
   holiness and Christian liberty, 269–70
   Holy Spirit and the church, 262–63
   inner testimony of the Holy Spirit, 270
   justification, 260

377

Spangenberg, Johann (*cont.*)
    the kingdom, 265
    office of the keys, 263–64
    person of the Holy Spirit, 251
    reception of the Holy Spirit, 257–58
    remission of sins, 270
    renewal, 266–69
    repentance, 258
    responses to the Holy Spirit, 271–72
    sacraments, 255–56
    teaching, 262
    work of the Holy Spirit, 335
spark of conscience (*synteresis*), 51–52
Spirit of doctrine, 174
Spirit of grace, 174, 267, 270, 291, 303
spiritual gifts, 135, 168–70, 265–66
spiritual knowledge, 119
Spiritus Creator (Prenter), 332
spoken word, 4, 109, 110
state, 265
Staupitz, Johann von, 30, 31–32, 33, 36–37
Steinmetz, David, 32, 36–37, 112
St. George, 25
St. Mary's Church, 152
St. Michael's Church, 236–38
Strigel, Victorin, 278
suffering, 11, 12, 50–51, 62, 79–85, 86–88, 145–46, 161–63
Swabian-Saxon Concord of 1575, 279
synergistic dispute, 202–7
Syngramma Suevicum (Brenz), 239, 255
Syntagma (Brenz), 262
synteresis (spark of conscience), 51–52

Tauler, Johan, 34–36, 76, 78, 158, 160
teaching, 112, 138, 145–46, 177, 212–13, 215, 261–62, 277–78, 308–10
Ten Commandments, 261, 267–68, 307
Teutonic Order of Sackshausen, 74
Theologia Germanica or *Theologia Deutsch* (*A German Theology*), 36, 65–66, 74–78
theologian of the cross, 63, 67–71, 79–80
theologians of glory, 12, 70–71, 79–81
theologians of the cross, 14–15, 71

theological breakthrough, 40–44
theology, 282–83
theology and music, 249
theology of definitions, 188–89
theology of glory, 11, 12, 14, 40, 52–53, 62, 66, 76, 80–81
theology of humility, 33–34, 40
theology of reality, 19–22, 34, 57, 68–69, 85, 88, 93, 105, 107, 110, 152, 158–59, 170, 217, 228
theology of the cross (*theologia crucis*), 10–15, 36, 64, 76–78, 178–81, 197–200, 210, 230, 249–50, 286–87, 332–33, 338
    conformity to Christ, 166
    cross and faith, 51
    cross and knowing God, 50–51
    cross and the Holy Spirit, 49–50
    cross and the law, 56
    cross and the word, 50
    cross story, 13–14
    doctrine of the Trinity, 89–90
    faith and reason, 52–53
    The Heidelberg Disputation (Luther), 79–83
    hidden God (*Deus absconditus*), 57–59
    Holy Spirit and faith, 171
    Holy Spirit and suffering, 161
    inner testimony of the Holy Spirit, 158–59
    lectures of 1532–33, 85–87
    Luther's formulation of, 65–88
    mysticism, 34–35
    Operationes on Psalmos (Luther), 85
    opposition to scholastic theology, 45, 46
    post-Reformation issues regarding, 16–17
    prayer, 178
    Seven Penitential Psalms, 67–74
    Spirit as *Spiritus Creator*, 155
    teaching, 39–40
    Theologia Germanica, 74–78
    Wittenberg New Theology, 76–77
    word of God, 105
"The Theology of the Cross" (Iwand), 34
Theology the Lutheran Way (Bayer), 118

NAME AND SUBJECT INDEX

Third Article of the Apostle's Creed, 20–22, 92–94, 102, 151, 156, 158, 172, 178, 300
Thomas Aquinas, 27, 42, 51
three causes of conversion, 202–7
"The Three Rules of Theology" (Luther), 117–18
Torgau conference, 286
To the Christian Nobility (Luther), 47, 149–51
To the Councilmen of all Cities in Germany (Luther), 47
Treatise on the New Testament (Luther), 148
Treatise on the Sacrament of Penance (Luther), 151
Trebonius, John, 25
Trigg, Jonathan, 123, 125, 136–37
Trinity
    action word of the Holy Spirit, 113
    baptism, 216
    divine essence in the, 333
    doctrine of the, 89–90
    Holy Spirit and the church, 311
    Luther's understanding of, 65
    office and work of the Holy Spirit, 93
    person and work of the Holy Spirit, 200
    person of the Holy Spirit, 251–52
    prayer and worship, 271
    procession of the Holy Spirit, 291
    worship of, 324–25
    See also God; Holy Spirit; Jesus Christ
true Catholic tradition, 1–2, 6, 48, 192
true worship, 178, 324–25, 339
Trutfetter von Eisenach, Jodocus, 27–28
Tübingen, 276–79, 285
Twelve Articles (Rhegius), 252
Twelve Articles of the Peasants (Brenz), 237
two kingdoms, 196–97, 211

understanding, 52
union with Christ, 100, 171–72, 211, 332
unity of God, 333
unity of the word and the Spirit, 98–99
University of Erfurt, 25–26, 27–28, 29, 30, 33, 247–48
University of Heidelberg, 186, 235–36
University of Leipzig, 48, 241
University of Rostock, 285
University of Tübingen, 187, 240–41
University of Wittenberg, 2, 27, 29–30, 31–32, 33, 36, 45–46, 187–88, 234, 280–84, 285
unmerited grace *(sola gratia)*, 20, 205
Usingen, Bartholomaeus Arnoldi von, 27–28

Vajta, Vilmos, 153, 178–79
via antiqua, 27
via moderna, 27–29, 33, 46
Virgin Mary, 251–52, 296, 298
visible church, 310–11, 338
Vulgate Bible, 37

Wartburg Castle, 85
water baptism, 99, 124–25
Wengert, Timothy, 186–90, 189–90, 195, 196–97, 198, 200, 209–10, 215, 218
Wessel, John, 187
wicked, 69–70
Wilhelm of Anhalt, 24
William of Occam, 27, 33, 45–46
will of God, 50, 52, 56, 70, 164–66, 180, 218, 266, 287, 300
will of man, 219
Winkelprediger, 312
Wittenberg Catechism, 284
Wittenberg Concord, 246
Wittenberg New Theology, 29–30, 36, 76–77
Wittenberg theology, 35, 189–90, 276
Wood, A. Skevington, 110
word and the Spirit, 108, 110, 114–15, 137, 177, 201, 203, 213–15, 294, 310, 335
word of God, 105–6, 332
    action words of the Holy Spirit, 112–13
    assurance of the Holy Spirit, 212, 223–24, 322, 336
    call to Christian ministry, 312–13

NAME AND SUBJECT INDEX

word of God (*cont.*)
  church of the pure doctrine, 194
  conversion, 202–7, 301–2
  and the cross, 50
  exclusivity of, 114–16
  external and internal word, 333
  external word and internal word, 109–10
  faith, 199, 259, 300–301
  faith and experience, 53–55
  faith and hope, 208
  Formula of Concord, 341
  gifts of the Holy Spirit, 169–70
  good works and the fruit of the Spirit, 325–27
  hearing of, 60, 81, 98, 110, 116, 117, 134, 199, 259, 301–2, 333, 341
  The Heidelberg Disputations (Luther), 81–83
  hidden reality of the Spirit, 161
  Holy Scriptures, 293–95
  and the Holy Spirit, 3–5
  Holy Spirit and faith, 171–74
  Holy Spirit and holiness, 159–60
  Holy Spirit and the church, 136–45, 262–63, 310–11, 336–38
  Holy Spirit and the kingdom, 322–23
  Holy Spirit and the kingdom of God, 133–36
  Holy Spirit and the priesthood of all believers, 150–52
  Holy Spirit as the author and interpreter of the, 106–8
  Holy Spirit in Law and Gospel, 217–21
  Holy Spirit inspires and teaches the, 117–27
  human will, 320
  inner testimony of the Holy Spirit, 156–59, 322
  and justification, 97–99, 195–96, 209, 260
  the Kingdom, 264–65
  life in the Spirit under the cross, 15
  Lord's Supper, 296
  means of the Holy Spirit, 213–15, 253–54, 292–93
  office and work of the Holy Spirit, 91–94
  office of the keys, 264, 313–14
  oral word and written word, 110–12
  person and reception of the Holy Spirit, 333–34
  person of the Holy Spirit, 287
  physical means of, 104–5
  prayer, 174, 176–78
  regeneration, 304–5
  renewal, 266–69
  repentance, 258
  sacraments, 119–23, 256
  sanctification, 210–11
  sin against the Holy Spirit, 272
  Sola Scriptura, 37–38
  synergistic dispute, 202–7
  teaching, 39, 261–62, 308–10
  theology of the cross, 287, 332–33
  unity of the word and the Spirit, 98–99
  work of the Holy Spirit, 297, 334–35, 334–36
  worship, 178–81, 228–30, 324–25
  See also preaching
work of Christ, 101, 111, 116, 193–94, 265, 326, 335
work of the Holy Spirit, 9, 17, 18, 20–21, 35, 48, 61, 64, 80, 81–82, 85, 87, 90–104, 100–101, 105, 118, 119, 127–30, 146, 155–56, 157–58, 159–60, 181, 196–97, 199–200, 200–213, 220, 229, 231–32, 252, 256, 258–62, 267, 297–310, 323–24, 328, 334–36
World War II, 64
worship, 178–81, 228–30, 271, 324–25, 338–39
written, Spirit's proclamation of God's word, 3, 139
written word, 4, 98, 110–12, 116
Württemberg Confession of 1559, 277

Zwingli, Ulrich, 239–40, 245–46
Zwinglians, 239–41, 256, 278, 284, 296

Scripture Index

OLD TESTAMENT

Genesis

1	38, 90, 92, 106–7, 290
1:2	9, 289, 290
1:3	112
1:26	297
2	106–7
2:7	15
3:15	130, 170
6:3	174
12	130
16:4	128
17:20	128
17:21	136
21:8–19	128
21:10	129
21:10–16	128
22:17–18	112
34	132
35:9–12	130
35:22	132
49:1–2	130
49:1–28	130
49:3	132
49:4	132
49:5–7	132
49:8–10	133
49:10	117
49:11–12	132

Exodus

4:1–3	312
19	149
19:5–6	147

Deuteronomy

8:3	130
30:2	183

Isaiah

6	288
11	314
45:15	82, 83
55:1	156
55:7	42
55:11	113
63:14	289
64:4	97
65:1	43

Jeremiah

23:21	312
31	257
31:33	303

Zechariah

7:12	290
12:10	323

SCRIPTURE INDEX

Psalms

1:1	42, 52
5:11	49, 84, 175
6	66
6:5	70
8:1	133
14:1	52
	32 66
32:2	72
32:8	68, 69, 70
32:9	70
32:35	106
33:6	9, 108, 290, 297
34	252
36:8	134
38	66
38:20	70, 72
45	107
51	44, 66, 106, 318
51:1:11–12	73
51:2	72, 97–99
51:4	106
51:6	3, 71
51:6b	72
51:7	72
51:10	168–69
51:11–13	100
68:18	315
69	39
74:3	52
102	66
104:30	9, 290
116	287
118:4	83
119	287
126:5	86
129:4	87
129:8	87
130	66
130:3	72
130:4–5	73
139:7	289
143	66, 73
143:7	73
143:10	69, 74
148:5b	112

Job

13:15	130

NEW TESTAMENT

Matthew

3:11	99
3:16	251
3:16–17	288
3:17	214, 216
4	3
5:11	145
5:12	146
7	155
7:15	302
9:38	312
10:19–20	200
10:20	77, 290
10:29–33	200
12	155
12:28	289
12:33	325
13:44	160
16:16–17	268
16:19	296
16:24	69
16:24–25	13, 50
16:24–26	10
18:15–20	144
19:4–6	146
26:26	126
26:41	83
28	252, 288
28:2	116
28:19	251, 289, 324

Mark

1:9–45	3
8:34	50
8:34b	161
8:34–35	10
16	288
16:16	104, 124, 228, 302
16:17–18	170, 337

Luke

1:41	289, 296
2:15	114
4:1	3
4:14	3
9:23	161
11:13	318, 323
11:20	289, 291
14:18	302
16:29	157

John

1	92, 106, 252, 297
1:33	99
2:27	291
3	155
3:5	295
3:6	96
3:19	302
4	263
5:17	297
6	182
6:8	342
6:28–29	181
7:39	289
8:47	302
10	257
10:26	302
10:30	126
12:25	163
14	252
14:9	126
14:16	289
14:16–17	288
14:23	137, 168, 289, 311
14:26	291
15	257
15:26	289, 297
16:3	50–51
16:8	92
17:17	100
20	264–65
20:22	289, 313
20:22–23	296
20:31	294

Acts

1:5	99
1:6–9	322
2	251, 252
2:1–4	318
2:4–6	315
2:10	293
2:38	15, 293
5	288
7:51	302
10	254
13:45–46	302
14:22	86
15	263
15:6–29	311
19:2	289–90
20:28	313

Romans

	164
1	81–82, 297
1:4	100
1:5	40, 93
1:16	142, 157, 322
1:17	44, 45
1:20	52
2:14–15	55
2:15	163
3:20	44
3:21	44
3:27	43
4:20	53
5	102
5:1–5	146
5:3–5	162
5:5	55, 56, 163
5:12	170
6	171
6:12	302
6:13–11	13, 69, 100
6:14	77
7	223, 267, 268, 270, 300, 306
7:5–6	170
7:22–23	83
7:22	322
7:24	102

Romans (cont.)

8	211, 259, 262, 267, 268, 270, 287, 336
8:1–16	100
8:2	185
8:5	195
8:5–11	289
8:9	155
8:10	267
8:11	15
8:13	302
8:13–14	164
8:14	77, 153
8:15	291
8:15–16	223
8:26	36, 43, 84, 158, 166, 167, 175, 323, 338
8:29	162
8:29–30	322
9:23	226
9:31–32	302
10:14–17	171–72
10:15	312
10:17	156, 292, 302
10:20	43
12	149
12:1	229
12:2–21	149
15:16	100
16:16	40
16:26	93

1 Corinthians

	315
1:21	81
1:30	95
1–2	10
2:6–10	3–4
2:9	97
2:10	97, 289
3:6	314
3:9	153
3:16	311
3:18	160
4:1	149
8:6	290
10:17	143
12	314
12:3	153
12:4–6	290
12:4–7	169
12:4–11	289
12:6	288
12:7	169
12:11	290, 316
12–14	170, 337
14:27–28	168
15:58	314

2 Corinthians

2:10	296
3:3	292
3:5	290
3:5–6	151
3:6	128, 289, 292, 294
3:8	292, 322
3:17	289
3:18	288, 292, 321
4	156
5:19–20	292
5:21	298
6:16	311
7:1	99
12:9	87
12:12	312
13:14	315

Galatians

2:15–16	44
2:20	13, 181
2:21	44
3:5–6	159
3:14	318
4:6	323
4:6–7	159, 166
4:21–31	128
4:29	128
5	156, 300, 316, 318
5:17	83, 170
5:24	96, 302
6:14	161

Ephesians

3:16–17	297
4	314
4:5	142
4:8	143, 312
4:11–12	312
6:17	253–54

Philippians

1:1–11	181

Colossians

1:16	108, 290
1:19	126
2	171
2:17	229
2:22	196

1 Timothy

1:9	184–85
4:5	142, 145
4:14	312–13

2 Timothy

1:6	312–13
2:2	313
3:12	161
4:2	92

Titus

2:12	96
3:5	142, 292
3:5–6	157
3:5–7	295, 296

Hebrews

1:2	290
1:3	290
4:7	302
6:4	311
10:29	303
11:1	53, 82
12:11	49

James

1:18	154

1 Peter

	152
1:2	229
1:11	86, 289
1:25	108
2	229
2:9	148, 151, 313
3:15	100
5	229

2 Peter

1:4	289, 315
2	303

1 John

3:24	289
4:13	289
5:7	251
16:13	289

CATHOLIC BIBLE

Wisdom

1:7	289

www.ingramcontent.com/pod-product-compliance
Lightning Source LLC
Chambersburg PA
CBHW071229290426
44108CB00013B/1350